Ancient Philosophy

Blackwell Readings in the History of Philosophy

Series Editors: *Fritz Allhoff and Anand Jayprakash Vaidya*

The volumes in this series provide concise and representative selections of key texts from the history of philosophy. Expertly edited and introduced by established scholars, each volume represents a particular philosophical era, replete with important selections of the most influential work in metaphysics, epistemology, moral and political philosophy, and the philosophy of science and religion.

1. *Ancient Philosophy: Essential Readings with Commentary*
Edited by Nicholas Smith with Fritz Allhoff and Anand Jayprakash Vaidya

2. *Medieval Philosophy: Essential Readings with Commentary*
Edited by Gyula Klima with Fritz Allhoff and Anand Jayprakash Vaidya

3. *Early Modern Philosophy: Essential Readings with Commentary*
Edited by A. P. Martinich with Fritz Allhoff and Anand Jayprakash Vaidya

4. *Late Modern Philosophy: Essential Readings with Commentary*
Edited by Elizabeth S. Radcliffe and Richard McCarty with Fritz Allhoff and Anand Jayprakash Vaidya

Forthcoming

5. *The Philosophy of Science: An Historical Anthology*
Fritz Allhoff, Marc Alspector-Kelly, and Timothy McGrew

Ancient Philosophy

Essential Readings with Commentary

Edited by

Nicholas Smith
with Fritz Allhoff and Anand Jayprakash Vaidya

Blackwell
Publishing

BLACKWELL PUBLISHING
350 Main Street, Malden, MA 02148-5020, USA
9600 Garsington Road, Oxford OX4 2DQ, UK
550 Swanston Street, Carlton, Victoria 3053, Australia

First published 2008 by Blackwell Publishing Ltd

Library of Congress Cataloging-in-Publication Data

Ancient philosophy : essential readings with commentary / edited by Nicholas Smith with
Fritz Allhoff and Anand Jayprakash Vaidya.
    p. cm. – (Blackwell readings in the history of philosophy ; 4)
    Includes bibliographical references and index.
    ISBN 978-1-4051-3562-7 (hardcover : alk. paper) – ISBN 978-1-4051-3563-4 (pbk. : alk. paper)
    1. Philosophy, Ancient. I. Smith, Nicholas D. II. Allhoff, Fritz. III. Vaidya, Anand.

B111.A534 2008
180–dc22

    2007024736

A catalogue record for this title is available from the British Library.

FSC
Mixed Sources
Product group from well-managed
forests and other controlled sources
Cert no. SGS-COC-2953
www.fsc.org
© 1996 Forest Stewardship Council

For further information on
Blackwell Publishing, visit our website at
www.blackwellpublishing.com

Contents

Acknowledgments

I am very grateful to Lloyd Gerson for advice on the selection of materials and on other matters relating to the production of this book.

List of Sources

The editor and publisher gratefully acknowledge the permission granted to reproduce the copyright material in this book:

Chronology: Mary Louise Gill and Pierre Pellegrin, eds., *Companion to Ancient Philosophy* (Oxford: Blackwell Publishing, 2006), pp. xvi–xxv, xxvi, xxvii, xxviii. © 2006 by Blackwell Publishing Ltd. Reprinted by permission of Blackwell Publishing.

7: Xenophon, *Recollections of Socrates and Socrates' Defense Before the Jury*, trans. Anna S. Benjamin (New York: Macmillan, 1985), books 1.4 and 4.3 (pp. 23–7, 117–20). © 1965. Reprinted by permission of Pearson Education, Inc., Upper Saddle River, NJ.

8: Plato, *Euthyphro*, trans. Thomas C. Brickhouse and Nicholas D. Smith, in *The Trial and Execution of Socrates: Sources and Controversies* (New York: Oxford University Press, 2002), pp. 25–41. © 2002 by Oxford University Press, Inc. Reprinted by permission of Oxford University Press, Inc.

9: Plato, *Apology of Socrates*, trans. Thomas C. Brickhouse and Nicholas D. Smith, in *The Trial and Execution of Socrates: Sources and Controversies* (New York: Oxford University Press, 2002), pp. 42–65. © 2002 by Oxford University Press, Inc. Reprinted by permission of Oxford University Press, Inc.

10: Plato, *Crito*, trans. Thomas C. Brickhouse and Nicholas D. Smith, in *The Trial and Execution of Socrates: Sources and Controversies* (New York: Oxford University Press, 2002), pp. 66–75. © 2002 by Oxford University Press, Inc. Reprinted by permission of Oxford University Press, Inc.

11: Plato, *Meno*, from R. E. Allen, *The Dialogues of Plato* (New Haven: Yale University Press, 1984), pp. 159–60, 162–71. © 1984 by Yale University. Reprinted by permission of Yale University Press.

12: Plato, *Phaedo*, from David Gallop, *Plato, Phaedo* (Oxford: Clarendon Press, 1988), pp. 8–15, 19–26, 54–62, and from *Phaedo*, trans. Thomas C. Brickhouse and Nicholas D. Smith, in *The Trial and Execution of Socrates: Sources and Controversies* (New York: Oxford University Press,

13: Plato, *Symposium*, from R. E. Allen, *The Dialogues of Plato* (New Haven: Yale University Press, 1984), pp. 144–57. © 1984 by Yale University. Reprinted by permission of Yale University Press.

14: Plato, *Republic*, from Allen Bloom, *The Republic of Plato*, 2nd edn. (New York: Basic Books, 1991), pp. 36–40, 45–57, 91–6, 105–25, 153–61, 182–92, 193–200. © 1968 by Allan Bloom. Reprinted by permission of Basic Books, a member of Perseus Books Group.

15: Plato, *Parmenides*, from R. E. Allen, *Plato's Parmenides* (New Haven: Yale University Press, 1997), pp. 4–15. © 1987 by Yale University. Reprinted by permission of Yale University Press.

16: Plato, *Timaeus*, from F. M. Cornford, *Plato's Cosmology: The Timaeus of Plato Translated with a Running Commentary* (New York: Humanities Press [Routledge], 1937), sections 27c–35a, 51d–52d. © 1937. Reprinted by permission of Taylor & Francis Books UK.

17: Aristotle, *Categories*, from *Aristotle: Selected Works*, 3rd edn., ed. and trans. H. G. Apostle and L. P. Gerson (Des Moines, IA: Peripatetic Press, 1991), pp. 29–35. Reprinted by permission of Peripatetic Press.

18: Aristotle, *On Interpretation*, from *Aristotle: Selected Works*, 3rd edn., ed. and trans. H. G. Apostle and L. P. Gerson (Des Moines, IA: Peripatetic Press, 1991), pp. 65–7. Reprinted by permission of Peripatetic Press.

19: Aristotle, *Physics*, from *Aristotle: Selected Works*, 3rd edn., ed. and trans. H. G. Apostle and L. P. Gerson (Des Moines, IA: Peripatetic Press, 1991), pp. 181–3, 185–8, 189–91, 192–7. Reprinted by permission of Peripatetic Press.

20: Aristotle, *On the Soul*, from *Aristotle: Selected Works*, 3rd edn., ed. and trans. H. G. Apostle and L. P. Gerson (Des Moines, IA: Peripatetic Press, 1991), pp. 259–62, 266–72. Reprinted by permission of Peripatetic Press.

21: Aristotle, *Metaphysics*, from *Aristotle: Selected Works*, 3rd edn., ed. and trans. H. G. Apostle and L. P. Gerson (Des Moines, IA: Peripatetic Press, 1991), pp. 334–9, 345–7, 351–6, 356–7, 362–5, 367–9, 371–4, 401–11. Reprinted by permission of Peripatetic Press.

22: Aristotle, *Nicomachean Ethics*, from *Aristotle: Selected Works*, 3rd edn., ed. and trans. H. G. Apostle and L. P. Gerson (Des Moines, IA: Peripatetic Press, 1991), pp. 419–23, 426–9, 438–42, 444–8, 534–43. Reprinted by permission of Peripatetic Press.

23, text 1: Aristotle, *Politics*, from *Aristotle: Selected Works*, 3rd edn., ed. and trans. H. G. Apostle and L. P. Gerson (Des Moines, IA: Peripatetic Press, 1991), pp. 547–50, 573–6. Reprinted by permission of Peripatetic Press; **text 2**: from *Aristotle's Politics*, trans. H. G. Apostle and L. P. Gerson (Des Moines, IA: Peripatetic Press, 1993), pp. 38–47. Reprinted by permission of Peripatetic Press.

24: Diogenes Laertius, *Life of Diogenes*, trans. C. D. Yonge, <http://classicpersuasion.org/pw/diogenes/dldiogenes.htm>.

25, text 1: Epicurus, *Letter to Herodotus*, from A. A. Long and D. N. Sedley, *The Hellenistic Philosophers*, vol. 1 (Cambridge: Cambridge University Press, 1987), selections from pp. 37–77. © 1987 by Cambridge University Press. Reprinted by permission of the authors and Cambridge

Chronology

History	Philosophy	Sciences, Arts, Religion
776–490 BCE: Archaic Period		776 BCE: First celebration of the Olympic games
753 BCE: Traditional founding of Rome		c.750–725 BCE?: Homeric poems fl. c.700 BCE: Hesiod
		Early or mid 7th century BCE: Archilochus (poet) Mid to late 7th century: Alcman (poet) b. 630 BCE: Sappho (poet)
594/3 BCE: Solon, chief archon in Athens	fl. 600–550 BCE: Thales of Miletus d. 547+ BCE: Anaximander of Miletus fl. 546–525 BCE: Anaximenes of Miletus	585 BCE: eclipse predicted by Thales fl. 544 BCE: Pherecydes of Syros
561/0–556/5; 550/49; 540/39–528/7 BCE: 3 periods of Peisistratus' rule in Athens	c.570–478 BCE: Xenophanes of Colophon c.570–490 BCE: Pythagoras of Samos (migrated to Croton c.530 BCE).	560–480 BCE: Hecataeus of Miletus (made map of the world; participated in Ionian Revolt 499 BCE)
c.524–459 BCE: Themistocles (statesman) 521–486 BCE: Darius king of Persia 508/7 BCE: Cleisthenes' political reforms in Athens	fl. c.490 BCE: Heraclitus of Ephesus *515–440s BCE: Parmenides of Elea	525/4–456/5 BCE: Aeschylus (tragic poet) 518–446+ BCE: Pindar (poet)

History	Philosophy	Sciences, Arts, Religion
499 BCE: Ionian Revolt *495–429 BCE: Pericles (statesman)	500–428 BCE: Anaxagoras c.492–432 BCE: Empedocles 5th century BCE: Zeno of Elea 5th century BCE: Melissus of Samos (Eleatic; participated in Samian defeat over Athens 441 BCE)	Early 5th century BCE: Hippasus of Metapontum (Pythagorean, mathematician, music theory) *496–406 BCE: Sophocles (tragic poet)
490–323 BCE: Classical Period 490–479 BCE: Persian Wars 490 BCE: Battle of Marathon	c.490–420 BCE: Protagoras (sophist) c.485–380 BCE: Gorgias (sophist) 5th century BCE: Hippias (sophist)	*485–420s BCE: Herodotus (historian) 480s–406 BCE: Euripides (tragic poet)
480 BCE: Battle of Salamis 478 BCE: Delian League established (Athenian alliance against the Persians)	c.470–390 BCE: Philolaus (Pythagorean) fl. 440–430 BCE: Diogenes of Apollonia	465–425 BCE: Phidias active (sculptor)
*460–403 BCE: Critias (poet, associate of Socrates and leader of the Thirty)	469–399 BCE: Socrates fl. late 5th century BCE: Antiphon (sophist) 5th century BCE: Leucippus (atomist) c.460–370 BCE: Democritus of Abdera (atomist)	c.469–399 BCE: Hippocrates of Chios (mathematician) 460s–399+ BCE: Theodorus of Cyrene (mathematician) c.460–370 BCE?: Hippocrates of Cos (medicine) 460/55–400 BCE: Thucydides (historian)
451/0–404/3 BCE: Alcibiades	c.450–380 or early 360s BCE: Euclides (Socratic/Megarian)	459/8–*380 BCE: Lysias (orator) *450–386 BCE: Aristophanes (comic poet) 2nd half 5th century BCE: Oinipides of Chios (mathematician)
443–429 BCE: Pericles general of Athens	*445–365 BCE: Antisthenes (Socratic/Cynic)	447–432 BCE: Construction of Parthenon 438 BCE: Statue of Athena Parthenos by Phidias
431–404 BCE: Peloponnesian War	c.430–355 BCE: Aristippus (Socratic/Cyrenaic) 429–347 BCE: Plato	436–338 BCE: Isocrates (orator, teacher) *430–355+ BCE: Xenophon (historian) 420s BCE?: Treatise contained in Derveni Papyrus (Orphic)

History	Philosophy	Sciences, Arts, Religion
411–410 BCE: Rule of Four Hundred in Athens 404–403 BCE: Rule of Thirty Tyrants in Athens	412/03–324/21 BCE: Diogenes of Sinope (the Cynic)	*415–369 BCE: Theaetetus (mathematician)
399 BCE: Trial and execution of Socrates	fl. c.400–350 BCE: Archytus (Pythagorian) 400/380 BCE?: Anonymous *Dissoi Logoi*	391/0–*340 BCE: Eudoxus (mathematician, astronomer) c.397–322 BCE: Aeschines (orator)
	387/6 BCE: Foundation of the Academy 384–322 BCE: Aristotle	384–322 BCE: Demosthenes (orator) c.384–322 BCE: Diocles of Carystus (medicine)
	372/70–288/86 BCE: Theophrastus (Peripatetic)	*370–?300 BCE: Aristoxenus (music)
367–357 BCE: Dionysius II tyrant of Syracuse (in exile 357–344, retired 344 BCE)	c.365–275 BCE: Pyrrho	
359–336 BCE: Philip II king of Macedon	347–339/8 BCE: Speusippus head of Academy 341–270 BCE: Epicurus	344/3–292/1 BCE: Menander (comic poet)
338 BCE: Defeat of Athens by Philip at Chaeronea	339/8–314 BCE: Xenocrates head of Academy 335 BCE: Foundation of the Lyceum	fl. 330 BCE: Callippus (mathematician, astronomer) Athenian calendar reform on basis of Callippus' astronomical theory
336–323 BCE: Alexander the Great, king of Macedon	2nd half 4th century BCE: Eudemus of Rhodes (Peripatetic, student of Aristotle)	
	2nd half 4th–early 3rd century BCE: Stilpo (Megarian)	
	4th–3rd century BCE: Diodorus Cronus and Philo of Megara (Megarians)	
331 BCE: Foundation of Alexandria	334/3–262/1 BCE: Zeno of Citium (founder of Stoicism; arrival in Athens 313 BCE) 331/0–230/29 BCE: Cleanthes (Stoic) c.331–278 BCE: Metrodorus of Lampsacus (Epicurean)	c.330–300 BCE: Derveni Papyrus c.330–260 BCE?: Herophilus (medicine) in Alexandria

History	Philosophy	Sciences, Arts, Religion
323–31 BCE: Hellenistic Period 323 BCE: Alexander's death followed by warfare among his generals and their successors	c.325–235 BCE: Timon (student of Pyrrho) 322/1–288/86 BCE: Theophrastus head of Lyceum fl. c.320–300 BCE: Dicaearchus (Peripatetic)	c.325–250 BCE: Euclid (mathematician)
317–307 BCE: Demetrius of Phaleron (student of Theophrastus) governs Athens	316/15–241/0 BCE: Arcesilaus (Academic) 314/13–270/69 BCE: Polemo head of the Academy 307/6 or 305/4 BCE: Foundation of the Epicurean school (the Garden)	c.315–240 BCE?: Erasistratus (medicine) in Alexandria
301 BCE: "Battle of the kings" at Ipsus Kingdoms of the successors: Antigonids in Macedonia Seleucids in Syria and Babylonia Ptolemies in Egypt	c.300 BCE: Foundation of the Stoa	Early 3rd century BCE: Foundation of the Museum and Library at Alexandria
	288/86–270/68 BCE: Strato head of Lyceum 280/76–208/4 BCE: Chrysippus (Stoic)	First half 3rd century BCE: Aristarchus of Samos (astronomer) *287–212/11 BCE: Archimedes (mathematician) c.276 BCE: *Phaenomena* by Aratus
	270/69–268/64 BCE: Crates head of Academy 270/68–226/24 BCE: Lyco head of Lyceum for 44 years	275/73–*194 BCE: Eratosthenes (scholar and head of Library in Alexandria)
264–241 BCE: First Punic War 247–183/2 BCE: Hannibal (Carthaginian general)	268/64–241/0 BCE: Arcesilaus head of Academy Mid 3rd century BCE: Aristo of Chios (Stoic)	
236–183 BCE: Scipio Africanus, poltician and conqueror of Spain	*230–140s BCE: Diogenes of Seleucia/Babylon (Stoic)	fl. c.205–184 BCE: Plautus (comic poet) 239–169 BCE: Ennius (comic poet)
218–201 BCE: Second Punic War	214/13–130/29 BCE: Carneades the Elder of Cyrene (Academic)	fl. 200 BCE: Apollonius of Perge (mathematician), author of *Conics*

History	Philosophy	Sciences, Arts, Religion
	2nd century BCE: Antipater of Tarsus (Stoic) 185/80–110/9 BCE: Panaetius of Rhodes (Stoic) 2nd century BCE: Critolaus head of Lyceum	c.200/170 BCE: *Successions* by Sotion of Alexandria c.200–118 BCE: Polybius (historian) 185–*159 BCE: Terence (comic poet)
	167/6–137/6 BCE: Carneades head of Academy 155 BCE: Carneades, Diogenes of Babylon, and Critolaus' embassy from Athens to Rome (bringing philosophy to Rome for the first time)	
149–146 BCE: Third Punic War 146 BCE: Destruction of Carthage 146 BCE: Greece becomes a Roman Province		147–127 BCE: Recorded observations of Hipparchus (astronomer)
133 BCE: Tiberius Gracchus, tribune of the people	137/6–131/0 BCE: Carneades the Younger head of Academy c.135–51 BCE: Posidonius (Stoic) c.130–68 BCE: Antiochus of Ascalon (Platonist)	
123 and 122 BCE: Gaius Gracchus, tribune of the people	127/6–110/9 BCE: Clitomachus head of Academy Late 2nd century BCE: Metrodorus of Stratonica (Academic)	
106–43 BCE: Cicero (orator, statesman, and philosopher) 100–44 BCE: Julius Caesar	110/9–84/3 BCE: Philo of Larissa last head of Academy *110–40/35 BCE: Philodemus (Epicurean) *94–50s BCE: Lucretius (poet, Epicurean)	
86 BCE: Sulla conquers Athens	Before 88 BCE?: Antiochus of Ascalon (Platonist) sets up his own Academy in Athens	c.86–35 BCE: Sallust (historian) c.84–54 BCE: Catullus (poet)

History	Philosophy	Sciences, Arts, Religion
	c.70–50 BCE: Andronicus of Rhodes head of Peripatetic school	70–19 BCE: Virgil (poet)
63 BCE–14 CE: Octavian (later Augustus)	1st century BCE?: Andronicus' publication of Aristotle's works 1st century BCE: Aenesidemus (Pyrrhonist) 1st century BCE?: Agrippa (Pyrrhonist)	65–8 BCE: Horace (poet) *64 BCE–21+ CE: Strabo (geographer and historian)
		59 BCE–17 CE: Livy (historian) 48 BCE: First fire in library of Alexandria
31 BCE: Battle of Actium: Egypt becomes a Roman Province 27 BCE: End of the Roman Republic	1st century BCE: Arius Didymus (doxographer) fl. c.25 BCE: Eudorus of Alexandia (Platonist)	1st century BCE–early 1st century CE: Vitruvius (architect)
27 BCE–476 CE **Imperial Rome** 27 BCE–14 CE: Augustus emperor 14–37 CE: Tiberius emperor	c.20 BCE–45 CE: Philo of Alexandria (Judaeus) (philosopher/theologian) 4 BCE/1 CE–65 CE: Seneca (poet and Stoic)	*8/4 BCE: birth of Jesus fl. 14–37 CE?: Celsus (Roman encyclopedist; medicine) d. 36 CE: Thrasyllus (editor of Plato and Democritus)
41–54 CE: Claudius emperor	c.40/50–110+ CE: Dio Chrysostom (orator and Cynic philosopher) c.45–125 CE: Plutarch of Chaeronea (Platonist, biographer, essayist)	*35–90s CE: Quintillian (orator)
54–68 CE: Nero emperor 69–79 CE: Vespasian emperor 70 CE: Titus takes Jerusalem 79 CE: Eruption of Mt. Vesuvius 79–81 CE: Titus emperor	50/60–*135 CE: Epictetus (Stoic) c.50–100 CE: Moderatus (Platonist) Late 1st century CE?: Aëtius (doxographer)	fl. 62 CE: Heron of Alexandria (mathematician), author of Mechanica *56–118+ CE: Tacitus (historian)
81–96 CE: Domitian emperor 95 CE: Domitian expels philosophers from Rome, including Epictetus		fl. c.100 CE: Nicomachus of Gerasa (mathematician and neo-Pythagorean)

History	Philosophy	Sciences, Arts, Religion
117–138 CE: Hadrian emperor	fl. *c*.120 CE: Hierocles (Stoic philosopher), author of *Elements of Ethics* *125–170+ CE: Apuleius (author and philosopher)	115/25–late 180s/early 190s CE: Lucian (satirist) 129–?199/216 CE: Galen (medicine)
138–161 CE: Antoninus Pius emperor	2nd century CE: Numenius (Platonist) 2nd century CE?: Alcinous (Platonist) *c*.150–200 CE: Atticus (Platonist)	fl. 146–*170 CE: Ptolemy (mathematician, astronomer) *150–211/16 CE: Clement of Alexandria (Christian theologian) 2nd century CE?: *Chaldaean Oracles* edited or composed by Julian (the sacred text of middle and late Platonists)
161–180 CE: Marcus Aurelius emperor	176 CE: Marcus Aurelius founds four chairs of philosophy in Athens	*c*.170–236 CE: Bishop Hippolytus (Christian theologian) 175/81 CE: *True Doctrine* by Celsus (anti-Christian) *c*.180 CE: *Attic Nights* by Aulus Gellius
193–211 CE: Septimius Severus emperor	fl. late 2nd century CE: Sextus Empiricus (Pyrrhonist) 198/209 CE: Alexander of Aphrodisias (commentator on Aristotle) appointed public teacher, probably in Athens	*c*.185–254 CE: Origen of Alexandria (Christian philosopher and exegete)
222–235 CE: Alexander Severus emperor	First half 3rd century CE: Diogenes Laertius, author of *Lives of Philosophers* 3rd century CE: Ammonius Saccas (Platonist in Alexandria, teacher of Plotinus, Origen, and Longinus) 205–270 CE: Plotinus (inaugurates Neoplatonism) *c*.213–273 CE: Longinus (rhetorician and philosopher) 234–*305 CE: Porphyry (Neoplatonist) 3rd century CE: Amelius (Platonist) *c*.245–325 CE: Iamblichus (founded a Neoplatonic school in Syria at Apamea)	fl. 250 CE: Diophantus, author of *Arithmetics*

History	Philosophy	Sciences, Arts, Religion
	273 CE: Longinus executed by the Romans	c.260–339 CE: Eusebius of Caesarea (theologian and historian)
284–305 CE: Diocletian emperor of Eastern empire 286–305 CE: Maximian rules West	c.300 CE: Porphyry publishes Plotinus' *Enneads*	
306–337 CE: Constantine the Great emperor (converts to Christianity) 313 CE: Edict of Milan (toleration of Christianity)	c.317–388 CE: Themistius (commentator on Aristotle)	fl. 320 CE: Pappus of Alexandria (mathematician)
	fl. c.350 CE: Calcidius (Christian translator and commentator on Plato's *Timaeus*)	c.328–373 CE: Athanasius bishop of Alexandria 329–389 CE: Gregory of Nazianz (theologian) c.330–379 CE: Basil of Caesarea (theologian) c.330–395 CE: Gregory of Nyssa (theologian)
361–363 CE: Reign of Julian (the Apostate), restoration of paganism		
379–395 CE: Reign of Theodosius 391 CE: Paganism outlawed	354–430 CE: Augustine, author of *Confessions* (c.397–400 CE) and *City of God* (c.413–426 CE)	374–397 CE: Ambrose bishop of Milan 398–403 CE: John Chrysostom bishop of Constantinople
411 CE: Alaric, king of the Visigoths, sacks Rome	After 400 CE: Neoplatonic schools in Athens and Alexandria 415 CE: Hypatia (mathematician and philosopher) murdered by Christians in Alexandria d. 432 CE (at a great age): Plutarch of Athens (Neoplatonist) d. c.437 CE: Syrianus (Neoplatonist) 412–485 CE: Proclus (Neoplatonist)	fl. early 5th century CE: Stobaeus (anthologist)

History	Philosophy	Sciences, Arts, Religion
455 CE: Rome sacked by Gaiseric, king of the Vandals	*440–517+ CE: Ammonius (Alexandria, teacher of Damascius, Philoponus, and Simplicius) 5th century CE: Hierocles of Alexandria (Neoplatonist)	
476 CE: Fall of the Western Empire Romulus Augustulus deposed by Odoacer, king of the Heruli	c.480–524 CE: Boethius (commentator and author of *Consolation of Philosophy*)	
493–526 CE: Theodoric Ostrogothic king of Italy	c.490–560 CE: Simplicius (Neoplatonist) c.490–570s CE: Philoponus (Christianized school in Alexandria) 495/505–565+ CE: Olympiodorus (Platonist)	
527–565 CE: Justinian emperor in Constantinople 529 CE: Justinian closes the Neoplatonic school in Athens	529 CE: Neoplatonists in Athens, including Damascius, Simplicius, and Priscian, flee to Persia (Ctesiphon) 532 CE: Simplicius' commentaries on Aristotle probably all written after this date 6th century CE: David and Elias (Alexandria) 2nd half 6th century CE: Anonymous *Introduction to Philosophy of Plato*	
570?–632 CE: Muhammad, prophet of Islam		c.580–662 CE: Maximus the Confessor (theologian)
7th century CE: Arab conquest of Syria, Jerusalem, Egypt, and elsewhere		c.640 CE: Destruction of library at Alexandria

c.   circa: around this/these date(s)
*   date approximate
?   date(s) uncertain or disputed
+   sometime after date listed
s   decade of
/   sometime within dates listed
fl. floruit: date(s) when person was active

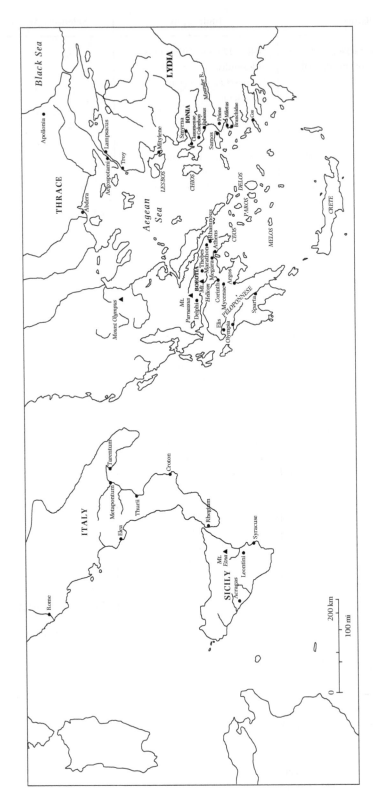

Map 1 The Greek World (6th–5th centuries BCE)

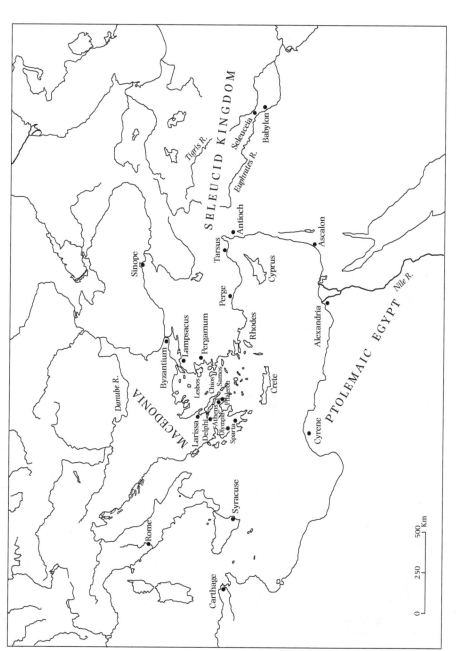

Map 2 The Hellenistic Period (323–31 BCE)

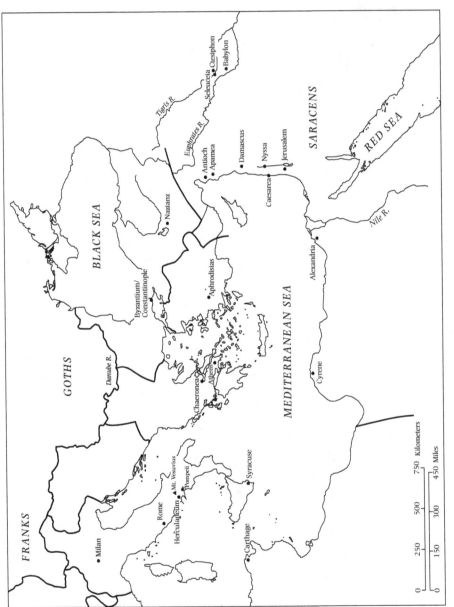

Map 3 The Late Roman Empire

General Introduction

I Introduction

> That it [wisdom] is not a productive science is also clear from those who began to philosophize, for it is because of wondering that men began to philosophize and do so now. First they wondered at the *difficulties* close at hand; then, advancing little by little, they discussed *difficulties* also about greater matters, for example, about the changing attributes of the Moon and of the Sun and of the stars, and about the generation of the universe. Now a man who is perplexed and wonders considers himself ignorant (whence a lover of myth, too, is in a sense a philosopher, for a myth is composed of wonders), so if indeed they philosophized in order to avoid ignorance, it is evident that they pursued science in order to understand and not in order to use it for something else. This is confirmed by what happened; for it was when almost all the necessities of life were supplied, both for comfort and for leisure, that such thinking began to be sought. Clearly, then, we do not seek this science for any other need; but just as a man is said to be free if he exists for his own sake and not for the sake of somebody else, so this alone of all the science is free, for only this science exists for its own sake.[1]

According to Aristotle, philosophy is unique among the many things that people think about, because philosophy alone is not dedicated to, and was not born out of, the desire to solve any practical problems. Instead, it derives from our sense of wonder. We observe the world about us, and as we think about all that we see and how it works . . . we find ourselves surrounded by *wonders*. But to find the world *wonderful*, as Aristotle says, is also to recognize ourselves as *ignorant*. We are rarely filled with wonder by those things we all understand fully. Our reactions to such things, on the contrary, are to take them for granted – we do not regard them with wonder; indeed, we mostly do not regard them at all. We simply use such things when we have need of them, and the rest of the time ignore them. Philosophy begins, then, not with what we *do* understand . . . but with what we *don't*. And it begins with the reaction of wonder, which in part reflects our own recognition that we do *not* understand something that we find wonderful.

1 Aristotle, *Metaphysics* I.2.982b12–28; trans. Apostle and Gerson.

II The History of Ancient Philosophy

What is now known as "ancient Greek philosophy" consists in writings by (and in some cases, writings about) thinkers who lived and worked in Greece or in Greek colonies all around the Mediterranean, extending roughly through the period from 600 BCE to 600 CE. In some cases, those whose work we include in this book were not Greek, and did not write in Greek, but in Latin; even so, the influence of the Greek thinkers on such writers is obvious.

Plainly, the people whose work we study in this book made their contributions a very long time ago, and their work has come down to us, in many cases, only in very fragmentary form, and in many other cases only via copies of copies of copies of the originals. The earliest originals were mostly written on papyrus, a kind of paper that is made from the Egyptian plant of the same name. After each piece was prepared in a more or less standardized size, it would be rolled into a scroll, which the Greeks called a *biblos* (book) from which our words "bibliography" and "Bible" derive.

Early in the Christian era, access to papyrus became more difficult in the West (possibly due to problems in Egypt), and so authors began to use goatskin or sheepskin, which was cut into sheets that would then be bound together in some way – hence our present "book" form. This technique was created in Pergamum, in what is now Turkey, and our word "parchment" comes from the Latin name for this city.

But papyrus and parchment, though quite durable, are biodegradable – so most papyri and parchment books from ancient times (other than a few that were preserved by very peculiar coincidences) rotted into dust long ago. Authors would write on these materials, but then these scrolls and books would be copied by hand (usually by slaves trained for such duties), and the copies would be available for students, or even for purchase. Great libraries came to exist through the purchases and collections of wealthy patrons, and those who gained the patrons' permission might come and make still further copies of the works there collected. Although many of these libraries were later destroyed (by natural disasters, such as the eruption of Vesuvius, by accidents, such as fires, and by human design, for example in wars or anti-intellectual pogroms), many copies were made of the most popular works, which is why as much as we have now has managed to survive. But those that have survived are mostly the result of very long traditions of copies – with very few exceptions, the earliest of these we now have available date to no earlier than the ninth century CE, and most date to several centuries later than that.

Once the printing press was invented, of course, it was possible to regularize the transmission of these materials, and scholars began to make great "editions" of the ancient works, based upon the different manuscripts available to them. After so many years of copying, however, these manuscripts might have slight differences – sometimes on points of significance to understanding the author's original intent. Later editors have had to decide which of the variant texts provided in the earliest manuscripts are most likely the correct ones, and this work continues even today. Most of the Greek texts scholars now study are the result of efforts (from the fifteenth century to the present) to compile the best and most accurate renderings on the basis of all of the known manuscripts of the various ancient works.

In addition to compiling editions of the ancient works in their original language, translations of these texts also began to appear, first into Latin and then into other European languages. (Other much earlier translations of Greek works can be found in several Middle Eastern languages, and in some cases provide our only access to otherwise lost Greek works.) Translations into English were first offered mainly in the late eighteenth century, and new translations of most of these works (sometimes several of them) now appear in each generation. By now, several translations of everything included herein can be found, and those who cannot read these texts in their original language would do well to consult a number of different translations, to see how great the difference can be in trying to render the sense of the ancient languages into contemporary English. Often, the differences in these translations are motivated by differences in the translators' interpretations of basic issues in the original text. Noting these differences can often allow a reader some insight into the various positions that have been taken within scholarly controversies about the text. There are obvious advantages enjoyed by those who can read the original languages – but even so, scholars can find themselves deeply divided over the specific meaning or intent of some ancient text. These problems, of course, are amplified for those who have to rely on a modern translation.

Other problems of interpretation derive from the fact that we do not have complete sets of works from any ancient authors other than Plato and Plotinus – and in the case of the former, there are debates over the authenticity of some of the works that have come down to us in his name. Only in the case of Plotinus can we be confident that we have all of his work, and that *only* his work is included in the body of writings attributed to him. In some cases, we only have ancient citations of an author, but nothing of his works has survived. In other cases, we have small fragments of work. It seems likely that only about 10 percent of the philosophical work done in the ancient Greco-Roman world is actually still available to us. In the case of some of the most important authors, the fact that work is missing makes interpretation of the philosopher's thought especially difficult. For example, in the case of Epicurus, we actually have only about 3 percent of the work attributed to him from antiquity. In the case of the great Stoic philosopher, Chrysippus, we are told that he wrote the equivalent of more than 8,400 modern pages of writing – yet we now have only fragments of his writings, and not a single complete work. We have no guarantee, moreover, that even the fragments that have survived – in the case of Chrysippus and every other ancient author – have been recorded entirely faithfully or accurately. And again, what has come down to us is the result of generations and generations of copied materials, where the abilities of those doing the copying may not always have been entirely reliable.

Thus it is that ancient scholarly work in this area is much like the work of archaeologists, who must reconstruct artifacts from small and disconnected bits of material. In some cases, we can confidently predict that scholarly debates about the meanings of these materials can never be resolved – or at any rate, will not be resolved unless and until some important new discovery is made by which lingering questions may be answered. Even so, among the texts that have survived, a certain body of work has enjoyed the attention of generations of scholars. In this collection, we present selections from the best known and most widely read authors and works from this era.

Every modern Western academic discipline derives from the works of these thinkers, including mathematics, all of the natural sciences, all of the social sciences, literary criticism, rhetoric, historiography, theology, and all of the fields still counted as philosophy. Obviously, there have been many significant developments in all of these areas since the time of the Greeks. Even so, it is not difficult to trace every modern academic discipline back to its roots in the Greek world.

III The Origins of Natural Science

It is often said that the origins of natural science may be found in ancient Greek philosophy, because of a certain lack of coherence – as well as a lack of authority – in ancient Greek religion. There is more than a little truth in this claim. The early Greeks certainly did have religious beliefs, but their religion placed greater emphasis on festivals and rituals than on any systematic theology or canonical sets of required beliefs. Unlike most of the rest of the world, the Greeks always regarded the stories that supplied the intellectual components of their religion with a certain degree of flexibility and without absolute conviction. These stories they called *muthoi* (myths), which literally means "stories," and which were generally regarded as some mix of supposition, edifying tale, and pure fiction. Only later did the Greeks come to regard those who doubted some detail or other as impious or offensive to the gods. In the beginning, the myths were simply tales told from one generation to the next, whose details could be modified along the way, as each teller found some new purpose or interest to include.

But this very flexibility not only allowed the stories to be subjected to critical scrutiny, it actually encouraged such scrutiny, by not requiring that they be accepted uncritically: give a populace the freedom to think for themselves, and that is precisely what they will do! Moreover, the myths themselves provided only very murky accounts (however colorful) of the origins of the world and of humankind, and so the Greeks could hardly look to these stories for convincing accounts of the most basic human questions: How did everything begin? How did human beings come into being? What is the meaning or purpose of anything?

Instead of accepting the dictates of religious authorities, then – since there really were none with the appropriate sort of authority to enforce the acceptance of specific beliefs – and instead of looking to their myths to provide answers to the most basic questions, the Greeks sought to understand the world in the ways we have now come to understand as scientific. The earliest Greek thinkers, and those who followed their interests later, became known among the Greeks themselves as the *phusiologoi* – those who argued or spoke about or explained (*logos*) nature (*phusis*). Just as we do, the Greeks distinguished the natural from the artificial, but this distinction, they quickly realized, may itself be questioned – just as birds build nests and other animals create other sorts of homes for themselves, might not some of human artifice actually reflect something deep within *human nature*?

The early Greek *phusiologoi* began, as Aristotle tells us, with wonder: they wondered whether nature was something we humans could understand and explain. The religious answer to such a question, for the most part, is "No": nature, instead, is the product of a being or beings so beyond human comprehension as to preclude any but the most superficial understanding by us. But the early Greek philosophers thought otherwise. They began by hypothesizing that the whole of nature was not a *chaos* (a word we get directly from ancient Greek), but instead a *cosmos* – that is, the universe conceived as orderly and unified. So one of the foundational questions of ancient Greek inquiry is this: How or in what way is the *cosmos* ordered? What orders it?

Even to get to this point is a remarkable achievement, for surely just observing the natural world does not necessarily convince one that the entirety of nature is *orderly*. It is true that observations of the movements of heavenly bodies would (mostly) give the impression of orderliness, but in other areas, nature seems much more chaotic – in the inevitability of death to living things, and in all the indefinite varieties of things that can kill them, in earthquakes and other natural disasters, in the unpredictability of the weather (Greece, being a maritime culture, was always painfully aware of how the sea could quickly become dangerous), and so on. But the early Greek thinkers were convinced that despite the enormous diversities in nature, and despite occasionally baffling occurrences, some order could be perceived, if only we look deeply enough into the underlying structure or structures of things.

Two linked issues soon became the primary focuses of early Greek philosophy: cosmogeny (or cosmogony) – from the words *cosmos* and *genesis* (birth or coming into being) – and cosmology (*cosmos* plus *logos*), the attempt to provide unified accounts of the structure of the *cosmos*. Not surprisingly, some of the earliest Greek thinkers tended to think that the present structure of the *cosmos* was a direct effect and reflection of its causal origins. At the beginning of ancient Greek thought, no significant distinctions were made between those parts of nature and the *cosmos* that were alive, and those we now suppose are not alive. The effect of this sometimes makes it seem as if the earliest thinkers supposed that the *cosmos* and/or all of its parts were somehow alive (a view generally regarded as quite primitive, known as "hylozoism") – and this supposition gets some support from the fact that the Greek word for nature (*phusis*) actually derives from the verb *phuein*, which means "to grow." But precisely because there was no clear distinction made between living and non-living things, it may be somewhat misleading to think of the earliest Greeks as hylozoists. After all, in order to think of the *cosmos* or all of its parts as "living things," one would need to have some concept of the very difference between *living* and *non-living* that these early thinkers seemed not to have!

Because the earliest theories of these matters inevitably identify structural foundations that are beneath the highly varied surfaces of things, the Greeks also soon found themselves confronting the distinction between the *appearance* of things and the *reality* of them. Many examples from sensation and perception, such as optical illusions or echoes, can convince us that the actual way we experience something may not reveal the way that thing *really is*. A problem that emerges as a result of these considerations is, then, to what degree we can rely on our senses, to tell us about the *cosmos*, and to what degree we must rely instead on pure theory, or what our own reasoning produces – even if that reasoning is at odds with our perceptions of things. From this same set of concerns, then, arises one of the areas still central to philosophy – epistemology, the study of knowledge and other forms of cognition. What do we (already) know, if anything? What (else) can we know? In what does knowledge consist, and what conditions must be satisfied for knowledge to be possible?

The earliest Greeks sought to understand the underlying unity of the *cosmos* in terms of some material, out of which all of the varieties of nature were formed. Debates among these philosophers developed because whatever substance or substances they hypothesized as fundamental, however much these substances might seem to help to explain the composition of things, always turned out to be inadequate to explain all that needed to be explained – particularly the many ways in which things can *change*. (Modern physics continues to develop such explanations to further and further levels, and does not yet seem entirely able to provide all of the explanation needed, though it has come a very long way from its ancient roots in the *phusiologoi*.) Moreover, along the way, philosophers began to notice that other forms of explanation were not only possible – they also seemed to be required for complete understandings of the *cosmos* and of nature generally.

Arguably, Aristotle was the Greek philosopher who was able to make the most sense of the varieties of explanation that would be required. So, for example, Aristotle complained about his predecessors that their theories were inadequate because they failed to recognize all of the most basic principles of explanation (which have come to be known as Aristotle's "four causes," though they are really more like four principles of explanation: matter, form, cause ("efficient cause"), and function ("final cause")). Even if we could know for certain what the underlying matter of a thing was (bronze, for example), that would not help us understand what *sort*, what *kind* of thing it was (for example, a statue of Zeus); for this, we would need to identify its Form or "formal cause," which identifies what a thing *is*, as opposed to what it is *made of*. Similarly, formal explanations – explanations of what a thing *is* – in no way provide answers to questions about the thing's causal ancestry, about how the thing came into being (that is, its cause, or "efficient cause"). These questions are related, of course – full understanding of what a thing is may also inform us about its causes in virtue of some natural laws, according to which things of such-and-such sorts come into being in certain specific ways: human beings come into being through sexual reproduction; trees come into being from seeds, and so forth. But complete explanations of things must include not only material explanations, but also formal and causal ones. And to this list, Aristotle (now very controversially) added a fourth, that of natural functioning (the "final cause") – what does the thing *do*? How does it characteristically function? One who knows full well that trees are made of wood may still be wholly ignorant of the ways in which trees function (e.g. by photosynthesis and by capillary action to bring nutrients up from the soil below).

Prior to Aristotle, the earlier Greek thinkers tended to offer explanations of the *cosmos* in terms of some, but not all, of these explanatory principles. As we will see, the earliest thinkers tended to explain things in terms of matter and (sometimes) cause. Later developments tended to focus more on form (as in Plato's famous theory of Forms, by which he sought to explain all things in terms of what they are, rather than in terms of what they are made of, or where they come from).

IV The Origins of Ethics, Psychology, and Political Theory

Aristotle was not the first to think of natural things as having certain natural functions. But what is the natural function of a human being? Do we even have such a function? If we do, then we might suppose that seeking to live in accordance with that natural function will be important for us, and that those who fail to live in accordance with that function will to that degree lead lives that are inherently stunted or frustrated in some way. The question of our own function, then, is critical to our understanding of our place in nature, in the cosmic order of things.

In order to understand our place in the world, the Greeks made observations about what made human beings *different* from other things in the world. One thing we can notice that distinguishes us from many other things is that we are *social* beings, preferring for various reasons to live together in groups. Other animals also do this, of course – and early Greek observers were struck by this similarity, and tended (apparently, generally correctly) to understand this commonality in terms of the basic needs of survival and flourishing. We do not do as well living on our own, and the same can be said for many other species.

But despite this similarity, human beings are still different from other creatures. Some natural differences (being both featherless and bipedal, for example), though absolutely distinguishing us from all other animals, do not seem to get to the most fundamental way or ways that we differ from other living things. What struck the Greeks as the true source of our fundamental difference was our capacity to *reason* – this is why Aristotle actually defines human beings as "rational animals." Our capacity for reasoning, moreover, is also not something that is primarily solitary – we communicate and share our reasoning with others in our social groups via language.

In fact, the Greeks did not clearly distinguish between reasoning, as such, and the language by which we communicate it – they used the same word to refer to both reason and language: *logos*. Reasoning about the *cosmos* (cosmology), accordingly, is one of the distinctively human things that we do. But we also reason socially, and we also reason *about* our social relationships with others. Is there some ultimate purpose or function in the way we reason and communicate? Is social interaction itself just a manifestation of something basic in human functioning?

Because we are social animals, we have a propensity to come into conflict with other members of our species. Were we disinclined to interact with one another, conflict might only arise if we were (unnaturally) brought into contact or forced into it. But because we live in groups, conflict seems inevitable. How, then, should we resolve the problems that conflicts can engender among us? Again, ancient Greek religion was poorly suited to provide authoritative answers to such questions (and later in this book, in Plato's *Euthyphro*, you will encounter a very strange Greek who thinks that Greek religion *does* provide the relevant answers, and as a result faces withering criticisms for the confusions that idea produces). From very early times in Greece, as a result, the shaping of social and political systems intended to manage the potential for conflict was a serious concern of intelligent people – and the idea of democracy, to which so many owe such a debt in the present day, is one of many Greek innovations in this area.

But might there not be a more fundamental question: What exactly is the most basic purpose or function of our lives, a purpose or function that social and political systems will, in the best instances, assist us in pursuing? Other cultures, with strong religious authorities providing the answers to such questions, have tended to formulate such answers in terms of rules of conduct – rules the religious authorities claim are mandated by God (or the gods), and which mere human beings are in no position to question or contravene (without predictable sanctions by God or the gods). The Greeks, by contrast, from the very beginning tended to focus less on the formulation of enforceable rules than on various understandings of what sorts of characteristics human beings should have, if they are to have good lives. We can see some of this even in the earliest works of ancient Greek authors. The characterization of the great Achilles in Homer's *Iliad*, for example, seems intended (among many things) to call our attention to the ways in which he is as great as he is – and also to the ways in which that greatness failed in certain obvious and painful ways to secure for him a life we would choose to emulate. Achilles did and did not lead an enviable life; so what would a fully enviable life consist in? What sort of person would one have to be to have a truly enviable life? And once we have an answer to that question, we can then return to the more broadly social and political questions: What sorts of social and political rules and structures would have the best chance of creating and sustaining enviable lives for those within them?

The most basic question of what makes an enviable life can be answered, obviously, in different ways. One might think, for example, that what makes a life enviable is simply the amassing of whatever one might desire – wealth, the satisfaction of appetites such as hunger, thirst, and lust, and the power over other human beings that would be required to amass and maintain the material necessities of such a life. But Homer's *Iliad* and many other Greek literary works, even before the philosophers got started, called this idea into question. In Book IX of the *Iliad*, Odysseus comes to Achilles and offers all of these sorts of things to Achilles in superabundance, but Achilles balks, recognizing that such things do not necessarily make one's life meaningful or secure. Later writers note that the more material wealth one requires, the more *insecure* one becomes – because one then has to take pains to preserve the great wealth on which one has come to rely.

By the time we get to the so-called classical period of Greece,[2] the Greeks generally agreed that our primary purpose in life was to live well and to be happy (*eudaimōn*), where by "being happy" they did not have transitory, purely subjective enjoyment in mind, but rather understood the state as one that was objectively good, and thus enviable for the right reasons. Drug addicts high on their drugs may *feel* happy, but cannot be happy in this objective sense – no one would reasonably envy the life-condition of the intoxicated addict, and we would prefer to live with less enjoyment, but greater self-control. The main question for Greek ethics, then, was: What sort of person should we seek to be or become, if we are to flourish and be happy in this objective way? But other questions also arise. For example, what is the relationship between being *good* and being *happy*? Some ancient Greeks questioned if there was any connection at all between morality and happiness, most notably some of the Sophists. But others, including particularly Socrates and all who followed him (not just Plato and Aristotle, but all the other later schools of Greek philosophers), emphatically argued that being ethically good, or virtuous, was the *only* way one could hope to be or to become objectively happy. And they emphasized that virtue was conducive to happiness precisely because it was, if rightly understood, the very actualization of our true human potential and natural function – the ultimate realization of our rational nature. To be happy, for a human being, was thus to be fully rational; and full rationality was thus both the guide to and the ultimate aim of the most ethical life.

The Greek notion of rationality, moreover, was not – as it is sometimes misunderstood by moderns – an ideal that wholly neglected or nullified the other aspects of human psychology. Socrates is sometimes still thought to have been guilty of such a blinkered version of what is called "intellectualism," which is roughly the view that the only thing that counts in a good life is intellect, but recent scholarship seems to be moving away from that assessment even in the case of Socrates. Plato and Aristotle, too, have sometimes been characterized as "intellectualists" because of their emphasis on the role of reason and rationality in the good and happy life. But close scrutiny of the ways in which these philosophers actually recommend we live the life of reason shows no failure to recognize the important role of our non-rational aspects, such as our appetites and passions. Socrates, Plato, and Aristotle all stress that we should not only recognize the effects of these elements of our psychology, but also understand how a successful life must achieve a kind of balance between our own internal and sometimes competing interests. Indeed, Plato famously argues, in the *Republic*, that justice consists in psychic harmony, the balancing of the rational and non-rational elements of our psychology.

Unlike the conceptions of morality that came after them, which were more indebted to the Judeo-Christian religious traditions than to Greek philosophy, the philosophers of Greece conceived of ethics not just in terms of our natural pursuit of happiness (rather than in divinely commanded duties and/or avoidance of sin), but also in terms of those personal characteristics they perceived as most conducive to becoming and being happy. This style of ethics, which for a long time afterwards was almost entirely abandoned and forgotten, is called "virtue theory," and has recently enjoyed a very strong resurgence of interest among philosophers. Instead of attempting to articulate first principles by which our moral obligations may be

---

2 Normally dated from 480 BCE to 323 BCE, the former date being when the Greeks finally repelled the Persian invasion of Greece, and the latter date being the date of Alexander the Great's death. Readers of this work might argue that we should list the end of this period a year later, in 322 BCE, the year Aristotle died.

systematized, the Greeks instead conceived of ethical theory in terms of human psychology and development, and sought to articulate which character traits could be developed on the basis of which the excellent or virtuous person would reliably exercise correct judgment in all cases. Rather than understanding a virtuous person simply as one who acted in accordance with the right rules of behavior (whether these be commanded by God or inferred from some first principle or principles), the virtue theorist understands right actions as *whatever* the virtuous person would do, in the relevant circumstances. In virtue theory, ethically relevant circumstances are innumerably many and indefinitely varied, and so few if any exceptionless rules can be given to guide all behavior under all circumstances. No doubt some reason for the Greek emphasis on rationality derives from this consequence of virtue theory: because the exercise of judgment is always required in the ethical life, and no simple (or even complex) rule-governed system can ever be wholly adequate, it is *ethically* required that we develop and exercise the intellect by which we make ethical judgments. The virtue theory approach also has important consequences in the ways in which the Greeks approached questions of political and educational theory. In politics, the primary concerns were not based on notions of obligation (such as rights), but instead upon the development of systems that would conduce to the development and practice of virtue. In education, too, the emphasis was more on the development of skills of judgment, and less on fact-learning or socialization by rules.

The Greek world changed greatly after Aristotle's time – in some ways, it had already undergone the very changes that would influence later thinkers, and it actually took philosophy some time to "catch up." The great power of democratic Athens, with its proud emphasis on freedom of speech, was waning – partly, no doubt, as a result of its aggressive and expansionist ways in the fifth century BCE, which led to its defeat by the Spartans and her allies in the Peloponnesian War, a defeat from which Athens really never fully recovered. Then, with the rise of Macedon, Athens increasingly found itself marginalized – though still a center for intellectuals and artists of all kinds, its time of political and military influence in the region was quickly passing into history. Increasingly, Greek philosophy confronted a world in which the pursuit of happiness seemed better focused on adapting to an intractable world, rather than on shaping that world in accordance to our will. Some of the philosophers after Aristotle (for example the Epicureans) found the primary operations of the world to be entirely random – merely the product of chaotic collisions of atoms in endless motion. Accordingly, the pursuit of happiness in such a world emphasizes reshaping our will in such a way as to eliminate or reduce as many of our desires as we possibly can, for in a random world there can be no guarantees that our desires will be satisfied. Others (for example the Stoics) went in the very opposite direction, and thought the world was bound by the adamant grip of necessity. In a deterministic world, all we can really shape with our will is our will itself, and so the Stoic Sage is one who seeks to mirror the necessities of nature with his own will – he wills all and only what nature makes necessary. These and other later philosophical movements reflect a conscious need for coping strategies – ways to deal with a world that seems indifferent, or even hostile, to our well-being.

V Cynicism, Epicureanism, Stoicism, Skepticism and Other Terms You Do Not Yet Understand

One delightful curiosity that readers of this collection will discover is how little certain terms and ideas that have come down to us from the Greeks really have anything much to do with their actual ancient antecedents. We will not here make any attempt to survey every possible one of these, but we encourage the reader to think about what is now meant by "Platonic love," when reading Plato's *Symposium*. What Plato has in mind in describing the erotic ascent to the Beautiful Itself plainly has virtually nothing to do with "Platonic relationships" or any such notion. The only connection, it seems, is that the Platonic lover that Plato himself describes is not focused upon sex or sexuality; the Platonic lover, however, is charged with and driven obsessively by erotic power – hardly "just friends" with the object of his love.

As you will see, each of the "schools" of philosophy listed in the title just above: Cynicism, Epicureanism, Stoicism, and Skepticism, are actually very poorly represented by our current uses of these terms – Diogenes became known as a "cynic" as a result of his having been called (perhaps by Plato) *kunikos* ("doglike"). He was highly critical of others, but was anything but "cynical" in our sense of the term. The Epicureans actually advocated the very *opposite* of excess in feasting and drinking, and most certainly did not savor luxuries; instead, they prescribed the most minimalistic of tastes, and would thoroughly approve of the man who might be completely satisfied by a diet of bread and water, and a life of similar simplicity in all other areas. The Stoics, too, did not emphasize passionless endurance of suffering so much as a profound understanding of nature, so that we might align our will with the way things are. In ancient Stoicism, the world was not merely to be calmly endured when it did not please us; we were supposed to learn how always to be pleased with it! Finally, we now think of a skeptic as one who doubts or disbelieves something that others do believe. Ancient skeptics also doubted the dogmas of others, but they did so only because they regarded any belief as a potential source of disappointment – and so they sought to avoid all such disappointment by withholding assent from *anything at all*, if possible. Modern skepticisms, by contrast, are usually motivated by reasons having to do with the evaluation of evidence only. In these and many other cases, as you read this book you will often begin with a sense of recognition, or of expectation, only to find that the ancient sources of many modern terms and ideas are actually quite different from what they have become today.

Part I

The Presocratics and Sophists

Introduction

The first group of philosophers to appear in Greece has come to be known as the "Presocratics," a term that is both misleading and uninformative. It is misleading because some of the Presocratics are actually not pre-Socratic, but were Socrates' contemporaries; it is uninformative, because there is nothing particularly unified about the philosophers unified under that title. The first of these philosophers got their start in Greek colonies in Asia Minor (now Turkey), and might best be thought of as early theoretical scientists. The works of these thinkers – or, at any rate, of those who wrote works – now survives mainly in fragments that appear as quotations in the writings of later philosophers or collectors (called "doxographers") of the works of earlier thinkers. Other evidence derives from (sometimes controversial or arguably tendentious) testimony given in later authors, perhaps without direct quotation offered. Scholars struggle to piece together the thinking of the different Presocratic authors from these fragments and testimonia.

The Sophists – most of them contemporaries of Socrates – were a group of paid teachers who often continued the scientific inquiries of their Presocratic predecessors, but who also added to these subjects those of political or forensic rhetoric, ethics, and political theory. Like the Presocratics, the Sophists – though generally vilified by Plato and Aristotle – did not present a unified view of their subjects, but were instead often highly individualistic.

Although certainly interesting in their own right, studying the Presocratics adds important insight into the intellectual milieu within which the really great thinkers of ancient Greece emerged. It is certainly no overstatement to say that much of what we find in Plato, in particular, is intended to supply some response to, or is influenced by, one or more of the Presocratics or Sophists.

Unless otherwise noted, the translations and commentaries that follow are all original, prepared by Nicholas D. Smith expressly for this collection.

1

The Milesians

The earliest Greek philosophers came from Miletus, one of the Greek colonies in the eastern part of the Greek world – the area called Ionia, on the western coastal regions of Asia Minor in the area that is now within the modern nation of Turkey. These Milesian philosophers wondered at how the great multiplicity and variety of nature might comprise a *cosmos*, which, as we said in the General Introduction, is the world conceived as a unified and orderly arrangement of parts. How or in what sense is the world a *cosmos*, rather than (another important Greek word) a *chaos*? Many things might exist within a *chaos*, but no sense could be made of them; no understanding of a chaotic world would be possible. Any wonder we might experience in witnessing events in such a world, accordingly, could never be relieved – in such a world, we would be doomed forever to the ignorance reflected in wonder. Indeed, we could not exist in such a world even to wonder at it – for the organization of our own bodily systems surely could not survive in such a world. The earliest Greek philosophers, accordingly, attempted to discern the underlying order within this *cosmos*.

Part of what makes the world *seem* chaotic, of course, is the fact that *things change*. Living plants grow out of what appeared to be dead earth; a bowl of water evaporates, leaving it empty; the heavenly bodies move through the skies, and so on. But how is change possible? The world would seem indeed to be chaotic if nothing remained stable – if, that is, there was nothing that remained in some sense *the same* before, during, and after the change. The earliest Greek thinkers, then, attempted to make sense of the *cosmos* and its changes by trying to recognize an enduring order deriving from some fundamental material, common to all of the great variety of nature. Thales of Miletus is generally credited with being the first philosopher.

Thales of Miletus

Thales left no writings behind; indeed, according to Diogenes Laertius' *Lives and Opinions of Eminent Philosophers*, he may never have written philosophy at all, though in some accounts he wrote two treatises (DL I.23). Ancient stories about Thales appear to confirm Aristotle's account of the birth of philosophy: Thales seems to have been quite the "wonderer," and though entirely capable of turning his impressive intellectual skills to profitable enterprises preferred a life of contemplating the wonders of the world.

I.1 Plato, *Theaetetus* 174a4–9 (= DK 11A9[1])
While Thales was doing astronomy and gazing up, he fell into a well. Some witty and clever Thracian servant-girl gave him a hard time, they say, because he was eager to know the things in the heavens, but couldn't see what was right at his feet.

The story is so familiar it has become a stereotype: the absent-minded professor. The point of the story (and the stereotype) is obviously that philosophical wonderers lack common sense. But another story shows that Thales' life of wonder was the product of choice, rather than the result of an inability to turn his attention to personal profit, as most people do.

I.2 Aristotle, *Politics* I.11.1259a9–18 (= DK 11A10; trans. Apostle and Gerson)
There is the story about the device which Thales of Miletus used to make money. This device is attributed to him because of his wisdom, but it happens to have universal application. He was reproached for his poverty, which indicated that philosophy was of no benefit to man. But, the story goes, from his knowledge of astronomy he perceived, while it was still winter, the coming of a great harvest of olives in the coming season, and, having procured a small sum of money, he made a deposit for the use of all of the olive presses of Miletus and Chios, which he rented at a low price since no one bid against him. When the harvest time came and there was a sudden and simultaneous demand for the use of the presses, he let these at whatever price he wished and made a fortune, thus pointing out that philosophers can easily become wealthy if they wish but that wealth is not their main pursuit in life.

A somewhat similar story of Thales making practical application of his philosophizing can be found in Herodotus (*Histories* 1.74 = DK 11A5), where Thales' prediction of an eclipse turned the tide of a military battle.

Whatever Thales' ingenuity in such things may have been, no doubt his most important contributions to the history of philosophy were in his attempts to understand the *cosmos* in terms of postulating water as the material first principle of all things. Aristotle, who thinks that complete explanations are not possible in only material terms, regarded as quite primitive theories of the sort Thales developed, but it is clear at least that Aristotle credits Thales with being the first and the founder of this sort of approach.

I.3 Aristotle, *Metaphysics* I.3.983b6–27 (= DK 11A2, excerpted; trans. Apostle and Gerson)
Most of those who first philosophized regarded the material kinds of principles as the principles of all things; for that of which things consist, and the first from which things come to be and into which they are finally resolved after destruction (this being the persisting *substance* of the thing, while the thing changes in its affections[2]), this they

---

1 References to DK are to H. Diels and W. Kranz, *Die Fragmente der Vorsokratiker*, 6th edn. (Berlin, 1952), the standard collection of fragments and testimonia, and indicate where a given citation appears in this edition.
2 By "affections," Aristotle means the often transitory properties that something just happens to have, which do not determine the exact sort of thing it is. The opposite of an "affection," in this sense, would be the thing's *essence*.

say is the element and the principle of things; and because of this they think that nothing is generated and nothing perishes, since such a nature is always preserved. [...] For there must be some nature, either one or more than one, which is preserved and from which the others are generated.

However, these thinkers do not all agree as to the number and kinds of such principles. Thales, the founder of such philosophy, said that this principle was *water* (and on account of this he also declared that the earth rests on water), perhaps coming to this belief by observing that all food is moist and that heat itself is generated from the moist and is kept alive by it (and that from which things are generated is the principle of all); and he came to this belief both because of this fact and because the seeds of all things have a moist nature, and water is the principle of the nature of moist things.

Much of Aristotle's testimony here is his own speculation as to what may have led Thales to his surmise that the first principle of everything is water. Whether or not Aristotle is right about this, it seems at least clear that Thales was indeed the first to try to explicate the *cosmos* in terms of an underlying unity of matter. Water really does seem a likely candidate, in some ways, as not only so important for life (as Aristotle notes), but also as the one natural substance readily observable in all three of the states of matter: solid, liquid, and gas. Of course, much remains *unexplained* by hypothesizing water to be the first material principle (e.g. colors). In particular, it seems obvious that another sort of principle must be introduced to explain why water undergoes the changes that it does, or what makes it do so – something Aristotle calls an "efficient cause," and which we would now call a causal principle. But is Aristotle right to suggest that Thales and those like him supposed that material principles were the only principles needed to explain the *cosmos*?

Aristotle's own testimony elsewhere would seem to refute this suggestion, but what he says raises more questions than it answers.

I.4 Aristotle, *On the Soul* I.2.405a19–21 (= DK 11A22)
It seems Thales, too, judging from what has been recorded about him, seems to have held soul to be a source of movement, if he said that magnetite has soul because it moves the iron.

I.5 Diogenes Laertius, *Lives of the Philosophers* I.24 (= DK 11A1)
Aristotle and Hippias claim that he [Thales] attributed soul even to soulless [lifeless] things, using magnetite and amber as evidence.

I.6 Aristotle, *On the Soul* I.5.411a7–8 (= DK 11A22)
Some say that it [the soul] is mixed in the whole of things, which is why, perhaps, Thales thought that all things are full of gods.

These texts are often taken as decisive evidence for attributing a kind of "hylozoism" to Thales[3] – the view we now generally regard as quite primitive, according to which many or all of the changes we see in the world are the result of animating principles within the things that change. Thales is counted as a hylozoist on the ground that (as per I.4 and I.5) he

---

3 See, for example, G. S. Kirk, J. E. Raven, and M. Schofield, *The Presocratic Philosophers: A Critical History with a Selection of Texts*, 2nd edn. (Cambridge, 1995), 95–8.

supposed that magnetite must have a soul because it can move iron. Although there is nothing impossible about the idea that Thales might have been a hylozoist, these texts hardly establish it. Aristotle's own commitment to the thesis that Thales attributed soul to magnetite (in I.4) is obviously tentative at best, and one can find no further evidence in Aristotle himself for the rather bolder claim we find in Diogenes (I.5). Even if Thales did associate "soul" with whatever the sources of movement within things might be, regarding this as evidence of hylozoism require that we conceive of Thales as holding an otherwise familiar conception of what a soul is – which is anything but assured by these texts. It seems rather more likely that Thales simply identified soul with *whatever* might count as a principle of change within a thing – without at all supposing that anything having such a principle or principles within it must *also* have other "psychological" attributes.

I.6 in particular would seem to support such a view. In I.6, notice, Aristotle is clear only in the attribution to Thales of the view that everything is full of gods – it is Aristotle's own hypothesis that links this idea with things having souls. Those most eager to attribute hylozoism to Thales manage to ignore the universality of Thales' view – not merely *some things* but *everything* is "full of gods."[4] We can, of course, elect to take this as evidence that Thales was guilty of a profound superstition of some sort. But Thales' view seems more plausibly understood as an attempt to articulate what modern physicists take to be the uncontroversial point that nothing in existence is absolutely *inert*, but instead all things have attributes that allow them to have causal effects on other things. If we use the words "soul" or "gods" to denote such attributes, it is only because the technical vocabulary of modern physics had yet to be invented.

At any rate, if we put this together with what Thales seems to have believed about water as the first material principle, we find an attempt to make sense of the world in terms of a single fundamental material, whose capacities for change are both numerous and also contained in everything that comes out of the fundamental water. If Thales had more to say about the nature(s) of these capacities, it seems to have been lost.

Anaximander of Miletus

Anaximander is said to have written several works, mostly on various topics in astronomy, but now only a small, obscure fragment remains (the quotation embedded within the following testimony):

I.7 Simplicius, *Commentary on Aristotle's Physics* 24.13–18 (= DK 12A9)[5]
Of those who say that it [the *cosmos*] is one, moving, indefinite, Anaximander, the son of Praxiades, a Milesian, the successor and student of Thales, said that the principle

---

4 Kirk, Raven, and Schofield conclude that Thales' actual view "approaches close to" a moderate sort of hylozoism, according to which "the world is interpenetrated by life, that many of its parts which appear inanimate are in fact animate" (ibid. 98). I.4 and I.5 are *compatible* with such an interpretation, but certainly do not compel it. I.6, however (and despite their complicated but irrelevant argument about what it means to say that something is "full of" something else), compels the view that whatever Thales means by "gods" *absolutely everything* is full of them.

5 Different versions of the same description, which seems originally to have come from Theophrastus, can be found in Hippolytus, *Refutation* 1.6.1–2 (= DK 12A11) and pseudo-Plutarch, *Stromata* 2 (= DK 12A10).

and element of things that are was the indefinite, and was the first to introduce this name [i.e. "indefinite" – *apeiron*] for the principle. He says that it is neither water nor any of the other things that are called elements, but is instead some other indefinite nature, and all the heavens and the worlds in them come out of this. And the source of coming into being for things that are is also that into which destruction occurs, "by necessity, for they pay penalty and retribution to each other for their wrongdoing, according to the arrangement of time," as he says in somewhat poetical language.

One of Anaximander's many contributions seems to have been to move away from Thales' conception of the first material principle as water, and to proclaim the material principle to be the "indefinite" instead. There continue to be debates about precisely what Anaximander meant by this term. The term itself is formed by adding what is called the "alpha privative" (which works like the prefix *a-* meaning "not") to the noun *peirar* or *peiras*, which means "limit" or "boundary." So, *apeiron* means something like "limitless" or "unbounded." But even though Anaximander thought of it as the material substance for all things, the idea of the *apeiron* seemed to be less that it was endless in special extent so much that it was *indefinite* in its characteristics and makeup.

There seem to have been two ways in which a substance might be called an *apeiron* among the early Greek thinkers, as Aristotle explains:

I.8 Aristotle, *Physics* I.4.187a12–23
The physical thinkers provide two sorts of explanation. Those who have made the underlying body one, either one of the three[6] or some other thing which is denser than fire and more rarified than air, and generate the other things by condensation and rarefaction, making many things [from the one body]. [. . .] The other [group of thinkers] claim that the opposites are in the one and separated out from it, as Anaximander says and all who say there are one and many, such as Empedocles and Anaxagoras; these also separate out other things from the mixture.

Some scholars have argued that we should understand Anaximander's *apeiron* as a kind of amorphous element that is somehow intermediate between the other elements, from which the other elements are generated.[7] But I.8 seems to make clear that Anaximander regarded the *apeiron* as a mixture of everything else, out of which all things are separated, and into which everything ultimately returns. Because he thought of the *apeiron* as everlasting and indestructible, Anaximander regarded this primordial substance as divine (Aristotle, *Physics* 3.4.203b13).

The way in which the process of separation occurs, for Anaximander, is some kind of never-ending motion (Hippolytus, *Refutation of All Heresies* 1.6.1 = DK12A11). According to Aristotle, those who talk about never-ending motion as the mechanism by which the *cosmos* is generated conceive of such motion as a vortex (the swirling motion of, for example, tornadoes).

I.9 Aristotle, *On the Heaven* II.13.295a7–14
But if in fact there is some natural motion, neither motion nor rest would be by force only; if, then, it is by force that the earth now remains in its place, it, too, came together

6 i.e. water, air, or fire. At *Metaphysics* A.988b30, and 989a5–6, Aristotle says that no one ever made earth the first material principle.
7 See e.g. Kirk, Raven, and Schofield, *The Presocratic Philosophers*, 111–13.

at the center because of the vortex. For this is the cause that everyone states, on the basis of what happens in water and in air; for in these the larger and heavier things are always carried to the center of the vortex. This is why all who generate the heavens say that the earth came together at the center.

Aristotle also suggests that Anaximander fixed the earth at the center of the *cosmos* by a kind of equilibrium of the surrounding (presumably vortex) forces. Anaximander's argument seems to have been that, once established at the center, it was "equally related" to all around it, and thus could not move in any direction without equal opposition from the others (Aristotle, *On the Heaven* 2.13.295b11–16).

Anaximander is also credited with many other theories, including what looks a bit like an early version of what physicists now call the "Big Bang" theory.

I.10 Pseudo-Plutarch, *Stromata* 2 (= DK 12A10)
He [Anaximander] says that what produces the hot and cold from the everlasting was separated off at the coming to be of this *cosmos*, and a kind of sphere of flame from this formed around the air surrounding the earth, like bark around a tree. When this was broken off and closed into certain circles, the sun and the moon and the stars were formed.

Anaximander also seems to have articulated a very early version of evolutionary theory, or at least an ancestor of such a theory, according to which animals derived from earlier life forms (Aetius 5.19.4 = DK12A30), and that human beings came into being from these other, earlier animals (Pseudo-Plutarch, *Stromata* 2 = DK 12A10; Censorinus, *On the Day of Birth* 4.7 = DK 12A30). According to one source (Pseudo-Plutarch), Anaximander reasoned that human beings would have to evolve from other animals, because whereas other animals do not require lengthy nurturing, human beings cannot take care of themselves for quite a long time after birth. So, human beings could not have survived unless the first human beings were born from, and preserved by, other species.

Anaximenes of Miletus

Anaximenes of Miletus was a student and associate of Anaximander. Although most scholars find Anaximenes somewhat less ingenious than his mentor, later Greeks often recalled Anaximenes' theories with obvious interest and respect. Rather than postulate some obscure "indefinite" (*apeiron*) as the material first principle, Anaximenes sought to explain the material source of the *cosmos* in terms of air. In keeping with Anaximander's insight that some explanation must be given for how everything else could come out of the material first principle, however, Anaximenes did not conceive of the air as a mixture of everything else, from which the rest would be "separated off," but instead conceived of the process of change-of-form as the product of condensation and rarefaction.

I.11 Theophrastus, quoted by Simplicius, *Commentary on Aristotle's Physics* 24.26–25.1 (= DK 13A5)
Anaximenes, son of Eurystratus of Miletus, an associate of Anaximander, like him also says that the underlying nature is one and indefinite [*apeiron*], but not indeterminate, as the latter held, but determinate, saying it was air. It differentiates in its substantial

forms by rarity and density. Becoming more rarefied, it becomes fire; being condensed, it becomes wind, then cloud, and when condensed yet further, water, then earth, then stones, and the rest come to be from these. He also makes motion everlasting and says that change also comes to be by it.

As Anaximander did before him, Anaximenes identified the material first principle with the divine (Cicero, *On the Nature of the Gods* 1.10.26 = DK 13A10). We do not know how Thales conceived of the way in which things came out of the primordial water. As we have seen, for Anaximander, the first material principle seems to have been a kind of mixture, where the process of separation into the more familiar substances derived from some sort of vortex motion. Even if Anaximenes' alternative explanations strike us as somewhat less magnificent in imagination, he provides them with the advantage of support from readily observable processes – and the ancient evidence supports that Anaximenes actually did offer direct empirical evidence for his views (see e.g. Plutarch, *The Principle of the Cold* 7.947F = DK 13B1).

Concluding Remarks about the Milesians

The earliest contributions to the history of thought helped to define intellectual inquiry in the West thereafter. As we have seen, these contributions included the formulation of cosmological systems based upon first material principles out of which all things came into being, and into which all things eventually returned. The forces by which cosmological changes came about were ubiquitous and though counted as "divine," it is their naturalistic (as opposed to supernatural) character that is most striking. Milesian speculation touched on much of what we now study in the natural sciences. But the move away from traditional religious explanations, implicit in the naturalistic accounts of the Milesians, and later explicit in Xenophanes, was, all by itself, a giant step in the history of philosophy.

2

Xenophanes, Heracleitus, and Pythagoras

Xenophanes of Colophon

One of the first philosophical figures for whom we have substantial (if quite fragmentary) surviving original writings is the poet Xenophanes, who was born *c.*570 BCE and who lived into his nineties. Born in the Ionian city of Colophon, Xenophanes was forced to flee his homeland by its fall to the Persians in 546 BCE. He ended up in Greek colonies in what is now southern Italy and Sicily. Like the Milesian philosophers before him, Xenophanes left some writings on natural subjects (astronomy and meteorology, in particular), but far better known are his criticisms of traditional religion – a theme that was only implicit in Milesian thought. (Consider the implications of Thales' "All things are full of gods," or Anaximander's and Anaximenes' insistence that the material first principle was the actual "divinity.") Xenophanes' critiques, however, are considerably more direct; the following is a sampling from his fragments:

> **I.12** Xenophanes, fr. 11[1]
> Homer and Hesiod have attributed to the gods all
> The actions that are a shame and a disgrace among human beings: Theft, adultery,
>   and deceiving one another.

> **I.13** Xenophanes, fr. 14
> But mortals suppose that the gods are born,
> And that they have clothing, and voices, and bodies [like those of mortals].

> **I.14** Xenophanes, fr. 15
> If cattle and horses and lions had hands,
> Or could draw with such hands and create works, as humans do,
> Horses would draw the forms of the gods like horses, and cattle like cattle
> And each would make the gods' bodies in the same form as they had themselves.

---

1 Fragments are numbered as per their appearance in DK (see p. 14, n. 1 above).

I.15 Xenophanes, fr. 16
Ethiopians say their gods are flat-nosed and black;
Thacians say theirs are blue-eyed and red-haired.

I.16 Xenophanes, fr. 34
No man knows or will ever
Know about the gods and the other things I speak of;
For even if one happened to speak the whole truth,
He himself would not know it. All things are wrought with appearance.

I.17 Xenophanes, fr. 35
May these things be believed as likened to truth . . .

I.18 Xenophanes, fr. 18
Indeed not from the beginning have the gods revealed all things to mortals,
But, in time, by seeking men find out more.

I.19 Xenophanes, fr. 38
If god had not created yellow honey, people
Would declare figs far sweeter.

I.20 Xenophanes, fr. 23
One god, among the gods and men the greatest
Not alike to men in body or in thought.

The effects of such critiques are plain enough: I.12 casts doubt on the ancient Greek myths that portray the gods as immoral and petty. I.13, I.14, and I.15 (and to some extent I.12, as well) all cast doubt on the way in which human beings conceive of their gods as images of themselves (so Africans conceive of their gods as black, whereas those who live north of Greece imagine that the gods are pale, red-haired, and blue-eyed). Such criticisms as these might lead someone to scorn all of religion as a sham. But Xenophanes' critiques were not those of an atheist – rather, he sought to reform religion, rather than to eliminate it. And as I.16, I.17, I.18, and I.19 show, the most important reform Xenophanes sought was to have people recognize their own ignorance about the subject – an ignorance that is a persistent part of the human condition. Xenophanes is not seeking to contrast his own supposedly certain knowledge of divinity with the faulty images of it provided in traditional accounts; rather, he doubts that the true nature of divinity is something any mere mortal can know.

Aristotle notes that Xenophanes seeks to replace the idea that the gods were born with the idea that the gods were immortal and everlasting:

I.21 Aristotle *Rhetoric* 2.23.1399b6–9 (= DK 21A12)
Xenophanes used to say that it is just as impious to claim that the gods were born as it is to claim that they die; for in both cases it follows that there was a time the gods did not exist.

Xenophanes also sought to replace the variety and anthropomorphism of the Greek gods with monotheism, in which the one God was wholly perfect, powerful, and unchanging (I.20; see also fragments 24–6).

Heracleitus of Ephesus

In many ways, Heracleitus is one of the most challenging of the Presocratics. Although we have many fragments of his work, he employed a very oracular style of writing that makes interpretation particularly difficult. Such complaints about Heracleitus, indeed, go back into antiquity. Timon of Phlius (c. third century BCE) called Heracleitus "the riddler" (DL IX.6); later, Cicero characterized Heracleitus as "the obscure" (*De finibus* II.5.15). Numerous (though not entirely reliable) biographical notices characterize Heracleitus as a highly idiosyncratic misanthrope. In spite of all such problems, however, Heracleitus' philosophical contributions were highly significant, and his influence on many later philosophers (particularly Plato) cannot be doubted.

Heracleitus is remembered as the author of a single book, *On Nature*, which was divided into three sections: on the *cosmos*, on politics, and on theology. In fact, however, many of the fragments that remain strongly suggest that the nature of Heracleitus' original work was probably less like a book in our sense, and more like a collection of enigmatic statements, perhaps intended more to stimulate thought than to create lucid understanding of any specific doctrines. Because later philosophers were influenced by their own understandings of Heracleitus' writings, however, we will arrange the fragments in topics, so as to highlight a few of the main themes to be found in what remains of this difficult figure.

(i) The *Logos* and human inadequacy

The Greek word *logos* can mean such a variety of things that it may be better in this case simply to leave it untranslated. In other contexts, the word is used in ways that suggest such translations as "reason," "account," "statement," "argument," "arrangement," "proportion," "logic" (which derives from the Greek word), "word," or "natural law."

I.22 Heracleitus, fr. 1
Of the *Logos*, which is always as I explain it, human beings always prove incapable of understanding, both before hearing it and when they have heard it the first time. For though all things happen according to this *Logos*, human beings are like inexperienced people, even when they experience such words and deeds as I explain, distinguishing each thing according to its nature and showing how it is. But other people fail to notice what they do after they wake up, just as they forget what they did while they were asleep.

I.23 Heracleitus, fr. 50
Listening not to me but to the *Logos* it is wise to agree that all things are one.

(ii) The truth is not obvious

I.24 Heracleitus, fr. 123
Nature loves to hide itself.

(iii) Self-examination

I.25 Heracleitus, fr. 101
I searched out myself.

(iv) Complaints about the faults of other putative sages

I.26 Heracleitus, fr. 40
Learning many things does not teach one intelligence; for it would have taught Hesiod and Pythagoras, and again Xenophanes and Hecataeus.

I.27 Heracleitus, fr. 42
Homer deserves to be thrown out of the contests, and whipped; and also Archilochus.

I.28 Heracleitus, fr. 57
Hesiod is the teacher of most human beings. They are convinced he knew most things – a man who could not recognize day and night; for they are one.

(v) "All things are one" (see I.23 above)

I.29 Heracleitus, fr. 8
What is in opposition is in agreement, and from things that differ the most beautiful harmony comes.

I.30 Heracleitus, fr. 10
Taken together things are wholes and not wholes, something that is brought together and brought apart, in tune and out of tune; from all things, one and from one, all things.

I.31 Heracleitus, fr. 60
The road up and down is the same.

I.32 Heracleitus, fr. 62
Immortals are mortal, mortals are immortal; each lives the other's death, and dies their life.

I.33 Heracleitus, fr. 88
The same thing is in us, both living and dead, awake and asleep, young and old; for the latter are transformed into the former, and the former are transformed again into the latter.

(vi) Endless change, the world as ever-changing fire

I.34 Heracleitus, fr. 12
Over those who step into the same river, different and again different waters flow.

I.35 Heracleitus, fr. 90
All things are an exchange for fire and fire for all things, as goods are exchanged for gold, and gold for goods.

I.36 Heracleitus, fr. 31
Fire's turnings: first, sea, and then of sea half is earth and half lightning . . . earth is dissolved as sea into the same *Logos* as it was before it became earth.

I.37 Heracleitus, fr. 30

This *cosmos* none of the gods nor human beings made, but it always was and is and will be an everliving fire, being lit in measures and extinguished in measures.

(vii) Criticisms of traditional religion

I.38 Heracleitus, fr. 5

They vainly purify themselves with blood when defiled by blood, like one who had stepped into mud trying to wash with mud. If anyone noticed him acting in this way, he would be thought insane. Furthermore, they pray to these statues, as if someone were to have a conversation with houses, for they do not know whosoever the gods are heroes are.

I.39 Heracleitus, fr. 14

The rituals practiced by human beings in the Mysteries are performed in an unholy way.

I.40 Heracleitus, fr. 15

For if it were not for Dionysos that they have processions and sing hymns to the shameful parts [the male sex organs], it would be a most shameless act; but Hades and Dionysos are the same, for whom they go crazy and celebrate Lenaian [Dionysian] rites.

(viii) Moralisms

I.41 Heracleitus, fr. 119

The character of a human being is his divinity [*daimōn*].

I.42 Heracleitus, fr. 29

The best people choose one thing instead of everything else: everlasting fame among mortals; but the many are satiated like cattle.

I.43 Heracleitus, fr. 43

Violent arrogance [*hubris*] should be extinguished even more than a fire.

I.44 Heracleitus, fr. 44

The people should fight for the law, as if for the city wall.

Concluding remarks about Heracleitus

Heracleitus' conception of a *cosmos* in which the opposites are in some way united, and for which the unifying arrangement of things (the *Logos*) somehow involved everlasting change, influenced later thinkers to seek novel ways to defend a primary role for reason within such a world – or, for others, to separate the realm of reason away from such a world. At any rate, Heracleitus' powerful images retain their potency for thinkers even now.

Pythagoras of Samos and his Followers

Originally born on the island of Samos (roughly a mile off the coast of Asia Minor), Pythagoras is said to have elected to leave his home because he could no longer accept the tyranny of its ruler (DK 14.8). He traveled to the other end of the Greek world, ending up on the western frontiers, in what is now Italy.

Pythagoras' intellectual influence in the Greek (and later, Roman) world is enormous, at least indirectly as a result of the works and clans of his followers, who continued to thrive for many centuries. The historical record is nearly impossible to penetrate, as later Pythagoreans attributed their own findings to Pythagoras himself. It is safest to infer, accordingly, that Pythagoras himself was more important for his evident charisma (see, e.g., DK 14, 8a) to such a degree that miracle stories about him are attributed to the usually sober and skeptical testimony of Aristotle (DK 14, 7). He seems to have used this immense charisma to persuade the people of Croton (on the "toe" of Italy) entirely to reform their society in accordance with Pythagoras' own theories. About these theories, one can find an impressive volume of scholarly speculation, but very reliable evidence on these matters is scarce. It may be safe to conclude that many of the features of the utopian state later depicted in Plato's *Republic* derive from Pythagorean origins, as many have argued, including greater inclusion of women in political life, and a special class of rulers. Plato's theory of Forms is probably also influenced by the Pythagorean metaphysics of numbers, and Plato's theories of reincarnation and learning as recollection from former lives also no doubt have their origins in Pythagoreanism.

(i) Religious doctrines

Although modern references to Pythagoras tend to focus on the mathematical discoveries by later Pythagoreans, it is doubtful that any of these go back to Pythagoras himself. Instead, Pythagoras's own teachings seem to have been more concerned with matters of religion and ethics. One doctrine closely associated with Pythagoras is the idea of reincarnation – the transmigration of souls, after death, into other life forms.

I.45 Porphyry, *Life of Pythagoras* 19 (= DK 14, 8a)
What he said to those around him, no one can say with confidence; so extraordinary was their silence. Nevertheless, the following became known by all: First, he says that the soul is immortal, and next, that it changes into other kinds of living things; also, that what happens recurs at certain intervals and nothing is absolutely new. And all things that come to have souls [be alive] should be recognized as beings of the same kind. It seems Pythagoras was the first to bring these doctrines into Greece.

Also associated with Pythagoras are various rules of abstinence. He enjoined his followers not to eat beans, nor could they touch white roosters, nor eat any fish deemed "sacred," or break loaves of bread – all for reasons our sources themselves do not seem to understand (see DL VIII.34–5 [= DK 58C3]). Some such prohibitions seem not to have been intended literally:

I.46 Aristotle fr. 197, Porphyry, *Life of Pythagoras* 42 (= DK 58C6)
There was another form of symbol, of this sort: "Do not step over a weigh-scale," meaning avoid excess; "Do not stir the fire with a sword," meaning do not annoy an angry man with sharp words; "Do not pluck at the crown," meaning make no offense against the laws, for they are the crowns of cities. Or again, "Do not eat heart," meaning do not pain yourself with grief; "Do not sit on the wheat ration," meaning

do not live lazily; "Do not turn back on a journey," meaning do not cling to this life when dying.

This way of understanding the many taboos and prohibitions associated with Pythagoreanism may be somewhat comforting to those of us who are impressed by the Pythagoreans' influences on later thinkers. Some of the restrictions recalled in our sources, however, seem more likely to have reflected purely religious – or even magical – beliefs.

(ii) The *akousmata*

The basic teachings of the Pythagoreans – perhaps originating with Pythagoras himself – seem to have been transmitted in what were called the *akousmata*, the "things heard." These included the prohibitions and other instructions by which one's life as a Pythagorean was to be shaped and guided.

I.47 Iamblichus, *Life of Pythagoras* 82 (= DK 58C4)
The *akousmata* referred to in this way are in three forms. Some of them signify what something is; some, what is the most of something; some, what should be done or should not be done. The following are of the what something is form: What are the Isles of the Blessed? Sun and Moon. What is the oracle at Delphi? Tetractus – which is the harmony in which the Sirens sing. Of the most of something form: What is the most just? To sacrifice. What is the wisest? Number; but second, the one who assigned names to things. What is the wisest of the things within our purview? Medicine. What is the most beautiful? Harmony. What is the most dominant? Knowledge. What is the best? Happiness. What is the truest thing said? That human beings are wicked.

There is quite a bit going on in this passage, so it will be worth our while to look at several things within it more closely. First, in the passage the "tetractus" is identified with the oracle at Delphi. We find out more about the tetractus elsewhere:

I.48 Sextus Empiricus, *Against the Professors* VII.94–5
By "Him that gave us [the tetractus]," [the Pythagoreans] meant Pythagoras (for they deified him). And by "the tetractus" [they meant] a certain number which, being composed of the four first numbers, produces the most perfect number, which is ten (for one plus two plus three plus four becomes ten). This number is the first tetractus and is called "the source of ever-flowing nature," because according to them the entire *cosmos* is organized according to harmony, and harmony is a system of three concords: the fourth, the fifth, and the octave. And the proportions of these three concords are found in the four numbers just mentioned: in the one, the two, the three, and the four.

The tetractus, accordingly, seems to have been the figure represented in this way:

•

•   •

•   •   •

•   •   •   •

Even if it seems reasonable to associate the tetractus with Pythagoras himself, the more sophisticated claims about harmony we find in I.43 are probably developments by later Pythagoreans, who seem to have taken Pythagoras' early mentions of harmony and developed them with the mathematical theories they discovered and put to use in many areas. These more scientific and intellectual Pythagoreans at first seem to have met with some resistance among the more traditional (and mostly religious) followers of Pythagoras and the *akousmata*.

(iii) The *akousmatikoi* and *mathematikoi*

I.49 Iamblichus, *On the Community of the Mathematical Sciences* 25.1–11
There are two forms of the Italian philosophy, which is called Pythagorean. For those who practiced it were also of two kinds: the *akousmatikoi* and the *mathematikoi*. Of these two groups, the *akousmatikoi* were acknowledged as Pythagoreans by the others, but they [the *akousmatikoi*] did not acknowledge the *mathematikoi*, claiming that their pursuits derived not from Pythagoras, but from Hippasus. [. . .] The philosophy of the *akousmatikoi* consists of unproven and unargued *akousmata* prescribing as appropriate certain ways of acting, and they try to preserve the other sayings of Pythagoras as divine dogma. They claim to say nothing innovative of their own, and claim that to innovate would be wrong. They consider the wisest among their number to be those who have learned the most *akousmata*.

These later testimonia suggest that perhaps references to harmony and the tetractus were included within the *akousmata*, but no serious inquiry into mathematics was a part of Pythagorean life until later, and then was pursued only by the *mathematikoi*. The original Pythagoreans were simply those who followed the guiding *akousmata* given to his followers by Pythagoras.

The *mathematikoi*, however, were undeterred by the skepticism their work received from their elders, and at least some of this work was directed at understanding in a more systematic way some of the teachings of Pythagoras himself, including especially those about harmony. As we saw in I.48, some of the Pythagoreans claimed that "the entire *cosmos* is organized according to harmony, and harmony is a system of three concords: the fourth, the fifth, and the octave. And the proportions of these three concords are found in the four numbers just mentioned: in the one, the two, the three, and the four." As those who play stringed instruments know, one can play a note that is an octave higher in pitch (from C to C′, for example) by fretting (or bridging) the string at exactly the halfway point between the fixed ends of the string (for example, between the neck and the bridge of a guitar). In relation to C, F is the fourth, and G is the fifth. These notes, too, are expressible entirely mathematically. The fourth will result from reducing (fretting or bridging) the length of the string (L) by a quarter, and the fifth will result by reducing the original length by a third. If the note of the original length (L) of the string is C, then, C′ can be expressed as $1/2 \, L$, G is $2/3 \, L$ and F is $3/4 \, L$. In these proportions, we can easily see the four first numbers: 1, 2, 3, and 4.

(iv) Numbers, opposites, and cosmogeny

Having discovered the mathematical relationships between these notes, it seems that the Pythagoreans made the bold deduction that literally everything might also be understood mathematically such that "the entire *cosmos* is organized according to harmony, and harmony is a system of three concords: the fourth, the fifth, and the octave." But other members of the *mathematikoi* seem to have perceived a need for more complicated theories about the relationships between the *cosmos* and numbers, and yet others among the Pythagoreans drew still different conclusions, as the following long quotation from Aristotle shows.

I.50 Aristotle, *Metaphysics* I.5 985b23–986b9 (= DK 58B4 and 58B5; trans. Apostle and Gerson)

Contemporaneously with these thinkers [Leucippus and Democritus, the atomists], and even before them, the so-called Pythagoreans, who were engaged in the study of mathematical objects, were the first to advance this study, and having been brought up in it, they regarded the principles of mathematical objects as the principles of all things. Since of mathematical objects numbers are by nature first, and (a) they seemed to observe in numbers, rather than in fire or earth or water, many likenesses to things, both existing and in generation (and so they regarded such and such an attribute of numbers as justice, such other as soul or intellect, another as opportunity, and similarly with almost all of the others), and (b) they also observed numerical *attributes* and ratios in the objects of harmonics; since, then, all other things appeared in their nature to be likenesses of numbers, and numbers to be first in the whole of nature, they came to the belief that the elements of numbers are the elements of all things and that the whole heaven is a harmony and a number. And whatever facts in numbers and harmonies could be shown to be consistent with the *attributes*, the parts, and the whole arrangement of the heaven, these they collected and fitted into a system; and if there was a gap somewhere, they readily made additions in order to make their whole system connected. I mean, for example, that since ten is considered to be complete and to include every nature in numbers, they said that the bodies that travel in the heavens are also ten; and since the visible bodies are nine,[2] they added the so-called "Counter-Earth" as the tenth body.

[. . .]

Indeed, these thinkers appear to consider numbers as principles of things, and in two senses: as matter and also as affections or possessions of things. The elements of a number are the *Even* and the *Odd*, the *Odd* being finite and the *Even* being infinite; the *One* is composed of both of these (for it is both even and odd); a number comes from the one; and, as we said, the whole heaven is numbers.

Other members of this same school declare that the principles are ten, that is, ten pairs arranged in two columns, opposite against opposite:

Finite–Infinite
Odd–Even
One–Many
Right–Left

2 Namely, Sun, Moon, Mercury, Venus, Earth, Mars, Jupiter, Saturn, and the fixed stars. Uranus, Neptune, and Pluto are not visible to the naked eye, and were thus discovered much later (1781, 1846, and 1930, respectively).

Male–Female
Resting–Moving
Straight–Curved
Light–Darkness
Good–Bad
Square–Rectangular

Alcmaion of Croton seems to have come to such a belief, and either he got it from them or they got it from him. For Alcmaion was in the prime of life when Pythagoras was old, and he expressed himself just about as they did; for he says that a great many things relating to men come to two, meaning and chance contraries (not a specific list like that given by the others), for example, white and black, sweet and bitter, good and bad, great and small, etc. Thus, Alcmaion gave indefinite hints about the rest, but the Pythagoreans stated both how many and which are the contraries.

From both of these schools, then, we can gather this much, that the principles of things are the contraries, and from the Pythagoreans we are told how many and which the contraries are. But these schools have not been clearly articulate as to how their principles can be grouped and related to our list of causes; however, they seem to place the elements under the material kind of cause; for they say that substances consist of or are fashioned out of these elements as out of constituents.

As for those Pythagoreans who conceived of the *cosmos* as deriving from numbers, we find the following account in Diogenes Laertius:

I.51 Alexander Polyhistor, *Pythagorean Notebooks*, quoted in DL VIII.25 (= DK 58B1a) From the unit and the undefined duo come numbers; and from numbers, points; and from these, lines, from which come plane figures; and from plane figures come solid figures; and from these come sensible bodies, for which the elements are four: fire, water, earth, air. These completely interchange and turn into each other; and from these come into being a *cosmos* that is ensouled [living], intelligent, spherical, with the earth – itself spherical and inhabited all around – at the center.

Aristotle, however, reports that the Pythagoreans accepted a heliocentric conception of the *cosmos*, rather than the geocentric conception reported in Diogenes.[3]

Given the variety of opinions about these issues even among the Pythagoreans themselves, it is almost certainly inappropriate to speak of "the Pythagorean view" of the *cosmos*. But rather than concern ourselves with trying to work out which of the views attributed to them are the "most Pythagorean," we should be alert to the many ways in which the various views associated with the Pythagoreans came to influence later philosophers.

3 Aristotle, *On the Heaven* 2.13 293a18–b8 (= DK 58B36). See also Aetius 2.7.7 (= DK 44A16).

3

The Eleatics

Parmenides of Elea

Parmenides is considered the central figure of the "Eleatic school" of philosophy, so called for Elea, a Greek colony in Italy and the birthplace of both Parmenides and his famous student and associate, Zeno. Parmenides is thought to have lived and flourished in the early or mid-fifth century BCE. Like many intellectuals of the period, he is thought to have traveled widely, especially through Greece and her colonies, but there is evidence for supposing his travels were not so extensive as to deprive him of an active (or perhaps even leading) role in the politics of Elea.

Unlike his philosophical predecessors, Parmenides wrote (only one work, according to DL I.16) in verse rather than prose, a style of philosophy that was, with one exception in the Greek world – Empedocles, in imitation of Parmenides – to begin and end with him. Far more durable was his method and the message he fashioned with it. Parmenides begins his philosophical investigation with the premise "it is," an assumption of Being and Truth from which he derives, by reason alone, a variety of startling conclusions. Not the least of these is the complete denial of motion and change, and this in turn leads Parmenides to dismiss the senses, which purport to reveal such things to us, as unsound measures of reality. The effects of his methods and doctrines are perhaps more substantial than those of any other single Presocratic philosopher: Zeno's commitment to them leads him to the paradoxes by which we know him; Empedocles and Anaxagoras find them so compelling that they attempt radically to revise traditional cosmology accordingly; whereas (implausibly) later Sophists claimed support in them for their rhetorical sleights of hand. But more significant yet were the effects of Parmenides' work on Plato, who undertook in his theory of participation to refashion the rational connection of Being to the world of sense that he took Parmenides to have severed. Clear indications of Plato's debt to Parmenides may be found in the central role of a changeless and timeless realm of Being in Plato's theories of knowledge and reality, in contrast to the inferior roles he assigns to sensation and the sensible world. Plato's respect for Parmenides is also evident both in the generous characterization of him in Plato's *Parmenides*, and no less by the "Eleatic Stranger" and his explicitly regretful revisions of Parmenidean doctrine in Plato's *Sophist*.

Parmenides' poem was presented in three parts: the Proem, or allegorical introduction, followed by the Way of Truth, and then the Way of Opinion. The first of these we appear to have in its entirety; the second is in fragments, though a few of these are substantial; the third part of the original is, unfortunately, largely lost. Each part of the poem holds a special interest for the student of early Greek culture and thought: the Proem for its rich texture of images; the Way of Truth for its radical philosophy and later effects; the Way of Opinion for its tantalizing suggestion of surprisingly sophisticated scientific knowledge, especially in the area of astronomy.

The order of the remaining fragments within the original poem is a matter of dispute among scholars, as is the specific sense of some of the more obscure lines. We follow the order of fragments given in DK, and include all but two of the remaining fragments.

(i) The Proem

I.52 Parmenides, fr. 1
The mares that bear me, as far as I may desire,
Were conducting me, when they set me on the famed way
Of the divinity, she who carries a knowing mortal through all places.
So I was borne along; for so the thoughtful mares bore me,
Straining the chariot, as young maidens guided the way.
The axle of the chariot, blazing in its socket,
Sang a piping note, for it was spun by the whirling
Wheels at each end, while the young maidens, daughters of Sun,
Leaving the realm of Night, hurried me to the light,
Having pushed back the veils from their heads with their hands.
There are the gates between the ways of Night and Day;
They have a lintel above and a stone threshold below.
These ethereal gates are fitted with great double doors,
But harsh punishing Justice holds the keys for them.
The young maidens, cajoling her with gentle words,
Wisely persuaded her to push back the bolt
Swiftly form the gates; and these
Made a wide vista of the doors being opened
Swinging their bronze hinge-pins in their respective sockets
Fastened with rivets and nails. So it was that the young maidens went
Straight through, guiding the mares and chariot along the wagon-way
And the goddess gave me a warm welcome, took
My right hand in hers, and spoke to me these words:
"O young one, kin to immortal charioteers, who
Comes to my home with the mares that bear you:
Welcome! It is no misfortune that has sent you
On this way (though indeed it is far from the normal path of humans)
But rather right and justice. And you must inquire into all things:
Both the unmoving heart of well-rounded truth
And the mere opinion of mortals, in which there is no genuine conviction.
But you will, at any rate, learn these things, how the appearances that pervade all things
    were bound to be accepted.

(ii) The Way of Truth

I.53 Parmenides, fr. 2

Come then, and I will tell you (and you must listen to the story and take it with
   you)
The only two ways of inquiry in thought:
The one, that it is and that it is impossible that "not-to-be" is;
The other that it is not and that it is necessary that "not-to-be" is,
Is the way of Conviction (for she accompanies Truth)

This I declare to you is a way wholly inscrutable;
For neither could you know What-Is-Not (for What-Is-Not is impossible)
Nor could you declare it.

I.54 Parmenides, fr. 3

. . . for the same thing is for thinking and for being.[1]

I.55 Parmenides, fr. 4

Behold: absent things are nevertheless securely present to the mind.
For What-Is is not cut off from holding to What-Is,
Neither all dispersed throughout the cosmos,
Nor united . . .

I.56 Parmenides, fr. 5

. . . it is of no consequence to me
Where I make my beginning, for there I shall return again.

I.57 Parmenides, fr. 6

It is necessary to say and to think What-Is, for to-be *is*
And nothing *is not*. These things I command you to consider.
For this I the first way from which [I hold you back][2]
But also, from this one, on which mortals knowing nothing
Wander, of two minds; for helplessness in their
Hearts guides aimless thought. They are borne along
Deaf and blind at the same time; astounded, uncritical tribes,
By whom to-be and not-to-be are thought the same
And not the same; and for whom the way of everything is reversed.

1 The literal translation of this fragment is "for to think and to be are the same thing." Despite its
potential appeal, however, literality must be avoided in this case. To insist upon it would be to under-
cut what is plain Parmenidean doctrine, since What-Is, or Being, is utterly static on Parmenides' view,
whereas thinking requires change. In context, the point is clear – only that which is can be thought
(or alternatively, the highest type of cognition, *nous*, can only be applied to What-Is; cf. fr. 2, lines 7–8,
fr. 6, line 1, and fr. 8, lines 16–17, 34–7). In this translation, we have treated the infinitives ("to think"
and "to be") as substantives in the dative case, as is recommended by most contemporary scholars considering this fragment.
2 The verb in brackets was supplied by Diels to complete the line. Given the context, it seems certain
that this, or something very like it, would have been in the original.

I.58 Parmenides, fr. 7

For never will this prevail, that things that are not are.
But you must hold back your thought from this way of inquiry;
And do not let ingrained habit force you to this way,
Using an imprudent eye and sound-filled ear
And tongue, but judge by reason the much-contested argument
That has been given by me.

I.59 Parmenides, fr. 8, lines 1–49

. . . there is only one tale of a way left:
To tell that it is; on this way are signs –
So many! – that What-Is is ungenerated and imperishable,
Whole, uniform, unmoving, and without end
Neither *was it*, nor *will it be*, but rather *it is now*, altogether one, continuous,
For what coming-into-being will you seek of it?
How and from what did it grow? Nor will I permit you to say
Or to think, "from What-Is-Not," for it is not possible to say or think that it is not
What need would have urged it
Later or sooner, starting from What-Is-Not, to grow?
Thus it must either be or not-be.
Not will even the strength of conviction permit something to-come-into-being
  beside it.[3]
To come-into-being from What-Is-Not itself. Thus, neither coming-into-being
Nor perishing does Justice slacken her chains to permit;
Rather she holds it fast. And judgment concerning these things is in this:
It is or *it is not*; and it has been judged, as is necessary,
To eschew one as unthinkable and nameless (for it is not
A true way), and the other as being fully real and true.
How might What-Is later perish? And how might it come-into-being?
For if it came-into-being [in the past], or if it will be [in the future], it *is* not.
Hence coming-into-being is extinguished and perishing unheard of
Nor is it divisible, since it is all alike;
And neither is there more in it (which would not allow it to hold together)
Nor less, but rather it is all full of What-Is.
It is all continuous, for What-Is is brought flush against What-Is
Moreover, changeless within the limits of great bonds,
It is without beginning and without end, since coming-into-being and perishing
Have driven far away, banished by genuine conviction.
And the same thing, remaining in the same state, it lies by itself.
Thus it remains firmly there; for strong Necessity
Holds it within the bonds of a limit, which confines it all around
Because it is not right that What-Is be incomplete;
For it does not lack – if it did, it would lack everything.
To think is the same as the thought that it is.[4]

---

3 Changing *mē* to *tou*.
4 The grammar of this line is anything but obvious, and has encouraged several interpretations.

For not without What-Is, in which what has been expressed is,
Will you find thought; for nothing either *is* or *will be*
Other than What-Is, since Fate has chained it
To be complete and changeless. Thus, all that mortals have proposed are [mere] names,
    convinced that they are true:
To come-into-being and to perish, to be and not,
As well as to change place and to vary in bright color.
Moreover, since there is a furthest limit, it is completed
On every side, like the bulk of a well-rounded ball,
From the center equally strong in all directions; for necessarily it cannot
Be more here and less there.
For neither is there What-Is-Not, which might stop it from reaching
Its like, nor is What-Is such that there could be
More of it here and less there, since it is all inviolable
Equal on every side, it attains its limits equally.

(iii) The Way of Opinion

I.60 Parmenides, fr. 8, lines 50–61 (continues I.52)
With this, I cease my trustworthy account and thought
About truth; from here on learn the opinions of mortals
Listening to the deceitful arrangement of my words.
For [humans] have decided to name two forms,
One of which is not necessary – in this they have gone astray –
And judged them as opposite in character, and assigned them marks
Different from one another; to one the ethereal flame of fire:
Gentle, very light, in every way identical with itself
But different from the other. But that other is, in itself,
The opposite: dark night, dense in character and heavy.
I tell you the entire apparent likely arrangement of these,
So that the judgment of mortals may never surpass you.

I.61 Parmenides, fr. 9
Moreover, once all things have been named Light and Night
And, according to their powers are applied to these things and to those,
All is at once full of light and obscure night –
Of both equally, since neither of them shares in nothingness.

I.62 Parmenides, fr. 10
You will learn the nature of the aether,[5] and in the aether all
The marks, and the annihilating deeds of the pure torch
Of the shining sun, and from where they came-into-being.
And you will know the wandering deeds of the round-faced moon
And its nature. You will also know from where the

---

5 "Aether" here probably refers to the sky.

Encompassing embrace of heaven arose, and how Necessity took it and chained it
To hold the limits of the stars.

I.63 Parmenides, fr. 11
. . . [You will learn] how the earth and the sun and the moon
And the common aether, and the Milky Way of heaven, and Olympus's
Heights, and the hot force of the stars were aroused
To come-into-being . . .

I.64 Parmenides, fr. 12
For the narrower orbits are filled with pure fire
And those next to them with night, though a share of flame is emitted.
In the middle of these is the divinity who governs all.
For everywhere she rules hateful birth and sexual union
Sending the female to unite with the male, and in turn the opposite,
Male with female . . .

I.65 Parmenides, fr. 13
First of all the gods she contrived was Erōs . . .

I.66 Parmenides, fr. 14
[The moon] wandering about the earth shining in the night with a light not its
   own . . .

I.67 Parmenides, fr. 15
[The moon] always looking at the beams of the sun . . .

I.68 Parmenides, fr. 16
According to which combination of the much-wandering parts of the body
Prevails at any time, so does thought come to human beings. For it is the same
Nature of parts of the body that thinks in human beings,
Each and all; for thought is that which is full.

I.69 Parmenides, fr. 19
Thus, according to opinion, were these things born and now are,
And from now on will grow, and will later perish.
And for each of these human beings proposed a distinguishing name.

Zeno of Elea

Little is known of Zeno's life other than that he was from Elea, a Greek colony in Italy, and
that he was a companion and student of the other great Eleatic philosopher, Parmenides.
Although the relevant evidence is scant, there is reason to believe that Zeno led an active
political life, once even plotting against a tyrant and suffering torture as a result (DK 19A1,
2, 6, 7, 8, and 9). If these stories are to be believed, Zeno distinguished himself in bravery
no less than in philosophy.

Zeno's philosophical importance lies wholly in his famous paradoxes. Determined to defend Parmenidean philosophy, Zeno adopted a style of argument in which he refuted opponents' views by showing that they led to absurd or contradictory conclusions, a style of reasoning known as *reductio ad absurdum* (or "indirect proof") later adapted and applied to ethics in the so-called "Socratic method" (the Socratic *elenchos*), and recognized as logically valid even today. Aristotle is said to credit Zeno with the discovery of dialectic (DL VIII.57).

(i) The paradox of parts

Zeno's paradoxes earned a good deal of respect; indeed, it is arguable that without them Parmenides' influence would not have been nearly as great as it was – especially given Parmenides' stylistic opacity. Unlike those of Parmenides, Zeno's arguments (for all their intricacy) have the virtue of plain logical structure. For example, against the pluralists (those who believe reality to be composed of many things, or parts, as opposed to the Parmenidean One – see Parmenides fr. 8 [I.59], line 6), Zeno proposes a dilemma (fragments 1 and 2: DK 29B1 and 29B2): if reality is composed of a plurality of things, then either the alleged parts of it have no size, or each part must be infinitely large. If composed of parts without size, everything is without size: adding nothing to nothing, no matter how many times, yields nothing. But if the parts reality is supposed to have are themselves made up of parts with size, then each must be infinitely divisible (at least in theory, if not in practice) into smaller parts of some finite size. But if this is the case, argues Zeno, each supposed part is infinitely large, for adding an infinite number of non-zero-sized things yields infinite size. A number of such arguments are credited to Zeno.

(ii) The paradoxes of space, time, and motion

Perhaps the effectiveness of Zeno's arguments is best shown by their durability; only by the invention of calculus were we finally able to circumvent Zeno's paradoxes of space, time, and motion – and by "circumvent," we do not mean "solve" or "refute," at least in any ordinary sense, for it is at least arguable that the concept of a limit, by which calculus redefines these problems, simply provides a different way to conceive the problem, rather than showing why Zeno's way is false. The fact remains that, given his assumptions, Zeno's logic is impeccable; and even if calculus is right in supplying new assumptions, those employed by Zeno remain compellingly intuitive even today – even if his conclusions remain as compellingly anti-intuitive as they have always been.

I.70 Aristotle, *Physics* VI.9.239b9–240a17
There are four arguments of Zeno about motion, which cause troubles to those trying to do away with them. The first says that there is no motion since the moving thing must get to the halfway point before reaching the end. [. . .]
    The second is called the "Achilles." It says that, when running, the slowest can never be caught by the swiftest; for the pursuer must first come upon the point from which the pursued began, and thus it is necessary for the slowest always to be ahead. This is the same argument as that involving bisection, except that what has to be gotten over successively is not divided in half. [. . .]
    The third [. . .] says that the flying arrow rests. This follows from supposing time to be made up of moments; if this is not granted, the argument will not work.

The fourth is about masses moving in opposite directions in a stadium, past masses equal to them, some from the end of the stadium, some from the curve, at equal speed; in this, he thinks it to follow that half a time is equal to its double. [. . .] Let the resting masses of equal size be A's, and let B's be those beginning from the middle of the A's, equal in number and size to these, and let C's begin from the end of the B's, equal in number and size to these, and equal in speed to the B's. It follows that the first B reaches the end of the A's at the same time as the first C does, moving equivalently. It also follows that this C has passed all of the B's, whereas the B has passed only half of the A's, so as to take half the time, for each of the two is equal to each. But at the same time it follows that the B's have passed all of the C's, for at the same time the first C and the first B will be at opposite ends, [the C's] taking an equal time to pass each of the B's and the A's, so he says, since it takes an equal time for each to pass the A's.

Happily, these arguments are also mentioned elsewhere in such a way as to allow us to interpret their content. The first two show the concept of motion to lead to absurdity by assuming the infinite divisibility of space and time. In brief, the first ("Stadium") shows that if space and time are extended and infinitely divisible, each example of motion will require the moving thing to traverse an infinite sequence of halfway points – half of the distance to the goal, and half of that distance, and half of that, and so on, *ad infinitum*. But the sum of an infinite sequence of non-zero extensions, Zeno argues, is infinite extension.[6] The second (the "Achilles") matches a faster runner with a slower one, where the slower is given a head start. For each interval where the faster runner gets to the place where the slower was at the start of that interval, the slower has moved ahead another interval. As the two runners continue to run, there will be an infinite (though decreasing in size each time) sequence of such intervals, each one including a finite length of space and each taking up a finite duration of time. The sum of these, again, will be infinite, according to Zeno, and so the faster runner can never overtake the slower.

The other two paradoxes show there to be no escape from the results of the first two in rejecting infinite divisibility. Again briefly, in the third ("Flying Arrow") a moving arrow is shown to occupy a certain extension of space larger than the space it occupies when at rest, for it moves from that space to another. Since velocity is distance (d) over time (t), let us say that the arrow is moving at a constant speed of d/t. We can show that it is absurd to

6 It is this inference that modern mathematics would reject. If we could define the distance between A and B as 1 unit in length, then each division would be half of the space divided. The sequence, then, would look something like this: $1/2, 1/4, 1/8, 1/16$ . . . Precisely because each of the next numbers in the sequence is only half of the former number, the total length – even if the sequence is iterated infinitely many times – will never be infinite in extension. Zeno could still object that any motion will have to accomplish the completion of an infinite series, whereas the series represented above is never "complete" – that is, it never sums to the "target" unit of length (the distance between A and B) – one unit of length. Moreover, the same reasoning would apply to each of the steps in the sequence: To complete any of the steps, one would first have to complete an infinite series, the "sum" of which would not be equal to the step in question, no matter how infinitesimally short in length we make the "target" step to be completed. Zeno might argue, accordingly, that under such circumstances, it seems that no matter how short we make the distance between the starting point and any "target," we will never be able to reach the target. If so, he might argue, motion is impossible, for by this reasoning, one could never traverse my extension of infinitely divisible length, no matter how small we make it.

imagine time to be composed of indivisible moments by showing that any supposedly indivisible interval (say, *t*), no matter how small, can be divided into half its size by recognizing that before moving all of *d*, the arrow would first have to go halfway. But then, if we ask how much time it would take to go that halfway, we will divide the interval that was suppose to be indivisible. Similarly, we can show that it is absurd to imagine space to be composed of indivisible minima, by showing that each extension of space (say, *d*) can be subdivided by recognizing the amount of space the arrow would fly in half of the time it took to cover *d*. Similar reasoning applies in the final paradox ("Moving Rows"). If we take three rows of objects – one stationary and two moving in opposite directions at the same speed – we can show that it is absurd to suppose that time is indivisible, because if we stipulate a supposedly indivisible interval of time as the time it takes one of the moving objects to pass one of the stationary ones, we will see that in that same interval, each moving object will pass two of the other moving objects, as they are moving at the same speed in opposite directions. But then if we ask how much time it will take for each moving object to pass *only one* of the other moving objects, we will divide the supposedly indivisible moment of time. Equally, if we try to suppose that space is not infinitely divisible, and suppose that each of the objects in the rows is one single minimum of space, then if we ask how many of the stationary objects each moving object will pass when it passes *only one* of the other moving objects, we will divide the supposedly indivisible minima of space.

The four paradoxes together yield the following argument schema:

1   Assume that motion is possible. (Assumption for indirect proof)
2   Motion requires there to be extended space and time. (Premise)
3   Either extended space and time are infinitely divisible, or they are not. (Law of excluded middle)
4   If space and time are infinitely divisible, the concept of motion is absurd. (From the first – "Stadium" – and second – "Achilles" – paradoxes)
5   But it is also absurd to suppose that space and time are extended, but not infinitely divisible. (From the third – "Flying Arrow" – and fourth – "Moving Rows" – paradoxes)
6   Therefore, the possibility of motion must be rejected.

It is simple enough to see how Zeno would use this argument structure as a foundation for his affirmation of a variety of Parmenidean conclusions: rejecting extended space and time as contributing to these paradoxes, rejecting the senses as purporting to reveal the impossible (e.g. motion) to us, and so forth.

Melissus of Samos

The philosophy of the Eleatic philosophers, Parmenides and Zeno, was enormously influential, and philosophers all over the Greek world – from Italy to Asia Minor (now Turkey) read and emulated the Eleatics. One such philosopher, on the other side of the Greek world (on the island of Samos, just off the Ionian coast of Asia Minor), was Melissus, who is recalled (DL I.16) as writing only one book of philosophy: *On Nature or On What Is* (Simplicius, *Commentary on Aristotle's Physics* 70.16 (= DK 30A4). But Melissus was no mere follower of the Eleatic view. He did accept and argued for the Eleatics' claim that being must be ungenerated and indestructible.

I.71 Melissus, fr. 1

It always was what it was and always will be. For if it had come into being, necessarily before it came into being there was nothing. But if there was nothing, in no way could something come into being from nothing.

But Melissus could not accept the Eleatic rejection of extended space and time. In Melissus' view, being must have limitless extension in both space and time.

I.72 Melissus, fr. 2

Since, therefore, it did not come into being, but is, it always was and always will be, and has no beginning nor end, but is limitless [*apeiron*]. For if it had come into being, it would have a beginning (for it would have begun coming into being at some time) and an end (for it would have ended coming into being at some time). But since it neither began nor ended, it always was and always will be, and has no beginning nor end; for what is not always cannot be complete.

I.73 Melissus, fr. 3

But since it always is, so too it must be limitless in size.

I.74 Melissus, fr. 4

Nothing that has a beginning and an end is either everlasting or limitless.

Several other fragments seek to draw out further conclusions from the original premises Melissus borrowed from Eleatic philosophy. Perhaps the most interesting of these serves as a challenge to the efforts of post-Parmenidean philosophers (such as Empedocles or Anaxagoras) who sought to make some application of the Eleatic philosophy of being in their cosmologies.

I.75 Melissus, fr. 8

If things were many, they would have to be such as I say the one is. For if there is earth and water and air and fire and iron and gold, and what's alive and what's dead, and black and white, and the other things people say really exist – if these things exist, and we see and hear correctly, each one of these must be such as it seemed to us at first, and can neither be changed nor become different, but each thing must always be such as it is. But now, we say that we see and hear and understand correctly, yet we believe that what is hot becomes cold and the cold, hot, and the hard, soft, and the soft, hard, and what's alive dies, and comes into being from what is not alive, and that all things are changed, and that what was and what now is are not the same, but iron, which is hard, is worn away by contact with the finger, and gold and stone and the other things as seem to us to be completely strong, and from water, earth and stone come into being. So it turns out that we neither see nor know existing things. These are therefore inconsistent with each other. For we say there are many things that are both everlasting and have forms and strength of their own, but it seems to us they all change from what we see each time. Plainly, therefore, that we did not see correctly, nor do we believe correctly that they are many. For they would not change if they were real, but each would be just as it seemed to be; for nothing is stronger that what really is. But if it has changed, what is has been destroyed and what is not has come into being. As a result, therefore, if there are many things, they would have to be such as the one.

As we will now see, this is precisely what later pluralists say about the many things that appear in their cosmologies – the basic elements themselves will be changeless, and all apparent change will simply be changes in the way the basic elements are configured relative to one another.

4

The Pluralists

Empedocles of Acragas

I.76 Simplicius, *Commentary on Aristotle's Physics* 25.19 (quoting Theophrastus; = DK 31A7)

Empedocles the Acragantian was born not long after Anaxagoras, and was an emulator and disciple of Parmenides, and even more of the Pythagoreans.

Such associations are commonly made by later sources, but often are contradicted by others.

I.77 Diogenes Laertius, VIII.55–6

Theophrastus says he emulated Parmenides and imitated him in his poetry. [. . .] But according to Hermippus, it was not Parmenides but Xenophanes whom he emulated and with whom he lived and whose poetry he imitated. He met with the Pythagoreans later.

Empedocles is said to have been trained as a physician, and supposedly wrote a discourse on medicine, though none of this work has survived. He may also have written as many as forty-three tragedies (DL VIII.58) and other works of various kinds, which are also lost. Quite a number of fragments of his writings (traditionally said to consist of two works, *On Nature* or *On the Nature of Things* and *Purifications*, though they are probably one work) have survived, however. Given the nature of the poetry, it can also sometimes be somewhat difficult to discern its meaning, or to reconstruct a thread of argument from what remains. In what follows, we seek only to provide a sample of the remaining fragments which reveals Empedocles' best-known views.

(i) The four elements (or "roots")

I.78 Empedocles, fr. 6

Hear first the four roots of all things!

Zeus shining, Hera bringer of life, Aidoneus [Hades]
And Nestis, whose tears moisten mortal springs.

According to Aristotle (*Metaphysics* I.4 985a31–3; = DK 31A37), we are supposed to understand these gods' names as references to the four elements, presumably fire, air, earth, and water, respectively (see Aetius 1.3.20). Empedocles declared that none of these comes into being, nor does any ever cease to exist (frr. 8, 11, 12, among others; presumably following Parmenides in this). Instead, things undergo change in form only, through separation and combination (thus allowing change, where the Eleatics had wholly denied it).

(ii) Strife separates things; Love brings them together (and creates living things)

I.79 Empedocles, fr. 17 (lines 16–20)
A double tale I tell: At one time they grew to be one, alone
From many. And at another time they grow apart to be many, from one:
Fire and water and earth and enormously high air,
And accursed Strife apart from them, alike everywhere
And Love among them, equal in length and width.

I.80 Empedocles, fr. 21 (lines 7–8)
In Anger, all things are of different shapes and separate;
But in Love they come together and long for each other.

I.81 Empedocles, fr. 35 (lines 3–11)
When Strife got to the lowest depth
Of the eddy, and Love comes to be in the middle of the whirl,
It is there that all these come together to be one alone.
Not suddenly, but willingly coming together – different ones from different places,
And as they mixed, myriads of tribes of mortal things poured forth,
But many remained unmixed, alternating with those being mixed:
Those that Strife restrained from above, for it had not blamelessly
Withdrawn completely to the furthest limits of the circle,
But some of its limbs remained within, and others had departed.

(iii) Before love joins them, separate parts and organs lived apart from others

I.82 Empedocles, fr. 57
Many heads sprang up, without necks
And arms were wandering, unattached, without shoulders
And eyes were roaming about alone, needing foreheads.

(iv) As these parts come together, random combinations form organisms

I.83 Empedocles, fr. 59
But when divinity was mixed with divinity to a greater degree,
These things fell together, however they chanced to meet each other,
And many other things besides them were constantly coming into being.

I.84 Empedocles, fr. 61
Many were born with faces and breasts on both sides,
Man-faced offspring of oxen, and some of the opposite sort:
Ox-faced offspring of men, combined partly from men
And partly from women, fitted with shadowy parts.

(v) Transmigration of souls and (presumably related) food prohibitions

I.85 Empedocles, fr. 117
For already I have been a boy, a girl,
A shrub, a bird, and a fish coming from the sea.[1]

I.86 Empedocles, fr. 139
Oh, woe that pitiless day did not destroy me first
Before I conceived the wicked deeds of eating flesh with my lips!

I.87 Empedocles, fr. 141
Wretches, utter wretches, keep your hands off beans!

Anaxagoras of Clazomenae

Anaxagoras seems actually to have been older than Empedocles, but is generally considered to be a later philosopher, on the basis of testimony from Aristotle:

I.88 Aristotle, *Metaphysics* I.3.984a11
Anaxagoras the Clazomenian, though older than Empedocles, was later in his works.

Though born in Clazomenae (a small island off the coast of Asia Minor), Anaxagoras seems to have relocated to Athens and began and continued his philosophical career there, leaving Athens only after being put on trial for atheism,[2] whereupon he moved again to Lampascus (on the coast of Asia Minor, some distance north of Clazomenae), where he lived for some time until his death early in the 420s BCE. It is unclear whether Anaxagoras ever read or responded to Melissus or Empedocles, though their works seem to have been created before those of Anaxagoras. Like Parmenides and Melissus, Anaxagoras seems to have written just a single book of philosophy (DL I.16), but the work was very important. The great Athenian leader Pericles was supposed to be a close companion – and perhaps student – of Anaxagoras, whose intellectual influence can be seen in the works of Archelaus of Athens, and in direct and indirect references in Plato.

(i) Mixture and plurality

Like Anaximander and Empedocles, Anaxagoras understood cosmology as deriving from a primeval mixture of everything, though unlike Anaximander and more like Empedocles,

---

1 The last words are speculative – the text is corrupt here.
2 Presumably, for claiming that the sun and moon were not divinities. He said the sun was a glowing stone and the moon was made of earth, which glowed by reflecting the sun's light (fr. 18; see also Hippolytus, *Refutation of All Heresies* 1.8.3–10 [= DK 59A42]; Plato, *Apology* 26d4–9).

Anaxagoras did not understand the primeval mixture as the material principle itself, but rather simply as a mixture of the basic elements.

I.89 Anaxagoras, fr. 1
All things were together, limitless both in number and in smallness. For the small was also limitless. And because all were together, nothing was distinguishable because of its smallness, for air and aether dominated all things, both being limitless. For these are the most important things in the complete mixture, both in number and in size.

Whereas the fundamental elements in Empedocles are four, however, Anaxagoras envisioned innumerably many – one for every sort of thing we find in nature. Following the Eleatic influence of the time, however, Anaxagoras held each of the elemental building blocks to be a changeless one – essentially as Melissus had insisted they must be – for there to be a plurality.

I.90 Anaxagoras, fr. 4
And this being how things are, one must believe that there are many things of all sorts in all things that are composite – seeds of all things, having all sorts of shapes and colors and flavors. And human beings have been put together, and the other animals with life [*psuchēn*]. And the human beings have both inhabited cities and constructed works, just as we do, and they had the sun, and moon and the other things, just as we do; and the earth produced for them many different kinds of crops, of which they gather the best and use them in their homes. This I have said about separating off – that not only with us does separation off occur, but also elsewhere.

But before these things were separated off, when all things were together, no color was distinguishable (for the mixture of all things prevented it) of the moist and the dry, the hot and the cold, and the bright and the dark, and there was much earth in the mixture and seeds limitless in number and in no way like each other. For none of the other things either are like each other. Being like this, one must believe that all things were in the whole.

(ii) Mind

If the *cosmos* originated in a mixture of everything, something must have begun the process of separating everything out of the mixture, as plainly today's world is not a great cosmic mixture of everything with everything else. According to Anaxagoras, it is Mind that began this process.

I.91 Anaxagoras, fr. 12
Other things have a portion of everything, but Mind is limitless and self-ruled, and is mixed with nothing, but is alone by itself. For if it were not by itself, but were mixed with anything else, it would have a share of all things, if it were mixed with anything. For in everything, there is a portion of everything, as I have said earlier. And the things mixed with it would impede it, so that it would rule nothing as it actually does by being alone by itself. For it is the finest of all things and the purest, and has complete knowledge about everything and the greatest power. And over whatever has soul [or is alive – *psuchēn*], both in greater and smaller amounts, mind rules. And over the entire

rotation mind ruled, so that it rotated in the beginning. And first it began to rotate from a small area, then rotates over a larger, and will rotate over larger yet. And what is mixed, separated off, and distinguished are all known by Mind. And whatever was to be – whatever was and whatever is now and whatever will be, all Mind arranged, also this rotation in which are now rotating the stars and the sun and the moon, and the air and the aether that are being separated off. This rotation caused the separating off. And the dense is being separated off from the rare, and the hot from the cold, and the bright from the dark and the dry from the moist. But there are many portions of many things, and nothing is being completely separated off nor distinguished one from the other except Mind. Mind is all alike, both the larger and smaller. Nothing else is like anything else, but each single thing is and was most clearly those things it contains the most.

(iii) "Seeds of all things," "seeds limitless in number"

In fragment 4 (I.90, above), we are told that within the primeval mixture there were "seeds of all things," and "seeds limitless in number." And in fragment 12 (I.91), we are told that "each single thing [except Mind] is an was most clearly those things it contains the most." Unlike the atomists, whom we will discuss momently, Anaxagoras stipulated (against the Eleatics) that the composition of the *cosmos* was infinitely divisible.

I.92 Anaxagoras, fr. 3
Neither of what is small is there a smallest, but always a smaller (for what is cannot not-be) – but also of the large there is always larger. And it is equal to what is small in number; but in relation to itself, each is both great and small.

Despite its infinite divisibility, however, once things begin to be separated off from the mixture, they begin to take the forms we recognize today, and the reason for this is that these recognizable forms have their character in virtue of what they contain the most. For "in everything there is a portion of everything, except Mind" (fr. 12 [I.91], above), though some things (presumably intelligent beings) also have a portion of Mind (fr. 11). These "seeds" or portions, when enough of the same sort are sufficiently concentrated in a thing, explain why all of the different things in the world (all except Mind containing portions of everything else nonetheless) seem different from one another.

I.93 Anaxagoras, fr. 10
For how could hair come from what is not hair and flesh from not flesh?

Aristotle helps us to understand how Anaxagoras' view worked differently from that of Empedocles.

I.94 Aristotle, *On the Heaven* III.3.302a28–b4 (see also *Physics* I.4.187a23–b7)
Anaxagoras and Empedocles say opposing things about the elements. Empedocles said that fire and earth and the other things of that order are the elements of bodies and that everything is composed of these, but Anaxagoras opposes this. He maintains that the homeomeries [the "seeds" or portions whose predominance give different things their recognizable forms] are elements (I mean flesh and bone and such other things),

whereas air and fire are mixtures of these and all the other seeds; for each of them consists of invisible homeomeries all combined.

Apparently, one advantage Anaxagoras saw in his conception of innumerably many elements (as opposed to the traditional four: earth, water, air, and fire) is that he could better explain phenomena such as nutrition. Water may quench our thirst, but we cannot receive adequate nutrition from any (or any combination) of the other traditional elements (see fr. 10 [I.93]; also, Aetius 1.3.5).

Anaxagoras is also credited with having made many other scientific discoveries, providing quite modern explanations of eclipses, for example (Hippolytus, *Refutation of All Heresies* 1.8.3–10 = DK 59A42), and hypothesizing that the first animals arose in moisture via natural processes (*Refutation* 1.8.12 = DK 59A42), presumably via the seeds contained in the air once it is separated off from the primeval mixture (Theophrastus, *History of Plants* 3.1.4).

5

The Atomists

Leucippus of Elea (or Miletus) and Democritus of Abdera

(i) Atoms and void

The first expressions of atomist philosophy, later claimed as his own by Epicurus, are associated with Leucippus and Democritus. Of these, we know very little about the former, except that he is credited by Aristotle and Aristotle's students as having been the founder of atomism.

> **I.95** Simplicius, *Commentary on Aristotle's Physics* 28.4–26 (= DK67A8, 68A38)
> Leucippus the Eleatic or Milesian (for both are claimed about him) had associated with Parmenides in philosophy, but in regard to the things that are did not follow the same path as Parmenides and Xenophanes, but the opposite, it seems. For whereas they made the *cosmos* one, immobile, ungenerated, and limited and did not even allow the investigation of what is not, he postulated the atoms as limitless and always moving elements, and limitlessly many shapes among them, on the ground that they are no more like this than like that, since he noted that coming into being and motion [or change] are never-ending in things that are. He also claimed that what is exists no more than what is not, and both are equal as causes of what comes into being. For supposing the content of the atoms to be compact and full, he said that it is Being, and moves in the void, which he called Not-Being. For by supposing the atoms are matter for things that are, they generate the rest by means of differences [in the ways the atoms combine]. These are three: rhythm, turning, and touching – that is, shape, position, and arrangement. For what is like is naturally moved by like, and things of the same sort move towards each other, and each of the shapes produces a different compound when arranged in a different combination. Hence, because the principles are limitless, they could plausibly account for all properties and substances: how and by what cause anything comes into being. This is why they say that only those who make the elements limitless account plausibly for everything. They say that the plurality of the shapes of atoms is limitless on the ground that they are no more like this than like that. For they assign this themselves as a cause of the limitlessness.

Democritus and Epicurus seem to have accepted the basic atomist theory offered by Leucippus, and then put that theory to several of their own original uses. But their atomism in itself led most sources simply to identify all of them as holding the same view.

I.96 Simplicius, *Commentary on Aristotle's On the Heaven* 242.18–26
For they [Leucippus, Democritus, and Epicurus] said that in number the first principles were limitless, and thought they were atoms and indivisible and incapable of being changed because of being compact, and with no share of void. They said that it is because of void in bodies that division comes about. These atoms in the limitless void – separate from one another and different in shape and size and position and arrangement – move in the void, and collide when they overtake one another, and some rebound in whatever chance direction, but others become entangled due to the congruity between their shapes and sizes and positions and arrangements, and stay together, and this is how things that are compounds are generated.

The atomists, then, accepted the non-infinite divisibility of matter, though they have changed the original meaning of "divisible" from the arithmetic or geometric notion (apparently intended in Zeno's work and also in that of Anaxagoras) to the idea of actual cutting or breaking up of things: the very word, "atom," derives from the Greek word "to cut" (*tomein*) with the negating "alpha privative"; hence, an "atom" is something that cannot be *cut* or broken into pieces – for, as Simplicius puts it, "it is because of void in bodies that division comes about." The atoms themselves contain no void. Similarly, by characterizing the atoms as "Being" and the void as "Not-Being," the atomists formulate an answer to the Eleatic denial of non-being, essentially by providing a new meaning to the term. "What is" becomes "what is an atom"; "what is not" becomes "the void."

All of the things we encounter in the world come into being from atoms and void because the atoms move constantly through the void, and sometimes become entangled into different larger forms. Even in such entanglements, however, there remain gaps between the entangled atoms – gaps occupied by void. Such larger compound entities, accordingly, can be partitioned or dissolved by separating the clinging atoms at these gaps in their connections. Everything comes into being and passes away, then, as a result of the random connection and disconnection of atoms colliding in the void.

(ii) Perception

Given such a simplified cosmology (limited to atoms and void), the atomists needed to explain sensation as the product of streams of atoms colliding with our sense-organs. This view did not much impress Aristotle:

I.97 Aristotle, *On Sensation* 4.442a29–31
Democritus and the majority of the nature-philosophers who talk about perception commit a huge error; for they regard all perception as being by touch.

Differences of perception were the result of differences in the kinds of atoms ricocheting off our sense organs (see Theophrastus *On Sensation* 66 [= DK 68A135] and *Causes of Plants* 6.1.6 [= DK 68A129]). This "particle theory" of perception was enormously influential throughout the ancient (and even into the medieval) period.

(iii) Skepticism about human judgment

We have many remaining fragments of Democritus' work, though only a very small fraction of what he was said to have written (some fifty-two works, according to DL IX.45 [= DK 68A33]). The majority of these remaining fragments are on ethics or are criticisms of human judgment (which thinks of things as large in size, and not as random combinations of atoms and void), and many of the fragments show no obvious application of atomist cosmology. But in some, it is clear that Democritus sought to make this connection.

> I.98 Democritus, fr. 9
> By convention, sweet; by convention, bitter; by convention, hot; by convention, cold; by convention color; but in reality, atoms and void.

> I.99 Democritus, fr. 8
> But it will be clear that to know really what each thing is, is perplexing.

Aristotle explains these points in terms of differences in perception between different animals and even between different human beings.

> I.100 Aristotle, *Metaphysics* III.5.1009b7–12
> And also the same things appear in opposite ways to many animals when they are in good health as they do to us, and even about the same things, one does not always believe the same things as a result of perception. Which, therefore, is true or false is unclear; for these are no more true than those, but equal. This is why Democritus, at any rate, says that either nothing is true, or else to us it is unclear.

(iv) Ethics

Most of the ancient Greek philosophers up through and including Aristotle conceived of the aim or goal of human life, or the highest human good, as *eudaimonia* – typically translated as "happiness," but which some have also translated as "human flourishing." But Democritus offered a somewhat different view:

> I.101 Diogenes Laertius IX.45 (DK 68A1)
> The aim [of human life] is cheerfulness [*euthumia*], which is not the same as pleasure, as some by misinterpretation have incorrectly supposed, but a state in which the soul continues calmly and steadily, not disturbed by fear or superstition or any other emotion. He also calls it well-being [*euestō*] and many other names.

It is not clear whether one of the names he used was the *eudaimonia* – happiness. At any rate, Democritus is clear in distinguishing cheerfulness from pleasure. The later atomist, Epicurus, as we will see, did accept a form of hedonism.

Democritus' view of cheerfulness also seemed to have some relationship to his cosmology of atoms randomly moving and colliding in the void. In such a world, no one is immune to chance; no one really controls their own destiny. It is best, then, to scale back one's desires and wishes to where one will not be frustrated and disturbed by overreaching.

I.102 Democritus, fr. 3

One who is to be cheerful must not do too much, whether in private or in public, nor, in whatever he does seek to go beyond his natural capacity. Instead, he must take special care that even when luck comes to him and promises more, in his judgment he can set it aside and not attempt more than those things within his capacities. The right load is better than a great load.

I.103 Democritus, fr. 191 (in part)

For cheerfulness comes to people by measured enjoyment and a proportioned life. Deficiencies and excesses love to turn around and make large motions in the soul. Those souls that undergo large motions neither do well nor are they cheerful. One should fix one's mind, therefore, on what is within one's powers and to be satisfied with what is at hand, giving slight notice to those who are envied or admired, and not attending to them in thought. Rather, one should consider the lives of those with troubles, and realize how great their suffering is. In this way, the things at hand and which you control will appear great and enviable, and no more will your soul suffer from desire for more.

Democritus also seems to have accepted some form of the idea that the best way to pursue the aim of human life was by mastering the potential that pleasure has to control one's life. This same view was argued in several ways by Socrates, Plato, and Aristotle.

I.104 Democritus, fr. 214

Not only is he who masters the enemy courageous, but also he who masters pleasures. Some are masters of cities, but slaves of women.

The advice we find in Democritus' surviving fragments may seem somewhat trite, in the light of the great and sophisticated theories that later ancient authors provided. Nonetheless, quite typical features of the later Greek theories may already be found here: conceiving of human life as having a single, overarching good at which we should aim, approaching that aim with moderation and prudence, and avoiding damaging and dangerously bewitching pleasures.

6

The Sophists

"Sophist" comes from the Greek word *sophistēs* which simply means "wise person," but came to be the term used to identify professional teachers who traveled around Greece offering courses and writing works on various subjects – including natural science, religion, and rhetoric (persuasive speaking) – in the latter part of the fifth and into the fourth century BCE. In natural science, the Sophists continued the research of the Presocratics whose work we have already introduced. Their main legacy, however, is in the various fields of rhetoric. Especially in ancient Athens, in which all legal and political speech was by citizens (rather than advocates, such as lawyers or paid prosecutors), if one wished to prosecute a legal case (there was effectively no difference between criminal and civil cases), one would have to undertake the prosecution oneself, and the same went for offering a defense if one were charged, and for any other public speaking – in the Assembly or Council or any other government body, in which one would serve either as a volunteer (e.g. in the Assembly) for modest pay, or for which one might be selected to serve by lot. Effective public speaking and persuasion was, in Athens and other Greek democracies, essentially a life-skill as a result. The Sophists generally charged high fees, however, so only the wealthy could afford their services. One could pay to have a defense or prosecution speech written on one's behalf, of course, and then memorize it. Or, if the orator was sympathetic to one's cause, one could arrange to have him serve as a *sunēgoros* (supporting speaker) in a legal trial. Among the Athenian citizens themselves, the great speech-writers themselves often became important statesmen. (Non-citizens could not participate, but could provide speeches to those who were able to participate.)

Some of the actual texts (and fragments) by the Sophists that have survived, however, are not actual speeches given by litigants or in government, but are "model orations" (*epideixeis*), whose main purpose seems to have been to advertise the cleverness and skill of the speech-maker, presumably to attract the business of students who would pay handsomely for the opportunity to learn from the Sophist. The interpretation of these "model orations" continues to be disputed, and there may not be a single correct way to approach all of them. Did their authors intend for us to take the points and arguments (including in some cases, important historical claims) made in them very seriously, or were they more simply displays of adroitness in argumentation, whose actual truth or falsehood was never intended to be at issue?

We know the names of many of the Sophists, but have texts and fragments from only a few. Several different Sophists are named or appear as speaking characters in Plato's dialogues. Those that do speak are inevitably portrayed as faltering under pressure from Socrates' questioning, and in any case Plato's hostility towards the Sophists and their teachings make him a very unreliable source. For our purposes here, then, we will include just a few representative writings from three of the most famous Sophists: Protagoras of Abdera, Gorgias of Leontini, and Antiphon (probably) of Athens.

Protagoras of Abdera (fl. c.444–441 BCE)

I.105 Diogenes Laertius IX.50–6 (excerpted)

Protagoras . . . was from Abdera. He . . . gave public speeches for which fees were charged . . . Protagoras studied under Democritus . . . [He] was the first to claim that there are two opposing arguments for every issue, and he was also the first to argue in this way. In addition, he began a work in this way

[Fragment 1]: "Man is the measure of all things, of things that are that they are, and of things that are not that they are not."

He said that that soul is nothing other than the senses . . . and that everything is true. In another work he began thus [Fragment 4]:

"About the gods, I cannot know whether they exist or do not exist. For many are the obstructions to knowledge, both the obscurity of the issue and the brevity of human life." Because of this introduction to his book the Athenians exiled him, and they burned his books in the marketplace, after sending around a messenger to collect them from everyone who had them.

He was the first to charge a hundred minae [for his teaching] . . . He was the originator of the kind of combative disputants now so much in fashion. He also first introduced the Socratic kind of argument . . . and the first to explain how to attack and refute any thesis. [. . .]

It is told that once, when he asked for his fee from his disciple Euathlus [who had studied with him and agreed to pay if and only if he won his first case at law], the latter replied, "But I haven't yet won a case." "But," he [Protagoras] said, "if I win this case I must get the fee, because I won; and if you win [I should get the fee] because you [won it]."

Euathlus, however, turned the tables on Protagoras by pointing out that, on the contrary, he owed nothing either way: if Euathlus should win the suit he is cleared by the court; if not, then he is relieved of the debt by his agreement with Protagoras.

Fragment 1 is certainly the most important of Protagoras' surviving fragments, and receives extensive consideration (and both explicit and implicit criticism) by Socrates, Plato, and Aristotle, all of whom argue against Protagoras' relativism and advocate instead non-relativistic conceptions of both ethics and reality. Somewhat less certain is Diogenes' claim that Protagoras was the first to teach competitive argumentation, though there can be no doubt that this style of argumentation had become a very popular subject by Plato's time (one that Plato subjects to withering criticism in several of his works, and which he is very careful to contrast with the Socratic style). Diogenes' tale about Protagoras' expulsion from Athens and his books being burned is not at all corroborated by anything else we know from this period, and is thus almost certainly apocryphal. But the agnosticism Protagoras expresses about the gods seems a more secure association, and seems to have become associated with the entire sophistical movement – eventually to become one of the stereotypes with which Socrates (fittingly or unfittingly) was impugned before and during his trial for impiety.

Gorgias of Leontini (c.480–390 BCE)

The surviving works of Gorgias include mere lines of several longer works, a part of a funeral oration given in praise of the Athenian war dead, and at least parts of two longer *epideixis* speeches, both of which must surely not be taken seriously as expressions of Gorgias' actual views, but instead are examples of clever arguments for positions that would on their face be taken as absurd. The more absurd the thesis, the more clever arguments must be to appear to make that thesis plausible. The two surviving *epideixeis* by Gorgias plainly demonstrate his rhetorical skills, accordingly. In one, he offers a defense for the notorious adulteress, Helen – whose running away with the Trojan prince Paris is what launched Greece into the Trojan War. In the other, which we offer below, Gorgias offers seductively logical-seeming arguments for the astonishing claim that nothing exists. Gorgias' manipulations of Parmenidean and Zenonian arguments should be obvious to readers. His burlesque of philosophical arguments may well have been precisely intended to make all such arguments appear foolish and ultimately pointless.

> **I.106** Gorgias, "Nothing Is" (= DK 82B3)
>
> If anything is, either it is what is or what is not, or both what is and what is not. But neither is it what is, as he will show,[1] nor is it what is not, as he will explain, nor what is and what is not, as he will also teach. Therefore, it is not. Indeed, what is not, is not. For if what is not, is, it will at the same time be and not be. For conceived as not being, it will not be, whereas in *being* what it not, contrarily, it will be. But it is completely absurd for something to be and not to be at the same time. Therefore, it is not the case that what is not, is. And besides, if what is not, is, what is will not be – for they are opposites, and if being is a property of what is not, then not being will be a property of what is. But certainly, it is not the case that what is, is not; so neither will what is not, be. Neither is it the case that what is, is. For if what is, is, it is either everlasting or generated, or everlasting and generated at the same time. But it is neither everlasting nor generated nor both, as we will show. Therefore, it is not the case that what is, is. For if what is, is everlasting (for we must begin here), it does not have any beginning; for everything that comes into being has some beginning, but what is everlasting, and accordingly ungenerated, did not have a beginning. If it does not have a beginning, it is limitless. And if it is limitless, it is nowhere, for if it is anywhere, the place it is in, is different from it, and so what is will no longer be limitless because it

---

1 This selection is treated as an actual fragment of Gorgias' work, but the third-person verb here and the direct reference to Gorgias later make it clear that the argument given here is at best a close paraphrase. The passage comes from Sextus Empiricus, *Against the Learned* 7.65–86. A somewhat different version of the argument appears in summary form in pseudo-Aristotle, *On Melissus, Xenophanes, and Gorgias*, chs. 5–6.

is enclosed in something. For what encloses is larger than what is enclosed; but nothing is larger than what is limitless, so what is limitless is not anywhere. Moreover, it is not enclosed by itself. For in that case, what contains and what is contained will be the same, and what is will become two – place and body (for what contains is place, and what is contained is body). But this is absurd; so what is does not contain itself either. Therefore, if what is, is everlasting, it is limitless, and if limitless, it is nowhere, and if it is nowhere, it is not. So if what is, is everlasting, it is not at all. Moreover, what is cannot be generated. For if it came into being, it either came from something that is, or from something that's not. But it neither came into being from what is – for if it is something that is, it has not come into being, but already is – nor from what is not – for what is not cannot generate something, since what generates something must necessarily share in existence. Therefore, it is not the case that what is, is generated. In the same ways, it is not both everlasting and generated at the same time. For these are antithetical to one another, and if what is, is everlasting, it has not come into being, and if it has come into being, it is not everlasting. So if what is, is neither everlasting nor generated nor both, what is would not be. And besides, if it is, it is either one or many. But it is neither one nor many, as will be shown. Therefore, it is not the case that what is, is. For if it is one, it is either a discrete quantity, or a continuum, or a magnitude, or a body. And if it is any of these, it is not one – but a discrete quantity is divisible, and a continuum can be cut. Similarly, if conceived as a magnitude, it will not be indivisible, whereas if it should happen to be a body it will be triple – for it will have length, breadth, and depth. But it is absurd to say that what is, is none of these. Therefore, it is not the case that what is, is one. Moreover, it is not many. For if it is not one, neither is it many. For the many are a compound of ones, and since the one is refuted, the many are refuted along with it. From this, it is patent that neither what is, is, nor what is not, is. That it is not the case that both are – what is and what is not – is easily proven. For if what is not, is, and what is, is, then what is not will be the same as what is in regard to being. And as a result neither of them is. For this much is agreed: what is not, is not, and what is has been shown to be the same as this. So it will also not be. Also, if what is, is the same as what is not, it is not possible for both to be. For if both are, then they are not the same; and if they are the same, they can't both be. It follows that nothing is. For if neither what is, is, nor what is not, nor both, and nothing other than these is conceived of, nothing is.

The next thing in order is to demonstrate that even if something is, it is unknowable and inconceivable by human beings. For if what is thought of, says Gorgias, are not things that are, then what is, is not thought. And this is reasonable. For just as if things thought of have the property of being white, being thought of would be a property of white things, so if things thought of have the property of not being things that are, then necessarily not to be thought of will be a property of things that are. This is why it is sound and preserves the consistency of the argument to say, "If the things thought of are not things that are, what is, is not thought of." But things that are thought of (for we must assume this) are not things that are, as we will show. It is not the case, therefore, that what is, is thought of. And in fact it is completely plain that the things thought of are not things that are. For if things thought of are things that are, then all things thought of are – however anyone thinks of them. But this is obviously false. For just because someone thinks that a person flies or chariots ride on the sea, it doesn't follow that a person flies or chariots riding ride on sea. Accordingly, it is not the case that things thought of are things that are. In addition to this, if things thought of are things that are, things that are not will not be thought of. For opposites have opposite properties, and what is not is opposite to what is. Because of this, it is certain that if being thought of is a property of what is, not being thought of will be a property of what is not. But this is absurd. For Scylla and Chimaera and many things that are not are thought of. Therefore, it is not the case that what is, is thought of. And just as things that are seen are called visible because they are seen, and things that are heard are called audible because they are heard, and we do not reject the visibles because they are not heard, nor dismiss the audibles because they are not seen (for each should be judged by it's own perception and not by another), so things thought of, even though not seen by vision and not heard by hearing, will be, because they are grasped by the appropriate criterion. So if someone thinks chariots ride on the sea, even if he doesn't see them, he should believe that there are chariots riding on the sea. But this is absurd. Therefore, it is not the case that what is, is thought of and apprehended.

Even if it were apprehended, it is incommunicable to another. For if things that are, are visible and audible and perceptible generally, as essentially external objects, and of these the visible are apprehended by vision and the audible by hearing and not the other way around, how can these be communicated to another? For we communicate by language [*logos*], but language is not the objects and the things that are. Therefore, it is not the case that that we communicate things that are to our neighbors, but language, which is different from the objects. Just as the visible could not become audible and vice versa, therefore, so, since whatever is, is an external object, it could not become our language. But if it were not language, it would not have been revealed to another. Language, in fact, he says, is composed of external things – perceivable things – contacting us. For from coming upon flavor, there comes to be in us the language used to express this quality, and from the incidence of color, the language used to express color. But if this is so, it is not the case that language reveals the external object, but the external object comes to explain language. Moreover, it can't be said that, as visible and audible things are, so too is language an object, so that objects that are can be communicated by it, which is an object that is. For, he says, even if language is an object, in any case it differs from all other objects, and visible bodies differ most of all from language. For the visible is grasped by one organ and language by a different one. Therefore it is not the case that language reveals the large number of objects, just as they do not make clear each other's nature.

Antiphon (latter part of the fifth century BCE)

One of the main features of philosophy associated with the Sophists was the contrast between *nomos* – law or custom – and *phusis* – nature. Moral rules, legal codes and other rules of conduct, they held, were merely customary – in more extreme versions of this view, they were actually just arbitrary and were in any case relative from place to place. At least in the matter of *nomos*, then, the Protagorean dictum that "mean is the measure" was certainly true. This view was later vehemently attacked by Socrates, Plato, and Aristotle. A particularly vivid (though not the most extreme) version of this distinction may be found in the longest fragment from Antiphon, of which we give only a portion of the first part:

I.107 Antiphon, fr. 44

Justice, then, is not violating the laws [*nomoi*] of the city in which you are a citizen. A person would gain most advantage for himself if he treated the laws as important when in the presence of witnesses, and treated the edicts of nature [*phusis*] when alone with no witnesses present. For the edicts of the laws are artificial, whereas those of nature are necessary; those of the laws are the results of agreement, not of natural growth, whereas those of nature are the products of natural growth, not of agreement. If those who made the agreement do not notice a person violating the dictates of the laws, he is free from both disgrace and penalty, and not so, otherwise. But if, as is not possible, anyone violates any of the things that are ingrained in nature, the evil is no less if no one notices him and no greater if all see him. For he does not suffer harm on account of opinion, but because of truth.

As we will soon see, Socrates, Plato, and Aristotle would all dispute this point, in different ways and to different degrees. In Plato's *Crito*, we will find Socrates arguing that disobedience of the laws of the state is morally wrong, and that all moral wrongs *as a matter of human nature* damage the soul of the wrongdoer. In Plato and Aristotle, too, we find various defenses of the *naturalness* of morality and law. Indeed, perhaps the Sophists' greatest achievement, for the history of philosophy, was in the reactions their views provoked from their peer, Socrates, and from his follower and student, Plato, and later, by Plato's student, Aristotle.

Part II

Xenophon (c.430–c.354 BCE)

Introduction

Xenophon was an Athenian historian, philosopher, and military adventurer. He was perhaps a year older than Plato, and these two men provide our most important sources on the life and philosophy of Socrates. Quite remarkably, all of the works of Xenophon mentioned by other writers in antiquity have survived. These include three very important historical works, the *Hellenica*, *Anabasis*, and (pseudo-historical, but still important) *Cyropaedia*, a few minor works in which Xenophon treats various issues related to warcraft and hunting, a few mostly political works, and then four Socratic works – works, that is, in which the philosopher Socrates is recalled or appears as a speaking character: the *Apology of Socrates* (or *Defense of Socrates*), the *Memorabilia* (or *Socratic Memoirs*), the *Symposium*, and the *Oeconomicus* (or *Home Economics*). Each of these works contains much of interest to a student of ancient Greece, but in the history of philosophy only Xenophon's portrait of Socrates has had much influence – and even there, most scholars have given more credence to the picture of Socrates given in Plato's Socratic works. We follow this judgment by including only two short pieces from Xenophon's *Memorabilia* in this collection.

Much has been said about the differences between Xenophon's and Plato's characterizations of Socrates and Socratic philosophy. In particular, the two authors provide very different accounts of several important details in Socrates' speeches and other behavior at his trial for impiety (in 399 BCE). Recent scholarship, however, has begun to reveal important consistencies in the accounts our two main sources provide – for example, in portraying Socrates as committed to obedience to law and legal authority (see Plato's *Crito*, included in this collection), and in the moral psychology both authors attribute to Socrates.

For the purposes of the history of philosophy, Xenophon can be credited with one of the earliest versions of what has come to be known as the "teleological argument" for the existence of God. The gist of this argument is that certain aspects of the way the *cosmos* is provide evidence that it is not the result of random chance (as some Presocratic philosophers had claimed), but is instead the result of a rational plan – a plan that is decidedly "anthropophilic" (friendly to human beings) in character. This argument has enjoyed widespread popularity among philosophical theists, and has been offered in many forms. But the first instance of such an argument in the history of philosophy is that made by Xenophon.

Xenophon (c430–c354 BC)

Introduction

7

Memorabilia

I.4 Conversations with Aristodemus on Religion

If any think, as some write and say on the basis of mere conjecture, that Socrates was extremely 1
influential in exhorting men to virtue yet powerless to lead them to it, they should examine not only the punishment he dealt out in cross-examining the men who thought they knew
everything, but also the conversations in which he passed the time of day with his friends.
Then let them judge whether he was capable of making his companions better. I shall first 2
tell what I once heard him say about divinity, in the course of a discussion with Aristodemus
"the Small," as he was nicknamed. When Socrates discovered that Aristodemus did not sacrifice
to the gods or consult oracles, but even mocked such things, he said, "Tell me, Aristodemus,
aren't there any men whom you admire for their wisdom?"

"Yes, there are."

"Who? Tell me their names," said Socrates.

"In epic poetry, I admire Homer most of all; in dithyramb, Melanippides; in tragedy, 3
Sophocles. In sculpture, Polyclitus; in painting, Zeuxis."

"Who do you think deserves more admiration? Those who create images without sense 4
or power to move, or those who create living beings able to think and act?"

"By Zeus, of course those who create living beings, provided they come into being
through design, not by some chance."

"Suppose there are things which give no hint as to the purpose of their existence, and also
things which clearly serve a useful purpose. Which do you judge to be works of chance and
which works of design?"

"Works that serve a useful end must be works of design."

"Don't you think that, from the very first, the creator of men endowed us with senses for 5
a useful purpose? With eyes to see visible objects, and ears to hear sounds? What use would
odors be to us if we had no nose? Would we taste sweet, bitter, and all the delights of the
palate if our tongue had not been made to taste them? Besides, don't you think that other 6
things, too, are likely to be the result of forethought? The sense of sight is weak, for example, and therefore the eyes are given eyelids which, like doors, open wide when we have
to use our eyes and close when we sleep. Eyelashes grow, like screens, so that the wind does

not hurt our eyes. Above the eyes, eyebrows project like cornices to prevent harm from the sweat of the brow. There is also the fact that ears receive all sounds, but never are clogged up. The front teeth in all living beings are designed to cut; the molars to receive food from the incisors and to grind it. The mouth, through which enter the things that living beings desire, was placed near the eyes and nose. Since excrements are unpleasant, the ducts that get rid of them are as far as possible from the sense organs. When these have been made with so much foresight, are you at a loss to say whether they are the works of chance or of design?"

7   "No, by Zeus!" replied Aristodemus. "When I look at it that way, they do appear to be the works of a wise and loving creator."

"What of the desire to beget children, the mother's desire to raise her children, the children's longing to live, and the great fear of death?"

"To be sure, they seem to be the contrivances of someone who planned for living creatures to exist."

"Do you think that you have any prudence?" asked Socrates.

8   "Ask and I shall reply!"[1]

"Do you think that prudence exists nowhere else? Even though you know that you have in your body only a tiny part of the earth that exists in great quantity, and only a drop of all the abundant waters that exist, and that your body is compounded of just a small part of each of the other elements that are, surely, abundant – do you think that you somehow, by luck, snatched up the only bit of mind that, it seems, exists nowhere else? That these masses, huge and infinite in number, are well arranged, as you suppose, through some absurdity?"

9   "Yes, by Zeus!" replied Aristodemus. "For I do not see the masters as I see the men who make things here on earth."

"Nor do you see your soul, which is master of your body! By your reasoning, then, you could say that nothing you do is by design, but everything is by chance."

10   Aristodemus said, "Socrates, I don't really despise deity; I simply think that it is too great to need my services."

Socrates replied, "Surely the greater the power that condescends to serve you, the more honor it deserves."

11   "You must know," he said, "that if I thought the gods cared at all about men, I would not neglect them."

"Then you don't think that they care? First of all, they made man the only one of living creatures to stand erect, and this upright position makes it possible for him to see farther in front of him, to look more easily above him, and to suffer less harm; they also gave him sight, hearing, and a mouth. Secondly, while to creatures who walk on all fours the gods gave feet, which are good only for locomotion, they gave to man hands, which do most of the things that make us happier than beasts."

12   While it is true that all animals have a tongue, the gods made only the tongue of man able, by touching the different parts of the mouth, to create sounds, and to communicate to other people what we wish. They limited the season of the year in which they gave other animals the pleasures of sexual intercourse, but to us they granted these continuously until old age.

1 It is not certain whether Aristodemus' reply means a modest "Yes," or "Judge for yourself from my answers," or "Continue asking, and I shall answer later."

Not only was the god pleased to take care of the body, but what is most important, he 13 has planted in man the soul which is man's most powerful part. What other creature possesses a soul that, first of all, perceives the existence of the gods, who have established the greatest and most wonderful order? What species, except man, worships gods? What soul is more capable than the human soul in taking precautions against hunger, thirst, heat, and cold, or in preventing diseases, exercising bodily strength, working hard for knowledge; what species is better able to remember what it hears, sees, or learns? Don't you see that in com- 14 parison with other living creatures, men live like gods and are naturally superior in body and soul? Even if he had the body of an ox and the mind of a man, a man could not do what he wanted. If he had hands and not reason, he still would have no advantage. Even though you have received both hands and reason, gifts of the greatest worth, do you think that the gods have no concern for you? What must they do before you will believe that they take care of you?

"When, as you say they do, they send advisers as to what we should and should not do," 15 replied Aristodemus.

Socrates continued, "But when they give answers to the Athenians who ask something through divination, don't you think that they are answering them, or when they send omens to warn the Greeks, or all men? Are you the only one they have singled out and selected for neglect? Do you think that the gods would plant in men the belief in their power to do 16 good and evil, unless they were able to do so? Do you think that men would never have perceived the deception? Don't you see that the oldest and wisest of human institutions, city-states and nations, are the most reverent toward the gods, and that the most prudent periods of man's life are the most concerned with gods? My dear sir," Socrates continued, "you 17 should understand that your mind within deals with your body as it wants. You therefore should realize that universal thought [*tēn en tōi panti phronēsin*] disposes of everything as it pleases. Do not think that your eye can see many miles and the god's eye cannot see the universe all at once, or that your soul can be concerned with things here, and in Egypt and Sicily as well, while the god's mind [*tēn tou theou phronēsin*] is unable to take care of the uni-verse all at once. Just as by serving men you discover who is willing to serve you in return, 18 and by doing a favor who will return the favor, and by taking advice you discover who is prudent – so you should make trial of the gods by serving them to see if they want to coun-sel you about matters hidden to men. You will know that the divine is so great and of such a nature that it sees and hears everything at once, is present everywhere, and is concerned with everything."

I thought that Socrates, by saying things like this, kept his companions from doing unholy, 19 unjust, or evil acts, not only when they could be seen by men, but even in a desert; for they would believe that nothing they might do would escape the notice of the gods.

* * *

IV.3 Socrates Converses with Euthydemus on Religion

Socrates was in no hurry to make his companions eloquent speakers, or men of action, or 1 inventive geniuses. He thought that they should first possess temperance. Men who had these abilities without temperance only became more unjust and more able to work evil, he believed. First of all he tried to make his companions moderate in regard to the gods. Other men who 2 were witnesses as he talked on this topic with various people have told their stories. I myself was present when he spoke as follows with Euthydemus:

3   "Tell me, Euthydemus, have you ever come to observe how carefully the gods have prepared the needs of man?"

"By Zeus, I have not!"

"But don't you know that first and foremost we need light, which the gods give us?"

"Yes, by Zeus, if we did not have light we would be like blind men, as far as our eyes are concerned."

"And because we need rest they give us lovely night for our rest."

"This too is a gift worth our gratitude," said Euthydemus.

4   "Because the sun shines and sheds light upon our daytime hours and all of our activities, whereas the night obscures everything in darkness, they made stars shine in the night; these mark the hours of the night, and enable us to do many of the things we must do."

"This is so," he said.

"The moon marks for us the time not only of the night, but also of the month."

"Yes," said Euthydemus.

5   "What of this? When we need food, the gods give food to us from the earth, and have arranged the seasons to furnish abundantly not only all sorts of necessities but even delights."

"This, too," replied Euthydemus, "shows their love of mankind."

6   Socrates continued, "What of the fact that they give us water – which is so valuable that, with the aid of the earth and the seasons, it produces all that is useful to us? Water even nourishes us and, when mixed with all the things that give us nourishment, it makes them more digestible, more beneficial, and more palatable. Because we need water above everything else, they furnish it most abundantly."

"This too," said Euthydemus, "reveals their forethought."

7   "Haven't they given us fire, a defense against cold and darkness, a fellow worker, as it were, in every art and in the preparation of every artifact that man uses? In short, man makes nothing worthwhile and useful in life without fire."

"This is the supreme instance of their love of mankind!" replied Euthydemus.

8   "Consider how, when the sun crosses the winter solstice and approaches, some fruits ripen and others wither because their season is over. When the sun's work is accomplished, doesn't it stop drawing nearer and turn away, to avoid harming us by heating us more than we need? When the sun withdraws to the point where, clearly, we would be frozen with cold if it went farther off, doesn't it turn again, advance, and traverse the part of the heavens where it may benefit us most?"

"By Zeus," exclaimed Euthydemus, "all of this, as well, seems to have been brought about for man's sake!"

9   Socrates continued, "Since we clearly could not endure heat or cold if it occurred suddenly, do you see how the sun approaches and withdraws little by little, so that we fail to notice how we arrived at either extreme?"

"Now I wonder," said Euthydemus, "if there is any other function for the gods except to serve man. But what prevents me from thinking this is the fact that all animals share these benefits."

10   "Isn't it also clear," said Socrates, "that animals are born and raised for the sake of man? What other living being except man enjoys so many goods from goats, sheep, cattle, horses,

and asses, among other animals? For I think that man derives more goods from animals than from plants; or, at any rate, men are nourished and enriched no less from animals than from plants. Many men do not use the fruits of the earth for food, but live upon the milk, cheese, and meat from their livestock. All men tame and domesticate useful animals and use them for war and many other purposes."

"I agree with you, Socrates, because I see animals much stronger than man so dominated by man as to be used as men wish."

"Consider the many different kinds of beautiful and useful things. Hasn't man been 11 endowed with perceptions suited to this variety through which we can enjoy every kind of good? The gods have endowed us with reason, by which we think about what we perceive, remember it, and come to understand how it is useful. Then we contrive many ways of enjoying good and of avoiding evil. They give us the power of speech, by which we share all the 12 good things with one another through teaching, and by which we form communities, pass laws, and become citizens of a state."

"Socrates, the gods truly seem to show great concern for men in all these respects."

Socrates continued, "What of the fact that, whereas we are powerless to foresee what will be of advantage in the future, the gods themselves, when we inquire, aid us by revealing through divination what will come about, and by teaching us how events may turn out in the best way possible?"

"They seem to treat you, Socrates, with more love than they treat other men, if it is true that they tell you what to do and what not to do without your asking."

"You yourself will realize that I speak the truth, if you do not wait until you see their out- 13 ward and visible forms, but, because you see their works, are satisfied to revere and to honor the gods. Note that the gods themselves teach this by their example, for when they give us gifts, the other gods do not present them in person, nor does the one god, who controls and orders the whole universe in which everything is good and beautiful, and who offers, for our use, goods that are fresh, whole, and new – goods which, quicker than thought, serve us unerringly. This god is manifest in performing these great works, and yet while he administers them he is invisible to us. Note also that even the sun, which seems to appear to all, 14 does not allow men to look at it carefully. If someone tries to stare boldly at the sun he will lose his sight. You will find that the god's agents are also invisible: The thunderbolt, for example, clearly comes from on high and overpowers all whom it strikes. Yet we cannot see it come or strike or go away. Not even the winds are visible, yet their effects are obvious and we perceive them as they come. Indeed, even the soul of man – which, more than all else that is human, shares in the divine – cannot be seen; yet clearly the soul rules us. We must understand this and not despise what we cannot see; and, realizing their power from its effects, we must honor the divine.

"Socrates," said Euthydemus, "I know clearly that I shall by no means neglect the divine, 15 but I feel discouraged when I realize that no one can ever return thanks worthy of the gods' benefits."

"Don't be discouraged, Euthydemus. For you see that when someone asked the god at 16 Delphi how he might return thanks to the gods, the god replied, 'According to the law of the state.' Surely the law everywhere is that a man should propitiate the gods with sacrifices according to his power. How then would anyone honor the gods more excellently or more reverently than by doing as the gods themselves command? But he must not do less than is 17 in his power; otherwise, when someone does less than he can, he is clearly not honoring the gods. Therefore, when a man does all in his power to honor the gods, he should take heart and hope for the greatest goods. A man could be called temperate when he does not hope for greater goods from anyone except from those who are able to bestow the greatest benefits, and there is no other way to achieve this except by pleasing them. How could he better please the gods than by obeying them as best he can?" By such words and deeds, Socrates made his companions more reverent and more temperate.

Part III

Plato (c.428–c.348/7 BCE)

Introduction

Life

Not much is known about Plato's early life. His parents were Ariston and Perictione (or Potone – see DL III.1[1]). Plato had two older brothers, Glaucon and Adeimantus, who appear as speaking characters in Plato's *Republic*, and a sister, Potone, by the same parents (see DL III.4). After Ariston's death, Plato's mother married her uncle, Pyrilampes, with whom she had another son, Antiphon, Plato's half-brother (see Plato, *Parmenides* 126a–b).

Plato came from one of the wealthiest and most politically active families in Athens. Their political sympathies lay strongly with the city's oligarchic faction: one of Plato's uncles (Charmides) was a member of the notorious "Thirty Tyrants," who overthrew the Athenian democracy in 404 BCE and Charmides' own uncle, Critias, was the leader of the Thirty. Plato's stepfather, Pyrilampes, however, was said to have been a close associate of the great democratic leader, Pericles.

Plato's birth name was apparently Aristocles, after his grandfather. "Plato" seems to have started as a nickname (for *platos*, or "broad"), perhaps first given to him by his wrestling teacher for his physique, or for the breadth of his style, or even the breadth of his forehead (all given in DL III.4).

When Socrates died, Plato left Athens and traveled to several spots in the western parts of the Greek world (in what is now Italy), and perhaps also to Egypt. During this time, Plato came into close contact with the Pythagorean communities and seems to have been much impressed with their teachings. When he returned to Athens he founded a school, known as the Academy (from which we get our word, "academic," but which got its name from its location, a grove of trees sacred to the hero Academus – or Hecademus: see DL III.7), a mile or so outside the Athenian walls. Except for two more trips to Sicily, the Academy seems to have been Plato's home base for the remainder of his life. According to Diogenes, Plato was

---

1 DL: Diogenes Laertius, *Lives and Opinions of Eminent Philosophers*.

buried at the school he founded (DL III.41). However, archaeological investigation has so far failed to discover his grave.

Understanding Plato's Dialogues

Unlike most other philosophers whose works we include in this book, Plato wrote entirely – or almost entirely – in the form of dialogues. Nearly 30 of these have survived, as well as over 30 other works – not all of them dialogues – which were attributed to Plato in antiquity, but which scholars now either regard as doubtful or reject altogether as having been written by Plato.

Plato's interest in Socrates is patent from the fact that Socrates appears as the main speaking character in many of his dialogues. But this presents a problem of interpretation: (1) is the Socrates who speaks in Plato's dialogues (or perhaps some identifiable subset of them) supposed to be a reasonably reliable portrait of the historical Socrates, or (2) does Socrates (in some or all of the dialogues) merely express Plato's own views, or (3) is this Socrates (and perhaps every other character who appears in Plato's writings) simply a fictional construction?

Scholars have been divided over these possibilities, and we do not wish in this collection to force any of the above interpretations upon our readers. Our presentation of the dialogues, however, betrays at least some of the sympathy we feel for the different versions of the view that Plato's dialogues show some progression in his thought – either from trying to represent Socrates more or less accurately, as per (1) above, to putting his own words more freely into Socrates' mouth, or, as per (2) above, in always expressing his own views through Socrates, but having his own views change significantly during his long career as a philosophical writer. We thus begin with the *Euthyphro*, *Apology*, and *Crito*, which have been generally treated as among Plato's earliest works; these dialogues, as well, are regularly employed by scholars seeking to understand the life and thought of Socrates. The *Meno* and *Phaedo* (in that order) are generally considered as somewhat later works, in which Plato's own views (and not those of Socrates) begin increasingly to be expressed by the character, Socrates. *Symposium* and *Republic* are among those dialogues in which Plato comes to express his own philosophy, which, though much influenced by his association with Socrates, also shows Plato's intellectual engagement with works by the Presocratics and the Sophists, and provides ingenious and original solutions to problems with which Socrates himself does not seem to have been at all concerned. The *Parmenides* seems to subject some of the views for which Plato argues in the *Phaedo* and *Republic* (particularly, Plato's most famous theory of Forms) to searching criticism and correction, and the *Timaeus* (often supposed to have been written fairly late in Plato's life) provides new theories of cosmic and biological origin and construction. Those who do not wish to read these dialogues as indicative of Platonic development during his long career may read them in any order they choose. No doubt the next generation of scholars will conceive of still new ways to organize and understand Plato's writings. No matter in what order one reads them, one will find much in each one to stimulate thought – and, perhaps, wonder.

Texts and Notations

All of Plato's texts – other than the *Timaeus* – were lost to the West until the medieval period. Fortunately, copies were maintained and studied by scholars in the Muslim world, and they reentered the West from here. In 1578 Henri Estienne (under his Latinized name, Stephanus) published a collection of the Platonic works that had been recovered in the West. Stephanus' copy divided each page of the Greek into five sections (labeled a, b, c, d, and e). Standard references to Plato, accordingly, provide the Stephanus page and section numbers. Those who wish to refer more specifically to individual lines in the Greek text itself add to the Stephanus page and section numbers a further number at the end of the citation – this number indicates the line number as it appears in the Oxford Classical Texts edition of Plato's works in the original Greek. Those relying on translations, however, simply provide the Stephanus page and section numbers. As is customary, we have provided these in our translations, and we use them, as well, in referring to various texts in our introductions to each work.

8

Euthyphro

Plato sets the *Euthyphro* near the entrance to the king-archon's office. Socrates is waiting there to find out why he has been charged with impiety. Euthyphro is there to charge his own father with murder, on highly dubious grounds. Socrates' probing questions bring out many of the confusions in Euthyphro's thinking, and, after suffering many reversals of his claims, Euthyphro beats a hasty retreat from the conversation.

The arguments provided in this dialogue continue to shed important light on many of the questions raised by any view that holds the relationship of ethics to divinity to be a *defining* one. Even if there is no disagreement among the divinity or divinities to be consulted, we must ask whether divinity accepts ethical principles *because* they are ethical (thus leaving their ethical status logically independent of divine acceptance, as prior to it), or whether it is the dictates of divinity that *define* those principles as ethical (leaving the strange result that the divinity had no reason to pick any ethical principle over any other, in which case even if our ethical decisions are not arbitrary – as guided by divine commandment – those made by divinity itself are wholly arbitrary).

EUTHYPHRO:[1] What's happened, Socrates, that would make you leave your regular place in 2a the Lyceum, and hang around here at the King's stoa?[2] Surely you don't have a suit before the King archon,[3] as I do.

---

1 Euthyphro's name means "straight thinker," which he plainly proves *not* to be in this dialogue. Despite the irony of his name in this conversation, it is likely that there actually was an Athenian named Euthyphro and that he was known for his religious convictions and, perhaps, his interest in the origins of religious words. Plato portrays him in this dialogue as familiar with Socrates, although whether or not he ever actually discussed the nature of piety with Socrates we cannot say.

2 The King's stoa was located in a corner of the agora and in front of the office of the King archon (see note 3).

3 The King archon was one of nine Athenian magistrates. His primary function was to oversee charges of violations of religious law. Before a case was actually brought to trial, a preliminary hearing was held before the King archon whose purpose was to ensure that the accusations being made did in fact amount to legal charges.

SOCRATES: As a matter of fact, Euthyphro, the Athenians don't call it a suit – they call it an indictment.[4]

2b EUTHYPHRO: What are you saying? I guess someone has indicted you; for I just won't believe that you're indicting someone else.

SOCRATES: I'm not.

EUTHYPHRO: So someone else is indicting you.

SOCRATES: Right.

EUTHYPHRO: Who is this person?

SOCRATES: I myself don't even know much about the man, Euthyphro. He seems to me to be young and not well known. At any rate, they call him Meletus,[5] I think. He's from the deme of Pittheus,[6] if you recall a Meletus of Pittheus, who has straight hair and only a slight beard and a somewhat hooked nose.

c EUTHYPHRO: I don't recall him, Socrates. But now what's he indicted you for?

SOCRATES: What sort of indictment is it? I think it's not trivial. For it's no small achievement for a young man to be knowledgeable about a matter such as this. For that man, so he says, knows how the youth are corrupted and who the corruptors are. And he's likely to be someone who's wise, and having noticed that, in my ignorance, I corrupt those who are his age, he's coming before the city to prosecute me, as if he were their mother. And he seems to me to be alone among the politicians to be starting in the right place. For he's right to care first and foremost that the young be as good as possible, just like a good farmer is likely to make the young plants his first concern, and after them he turns to the others. And Meletus is really starting by weeding out those of us who are ruining the young seedlings, as he says. Then after this, it's clear that when he takes care of the older people, he'll be the cause of many great goods for the city, at least that's the reasonable outcome for someone who begins in this way.

d

3a

EUTHYPHRO: I'd hope so, Socrates, but I'm afraid that just the opposite will happen. For it seems to me that by trying to wrong you, he's really beginning by harming the very heart of the city. So tell me, what does he say you're doing to corrupt the youth?

b SOCRATES: Absurd things at first hearing, my wonderful friend. For he says that I'm a maker of gods, and because I make new gods but don't believe in the old ones, he has indicted me, or so he says.

4 The distinction corresponds roughly to our distinction between a crime and a civil action, although many actions that we would consider to be crimes the Athenians would consider matters between private individuals.

5 The Athenian legal system did not provide for a state prosecutor. Instead, crimes were prosecuted by private individuals. The charges against Socrates were brought by the man mentioned here, Meletus, about whom nothing is really known. He may have been the son of a poet of the same name and [. . .] he may have been the Meletus who spoke against Andocides in an impiety trial that took place in the same year as Socrates trial, 399. One problem with identifying the Meletus who brought the charges against Socrates with the Meletus who spoke against Andocides is that Andocides says that Meletus was one of the four who participated in the arrest of Leon of Salamis. Were they the same person, Socrates could hardly say that Meletus is unknown to him, as he does at this point in the *Euthyphro*, since Socrates implies in the *Apology* (32c–d) that he knew those ordered to arrest Leon.

6 One of the 139 political districts into which Athens had been divided since the end of the sixth century.

EUTHYPHRO: I see, Socrates. It's because you say that your spiritual voice[7] comes to you from time to time. So because you make innovations about divine matters, he's written this indictment, and he's taking it to court, of course, to slander you, knowing that it's easy to slander before most people. In fact, even for me, whenever I say anything in the Assembly c about divine matters, foretelling what's to happen to them, they laugh like I'm crazy. And yet there's nothing that I've foretold that wasn't true. Even so, they're jealous of everyone like us. But we shouldn't worry about them; instead, we should take them on.

SOCRATES: Dear Euthyphro, being laughed at probably doesn't matter. It seems to me that the Athenians don't really care if they think someone is clever as long as he doesn't teach his wisdom. But they get angry with one who they think is making others wise, whether d out of jealousy, as you say, or because of something else.

EUTHYPHRO: I don't really care to test out what they think of me on this issue.

SOCRATES: Perhaps you seem to hold yourself aloof and don't want to provide instruction about your wisdom. I, on the other hand, am afraid that because of my good-hearted nature, they think that I've been eager to speak to everyone, only without taking a fee, but instead gladly paying if anyone would want to listen to me. If, then, as I was saying just now, they were really going to laugh at me, as you say they laugh at you, it wouldn't be an e unpleasant way at all to spend my time in court – laughing and joking. But if they're going to be serious, it's not clear how it'll turn out except to you soothsayers.

EUTHYPHRO: Surely it won't be a problem, and you'll conduct your trial intelligently and, I think, I will do so with mine.

SOCRATES: So now what's your case about, Euthyphro? Are you defending or prosecuting?

EUTHYPHRO: I'm prosecuting.

SOCRATES: Whom?

EUTHYPHRO: Someone whom I seem, again, to be crazy for prosecuting.   4a

SOCRATES: Why? Are you prosecuting someone who can fly away?

EUTHYPHRO: He can hardly fly away; he's already quite old.

SOCRATES: Who is he?

EUTHYPHRO: My father.

SOCRATES: Your father!

EUTHYPHRO; Absolutely.

SOCRATES: What's the charge, and what is the trial about?

EUTHYPHRO: Murder.

SOCRATES: By Heracles! Surely most people *don't* see how that's right! Indeed, I don't think this would be done correctly by just anyone, but I suppose it takes someone *far* advanced b in wisdom.

EUTHYPHRO: Far, indeed, by god.

SOCRATES: But surely the one killed by your father is a member of your family. Of course, that's obvious. I suppose you wouldn't prosecute him for the murder of someone outside the family.

EUTHYPHRO: It's funny, Socrates, that you think it makes a difference whether the dead man's a stranger or a member of the family and it's not necessary to guard against this one thing

---

7 That Socrates claimed to hear something divine, which Euthyphro here calls a "spiritual voice," was apparently well known. In the *Apology* (31c–d and 40a), Socrates tells the jury that it comes to him often and that he has heard it from childhood. It never advises him to *do* anything, but when it comes to him, it always "turns him away from" doing something that would be bad for him.

4c – whether the killing took place justly or not, and if justly, let it go, but if not, prosecute, even if the killer shares your hearth and table. For the pollution's[8] the same either way if you knowingly associate with such a person and don't purify both yourself and him by going to court.

At any rate the one who was killed was a laborer of mine, and when we were working our farm on Naxos,[9] he was there as a worker hired by us. He got drunk and angry with one of our slaves and cut his throat. So my father bound his hands and feet, threw him in a ditch and sent a man here to inquire of the Religious Counselor[10] what should be done.

d During this time, he paid little attention to the captive and really didn't care much if he did die because he was a murderer, which is just what happened. He died from hunger and cold and being bound up before the messenger got back from the Religious Counselor. So that's what's upsetting my father and my relatives – because I'm prosecuting my father for murder on behalf of the one who was murdered. He didn't even kill him, so they claim, and even if he did, because the one who died was a murderer, we shouldn't e be concerned on behalf of such a person, for it's unholy for a son to prosecute his father for murder – they know so little of the divine point of view concerning the pious and the impious.[11]

SOCRATES: Before god, Euthyphro, do you really think you know so exactly how things are concerning the gods, and about pious and impious matters that when things have happened as you say they have, you're not afraid that in bringing the case against your father, you're not also doing something impious?

5a EUTHYPHRO: Then I'd be useless and Euthyphro wouldn't be better than most people unless I had precise knowledge of all things of this sort.

SOCRATES: Well, then, most amazing Euthyphro, it's best that I become your pupil, and, before the court fight with Meletus, challenge him about this very thing, telling him that in the past I've thought that it's important to know about divine matters, and I do so now, when that man says I've committed a grave offense by speaking ill-advisedly and by introducing innovations about divine matters, I've, in fact, become your pupil. "And if, Meletus," b I'd say, "you agree that Euthyphro is wise about such matters, then you should accept that I too am thinking correctly and don't bring me to trial. But if you don't agree, bring the suit first against him, my teacher, rather than me on the ground that he's corrupting his elders, both me and his father, by teaching me, on the one hand, and humiliating and punishing him, on the other." And if I don't persuade him to drop his case or to indict

---

8 The notion refers to a kind of guilt that anyone who gives aid to someone who has offended to the gods would thereby take on. One of the oldest Greek religious notions held that anyone who becomes "polluted" in this way will receive some terrible punishment from the gods. Euthyphro wants to "cleanse" himself of any such pollution by prosecuting his father.

9 An island in the middle of the Aegean. From this distance, it would take quite a long time to send a question to the Religious Counselor in Athens (see next note) and receive an answer.

10 According to Burnet, Euthyphro is referring to one of three officials whose function it was to provide official interpretations of various religious laws and rules governing ceremonies.

11 Socrates uses *hosiotes* and *eusebeia* and their cognates interchangeably. Although they are often translated as "holiness" and "piety," respectively, we have followed the reverse of this practice here to preserve better what ancient readers would have recognized clearly – the connection between the topic of the conversation here and the trial of Socrates.

you instead of me, it's best for me to use the same argument in court with which I have challenged him.

EUTHYPHRO: Yes, by god, Socrates, but if he tried to indict me, I think I'd uncover where c he's weak, and our discussion in court would be about him long before it was about me.

SOCRATES: And indeed, dear friend, because I understand this, I'm eager to become your student, knowing also that this Meletus and everyone else, I suppose, never seems to notice you, whereas he observes me so keenly and easily that he indicted me for impiety. So now, before God, tell me what you claimed just now to know clearly: What sort of thing do you say piety and impiety are as they apply to murder and to other things, or isn't the d pious the same thing in every action, and isn't impiety in turn the complete opposite of impiety, but in itself the same as itself, and doesn't all that is going to be impious, in fact, have a certain distinctive feature of impiousness?

EUTHYPHRO: Without any doubt, Socrates.

SOCRATES: So, tell me, what do you say the pious and the impious are?

EUTHYPHRO: I'll tell you right now that the pious is what I'm doing now, prosecuting the wrongdoer – whether it's for murder or for robbing temples – or one who has committed an offense in any other way such as these, whether it happens to be one's father or e mother, or anyone else at all; and not prosecuting is impious. Moreover, notice that I have powerful evidence that this is how the law is – just what I have already said to others – that what has happened is as it should be, namely, not to give in to one who is unholy, no matter who he happens to be. These very people think that Zeus is the best and most just of the gods, and they agree that he bound his father because he unjustly swallowed his 6a sons, and that Zeus' father, in turn, castrated *his* father for some other such reasons.[12] But they condemn me because I'm prosecuting my father when he is a wrongdoer, and in this way they say contradictory things about the gods and me.

SOCRATES: Is *this*, Euthyphro, why I'm being indicted – because whenever someone says such things about the gods, I have trouble accepting it for some reason? Surely it's for this reason that some, it seems, will say that I've committed a crime. Now if these things seem right to you, who has a thorough knowledge about such things, surely it's neces- b sary, it seems, for the rest of us to concur. What can those of us who agree that we know nothing about such things say? So tell me, in the name of Friendship,[13] do you really believe these things happened in this way?

EUTHYPHRO: And still more marvelous things than these, Socrates, which most people don't know about.

SOCRATES: Then you believe that the gods really do war among themselves, and that there are terrible feuds and battles and many other such things, the sorts of things the poets talk about and as other sacred things are adorned by our good artists, and especially the c robe filled with these adornments that's carried during the Great Panathenaea[14] up the Acropolis? Shall we say these things are true, Euthyphro?

---

12 Euthyphro is referring to story told by Hesiod of Cronus's castration of Ouranus, and Zeus's later imprisonment of Cronus.

13 This is an oath to Zeus, the patron god of friendship.

14 One of the great religious festivals held every four years in Athens. The festival culminated in the placement of an elaborately embroidered robe on a statue of Athena Polias ("Athena of the City") in the Erechtheion, one of the temples on the Athenian Acropolis.

EUTHYPHRO: Not only that, Socrates, but as I was saying just now, I'll describe many other things about divine matters for you, if you wish, which I'm certain will amaze you when you hear them.

SOCRATES: I wouldn't be surprised. But you can go through them for me another time when we have time. For now, try to say more clearly what I asked you just now. For in the first thing you said, you didn't instruct me well enough when I asked what piety is, but you were telling me that piety happens to be what you're doing now – prosecuting your father for murder.

EUTHYPHRO: And indeed I was right to say that, Socrates.

SOCRATES: Perhaps. But yet you say that there are many other pious things, as well.

EUTHYPHRO: Indeed, there are.

SOCRATES: Recall then that this isn't what I requested of you – to instruct me about one or two of the many thing that are pious, but that form[15] by which all pious things are pious. You were saying, weren't you, that all impious things are impious and all pious things are pious by reason of a single characteristic. Or don't you recall?

EUTHYPHRO: Indeed, I do.

SOCRATES: Instruct me then about what this very characteristic is in order that by looking at it and using it as a standard, I can say what either you or someone else might do is the sort of thing that is pious and that what is not of this sort I can say it is not pious.

EUTHYPHRO: Well, if you want it put this way, I'll put it this way for you.

SOCRATES: Indeed, I do want it.

EUTHYPHRO: What's pleasing to the gods is pious, then, and what isn't pleasing to the gods is impious.

SOCRATES: Excellent, Euthyphro. You are answering now in the way 1 was looking for. I don't know yet if you're right, but it's clear that you're going on to show that what you say is true.

EUTHYPHRO: Of course.

SOCRATES: Come, then, and let's consider what we're saying. Both what is beloved by the gods and the one who's beloved by the gods are pious, but what's hateful to gods and the person hated by the gods are impious. They're not the same but complete opposites – the pious and the impious. Is that it?

EUTHYPHRO: That's it.

SOCRATES: And does this appear to be right?

EUTHYPHRO: I think so.

SOCRATES: Then, Euthyphro, is it right that the gods fight and disagree with each other and that there is hatred among them for each other?

15 The term used here is the same as the one Plato later uses in metaphysical discussions to refer to the Forms (or what we now call the Platonic Forms) – pure essences which exist in a nonphysical realm, and which concrete particular objects in this realm "imitate" or "participate in" or "share in" in such a way as (temporary and imperfectly) to have whatever characteristics they happen to have. Aristotle claims that Socrates did not separate forms from particulars but that it was Plato and his followers who first did so (Aristotle, *Metaphysics* M.4.1079b17–32; see also *Metaphysics* A.6.987a32–b12), and most scholars agree that there is no reason to see this metaphysical theory underlying Socrates' remark here, for the same term can be used – as it seems to be here – to identify the common character among many things said to share a characteristic. The "form" of piety, in this case, simply refers to whatever it is that makes all pious things pious – whatever it is that is common to all pious things. This does not require the positing of Forms that are separate from individual particular things that have common characteristics.

EUTHYPHRO: Yes.

SOCRATES: Is there disagreement about what things create the hatred and anger? Let's look at it this way: If you and I were to disagree about which number is greater, would the disagreement make us enemies and make us angry with each other, or would we quickly get rid of disagreement by resorting to calculation about these sorts of things?　　c

EUTHYPHRO: Of course.

SOCRATES: Then if we were disagreeing about the larger and the smaller, by resorting to measurement, would we quickly put an end to the disagreement?

EUTHYPHRO: That's true.

SOCRATES: And by resorting to the scale, could we judge the heavier and the lighter?

EUTHYPHRO: Of course.

SOCRATES: But then about what sort of thing are we enemies and become angry with each other when we've differed and haven't been able to find an answer? Perhaps it is not at the tip of your tongue, but consider what I'm saying – that it's the just and the unjust,　d noble and disgraceful, and good and bad. Isn't it when we disagree and aren't able to come to a sufficient answer that we become enemies to each other, whenever we do, I and you and everyone else?

EUTHYPHRO: Why, yes, Socrates, the disagreement's about just these things.

SOCRATES: What about the gods, Euthyphro? If indeed they disagree about anything, won't it be on account of these same things?

EUTHYPHRO: Absolutely.

SOCRATES: And about the gods, noble Euthyphro, according to your argument, don't they　e believe different things are just, noble and disgraceful, and good and bad. I don't suppose they fight with each other unless they disagree about these things? Isn't that so?

EUTHYPHRO: You're right.

SOCRATES: Therefore, what each believes to be noble and good and just, they love. But the opposites of these, they hate.

EUTHYPHRO: Certainly.

SOCRATES: So, according to you, the same things are believed to be just by some and believed to be unjust by others, and it's when they disagree about these that they fight and make　8a war on each other. Isn't it so?

EUTHYPHRO: It is.

SOCRATES: So the same things, it seems, are hated by the gods and loved by gods, and the same things are hateful to gods and beloved by the gods.

EUTHYPHRO: It would seem.

SOCRATES: And, then, the same things would be pious and impious, Euthyphro, by this argument.

EUTHYPHRO: So it turns out.

SOCRATES: Then you haven't answered what I asked, as impressive as you are. For I wasn't asking what happens to be both pious and impious; yet what would be beloved of gods is hateful to the gods, it seems. The result, Euthyphro, is that it wouldn't be at all sur-　b prising if what you're doing now in punishing your father is pleasing to Zeus but hateful to Cronus and Ouranos, and dear to Hephaestus and hateful to Hera, and the same thing applies if any of the other gods differ with each other about this.

EUTHYPHRO: But I think, Socrates, that about this matter none of the gods differ with each other, namely, that the one who has killed someone unjustly needn't pay the penalty for it.

SOCRATES: What about human beings, Euthyphro? Have you ever heard someone disputing
8c   the claim that one who kills unjustly or who does anything else whatever unjustly needn't
pay the penalty for it?

EUTHYPHRO: They never stop disputing about these things in the courts and elsewhere. For
they commit all sorts of wrongs and then do and say everything to avoid paying the penalty.

SOCRATES: Is it that they agree, Euthyphro, that they've been unjust, and having agreed to
that, they nevertheless say that they don't need to pay the penalty?

EUTHYPHRO: It is never *this*.

SOCRATES: Then they don't do and say exactly everything. I don't think that they would dare
say that if indeed they have acted unjustly, they shouldn't pay the penalty. Rather, I think
d   they say they've not acted unjustly. Isn't that so?

EUTHYPHRO: You're right.

SOCRATES: So, then, they don't dispute that the one who acts unjustly must pay the penalty.
Rather, they dispute who the wrongdoer is, what he did, and when?

EUTHYPHRO: You're right.

SOCRATES: Then, do the same things occur to the gods, if indeed they fight about matters of
justice and injustice, according to your account – one saying that the other is unjust and
e   the other denying it? For surely neither god nor man would dare say that the wrongdoer
need not pay the penalty!

EUTHYPHRO: Yes, Socrates, you've made just the right point.

SOCRATES: So when gods and men dispute – if the gods dispute – they dispute about each
action that's been performed. And when they dispute about some action, some say that
it was done justly and others that it was done unjustly. Isn't that so?

EUTHYPHRO: Of course.

9a   SOCRATES: Come now, dear Euthyphro, so that I may become wiser, instruct me about your
proof that all the gods think that one has died unjustly when he was a worker and became
a murderer and was bound by the dead man's master and who died from being tied up
before the one who bound him could learn from the Religious Counselors what he needed
to do about him. Show me how, on behalf of such a person, it's right for a son to prosecute his father and to bring against him a charge of murder. Come, then, and try to make
b   this clear to me that all of the gods unquestionably agree that this is the right course of
action. If you would make this sufficiently clear to me, I'll never stop praising you for
your wisdom.

EUTHYPHRO: Well, that's perhaps no small task, though I could show you quite clearly.

SOCRATES: I understand. That's because I seem to you to be slower than the jurors, since it
is clear that you'll show them that such acts are unjust and that all the gods hate such
acts.

EUTHYPHRO: It'll be quite clear, if, in fact, they'll listen to what I say.

c   SOCRATES: They *will* listen if indeed you seem to be speaking well. In any case, I was thinking while you were talking and I put this question to myself: "Even if Euthyphro shows
me convincingly that all of the gods believe that such a death is unjust, what more have
I learned from Euthyphro about both the pious and the impious? This deed, it seems, would
then be hateful to the gods. But it was revealed just now that the impious and the impious are not defined in this way, for what is hateful to the gods was manifestly what is
beloved of gods." So I'll release you from this point, Euthyphro. If you want, let all the
d   gods believe this is unjust and let all the gods hate it. Well, then, is this what we're now
correcting in our account – that what all of the gods hate is impious and what all of the

gods love is pious, and what some love and some hate is neither or both? Do you then want us to define the pious and impious in this way?

EUTHYPHRO: What's to stop us, Socrates?

SOCRATES: Nothing at all is to stop *me*, Euthyphro, but consider your view to see if in setting it down in this way you'll most easily instruct me about what you promised.

EUTHYPHRO: I'd say that the pious is what all of the gods love, and the opposite of this – e what all of the gods hate – is the impious.

SOCRATES: Should we consider this next then, Euthyphro, to see if you're right, or should we just allow it and accept what we ourselves or other people say, if someone only says it is, and concede that it's so? Or should we look into what the speaker says?

EUTHYPHRO: We should look into it. However, I think that this time I'm right.

SOCRATES: We'll know better in a minute, my good man. But first think about this: Is the 10a pious loved by the gods because it is pious, or is it pious because it is loved?

EUTHYPHRO: I don't know what you mean, Socrates.

SOCRATES: Then I'll try to say it more clearly. We talk about something's being carried and carrying, being led and leading, being seen and seeing; and do you understand that all such things are different from each other and in what way they are different?

EUTHYPHRO: I think I understand.

SOCRATES: Therefore, there is what is loved and it is different from what loves?

EUTHYPHRO: Of course.

SOCRATES: Tell me now: Is what's being carried something carried *because it's being carried*, b or is it a thing that's carried for some other reason?

EUTHYPHRO: No, it's for this reason.

SOCRATES: And then a thing that's led is a led thing because it's being led, and a seen thing because it's being seen?

EUTHYPHRO: Of course.

SOCRATES: Therefore, it's not because it's a seen thing that it's being seen, but the opposite: It's because it is being seen that it's a seen thing. Nor is it because it's a led thing that it's being led, but it's because it's being led that it's a led thing. Nor is it because it's a carried thing that it's being carried, but it's because it's being carried that it's a carried thing. So, is what I want to say clear? I want to say this: If something becomes or undergoes any- c thing, it does not become what it does because it's what becomes that, but rather it's what becomes that because it becomes what it does. Nor does it undergo what it does because it's what undergoes that, but it's what undergoes that, because it undergoes what it does. Or, don't you concede this?

EUTHYPHRO: I do.

SOCRATES: Then is a loved thing either what's become something or undergoes something by something?

EUTHYPHRO: Of course.

SOCRATES: And is it just as it was with the previous items? It's not because it's a loved thing that it's loved by whom it's loved; rather, because it's loved, it's a loved thing.

EUTHYPHRO: Necessarily.

SOCRATES: So then – what are we saying about the pious, Euthyphro? Is it anything other d than what's loved by all the gods, according to your account?

EUTHYPHRO: Yes.

SOCRATES: Then it's in virtue of this – because it's pious – or for some other reason?

EUTHYPHRO: No, that's why.

SOCRATES: Then is it loved because it's pious, but it's not pious because it's loved?

EUTHYPHRO: It seems so.

SOCRATES: But it's because it's loved by the gods that it's a loved thing and beloved of gods.

EUTHYPHRO: Of course.

SOCRATES: Then what's beloved of gods isn't pious and the pious isn't what's beloved of gods, as you're claiming, but the one is different from the other.

10e EUTHYPHRO: How's that, Socrates?

SOCRATES: Because we agree that the pious is loved because it's pious, but it's not pious because it's loved. Isn't that right?

EUTHYPHRO: Yes.

SOCRATES: But the thing that's beloved of gods is beloved of gods *by this very being loved*, that is, *because* it is loved by the gods. But it is not because it is beloved of gods that it is being loved.

EUTHYPHRO: You're right.

SOCRATES: But if being a thing beloved of gods and being pious were indeed the same thing,

11a Euthyphro, and the pious is loved in virtue of its being pious, then the thing that's beloved of gods would be loved by them in virtue of being a thing beloved of gods. And if the thing beloved of gods is beloved of gods in virtue of being loved by the gods, then the pious would be pious in virtue of being loved. But now you see that the opposite holds for them, since they are completely different from each other. The one is the loved sort of thing because the gods love it; in the other case, the gods love it because it is the loved sort of thing. When you were asked what the pious is, it turned out, Euthyphro, that you didn't want to make its essential nature clear to me, but you mentioned a feature that

b *happens* to the pious – namely being loved by all the gods.[16] But what it is, you haven't yet said. So please don't hide it from me, but again, tell be from the beginning what the pious is – whether it's loved by the gods or whatever it takes on, for we don't differ about this – but tell me earnestly what the pious and the impious are?

EUTHYPHRO: But Socrates, I can't tell you what I know. What we propose somehow always moves around us and doesn't want to stay where we set it down.

SOCRATES: What you've said seems to have come from my ancestor, Daedalus.[17] If I were

c saying this and proposing these things, you would probably make fun of me since the results of my arguments run around and don't want to stay where they're put, on account of my relationship to him. But as it is, they're your claims. We really need another joke, because, as you yourself think, it's for *you* that they don't want to stay put.

16 A similar consideration from a more modern viewpoint might help us to understand Socrates' argument. Consider what God wants us to do. If we say, as most contemporary theists do, that God wants us to do all and only good things, and (as an omnibenevolent being) that it is for this very reason – that they are good – that God wants us to do them, then even if it is true that all good things are, as a matter of fact, wanted from us by God, we cannot say they are good *because* they are the things God wants from us – that cannot be what *makes them good* – for that would make the property they needed to have *in order to be* wanted from us by God turn out to be *the result* of God's wanting them, rather than the *condition of* God's wanting them.

17 One of the stories that made up Greek folklore claimed that Daedalus' statues were so lifelike that they would actually move around. It is not clear why Socrates would claim that Daedalus was his ancestor. Some ancient writers claimed that Socrates' father was a stone worker. If so, Socrates would probably have been trained in his father's occupation. However, there is no credible evidence that such was indeed his father's occupation.

EUTHYPHRO: I think the same joke fits what's been said, for I'm not the one making them moving around and not staying put in the same place. But you strike me as the Daedalus, d since it's because of you that they don't stay put in this way.

SOCRATES: I'm afraid, then, that I'm a more clever artist than he was, in so far as he only made his own creations move about, whereas I, it seems, make others' move about – as well as my own. Indeed, this is the most incredible aspect of my craft – that I'm wise unwillingly. For I wanted my arguments to stay put and remain settled more than to have the riches of Tantalus in addition to the wisdom of Daedalus. But enough of this. Since you e seem not to be up to it, I'll be delighted to share my eagerness with you how you can instruct me about what the pious is. So don't give up on the task. See if it doesn't seem necessary to you that all of the pious is just.

EUTHYPHRO: That seems right to me.

SOCRATES: Then is all of the just pious? Or is all of the pious just but not all of the just is 12a pious, but some of it is and some of it is something else?

EUTHYPHRO: I'm not following what you're saying, Socrates.

SOCRATES: And yet you're wiser than I am, just as you're younger than I am. What I'm saying is that you've grown soft because of your wealth of wisdom. But, blessed one, steel yourself. For it's not difficult to grasp what I'm saying. I mean the opposite of what the poet meant when he wrote:

One doesn't want to dispute with Zeus, the creator, who brought all things about. For where   b
there is fear, there is reverence.

Thus, I disagree with this poet. Shall I tell you in what way?

EUTHYPHRO: Of course.

SOCRATES: Well, then, it doesn't seem to me that "where there is fear, there is reverence"; for many people who are afraid seem to me to fear sickness, poverty, or many other such things, but they don't have reverence for what they fear. Doesn't it seem that way to you?

EUTHYPHRO: Of course.

SOCRATES: But where there is reverence, there is fear, since hasn't whoever revered and felt ashamed about something at the same time both feared and worried about a bad c reputation?

EUTHYPHRO: He'd surely be worried about it.

SOCRATES: Then it isn't right to say that "where there is fear, there is reverence," but where there is reverence, there is fear; however, it's not the case that everywhere there's fear, there's reverence. For I think that fear's more extensive than reverence, for reverence is a part of fear – just as odd is a part of, so that it's not that wherever there's number, there's odd number, but wherever there's odd number, there's number. Surely you follow now.

EUTHYPHRO: Of course.

SOCRATES: This is the sort of thing I was asking about when I was talking back then: Is it that where there's justice, there's also piety, or that where there's piety, there's also justice, d but piety isn't wherever justice is? For piety is a part of justice. Should we say this, or does it seem to you to be otherwise?

EUTHYPHRO: No, this appears to me to be the right way.

SOCRATES: See now what follows: If the pious is a part of justice, we should, it seems, discover the sort of part of justice the pious is. Thus, if you asked me about one of the things we were discussing just now – for example, what sort of part of number is the even, and what sort of number this happens to be, I'd say that it is not the scalene triangle but the isosceles.[18] Or doesn't that seem to you to be that way?

EUTHYPHRO: It does.

12e SOCRATES: Try to instruct me then about what sort of part of justice the pious is so that we may tell Meletus not to be unjust to us any longer and not to indict us for impiety since I've learned enough from you about what's holy and pious and what's not.

EUTHYPHRO: The part of justice that seems to me to be both holy and pious is what concerns service to the gods, and the remaining part of justice is what concerns service to men.

SOCRATES: It appears to me that you're right, Euthyphro. But I still need one little thing.

13a I don't yet understand what you're calling "service." You probably don't mean one like services concerning other things. This is what we mean, for example, when we say that not everyone knows how to take care of horses, but the horse trainer does. Isn't that right?

EUTHYPHRO: Of course.

SOCRATES: For horsemanship is, I suppose, the service concerning horses?

EUTHYPHRO: Yes.

SOCRATES: And not everyone knows how to care for dogs, but the hunter does.[19]

EUTHYPHRO: Just so.

SOCRATES: And isn't huntsmanship, I suppose, the service concerning dogs?

b EUTHYPHRO: Yes.

SOCRATES: Isn't herdsmanship the service concerning cattle?

EUTHYPHRO: Of course.

SOCRATES: And now are piety and holiness a service concerning the gods, Euthyphro? Do you mean this?

EUTHYPHRO: I do.

SOCRATES: Doesn't every service achieve the same thing? For example, this sort of thing: It's for some good or benefit of what is served, just as you see when horses that are served by the art of horsemanship are benefited and become better. Or doesn't it seem that way to you?

EUTHYPHRO: It does to me.

SOCRATES: So are dogs benefited by the craft of the hunter, and cattle by herdsmanship, and
c all other things in the same way? Or do you think that the service is to the detriment of what is served?

EUTHYPHRO: By Zeus, I don't think so.

SOCRATES: But it's for their benefit?

EUTHYPHRO: Certainly.

SOCRATES: Then can it be the case that piety – since it's a service to the gods – is both a benefit to the gods and makes the gods better? Would you concede that whenever you do something pious, you accomplish a good for the gods?

EUTHYPHRO: By god, I don't agree.

SOCRATES: Nor did I think you meant this – far from it – and, in fact, that's why I asked you what
d you meant by "service to the gods," since I didn't think you meant that sort of thing.

---

18 The Greek word *isoskeles* means "having equal legs." An isosceles triangle, then, is one with equal sides. The Greeks must have used the isosceles triangles to refer to even numbers and scalene triangles – which have uneven sides – to refer to uneven numbers.

19 The ancient Greeks did not own dogs simply as pets. Dog owners would have the animals only for their usefulness in hunting. This is why Socrates says that the service concerning dogs is huntsmanship – and not, as we would say, the business of the veterinarian.

EUTHYPHRO: And you're right, Socrates. I don't mean that sort of thing.

SOCRATES: Well then, what service to the gods is piety?

EUTHYPHRO: The very one, Socrates, by which slaves serve their masters.

SOCRATES: I understand. It is a kind of assistance given to the gods.

EUTHYPHRO: Absolutely.

SOCRATES: Can you tell me this: What is accomplished as a result of assistance given to physicians? Don't you think it's health?

EUTHYPHRO: I do.

SOCRATES: What about the assistance given to ship builders? What result does this assistance e seek to accomplish?

EUTHYPHRO: It's clear that it's a ship.

SOCRATES: And, I suppose, the service rendered for house builders is for a house.

EUTHYPHRO: Yes.

SOCRATES: Tell me now, best one. The assistance to the gods is assistance for the accomplishment of what end? It's clear that you know, especially since you say that you know divine matters best of all men.

EUTHYPHRO: And I'm right, Socrates.

SOCRATES: So say, by Zeus, what is this all-glorious result which the gods accomplish by using our assistance?

EUTHYPHRO: Many wonderful things.

SOCRATES: And so do generals, friend. But all the same, can you easily say what the point of 14a their assistance is, namely, that they accomplish victory in war, or can't you say that?

EUTHYPHRO: Of course.

SOCRATES: And farmers, I think, accomplish many good things. But all the same raising food from the earth is the point of their accomplishment.

EUTHYPHRO: Absolutely.

SOCRATES: So what about the many good things that the gods accomplish? What is the point of their work?

EUTHYPHRO: And I told you a little earlier, Socrates, that it's quite a task to learn exactly how it is with all these matters. I'll simply tell you this: If anyone knows how to say and do b what pleases the gods through praying and sacrificing, these are pious, and these things preserve private households and the common good of cities. And the opposite of what pleases the gods is unholy, which then overturns and destroys all things.

SOCRATES: You could have told me the point of what I was asking about much more quickly, Euthyphro, if you had wanted. But you're not eager to teach me; that's clear, for now c just when you were right on top of it, you turned away. If you had answered that, I'd have learned all I needed from you about what piety is. But it's necessary for the questioner to follow the one who is questioned wherever he leads. So, again, what do you say the piety and piety is: Isn't it a kind of knowledge of sacrifice and prayer?

EUTHYPHRO: I think so.

SOCRATES: Then is sacrificing giving to the gods and prayer asking of the gods?

EUTHYPHRO: Obviously.

SOCRATES: By this account, the knowledge of asking and giving to the gods is piety. d

EUTHYPHRO: You understand what I'm saying quite well, Socrates.

SOCRATES: I'm eager for your wisdom and I'm concentrating so that what you're saying won't be lost. So tell me: What's this service to the gods? You say it's asking them and giving to them.

EUTHYPHRO: I do.

SOCRATES: And isn't asking them for these things a matter of correctly asking what we need from them?

EUTHYPHRO: What else?

14e SOCRATES: And next is giving back to them in return giving correctly what they happen to need from us. For I suppose it wouldn't be very craftsmanlike to give to someone what isn't needed.

EUTHYPHRO: You're right, Socrates.

SOCRATES: So, the craft of piety is a kind of commercial business that men and gods engage in with each other.

EUTHYPHRO: A commercial business, if you like calling it that.

SOCRATES: I don't like calling it that unless it's true. But tell me, what benefit do the gods happen to get from the gifts they receive from us? What they give is clear to everyone.

15a For we have nothing good that they don't provide us. But how are they benefited by what they get from us? Or do we get so much more from them from this business, that we get all good things from them but they get nothing good from us?

EUTHYPHRO: Do you believe that the gods benefit from what they get from us?

SOCRATES: Well then, Euthyphro, what in the world are these gifts from us to the gods?

EUTHYPHRO: Do you think it's anything but honor and respect and, as I was saying just now, gratitude?

b SOCRATES: Then is the pious what gratifies but isn't beneficial or even loved by the gods?

EUTHYPHRO: I think that this is what's loved above all by the gods!

SOCRATES: Then the pious is, it seems, what's loved by the gods.

EUTHYPHRO: Absolutely.

SOCRATES: Would you be surprised, then, having said these things, if what you say doesn't stay put but walks around? And you accuse me of being the Daedalus who makes them walk when you're really much more skillful than Daedalus in making them go around in a circle? Or don't you see that, having gone around, our account comes back around to

c the same spot? You remember, surely, that earlier the pious and what is loved by the gods didn't appear to be the same thing but appeared different from each other. Or don't you remember?

EUTHYPHRO: I remember.

SOCRATES: Don't you realize that you're saying that what's loved by the gods is pious? But isn't this the same thing you were saying before?

EUTHYPHRO: Of course.

SOCRATES: Then either our agreement earlier wasn't a good one, or if it was, then what we are establishing just now isn't right.

EUTHYPHRO: It seems so.

SOCRATES: Then we must go back to the beginning to consider what the pious is, since I won't

d back off from this voluntarily until I understand. So, don't ignore me, but by all means set your mind to it and tell me the absolute truth. For you know if anyone does and you mustn't, like Proteus,[20] be set free before you say what it is. For if you didn't know clearly

---

20 Proteus, a god of the sea, who could change shape at will. According to Homer's *Odyssey* (IV, 384–93), Proteus promised that he would tell the truth to anyone who could hold him down and keep him from transforming himself. Socrates, then, is threatening to hold on to Euthyphro and not let him go until he tells Socrates the right definition of piety.

what the pious and the impious are, you couldn't possibly be trying to prosecute your elderly father for murder on behalf of a servant, and you'd fear that you'd be at risk with respect to the gods that you would be wrong in doing this and would be held in contempt by men. But now I'm quite confident that you think you know what the pious and the e impious are. So tell me, good Euthyphro, and don't hide what you believe it is.

EUTHYPHRO: Another time, Socrates. I must hurry off somewhere, and it's time for me to get out of here.

SOCRATES: What are you doing, friend? By leaving, you're tossing out my great hope that I'd learn from you what things are pious and what aren't and I could escape from Meletus' indictment by showing him that I've become wise about divine matters through Euthyphro 16a and no longer speak off-handedly from ignorance or make innovations about them, and, especially, that I'd be a better person for the rest of my life.

9

Apology

The Greek word *apologia*, from which this dialogue takes its name, really means "defense" and not "apology," and the actual defense Plato has Socrates give in this work is hardly apologetic in tone. The *Apology* is divided into three parts: Socrates' defense, his deliberation about what to offer as a counter-penalty, and his closing words to his jurors. Athenian law set no specific penalty for impiety. Prosecutors, therefore, would not only specify in what ways the defendant was supposed to be guilty, but would also propose a penalty in the indictment itself. If a defendant in cases of this sort was found guilty by a majority, then he would make a second speech in which he would propose a penalty that was supposed to be more suitable than the one proposed by the prosecution. This is what Socrates does in his second speech. In the third speech, Socrates first addresses the jurors who voted against him, and then seeks to reassure those who had voted in his favor. As we mentioned in our introduction to part III, scholars are divided over how much we can rely upon the historical accuracy of Plato's depiction of Socrates at his trial.

17a I don't know what effect my accusers[1] have had on you, Athenians, but they were speaking so persuasively that I myself almost forgot who I am. And yet they said virtually nothing that's true. Of their many lies, one surprised me most of all: When they said you needed to

b be on your guard against getting tricked by me, because I'm a clever speaker. Their not being ashamed of that seems to me to be the worst thing they did, because I'm immediately going to refute them by what I do – as soon as I show that I'm not a clever speaker at all – unless they call a clever speaker one who tells the truth. If this is what they mean, I'd agree that I'm an orator, though not the way they are. As I say, they've said almost nothing that's true.

---

1 The speeches given by Socrates' accusers took place during the morning of the trial. Meletus was the man who actually brought the formal charges against him. But it was not uncommon to ask others to speak in court, as part of the presentations of the prosecution or the defense to the jurors. Apparently, speaking in support of Meletus' indictment were two others, Anytus and Lycon, which is why Socrates refers to more than one accuser. It does not appear that Socrates had anyone else give a speech as part of his defense.

But you'll hear only the truth from me, and yet not, by god, Athenians, in beautifully crafted language like theirs, carefully arranged with words and phrases. Instead, you'll hear things c said by me without any planning, in words as they occur to me – for I assume that what I say is just – and none of you should expect anything else. Nor would it be appropriate, I suppose, men, for someone at my age to come before you like a boy planning out what he's going to say. I really implore you to grant me one thing: If you hear me making my defense with the same language I'm used to using in the marketplace at the merchants' tables, where many of you have heard me, and elsewhere, don't be surprised and don't make a disturbance because of it. The truth is this: Now is the first time I've come before a court, although d I'm seventy years old. I'm a complete stranger to the language used here.[2] So just as if I really were a stranger, you would surely forgive me if I spoke in that dialect and manner of speaking in which I had been brought up, so what I am now asking is fair, it seems to me, 18a namely, that you ignore the way I speak – it's not important – and you pay attention to and concentrate on this one thing: if what I say is just or not. This is the virtue of a judge; the virtue of a speaker is to tell the truth.

First, then, it's right for me to make my defense, Athenians, against the first of the false accusations made against me and against my first accusers, and then against the later ones and the later accusers. Many have accused me before you, and have done so for a long time b now, though they didn't say anything that's true. I'm more afraid of them than I am of Anytus and those with him, although they do worry me. But the earlier ones worry me more, men, who having gotten hold of many of you when you were children, convinced you with accusations against me that weren't any truer than the ones I now face. They said that there's a certain Socrates, a wise man, who thinks about what's in the heavens and who has investigated all the things below the earth and who makes the weaker argument appear to be the stronger. Those who spread this rumor, Athenians, are the accusers who worry me. For the c people who hear such things believe that those who inquire about such topics also don't believe in the gods. There are lots of these accusers and they've been at it for a long time already, telling you these things when you were still at an age when you were most apt to believe them, when some of you were children and others were adolescents, and they made their case when absolutely no one presented a defense. But the most unreasonable part of all is that it's impossible to know and say their names, except one who happens to be a d certain writer of comedies.[3] Those who persuaded you by using malice and slander, and some who persuaded others after they themselves had been persuaded – all are very hard to deal with. It isn't even possible to bring any of them up here and to question them, and it's absolutely necessary in making my defense to shadow-box, as it were, and to ask questions when no one answers. Trust me, then, that, as I say, two groups of accusers have arisen against me: the ones who are accusing me right now and the others who I say have been accusing me for quite a while. And please understand that I should defend myself against e

---

2 Socrates is not claiming not to know how people speak or act in courtrooms, for later he shows that he does have some knowledge of such things (see 32a and 34c). His claim is only that he has never before been a litigant in a courtroom. In Athens' participatory democracy, those who did fancy themselves clever speakers would be very likely to have direct experience in litigation. Here and elsewhere, Socrates emphasizes the fact that he has not engaged in the sorts of political activities one would expect from him, if indeed he were the sort of "clever speaker" his accusers have made him out to be.

3 Socrates is referring to Aristophanes, the comic playwright. He refers to Aristophanes explicitly below, at 19c.

the latter group first. After all, you heard them accusing me earlier and with much more intensity than the ones who came later.

19a Well, then, I must make my defense, Athenians, and try to remove from your minds in such a short time the slander you accepted for a long time. I'd hope this happens, if it's better for you and for me, and that in making my defense I do it successfully. But it's not lost on me that this sort of task I'm facing will be difficult. In any case, let this turn out as the god wants; I must obey the law and make a defense.

b Let's take up from the beginning what the accusation against me is from which the slander about me arose – the one that Meletus in particular put his faith in when he brought this indictment against me. Well, what did the slanderers say? I must read it as if it were the sworn statement of accusers: "Socrates does wrong and is too concerned with inquiring about

c what's in the heavens and below the earth and to make the weaker argument appear to be the stronger and to teach these same things to others" – something like this. For you your-selves saw these things in the comedy by Aristophanes: a Socrates being carried around there, saying that he's walking on air and all kinds of other nonsense which I don't understand at all.[4] And I don't mean to disparage knowledge of this sort, if anyone is wise about such things

d (may I not have to answer such charges by Meletus as that!), but, as a matter of fact, I don't possess a bit of that wisdom, Athenians. I'm supplying many of you as my witnesses, and I ask you to talk to and inform each other, as many of you as ever heard me carrying on a discussion – and there are many of you in this category – tell each other whether any of you have ever heard me discussing anything at all about things of this sort. And from this you'll know that the other things that most people say about me are no different.

In fact there's nothing to these claims, not even if you've heard someone say that I try to

e instruct people and make money that way. No, not even this is true. Although as a matter of fact I think it's impressive if anyone is able to instruct people in the way Gorgias of Leontini, Prodicus of Ceos, and Hippias of Elis pretend to do.[5] Each of them is able to go into any

20a city and persuade the young – who can associate for free with any of their own citizens they want to – to abandon their associations with the local people and to associate instead with them and pay them and to thank them for it on top of it all. And then there's another wise man, a Parian, who I learned was living here. For I happened to run into Callias, the son of Hipponicus, a man who had paid more money to the sophists than anyone else. So I asked him – he has two sons – "Callias," I said, "if your two sons were two colts or two calves,

b and we could get hold of and hire an expert for them, who would make them admirable and good in the appropriate virtue? This person would be knowledgeable either about horses or farming. But now, since they're men, what expert do you have in mind to get for them? Who's knowledgeable about this sort of virtue, that of a human being and a citizen? I imag-ine you've looked into it, because you have two sons. Is there someone," I said, "or not?" "Of course," he said. "Who is he," I said, "and where does he come from, and how much does he charge for instruction?" "Evenus," he said, "a Parian, and 5 minas." And I called Evenus

---

4 The reference is to Aristophanes' play, the *Clouds*, which was first produced in 423 BCE. A central character named "Socrates" is made to look mischievous and silly to achieve a comic effect.

5 Each was a prominent sophist. The sophists were teachers who traveled throughout Greece. It is difficult to generalize about the various subjects they professed to teach, but the most prominent of the sophists taught forensic and public speaking. Because some made extravagant claims about improving the character of their students, they were viewed with suspicion and outright contempt by many Athenians, who saw moral education as the province of the family and state (see 24d–25a).

blessed, if he really has such a skill and teaches for such a reasonable fee.[6] I myself would c certainly be pretty puffed up and would act like a bigshot if I knew these things. But the fact is that I don't know them, Athenians.

One of you, perhaps, might respond: "So what's the matter with you, Socrates? Where did these accusations come from? For surely if you weren't engaged in something unusual but were only doing something different from most people, these rumors and talk about d you wouldn't have gotten started. So tell us what it is, so that we don't reach a hasty judgment about you." I think this is a fair question, and I'll try to show you what produced both my reputation and the slander. So listen. No doubt, I'll seem to some of you to be joking. Rest assured, however, that I'll say only what's true. Athenians, I acquired this reputation on account of nothing other than a sort of wisdom. Well, what sort of wisdom is this? It is, surely, just human wisdom. It's likely that I really am wise in that sense. These men, to whom e I was referring just now, might perhaps be wise in a way that's greater than human, or else I don't know what to call it. For I'm certainly not wise in that way, and whoever says I am is either lying or saying it to slander me. And don't interrupt me with your jeering, Athenians, not even if I seem to you to be bragging. The story I'm about to tell you isn't mine, but I refer you to a speaker you trust. About my wisdom, if it really is wisdom and what sort of wisdom it is, I'll produce as a witness the Delphic god.[7] I suppose you know Chairephon. He was both my friend ever since we were young, and also a friend to your 21a democratic faction, and he took part in your faction's exile, and he came back into the city with you.[8] And you know what sort of person Chairephon was and how impulsive he was about whatever he had an urge to do. Once, in particular, he had the nerve to go to Delphi and ask the oracle this question – and, as I say, don't interrupt me, men – he really did ask if anyone is wiser than I am. Then the Pythia responded that no one is wiser. His brother here will serve as a witness for you about these matters, since Chairephon is dead.

Consider why I'm telling you this. I'm about to explain to you how the slandering of me b came about. When I heard about what the oracle told Chairephon, here's what I thought about it: "What's the god saying and what's he hinting at? For I'm aware that, in fact, I'm not wise at all. What then does he mean in saying that I'm the wisest? He certainly isn't lying. That isn't divinely sanctioned for him." And for a long time I was puzzled about what he meant. And then, and with great reluctance, I undertook a search for its meaning in this way: I went to one of those who's reputed to be wise in order there, if indeed anywhere, to c refute the oracle's response and show the oracle: "This person here is wiser than I am, but

6 A mina was equal to 100 silver drachmae. One drachma was the average daily wage for a worker in Athens at this time, and so a single mina was equivalent to 100 days' wages for many Athenian workers. Even though 5 minas is, then, a considerable sum of money, Socrates is being sincere when he says that it is really quite reasonable if Evenus can indeed do what he claims, namely provide Callias with sons of good character.

7 The Greek god Apollo was believed to communicate to humans through the oracle at Delphi. Delphi is located in the mountains, about seventy miles northwest of Athens.

8 At the end of the Peloponnesian War, a commission of thirty men was established to rewrite the laws of Athens. The group soon became known as the Thirty Tyrants, for they soon made it clear that they had no interest in recognizing the rights most Athenians enjoyed under democratic rule (see also note 18, below). Many who wanted to see democracy reestablished in Athens left the city and later retook the city by force from those loyal to the Thirty. Socrates' friend, Chairephon, was one who fought on the side of the democrats.

you claimed that I'm the wisest man." Then after thoroughly examining him – I needn't mention his name, Athenians, but he was one of the politicians that I had this sort of experience with. After conversing with him, I thought that this guy seems to be wise to many other people and, most of all, to himself, yet he isn't. And then I tried to show him that he

21d thought he is wise, but he isn't. And so, as a result, I became hated by him and by many of those who were there. So, as I went away from him, I concluded to myself that I'm, indeed, wiser than this guy. I'm afraid that neither of us knows anything admirable and good, but this guy thinks he knows something when he doesn't, whereas I, just as I don't know, don't even think I know. At least, then, I seem to be wiser in this small way than this guy, because I don't even think I know what I don't know. From him, I went to someone else, one of those reputed to be wiser than the first guy, and the very same thing seemed to me to be

e true, and at that point I became hated by that guy and by many others too.

After that I went from one person to the next, and although I was troubled and fearful when I saw that I had become hated, nevertheless I thought I had to make the god's business the most important thing. In searching for the meaning of the oracle, I had to proceed

22a on to all who had a reputation for knowing something. And, by the Dog,[9] Athenians – for I must tell you the truth – the fact is that I experienced something of this sort: Those who enjoyed the greatest reputation seemed to me, as I searched in accordance with the god, to be pretty much the most lacking, whereas those who were reputed to be less worthy of consideration were better men when it came to having good sense.

Now, I must instruct you about my wandering, undertaken like labors, which resulted in my not refuting the oracle. After the politicians I went to the poets – those who write tragedies,

b dithyrambs, and the others, so that right in the very act of questioning them, I would catch myself being more ignorant than they are. Then when they read their poetry, which I thought they had really worked at, I asked them what they meant in order to learn something from them. Now I'm embarrassed to tell you the truth, but I must say it. Virtually everyone present could have given a better account of what they had written. After a little while, I realized this about the poets: They composed what they did, not out of wisdom but by some

c kind of natural ability and because they were divinely inspired, just like seers and prophets. For even though they in fact say many fine things, they don't know what they're saying. It was evident to me that the poets had been affected in some way like this. I found out that because of their poetry, they thought they were the wisest of people in other ways as well, which they weren't. So I left them, thinking that I'm superior to them in just the way that I'm superior to the politicians.

And then finally, I went to the craftsmen. I was aware that I knew virtually nothing, but

d I also knew that I'd discover that they knew many admirable things. I wasn't deceived about this: They did know what I didn't know, and in that way they were wiser than I am. But, Athenians, the good craftsmen also seemed to me to make the same mistake the poets committed. Because of practicing his craft well, each one believed he was supremely wise in other things, the most important things – and this very mistake of theirs seemed to me to over-

e shadow that wisdom they did have. So I asked myself on behalf of the oracle whether I would prefer to be simply as I am, neither being wise in their sort of wisdom, nor ignorant in the way they are ignorant, or to be in both ways as they are. Then I answered myself and the oracle that I'd be better off being simply as I am.

---

9 The expression is uncommon. Socrates is clearly using it to signal to the jury the importance of what he is about to say.

This very investigation, Athenians, has generated for me a great deal of hatred, which is most difficult to handle and hard to bear, and the result has been a lot of slandering, and the 23a claim made that I'm "wise." It's because every time the people present think that I'm wise about the subject I refute someone else on. But what's likely, men, is that the god is really wise and that in this oracle he means that human wisdom is of little or no value. And he appears to mean that such a person is Socrates and to have used my name, taking me as an b example, as if to say, "This one of you, O human beings, is wisest, who – as Socrates does – knows that he's in truth worthless with respect to wisdom." And so even now I go around searching and questioning, in keeping with the god, any citizen or stranger whom I think is wise. And when he doesn't seem to me to be so, I help the god out and show that he isn't wise. It's because of this occupation that I have no leisure time worth mentioning to do any-thing for the city or for my family, but instead I'm in complete poverty on account of my c service to the god.

But in addition to this, the young who follow me around, doing so of their free will, who have complete leisure – the sons of the richest people – enjoy hearing people examined, and they often imitate me, and then try to examine others. And then, I imagine, they find an abundance of people who think they know something but know virtually nothing. That's why those who are examined by them get angry with me and not with them, and say that a certain Socrates completely pollutes[10] the land and corrupts the youth. And when anyone d asks them what I do and what I teach, they have nothing to say and draw a blank, but so they don't appear to be confused, they say what's commonly said against all philosophers – "what's in the heavens and below the earth," "doesn't believe in gods," and "makes the weaker argument the stronger." But I think they wouldn't want to say what's true, that they're plainly pretending to know, and they don't know anything. In so far, then, as they are, I think, con-cerned about their honor, and are zealous, and numerous, and speak earnestly and per- e suasively about me, they've filled your ears for a long time by vehemently slandering me. It was on this account that Meletus, Anytus, and Lycon came after me: Meletus, angry on behalf of the poets; Anytus, on behalf of the craftsmen and politicians;[11] and Lycon, on behalf of 24a the orators. The result is that, as I was saying when I began, I'd be amazed if I were able to refute in such a little time this slander you accept and that has gotten out of hand. There you have the truth, men of Athens, and in what I'm saying, I'm neither hiding nor even shading anything large or small. And yet I know pretty well that in saying these things, I'm making myself hated, which is evidence that I'm telling the truth and that such is the slander against me and that these are its causes. And whether you investigate these things now or later, you'll discover that they're so.   b

Let this be enough of a defense for you about what my first accusers accuse me of. But regarding the good and patriotic Meletus, as he says, and the later accusers, I'll try to pre-sent a defense next. Just as if they were in fact a different group of accusers, let's take up their sworn statement in turn. It goes, I suppose, like this: They're saying that Socrates does

10 An ancient Greek notion that one who commits offenses against the gods "pollutes" the surrounding land and makes himself and everyone who inhabits the area liable to divine punishments until the land is "cleansed" by having the one who has offended undergo the proper punishment for the offense.

11 Anytus was a craftsman who became one of the leading members of the democratic faction in Athens. Nothing is known about Lycon other than his participation as one who spoke against Socrates at his trial.

wrong because he corrupts the youth and doesn't believe in the gods that the city believes
24c in, but believes in other new divinities. Such is the charge. But let's examine each part of this accusation.

He says that I do wrong because I corrupt the young. But I say, Athenians, that *he* does wrong, because he's playing around in what's serious business, thoughtlessly putting people on trial, while pretending to be serious and troubled about matters which he has never cared about at all.[12] I'll try to show you this is so.

Come here, Meletus, and tell me. Isn't it true that you take it to be very important that
d the young be as good as possible?

I do.

Come on now and tell these people: Who improves them? It's clear that you know; at least it's a matter of concern to you. Since you've discovered me as the one who corrupts them, as you say, and you're bringing me to trial before these people here and you're accusing me. Come and tell us who improves them and show these people who he is. Do you notice, Meletus, that you're silent and can't say anything? And yet doesn't it seem to you to be disgraceful and sufficient proof of what I'm talking about, that none of this has mattered to you? But tell me, my good man, who improves them?

The laws.

e I'm not asking you that. But who's the person who knows the laws to begin with?

These men, Socrates, the jurors.

What're you saying, Meletus – that they're able to educate the young and improve them?

Absolutely.

And which is it? All of them, or is it that some are able to do so and others not?

Everyone is.

What good news, by Hera! There's no shortage of those who provide help! But what about
25a this? Do those who are here listening to the trial improve them or not?

They do, too.

What about the members of the Council?[13]

The members of the Council do, too.

But, then, Meletus, do those in the Assembly, its members, corrupt the youth, or do all of those people improve them?

They do, too.

Therefore, it seems, all Athenians except me make the youth admirable and good, but I alone corrupt them. Is this what you're saying?

That's exactly what I'm saying.

You've condemned me to a terrible fate! But tell me this: Don't you think this also holds
b with horses? Everyone improves them and an individual corrupts them? Or isn't it just the opposite of this, that one person or only a few are able to improve them – the horse trainers – whereas most people, if in fact they're around and use horses, corrupt them? Isn't that true, Meletus, both with horses and with all other animals? It's absolutely clear that it is,

---

12 Socrates is punning on the Meletus' name. "Meletus" sounds like *melein*, a Greek verb that means "to care about."

13 The Council was the body of 500, selected by lot and rotated among the citizens, whose primary responsibility was the preparation of the agenda for the Athenian Assembly, the law-making body that all citizens could attend.

whether you and Anytus say so or not! The young would be fortunate indeed if only one c person corrupts them and the others improve them! But the fact is, Meletus, that you're making it quite clear that you've never even thought about the young, and you're making your lack of concern readily apparent, because you haven't been concerned at all about what you're bringing me to trial for.

Anyway, tell me, in the name of Zeus, whether it's better to live among good citizens or bad? Answer, my good man, for I'm not asking you anything difficult! Don't bad people always do something bad to those who happen to be closest to them, whereas good people do something good for those who are closest to them?

Of course.

Then is there anyone who'd rather be harmed by those they're around instead of d benefited? Answer, my good man, for the law commands you to answer! Is there anyone who wishes to be harmed?

Clearly not.

Come then. Are you putting me on trial here on the ground that I corrupt the youth and make them worse voluntarily or involuntarily?

I say you do it voluntarily.

What's that, Meletus? Are you at your age so much wiser than I am at mine that you knew that bad people always do something evil to those who are their closest neighbors, whereas good people always do something good, but I've reached the point of such e ignorance that I don't know this, because if I make someone I'm with bad, I'm likely to receive something bad from him, and so I'm doing such an evil voluntarily, as you say? I'm not persuaded by you about these things, Meletus, nor do I think anyone else is! Either I don't corrupt them, or if I do corrupt them, I do so involuntarily, so that, either way, you're not 26a telling the truth! If I corrupt them involuntarily, however, the law here isn't to bring people to trial for errors of this sort but to take them aside in private to teach and admonish them. For it's clear that once I understand, I'll stop what I'm doing involuntarily. But you've avoided associating with me and you didn't want to instruct me, and instead wanted to bring me here to trial where it's the law to try those who need punishment, not instruction.

Well, anyway, Athenians, what I was saying is obvious, namely, that Meletus has never b cared anything at all about these things. Nevertheless, tell us now: How do you say that I corrupt the youth, Meletus? Isn't it in fact clear according to the indictment you wrote that I do so by teaching the young not to believe in the gods that the city believes in but instead to believe in other new divinities? Aren't you claiming that it's by teaching that I corrupt them?

That's exactly what I'm claiming!

In the name of these very gods that we're arguing about, Meletus, tell me and these men here still more clearly. I'm not able to understand whether you're saying that I teach people c not to believe that some gods exist – and therefore that I myself believe gods exist and am not a complete atheist, nor am not a wrongdoer in that way – and yet I do not believe in the ones that the city believes in, but others, and this is what you're accusing me of, because I believe in the others? Or are you saying that I don't believe in gods at all and that I teach others such things?

I'm saying that you don't believe in the gods at all.

Wonderful Meletus, why are you saying these things? Don't I even believe that the sun d and the moon are gods, as other people do?

No, by god, jurymen, since he says that the sun is a stone and the moon is earth.

Do you think you are prosecuting Anaxagoras,[14] Meletus? Are you being contemptuous of these men, and do you think they're so illiterate that they don't know that Anaxagoras of Clazomenae's books are full of these sayings? And, indeed, do you think the young learn 26e from me what they can sometimes buy for at most a drachma in the stalls in the market-place, and laugh at Socrates, if he pretends they're his own, especially since they're so absurd! In the name of Zeus, do you really think this about me, that I don't believe in any god?

No, by Zeus, you don't, not at all.

You're not to be believed, Meletus – and what's more, I think, not even to yourself! He seems to me, Athenians, to be completely insolent and out of control and this indictment is 27a just the result of insolence, lack of self-restraint, and immaturity. He seems to be testing me by making a riddle, as it were. "Will the wise Socrates recognize that I'm fooling around and contradicting myself, or will I trick him and the others who are listening?" He seems to be saying contradictory things in his indictment, as if he were saying: Socrates is guilty since he doesn't believe in the gods, but he does believe in the gods. And this is the sort of thing someone says when he's fooling around.

So let's consider together, men, in what sense he appears to me to mean what he's say-
b ing. Answer us, Meletus; and you, members of the jury, as I requested at the beginning, bear in mind that you're not to interrupt me if I present my arguments in the way I'm used to.

Is there anyone, Meletus, who believes in what is associated with human beings, but who doesn't believe in human beings? Let him answer, men, and don't keep on interrupting. Is there anyone who doesn't believe in horses but who believes in what's associated with horses? Or is there anyone who doesn't believe in flute-players but who believes in what's associated with flute-players? There is not, O best of men! If you don't want to answer, I'll give the answer to you and to the others here. But answer the next one at least: Is there anyone who
c believes in the existence of what's associated with spiritual things, but who doesn't believe in spirits?

There isn't.

How helpful it was that you answered so reluctantly when you were forced to by the jurors here! Aren't you saying that I believe in and teach that there are spiritual things, whether new or old, and I believe in spiritual things, at least according to your argument, and you swore to that in your indictment. But if I believe in spiritual things, surely it absolutely has to be true that I believe in spirits. Isn't that so? Of course it is! I take it that you agree with me, since you're not answering. But don't we believe that spirits are at least either gods or
d the children of gods? Do you say so or not?

Of course.

Then if I believe in spirits, as you're saying, and if spirits are gods, then this is what I'm saying that you're making a riddle of and fooling around about when you say that I don't believe in gods and then in addition to that, that I do believe in gods, since at least I believe in spirits. But if spirits are the illegitimate children of gods, either from nymphs or any others from whom it's also said they come, could someone believe that the children gods had with
e human beings exist, but not believe that gods exist? It would be similarly absurd if someone believed in the children of horses and donkeys, that is, mules, but didn't believe in horses and donkeys. Meletus, isn't it true that you wrote this indictment either to test us out or

14 A nature-philosopher who was at one time on friendly terms with Pericles and who may have been exiled. His views about natural change put him at odds with those who held traditional views about the way the gods cause many natural changes.

because you were confused about what actual wrongdoing you could accuse me of! It just isn't possible that you could persuade anyone who has even a little sense that the same person could believe in spiritual and divine things and yet for the same person not to believe in spirits, gods, and heroes! 28a

Well anyway, Athenians, that I'm not guilty according to Meletus's indictment doesn't seem to me to need much of a defense, and what I've said about it is enough. But what I was saying earlier – that there's great deal of hatred directed at me and by many people, you may be sure that's true. And it's this that'll convict me, if indeed I'm going to be convicted – not Meletus nor even Anytus but the prejudice and ill will of most people. This is what's b convicted many other good men and, I think, it'll do so in the future. And we needn't fear that it'll end with my case.

Perhaps someone could say, "But then aren't you ashamed, Socrates, of having been devoted to such a pursuit that's likely to lead to death at this time?" I should respond to this person as follows: "You're wrong, sir, if you think that a person who has any merit needs to consider the likelihood of life or of death and not to look only to this when he acts: Is he acting justly or unjustly and performing the deeds of a good or a bad person? By your c argument, all those demigods who died at Troy would be worthless people, and especially the son of Thetis,[15] who scorned such danger when the choice was to endure disgrace, so that his mother, who's a goddess, spoke to him when he was eager to kill Hector, I suppose, in this fashion. 'My child, if you avenge the killing of your friend Patroclus and kill Hector, you yourself will die – for right away,' she says, "after Hector, your death awaits you." But when he heard this, Achilles thought little of danger and death, but instead since he had a much greater fear of living as a bad man and not of avenging his friends, he says, 'may I die d after I dispense justice to the unjust in order that I not remain here, a laughingstock, beside the curved ships, a burden of the earth?' You don't really think *he* considered death and danger, do you?"

For it really is this way, Athenians, that wherever someone stations himself, believing it to be best or where someone has been stationed by his commander, I think, he must remain there to face danger, not weighing death or anything else more than disgrace.

Thus, I would have done a terrible thing, Athenians, if, when my commanders, whom e you elected to command me, stationed me at Potidaia, and Amphipolis, and Delium, and then remained where they stationed me, like anyone else, and risked death and yet when the god ordered – as I believed and understood myself to have been so ordered – that I must spend my life philosophizing and examining myself and others, I would have abandoned my position through fear of death or any other concern whatsoever. That would be terrible and 29a then someone might really bring me to court justly on the ground that I don't believe the gods exist, since I disobey the oracle, fear death, and think I'm wise when I'm not. In truth, the fear of death, men, is nothing but thinking you're wise when you're not, for you think you know what you don't. For no one knows whether death happens to be the greatest of all goods for humanity, but people fear it because they're completely convinced that it's the greatest of evils. And isn't this ignorance, after all, the most shameful kind: thinking you know b what you don't? But in this respect, too, men, I'm probably different from most people. If, then, I'd say that I'm wiser than someone in some way, it would be in this way: While I

---

15 The son of Thetis was Achilles, the Greek hero who, believing that it was right for him to avenge the death of his friend, Patroclus, went forth in battle to kill Hector, even though Achilles knew that the killing of Hector would eventually result in his own death.

don't really know about the things in Hades, I don't think I know. But I do know that it's evil and disgraceful to do what's wrong and to disobey one's superior, whether god or man.

29c Rather than those things that I know are bad, I'll never run from nor fear those things that may turn out to be good. The upshot is that even if you let me go because you don't believe Anytus – who said that either you shouldn't bring me here in the first place or since you've done so, you have to kill me, telling you that if I were acquitted, all of your sons will be completely corrupted by spending their time practicing what Socrates teaches – well, if you'd respond to me: "Socrates, this time we won't do as Anytus says. We'll let you go, but on this condition, that you stop spending your time in this inquiry of yours and philosophizing.

d But if you're caught still doing so, you'll die." Thus, if, as I was saying, you were to let me go on this condition, I'd tell you, "Athenians, I respect and I love you, but I'll obey the god rather than you, and as long as I breathe and am able, I won't stop philosophizing and exhorting you and pointing out to any of you I ever happen upon, saying just what I usually do, 'Best of men, since you're an Athenian, from the greatest city with the strongest reputation for wisdom and strength, aren't you ashamed that you care about having as much money,

e fame, and honor as you can, and you don't care about, or even consider wisdom, truth, and making your soul as good as possible?' " And if any of you disputes me on this and says he does care, I won't immediately stop talking to him and go away, but I'll question, examine,

30a and try to refute him. And if he doesn't appear to me to have acquired virtue but says he has, I'll shame him because he attaches greater value to what's of less value and takes what's inferior to be more important. And I'll do this for whomever I come upon, young and old, foreigner and citizen, but I'll be more concerned with citizens insofar as you're more closely related to me.

You may be sure that the god has commanded this, and I think that there's no greater good for the city than my service to the god. For the only thing I do is to go around trying

b to persuade you, young and old, not to care more about either your bodies or money, nor so passionately as you do about the perfection of your souls, saying, "Virtue doesn't come from money, but money and all other good things for human beings, both in private and in public, come from virtue." If I corrupt the young by saying these things, then this would be harmful. But if anyone maintains that I say anything else, he's lying. "Therefore," I would say, "Athenians, be persuaded by Anytus or not, let me go or not, because I won't do any-

c thing else, even if I have to die many times."

Don't interrupt me, but stick to what I asked you to do. Listen to what I'm saying and don't interrupt. I think you'll benefit by listening. For I'm about to tell you some other things that'll probably cause you to yell out. But don't ever do this. Rest assured that if you kill me – since I am the person I say I am – you won't harm me more than you harm yourselves. Neither Meletus nor Anytus could do anything to harm me; it isn't even possible. For I don't

d think it's divinely sanctioned for a better man to be harmed by a worse. Doubtless, he could kill me, or send me into exile, or take away my rights, and doubtless he and others also think these things are great evils. But I don't. In fact, I think that what he's doing now – trying to kill a man unjustly – is a much greater evil. Athenians, at this point I'm far from making this defense on my behalf, as one might think, but instead I'm making it on yours, so that by condemning me you don't make a terrible mistake regarding the gift the god has

e given you. For if you kill me, you won't easily find another person like me, simply put, even if it's funny to say so, who's been attached to the city by the god as if it were a large and well-bred horse, though one that's somewhat sluggish on account of its size and that needs to be disturbed by a gadfly. In some such way as this I think the god has attached me to the city – such a person who disturbs you and stirs you up and shames each one of you, I never stop landing on you everywhere all day long. Another one like me won't quickly come to you, men, and if you're persuaded by me, you'll spare me. But it's more likely that you'll 31a be angry, like those who are disturbed when they're drowsy, and swat me – having been persuaded by Anytus – and easily kill me, then you'd spend the rest of your life asleep, unless the god, in his concern for you, were to send someone else to you. That I am the sort of person who's been given to the city by the god, you'll see from what I'm about to say. For it doesn't seem to be human nature for me to have neglected all of my own affairs and endured b not caring for my family's concerns all these years, and instead to have always done what's in your interest, coming to each of you individually like a father or an older brother, trying to persuade you to care about virtue. If I profited at all from these things and gave advice for a fee, it would make some sense. But now you yourselves see that my accusers, while accusing me of everything else in such a shameless way, couldn't bring themselves to be so shameless as to produce witnesses that I ever made money from anyone or that I asked for c any. I think that I'm producing a sufficient witness that I'm telling the truth: my poverty.

Perhaps it would seem odd that I go around giving advice in private and sticking my nose into other people's business but don't dare step up and give the city advice about your concerns in public. The reason for this is the one you've often heard me give in many places, namely, something divine and spiritual comes to me, and it's this that Meletus made fun of d in the indictment he wrote. It's come to me since childhood – this voice – and whenever it comes, it always turns me away from what I'm about to do but never turns me toward anything. This is what opposes my engaging in politics, and I think it's wonderful that it's done so. For you can be sure, Athenians, that if I'd tried to engage in politics earlier, I'd have been put to death earlier, and neither you nor I would've benefited. Don't be upset at me for e telling the truth: No one will survive who genuinely opposes you or any other populace and tries to prevent many unjust and illegal things from happening in the city. Instead, one who 32a really fights for what's just, if he's to survive even for a little while, must live as a private and not as a public man.

I'm going to provide you with compelling evidence of this, not just talk, but what you respect – actions. Listen now to what happened to me so that you'll know that I'd give in to no one, under any conditions, out of fear of death, contrary to what's just, even if by not giving in I'd die right away. I'm going to tell you some of the things one commonly hears in law courts, but they're true nonetheless. Athenians, I never held any other office in the b city, but I was a member of the Council. My district, Antiochis, was in charge of the Council,[16] when you wanted to judge as a group the ten generals who failed to pick up those who died in the sea battle.[17] What you wanted though was against the law, as you all realized some time later on. At that time, I was the only one of the Councilors in charge who opposed you, urging you to do nothing against the law, and I voted in opposition. And though the orators were ready to denounce me and arrest me, and though you urged them to do so by your shouting, with the law and justice on my side I thought that, though I feared imprison- c ment or death, I should run the risk rather than to join with you, since you wanted what's

16 Each district had fifty representatives (selected by rotation and lot) on the Council (see note 13, above) each year and each group of fifty took a turn being in charge of the Council.
17 Socrates is referring to the sea battle at Arginusae, which took place in 406 BCE, just two years before the end of the Peloponnesian War. The Athenian generals were charged as a group with a failure to retrieve the bodies of those Athenians who died during the battle.

not just. These things happened when the city was still a democracy. But when the oligarchy came to power, the Thirty summoned me and four others to the Rotunda and ordered us to bring Leon from Salamis to be put to death.[18] They often ordered many others to do such things, since they wanted to implicate as many as possible in their causes. At that time I made

32d it clear once again, not by talk but by action, that I didn't care at all about death – if I'm not being too blunt to say it – but it mattered everything that I do nothing unjust or impious, which matters very much to me. For though it had plenty of power, that government didn't frighten me into doing anything that's wrong. So when we left the Rotunda, the other four went to Salamis and arrested Leon, and I left and went home. I suppose I'd have been killed for doing so if that regime hadn't been deposed shortly thereafter. You can also have many

e witnesses to these things.

So do you think I could've lasted all these years if I had been engaging in politics and by acting in a way that's worthy of a good man I had supported the right causes and, as one must, attached the greatest importance to this? Far from it, men of Athens. Nor could any-

33a one else. For my whole life shows that I am this sort of person whether I did anything in public or in private, namely one who never gave in to anyone at all contrary to what's just, nor to any of those whom my accusers say are my students. I've never been anyone's teacher. But if anyone, young or old, wants to hear me talking or carrying out my own work, I never refused him, nor do I carry on a conversation when I get paid but not when I don't get paid.

b Instead, I make myself question rich and poor and by answering if anyone wants to hear what I have to say. And if any of those who listen becomes good or not, I couldn't rightly be held to be the cause, since I've never promised any of them any knowledge, nor have I ever taught anyone anything. If anyone says that he's ever learned anything from me or heard in private something that everyone else hasn't heard, you can be sure he's not telling the truth.

c Why then do some enjoy spending so much time with me? Listen, Athenians, I'm telling you the whole truth. They enjoy hearing me examine those who think they're wise when they're not. It's not unpleasant. But, as I say, I've been ordered to do this by the god through dreams and oracles and in every way in which divine providence has ever ordered a human being to do anything whatever.

This, Athenians, is the truth, and it's easily tested. If indeed I am corrupting some of

d the young and have corrupted others, then surely some of them who have grown up and recognized that I encouraged them to do wrong when they were younger ought to accuse me and take their revenge by coming forward. And if they don't want to, some of their relatives – their fathers and brothers and others who are close to them, if in fact any of their relatives suffered any harm from me – should make their complaint now and take their revenge. In any case, I see quite a few of them present here. First, there's Crito here, who's

e my age and from the same part of the city, the father of Critoboulus; then, there's Lysanias of Sphettus, the father of Aeschines here; and also Antiphon of Cephisus, the father of Epigenes, is here; and others still, whose brothers kept my company: Nicostratus, the son of Theozotides and brother of Theodotus – Theodotus is dead and so he couldn't beg his father not to accuse me – and Paralius there, the son of Demodocus, whose brother was

34a Theages. There's Adeimantus, the son of Ariston, whose brother is Plato here; and Ainantodorus, whose brother is Apollodorus here. And I can name many others for you,

---

18 The arrest of Leon was by no means the only such illegal arrest that took place during the reign of the Thirty Tyrants, but it must have been especially egregious in the eyes of many Athenians.

some of whom Meletus certainly should've called as witnesses when he gave his speech. If he forgot, let him call them – I yield up the time – and let him speak if he has anything of this sort to say. You'll find, however, that just the opposite's the case, men. All of those related to those I "corrupted" are ready to help me, the guy who did "bad things" to their relatives, according to Meletus and Anytus. Those who've been corrupted would probably have some b reason to help me. But what reason could those who haven't been corrupted and who are already older men – their relatives – have except the correct and right one, namely, that they know Meletus is lying and I'm telling the truth?

Well then, men, this and perhaps other things like it are about all I can say in my defense. Perhaps some one of you may be angry when he thinks about himself if he went to trial on c a less serious matter than this and he begged and pleaded with lots of tears with the members of the jury, and brought in his children, as well as many other relatives and friends in order to be shown as much pity as possible. But I'll do none of these things, and although in doing this, I appear to him to be running the ultimate risk. Then perhaps when some d of you consider this, you'll become more closed-minded about me and, having become angry, will cast your vote in anger. If indeed any of you is so disposed – I don't expect it of you, but if there is anyone – I think it's fair for me to say to this person, "I have a family, too, sir. This is just what Homer said: 'not from oak or rock' was I born, but from human beings. And so I do have a family, and sons, three of them, one in adolescence and two in childhood. Nevertheless, I won't bring them in here and beg you to acquit me." Why won't I? Not because I'm indifferent, Athenians, nor out of disrespect for you. But whether I'm coura- e geous in the face of death or not is another matter; but it seems to me not a good thing – for the reputation of me and you and of the whole city – for me at my age and with this reputation to do any of these things. Whether it's true or not, there's a view that Socrates 35a is superior in some way to most people. If those of you who think they're superior – whether in wisdom or courage or in any virtue whatsoever – would act in that way, it would be disgraceful. I've often seen certain people put on trial, who, though they are reputed to be important, do surprising things, because they think their death is something terrible, as if they would be immortal if you didn't kill them. But I think they are bringing disgrace to the city, so that a foreigner would suppose that those Athenians who're superior in virtue, whom they judge b from among themselves to be worthy of getting offices and other honors, are no better than women. Such things, Athenians, those of you who seem to be important in any way whatever shouldn't do; nor, if we do them, should you allow it. But you should make this very thing clear: You'll do much better to condemn one who makes these pitiable scenes and who makes a laughingstock of the city than one who maintains his composure.

But apart from the issue of one's reputation, it doesn't seem to me right to beg the members of the jury, nor to grant acquittal to the one who asks, but instead it's right to try to instruct c and persuade. For the member of the jury doesn't sit for this reason – to make gifts out of what's just – but to judge what's just. He's taken an oath not to make gifts to whom he wants but to judge according to the laws. Therefore, we shouldn't get you in the habit of breaking your oaths, nor should you get in the habit of doing so. That wouldn't be pious for either of us. So please don't think that I, Athenians, should do for you what I believe d isn't noble, or just, or pious, and especially, by Zeus, when I'm being prosecuted by Meletus here for impiety. For it's clear that if I should persuade you and force you by begging when you have taken oaths, I'd be teaching you not to believe the gods exist, and in presenting a defense, I'd have simply made the charge against myself that I don't believe in the gods. But that's far from the truth. For I do believe in them, Athenians, as none of my accusers do, and I leave it to you and to the god to judge in what way it's going to be best for you and for me.[19]

• • •

35e Many things contribute to my not being angry at what's happened – that you voted against
36a me – and the result was not unexpected by me, but I was much more surprised by the total number of votes on each side. For I didn't think it would be such a small majority. I thought it would be much larger. Now, it seems, if only thirty votes had gone the other way, I'd have been acquitted.[20] I think that as far as Meletus is concerned, I've now been acquitted, and not only have I already been acquitted, but isn't it obvious to everyone that if Anytus
b and Lycon hadn't come forward to prosecute me, he would have incurred a 1000 drachma fine for not having received one-fifth of the votes?[21]

So the gentleman [Meletus] asks that the penalty be death. Well, what should I propose for you as a counterpenalty? Isn't it clear that it should be what I deserve? So, what would that be? What do I deserve to suffer or to pay for not having led an inactive life and for not caring about what most people care for – making money, managing my affairs, being a general or a political leader and any of the different offices and parties and factions that
c come about in the city? I believed that I was really too good to go down that path and sur-vive. I didn't go where I would've been no help at all to you or to me, but went, instead, to each one of you in private to do the greatest good. As I say, I went there, undertaking to persuade each of you not to care about your possessions before you care about how you will be the best and wisest you can be, nor to care about what the city has, before you care
d about the city itself, and to care about other things in just the same way. Being this sort of person, what do I deserve to suffer? Something good, Athenians, if indeed I should truly assess my penalty according to what I deserve! Yes, and the sort of good thing that would be appro-priate for me. What's appropriate for a poor man who's your benefactor and who needs to have the leisure to exhort you? There's nothing more appropriate, Athenians, than that such a person be given meals in the Prytaneum;[22] in fact, it's much more appropriate than for one of you who had won at Olympia with either a pair or a team of horses. For he makes you think you are happy, but I make you happy, and he doesn't need the food, but I do. So if
e
37a I'm supposed to propose a penalty in accordance with what I deserve, I propose to be given meals at the Prytaneum.[23]

In speaking in this way I probably strike some of you as speaking impudently pretty much as I did when I spoke about wailing and begging. But it isn't this sort of thing at all, Athenians,

19 The jury now votes on whether or not to convict Socrates. He begins his next speech after the number of votes for guilt and for innocence is announced. For violations of this sort, the trial proce-dure was called an *agon timētos*, which meant that the law itself did not set the penalty for a con-viction, leaving it for the defendant to propose a counterpenalty to whatever penalty had already been proposed by the prosecutor (in the indictment itself). Meletus had called for the death penalty. In this section of the *Apology*, Socrates explains why he chooses to propose the counterpenalty he does.

20 Plato does not tell us exactly how large the jury was, but it is likely that the jury consisted of 500 citizens, in which case, 280 jurors voted to convict and 220 voted to acquit.

21 Imposing this fine, which was quite substantial, served to discourage frivolous prosecutions.

22 The Prytaneum was a building in which various Athenian heroes, Olympic victors, generals, and others were given meals at public expense. The privilege was, perhaps, the highest honor Athens bestowed on anyone.

23 Socrates does not actually propose "free meals at the Prytaneum" as his counterpenalty; he only says that this is what he should propose, if he were to propose what he really deserves.

but in fact it's more like this: I'm convinced that I've never willingly wronged anyone, but I haven't convinced you of this. For we've conversed with each other for just a little while. What I mean is, I think that if you had a law, as other people do, about not judging death-penalty cases in a single day but over many, you'd have been persuaded by me. But as it is, it isn't easy to destroy widespread slanders in a short time. Since I'm convinced that I've b never been unjust, I'm not about to treat myself unjustly and to say of myself that I deserve something evil and to propose that sort of penalty for myself. Why should I? Can it be that I should suffer the penalty that Meletus proposes, which I say that I don't know whether it's good or not? Or should I choose what I'm convinced is an evil, making this my counter-proposal instead? Imprisonment? Why should I live obedient to those who happen to hold c the office of the eleven prison commissioners? Or a fine, and be imprisoned until I pay it? But that's the same thing I was just talking about, for I have no money to pay it with. Shall I now offer exile? Perhaps you'd impose that as my penalty. I'd really have to be in love with living, men of Athens, to be so illogical as not to be able to see that if you, who are my fellow citizens, weren't able to bear my activities and arguments – but they became so d burdensome and hateful that you're now seeking to be free of them – yet others will endure them easily. I think that's pretty unreasonable, Athenians. A fine life I'd have to live, a man of my age, after going into exile, going from one city to the next, always being sent into exile? You can be sure that wherever I'd go, young people will listen to what I have to say, just as they do here. If I drive them away, they themselves will send me into exile by persuading their elders. But if I don't drive them away, their fathers and relatives will send e me into exile for their sakes.

Perhaps some of you might say, "Can't you leave us to live in exile and keep quiet and not talk?" This is the most difficult thing to convince some of you of. If I say that this is dis-obedience to the god and that's why it's impossible to keep quiet, you'll think I'm not being 38a sincere. And if I say that this really is the greatest good for human beings – to engage in dis-cussion each day about virtue and the other things which you have heard me talking about and examining myself and others, and the unexamined life is not worth living for a human being – you'll be persuaded even less by what I say. These things are true, as I say, but it's not easy to persuade you. At the same time, I'm not in the habit of thinking that I deserve anything bad. If I had money, I'd offer what I could afford to pay; for I wouldn't be harm- b ing anything. But as it is, that isn't possible, unless you want to impose a penalty on me that I can pay. I suppose I could probably offer to pay you a mina of silver.[24] So I offer this amount.

Plato, here, Athenians, and Crito, Critobulus, and Apollodorus bid me to pay a penalty of 30 minas, and they'll guarantee that it's paid. I offer that much, then, and they'll be guarantors of the silver for you; they're good for it.[25]

• • •

24 See note 6 above. Because Socrates insists that he is at this point in his life a poor man and because he refuses to go to prison until money can be raised, it is reasonable to think that one mina is all that he could pay as a fine.

25 See note 6, above. Thirty minas was the equivalent of 3000 days wages for an ordinary Athenian worker – hence, quite a substantial sum of money. It was not uncommon for others to provide assistance to those required to pay large fines – those who could not find sufficient resources to pay their fines would have all of their property confiscated and would be sent into exile. The four who encourage Socrates to raise the amount of his proposed fine to the much higher amount all come from some of the wealthiest families in Athens.

38c Just to gain a little time, Athenians,[26] you'll be notorious and blamed by those who want to revile the city because you killed Socrates, a wise man – for those who want to hold you in contempt will say that I am in fact wise, even if I'm not. If you had held off for a little while, you'd have gotten what you wanted without having to do anything. For you see that

d I'm far along in life and that death is near. I say this not to all of you, but to those of you who voted for my execution. To them I have this to say: "Men, perhaps you think that I was convicted because of a failure to understand what words would have persuaded you, if I thought I should do and say anything that would gain my acquittal. That's far from accurate. I was convicted, not because of a failure to understand what to say, but because of not being brazen and shameless and because of not wanting to say the things you'd most like to hear – wailing and crying out and doing and saying many other unworthy things, which

e indeed, as I say, you're used to hearing from others. Nor did I think then that I should simply do anything slavish on account of the danger I was in, nor am I sorry that I've defended myself in this way, but I'd much rather choose to die having defended myself in the way I have than to live on in that other way. Neither in the law court nor in war should I or any

39a other person try to come up with plans to avoid death by doing anything we can. In battles it often becomes clear that one could avoid death by throwing down his weapons and turning to plead with his pursuers. And there are many other ways in each sort of danger to escape death if one would resort to doing and saying anything. For, men, it's surely not difficult

b to flee from death, but it's much more difficult to flee from evil; for evil runs faster than death. And now, being slow and old, I'm caught by the slower one, but my accusers, being clever and sharp-witted are caught by the faster one, evil. And now I go away, having been sentenced by you to death and they go away, sentenced by the truth to evil and injustice. I'll stand by my penalty and they, by theirs. I suppose it had to be this way, and I think it's appropriate.

c Next I want to prophesy to those of you who voted against me. For I'm already here at that point at which people most often make their prophesies, when they're just about to die. I say, you who are putting me to death, that immediately after my death you'll have a much worse penalty, by Zeus, than the one you've imposed me by killing me. For you're achieving this now, thinking that you'll get off from having your life tested, exactly the

d opposite will happen to you, so I claim. There'll be more people who'll examine you – people I've held in check, but you didn't see it. And they'll be harder to deal with, in as much as they're younger, and you'll find them more irritating. If you think that by killing people you'll put a stop to anyone criticizing you because you don't live as you should, you're not thinking clearly. Escape is neither really possible nor admirable; the best and easiest course is not to restrain others, but instead to do what you need to do to be as good as possible. Now that I have made these prophesies to those of you who voted against me, I make my escape.

e But to those who voted for me, I'd enjoy talking about what's just happened while the officers are taking a break and I'm not yet going to the place where I have to go to die. Stay with me during this time. For nothing prevents us from conversing while we can. As my

40a friends, I want to show you the meaning of what's happened to me just now. Judges – for

---

26 A third speech of the sort Socrates now gives was not called for by Athenian legal procedure. If he spoke to the jury at all after the vote to execute him, he must have done so as they were preparing to leave the court.

in calling you judges I'm referring to you as I should[27] – something wonderful has happened to me. In the past, the usual oracular voice of the spiritual thing has always come very quickly and has opposed me on quite trivial matters if I was about to do something that wasn't right. But now, as you can see for yourselves, what might well be thought – and is generally considered to be – the greatest of evils has befallen me. Yet this sign from the god didn't oppose b me when I left home at dawn, nor when I came here to court, nor when I was about to say anything at all in my speech. And yet often at other times when I was talking, it held me back when I was in the middle of what I was saying. But today, concerning this matter, it hasn't opposed me at any point in what I was doing or saying. What, then, do I take to be the explanation? I'll tell you. What's happened to me will probably be something good, and it can't be that we're right in supposing that death's an evil. I've got strong evidence c that this is so. It can't be that I haven't been opposed by my usual sign unless I'm about to have good luck.

Let's also consider that we have good reason to be hopeful that this is a good thing. Death is one of two things. Either it's like nothingness and the dead have no awareness of anything, or it's, as they say, a change and the soul migrates from this place to another place. If it's the absence of sentience and is like sleep, as when someone sleeps and doesn't even d dream, death would be a wonderful gain. For I think that anyone who picked a night in which he slept so soundly that he didn't even dream and put it up against the other days and nights of his life, and after thinking about it, had to say how many days and night were better and more pleasant in his life than this night, why I think that not just a private individual but even the great king[28] would discover that such nights are easily counted com- e pared to the other days and nights. If death's like this, I say it's a gain; for the whole of time seems no more than a single night.

If, on the other hand, death's like taking a journey from here to another place, and what they say is true, that all the dead are there, what greater good could there be than this, judges? For if anyone who arrives in Hades, having escaped those who claim to be judges here, will 41a discover real judges, who are said to sit in judgment there, Minos and Rhadamanthus, and Aeacus and Triptolemus, and the other demigods who lived just lives, would the journey be a bad one? Or, in addition, how much would any of you give to be with Orpheus and Musaeus and Hesiod and Homer? I'd want to die many times if this is true! It would be wonderful for me personally to spend time there, since I could fall in with Palamedes and b Ajax, the son of Telemon, and any of the other ancients who died on account of an unjust verdict, as I compare my suffering with theirs – I think it wouldn't be unpleasant – and what's the greatest part of all, to spend my time testing and examining those who are there, just as I do those who live here, to see if any of them is wise and to see if any thinks he's wise when he's not. How much would one pay, members of the jury, to examine the leader of the great army at Troy,[29] or Odysseus, or Sisyphus, or countless other people one could mention, c men and women? Wouldn't it be unimaginable happiness to converse and associate with,

---

27 Prior to this point in any of Socrates' speeches, he addressed his jurors only as "men," or "Athenians," reserving their formal title (*dikastai*, which we have translated as "judges") only for the subgroup of the jurors to whom he now speaks – those, that is, whom he thinks actually performed their duty as judges in the correct manner.

28 This is a common way of referring to the King of Persia.

29 Socrates is referring to Agamemnon, the legendary King of Mycenae and leader of the Greek force that attacked Troy.

and examine those who are there? Surely those who are there don't kill people for that! For in addition to being happier than those who live here, those who are there are now death-less for eternity, if indeed what they say is true.

And so, members of the jury, you should be optimistic about death and think about this
41d one truth, that no harm comes to a good man in life or in death, and his problems are not neglected by the gods. And what's happened to me now hasn't come about by chance, but it's clear to me that dying now and escaping these problems is better for me. This is why my sign hasn't turned me away from anything, and I'm not at all angry with those who con-
e demned me or with my accusers. Yet, it wasn't with that in mind that they were condemning and accusing me, but instead they thought they'd injure me. They deserve to be blamed for that. At any rate, I do ask this of them. When my sons come of age, "punish" them, men, by disturbing them with the same things by which I disturbed you, if they seem to you to care about money or anything more than virtue. And if they think they've amounted to anything when they haven't, reproach them as I've reproached you because they don't care about what they should and because they think they've amounted to something when they're
42a worthless. If you'd do this, I myself and my sons will have been treated justly by you. But now the time has come to leave, me to die and you to live on; which of us is going to the better fate is unclear to anyone except the god.

10

Crito

Plato's *Crito* is set in the Athenian jail, as Socrates awaits the end of the Delian festival (during which Athens would carry out no executions). Crito wishes to bribe the guard and spirit Socrates away to Thessaly, thus sparing his friend's life. Socrates insists that they should not take action until they have deliberated about the issues involved. In the deliberations that ensue, Socrates offers several reasons why he is convinced that escaping from prison would be wrong and unjust.

    This dialogue addresses one of the most fundamental questions of political philosophy: To what extent is the authority of the state over its citizens morally legitimate? Socrates and Crito are convinced that Socrates has been unjustly condemned to death. Socrates and his friend have no quarrel with the legal system by which this outcome was reached – their dispute is with the judgments of those jurors who made the decision. If the law is followed but the outcome is incorrect, is it acceptable for a private citizen to disobey?

SOCRATES: Why have you come at this hour, Crito? Isn't it still early?   43a
CRITO: Of course it is.
SOCRATES: Just what time is it?
CRITO: Right before dawn.
SOCRATES: I'm surprised that the prison guard was willing to answer your knock.
CRITO: Oh, he's well acquainted with me by now, Socrates, since I come here so often and
    I've taken good care of him.
SOCRATES: Have you come just now or did you come earlier?
CRITO: A bit earlier.
SOCRATES: Then why didn't you wake me immediately instead of sitting quietly beside me? b

It appears that Crito and Socrates came from the same deme, or precinct, in Athens. Unlike Socrates, however, Crito seems to have been a wealthy man. He was one of the four who guaranteed the fine of 30 minas that Socrates offered as his counterpenalty at his trial (see *Apology* 38b). Whether or not Crito urged Socrates to escape from prison or whether Socrates responded with the arguments Plato attributes to him, we cannot say. Xenophon, however, does confirm in his *Apology* (23) that some of Socrates' companions urged him to escape before he could be executed.

CRITO: By the god, Socrates, I didn't want to. I wish I weren't so upset and unable to sleep. And I was amazed just now when I saw how peacefully you were sleeping. So I didn't disturb you on purpose so that you'd go on sleeping as peacefully as possible. Before now I've often thought you had a happy character throughout your whole life; but now, in this present disaster, I think so more than ever, since you are handling it easily and calmly.

SOCRATES: Well, Crito, it would be inappropriate for me at my age[1] to be worried if I have to die soon.

43c CRITO: Others who are your age have been caught up in similar calamities, but their age doesn't free them at all from being worried about the problems they face.

SOCRATES: That's true. But why have you come so early?

CRITO: I've got bad news, Socrates – not for you, so it would seem – but bad and depressing news for me and all your companions . . . and hardest of all, I think, for me to bear.

d SOCRATES: What is it? Has the boat arrived from Delos? For when it arrives, I have to die.[2]

CRITO: It hasn't yet arrived, but I have to think it'll arrive today, from what those who've come from Sounion[3] say, which is where they left it. And it's clear from what they've said that it'll be here today. And then, Socrates, on the next day your life must end.

SOCRATES: Well, Crito, may it turn out for the best. If that's what the gods want, so be it. And yet I don't think it'll come today.

44a CRITO: What makes you think it won't?

SOCRATES: I'll tell you. I gather I'm supposed to die the day after the boat arrives.

CRITO: Well, that's what the authorities say, at any rate.

SOCRATES: Well then, I don't think that it'll come today but tomorrow. I think this because of a dream I had a little earlier in the night.[4] You probably didn't disturb me at a crucial time.

CRITO: And what was the dream?

SOCRATES: I dreamed that a beautiful and graceful woman, wearing a white cloak, came toward
b me and called to me, saying: "Socrates, on the third day you will come to fertile Phthia."[5]

CRITO: What a mysterious dream, Socrates!

SOCRATES: On the contrary; I think it's clear, Crito.

CRITO: Too much so, it seems. Yet, Socrates, you incredible man, even so, be persuaded by me and be saved. Since it's not just one disaster for me if you die, but apart from having been robbed of a companion such as I'll never find again, I'll appear to most people, who
c don't know you and me well, not to care – since I could've saved you had I been willing to part with the money. And indeed what could be more disgraceful than a reputation for

---

1 In the *Apology* (17d) Socrates indicates that he is seventy years old. See also *Crito* 52e.

2 Delos is a small island in the Aegean. Every year a ship was sent on a voyage to the island to commemorate the return of Theseus to Athens. During the time that the ship was en route, no executions could take place in Athens. Thus, in effect, Socrates was given a month's reprieve. According to Plato, he used this time to converse with his companions (see *Phaedo* 59d ff.)

3 Ships coming back to Athens from the island of Delos would have to sail by Sounion, on the tip of the peninsula of land leading back toward Athens.

4 It is likely that Plato intends the reader to take this remark seriously, for in the *Apology* (33c–d) Socrates indicates that he thinks dreams can indeed be a way in which divinities communicate with human beings.

5 Phthia is the home of the great warrior Achilles, the central figure in Homer's *Iliad*. Many readers of Plato's time would have instantly recognized the allusion and would have seen that Socrates is suggesting that death will be a kind of homecoming for his soul and, hence, not something to be feared. Socrates also compares himself to Achilles in the *Apology* (28c–d).

thinking that money is more important than friends? Most people won't be persuaded that you yourself didn't want to leave when we encouraged you to do it.

SOCRATES: But what do we care about what most people think, Crito? The most sensible people – the ones we ought to hold in higher regard – will think the matter's been handled just as it should've been.

CRITO: But surely you see, Socrates, that it's necessary to care about what most people think. d The circumstances we're in now make it clear that most people are able to do not just the smallest evils but virtually the greatest if someone's been slandered when they're around.

SOCRATES: I only wish, Crito, that most people were capable of the greatest evils so that they'd be capable of the greatest goods. That would be fine. But as things are, they're able to do neither. For they're not able to make anyone wise or ignorant, but they do whatever strikes them.

CRITO: I grant that. But, Socrates, tell me this. Surely your concern about me and your other e companions isn't that if you leave this place, the blackmailers[6] will cause trouble for us for having sneaked you out of here, and we would then be forced to forfeit either all our property or quite a bit of money, or suffer something else in addition to these things? If you're afraid of something like this, don't give it a thought. We're doing the right thing 45a to run this risk in rescuing you and, if need be, to run an even greater one. So be persuaded by me and do nothing else.

SOCRATES: But I *am* concerned about these things, Crito, and about many others too.

CRITO: Don't worry about these things now – what people want to be paid to save you and get you out of here doesn't amount to much money. Anyway, don't you see how cheap these blackmailers are and that one wouldn't need much money for them? My money is enough, I think, and what's mine is yours. Furthermore, if, in your concern for me, you b think I shouldn't spend my own money, these foreigners here are ready to spend theirs. One of them – Simmias, the Theban[7] – has brought enough money for this very thing. He's prepared, as is Cebes and a great many others, as well. So, as I say, don't back away from saving yourself out of fear of these things.

Nor should what you said in court bother you, namely, that you couldn't go into exile because you wouldn't know what to do with yourself.[8] People will welcome you in many c of the places you may go. If you wish to go to Thessaly,[9] I have friends there and they'll provide for your safety and do many things for you so that none of the Thessalians will bother you.

Moreover, Socrates, it doesn't seem right to me to undertake what you're doing – betraying yourself when it's possible to save yourself – and you're speeding up for yourself what

6 The Greek word which we are here translating as "blackmailers" is *sukophantoi*, from which we get the English word "sycophant." The Athenian legal system did not allow for public prosecutors. Instead, prosecutions for crimes were left to private individuals to pursue. Some individuals, however, made it their business to find out about allegations of crimes and, then, threatened the alleged perpetrators with prosecution unless they were paid a fee. Hence, the *sucophantoi* were blackmailers.

7 Simmias and Cebes, referred to in the next line, were young men from Thebes, both devoted companions of Socrates. Plato chooses them to be Socrates' principal interlocutors in the *Phaedo*, the dialogue set in prison on the last day of Socrates' life and in which Plato discusses various arguments about the immortality of the soul.

8 Crito is referring to Socrates' refusal to suggest exile as a counterpenalty the jury could impose on him. See *Apology* 37c–d.

9 Thessaly was a large remote region north of Athens.

45d your enemies would be hurrying to do and what they've done their best to expedite in their desire to destroy you. In addition to these things, it seems to me that you're betraying your sons, whom you'll have left behind and abandoned, when it's possible for you to raise and educate them, and as far as you're concerned, they'll have to take whatever happens to them. And what'll happen to them, it seems likely, are the very sorts of things that usually happen to orphans. Either you shouldn't have children or you should share in their lives by nurturing and educating completely. You seem to me to be choosing the laziest way out. One should choose what a good and courageous man would choose, especially one who spends his whole life talking about caring for virtue. I'm ashamed for you

e and for us, your companions, that this whole matter involving you will seem to have been conducted with a certain lack of courage on our part – how the case was brought to court, when it was possible for it not to be; how the case itself was conducted; and last of all, there's this: As if we're making a joke of the matter, the opportunity appears to have escaped

46a us through some fault and cowardice on our part – we, who didn't save you, and you, who didn't save yourself – when it was entirely possible to have done so if we'd been of any use at all. See to it then, Socrates, that this doesn't end badly and disgracefully for you and for us. So consider – or actually the time is past for considering but we need to have already settled on – a single plan. All these things need to have been done this very night; but if we're still waiting around, it'll be completely impossible. So by all means, Socrates, be persuaded by me and don't do anything else.

b SOCRATES: My friend, Crito, your concern will be worth a great deal if it is on the right side of this issue. But if not, the greater it is, the more difficult it makes things. So we need to consider whether we must do this or not. Because I'm not just now but in fact I've always been the sort of person who's persuaded by nothing but the reason that appears to me to be best when I've considered it. I can't now, when I'm in my present circumstance, set aside reasons I was giving earlier. If they seem to me to be virtually the same, I'll respect

c and honor the ones I did before. Unless we can come up with something better in the present circumstance than these, rest assured that I won't give in to you. Nor should the majority of people have any greater power to scare us in this present circumstance, like we were children by sending us to prison and death and confiscating our money.

What, then, is the most reasonable way to take up the matter? We could first take up

d the argument you were giving about opinions. Were we right or not each time we said that one ought to pay attention to the opinions of some but not of others? Or were we right before I was obliged to die, but now it's become clear after all that it was all done merely for the sake of argument and was really just for play and fooling around? I'm eager to investigate it together with you, Crito, to see if the reasoning seems different in any way to me since I'm in this circumstance or does it seem to be the same? Should we let it go or be persuaded by it?

I think that people who always think they have something to say, maintain, as I was

e saying just now, that, among the opinions people hold, one ought to think highly of some and not others. By the gods, Crito, doesn't this seem to you to be right? For you, in all

47a probability, are *not* about to die tomorrow, and my present misfortune shouldn't skew *your* judgment. Consider then: Doesn't it seem to you to be correct that one shouldn't respect all the opinions people have but some and not others, nor the opinions of all people, but some and not others? What do you say? Is this right or not?

CRITO: It's right.

SOCRATES: Then should we respect the good ones but not the bad ones?

CRITO: Yes.

SOCRATES: Aren't the good ones are the opinions of the wise, and the bad ones the opinions of the foolish?

CRITO: Of course.

SOCRATES: Come, then. What did we used to say about these things? Does the trained athlete and one who's involved in such things pay attention to the praise and censure and b opinion of everyone or of that one only who happens to be a doctor or a trainer?

CRITO: Of the one only.

SOCRATES: Therefore, we should fear the censure and welcome the praise of that one – but not the censure and praise of the many?

CRITO: That's quite clear.

SOCRATES: So one should act and exercise and eat and drink in the way that would seem best to him – to the one person, the one who has knowledge and expertise – rather than in the way that seems best to all the others?

CRITO: That's right.

SOCRATES: Well then. If one disobeyed the one and disdained his opinion and what he encour- c ages, but respected those of the many, who understand nothing, won't he suffer some evil?

CRITO: Of course.

SOCRATES: What is this evil? Where does it achieve its effects and what part of the one who disobeys does it affect?

CRITO: Clearly, it's the body. It destroys it.

SOCRATES: You're right. Then in other areas too, Crito, isn't it this way as well? So that we don't have to run through them all, isn't it especially true that in what pertains to the just and unjust and the noble and good and evil – what we're now deliberating about – we should follow the opinion of most people and fear it, or that of the one, if there is any- d one who understands, whom one ought to respect and fear rather than all of the others? If we don't follow this one individual, won't we corrupt and destroy what becomes better through justice but is destroyed by injustice? Isn't this so?

CRITO: I think so, Socrates.

SOCRATES: Come then. If we ruin what becomes better by health but is destroyed by disease when we're persuaded by the opinion of those who lack expertise, is our life worth living when this has been corrupted? This is, surely, the body, isn't it? e

CRITO: Yes.

SOCRATES: Therefore, is our life worth living with a body in bad condition and corrupted?

CRITO: Certainly not.

SOCRATES: But is our life worth living with this thing being corrupted which injustice mutilates and justice improves? Or, do we believe that what justice and injustice concern – whatever it is of the things that makes us up – is inferior to the body? 48a

CRITO: Certainly not.

SOCRATES: It is, rather, to be respected more?

CRITO: Much more.

SOCRATES: Well then, my good friend, we mustn't take very seriously what most people will say to us but rather what the one who understands justice and injustice will say – the one person, and truth itself. The upshot is that you didn't introduce the issue correctly when you started off by saying that one should consider most people's opinion about just, noble, and good things and their opposites. "But then surely," someone might say, "these 'most people' can kill us."

48b CRITO: Clearly, someone might say that, Socrates.

SOCRATES: You're right. But, my incredible friend, the argument we've gone through seems to me to be the same as before. Consider once more if we're still standing by it or not, namely, that one mustn't be much concerned with living, but with living well?

CRITO: We stand by it.

SOCRATES: And that living well and nobly and justly are the same – do we stand by it or not?

CRITO: We stand by it.

SOCRATES: Then from these agreements we must consider this: whether it's just or not for

c me to try to escape from here when the Athenians haven't released me. And if it seems just, we should attempt it; but if not, we should let the matter go. The considerations you mention – about the confiscation of money, reputation, and the raising of children – these, I'm afraid, are really the considerations of most people, who readily kill people and would bring them back to life if they could and would do so without even thinking about it. But since our reasoning requires this, we must consider only what we were saying just now: Would we, the ones who are escaping and the ones who are helping out, be doing what's

d just in paying our money and thanking those who'll get me out of here? Or would we really be acting unjustly by doing all of these things? If we'd clearly be bringing about an injustice, we shouldn't give any consideration to whether we need to remain behind to be killed and keep quiet about it or suffer anything at all rather than the injustice we'd be doing.

CRITO: I think what you said is right, Socrates, but think about what we should do.

SOCRATES: Let's consider it together, my good man, and if you can somehow refute what

e I'm saying, refute it, and I'll try to do the same for you. But if not, stop giving me the same old speech – that I ought to go away from here against the will of the Athenians. For I think it's important to persuade you to do this and not act against your wishes. Think about whether what we said at the beginning of our investigation satisfies you, and try

49a to answer what's put to you as you think best.

CRITO: I'll try.

SOCRATES: Do we say that we should by no means willingly do what's unjust, or do we say that we should act unjustly in some cases but not in others? Isn't injustice never good or noble, as we've often agreed before? Or, have all of our previous agreements been given up in these last few days, and have we, men at this age who have seriously discussed these

b matters with each other, failed to see long ago that we are no better than children? Or is it absolutely what we said it was then? Whether most people agree with us or not, and whether we have to suffer harsher or more lenient things than what's going on now, injustice is still evil and disgraceful in every way for the one who's unjust? Do we say this or not?

CRITO: We do.

SOCRATES: One should never do what's unjust.

CRITO: Clearly not.

SOCRATES: Nor retaliate when one's been treated unjustly, as most people say, since one should never do injustice?

c CRITO: It seems not.

SOCRATES: What follows then? Should we do evil, Crito, or not?

CRITO: Surely, we shouldn't, Socrates.

SOCRATES: What then? Is it just or not to do evil in return when one has suffered an evil, as most people say?

CRITO: Never.

SOCRATES: Treating men evilly does not differ from treating them unjustly.

CRITO: That's true.

SOCRATES: Therefore, we should neither retaliate nor treat anyone evilly, no matter what we have suffered from them. In agreeing to these things, Crito, make sure that you don't speak d contrary to what you think. For I know that these things seem and will seem true only to a few people. But to those to whom it has seemed right and to those to whom it hasn't, there is no common ground, but they can't avoid having disdain for each other when they see each other's conclusions. Consider very carefully then whether you agree and share the same opinion with me and let's begin by deliberating from that point, namely that it's never right to do what's unjust or to retaliate or for one who has suffered an evil to avenge it by retaliating wrongly, or do you reject this and not share my opinion about where to start? For it seems to be now the same as before, but if it has appeared to you to be otherwise, speak up and instruct me. But if you stand by what was said earlier, e listen to what follows.

CRITO: I do stand by it and it seems to me the same as before. Go on, then.

SOCRATES: I'll tell you what comes next, or rather, I'll ask: Should one do what one agrees to do for someone when it is just, or should one renege?

CRITO: One should do what one has agreed to.

SOCRATES: Now observe what follows. If we go away from here without having persuaded the city, would we be doing anything wrong to anyone, and what's more, would we be 50a doing it to those whom we ought least of all be doing it, or not? Do we stand by what we agreed is right, or not?

CRITO: I can't answer what you're asking, Socrates, because I don't understand.

SOCRATES: Well, think about it this way: Suppose the laws and the state, or however it should be called, came and confronting us as we were about to run away from here were to say: "Tell me, Socrates, what are you thinking about doing? Are you contemplating by this act that you're attempting anything other than the destruction of us, the laws, and the whole b city insofar as you can? Or, do you think that the city can still exist and not be destroyed when the decisions handed down in the courts have no force but are left without authority by private citizens and are destroyed?" What shall we say, Crito, to this and other things of the same sort? For someone, especially an orator, could say a lot on behalf of the law that has been destroyed which decrees that the decisions of the courts be authoritative. Or shall we say to them, "The city was unjust to us and did not judge my case correctly." c Shall we say this or what?

CRITO: That's what we'll say, by god, Socrates.

SOCRATES: Then what if the Laws should say: "Socrates, is this the agreement between us and you, or was it to stand by the judgments that the city hands down?" If at that point we'd be surprised when they said this, perhaps they'd say, "Socrates, don't be surprised at what we're saying, but answer, since you're accustomed to using question and answer. Come, then. What's the charge against us and the city that leads you to try to destroy us? d First, didn't we produce you, and through us didn't your father take your mother in marriage and give birth to you? And tell us, what complaint do you have against those of our laws that govern marriage?" "I have no complaint," I'd say. "And what about those laws concerning the raising of offspring and the education which you received? Or did our established laws for this not command the right thing in ordering your father to educate you in music and physical training?"[10] "It was well done," I'd say. "Well then, since you were e

10 Music and physical training were standard forms of education expected of all free male children in Athens.

born and raised and educated by us, could you say in the first place that you're not our offspring and slave, you and your ancestors? And if this is so, do you think that what's just for us and you is based on equality? And whatever we try to do to you, do you think it's right for you also to do in return? What's just for you in relation to your father, or to your master, if you happened to have one, wasn't based on equality so that you could do

51a in return the very thing you suffered, whether to talk back when criticized or to strike back when struck, and many other such things? Yet, on the other hand, you are empowered to do such things against your fatherland and the laws, so that if we try to destroy you in the belief that it's right, you'll try to destroy us, the laws, and the country in return in so far as you're able. And do you, who really cares about virtue, maintain that in doing this you're doing what's just? Or, are you so wise that it's escaped you that, compared to your father and mother and all of your ancestors, your country is more honorable, more

b revered, more sacred, and to be held in higher esteem by the gods and by people with sense, and that you should revere your country and yield to it and cajole it when it's angry more than your father, and either persuade or to do what it orders and you should suffer in silence if it orders you to suffer something, whether it's to be beaten or to be imprisoned, and whether it leads you into war to be wounded or killed, you must do this, and it's just that you do so, and you shouldn't yield, or retreat, and abandon your post, but in war and in court and everywhere, you must do what your city and country orders,

c or persuade it as to the nature of what's just. But it's impious to use force on your mother and father; it's much more impious still to use it on your country." What shall we say to this, Crito? Are the laws telling the truth or not?

CRITO: It seems to me they are.

SOCRATES: "Consider, then, Socrates," perhaps the laws would say, "if we're right, then what you're now trying to do isn't right. Although we produced you, and raised you, and edu-

d cated you, and gave all the other citizens and you, too, a share of all the good things we could, nonetheless we publically grant the power to an Athenian who wishes, as soon as he has been entered into citizenship[11] and sees the ways of the city and us the laws and who's not pleased with us, to pack up his belongings and go wherever he wants. Whether someone wishes to emigrate to a colony or to go somewhere else and live as an alien if we and the city should fail to please him, no law stands in his way or forbids him to go

e where he desires and keep his things. But he among you who stays, seeing the manner in which we dispense justice and conduct the affairs of the city in other ways, we say that this person has already agreed with us by his actions that he'll do what we command, and we say that the one who does not persuade us acts unjustly in three ways: because he doesn't obey us who produced him; because he doesn't obey those who raised him; and because, having agreed to obey us, he neither obeys nor persuades us if we're doing some-

52a thing that's not right, even though we offer him this alternative and don't order him about roughly to do what we command him to do. Although we permit him two options – either persuade us or do what we command – he does neither of these. We say that you, Socrates, will be ensnared by these charges if you do what you're thinking about, and of the Athenians

---

11 At age eighteen, Athenian males who wished to become citizens actually went through a formal procedure in which they had to prove their eligibility and to declare formally that they wished to become citizens.

you'll not be the least culpable, but among the most." If I were to say, "Why's that?" perhaps they would be right to attack me and say that I, more than any other Athenian, happened to have made this agreement with them. For they'd say, "Socrates, we have b strong evidence that we and the city were pleasing to you. For you wouldn't have stayed here more than all the other Athenians unless the city had been more pleasing to you. You never left the city to go to a festival, except once to go to the Isthmus,[12] nor to go to any other place except when you were serving in the army somewhere, nor did you ever make a trip abroad, as other people do, nor were you seized by a desire to know another city or other laws, but we and our city were enough for you. You emphatically c chose us and you agreed to be governed by us, and, in particular, you had children in it, because you were satisfied with the city. Besides, at the trial it was possible for you to have proposed exile as your counterpenalty if you wanted, and the very thing you're now attempting when the city is unwilling, it was possible for you to do then when the city was willing. You were trying to make yourself look good then by not being worried if you had to die, but you chose, as you were saying, death over exile. Now you aren't ashamed at those words. You don't even respect us, the laws, since in trying to destroy them you're doing just what the lowest slave would do, trying to run away in violation of the com- d pacts and agreements, according to which you agreed to be governed by us. First, answer this: Are we telling the truth or not when we say that you agreed – through your actions, not in words – to be governed by us, or aren't we telling the truth? What would we say to this, Crito? Do we agree or not?

CRITO: We have to agree, Socrates.

SOCRATES: "Isn't it also true," they'd say, "that you're breaking these compacts and agree-ments with us, though you weren't compelled to agree, and neither were you deceived e nor were you given only a short time to deliberate about it, but you had seventy years, in which it was possible for you to leave if you weren't satisfied with us or if the agree-ments didn't seem right to you? You preferred neither Sparta nor Crete, which you're always saying are well governed, nor any other Greek or foreign city, but you left the city less 53a than the lame, the blind, and other disabled people. So it's clear that the city and us, the Laws, pleased you more than other Athenians. Could anyone be satisfied with a city without being satisfied with its laws? Well do you not now stand by the agreements? You will if you're persuaded by us, Socrates; and you won't make yourself a laughingstock by leaving the city.

For consider: If you violate your agreements and commit any of these wrongs, what good will you be doing for yourself or for your companions? It's pretty clear that your b companions are likely to be prosecuted themselves and be deprived of the city or lose their property. But first, you yourself, if you go to any of the nearest cities, Thebes or Megara – for both are well governed – you'll arrive as an enemy, Socrates, to their state. Those who care about their cities will suspect you, thinking that you're someone who destroys laws. Further, you'll confirm for the members of the jury their opinion, so they'll c

---

12 Isthmus (near Corinth, west of Athens, in the small land connection – severed in modern times by a canal – between the Peloponnesus and the northern part of Greece) was the site of the Isthmian Games, a panhellenic athletic festival (similar to the now more famous Olympic Games) held every two years in April or May.

think they decided the case correctly. For whoever destroys the laws would probably seem to be someone who corrupts the young and who corrupts people who don't know any better. So, will you avoid well-governed cities and people who lead the most orderly lives? And in doing this will your life be worth living? Or will you approach these people and be so shameless as to discuss – what arguments, Socrates? Will you discuss the very ones

d you discuss here, that virtue and justice, and laws and customs are the most valuable things for people? Don't you think the 'Socrates affair' will appear unseemly? Surely you must think so. Or will you leave these places and go instead to Thessaly to be with Crito's friends? Now that place is filled with disorder and self-indulgence, and they might well enjoy hearing about you running comically from the prison, having put on a disguise and changing your appearance by wearing a leather hide or the other sorts of things that runaways use

e to disguise themselves. Is there no one who will say that you – an old man, who likely had only a short time left to live – dared to have such a greedy desire to live on in this way by breaking the greatest laws? Perhaps, if you don't disturb anyone. But if that's not the case, you'll hear many terrible things about yourself. You'll live a life of fawning and

54a serving all people – what will you do in Thessaly other than feasting? – as if you had traveled to Thessaly for dinner! And what'll happen to our arguments about justice and the other virtues? Or is it that you want to live for the sake of your children, to raise them and to educate them? But why? By leading them off to Thessaly, you'll raise and educate them after you have made them exiles, and that is supposed to benefit them too? But if instead of that, they're raised while you're alive, will they be better brought up and educated than if you're not with them? For your companions will take care of them. Or is it that if you go away to Thessaly they'll care for them, but if you go away to Hades they won't? One has to think so if indeed those who say they're your friends are to benefit

b them at all.

"So, Socrates, be persuaded by us who raised you, and don't put your concern for your children or your life or anything else before justice, so that when you go to Hades you can use all of these things in your defense before those who rule there. For neither will it appear that it was better or more just or more pious for you or for any of your companions here that you did this, nor will it be better for you in Hades when you arrive there. But instead, now you'll leave – if you do leave – having been unjustly

c treated not by us, the laws but by men. If you escape after so disgracefully retaliating and returning wrong for wrong, and having broken the agreements and compacts with us, and having mistreated those whom you ought least of all to harm – yourself, your friends, your country, and us – we'll deal harshly with you while you're alive, and our brothers, the laws of Hades, won't receive you kindly there, knowing that, for your part, you tried

d to destroy us. So then, don't let Crito persuade you to do what he says instead of what we say."

Rest assured, dear friend Crito, that I think I hear this, just like the Corybantic revelers[13] think they hear flutes, and the same sound of these arguments buzzes in me and keeps me from hearing anything else. Know that if you say anything contrary to what

---

13 Corybantic revelers participated through frenzied dancing in rites celebrating the goddess Cybele. Socrates is here comparing the force of the argument the "Laws" have presented to the drums the revelers listened to while dancing.

seems now to be true, you'll be speaking in vain. Nonetheless, if you think it'll do you some good, say it.

CRITO: I have nothing to say, Socrates.

SOCRATES: Let it be so then, Crito, and let's act in this way, since this is the way the god[14] is e leading.

---

14 Socrates' reference to the god in the singular is controversial. (For contrast, see the reference to what the [plural] gods want, at *Crito* 43d). It is unlikely that he is referring to the divinity who communicates with him through the "voice" he hears, for, as he tells us in the *Apology* (31d), the voice always turns him away from what he is about to do. It does not lead him. Zeus is the divine protector of sworn oaths (which would be sworn in his name), and since Socrates' argument refers to the fact that he has sworn oaths of allegiance to the laws of Athens, and since Zeus' will might well be thought to represent the will of all the gods (assuming that they all agree) on matters of justice (see *Euthyphro* 6a–8e), Socrates' reference to "the god" may simply refer to Zeus as representative of the generic divine will. It is also clear that Socrates' discussion with Crito (unlike so many other discussions in which we find Socrates, in Plato's dialogues), is a discussion between good friends – and this, too, is a significant feature of the premises on which they rely in the argument (see *Crito* 49d). If Socrates is referring to the god of friendship as the guide of this friendly conversation, his reference would again be to Zeus, the god of friendship (see *Euthyphro* 6b). In any case, it seems reasonable to suppose that Socrates' reference is to whichever god might be supposed to have led their argument.

11

Meno

At the beginning of the *Meno*, Socrates is asked: Can virtue can be taught, or is it the result of practice or perhaps inborn? Socrates defers this question to consider a prior one: What is virtue? In the first selection, Socrates defeats one of Meno's proposed definitions of virtue, arguing that no one actually wants what is bad; so whenever anyone pursues something bad, it must be that the person mistakenly takes the bad thing to be good. In the second passage, Meno challenges Socrates: If one doesn't know what something is (in this case virtue), how will one find out, and how would one even know when presented with the correct definition? Socrates questions a slave-boy to demonstrate his reply – all knowledge is innate, and when we "discover" something, we are merely recollecting knowledge we had in a prior life. Scholars count the *Meno* as "transitional," by which they mean that some of its features are Socratic, and some belong more to Plato than to Socrates. In the case of the two arguments we include herein, the first is regarded as Socratic; the second is regarded as Platonic.

77b MENO: Well, I think, Socrates, that as the poet says, virtue is "to rejoice in things beautiful and be capable of them."[1] And that, I claim, is virtue: desire for beautiful things and ability to attain them.

SOCRATES: Do you say that to desire beautiful things is to desire good things?

MENO: Yes, of course.

SOCRATES: Then do some men desire evils, and others goods? Does it not seem to you, my
c   friend, that *all* men desire goods?

MENO: No, it doesn't.

SOCRATES: Some desire evils?

MENO: Yes.

SOCRATES: Supposing the evils to be goods, you mean, or recognizing that they are evils and still desiring them?

MENO: Both, I think.

SOCRATES: You think, Meno, that anyone recognizes evils to be evils and still desires them?

---

1 Perhaps Simonides.

MENO: Certainly.

SOCRATES: What do you mean by "desire"? Desire to possess?

MENO: Why yes, of course.

SOCRATES: Believing that evils benefit, or recognizing that evils harm, those who possess them? d

MENO: Some believe evils benefit, others recognize that they harm.

SOCRATES: Does it seem to you that those who believe that evils benefit recognize evils to be evils?

MENO: No, I certainly don't think that.

SOCRATES: Then it is clear that these people, who do not recognize evils for what they are, do not desire evils; rather, they desire things they suppose to be good, though in fact those e things are evil. Hence, these people, not recognizing evils to be evils, and supposing them to be goods, really desire goods. Not so?

MENO: Yes, very likely it is.

SOCRATES: Now what about those who, as you claim, desire evils believing that evils harm their possessor. Surely they recognize they will be harmed by them?

MENO: They must.

SOCRATES: Don't they suppose that people who are harmed are made wretched to the degree 78a they are harmed?

MENO: Again, they must.

SOCRATES: And aren't the wretched unhappy?

MENO: I should think so.

SOCRATES: Now, does anyone wish to be wretched and unhappy?

MENO: I think not, Socrates.

SOCRATES: Then nobody wishes for evils, Meno, unless he wishes to be in that condition. For what else is it to be wretched, than to desire evils and get them?

MENO: You are very likely right, Socrates; nobody wishes for evils.   b

[. . .]

SOCRATES: For I don't cause perplexity in others while free of perplexities myself; the truth is rather that I cause perplexity in others because I am myself perplexed. And so it is now 80d with virtue. I don't know what it is, while you, who may have known before I touched you, are now in like way ignorant. Nevertheless, I wish to join with you in inquiring what it is.

MENO: And how will you inquire into a thing, Socrates, when you are wholly ignorant of what it is? What sort of thing among those you don't know will you set up as the object of your inquiry? Even if you happen to bump right into it, how will you know that it is the thing you didn't know?

SOCRATES: I understand what you want to say, Meno. Do you see what an eristical argument e you're spinning? It is thus impossible for a man to inquire either into what he knows, or into what he does not know. He cannot inquire into what he knows; for he knows it, and there is no need for inquiry into a thing like that. Nor would he inquire into what he does not know; for he does not know what it is he is to inquire into.

MENO: Well, don't you think that's a good argument, Socrates?   81a

SOCRATES: I do not.

MENO: Can you say why?

SOCRATES: Yes. For I have heard from men and women who are wise in things divine –

MENO: What was it they told?

SOCRATES: A noble truth, I think.

MENO: What was it? And who were they who told it?

SOCRATES: Some were priests and priestesses who wanted to explain their observances. But
81b   Pindar and as many other poets who are inspired have told it too. Here is their tale. See
if you think it true. They say that the soul of man is immortal, sometimes reaching an
end which men call dying, sometimes born again, but never perishing. Because this is so,
one must live his whole life in utmost holiness; for from whomsoever

> Persephone shall accept requital for her ancient grief,
> Returning their souls in the ninth year to the upper light,
> Their term of banishment to darkness done:
c > From them illustrious kings shall spring,
> Lords of rushing wisdom, and strength unsurpassed.
> In all remaining time they shall be known
> As heroes, and be sanctified by men.[2]

Seeing then that the soul is immortal, and has been born many times, and has beheld all
things in this world and the world beyond, there is nothing it has not learnt: so it is not
surprising that it can be reminded of virtue and other things which it knew before. For
d since the whole of nature is akin, and the soul has learned all things, there is nothing to
prevent someone, upon being reminded of one single thing – which men call learning –
from rediscovering all the rest, if he is courageous and faints not in the search. For learning and inquiry are then wholly recollection. Therefore we need not be persuaded by
the eristical argument, which would cause us to be idle; it is sweet only to the ear of the
e soft and weak, whereas this account induces industry and inquiry. I put my trust in its
truth, and ask you to join me in inquiring what virtue is.

MENO: Yes, Socrates, but what do you mean by saying that we do not learn, that what we
call learning is recollection? Can you teach me that this is so?

SOCRATES: Why Meno, I just said you were unscrupulous, and now you are asking me to
82a   teach you, when I claim there is no teaching but recollection, just so I can straightway
prove myself inconsistent.

MENO: No, no, Socrates, that was surely not my aim. I just spoke from habit. If you can
somehow prove it is as you say, please do so.

SOCRATES: Well, it is not easy, but still, for you I will make the effort. You have many of
b your attendants here. Summon for me whichever one you please for the demonstration.

MENO: Certainly. (*Beckoning to a slave boy.*) You there, come here.

SOCRATES: He's a Greek, I assume, and speaks Greek?

MENO: Oh yes, he was born and raised in our house.

SOCRATES: Then pay close attention. See whether it appears to you that he recollects, or learns
from me.

MENO: I certainly shall.

SOCRATES: (*Turning to the boy.*) Tell me, my boy. Do you recognize that this sort of figure is
a square? (*Socrates traces square ABCD in the sand at his feet.*)

---

2 The poet cited by Meno is Pindar.

BOY: I do.

SOCRATES: Now, a square figure is one having all four of these sides equal? (*Indicating the* c *sides.*)

BOY: Of course.

SOCRATES: And so is one having these lines drawn through the middle equal too? (*Socrates draws in transversals bisecting each side.*)

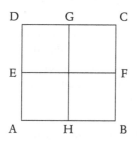

BOY: Yes.

SOCRATES: Now, a figure of this sort could be larger or smaller?

BOY: Of course.

SOCRATES: Now suppose that this side (AB) were two feet, and this one (AD) two feet. How many feet[3] would the whole be? Look at it this way: if it were two feet this way (AB) and only one foot that way (AE), wouldn't the figure be two feet taken once?

BOY: (*Inspecting ABFE*) Yes.

SOCRATES: But since it is also two feet that way (AD), doesn't it become twice two?   d

BOY: It does.

SOCRATES: Therefore it becomes twice two feet?

BOY: Yes.

SOCRATES: Now, how many is twice two feet? Count and tell me. (*The boy looks at ABCD and counts the squares it contains.*)

BOY: Four, Socrates.

SOCRATES: Now could there be another figure twice the size of this one, but similar to it – that is, having four sides equal to each other?

BOY: Yes.

SOCRATES: How many feet will it be?

BOY: Eight.

SOCRATES: Come then. Try and tell me how long each side of it will be. Each side of this one (ABCD) is two feet. What about the side of a figure double this?   e

BOY: Clearly it will be double, Socrates.

---

3 It is customary here and in what follows to translate "feet" in appropriate contexts as "square feet," a concept for which Greek mathematics had no special term. This lack, however, is no accident, for the Greek mathematicians used geometry to perform both arithmetical and algebraic operations. Thus for example, a side of three and a side of seven expressed as a rectangle yields the equation $3 \times 7 = 21$, and when the operation is viewed in this way, the distinction between feet and square feet obscures its point. I have therefore kept to Greek usage because of the geometrical algebra which explains the use. For further discussion, see T. L. Heath, *The Thirteen Books of Euclid's Elements*, vol. 1 (New York, 1960), pp. 372–4.

SOCRATES: Do you see, Meno, that I am teaching him nothing but am asking him all these things? And now he thinks he knows the length of the side from which the eight-foot figure will be generated. Do you agree?

MENO: I do.

SOCRATES: Well, does he know?

MENO: Of course not.

SOCRATES: He merely thinks it is generated from the doubled side?

MENO: Yes.

SOCRATES: Now watch him recollect serially and in order, as is necessary for recollection.

83a (*Turning to the boy*) Tell me: are you saying that the doubled figure is generated from the doubled side? The figure I mean is not to be long one way and short the other; it is to be equal on all sides, as this one (ABCD) is, but double it, eight feet. See if you still think it will result from double the side.

BOY: I do.

SOCRATES: Now, this line (AB) becomes double (AX) if we add another of the same length here?

BOY: Of course.

SOCRATES: So there will be an eight-foot figure from it, you say, if four such sides are generated?

b BOY: Yes.

SOCRATES: Then let us inscribe four equal sides from it. (*Socrates, beginning with base AX, inscribes AXYZ.*)

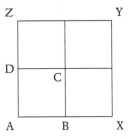

You say this would be eight feet?

BOY: Of course.

SOCRATES: Now, there are four squares in it, each of which is equal to this four-foot figure (ABCD)? (*Socrates completes the transversals begun by DC and BC above.*)

BOY: Yes.

SOCRATES: Then how big has it become? Four times as big?

BOY: Certainly.

SOCRATES: Now, is four times the same as double?

BOY: Surely not.

SOCRATES: How many?

BOY: Fourfold.

c SOCRATES: Then from double the line, my boy, not a double but a four-fold figure is generated.

BOY: True.

SOCRATES: Since four times four is sixteen. Right?

BOY: Yes.

SOCRATES: Well, then, an eight-foot figure will be generated from what line? That one (AX) gave us a four-fold figure, didn't it? (i.e., AXYZ)

BOY: Yes.

SOCRATES: But half of it (AB) gave us four feet? (i.e., ABCD)

BOY: I agree.

SOCRATES: Very well. But an eight-foot figure is double this (ABCD), and half that (AXYZ)?

BOY: Yes.

SOCRATES: Then it will be from a side greater than this (AB) but smaller than that one there (AX), won't it?   d

BOY: Yes, I think so.

SOCRATES: Excellent. Always answer what you think. Now tell me: wasn't this line (AB) two feet, and that one (AX) four?

BOY: Yes.

SOCRATES: So the side of an eight-foot figure must be greater than this two-foot side here, but smaller than the four-foot side?

BOY: It must.

SOCRATES: Try and tell me how long you'd say it is.   e

BOY: Three feet.

SOCRATES: Now, if it is to be three feet, we'll add (to AB) half of this (BX), and it will be three feet; for this (AB) is two, and that (BM) is one. And in the same way over here, this (AD) is two and that (DN) is one; and the figure you speak of is generated. (*Socrates as he speaks marks M and N on BX and DZ, and then completes the square.*)

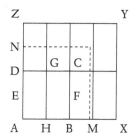

BOY: Yes.

SOCRATES: Now if this (AM) is three and that (AN) is three, the whole figure generated is thrice three feet?

BOY: That follows.

SOCRATES: And how many is thrice three?

BOY: Nine.

SOCRATES: But the double (of the original square) had to be how many feet?

BOY: Eight.

SOCRATES: So somehow the eight foot figure is not generated from the three-foot side either.

BOY: It certainly isn't.

SOCRATES: But from what, then? Try and tell us exactly. If you don't want to count it out, just point to it.   84a

BOY: Socrates, I really don't know.

SOCRATES: (*Turning to Meno.*) Here again, Meno, do you see the progress in recollection he's made so far? At first he didn't know the side required for an eight-foot figure – and he still doesn't. But earlier he supposed he knew and answered confidently, and did not believe
84b he was in perplexity. But now he *does* believe it, and as he doesn't know, neither does he suppose he knows.

MENO: You are right.

SOCRATES: So he is now better off with respect to the thing which he did not know?

MENO: I agree.

SOCRATES: Well, did we harm him any by numbing him like a stingray and making him aware of his perplexity?

MENO: I think not.

SOCRATES: We have at any rate done something, it seems, to help him discover how things are, for in his present condition of ignorance, he will gladly inquire into the matter, whereas before he might easily have supposed he could speak well, and frequently, and before large
c audiences, about doubling the square and how the side must be double in length.

MENO: So it seems.

SOCRATES: Well, do you think he would undertake to inquire into or learn what he thought he knew and did not, before he fell into perplexity and became convinced of his ignorance and longed to know?

MENO: I think not, Socrates.

SOCRATES: So numbing benefited him?

MENO: Yes.

SOCRATES: Then please observe what he will discover from this perplexity as he inquires with
d me – even though I will only ask questions and will not teach. Be on guard lest you find that I teach and explain to him, instead of questioning him about his own opinions. (*Socrates at this point rubs out the figures in the sand at his feet, leaving only rectangle ABCD, and turns to the boy.*) Now back to you. We've got this figure of four feet, don't we? Do you follow?

BOY: I do.

SOCRATES: And we can add here another equal to it? (*Inscribes it*)

BOY: Yes.

SOCRATES: And a third here, equal to each of those? (*Inscribes it*)

BOY: Yes.

SOCRATES: Now, we can fill in the one here in the corner? (*Inscribes it*)

BOY: Of course.

SOCRATES: So these four equal figures would be generated?

e BOY: Yes.

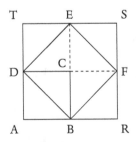

SOCRATES: Now then. How many times larger than this (ABCD) does this whole (ARST) become?

BOY: Four times.

SOCRATES: But we had to generate double. Do you recall?

BOY: Of course.

SOCRATES: Now take this line from corner to corner. (*Socrates inscribes BFED.*) Does it cut each of these figures in two? 85a

BOY: Yes.

SOCRATES: Now, have we generated four equal lines here (BD, DE, EF, FB), enclosing this figure (BFED)?

BOY: We have.

SOCRATES: Then consider: how large is this figure?

BOY: I don't understand.

SOCRATES: Hasn't each of these lines cut off the inner half of these four squares?

BOY: Yes.

SOCRATES: Then how many (halves) of that size are in this (BFED)?

BOY: Four.

SOCRATES: And how many in this one (ABCD)?

BOY: Two.

SOCRATES: What is four to two?

BOY: Double.

SOCRATES: So this becomes how many feet? b

BOY: Eight feet.

SOCRATES: From what line?

BOY: That one (BD).

SOCRATES: That is, from the line stretching from corner to corner of the four-foot figure?

BOY: Yes.

SOCRATES: Students of the subject call that the diagonal. So if that is the name for it, then you, Meno's slave, are stating as your view that the double figure would be generated from the diagonal.

BOY: Yes, certainly, Socrates.

SOCRATES: (*Turning to Meno*) Well, Meno, what do you think? Did he reply with any opinion not his own?

MENO: No, they were his. c

SOCRATES: Yet he didn't *know*, as we were saying a little earlier.

MENO: True.

SOCRATES: Yet these opinions were *in* him, weren't they?

MENO: Yes.

SOCRATES: Therefore, while he is ignorant of these things he does not know, there are true opinions in him about these very things?

MENO: That follows.

SOCRATES: For the moment, these opinions have been stirred up in him as in a dream; but if he were repeatedly asked these same questions in different ways, you may rest assured that eventually he would know about these things as accurately as anyone. d

MENO: It seems so.

SOCRATES: Then he will know without being taught but only questioned, recovering knowledge out of himself?

MENO: Yes.

SOCRATES: And his recovering knowledge which is in him is recollection?

MENO: Yes.

SOCRATES: The knowledge he now has he either gained at some time or always had?

MENO: Yes.

SOCRATES: Well, if he always had it, he always knew. And if he gained it at some time, he

85e surely didn't do so in his present life. Or did someone teach him geometry? For he will do the very same thing all through geometry, and every other study. Is there anyone who has taught him all this? You ought to know, especially since he was born in your house and raised there.

MENO: I do know: no one ever taught him.

SOCRATES: But he has these opinions, does he not?

MENO: It appears he must, Socrates.

SOCRATES: Well, if he did not get them in his present life, is it not at this point clear he got

86a and learned them at some other time?

MENO: It appears so.

SOCRATES: A time when he was not in human form?

MENO: Yes.

SOCRATES: So if we are to say that there are true opinions present in him both during the time when he is and is not a man, and that those opinions become knowledge when roused by questioning, then his soul will ever be in a state of having learned. For it is clear that through all time he either is or is not a man.

MENO: That follows.

b SOCRATES: Now, if the truth of things is always in our soul, the soul is immortal. So it is right to try boldly to inquire into and recollect what you do not happen to know at present – that is, what you do not remember.

12

Phaedo

The *Phaedo* purportedly recounts a discussion held in the jail on the day of Socrates' execution. Socrates' friends are naturally distraught at the imminent death of their dear friend and mentor. But Socrates tells his friends that their concern and grief are unfounded: he will survive death, he contends, and the discussion provides a series of arguments and counter-arguments on the question of the immortality of the soul. Many scholars regard the *Phaedo* as perhaps the first complete work in which Plato finally feels entirely free to put his own views into Socrates' mouth. It is easy enough to see why scholars believe this, if we take the expression of agnosticism about death that Socrates makes in the *Apology* (29b) to be better suited to the historical Socrates. Plato's famous theory of Forms also makes its appearance in the *Phaedo*, also perhaps for the first time. At any rate, Plato's arguments for the immortality of the soul continue to provoke philosophical controversy, and the death scene with which the dialogue closes has its own special power for us all.

'Let him be,' [Socrates] said. 'Now then, with you for my jury I want to give my defence, and show with what good reason, as it seems to me, a man who has truly spent his life in philosophy feels confident when about to die, and is hopeful that, when he has died, he will 64a win very great benefits in the other world. So I'll try, Simmias and Cebes, to explain how this could be.

'Other people may well be unaware that all who actually engage in philosophy aright are practising nothing other than dying and being dead. Now if this is true, it would be odd indeed for them to be eager in their whole life for nothing but this, and yet to be resentful when it comes, the very thing they'd long been eager for and practised.'

Simmias laughed at this and said: 'Goodness, Socrates, you've made me laugh, even though I wasn't much inclined to laugh just now. I imagine that most people, on hearing that, would b think it very well said of philosophers – and our own countrymen would quite agree – that they are, indeed, verging on death, and that they, at any rate, are well aware that this is what philosophers deserve to undergo.'

'Yes, and what they say would be true, Simmias, except for their claim to be aware of it themselves; because they aren't aware in what sense genuine philosophers are verging on death and deserving of it, and what kind of death they deserve. Anyway, let's discuss it among c ourselves, disregarding them: do we suppose that death *is* something?'

'Certainly,' rejoined Simmias.

'And that it is nothing but the separation of the soul from the body? And that being dead is this: the body's having come to be apart, separated from the soul, alone by itself, and the soul's being apart, alone by itself, separated from the body? Death can't be anything else but that, can it?'

'No, it's just that.'

'Now look, my friend, and see if maybe you agree with me on these points; because through 64d them I think we'll improve our knowledge of what we're examining. Do you think it befits a philosophical man to be keen about the so-called pleasures of, for example, food and drink?'

'Not in the least, Socrates,' said Simmias.

'And what about those of sex?'

'Not at all.'

'And what about the other services to the body? Do you think such a man regards them as of any value? For instance, the possession of smart clothes and shoes, and the other bodily adornments – do you think he values them highly, or does he disdain them, except e in so far as he's absolutely compelled to share in them?'

'I think the genuine philosopher disdains them.'

'Do you think in general, then, that such a man's concern is not for the body, but so far as he can stand aside from it, is directed towards the soul?'

'I do.'

'Then is it clear that, first, in such matters as these the philosopher differs from other men 65a in releasing his soul, as far as possible, from its communion with the body?'

'It appears so.'

'And presumably, Simmias, it does seem to most men that someone who finds nothing of that sort pleasant, and takes no part in those things, doesn't deserve to live; rather, one who cares nothing for the pleasures that come by way of the body runs pretty close to being dead.'

'Yes, what you say is quite true.'

'And now, what about the actual gaining of wisdom? Is the body a hindrance or not, b if one enlists it as a partner in the quest? This is the sort of thing I mean: do sight and hearing afford men any truth, or aren't even the poets always harping on such themes, telling us that we neither hear nor see anything accurately? And yet if these of all the bodily senses are neither accurate nor clear, the others will hardly be so; because they are, surely, all inferior to these. Don't you think so?'

'Certainly.'

'So when does the soul attain the truth? Because plainly, whenever it sets about examining anything in company with the body, it is completely taken in by it.'

c 'That's true.'

'So isn't it in reasoning, if anywhere at all, that any of the things that *are* become manifest to it?'

'Yes.'

'And it reasons best, presumably, whenever none of these things bothers it, neither hearing nor sight nor pain, nor any pleasure either, but whenever it comes to be alone by itself as far as possible, disregarding the body, and whenever, having the least possible communion and contact with it, it strives for that which is.'

'That is so.'

'So there again the soul of the philosopher utterly disdains the body and flees from it, d seeking rather to come to be alone by itself?'

'It seems so.'

'Well now, what about things of this sort, Simmias? Do we say that there is something *just*, or nothing?'

'Yes, we most certainly do!'

'And again, something *beautiful*, and *good*?'

'Of course.'

'Now did you ever yet see any such things with your eyes?'

'Certainly not.'

'Well did you grasp them with any other bodily sense-perception? And I'm talking about them all – about largeness, health, and strength, for example – and, in short, about the Being of all other such things, what each one actually is; is it through the body that their truest e element is viewed, or isn't it rather thus: whoever of us is prepared to think most fully and minutely of each object of his inquiry, in itself, will come closest to the knowledge of each?'

'Yes, certainly.'

'Then would that be achieved most purely by the man who approached each object with his intellect alone as far as possible, neither adducing sight in his thinking, nor dragging in any other sense to accompany his reasoning; rather, using his intellect alone by itself and 66a unsullied, he would undertake the hunt for each of the things that are, each alone by itself and unsullied; he would be separated as far as possible from his eyes and ears, and virtually from his whole body, on the ground that it confuses the soul, and doesn't allow it to gain truth and wisdom when in partnership with it: isn't it this man, Simmias, who will attain that which is, if anyone will?'

'What you say is abundantly true, Socrates,' said Simmias.

'For all these reasons, then, some such view as this must present itself to genuine philo- b sophers, so that they say such things to one another as these: "There now, it looks as if some sort of track is leading us, together with our reason, astray in our inquiry: as long as we possess the body, and our soul is contaminated by such an evil, we'll surely never adequately gain what we desire – and that, we say, is truth. Because the body affords us countless distractions, owing to the nurture it must have; and again, if any illnesses befall it, they hamper c our pursuit of that which is. Besides, it fills us up with lusts and desires, with fears and fantasies of every kind, and with any amount of trash, so that really and truly we are, as the saying goes, never able to think of anything at all because of it. Thus, it's nothing but the body and its desires that brings wars and factions and fighting; because it's over the gaining of wealth that all wars take place, and we're compelled to gain wealth because of the body, enslaved as we are to its service; so for all these reasons it leaves us no leisure for philo- d sophy. And the worst of it all is that if we do get any leisure from it, and turn to some inquiry, once again it intrudes everywhere in our researches, setting up a clamour and disturbance, and striking terror, so that the truth can't be discerned because of it. Well now, it really has been shown us that if we're ever going to know anything purely, we must be rid of it, and must view the objects themselves with the soul by itself; it's then, apparently, that the thing e we desire and whose lovers we claim to be, wisdom, will be ours – when we have died, as the argument indicates, though not while we live. Because, if we can know nothing purely in the body's company, then one of two things must be true: either knowledge is nowhere to be gained, or else it is for the dead; since then, but no sooner, will the soul be alone by 67a itself apart from the body. And therefore while we live, it would seem that we shall be closest to knowledge in this way – if we consort with the body as little as possible, and do not commune with it, except in so far as we must, and do not infect ourselves with its nature,

but remain pure from it, until God himself shall release us; and being thus pure, through separation from the body's folly, we shall probably be in like company, and shall know through
67b our own selves all that is unsullied – and that, I dare say, is what the truth is; because never will it be permissible for impure to touch pure." Such are the things, I think, Simmias, that all who are rightly called lovers of knowledge must say to one another, and must believe. Don't you agree?'

'Emphatically, Socrates.'

'Well then, if that's true, my friend,' said Socrates, 'there's plenty of hope for one who arrives where I'm going, that there, if anywhere, he will adequately possess the object that's been our great concern in life gone by; and thus the journey now appointed for me may
c also be made with good hope by any other man who regards his intellect as prepared, by having been, in a manner, purified.'

'Yes indeed,' said Simmias.

'Then doesn't purification turn out to be just what's been mentioned for some while in our discussion – the parting of the soul from the body as far as possible, and the habituating of it to assemble and gather itself together, away from every part of the body, alone by
d itself, and to live, so far as it can, both in the present and in the hereafter, released from the body, as from fetters?'

'Yes indeed.'

'And is it just this that is named "death" – a release and parting of soul from body?'

'Indeed it is.'

'And it's especially those who practise philosophy aright, or rather they alone, who are always eager to release it, as we say, and the occupation of philosophers is just this, isn't it – a release and parting of soul from body?'

'It seems so.'

'Then wouldn't it be absurd, as I said at the start, for a man to prepare himself in his life
e to live as close as he can to being dead, and then to be resentful when this comes to him?'

'It would be absurd, of course.'

'Truly then, Simmias, those who practise philosophy aright are cultivating dying, and for them least of all men does being dead hold any terror. Look at it like this: if they've set themselves at odds with the body at every point, and desire to possess their soul alone by itself, wouldn't it be quite illogical if they were afraid and resentful when this came about – if, that
68a is, they didn't go gladly to the place where, on arrival, they may hope to attain what they longed for throughout life, namely wisdom – and to be rid of the company of that with which they'd set themselves at odds? Or again, many have been willing to enter Hades of their own accord, in quest of human loves, of wives and sons who have died, led by this hope, that there they would see and be united with those they desired; will anyone, then, who truly longs for wisdom, and who firmly holds this same hope, that nowhere but in Hades will he
b attain it in any way worth mentioning, be resentful at dying; and will he not go there gladly? One must suppose so, my friend, if he's truly a lover of wisdom; since this will be his firm belief, that nowhere else but there will he attain wisdom purely. Yet if that is so, wouldn't it, as I said just now, be quite illogical if such a man were afraid of death?'

'Yes, quite illogical!'

'Then if you see a man resentful that he is going to die, isn't this proof enough for you that he's no lover of wisdom after all, but what we may call a lover of the body? And this
c same man turns out, in some sense, to be a lover of riches and of prestige, either one of these or both.'

'It's just as you say.'

'Well now, Simmias, isn't it also true that what is named "bravery" belongs especially to people of the disposition we have described?'

'Most certainly.'

'And then temperance too, even what most people name "temperance" – not being excited over one's desires, but being scornful of them and well-ordered – belongs, doesn't it, only to those who utterly scorn the body and live in love of wisdom?'

'It must.'   d

'Yes, because if you care to consider the bravery and temperance of other men, you'll find it strange.'

'How so, Socrates?'

'You know, don't you, that all other men count death among great evils?'

'Very much so.'

'Is it, then, through being afraid of greater evils that the brave among them abide death, whenever they do so?'

'It is.'

'Then, it's through fearing and fear that all men except philosophers are brave; and yet it's surely illogical that anyone should be brave through fear and cowardice.'

'It certainly is.'   e

'And what about those of them who are well-ordered? Aren't they in this same state, temperate through a kind of intemperance? True, we say that's impossible; but still that state of simple-minded temperance does turn out in their case to be like this: it's because they're afraid of being deprived of further pleasures, and desire them, that they abstain from some because they're overcome by others. True, they call it "intemperance" to be ruled by   69a pleasures, but still that's what happens to them: they overcome some pleasures because they're overcome by others. And this is the sort of thing that was just mentioned: after a fashion, they achieve temperance because of intemperance.'

'Yes, so it seems.'

'Yes, Simmias, my good friend; since this may not be the right exchange with a view to goodness, the exchanging of pleasures for pleasures, pains for pains, and fear for fear, greater for lesser ones, like coins; it may be, rather, that this alone is the right coin, for which one should exchange all these things – wisdom; and the buying and selling of all things for that,   b or rather with that, may be real bravery, temperance, justice, and, in short, true goodness in company with wisdom, whether pleasures and fears and all else of that sort be added or taken away; but as for their being parted from wisdom and exchanged for one another, goodness of that sort may be a kind of illusory facade, and fit for slaves indeed, and may have nothing healthy or true about it; whereas, truth to tell, temperance, justice, and bravery may in fact be a kind of purification of all such things, and wisdom itself a kind of purifying rite.   c So it really looks as if those who established our initiations are no mean people, but have in fact long been saying in riddles that whoever arrives in Hades unadmitted to the rites, and uninitiated, shall lie in the slough, while he who arrives there purified and initiated shall dwell with gods. For truly there are, so say those concerned with the initiations, "many who bear the wand, but few who are devotees". Now these latter, in my view, are none other than   d those who have practised philosophy aright. And it's to be among them that I myself have striven, in every way I could, neglecting nothing during my life within my power. Whether I have striven aright and we have achieved anything, we shall, I think, know for certain, God willing, in a little while, on arrival yonder.

'There's my defence, then, Simmias and Cebes, to show how reasonable it is for me not
69e to take it hard or be resentful at leaving you and my masters here, since I believe that there
also, no less than here, I shall find good masters and companions; so if I'm any more convincing in my defence to you than to the Athenian jury, it would be well.'

[. . .]

'Yes, and besides, Socrates,' Cebes replied, 'there's also that theory you're always putting
forward, that our learning is actually nothing but recollection; according to that too, if it's
true, what we are now reminded of we must have learned at some former time. But that
73a would be impossible, unless our souls existed somewhere before being born in this human
form; so in this way too, it appears that the soul is something immortal.'

'Yes, what are the proofs of those points, Cebes?' put in Simmias. 'Remind me, as I don't
recall them very well at the moment.'

'One excellent argument,' said Cebes, 'is that when people are questioned, and if the
questions are well put, they state the truth about everything for themselves – and yet unless
knowledge and a correct account were present within them, they'd be unable to do this;
b thus, if one takes them to diagrams or anything else of that sort, one has there the plainest
evidence that this is so.'

'But if that doesn't convince you, Simmias,' said Socrates, 'then see whether maybe you
agree if you look at it this way. Apparently you doubt whether what is called "learning" is
recollection?'

'I don't *doubt* it,' said Simmias; 'but I do need to undergo just what the argument is about,
to be "reminded". Actually, from the way Cebes set about stating it, I do almost recall it and
am nearly convinced; but I'd like, none the less, to hear now how you set about stating it
yourself.'

c 'I'll put it this way. We agree, I take it, that if anyone is to be reminded of a thing, he
must have known that thing at some time previously.'

'Certainly.'

'Then do we also agree on this point: that whenever knowledge comes to be present in
this sort of way, it is recollection? I mean in some such way as this: if someone, on seeing
a thing, or hearing it, or getting any other sense-perception of it, not only recognizes that
thing, but also thinks of something else, which is the object not of the same knowledge but
of another, don't we then rightly say that he's been "reminded" of the object of which he
d has got the thought?'

'What do you mean?'

'Take the following examples: knowledge of a man, surely, is other than that of a lyre?'

'Of course.'

'Well now, you know what happens to lovers, whenever they see a lyre or cloak or anything else their loves are accustomed to use: they recognize the lyre, and they get in their
mind, don't they, the form of the boy whose lyre it is? And that is recollection. Likewise,
someone seeing Simmias is often reminded of Cebes, and there'd surely be countless other
such cases.'

'Countless indeed!' said Simmias.

e 'Then is something of that sort a kind of recollection? More especially, though, whenever
it happens to someone in connection with things he's since forgotten , through lapse of time
or inattention?'

'Certainly.'

'Again now, is it possible, on seeing a horse depicted or a lyre depicted, to be reminded of a man; and on seeing Simmias depicted, to be reminded of Cebes?'

'Certainly.'

'And also, on seeing Simmias depicted, to be reminded of Simmias himself?'

'Yes, that's possible.'   74a

'In all these cases, then, doesn't it turn out that there is recollection from similar things, but also from dissimilar things?'

'It does.'

'But whenever one is reminded of something from similar things, mustn't one experience something further: mustn't one think whether or not the thing is lacking at all, in its similarity, in relation to what one is reminded of?'

'One must.'

'Then consider whether this is the case. We say, don't we, that there is something *equal* – I don't mean a log to a log, or a stone to a stone, or anything else of that sort, but some further thing beyond all those, the equal itself: are we to say that there *is* something or nothing?'

'We most certainly are to say that there *is*,' said Simmias; 'unquestionably!'   b

'And do we know *what it is*?'

'Certainly.'

'Where did we get the knowledge of it? Wasn't it from the things we were just mentioning: on seeing logs or stones or other equal things, wasn't it from these that we thought of that object, it being different from them? Or doesn't it seem different to you? Look at it this way: don't equal stones and logs, the very same ones, sometimes seem equal to one, but not to another?'

'Yes, certainly.'

'But now, did the equals themselves ever seem to you unequal, or equality inequality?'   c

'Never yet, Socrates.'

'Then those equals, and the equal itself, are not the same.'

'By no means, Socrates, in my view.'

'But still, it is from *those* equals, different as they are from *that* equal, that you have thought of and got the knowledge of it?'

'That's perfectly true.'

'It being either similar to them or dissimilar?'

'Certainly.'

'Anyway, it makes no difference; so long as on seeing one thing, one does, from this sight,   d think of another, whether it be similar or dissimilar, this must be recollection.'

'Certainly.'

'Well now, with regard to the instances in the logs, and, in general, the equals we mentioned just now, are we affected in some way as this: do they seem to us to be equal in the same way as *what it is* itself? Do they fall short of it at all in being like the equal, or not?'

'Very far short of it.'

'Then whenever anyone, on seeing a thing, thinks to himself, "this thing that I now see seeks to be like another of the things that are, but falls short, and cannot be like that object: e it is inferior", do we agree that the man who thinks this must previously have known the object he says it resembles but falls short of?'

'He must.'

'Now then, have we ourselves been affected in just this way, or not, with regard to the equals and the equal itself?'

'Indeed we have.'

'Then we must previously have known the equal, before that time when we first, on seeing 75a the equals, thought that all of them were stritving to be like the equal but fell short of it.'

'That is so.'

'Yet we also agree on this: we haven't derived the thought of it, nor could we do so, from anywhere but seeing or touching or some other of the senses – I'm counting all these as the same.'

'Yes, they are the same, Socrates, for what the argument seeks to show.'

'But of course it is *from* one's sense-perceptions that one must think that all the things in b the sense-perceptions are striving for *what equal is*, yet are inferior to it; or how shall we put it?'

'Like that.'

'Then it must, surely, have been before we began to see and hear and use the other senses that we got knowledge of the equal itself, of *what it is*, if we were going to refer the equals from our sense-perceptions to it, supposing that all things are doing their best to be like it, but are inferior to it.'

'That must follow from what's been said before, Socrates.'

'Now we were seeing and hearing, and were possessed of our other senses, weren't we, just as soon as we were born?'

'Certainly.'

c 'But we must, we're saying, have got our knowledge of the equal *before* these?'

'Yes.'

'Then it seems that we must have got it before we were born.'

'It seems so.'

'Now if, having got it before birth, we were born in possession of it, did we know, both before birth and as soon as we were born, not only the equal, the larger and the smaller, but everything of that sort? Because our present argument concerns the beautiful itself, and d the good itself, and just and holy, no less than the equal; in fact, as I say, it concerns everything on which we set this seal, "*what it is*", in the questions we ask and in the answers we give. And so we must have got pieces of knowledge of all those things before birth.'

'That is so.'

'Moreover, if having got them, we did not on each occasion forget them, we must always be born knowing, and must continue to know throughout life: because this is knowing – to possess knowledge one has got of something, and not to have lost it; or isn't loss of knowledge what we mean by "forgetting", Simmias?'

e 'Certainly it is, Socrates.'

'But on the other hand, I suppose that if, having got them before birth, we lost them on being born, and later on, using the senses about the things in question, we regain those pieces of knowledge that we possessed at some former time, in that case wouldn't what we call "learning" be the regaining of knowledge belonging to us? And in saying that this was being reminded, shouldn't we be speaking correctly?'

'Certainly.'

76a 'Yes, because it did seem possible, on sensing an object, whether by seeing or hearing or getting some other sense-perception of it, to think from this of some other thing one had forgotten – either a thing to which the object, though dissimilar to it, was related, or else something to which it was similar; so, as I say, one of two things is true: *either* all of us were born knowing those objects, and we know them throughout life; *or* those we speak of as "learning" are simply being reminded later on, and learning would be recollection.'

'That's quite true, Socrates.'

'Then which do you choose, Simmias? That we are born knowing, or that we are later reminded of the things we'd gained knowledge of before?'   b

'At the moment, Socrates, I can't make a choice.'

'Well, can you make one on the following point, and what do you think about it? If a man knows things, can he give an account of what he knows or not?'

'Of course he can, Socrates.'

'And do you think everyone can give an account of those objects we were discussing just now?'

'I only wish they could,' said Simmias; 'but I'm afraid that, on the contrary, this time tomorrow there may no longer be any man who can do so properly.'

'You don't then, Simmias, think that everyone knows those objects?'   c

'By no means.'

'Are they, then, reminded of what they once learned?'

'They must be.'

'When did our souls get the knowledge of those objects? Not, at any rate, since we were born as human beings.'

'Indeed not.'

'Earlier, then.'

'Yes.'

'Then our souls did exist earlier, Simmias, before entering human form, apart from bodies; and they possessed wisdom.'

'Unless maybe, Socrates, we get those pieces of knowledge at the very moment of birth; that time still remains.'

'Very well, my friend; but then at what other time, may I ask, do we lose them? We aren't d born with them, as we agreed just now. Do we then lose them at the very time at which we get them? Or have you any other time to suggest?'

'None at all, Socrates. I didn't realize I was talking nonsense.'

'Then is our position as follows, Simmias? If the objects we're always harping on exist, a beautiful, and a good and all such Being, and if we refer all the things from our sense-perceptions to that Being, finding again what was formerly ours, and if we compare these e things with that, then just as surely as those objects exist, so also must our soul exist before we are born. On the other hand, if they don't exist, this argument will have gone for nothing. Is this the position? Is it equally necessary that those objects exist, and that our souls existed before birth, and if the former don't exist, then neither did the latter?'

'It's abundantly clear to me, Socrates,' said Simmias, 'that there's the same necessity in either case, and the argument takes opportune refuge in the view that our soul exists before 77a birth, just as surely as the Being of which you're now speaking. Because I myself find nothing so plain to me as that all such objects, beautiful and good and all the others you were speaking of just now, *are* in the fullest possible way; so in my view it's been adequately proved.'

'And what about Cebes?' said Socrates. 'We must convince Cebes too.'

'It's adequate for him, I think,' said Simmias; 'though he's the most obstinate of people when it comes to doubting arguments. But I think he's been sufficiently convinced that our

77b soul existed before we were born. Whether it will still exist, however, after we've died, doesn't seem, even to me, to have been shown, Socrates; but the point Cebes made just now still stands – the popular fear that when a man dies, his soul may be dispersed at that time, and that that may be the end of its existence. Because what's to prevent it from coming to be and being put together from some other source, and from existing before it enters a human body, yet when it has entered one, and again been separated from it, from then meeting its end, and being itself destroyed?'

c 'You're right, Simmias,' said Cebes. 'It seems that half, as it were, of what is needed has been shown – that our soul existed before we were born; it must also be shown that it will exist after we've died, no less than before we were born, if the proof is going to be complete.'

'That's been proved already, Simmias and Cebes,' said Socrates, 'if you will combine this argument with the one we agreed on earlier, to the effect that all that is living comes from d that which is dead. Because if the soul does have previous existence, and if when it enters upon living and being born, it must come from no other source than death and being dead, surely it must also exist after it has died, given that it has to be born again? So your point has been proved already.

[. . .]

PHAEDO: 'As I recall, when these points had been granted him, and it was agreed that each 102b of the forms *was* something, and that the other things, partaking in them, took the name of the forms themselves, he next asked: 'If you say that that is so, then whenever you say that Simmias is larger than Socrates but smaller than Phaedo, you mean then, don't you, that both things are in Simmias, largeness and smallness?'

'I do.'

'Well anyhow, do you agree that Simmias' overtopping of Socrates isn't expressed in those c words according to the truth of the matter? Because it isn't, surely, by nature that Simmias overtops him, by virtue, that is of his being Simmias, but by virtue of the largeness that he happens to have. Nor again does he overtop Socrates because Socrates is Socrates, but because of smallness that Socrates has in relation to his largeness?'

'True.'

'Nor again is he overtopped by Phaedo in virtue of Phaedo's being Phaedo, but because of largeness that Phaedo has in relation to Simmias' smallness?'

'That is so.'

'So that's how Simmias takes the name of being both small and large; it's because he's d between the two of them, submitting his smallness to the largeness of the one for it to over-top, and presenting to the other his largeness which overtops the latter's smallness.'

At this he smiled, and added: 'That sounds as if I'm going to talk like a book. But any-way, things are surely as I say.'

He agreed.

'My reason for saying this is that I want you to think as I do. Now it seems to me that not only is largeness itself never willing to be large and small at the same time, but also that the largeness in us never admits the small, nor is it willing to be overtopped. Rather, one of two things must happen: either it must retreat and get out of the way, when its opposite, e the small, advances towards it; or else, upon that opposite's advance, it must perish. But what it is not willing to do is to abide and admit smallness, and thus be other than what it was.

Thus I, having admitted and abided smallness, am still what I am, this same individual, only small; whereas the large in us, while being large, can't endure to be small. And similarly, the small that's in us is not willing ever to come to be, or to be, large. Nor will any other of the opposites, while still being what it was, at the same time come to be, and be, its own 103a opposite. If that befalls it, *either* it goes away *or* it perishes.'

'I entirely agree,' said Cebes.

On hearing this, one of those present – I don't remember for sure who it was – said: 'But look here, wasn't the very opposite of what's now being said agreed in our earlier discussion: that the larger comes to be from the smaller, and the smaller from the larger, and that coming-to-be is, for opposites, just this – they come to be from their opposites. Whereas now I think it's being said that this could never happen.'

Socrates turned his head and listened. 'It's splendid of you to have recalled that,' he said; 'but you don't realize the difference between what's being said now and what was said then. b It was said then that one opposite *thing* comes to be from another opposite *thing*; what we're saying now is that the opposite *itself* could never come to be opposite to itself, whether it be the opposite in us or the opposite in nature. Then, my friend, we were talking about things that *have* opposites, calling them by the names they take from them; whereas now we're talking about the opposites themselves, from whose presence in them the things so called c derive their names. It's these latter that we're saying would never be willing to admit coming-to-be from each other.'

With this he looked towards Cebes and said: 'Cebes, you weren't troubled, I suppose, by any of the things our friend here said, were you?'

'No, not this time,' said Cebes; 'though I don't deny that many things do trouble me.'

'We've agreed, then, unreservedly on this point: an opposite will never be opposite to itself.'

'Completely.'

'Now please consider this further point, and see if you agree with it. Is there something you call hot, and again cold?'

'There is.'

'Do you mean the same as snow and fire?'

'No, most certainly not.'   d

'Rather, the hot is something different from fire, and the cold is something different from snow?'

'Yes.'

'But this I think you will agree: what is snow will never, on the lines of what we were saying earlier, admit the hot and still be what it was, namely snow, and also hot; but at the advance of the hot, it will either get out of the way or perish.'

'Certainly.'

'And again fire, when cold advances, will either get out of the way or perish; but it will never endure to admit the coldness, and still be what it was, namely fire and also cold.'

'That's true.'   e

'The situation, then, in some cases of this kind, is as follows: not only is the form itself entitled to its own name for all time; but there's something else too, which is not the same as the form, but which, whenever it exists, always has the character of that form. Perhaps what I mean will be clearer in this further example: the odd must, surely, always be given this name that we're now using, mustn't it?'

'Certainly.'

'But is it the only thing there is – this is my question – or is there something else, which
104a is not the same as the odd, yet which one must also always call odd, as well as by its own
name, because it is by nature such that it can never be separated from the odd? I mean the
sort of thing that happens to threeness, and to many other instances. Consider the case of
threeness. Don't you think it must always be called both by its own name and by that of
the odd, although the odd is not the same as threeness? They aren't the same, yet threeness
b and fiveness and half the entire number series are by nature, each of them, always odd, although
they are not the same as the odd. And again, two and four and the whole of the other row
of numbers, though not the same as the even, are still, each of them, always even. Do you
agree or not?'

'Of course.'

'Look closely then at what I want to show. It is this: apparently it's not only the opposites we spoke of that don't admit each other. This is also true of all things which, although
not opposites to each other, always have the opposites. These things too, it seems, don't
admit whatever form may be opposite to the one that's in them, but when it attacks, *either*
c they perish *or* they get out of the way. Thus we shall say, shan't we, that three will sooner
perish, will undergo anything else whatever, sooner than abide coming to be even, while
remaining three?'

'Indeed we shall,' said Cebes.

'Moreover, twoness isn't opposite to threeness.'

'Indeed not.'

'Then not only do the forms that are opposites not abide each other's attack; but there
are, in addition, certain other things that don't abide the opposites' attack.'

'Quite true.'

'Then would you like us, if we can, to define what kinds these are?'

'Certainly.'

d   'Would they, Cebes, be these: things that are compelled by whatever occupies them to
have not only its own form, but always the form of some opposite as well?'

'What do you mean?'

'As we were saying just now. You recognize, no doubt, that whatever the form of three
occupies must be not only three but also odd.'

'Certainly.'

'Then, we're saying, the form opposite to the character that has that effect could never
go to a thing of that kind.'

'It couldn't.'

'But it was that of odd that had that effect?'

'Yes.'

'And opposite to this is that of the even?'

'Yes.'

e   'So that of the even will never come to three.'

'No, it won't.'

'Three, then, has no part in the even.'

'No part.'

'So threeness is uneven.'

'Yes.'

'So what I was saying we were to define, the kind of things which, while not opposite to
a given thing, nevertheless don't admit it, the opposite in question – as we've just seen that

threeness, while not opposite to the even, nevertheless doesn't admit it, since it always brings up its opposite, just as twoness brings up the opposite of the odd, and the fire brings up the opposite of the cold, and so on in a great many other cases – well, see whether you would 105a define them thus: it is not only the opposite that doesn't admit its opposite; there is also that which brings up an opposite into whatever it enters itself; and that thing, the very thing that brings it up, never admits the quality opposed to the one that's brought up. Recall it once more: there's no harm in hearing it several times. Five won't admit the form of the even, nor will ten, its double, admit that of the odd. This, of course, is itself also the opposite of something else; nevertheless, it won't admit the form of the odd. Nor again will one-and-a b half, and the rest of that series, the halves, admit the form of the whole; and the same applies to a third, and all that series. Do you follow and agree that that is so?'

'I agree most emphatically, and I do follow.'

'Then please repeat it from the start; and don't answer in the exact terms of my question, but in imitation of my example. I say this, because from what's now being said I see a different kind of safeness beyond the answer I gave initially, the old safe one. Thus, if you were to ask me what it is, by whose presence in a body, that body will be hot, I shan't give you c the old safe, ignorant answer, that it's *hotness*, but a subtler answer now available, that it's *fire*. And again, if you ask what it is, by whose presence in a body, that body will ail, I shan't say that it's *illness*, but *fever*. And again, if asked what it is, by whose presence in a number, that number will be odd, I shan't say *oddness*, but *oneness*; and so on. See whether by now you have an adequate understanding of what I want.'

'Yes, quite adequate.'

'Answer then, and tell me what it is, by whose presence in a body, that body will be living.'

'Soul.'

'And is this always so?'   d

'Of course.'

'Then soul, whatever it occupies, always comes to that thing bringing life?'

'It comes indeed.'

'And is there an opposite to life, or is there none?'

'There is.'

'What is it?'

'Death.'

'Now soul will absolutely never admit the opposite of what it brings up, as has been agreed earlier?'

'Most emphatically,' said Cebes.

'Well now, what name did we give just now to what doesn't admit the form of the even?'

'Un-even.'

'And to that which doesn't admit the just, and to whatever doesn't admit the musical?'

'Un-musical, and un-just.'   e

'Well then, what do we call whatever doesn't admit death?'

'Im-mortal.'

'But soul doesn't admit death?'

'No.'

'Then soul is immortal.'

'It's immortal.'

'Very well. May we say that this much has been proved? Or how does it seem to you?'

'Yes, and very adequately proved, Socrates.'

'Now what about this, Cebes? If it were necessary for the uneven to be imperishable, three
106a would be imperishable, wouldn't it?'

'Of course.'

'Or again, if the un-hot were necessarily imperishable likewise, then whenever anyone brought hot against snow, the snow would get out of the way, remaining intact and unmelted? Because it couldn't perish, nor again could it abide and admit the hotness.'

'True.'

'And in the same way, I imagine, if the un-coolable were imperishable, then whenever something cold attacked the fire, it could never be put out nor could it perish, but it would depart and go away intact.'

'It would have to.'

b 'Then aren't we compelled to say the same thing about the im-mortal? If the immortal is also imperishable, it's impossible for soul, whenever death attacks it, to perish. Because it follows from what's been said before that it won't admit death, nor will it be dead, just as we said that three will not be even, any more than the odd will be; and again that fire will not be cold, any more than the hotness in the fire will be. "But", someone might say, "what's to prevent the odd, instead of coming to be even, as we granted it didn't, when the even
c attacks, from perishing, and there coming to be even in its place?" Against one who said that, we could not contend that it doesn't perish; because the uneven is not imperishable. If that had been granted us, we could easily have contended that when the even attacks, the odd and three depart and go away. And we could have contended similarly about fire and hot and the rest, couldn't we?'

'Certainly we could.'

'So now, about the immortal likewise: if it's granted us that it must also be imperishable,
d then soul, besides being immortal, would also be imperishable; but if not, another argument would be needed.'

'But there's no need of one, on that score at least. Because it could hardly be that anything else wouldn't admit destruction if the immortal, being everlasting, is going to admit destruction.'

'Well God anyway,' said Socrates, 'and the form of life itself, and anything else immortal there may be, never perish, as would, I think, be agreed by everyone.'

'Why yes, to be sure; by all men and still more, I imagine, by gods.'

e 'Then, given that the immortal is also indestructible, wouldn't soul, if it proves to be immortal, be imperishable as well?'

'It absolutely must be imperishable.'

'Then when death attacks a man, his mortal part, it seems, dies; whereas the immortal part gets out of the way of death, departs, and goes away intact and undestroyed.'

'It appears so.'

'Beyond all doubt then, Cebes, soul is immortal and imperishable, and our souls really
107a will exist in Hades.'

'Well, Socrates, for my part I've no further objection, nor can I doubt the arguments at any point. But if Simmias here or anyone else has anything to say, he'd better not keep silent; as I know of no future occasion to which anyone wanting to speak or hear about such things could put it off.'

'Well no,' said Simmias; 'nor have I any further ground for doubt myself, as far as the
b arguments go; though in view of the size of the subject under discussion, and having a low regard for human weakness, I'm bound to retain some doubt in my mind about what's been said.'

'Not only that, Simmias,' said Socrates; 'what you say is right, so the initial hypotheses, even if they're acceptable to you people, should still be examined more clearly: if you analyse them adequately, you will, I believe, follow the argument to the furthest point to which man can follow it up; and if you get that clear, you'll seek nothing further.'

'What you say is true.'

'But this much it's fair to keep in mind, friends: if a soul *is* immortal, then it needs care, c not only for the sake of this time in which what we call "life" lasts, but for the whole of time; and if anyone is going to neglect it, now the risk *would* seem fearful. Because if death were a separation from everything, it would be a godsend for the wicked, when they died, to be separated at once from the body and from their own wickedness along with the soul; but since, in fact, it is evidently immortal, there would be no other refuge from ills or d salvation for it, except to become as good and wise as possible. For the soul enters Hades taking nothing else but its education and nurture, which are, indeed, said to do the greatest benefit or harm to the one who has died, at the very outset of his journey yonder.'

[...]

PHAEDO: [Socrates] got up and went to a room to bathe and Crito followed him in and told 116a us to stay put. And so as we waited by ourselves we talked and thought about what had been said, and then we discussed the catastrophe that had happened to us, since we absolutely believed that we would have to spend the rest of our lives just like orphans who had lost a father. And when he had bathed, his children were brought to him – he had two small b sons and an older one – and the women of the house came, and when he had spoken to them in front of Crito and had instructed them about what he wanted, he told the women and children to leave, and he came back in with us. The sun was already near setting. He had spent a long time within. After bathing, he came out and sat down and didn't say much after that, and the servant of the Eleven came and stood near him and said, 'Socrates, I won't c think of you the way I think of others, because they made it difficult for me and cursed at me when I gave the order to drink the poison when the officers required it. But I know you to be the noblest and gentlest man who's ever come here. And now especially I know that you're not going to be upset with me – for you know who's responsible – but at them. So now you know what I came to tell you. Farewell and try to bear what you must endure as easily as possible.' With tears in his eyes, he turned around and went out.   d

And Socrates looked up at him and said, 'Farewell to you and we'll do what you say.' And at the same time he said to us, 'How kind this man is. Throughout my whole time here, he put up with me and talked with me sometimes, and couldn't have been better. And now how genuinely he's weeping for me! But come, Crito, let's obey him and let someone bring the poison if it's been ground up. If not, let the man go ahead and grind it up.'

And Crito said, 'But, Socrates, I think that the sun is still on the mountains and hasn't e gone down yet. And I know that others wait until well after they have been ordered to drink the poison, eating and drinking all they want, and even having sex with their lovers. Don't be in a hurry. There's still time.' Socrates said, 'It's understandable, Crito, that they do the things you're talking about, for they think that in doing them they're benefiting from it. But it wouldn't be a reasonable thing for me to do. For I think that by drinking the poison a 117a little later, I'll have nothing to show for it but looking ridiculous in my own eyes, hanging on to life and being "stingy with the cup when there is nothing in it." So, come, he said, obey, and don't refuse me.'

And when Crito heard this, he motioned to a slave who was nearby, and after he'd delayed quite a while, he came, leading the one who was to deliver the poison, carrying what had been ground up in a drinking cup. And when Socrates saw the man, he said, 'My good man, since you know about these things, what should I do?'

117b 'Nothing but drink it and move around until your legs get heavy, and lie down. It'll do its work.' And then he offered the cup to Socrates.

And he took it quite gratefully, and without any fear and without changing the color or the expression on his face, looking at the man in his familiar bull-like way, he said, 'What do you say about pouring a libation from the drink? Is it permitted or not?'

'We ground out, Socrates,' he said, 'what we think is the right amount to drink.'

c 'I understand,' he said, 'but surely it is possible – and indeed one ought to say a prayer to the gods that the journey from here to there will be a happy one. That's what I pray and may it turn out to be so.' And as he said these things and was holding the cup, he drank it down quite easily and calmly. Most of us had been able to keep from crying reasonably well up 'til then, but when we saw him drinking and then after he had drunk, we were no longer able to do hold back. My tears came flooding out uncontrollably, so when I had bowed my

d head, I was weeping – not at all for him – but for my misfortune, such a companion was I losing. Crito got up before me, since he wasn't able to hold back his tears. And Apollodoros had been crying all along and especially at this point exploded with wailing and anger and made everyone present break down except Socrates. 'What are you doing?' he said. 'That's

e just why I sent the women away, so that I wouldn't have to put up with that! For I've heard that one should die in solemn silence. So keep quiet and bear up!' And when we heard this, we kept quiet and held back our tears. He walked around and when he said that his legs were heavy, he lay down on his back, for that's what the man told him to do. And then the one who administered the poison touched him, and after a time examined his feet and legs and after pressing hard on his foot, he asked him if he could feel anything. And he said that

118a he couldn't. Next he touched his calves and going up in this way he demonstrated to us that they were cold and stiff. And then he touched him and said that when it, the coldness, reaches his heart, he'll be gone.[1] And then the coldness was almost to his abdomen, and he uncovered his head – for he had covered it and he said his last words, 'Crito, we owe a cock to Asclepius. Pay it and don't neglect it.' Crito said, 'It'll be done. Tell us if you want anything else.' And after Crito said this, Socrates didn't answer. After a little while he moved, the man uncovered him, and his eyes were fixed. When Crito saw this, he closed his mouth and eyes. Such Echecrates was the end of our companion – a man, we could say, who was of those we knew living at that time the best and also the wisest and most just.

1 The symptoms of hemlock poisoning described here have been much disputed by scholars, with some even claiming that Plato's description here is entirely misleading and inaccurate. However, it is anything but obvious what Plato would hope to gain by having the prison attendant explain the working of the most common form of execution at this period in a way that was patently (and demonstrably) false. In any case, the most recent work on this subject strongly supports Plato's accuracy.

13

Symposium

The *Symposium* is set in Agathon's house, to celebrate his recent victory in the drama competition. There has been quite a drunken bash the night before, leaving the celebrants on this next evening still hung over and somewhat leery of another long night of drinking. So one of the assembled company proposes that the evening should be spent making speeches in praise of *erōs* (somewhat misleadingly, but inevitably translated as "love"). Most ancient Greek literature characterizes *erōs* quite negatively: it is said to be painful, maddening, and sometimes deadly. But in this dialogue the proposal is made that praising it would be to show proper reverence for an ancient god. The result is a series of speeches, each one more clever than the last, and culminating in a remarkable speech by Socrates, who attributes all he has to say to a prophetess named Diotima. In this speech, Plato has Socrates explicate what has come to be known as "Platonic love." All love is motivated by our innate desire for Beauty; but the most common expressions of love are incomplete: the true lover will climb the "ladder of love," seeking to make intellectual contact with Beauty itself.

And now I'll let you[1] go. But the account of Eros I once heard from a Mantinaean woman, 201d Diotima, who was wise in this and many other things – she once caused the Athenians, when they offered sacrifices before the Plague,[2] a ten-year delay in the onset of the disease, and it was she who instructed me in the things of love – well, the account she used to give I will myself try to describe to you[3] on my own, from the agreements which Agathon and I have reached, as best I can.

It is necessary then, Agathon, as you explained, first to recount who Eros is and of what e sort, and his works afterwards.[4] Now, I think I can most easily recount it as she used to do in examining me. For I used to say pretty much the same sort of thing to her that Agathon was saying now to me, that Eros would be a great god, but of beautiful things; but she refuted me by these arguments I offered him, that Eros by my account would be neither beautiful nor good.

1 Singular, addressed to Agathon.
2 In 430 BC. See Thucydides II 47.
3 Plural. Socrates is now addressing the company.
4 Socrates loosely repeats Agathon's formula at 195a, but with significant emphasis on who Eros is.

And I said, How do you mean, Diotima? Eros then is ugly and bad?

And she said, Hush, don't blaspheme! Or do you suppose that whatever is not beautiful is necessarily ugly?

202a Yes, of course.

And not wise, ignorant? Are you not aware that there is something intermediate between wisdom and ignorance?

What is it?

Don't you know, she said, that right opinion without ability to render an account is not knowledge – for how could an unaccountable thing be knowledge? – nor is it ignorance – for how could what meets with what is be ignorance? Right opinion is surely that sort of thing, intermediate between wisdom and ignorance.

True, I said.

b Then don't compel what is not beautiful to be ugly, nor what is not good to be bad. So too for Eros, since you yourself agree that he is neither good nor beautiful, do not any the more for that reason suppose he must be ugly and bad, she said, but rather something between these two.

And yet, I said, everybody agrees he is a great god.

You mean everybody who doesn't know, or also those who know? she said.

Why, absolutely everybody.

She laughed and said, And how would he be agreed to be a great god, Socrates, by those

c who say he is not even a god at all?

Who are these people?, I said.

You're one, she said, and I'm another.

And I said, How can you say that?

Easily, she replied. For tell me: don't you claim that all gods are happy and beautiful? Or would you dare deny that any god is beautiful and happy?

Emphatically not, I said.

But you say that it is those who possess good and beautiful things who are happy?

Of course.

d Moreover, you have agreed that Eros, by reason of lack of good and beautiful things, desires those very things he lacks.

Yes, I have.

How then would what is without portion of beautiful and good things be a god?

In no way, it seems.

Then you see, she said, that even you do not acknowledge Eros to be a god?

Then what is he? I said. A mortal?

Hardly.

But what, then?

As I said before, she said, intermediate between mortal and immortal.

What is he, Diotima?

A great divinity, Socrates; for in fact, the whole realm of divinities is intermediate

e between god and mortal.

Having what power? I said.

Interpreting and conveying things from men to gods and things from gods to men, prayers and sacrifices from the one, commands and requitals in exchange for sacrifices from the other, since, being in between both, it fills the region between both so that the All is bound together with itself. Through this realm moves all prophetic art and the art of priests

having to do with sacrifices and rituals and spells, and all power of prophecy and enchantment. God does not mingle with man, but all intercourse and conversation of gods with 203a
men, waking and sleeping, are through this realm. He who is wise about such things as this
is a divine man, but he who is wise about any other arts or crafts is a mere mechanic.[5] These
divinities, then, are many and manifold, and one of them is Eros.

Who is father and mother?[6] I said.

It's a rather long story, she replied; nevertheless, I will tell you. When Aphrodite was born, b
the gods banqueted, both the others and Poros, Resourcefulness, son of Metis, Wisdom. When
they dined, Penia, Want, came to beg, as one would expect when there is a feast, and hung
about the doors. Well, Poros got drunk on nectar – for there was as yet no wine – and went
into the garden of Zeus where, weighed down by drink, he slept. So Penia plotted to have
a child by Poros by reason of her own resourcelessness, and lay with him and conceived c
Eros. This is why Eros has been a follower and servant of Aphrodite, because he was begotten on the day of her birth,[7] and at the same time it is why he is by nature a lover of beauty,
since Aphrodite is beautiful.

Because then Eros is son of Poros and Penia, this is his fortune: first, he is ever poor, and
far from being delicate and beautiful, as most people suppose, he on the contrary is rough
and hard and homeless and unshod, ever lying on the ground without bedding, sleeping in d
doorsteps and beside roads under the open sky. Because he has his mother's nature, he dwells
ever with want. But on the other hand, by favor of his father, he ever plots for good and
beautiful things, because he is courageous, eager and intense, and clever hunter ever
weaving some new device, desiring understanding and capable of it, a lover of wisdom
through the whole of life, clever at enchantment, a sorcerer and a sophist.[8] And he is by
nature neither mortal nor immortal, but sometimes on the same day he lives and flourishes, e
whenever he is full of resource, but then he dies and comes back to life again by reason of
the nature of his father, though what is provided ever slips away so that Eros is never rich
nor at a loss and on the other hand he is between wisdom and ignorance. For things stand
thus: no god loves wisdom or desires to become wise – for he is so; nor, if anyone else is 204a
wise, does he love wisdom. On the other hand, neither do the ignorant love wisdom nor
desire to become wise; for ignorance is difficult just in this, that though not beautiful and
good, nor wise, it yet seems to itself to be sufficient. He who does not think himself in need
does not desire what he does not think he lacks.

Then who are these lovers of wisdom, Diotima, I said, if they are neither the wise nor
the ignorant?

Why, at this point it's clear even to a child, she said, that they are those intermediate between 204b
both of these, and that Eros is among them. For wisdom is surely among the most beautiful of things, but Eros is love of the beautiful, so Eros is necessarily a philosopher, a lover
of wisdom, and, being a philosopher, intermediate between wisdom and ignorance. His birth

---

5 Cf. *Republic* VI 495d–e.

6 The question arises from the fact that Eros is a "divinity," and so either a god or a child of gods.

7 Dover, *Symposium*, remarks on this passage: "Hesiod's injunction (*WD* 735 f.) 'do not beget offspring
when you have come home from a funeral, but from a festival of the immortals,' shows the existence
of a belief in some kind of connection between the character or fortunes of a child and the occasion
of his or her conception."

8 Diotima is herself said to be "most wise," and her mode or reply compared to "an accomplished
sophist" at 208b–c.

is the cause of this too: for he is of a wise and resourceful father, but of an unwise and resource-less mother.

c This then is the nature of the divinity, my dear Socrates; but there is nothing surprising about what you thought Eros is. You thought, as I gather from what you say, that Eros is what is loved, not the loving. That is why, I think, Eros seemed utterly beautiful to you. In fact, it is what is beloved that is really beautiful and charming and perfect and deemed blessed; but loving has this other character, of the sort I described.

And I said: Very well then, my dear lady; you speak beautifully. But if Eros is of this sort, what usefulness does he have for men?

d That's the next thing I will try to teach you, Socrates, she said. For since Eros is of this sort and this parentage, he is of beautiful things, as you say. But suppose someone asked us, Why is Eros of beautiful things, Socrates and Diotima? I will ask still more clearly: Why does he who loves, love beautiful things?

And I replied, To possess them for himself.

But the answer still longs for the following kind of question, she said: What will he have who possesses beautiful things?

I still can't quite readily answer that question, I said.

e But suppose someone changed "beautiful" to "good," she said, and then inquired: Come, Socrates, he who loves, loves good things. Why does he love them?

To possess them for himself.

And what will he have who possesses good things?

This I can answer more easily, I said. He will be happy.

205a Yes, she said; for the happy are happy by possession of good things, and there is no need in addition to ask further for what purpose he who wishes to be happy wishes it. On the contrary, the answer seems final.

True, I replied.

Do you think this wish and this love are common to all men, and that everyone wishes to possess good things for themselves forever?

Yes, I said: it is common to everyone.

Why is it then, Socrates, she said, that we do not say that everyone loves, if indeed every-

b one loves the same things, and always, but we rather say that some love and some do not?

I'm also surprised myself, I said.

Don't be, she said. It is because we subtract a certain species of eros and name it Eros, applying the name of the whole, but we use other names for the others.

As what? I said.

As this. You know that making [poiēsis] is something manifold; for surely the cause of passing from not being into being for anything whatever is all a making, so that the pro-

c ductions of all the arts are makings, and the practitioners of them are all makers [poiēsis].

True.

But nevertheless, she said, you know that they are not called makers [poiēsis] but have other names, while from all making one single part has been subtracted, that concerned with music[9] and meter, and given the name of the whole. For this alone is called poetry [poiēsis], and those who have this part of making are called poets [poiēsis].

True, I said.

9 *Mousikē* was any art over which the Muses preside, but especially poetry, which was sung. Cf. *Republic* II 376e.

So also then for Eros. In general, it is every desire for good things and happiness, "Eros   d
most great, and wily[10] in all"; but those who turn to him in various other ways, either money-
making or athletics or philosophy, are neither said to love nor to be lovers, while those who
sedulously pursue one single species get the name of the whole, Eros, and are said to love
and be lovers.

Very likely true, I said.

Yes, and a certain story is told, she said, that those in love are seeking the other half of
themselves. But my account is that love is of neither half nor whole, my friend, unless it   e
happens to be actually good, since people are willing to cut off their own hands and feet if
they think these possessions of theirs are bad. For they each refuse, I think, to cleave even
to what is their own, unless one calls what is good kindred and his own, and what is bad
alien; because there is nothing else that men love than the good. Do you agree?   206a

I most certainly do, I said.

Then one may state without qualification that men love the good? she said.

Yes, I said.

Really? Is it not to be added, she said, that they also love the good to be their own?

It must.

And not only to be theirs, she said, but also to be theirs forever?

This too is to be added.

In sum, then, she said, Eros is of the good, being his own forever.

Very true, I replied.

Then given that Eros is ever this, she said, in what way, and in what activity, would eager-   b
ness and effort among those pursuing it be called Eros? What does this work happen to be?
Can you say?

No, I said. If I could, I would not admire your wisdom so much, Diotima, and keep coming to you to learn these very things.

But I will tell you, she said: this work is begetting[11] in beauty, in respect to both the body
and the soul.

What you say needs divination, I said, and I don't understand.

Why, I'll put it more clearly, she said. All men are pregnant in respect to both the body   c
and the soul, Socrates, she said, and when they reach a certain age, our nature desires to
beget. It cannot beget in ugliness, but only in beauty. The intercourse of man and woman
is a begetting. This is a divine thing, and pregnancy and procreation are an immortal element in the mortal living creature. It is impossible for birth to take place in what is discordant. But ugliness is in discord with all that is divine, and beauty concordant. So the Goddess   d
of Beauty is at the birth Moira, Fate, and Eilithyia, She Who Comes in Time of Need. That
is why, when what is pregnant draws near to the beautiful, it becomes tender and full of
gladness and pours itself forth and begets and procreates; but when it draws near to the ugly,
it shrivels in sullen grief and turns away and goes slack and does not beget, but carries with
difficulty the conception within it. Whence it is that one who is pregnant and already swollen
is vehemently excited over the beautiful, because it releases its possessor from great pangs.   206e
For Socrates, she said, Eros is not, as you suppose, of the beautiful.

But what, then?

---

10 *Doleros*. The adjective is otherwise rare in Plato, but applied at *Hippias Minor* 365c to Odysseus. See
above, 203d.

11 Or bearing children.

It is of procreation and begetting of children in the beautiful.

Very well, I said.

207a To be sure, she said. But why of procreation? Because procreation is everlasting and immortal as far as is possible for something mortal. Eros necessarily desires immortality with the good, from what has been agreed,[12] since its object is to possess the good for itself forever. It necessarily follows from this account, then, that Eros is also love of immortality.

All these things she taught me at various times when she discoursed about matters of love. Once she asked, Socrates, what do you think is cause of this love and desire? Or are you not aware how strangely all beasts are disposed, footed and winged, when they desire to

b reproduce – all sick and erotically disposed, first for intercourse with each other and next for the nurture of the offspring? In their behalf the weakest are ready to do battle with the strongest, to die in their behalf, to be racked with hunger themselves so as to feed them, to do anything else. One might suppose, she said, that men do these things on the basis of reflection;

c but what is the cause of beasts being erotically disposed this way? Can you tell?

And I again used to say I didn't know.

She said, Then do you think you'll ever become skilled in the things of love if you don't understand this?

Why, that's why I keep coming to you, Diotima, as I just now said,[13] knowing I need instruction. Please tell me the cause of this, and other things concerning matters of love.

If then you are persuaded, she said, that love is by nature of what we have often agreed,

d do not be surprised. For here, in the animal world, by the same account as before, the mortal nature seeks so far as it can to exist forever and be immortal. It can do so only in this way, by giving birth, ever leaving behind a different new thing in place of the old, since even in the time in which each single living creature is said to live and to be the same – for example, as a man is said to be the same from youth to old age – though he never has the same things in himself, he nevertheless is called the same, but he is ever becoming new while otherwise perishing, in respect to hair and flesh and bone and blood and the entire body.

e And not only in respect to the body but also in respect to the soul,[14] its character and habits, opinions, desires, pleasures, pains, fears are each never present in each man as the same, but some are coming to be, others perishing. Much more extraordinary still, not only

208a are some kinds of knowledge coming to be and others perishing in us, and we are never the same even in respect to the kinds of knowledge, but also each single one among the kinds of knowledge is affected in the same way. For what is called studying exists because knowledge leaves us; forgetting is departure of knowledge, but study, by introducing again a new memory in place of what departs, preserves the knowledge so that it seems to be the same.[15]

For it is in this way that all that is mortal is preserved: not by being ever completely the

b same, like the divine, but by leaving behind, as it departs and becomes older, a different new thing of the same sort as it was. By this device, Socrates, she said, what is mortal has a share of immortality both body and everything else; but what is immortal by another device. Do not be surprised, then, if everything by nature values its own offshoot; it is for the sake of immortality that this eagerness and love attend upon all.

---

12 206a.

13 206b.

14 Application of the claim to the second case distinguished at 206b.

15 Compare Aristotle's account of perception, memory, and experience at *Metaphysics* I 980a 29ff., *Posterior Analytics* II 99b 35ff.

When I heard this account I was surprised and said, Why really, my most wise Diotima, are these things actually true?

And she replied as the accomplished sophists do, Know it well, Socrates. Since indeed if c you will look to the love of honor among men, you'd be surprised by the unreasonableness of which I've spoken, unless you keep in mind and reflect on how strangely disposed men are by Eros to make a name and "lay up store of immortal glory for everlasting time"; for this they are ready to run every risk, even more than for their children, to spend money, to d perform labors of every sort, to die for it. Do you think, she said, that Alcestis would have died for Admetus, or Achilles after Patroclus, or our own Cadmus for his children's king-doms, if they had not thought the fame of their own virtue, which we now cherish, would be immortal? Far from it, she said; rather, I think, it is for immortal virtue and the sort of fame which brings glory that everyone does everything, and the more insofar as they are better. For they love the immortal. e

Some men are pregnant in respect to their bodies, she said, and turn more to women and are lovers in that way, providing in all future time, as they suppose, immortality and hap-piness for themselves through getting children. Others are pregnant in respect to their soul – for there are those, she said, who are still more fertile in their souls than in their bodies 209a with what it pertains to soul to conceive and bear. What then so pertains? Practical wisdom and the rest of virtue – of which, indeed, all the poets are procreators, and as many crafts-men as are said to be inventors. But the greatest and most beautiful kind of practical wisdom by far, she said, is that concerned with the right ordering of cities and households, for which the name is temperance and justice.

On the other hand, whenever one of them is pregnant of soul from youth, being divine, and reaches the age when he then desires to bear and beget, he too then, I think, goes about b seeking the beautiful in which he might beget; for he will never beget in the ugly. Now, because he is fertile, he welcomes beautiful rather than ugly bodies, and should he meet with a beautiful and noble and naturally gifted soul, he welcomes the conjunction of both even more, and to this person he is straightway resourceful in speaking about virtue, and what sort of thing the good man must be concerned with and his pursuits; and he undertakes to educate him.

For I think that in touching the beautiful [person] and holding familiar intercourse with c it [him], he bears and begets what he has long since conceived, and both present and absent he remembers and nurtures what has been begotten in common with that [him],[16] so that people of this sort gain a far greater communion with each other than that of the sharing of children, and a more steadfast friendship, because they have held in common children more beautiful and more immortal. Everyone would prefer for himself to have had such children as these, rather than the human kind, and they look to Homer and Hesiod and the rest of d our good poets and envy offspring of the sort they left behind, offspring which, being such themselves, provide immortal fame and remembrance.

But if you wish, she said, look at the sort of children Lycurgus left behind in Sparta, saviors of Sparta and, one might almost say, of Greece.[17] Solon also is honored among you because

16 This sentence is purposefully ambiguous: it refers to the beloved, but also anticipates what will be said in the Greater Mysteries of Eros about Beauty itself.
17 Diotima speaks as a native of Mantinea, located in the Peloponnesus and allied with Sparta. Lycurgus, like Solon in Athenas, was supposed to have given laws to Sparta, and those laws are here regarded as his children.

of his begetting of the Laws,[18] and other men in other times and many other places, both in
209e Greece and among the barbarians, who have displayed many beautiful deeds and begotten
every sort of virtue; for whom, also, many temples and sacred rites have come into being
because of children such as these, but none because of children merely human.

Into these things of love, Socrates, perhaps even you may be initiated; but I do not know
210a whether you can be initiated into the rites of and revelations for the sake of which these
actually exist if one pursues them correctly. Well, I will speak of them and spare no effort,
she said; try to follow if you can.

It is necessary, she said, for him who proceeds rightly to this thing to begin while still
young by going to beautiful bodies; and first, if his guide[19] guides rightly, to love one single
body and beget there beautiful discourses; next, to recognize that the beauty on any body
b whatever is akin to that on any other body, and if it is necessary to pursue the beautiful as
it attaches to form, it is quite unreasonable to believe that the beauty on all bodies is not
one and the same. Realizing this, he is constituted a lover of all beautiful bodies and relaxes
this vehemence for one, looking down on it and believing it of small importance.

After this he must come to believe that beauty in souls is more to be valued than that in
the body, so that even if someone good of soul has but a slight bloom, it suffices for him,
c and he loves and cares and begets and seeks those sorts of discourses that will make the young
better, in order that he may be constrained in turn to contemplate what is beautiful in practices and laws and to see that it is in itself all akin to itself, in order that he may believe
bodily beauty a small thing.

After practices, he[20] must lead him to the various branches of knowledge, in order that
d he may in turn see their beauty too, and, looking now to the beautiful in its multitude, no
longer delight like a slave, a worthless, petty-minded servant, in the beauty of one single
thing, whether beauty of a young child or man or of one practice; but rather, having been
turned toward the multitudinous ocean of the beautiful and contemplating it, he begets many
beautiful and imposing discourses and thoughts in ungrudging love of wisdom, until, having at this point grown and waxed strong, he beholds a certain kind of knowledge which is
e one, and such that it is the following kind of beauty. Try, she said, to pay me the closest
attention possible.

He who has been educated in the things of love up to this point, beholding beautiful things
rightly and in due order, will then, suddenly, in an instant, proceeding at that point to the
end of the things of love, see something marvelous, beautiful in nature: it is *that*, Socrates,
for the sake of which in fact all his previous labors existed.

211a   First, it ever is and neither comes to be nor perishes, nor has it growth nor diminution.

Again, it is not in one respect beautiful but in another ugly, nor beautiful at one time but
not at another, nor beautiful relative to this but ugly relative to that, nor beautiful here but
ugly there, as being beautiful to some but ugly to others.

Nor on the other hand will it appear beautiful to him as a face does, or hands, or anything else of which body partakes, nor as any discourse or any knowledge does, nor as what
is somewhere in something else, as in an animal, or in earth, or in heaven, or in anything
b else; but it exists in itself alone by itself, single in nature forever, while all other things are

---

18 The Laws of Athens were often referred to as the Laws of Solon, though there had been (sometimes unacknowledged) changes since his time. Plato was a direct and lineal descendant of Solon.
19 Cf. 210c, e, 211c.
20 That is, the guide mentioned at 210a.

beautiful by sharing in *that* in such manner that though the rest come to be and perish, *that* comes to be neither in greater degree nor less and is not at all affected.

But when someone, ascending from things here through the right love of boys, begins clearly to see *that*, the Beautiful, he would pretty well touch the end. For this is the right way to proceed in matters of love, or to be led by another[21] – beginning from these beauti- c ful things here, to ascend ever upward for the sake of *that*, the Beautiful, as though using the steps of a ladder, from one to two, and from two to all beautiful bodies, and from beautiful bodies to beautiful practices, and from practices to beautiful studies, and from studies one arrives in the end at *that* study which is nothing other than the study of *that*, the Beautiful itself, and one knows in the end, by itself, what it is to be beautiful. It is there, if anywhere, dear Socrates, said the Mantinean Stranger, that human life is to be lived: in con- d templating the Beautiful itself. If ever you see it, it will not seem to you as gold or raiment or beautiful boys and youths, which now you look upon dumbstruck; you and many another are ready to gaze on those you love and dwell with them forever, if somehow it were pos- sible, not to eat nor drink but only to watch and be with them.

What then do we suppose it would be like, she said, if it were possible for someone to see the Beautiful itself, pure, unalloyed, unmixed, not full of human flesh and colors, and e the many other kinds of nonsense that attach to mortality, but if he could behold the divine Beauty itself, single in nature? Do you think it a worthless life, she said, for a man to look *there* and contemplate *that* with that by which one must contemplate it, and to be with it? 212a Or are you not convinced, she said, that there alone it will befall him, in seeing the Beautiful with that by which it is visible, to beget, not images of virtue, because he does not touch an image, but true virtue, because he touches the truth? But in begetting true virtue and nurturing it, it is given to him to become dear to god, and if any other among men is immortal, he is too.

These then, Phaedrus and you others, are the things Diotima said, and I am persuaded. Being b persuaded, I try also to persuade others that one would not easily get a better partner for our human nature in acquiring this possession than Eros. Therefore I say that every man should honor Eros, and I myself honor and surpassingly devote myself to the things of love and summon others to do so; now and always, I praise the power and courage of Eros so far as I am able. Consider this speech then, Phaedrus, if you will, an encomium to Eros, or c if you prefer, name it what you please.

---

21 Cf. 210a, c, e.

14

Republic

It is generally agreed that Plato's *Republic* is his greatest work – so great, indeed, that it is counted as one of the most important philosophical works of all time. The dialogue appears to have been written and revised over a number of years.

For reasons of space, we can only include a series of excerpts of important passages from the dialogue. Socrates is speaking with Plato's brothers, Adeimantus and Glaucon, who wish Socrates to provide a defense of justice against those (such as Thrasymachus in the first book of the *Republic*), who claim that justice is preferred to injustice only as a means to avoid punishments – and not as something desirable in itself. The defense that Socrates provides gets its start by comparing justice in the individual to justice in the state, with the result that a sketch of what Socrates calls a *kallipolis* (a "noble state") is provided and defended, and then compared to the workings of an individual soul. Many details of the proposed state remain extremely controversial today, but perhaps none is as radical as Socrates' proposal that philosophers should rule. When challenged to explicate this surprising theory, Plato has Socrates explain a theory of knowledge and reality that supports his view. These theories have come to be known as the very essence of Platonic philosophy.

Book II

358e "They say that doing injustice is naturally good, and suffering injustice bad, but that the bad in suffering injustice far exceeds the good in doing it; so that, when they do injustice to one another and suffer it and taste of both, it seems profitable – to those who are not able to
359a escape the one and choose the other – to set down a compact among themselves neither to do injustice nor to suffer it. And from there they began to set down their own laws and compacts and to name what the law commands lawful and just. And this, then, is the genesis and being of justice; it is a mean between what is best – doing injustice without paying the penalty – and what is worst – suffering injustice without being able to avenge oneself. The just is in the middle between these two, cared for not because it is good but because it is
b honored due to a want of vigor in doing injustice. The man who is able to do it and is truly a man would never set down a compact with anyone not to do injustice and not to suffer

it. He'd be mad. Now the nature of justice is this and of this sort, and it naturally grows out of these sorts of things. So the argument goes.

"That even those who practice it do so unwillingly, from an incapacity to do injustice, we would best perceive if we should in thought do something like this: give each, the just man c and the unjust, license to do whatever he wants, while we follow and watch where his desire will lead each. We would catch the just man red-handed going the same way as the unjust man out of a desire to get the better; this is what any nature naturally pursues as good, while it is law which by force perverts it to honor equality. The license of which I speak would best be realized if they should come into possession of the sort of power that it is said the ancestor of Gyges, the Lydian, once got. They say he was a shepherd toiling in the service d of the man who was then ruling Lydia. There came to pass a great thunderstorm and an earthquake; the earth cracked and a chasm opened at the place where he was pasturing. He saw it, wondered at it, and went down. He saw, along with other quite wonderful things about which they tell tales, a hollow bronze horse. It had windows; peeping in, he saw there was a corpse inside that looked larger than human size. It had nothing on except a gold ring on its hand; he slipped it off and went out. When there was the usual gathering of the shep- e herds to make the monthly report to the king about the flocks, he too came, wearing the ring. Now, while he was sitting with the others, he chanced to turn the collet of the ring to himself, toward the inside of his hand; when he did this, he became invisible to those sitting by him, and they discussed him as though he were away. He wondered at this, and, finger- 360a ing the ring again, he twisted the collet toward the outside; when he had twisted it, he became visible. Thinking this over, he tested whether the ring had this power, and that was exactly his result: when he turned the collet inward, he became invisible, when outward, visible. Aware of this, he immediately contrived to be one of the messengers to the king. When he arrived, he committed adultery with the king's wife and, along with her, set upon the king b and killed him. And so he took over the rule.

"Now if there were two such rings, and the just man would put one on, and the unjust man the other, no one, as it would seem, would be so adamant as to stick by justice and bring himself to keep away from what belongs to others and not lay hold of it, although he had license to take what he wanted from the market without fear, and to go into houses and have intercourse with whomever he wanted, and to slay or release from bonds whom- c ever he wanted, and to do other things as an equal to a god among humans. And in so doing, one would act no differently from the other, but both would go the same way. And yet, someone could say that this is a great proof that no one is willingly just but only when com- pelled to be so. Men do not take it to be a good for them in private, since wherever each supposes he can do injustice, he does it. Indeed, all men suppose injustice is far more to their private profit than justice. And what they suppose is true, as the man who makes this kind d of an argument will say, since if a man were to get hold of such license and were never will- ing to do any injustice and didn't lay his hands on what belongs to others, he would seem most wretched to those who were aware of it, and most foolish too, although they would praise him to each others' faces, deceiving each other for fear of suffering injustice. So much for that.

"As to the judgment itself about the life of these two of whom we are speaking, we'll be e able to make it correctly if we set the most just man and the most unjust in opposition; if we do not, we won't be able to do so. What, then, is this opposition? It is as follows: we shall take away nothing from the injustice of the unjust man nor from the justice of the just man, but we shall take each as perfect in his own pursuit. So, first, let the unjust man act

like the clever craftsmen. An outstanding pilot or doctor is aware of the difference between
361a what is impossible in his art and what is possible, and he attempts the one, and lets the other
go; and if, after all, he should still trip up in any way, he is competent to set himself aright.
Similarly, let the unjust man also attempt unjust deeds correctly, and get away with them,
if he is going to be extremely unjust. The man who is caught must be considered a poor
chap. For the extreme of injustice is to seem to be just when one is not. So the perfectly
unjust man must be given the most perfect injustice, and nothing must be taken away; he
must be allowed to do the greatest injustices while having provided himself with the great-
b est reputation for justice. And if, after all, he should trip up in anything, he has the power
to set himself aright; if any of his unjust deeds should come to light, he is capable both of
speaking persuasively and of using force, to the extent that force is needed, since he is courageous and strong and since he has provided for friends and money. Now, let us set him
down as such, and put beside him in the argument the just man in his turn, a man simple
and noble, who, according to Aeschylus, does not wish to seem, but rather to be, good. The
c seeming must be taken away. For if he should seem just, there would be honors and gifts
for him for seeming to be such. Then it wouldn't be plain whether he is such for the sake
of the just or for the sake of the gifts and honors. So he must be stripped of everything except
justice, and his situation must he made the opposite of the first man's. Doing no injustice,
let him have the greatest reputation for injustice, so that his justice may be put to the test
to see if it is softened by bad reputation and its consequences. Let him go unchanged till
d death, seeming throughout life to be unjust although he is just, so that when each has come
to the extreme – the one of justice, the other of injustice – they can be judged as to which
of the two is happier."

"My, my," I said, "my dear Glaucon, how vigorously you polish up each of the two men
– just like a statue – for their judgment."

"As much as I can," he said. "With two such men it's no longer hard, I suppose, to complete the speech by a description of the kind of life that awaits each. It must be told, then.
e And if it's somewhat rustically told, don't suppose that it is I who speak, Socrates, but rather
362a those who praise injustice ahead of justice. They'll say that the just man who has such a disposition will be whipped; he'll be racked; he'll be bound; he'll have both his eyes burned
out; and, at the end, when he has undergone every sort of evil, he'll be crucified and know
that one shouldn't wish to be, but to seem to be, just. After all, Aeschylus' saying applies far
more correctly to the unjust man. For really, they will say, it is the unjust man, because he
pursues a thing dependent on truth and does not live in the light of opinion, who does not
wish to seem unjust but to be unjust,

> Reaping a deep furrow in his mind
> b   From which trusty plans bear fruit.

First, he rules in the city because he seems to be just. Then he takes in marriage from whatever station he wants and gives in marriage to whomever he wants; he contracts and has
partnerships with whomever he wants and, besides benefiting himself in all this, he gains
because he has no qualms about doing injustice. So then, when he enters contests, both private and public, he wins and gets the better of his enemies. In getting the better, he is wealthy
c and does good to friends and harm to enemies. To the gods he makes sacrifices and sets
up votive offerings, adequate and magnificent, and cares for the gods and those human
beings he wants to care for far better than the just man. So, in all likelihood, it is also more

appropriate for him to be dearer to the gods than is the just man. Thus, they say, Socrates, with gods and with humans, a better life is provided for the unjust man than for the just man."

[...]

Glaucon and the others begged me in every way to help out and not to give up the argu- 368c ment, but rather to seek out what each is and the truth about the benefit of both. So I spoke my opinion.

"It looks to me as though the investigation we are undertaking is no ordinary thing, but one for a man who sees sharply. Since we're not clever men," I said, "in my opinion we d should make this kind of investigation of it: if someone had, for example, ordered men who don't see very sharply to read little letters from afar and then someone had the thought that the same letters are somewhere else also, but bigger and in a bigger place, I suppose it would look like a godsend to be able to consider the littler ones after having read these first, if, of course, they do happen to be the same."

"Most certainly," said Adeimantus. "But, Socrates, what do you notice in the investigation of the just that's like this?"   e

"I'll tell you," I said. "There is, we say, justice of one man; and there is, surely, justice of a whole city too?"

"Certainly," he said.

"Is a city bigger than one man?"

"Yes, it is bigger;" he said.

"So then, perhaps there would be more justice in the bigger and it would be easier to observe closely. If you want, first we'll investigate what justice is like in the cities. Then, 369a we'll also go on to consider it in individuals, considering the likeness of the bigger in the *idea* of the littler?"

"What you say seems fine to me," he said.

"If we should watch a city coming into being in speech," I said, "would we also see its justice coming into being, and its injustice?"

"Probably," he said.

"When this has been done, can we hope to see what we're looking for more easily?"

"Far more easily."   b

"Is it resolved that we must try to carry this out? I suppose it's no small job, so consider it."

"It's been considered," said Adeimantus. "Don't do anything else."

"Well, then," I said, "a city, as I believe, comes into being because each of us isn't self-sufficient but is in need of much. Do you believe there's another beginning to the founding of a city?"

"None at all," he said.

"So, then, when one man takes on another for one need and another for another need, c and, since many things are needed, many men gather in one settlement as partners and helpers, to this common settlement we give the name city, don't we?"

"Most certainly."

"Now, does one man give a share to another, if he does give a share, or take a share, in the belief that it's better for himself?"

"Certainly."

"Come, now," I said, "let's make a city in speech from the beginning. Our need, as it seems, will make it."

"Of course."

369d "Well, now, the first and greatest of needs is the provision of food for existing and living."

"Certainly."

"Second, of course, is housing, and third, clothing, and such."

"That's so."

"Now wait," I said. "How will the city be sufficient to provide for this much? Won't one man be a farmer, another the housebuilder, and still another, a weaver? Or shall we add to it a shoemaker or some other man who cares for what has to do with the body?"

"Certainly."

"The city of utmost necessity would be made of four or five men."

e "It looks like it."

"Now, what about this? Must each one of them put his work at the disposition of all in common – for example, must the farmer, one man, provide food for four and spend four times as much time and labor in the provision of food and then give it in common to the others; or must he neglect them and produce a fourth part of the food in a fourth part of

370a the time and use the other three parts for the provision of a house, clothing, and shoes, not taking the trouble to share in common with others, but minding his own business for himself?"

And Adeimantus said, "Perhaps, Socrates, the former is easier than the latter."

"It wouldn't be strange, by Zeus," I said. "I myself also had the thought when you spoke that, in the first place, each of us is naturally not quite like anyone else, but rather differs in his

b nature; different men are apt for the accomplishment of different jobs. Isn't that your opinion?"

"It is."

"And, what about this? Who would do a finer job, one man practicing many arts, or one man one art?"

"One man, one art," he said.

"And, further, it's also plain, I suppose, that if a man lets the crucial moment in any work pass, it is completely ruined."

"Yes, it is plain."

"I don't suppose the thing done is willing to await the leisure of the man who does it; but it's necessary for the man who does it to follow close upon the thing done, and not as a

c spare-time occupation."

"It is necessary."

"So, on this basis each thing becomes more plentiful, finer, and easier, when one man, exempt from other tasks, does one thing according to nature and at the crucial moment."

"That's entirely certain."

"Now, then, Adeimantus, there's need of more citizens than four for the provisions of which we were speaking. For the farmer, as it seems, won't make his own plow himself, if

d it's going to be a fine one, or his hoe, or the rest of the tools for farming; and the housebuilder won't either – and he needs many too. And it will be the same with the weaver and the shoemaker, won't it?"

"True."

"So, carpenters, smiths, and many other craftsmen of this sort become partners in our little city, making it into a throng."

"Most certainly."

"But it wouldn't be very big yet, if we added cowherds, shepherds, and the other kinds

e of herdsmen, so that the farmers would have oxen for plowing, the housebuilders teams to use with the farmers for hauling, and the weavers and cobblers hides and wool."

"Nor would it be a little city," he said, "when it has all this."

"And, further," I said, "just to found the city itself in the sort of place where there will be no need of imports is pretty nearly impossible."

"Yes, it is impossible."

"Then, there will also be a need for still other men who will bring to it what's needed from another city."

"Yes, they will be needed."

"Now, if the agent comes empty-handed, bringing nothing needed by those from whom they take what they themselves need, he'll go away empty-handed, won't he?"   371a

"It seems so to me."

"Then they must produce at home not only enough for themselves but also the sort of thing and in the quantity needed by these others of whom they have need."

"Yes, they must."

"So our city needs more farmers and other craftsmen."

"It does need more."

"And similarly, surely, other agents as well, who will import and export the various products. They are merchants, aren't they?"

"Yes."

"Then, we'll need merchants too."

"Certainly."

"And if the commerce is carried on by sea, there will also be need of throngs of other men who know the business of the sea."   b

"Throngs, indeed."

"Now what about this? In the city itself, how will they exchange what they have produced with one another? It was for just this that we made a partnership and founded the city."

"Plainly," he said, "by buying and selling."

"Out of this we'll get a market and an established currency as a token for exchange."

"Most certainly."

"If the farmer or any other craftsman brings what he has produced to the market, and he c doesn't arrive at the same time as those who need what he has to exchange, will he sit in the market idle, his craft unattended?"

"Not at all," he said. "There are men who see this situation and set themselves to this service; in rightly governed cities they are usually those whose bodies are weakest and are useless for doing any other job. They must stay there in the market and exchange things for d money with those who need to sell something and exchange, for money again, with all those who need to buy something."

"This need, then, produces tradesmen in our city," I said. "Don't we call tradesmen those men who are set up in the market to serve in buying and selling, and merchants those who wander among the cities?"

"Most certainly."

"There are, I suppose, still some other servants who, in terms of their minds, wouldn't e be quite up to the level of partnership, but whose bodies are strong enough for labor. They sell the use of their strength and, because they call their price a wage, they are, I suppose, called wage earners, aren't they?"

"Most certainly."

"So the wage earners too, as it seems, go to fill out the city."

"It seems so to me."

"Then has our city already grown to completeness, Adeimantus?"

"Perhaps."

"Where in it, then, would justice and injustice be? Along with which of the things we considered did they come into being?"

372a "I can't think, Socrates," he said, "unless it's somewhere in some need these men have of one another."

"Perhaps what you say is fine," I said. "It really must be considered and we mustn't back away. First, let's consider what manner of life men so provided for will lead. Won't they make bread, wine, clothing, and shoes? And, when they have built houses, they will work in the summer, for the most part naked and without shoes, and in the winter adequately

b clothed and shod. For food they will prepare barley meal and wheat flour; they will cook it and knead it. Setting out noble loaves of barley and wheat on some reeds or clean leaves, they will stretch out on rushes strewn with yew and myrtle and feast themselves and their children. Afterwards they will drink wine and, crowned with wreathes, sing of the gods. So they will have sweet intercourse with one another, and not produce children beyond their

c means, keeping an eye out against poverty or war."

And Glaucon interrupted, saying: "You seem to make these men have their feast without relishes."

"What you say is true," I said. "I forgot that they'll have relishes, too – it's plain they'll have salt, olives, cheese; and they will boil onions and greens, just as one gets them in the country. And to be sure, we'll set desserts before them – figs, pulse and beans; and they'll roast myrtle-berries and acorns before the fire and drink in measure along with it. And so

d they will live out their lives in peace with health, as is likely, and at last, dying as old men, they will hand down other similar lives to their offspring."

And he said, "If you were providing for a city of sows, Socrates, on what else would you fatten them than this?"

"Well, how should it be, Glaucon?" I said.

"As is conventional," he said. "I suppose men who aren't going to he wretched recline on

e couches and eat from tables and have relishes and desserts just like men have nowadays."

"All right," I said. "I understand. We are, as it seems, considering not only how a city, but also a luxurious city, comes into being. Perhaps that's not bad either. For in considering such a city too, we could probably see in what way justice and injustice naturally grow in cities. Now, the true city is in my opinion the one we just described – a healthy city, as it were. But, if you want to, let's look at a feverish city, too. Nothing stands in the way. For these

373a things, as it seems, won't satisfy some, or this way of life, but couches, tables, and other furniture will be added, and, of course, relishes, perfume, incense, courtesans and cakes – all sorts of all of them. And, in particular, we can't still postulate the mere necessities we were talking about at first – houses, clothes, and shoes; but painting and embroidery must also be set in motion; and gold, ivory, and everything of the sort must be obtained. Isn't that so?"

b "Yes," he said.

"Then the city must be made bigger again. This healthy one isn't adequate any more, but must already be gorged with a bulky mass of things, which are not in cities because of necessity – all the hunters and imitators, many concerned with figures and colors, many with music; and poets and their helpers, rhapsodes, actors, choral dancers, contractors, and craftsmen of

c all sorts of equipment, for feminine adornment as well as other things. And so we'll need more servants too. Or doesn't it seem there will be need of teachers, wet nurses, governesses, beauticians, barbers, and, further, relish-makers and cooks? And, what's more, we're in addition going to need swineherds. This animal wasn't in our earlier city – there was no need – but in this one there will be need of it in addition. And there'll also be need of very many other fatted beasts if someone will eat them, won't there?"

"Of course."

"Won't we be in much greater need of doctors if we follow this way of life rather than d the earlier one?"

"Much greater."

"And the land, of course, which was then sufficient for feeding the men who were then, will now be small although it was sufficient. Or how should we say it?"

"Like that," he said.

"Then must we cut off a piece of our neighbors' land, if we are going to have sufficient for pasture and tillage, and they in turn from ours, if they let themselves go to the unlimited acquisition of money, overstepping the boundary of the necessary?"

"Quite necessarily, Socrates," he said.   e

"After that won't we go to war as a consequence, Glaucon? Or how will it be?"

"Like that," he said.

"And let's not yet say whether war works evil or good," I said, "but only this much, that we have in its turn found the origin of war – in those things whose presence in cities most of all produces evils both private and public."

"Most certainly."

"Now, my friend, the city must be still bigger, and not by a small number but by a whole army, which will go out and do battle with invaders for all the wealth and all the things we 374a were just now talking about."

"What," he said, "aren't they adequate by themselves?"

"Not if that was a fine agreement you and all we others made when we were fashioning the city," I said. "Surely we were in agreement, if you remember, that it's impossible for one man to do a fine job in many arts."

"What you say is true," he said.

"Well then," I said, "doesn't the struggle for victory in war seem to be a matter for art?" b

"Very much so," he said.

"Should one really care for the art of shoemaking more than for the art of war?"

"Not at all."

"But, after all, we prevented the shoemaker from trying at the same time to be a farmer or a weaver or a housebuilder; he had to stay a shoemaker just so the shoemaker's art would produce fine work for us. And in the same way, to each one of the others we assigned one thing, the one for which his nature fitted him, at which he was to work throughout his life, exempt from the other tasks, not letting the crucial moments pass, and thus doing a fine job. c Isn't it of the greatest importance that what has to do with war be well done? Or is it so easy that a farmer or a shoemaker or a man practicing any other art whatsoever can be at the same time skilled in the art of war, while no one could become an adequate draughts or dice player who didn't practice it from childhood on, but only gave it his spare time? Will a man, if he picks up a shield or any other weapon or tool of war, on that very day be an d adequate combatant in a battle of heavy-armed soldiers, or any other kind of battle in war, even though no other tool if picked up will make anyone a craftsman or contestant, nor will it even be of use to the man who has not gained knowledge of it or undergone adequate training?"

"In that case," he said, "the tools would be worth a lot."

"Then," I said, "to the extent that the work of the guardians is more important, it would
374e require more leisure time than the other tasks as well as greater art and diligence."

"I certainly think so," he said.

"And also a nature fit for the pursuit?"

"Of course."

"Then it's our job, as it seems, to choose, if we're able, which are the natures, and what
kind they are, fit for guarding the city."

"Indeed it is our job."

"By Zeus," I said, "it's no mean thing we've taken upon ourselves. But nevertheless, we
mustn't be cowardly, at least as far as it's in our power."

375a   "No," he said, "we mustn't."

"Do you suppose," I said, "that for guarding there is any difference between the nature
of a noble puppy and that of a well-born young man?"

"What do you mean?"

"Well, surely both of them need sharp senses, speed to catch what they perceive, and,
finally, strength if they have to fight it out with what they have caught."

"Yes, indeed," he said, "both need all these things."

"To say nothing of courage, if they are to fight well."

"Of course."

"Then, will horse or dog – or any other animal whatsoever – be willing to be courageous
b if it's not spirited? Haven't you noticed how irresistible and unbeatable spirit is, so that its
presence makes every soul fearless and invincible in the face of everything?"

"Yes, I have noticed it."

"As for the body's characteristics, it's plain how the guardian must be."

"Yes."

"And as for the soul's – that he must be spirited."

"That too."

"Glaucon," I said, "with such natures, how will they not be savage to one another and
the rest of the citizens?"

"By Zeus," he said, "it won't be easy."

c   "Yet, they must be gentle to their own and cruel to enemies. If not, they'll not wait for
others to destroy them, but they'll do it themselves beforehand."

"True," he said.

"What will we do?" I said. "Where will we find a disposition at the same time gentle and
great-spirited? Surely a gentle nature is opposed to a spirited one."

"It looks like it."

"Yet, if a man lacks either of them, he can't become a good guardian. But these condi-
d tions resemble impossibilities, and so it follows that a good guardian is impossible."

"I'm afraid so," he said.

I too was at a loss, and, looking back over what had gone before, I said, "It is just, my
friend, that we're at a loss. For we've abandoned the image we proposed."

"How do you mean?"

"We didn't notice that there are, after all, natures such as we thought impossible, possessing these opposites."

"Where, then?"

"One could see it in other animals too, especially, however, in the one we compared to
e the guardian. You know, of course, that by nature the disposition of noble dogs is to be as

gentle as can be with their familiars and people they know and the opposite with those they don't know."

"I do know that."

"Then," I said, "it is possible, after all; and what we're seeking for in the guardian isn't against nature."

"It doesn't seem so."

"In your opinion, then, does the man who will be a fit guardian need, in addition to spiritedness, also to be a philosopher in his nature?"

"How's that?" he said. "I don't understand."   376a

"This, too, you'll observe in dogs," I said, "and it's a thing in the beast worthy of our wonder."

"What?"

"When it sees someone it doesn't know, it's angry, although it never had any bad experience with him. And when it sees someone it knows, it greets him warmly, even if it never had a good experience with him. Didn't you ever wonder about this before?"

"No, I haven't paid very much attention to it up to now. But it's plain that it really does this."

"Well, this does look like an attractive affection of its nature and truly philosophic."   b

"In what way?"

"In that it distinguishes friendly from hostile looks by nothing other than by having learned the one and being ignorant of the other," I said. "And so, how can it be anything other than a lover of learning since it defines what's its own and what's alien by knowledge and ignorance?"

"It surely couldn't be anything but," he said.

"Well," I said, "but aren't love of learning and love of wisdom the same?"

"Yes, the same," he said.

"So shall we be bold and assert that a human being too, if he is going to be gentle to his own and those known to him, must by nature be a philosopher and a lover of learning?"   c

"Yes," he said, "let's assert it."

"Then the man who's going to be a fine and good guardian of the city for us will in his nature be philosophic, spirited, swift, and strong."

"That's entirely certain," he said.

"Then he would be of this sort to begin with. But how, exactly, will they be reared and educated by us? And does our considering this contribute anything to our goal of discerning that for the sake of which we are considering all these things – in what way justice and d injustice come into being in a city? We don't want to scant the argument, but we don't want an overlong one either."

And Glaucon's brother said, "I most certainly expect that this present consideration will contribute to that goal."

"By Zeus," I said, "then, my dear Adeimantus, it mustn't be given up even if it turns out to be quite long."

"No, it mustn't."

"Come, then, like men telling tales in a tale and at their leisure, let's educate the men in speech."

"We must."   e

"What is the education? Isn't it difficult to find a better one than that discovered over a great expanse of time? It is, of course, gymnastic for bodies and music for the soul."

"Yes, it is."

"Won't we begin educating in music before gymnastic?"

"Of course."

"You include speeches in music, don't you?" I said.

"I do."

"Do speeches have a double form, the one true, the other false?"

"Yes."

377a "Must they be educated in both, but first in the false?"

"I don't understand how you mean that," he said.

"Don't you understand," I said, "that first we tell tales to children? And surely they are, as a whole, false, though there are true things in them too. We make use of tales with children before exercises."

"That's so."

"That's what I meant by saying music must be taken up before gymnastic."

"That's right," he said.

"Don't you know that the beginning is the most important part of every work and that b this is especially so with anything young and tender? For at that stage it's most plastic, and each thing assimilates itself to the model whose stamp anyone wishes to give to it."

"Quite so."

"Then shall we so easily let the children hear just any tales fashioned by just anyone and take into their souls opinions for the most part opposite to those we'll suppose they must have when they are grown up?"

"In no event will we permit it."

"First, as it seems, we must supervise the makers of tales; and if they make a fine tale, it c must be approved, but if it's not, it must be rejected. We'll persuade nurses and mothers to tell the approved tales to their children and to shape their souls with tales more than their bodies with hands. Many of those they now tell must be thrown out."

"Which sort?" he said.

"In the greater tales we'll also see the smaller ones," I said. "Both the greater and the smaller d must be taken from the same model and have the same power. Don't you suppose so?"

"I do," he said. "But I don't grasp what you mean by the greater ones."

"The ones Hesiod and Homer told us, and the other poets too. They surely composed false tales for human beings and used to tell them and still do tell them."

"But what sort," he said, "and what do you mean to blame in them?"

"What ought to be blamed first and foremost," I said, "especially if the lie a man tells isn't a fine one."

"What's that?"

e "When a man in speech makes a bad representation of what gods and heroes are like, just as a painter who paints something that doesn't resemble the things whose likeness he wished to paint."

"Yes, it's right to blame such things," he said. "But how do we mean this and what sort of thing is it?"

"First," I said, "the man who told the biggest lie about the biggest things didn't tell a fine lie – how Uranus did what Hesiod says he did, and how Cronos in his turn took revenge 378a on him. And Cronos' deeds and his sufferings at the hands of his son, not even if they were true would I suppose they should so easily be told to thoughtless young things; best would be to keep quiet, but if there were some necessity to tell, as few as possible ought to hear them as unspeakable secrets, after making a sacrifice, not of a pig but of some great offering that's hard to come by, so that it will come to the ears of the smallest possible number."

"These speeches are indeed harsh," he said.

"And they mustn't be spoken in our city, Adeimantus," I said. "Nor must it be said within b the hearing of a young person that in doing the extremes of injustice, or that in punishing the unjust deeds of his father in every way, he would do nothing to be wondered at, but would be doing only what the first and the greatest of the gods did."

"No, by Zeus," he said. "To say this doesn't seem fitting to me either."

"Above all," I said, "it mustn't be said that gods make war on gods, and plot against them and have battles with them – for it isn't even true – provided that those who are going to c guard the city for us must consider it most shameful to be easily angry with one another. They are far from needing to have tales told and embroideries woven about battles of giants and the many diverse disputes of gods and heroes with their families and kin. But if we are somehow going to persuade them that no citizen ever was angry with another and that to be so is not holy, it's just such things that must be told the children right away by old men and women; and as they get older, the poets must be compelled to make up speeches for d them which are close to these. But Hera's bindings by her son, and Hephaestus' being cast out by his father when he was about to help out his mother who was being beaten, and all the battles of the gods Homer made, must not be accepted in the city, whether they are made with a hidden sense or without a hidden sense. A young thing can't judge what is hidden sense and what is not; but what he takes into his opinions at that age has a tendency to become hard to eradicate and unchangeable. Perhaps it's for this reason that we must do e everything to insure that what they hear first, with respect to virtue, be the finest told tales for them to hear."

"That's reasonable," he said. "But if someone should at this point ask us what they are and which tales we mean, what would we say?"

And I said, "Adeimantus, you and I aren't poets right now but founders of a city. It's appropriate for founders to know the models according to which the poets must tell their 379a tales. If what the poets produce goes counter to these models, founders must not give way; however, they must not themselves make up tales."

"That's correct," he said. "But, that is just it; what would the models for speech about the gods be."

"Doubtless something like this," I said. "The god must surely always be described such as he is, whether one presents him in epics, lyrics, or tragedies."

"Yes, he must be."

"Then, is the god really good, and, hence, must he be said to be so?"   b

"Of course."

"Well, but none of the good things is harmful, is it?"

"Not in my opinion."

"Does that which isn't harmful do harm?"

"In no way."

"Does that which does not harm do any evil?"

"Not that, either."

"That which does no evil would not be the cause of any evil?"

"How could it be?"

"What about this? Is the good beneficial?"

"Yes."

"Then it's the cause of doing well?"

"Yes."

"Then the good is not the cause of everything; rather it is the cause of the things that are in a good way, while it is not responsible for the bad things."

379c   "Yes," he said, "that's entirely so."

"Then," I said, "the god, since he's good, wouldn't be the cause of everything, as the many say, but the cause of a few things for human beings and not responsible for most. For the things that are good for us are far fewer than those that are bad; and of the good things, no one else must be said to be the cause; of the bad things, some other causes must be sought and not the god."

[. . .]

Book III

412b "All right," I said. "After that, what would it be that we must determine? Isn't it who among these men will rule and who be ruled?"

c   "Of course."

"That the rulers must be older and the ruled younger is plain, isn't it?"

"Yes, it is."

"And that they must be the best among them?"

"That's plain, too."

"And the best of the farmers, aren't they the most skillful at farming?"

"Yes."

"Now since they must be the best of the guardians, mustn't they be the most skillful at guarding the city?"

"Yes."

"Mustn't they, to begin with, be prudent in such matters as well as powerful, and, moreover, mustn't they care for the city?"

d   "That's so."

"A man would care most for that which he happened to love."

"Necessarily."

"And wouldn't he surely love something most when he believed that the same things are advantageous to it and to himself, and when he supposed that if it did well, he too himself would do well along with it, and if it didn't, neither would he?"

"That's so," he said.

"Then we must select from the other guardians the sort of men who, upon our con-
e sideration, from everything in their lives, look as if they were entirely eager to do what they believe to be advantageous to the city and would in no way be willing to do what is not."

"Yes," he said, "they would be suitable."

"Then, in my opinion, they must be watched at every age to see if they are skillful guardians of this conviction and never under the influence of wizardry or force forget and thus banish the opinion that one must do what is best for the city."

"What do you mean by 'banishment'?" he said.

"I'll tell you," I said. "It looks to me as though an opinion departs from our minds either willingly or unwillingly; the departure of the false opinion from the man who learns other-
413a wise is willing, that of every true opinion is unwilling."

"I understand the case of the willing departure," he said, "but I need to learn about the unwilling."

"What?" I said. "Don't you too believe that human beings are unwillingly deprived of good things and willingly of bad ones? Or isn't being deceived about the truth bad, and to have the truth good? Or isn't it your opinion that to opine the things that are, is to have the truth?"

"What you say is correct," he said, "and in my opinion men are unwillingly deprived of true opinion."

"Don't they suffer this by being robbed, bewitched by wizards, or forced?"   b

"Now I don't understand again," he said.

"I'm afraid I am speaking in the tragic way," I said. "By the robbed I mean those who are persuaded to change and those who forget, because in the one case, time, in the other, speech, takes away their opinions unawares. Now you surely understand?"

"Yes."

"And, then, by the forced I mean those whom some grief or pain causes to change their opinions."

"I understand that too," he said, "and what you say is correct."

"And, further, the bewitched you too, I suppose, would say are those who change their   c
opinions either because they are charmed by pleasure or terrified by some fear."

"Yes," he said, "that's because everything that deceives seems to bewitch."

"Now then, as I said a while ago, we must look for some men who are the best guardians of their conviction that they must do what on each occasion seems best for the city. So we must watch them straight from childhood by setting them at tasks in which a man would most likely forget and be deceived out of such a conviction. And the man who has a memory and is hard to deceive must be, chosen, and the one who's not must be rejected,   d
mustn't he?"

"Yes."

"And again, they must be set to labors, pains, and contests in which these same things must be watched."

"Correct," he said.

"Then," I said, "we must also make them a competition for the third form, wizardry, and we must look on. Just as they lead colts to noises and confusions and observe if they're fearful, so these men when they are young must be brought to terrors and then cast in turn into   e
pleasures, testing them far more than gold in fire. If a man appears hard to bewitch and graceful in everything, a good guardian of himself and the music he was learning, proving himself to possess rhythm and harmony on all these occasions – such a man would certainly be most useful to himself and the city. And the one who on each occasion, among the children and youths and among the men, is tested and comes through untainted, must be appointed 414a
ruler of the city and guardian; and he must be given honors, both while living and when dead, and must be allotted the greatest prizes in burial and the other memorials. And the man who's not of this sort must be rejected. The selection and appointment of the rulers and guardians is, in my opinion, Glaucon," I said, "something like this, not described precisely, but by way of a model."

"That," he said, "is the way it looks to me too."

"Isn't it then truly most correct to call these men complete guardians? They can guard b
over enemies from without and friends from within – so that the ones will not wish to do harm and the others will be unable to. The young, whom we were calling guardians up to now, we shall call auxiliaries and helpers of the rulers' convictions."

"In my opinion," he said, "that is what they should be called."

"Could we," I said, "somehow contrive one of those lies that come into being in case of
414c   need, of which we were just now speaking, some one noble lie to persuade, in the best case,
even the rulers, but if not them, the rest of the city?"

"What sort of a thing?" he said.

"Nothing new," I said, "but a Phoenician thing, which has already happened in many
places before, as the poets assert and have caused others to believe, but one that has not
happened in our time – and I don't know if it could – one that requires a great deal of
persuasion."

"How like a man who's hesitant to speak you are," he said.

"You'll think my hesitation quite appropriate, too," I said, "when I do speak."

"Speak," he said, "and don't be afraid."

d   "I shall speak – and yet, I don't know what I'll use for daring or speeches in telling it –
and I'll attempt to persuade first the rulers and the soldiers, then the rest of the city, that
the rearing and education we gave them were like dreams; they only thought they were
undergoing all that was happening to them, while, in truth, at that time they were under
e   the earth within, being fashioned and reared themselves, and their arms and other tools being
crafted. When the job had been completely finished, then the earth, which is their mother,
sent them up. And now, as though the land they are in were a mother and nurse, they
must plan for and defend it, if anyone attacks, and they must think of the other citizens as
brothers and born of the earth."

"It wasn't," he said, "for nothing that you were for so long ashamed to tell the lie."

415a   "It was indeed appropriate," I said. "All the same, hear out the rest of the tale. 'All of you
in the city are certainly brothers,' we shall say to them in telling the tale, 'but the god, in
fashioning those of you who are competent to rule, mixed gold in at their birth; this is why
they are most honored; in auxiliaries, silver; and iron and bronze in the farmers and the other
craftsmen. So, because you're all related, although for the most part you'll produce offspring
b   like yourselves, it sometimes happens that a silver child will be born from a golden parent,
a golden child from a silver parent, and similarly all the others from each other. Hence the
god commands the rulers first and foremost to be of nothing such good guardians and to
keep over nothing so careful a watch as the children, seeing which of these metals is mixed
in their souls. And, if a child of theirs should be born with an admixture of bronze or iron,
c   by no manner of means are they to take pity on it, but shall assign the proper value to its
nature and thrust it out among the craftsmen or the farmers; and, again, if from these men
one should naturally grow who has an admixture of gold or silver, they will honor such ones
and lead them up, some to the guardian group, others to the auxiliary, believing that there
is an oracle that the city will be destroyed when an iron or bronze man is its guardian.' So,
have you some device for persuading them of this tale?"

d   "None at all," he said, "for these men themselves; however for their sons and their
successors and the rest of the human beings who come afterwards."

"Well, even that would be good for making them care more for the city and one
another," I said. "For I understand pretty much what you mean.

" Well, then, this will go where the report of men shall lead it. And when we have armed
these earth-born men, let's bring them forth led by the rulers. When they've come, let
them look out for the fairest place in the city for a military camp, from which they could
e   most control those within, if anyone were not willing to obey the laws, and ward off those
from without, if an enemy, like a wolf, should attack the flock. When they have made the

camp and sacrificed to whom they ought, let them make sleeping places. Or how should it be?"

"Like that," he said.

"Won't these places be such as to provide adequate shelter in both winter and summer?"

"Yes, of course," he said. "For you seem to me to mean houses."

"Yes," I said, "those of soldiers, not moneymakers."

"How," he said, "do you mean to distinguish the one from the other?"   416a

"I shall try to tell you," I said. "Surely the most terrible and shameful thing of all is for shepherds to rear dogs as auxiliaries for the flocks in such a way that due to licentiousness, hunger or some other bad habit, they themselves undertake to do harm to the sheep and instead of dogs become like wolves."

"Terrible," he said. "Of course."

"Mustn't we in every way guard against the auxiliaries doing anything like that to the   b citizens, since they are stronger than they, becoming like savage masters instead of well-meaning allies?"

"Yes," he said, "we must."

"And wouldn't they have been provided with the greatest safeguard if they have been really finely educated?"

"But they have been," he said.

And I said, "It's not fit to be too sure about that, my dear Glaucon. However, it is fit to be sure about what we were saying a while ago, that they must get the right education, what-   c ever it is, if they're going to have what's most important for being tame with each other and those who are guarded by them."

"That's right," he said.

"Now, some intelligent man would say that, in addition to this education, they must be provided with houses and other property such as not to prevent them from being the best possible guardians and not to rouse them up to do harm to the other citizens."   d

"And he'll speak the truth."

"Well, then," I said, "see if this is the way they must live and be housed if they're going to be such men. First, no one will possess any private property except for what's entirely necessary. Second, no one will have any house or storeroom into which everyone who wishes cannot come. The sustenance, as much as is needed by moderate and courageous men who are champions of war, they'll receive in fixed installments from the other citizens as a wage   e for their guarding, in such quantity that there will be no surplus for them in a year and no lack either. They'll go regularly to mess together like soldiers in a camp and live a life in common. We'll tell them that gold and silver of a divine sort from the gods they have in their soul always and have no further need of the human sort; nor is it holy to pollute the possession of the former sort by mixing it with the possession of the mortal sort, because many unholy things have been done for the sake of the currency of the many, while theirs 417a is untainted. But for them alone of those in the city it is not lawful to handle and to touch gold and silver, nor to go under the same roof with it, nor to hang it from their persons, nor to drink from silver or gold. And thus they would save themselves as well as save the city. Whenever they'll possess private land, houses, and currency, they'll be householders and farmers instead of guardians, and they'll become masters and enemies instead of allies   b of the other citizens; hating and being hated, plotting and being plotted against, they'll lead their whole lives far more afraid of the enemies within than those without. Then them-selves as well as the rest of the city are already rushing toward a destruction that lies very near. So, for all these reasons," I said, "let's say that the guardians must be provided with houses and the rest in this way, and we shall set this down as a law, shall we not?"

"Certainly," said Glaucon.

Book IV

[. . .]

427e "I suppose our city – if, that is, it has been correctly founded – is perfectly good."

"Necessarily," he said.

"Plainly, then, it's wise, courageous, moderate and just."

"Plainly."

"Isn't it the case that whichever of them we happen to find will leave as the remainder what hasn't been found?"

428a "Of course."

"Therefore, just as with any other four things, if we were seeking any one of them in something or other and recognized it first, that would be enough for us; but if we recognized the other three first, this would also suffice for the recognition of the thing looked for. For plainly it couldn't be anything but what's left over."

"What you say is correct," he said.

"With these things too, since they happen to be four, mustn't we look for them in the same way?"

"Plainly."

"Well, it's wisdom, in my opinion, which first comes plainly to light in it. And something
b about it looks strange."

"What?" he said.

"The city we described is really wise, in my opinion. That's because it's of good counsel, isn't it?"

"Yes."

"And further, this very thing, good counsel, is plainly a kind of knowledge. For it's surely not by lack of learning, but by knowledge, that men counsel well."

"Plainly."

"But, on the other hand, there's much knowledge of all sorts in the city."

"Of course."

"Then, is it thanks to the carpenters' knowledge that the city must be called wise and of good counsel?"

c "Not at all," he said, "thanks to that it's called skilled in carpentry."

"Then, it's not thanks to the knowledge that counsels about how wooden implements would be best that a city must be called wise."

"Surely not."

"And what about this? Is it thanks to the knowledge of bronze implements or any other knowledge of such things?"

"Not to any knowledge of the sort," he said.

"And not to the knowledge about the production of the crop from the earth; for that, rather, it is called skilled in farming."

"That's my opinion."

"What about this?" I said. "Is there in the city we just founded a kind of knowledge belonging to some of the citizens that counsels not about the affairs connected with some particular d thing in the city, but about how the city as a whole would best deal with itself and the other cities?"

"There is indeed."

"What and in whom is it?" I said.

"It's the guardian's skill," he said, "and it's in those rulers whom we just now named perfect guardians."

"Thanks to this knowledge, what do you call the city?"

"Of good counsel," he said, "and really wise."

"Then, do you suppose," I said, "that there will be more smiths in our city than these true e guardians?"

"Far more smiths," he said.

"Among those," I said, "who receive a special name for possessing some kind of knowledge, wouldn't the guardians be the fewest of all in number?"

"By far."

"It is, therefore, from the smallest group and part of itself and the knowledge in it, from the supervising and ruling part, that a city founded according to nature would be wise as a whole. And this class, which properly has a share in that knowledge which alone among the various kinds of knowledge ought to be called wisdom, has, as it seems, the fewest members 429a by nature."

"What you say," he said, "is very true."

"So we've found – I don't know how – this one of the four, both it and where its seat in the city is."

"In my opinion, at least," he said, "it has been satisfactorily discovered."

"And, next, courage, both itself as well as where it's situated in the city – that courage thanks to which the city must be called courageous – isn't very hard to see."

"How's that?"

"Who," I said, "would say a city is cowardly or courageous while looking to any part other b than the one that defends it and takes the field on its behalf?"

"There's no one," he said, "who would look to anything else."

"I don't suppose," I said, "that whether the other men in it are cowardly or courageous would be decisive for its being this or that."

"No, it wouldn't."

"So a city is also courageous by a part of itself, thanks to that part's having in it a power that through everything will preserve the opinion about which things are terrible – that they c are the same ones and of the same sort as those the lawgiver transmitted in the education. Or don't you call that courage?"

"I didn't quite understand what you said," he said. "Say it again."

"I mean," I said, "that courage is a certain kind of preserving."

"Just what sort of preserving?"

"The preserving of the opinion produced by law through education about what – and what sort of thing – is terrible. And by preserving through everything I meant preserving that opinion and not casting it out in pains and pleasures and desires and fears. If you wish I'm d willing to compare it to what I think it's like."

"But I do wish."

"Don't you know," I said, "that the dyers, when they want to dye wool purple, first choose from all the colors the single nature belonging to white things; then they prepare it beforehand and care for it with no little preparation so that it will most receive the color; and it is
429e only then that they dye? And if a thing is dyed in this way, it becomes color-fast, and washing either without lyes or with lyes can't take away its color. But those things that are not so dyed – whether one dyes other colors or this one without preparatory care – you know what they become like."

"I do know," he said, "that they're washed out and ridiculous."

"Hence," I said, "take it that we too were, to the extent of our power, doing something
430a similar when we selected the soldiers and educated them in music and gymnastic. Don't think we devised all that for any other purpose than that – persuaded by the laws – they should receive them from us in the finest possible way like a dye, so that their opinion about what's terrible and about everything else would be color-fast because they had gotten the proper nature and rearing, and their dye could not be washed out by those lyes so terribly effective at scouring, pleasure – more terribly effective for this than any Chalestrean soda and alkali;
b and pain, fear, and desire – worse than any other lye. This kind of power and preservation, through everything, of the right and lawful opinion about what is terrible and what not, I call courage; and so I set it down, unless you say something else."

"But I don't say anything else," he said. "For, in my opinion, you regard the right opinion about these same things that comes to be without education – that found in beasts and slaves – as not at all lawful and call it something other than courage."

c   "What you say," I said, "is very true."

"Well, then, I accept this as courage."

"Yes, do accept it, but as political courage," I said, "and you'd be right in accepting it. Later, if you want, we'll give it a still finer treatment. At the moment we weren't looking for it, but for justice. For that search, I suppose, this is sufficient."

"What you say is fine," he said.

"Well, now," I said, "there are still two left that must be seen in the city, moderation and
d that for the sake of which we are making the whole search, justice."

"Most certainly."

"How could we find justice so we won't have to bother about moderation any further?"

"I for my part don't know," he said, "nor would I want it to come to light before, if we aren't going to consider moderation any further. If you want to gratify me, consider this before the other."

e   "But I do want to," I said, "so as not to do an injustice."

"Then consider it," he said.

"It must be considered," I said. "Seen from here, it's more like a kind of accord and harmony than the previous ones."

"How?"

"Moderation," I said, "is surely a certain kind of order and mastery of certain kinds of pleasures and desires, as men say when they use – I don't know in what way – the phrase 'stronger than himself'; and some other phrases of the sort are used that are, as it were, its tracks. Isn't that so?"

"Most surely," he said.

"Isn't the phrase 'stronger than himself' ridiculous though? For, of course, the one who's stronger than himself would also be weaker than himself, and the weaker stronger. The same
431a 'himself' is referred to in all of them."

"Of course it is."

"But," I said, "this speech looks to me as if it wants to say that, concerning the soul, in the same human being there is something better and something worse. The phrase 'stronger than himself' is used when that which is better by nature is master over that which is worse. At least it's praise. And when, from bad training or some association, the smaller and better part is mastered by the inferior multitude, then this, as though it were a reproach, is blamed b and the man in this condition is called weaker than himself and licentious."

"Yes," he said, "that's likely."

"Now, then," I said, "take a glance at our young city, and you'll find one of these conditions in it. For you'll say that it's justly designated stronger than itself, if that in which the better rules over the worse must be called moderate and 'stronger than itself.' "

"Well, I am glancing at it," he said, "and what you say is true."

"And, further, one would find many diverse desires, pleasures, and pains, especially in children, women, domestics, and in those who are called free among the common many." c

"Most certainly."

"But the simple and moderate desires, pleasures and pains, those led by calculation accompanied by intelligence and right opinion, you will come upon in few, and those the ones born with the best natures and best educated."

"True," he said.

"Don't you see that all these are in your city too, and that there the desires in the common many are mastered by the desires and the prudence in the more decent few?" d

"I do," he said.

"If, therefore, any city ought to be designated stronger than pleasures, desires, and itself, then this one must be so called."

"That's entirely certain," he said.

"And then moderate in all these respects too?"

"Very much so," he said.

"And, moreover, if there is any city in which the rulers and the ruled have the same opinion about who should rule, then it's this one. Or doesn't it seem so?" e

"Very much so indeed," he said.

"In which of the citizens will you say the moderation resides, when they are in this condition? In the rulers or the ruled?"

"In both, surely," he said.

"You see," I said, "we divined pretty accurately a while ago that moderation is like a kind of harmony."

"Why so?"

"Because it's unlike courage and wisdom, each of which resides in a part, the one making the city wise and the other courageous. Moderation doesn't work that way, but actually 432a stretches throughout the whole, from top to bottom of the entire scale, making the weaker, the stronger and those in the middle – whether you wish to view them as such in terms of prudence, or, if you wish, in terms of strength, or multitude, money or anything else whatsoever of the sort – sing the same chant together. So we would quite rightly claim that this unanimity is moderation, an accord of worse and better, according to nature, as to which must rule in the city and in each one."

"I am," he said, "very much of the same opinion." b

"All right," I said. "Three of them have been spied out in our city, at least sufficiently to form some opinion. Now what would be the remaining form thanks to which the city would further partake in virtue? For, plainly, this is justice."

"Plainly."

"So then, Glaucon, we must, like hunters, now station ourselves in a circle around the thicket and pay attention so that justice doesn't slip through somewhere and disappear into 432c obscurity. Clearly it's somewhere hereabouts. Look to it and make every effort to catch sight of it; you might somehow see it before me and could tell me."

"If only I could," he said. "However, if you use me as a follower and a man able to see what's shown him, you'll be making quite sensible use of me."

"Follow," I said, "and pray with me."

"I'll do that," he said, "just lead."

"The place really appears to be hard going and steeped in shadows," I said. "At least it's dark and hard to search out. But, all the same, we've got to go on."

d "Yes," he said, "we've got to go on."

And I caught sight of it and said, "Here! Here! Glaucon. Maybe we've come upon a track; and, in my opinion, it will hardly get away from us."

"That's good news you report," he said.

"My, my," I said, "that was a stupid state we were in."

"How's that?"

"It appears, you blessed man, that it's been rolling around at our feet from the beginning and we couldn't see it after all, but were quite ridiculous. As men holding something in their e hand sometimes seek what they're holding, we too didn't look at it but turned our gaze somewhere far off, which is also perhaps just the reason it escaped our notice."

"How do you mean?" he said.

"It's this way," I said. "In my opinion, we have been saying and hearing it all along without learning from ourselves that we were in a way saying it."

"A long prelude," he said, "for one who desires to hear."

433a "Listen whether after all I make any sense," I said. "That rule we set down at the beginning as to what must be done in everything when we were founding the city – this, or a certain form of it, is, in my opinion, justice. Surely we set down and often said, if you remember, that each one must practice one of the functions in the city, that one for which his nature made him naturally most fit."

"Yes, we were saying that."

"And further, that justice is the minding of one's own business and not being a busybody, b this we have both heard from many others and have often said ourselves."

"Yes, we have."

"Well, then, my friend," I said, "this – the practice of minding one's own business – when it comes into being in a certain way, is probably justice. Do you know how I infer this?"

"No," he said, "tell me."

"In my opinion," I said, "after having considered moderation, courage, and prudence, this is what's left over in the city; it provided the power by which all these others came into being; and, once having come into being, it provides them with preservation as long as it's c in the city. And yet we were saying that justice would be what's left over from the three if we found them."

"Yes, we did," he said, "and it's necessarily so."

"Moreover," I said, "if one had to judge which of them by coming to be will do our city the most good, it would be a difficult judgment. Is it the unity of opinion among rulers and ruled? Or is it the coming into being in the soldiers of that preserving of the lawful opinion d as to which things are terrible and which are not? Or is it the prudence and guardianship present in the rulers? Or is the city done the most good by the fact that – in the case of child, woman, slave, freeman, craftsman, ruler and ruled – each one minded his own business and wasn't a busybody?"

"It would, of course," he said, "be a difficult judgment."

"Then, as it seems, with respect to a city's virtue, this power that consists in each man's minding his own business in the city is a rival to wisdom, moderation and courage."

"Very much so," he said.

"Wouldn't you name justice that which is the rival of these others in contributing to a city's virtue?"   e

"That's entirely certain."

"Now consider if it will seem the same from this viewpoint too. Will you assign the judging of lawsuits in the city to the rulers?"

"Of course."

"Will they have any other aim in their judging than that no one have what belongs to others, nor be deprived of what belongs to him?"

"None other than this."

"Because that's just?"

"Yes."

"And therefore, from this point of view too, the having and doing of one's own and what belongs to one would be agreed to be justice."   434a

"That's so."

"Now see if you have the same opinion as I do. A carpenter's trying to do the job of a shoemaker or a shoemaker that of a carpenter, or their exchanging tools or honors with one another, or even the same man's trying to do both, with everything else being changed along with it, in your opinion, will that do any great harm to the city?"

"Not much," he said.

"But, I suppose, when one who is a craftsman or some other kind of money-maker by nature, inflated by wealth, multitude, strength, or something else of the kind, tries to get b into the class of the warrior, or one of the warriors who's unworthy into that of the adviser and guardian, and these men exchange tools and honors with one another; or when the same man tries to do all these things at once – then I suppose it's also your opinion that this change in them and this meddling are the destruction of the city."

"That's entirely certain."

"Meddling among the classes, of which there are three, and exchange with one another is the greatest harm for the city and would most correctly be called extreme evil-doing."   c

"Quite certainly."

"Won't you say that the greatest evil-doing against one's own city is injustice?"

"Of course."

"Then, that's injustice. Again, let's say it this way. The opposite of this – the money-making, auxiliary, and guardian classes doing what's appropriate, each of them minding its own business in a city – would be justice and would make the city just."

"My opinion," he said, "is also that and no other."   d

"Let's not assert it so positively just yet," I said. "But, if this form is applied to human beings singly and also agreed by us to be justice there, then we'll concede it. What else will there be for us to say? And if not, then we'll consider something else. Now let's complete the consideration by means of which we thought that, if we should attempt to see justice first in some bigger thing that possessed it, we would more easily catch sight of what it's

434e like in one man. And it was our opinion that this bigger thing is a city; so we founded one as best we could, knowing full well that justice would be in a good one at least. Let's apply what came to light there to a single man, and if the two are in agreement, everything is fine. But if something different should turn up in the single man, we'll go back again to
435a the city and test it; perhaps, considering them side by side and rubbing them together like sticks, we would make justice burst into flame, and once it's come to light, confirm it for ourselves."

"The way to proceed is as you say," he said, "and it must be done."

"Then," I said, "is that which one calls the same, whether it's bigger or smaller, unlike or like in that respect in which it's called the same?"

"Like," he said.

b "Then the just man will not be any different from the just city with respect to the form itself of justice, but will be like it."

"Yes," he said "he will be like it."

"But a city seemed to be just when each of the three classes of natures present in it minded its own business and, again, moderate, courageous, and wise because of certain other affections and habits of these same classes."

"True," he said.

"Then it's in this way, my friend, that we'll claim that the single man – with these same
c forms in his soul – thanks to the same affections as those in the city, rightly lays claim to the same names."

"Quite necessarily," he said.

"Now it's a slight question about the soul we've stumbled upon, you surprising man," I said. "Does it have these three forms in it or not?"

"In my opinion, it's hardly a slight question," he said. "Perhaps, Socrates, the saying that fine things are hard is true."

"It looks like it," I said. "But know well, Glaucon, that in my opinion, we'll never get a
d precise grasp of it on the basis of procedures such as we're now using in the argument. There is another longer and further road leading to it. But perhaps we can do it in a way worthy of what's been said and considered before."

"Mustn't we be content with that?" he said. "It would be enough for me at present."

"Well, then," I said, "it will quite satisfy me too."

"So don't grow weary," he said, "but go ahead with the consideration."

e "Isn't it quite necessary for us to agree that the very same forms and dispositions as are in the city are in each of us?" I said. "Surely they didn't get there from any other place. It would be ridiculous if someone should think that the spiritedness didn't come into the cities from those private men who are just the ones imputed with having this character, such as those in Thrace, Scythia, and pretty nearly the whole upper region; or the love of learning,
436a which one could most impute to our region, or the love of money, which one could affirm is to be found not least among the Phoenicians and those in Egypt."

"Quite so," he said.

"This is so, then," I said, "and not hard to know."

"Surely not."

"But this now is hard. Do we act in each of these ways as a result of the same part of ourselves, or are there three parts and with a different one we act in each of the different ways? Do we learn with one, become spirited with another of the parts within us, and desire the pleasures of nourishment and generation and all their kin with a third; or do we act with

the soul as a whole in each of them once we are started? This will be hard to determine in b
a way worthy of the argument."

"That's my opinion too," he said.

"Now let's try to determine whether these things are the same or different from each other
in this way."

"How?"

"It's plain that the same thing won't be willing at the same time to do or suffer opposites
with respect to the same part and in relation to the same thing. So if we should ever find
that happening in these things, we'll know they weren't the same but many." c

"All right."

"Now consider what I say."

"Say on," he said.

"Is it possible that the same thing at the same time and with respect to the same part should
stand still and move?"

"Not at all."

"Now let's have a more precise agreement so that we won't have any grounds for
dispute as we proceed. If someone were to say of a human being standing still, but moving
his hands and his head, that the same man at the same time stands still and moves, I don't
suppose we'd claim that it should be said like that, but rather that one part of him stands
still and another moves. Isn't that so?" d

"Yes, it is."

"Then if the man who says this should become still more charming and make the subtle
point that tops as wholes stand still and move at the same time when the peg is fixed in the
same place and they spin, or that anything else going around in a circle on the same spot
does this too, we wouldn't accept it because it's not with respect to the same part of themselves that such things are at that time both at rest and in motion. But we'd say that they e
have in them both a straight and a circumference; and with respect to the straight they stand
still since they don't lean in any direction – while with respect to the circumference they
move in a circle; and when the straight inclines to the right, the left, forward, or backward
at the same time that it's spinning, then in no way does it stand still."

"And we'd be right," he said.

"Then the saying of such things won't scare us, or any the more persuade us that something that is the same, at the same time, with respect to the same part and in relation to the
same thing, could ever suffer, be, or do opposites." 437a

"Not me at least," he said.

"All the same," I said, "so we won't be compelled to go through all such objections and
spend a long time assuring ourselves they're not true, let's assume that this is so and go ahead,
agreed that if it should ever appear otherwise, all our conclusions based on it will be
undone."

"That," he said, "is what must be done."

"Then, would you set down all such things as opposites to one another," I said, "accept- b
ance to refusal, longing to take something to rejecting it, embracing to thrusting away, whether
they are actions or affections? That won't make any difference."

"Yes," he said, "they are opposites."

"What about this?" I said. "Being thirsty and hungry and generally the desires, and further, willing and wanting – wouldn't you set all these somewhere in those classes we just c
mentioned? For example, won't you say that the soul of a man who desires either longs for

what it desires or embraces that which it wants to become its own; or again, that, insofar as the soul wills that something be supplied to it, it nods assent to itself as though it had posed a question and reaches out toward the fulfillment of what it wills?"

"I shall."

"And what about this? Won't we class not-wanting, and not-willing and not-desiring with the soul's thrusting away from itself and driving out of itself and along with all the opposites of the previously mentioned acts?"

437d   "Of course."

"Now since this is so, shall we assert that there is a form of desires and that what we call being thirsty and hungry are the most vivid of them?"

"Yes," he said, "we shall assert it."

"Isn't the one for drink and the other for food?"

"Yes."

"Insofar as it's thirst, would it be a desire in the soul for something more than that of which we say it is a desire? For example, is thirst thirst for hot drink or cold, or much or lit-tle, or, in a word, for any particular kind of drink? Or isn't it rather that in the case where

e   heat is present in addition to the thirst, the heat would cause the desire to be also for some-thing cold as well; and where coldness, something hot; and where the thirst is much on account of the presence of muchness, it will cause the desire to be for much, and where it's little, for little? But, thirsting itself will never be a desire for anything other than that of which it naturally is a desire – for drink alone – and, similarly, hungering will be a desire for food?"

"That's the way it is," he said. "Each particular desire itself is only for that particular thing itself of which it naturally is, while the desire for this or that kind depends on additions."

438a   "Now let no one catch us unprepared," I said, "and cause a disturbance, alleging that no one desires drink, but good drink, nor food, but good food; for everyone, after all, desires good things; if, then, thirst is a desire, it would be for good drink or for good whatever it is, and similarly with the other desires."

"Perhaps," he said, "the man who says that would seem to make some sense."

"However," I said, "of all things that are such as to be related to something, those that

b   are of a certain kind are related to a thing of a certain kind, as it seems to me, while those that are severally themselves are related only to a thing that is itself."

"I don't understand," he said.

"Don't you understand," I said, "that the greater is such as to be greater than something?"

"Certainly."

"Than the less?"

"Yes."

"And the much-greater than the much-less, isn't that so?"

"Yes."

"And, then, also the once-greater than the once-less, and the-going-to-be-greater than the-going-to-be-less?"

"Of course," he said.

c   "And, further, the more in relation to the fewer, the double to the half, and everything of the sort; and, again, heavier to lighter, faster to slower; and further, the hot to the cold, and everything like them – doesn't the same thing hold?"

"Most certainly."

"And what about the various sorts of knowledge? Isn't it the same way? Knowledge itself is knowledge of learning itself, or of whatever it is to which knowledge should be, related;

while a particular kind of knowledge is of a particular kind of thing. I mean something like d this. When knowledge of constructing houses came to be, didn't it differ from the other kinds of knowledge and was thus called housebuilding?"

"Of course."

"Wasn't this by its being a particular kind of thing that is different from the others?"

"Yes."

"Since it was related to a particular kind of thing, didn't it too become a particular kind of thing itself? And isn't this the way with the other arts and sorts of knowledge too?"

"It is."

"Well, then," I said, "say that what I wanted to say then, if you now understand after all, is that of all things that are such as to be related to something, those that are only themselves are related to things that are only themselves, while those that are related to things of a particular kind are of a particular kind. And I in no sense mean that they are such as e the things to which they happen to be related, so that it would follow that the knowledge of things healthy and sick is healthy and sick and that of bad and good is itself bad and good. But when knowledge became knowledge not of that alone to which knowledge is related but of a particular sort of thing, and this was health and sickness, it as a consequence also became of a certain sort itself; and this caused it not to be called knowledge simply any more but, with the particular kind having been added to it, medicine."

"I understand," he said, "and, in my opinion, that's the way it is."

"And then, as for thirst," I said, "won't you include it among those things that are related 439a to something? Surely thirst is in relation to . . ."

"I will," he said, "and it's related to drink."

"So a particular sort of thirst is for a particular kind of drink, but thirst itself is neither for much nor little, good nor bad, nor, in a word, for any particular kind, but thirst itself is naturally only for drink."

"That's entirely certain."

"Therefore, the soul of the man who's thirsty, insofar as it thirsts, wishes nothing other than to drink, and strives for this and is impelled toward it."   b

"Plainly."

"If ever something draws it back when it's thirsting, wouldn't that be something different in it from that which thirsts and leads it like a beast to drink? For of course, we say, the same thing wouldn't perform opposed actions concerning the same thing with the same part of itself at the same time."

"No, it wouldn't."

"Just as, I suppose, it's not fair to say of the archer that his hands at the same time thrust the bow away and draw it near, but that one hand pushes it away and the other pulls it in."

"That's entirely certain," he said.   c

"Now, would we assert that sometimes there are some men who are thirsty but not willing to drink?"

"Surely," he said, "many and often."

"What should one say about them?" I said. "Isn't there something in their soul bidding them to drink and something forbidding them to do so, something different that masters that which bids?"

"In my opinion there is," he said.

"Doesn't that which forbids such things come into being – when it comes into being – from calculation, while what leads and draws is present due to affections and diseases?"   d

"It looks like it."

"So we won't be irrational," I said, "if we claim they are two and different from each other, naming the part of the soul with which it calculates, the calculating, and the part with which it loves, hungers, thirsts and is agitated by the other desires, the irrational and desiring, companion of certain replenishments and pleasures."

439e "No, we won't," he said. "It would be fitting for us to believe that."

"Therefore," I said, "let these two forms in the soul be distinguished. Now, is the part that contains spirit and with which we are spirited a third, or would it have the same nature as one of these others?"

"Perhaps," he said, "the same as one of them, the desiring."

"But," I said, "I once heard something that I trust. Leontius, the son of Aglaion, was going up from the Piraeus under the outside of the North Wall when he noticed corpses lying by the public executioner. He desired to look, but at the same time he was disgusted and made himself turn away; and for a while he struggled and covered his face. But finally, overpowered

440a by the desire, he opened his eyes wide, ran toward the corpses and said: 'Look, you damned wretches, take your fill of the fair sight.'"

"I too have heard it," he said.

"This speech," I said, "certainly indicates that anger sometimes makes war against the desires as one thing against something else."

"Yes," he said, "it does indicate that."

"And in many other places, don't we," I said, "notice that, when desires force someone

b contrary to the calculating part, he reproaches himself and his spirit is roused against that in him which is doing the forcing; and, just as though there were two parties at faction, such a man's spirit becomes the ally of speech? But as for its making common cause with the desires to do what speech has declared must not be done, I suppose you'd say you had never noticed anything of the kind happening in yourself, nor, I suppose, in anyone else."

"No, by Zeus," he said.

c "And what about when a man supposes he's doing injustice?" I said. "The nobler he is, won't he be less capable of anger at suffering hunger, cold or anything else of the sort inflicted on him by one whom he supposes does so justly; and, as I say, won't his spirit be unwilling to rouse itself against that man?"

"True," he said.

"And what about when a man believes he's being done injustice? Doesn't his spirit in this case boil and become harsh and form an alliance for battle with what seems just; and, even if it suffers in hunger, cold and everything of the sort, doesn't it stand firm and con-

d quer, and not cease from its noble efforts before it has succeeded, or death intervenes, or before it becomes gentle, having been called in by the speech within him like a dog by a herdsman?"

"Most certainly, it resembles the likeness you make. And, of course, we put the auxiliaries in our city like dogs obedient to the rulers, who are like shepherds of a city."

"You have," I said, "a fine understanding of what I want to say. But beyond that, are you aware of this too?"

e "What?"

"That what we are now bringing to light about the spirited is the opposite of our recent assertion. Then we supposed it had something to do with the desiring part; but now, far from it, we say that in the faction of the soul it sets its arms on the side of the calculating part."

"Quite so," he said.

"Is it then different from the calculating part as well, or is it a particular form of it so that there aren't three forms in the soul but two, the calculating and the desiring? Or just as there were three classes in the city that held it together, money-making, auxiliary, and deliberative, is there in the soul too this third, the spirited, by nature an auxiliary to the calculating part, if it's not corrupted by bad rearing?" 441a

"Necessarily," he said, "there is the third."

"Yes," I said, "if it should come to light as something other than the calculating part, just as it has come to light as different from the desiring part."

"But it's not hard," he said, "for it to come to light as such. For, even in little children, one could see that they are full of spirit straight from birth, while, as for calculating, some seem to me never to get a share of it, and the many do so quite late." b

"Yes, by Zeus," I said, "what you have said is fine. Moreover, in beasts one could see that what you say is so. And to them can be added the testimony of Homer that we cited in that other place somewhere earlier,

> He smote his breast and reproached
> his heart with word . . .

Here, you see, Homer clearly presents that which has calculated about better and worse and c rebukes that which is irrationally spirited as though it were a different part."

"What you say is entirely correct," he said.

"Well," I said, "we've had a hard swim through that and pretty much agreed that the same classes that are in the city are in the soul of each one severally and that their number is equal."

"Yes, that's so."

"Isn't it by now necessary that the private man be wise in the same way and because of the same thing as the city was wise?"

"Of course."

"And, further, that a city be courageous because of the same thing and in the same way d as a private man is courageous, and that in everything else that has to do with virtue both are alike?"

"Yes, that is necessary."

"And, further, Glaucon, I suppose we'll say that a man is just in the same manner that a city too was just."

"This too is entirely necessary."

"Moreover, we surely haven't forgotten that this city was just because each of the three classes in it minds its own business."

"We haven't in my opinion forgotten," he said.

"Then we must remember that, for each of us too, the one within whom each of the parts minds its own business will be just and mind his own business." e

"Indeed," he said, "that must be remembered."

"Isn't it proper for the calculating part to rule, since it is wise and has forethought about all of the soul, and for the spirited part to be obedient to it and its ally?"

"Certainly."

"So, as we were saying, won't a mixture of music and gymnastic make them accordant, tightening the one and training it in fair speeches and learning, while relaxing the other with 442a soothing tales, taming it by harmony and rhythm?"

"Quite so," he said.

"And these two, thus trained and having truly learned their own business and been educated, will be set over the desiring – which is surely most of the soul in each and by nature most insatiable for money – and they'll watch it for fear of its being filled with the so-called pleasures of the body and thus becoming big and strong, and then not minding its own business, but attempting to enslave and rule what is not appropriately ruled by its class and subverting everyone's entire life."

442b

"Most certainly," he said.

"So," I said, "wouldn't these two do the finest job of guarding against enemies from without on behalf of all of the soul and the body, the one deliberating, the other making war, following the ruler, and with its courage fulfilling what has been decided?"

"Yes, that's so."

"And then I suppose we call a single man courageous because of that part – when his spirited part preserves, through pains and pleasures, what has been proclaimed by the speeches about that which is terrible and that which is not."

c

"Correct," he said.

"And wise because of that little part which ruled in him and proclaimed these things; it, in its turn, possesses within it the knowledge of that which is beneficial for each part and for the whole composed of the community of these three parts."

"Most certainly."

"And what about this? Isn't he moderate because of the friendship and accord of these parts – when the ruling part and the two ruled parts are of the single opinion that the calculating part ought to rule, and don't raise faction against it?"

d

"Moderation, surely," he said, "is nothing other than this, in city or in private man."

"Now, of course, a man will be just because of that which we are so often saying, and in the same way."

"Quite necessarily."

"What about this?" I said. "Has our justice in any way been blunted so as to seem to be something other than what it came to light as in the city?"

"Not in my opinion," he said.

"If there are still any doubts in our soul," I said, "we could reassure ourselves completely by testing our justice in the light of the vulgar standards."

e

"Which ones?"

"For example, if, concerning this city and the man who by nature and training is like it, we were required to come to an agreement about whether, upon accepting a deposit of gold or silver, such a man would seem to be the one to filch it – do you suppose anyone would suppose that he would be the man to do it and not rather those who are not such as he is?"

443a

"No one would," he said.

"And as for temple robberies, thefts, and betrayals, either of comrades in private or cities in public, wouldn't this man be beyond them?"

"Yes, he would be beyond them."

"And, further, he would in no way whatsoever be faithless in oaths or other agreements."

"Of course not."

"Further, adultery, neglect of parents, and failure to care for the gods are more characteristic of every other kind of man than this one."

"Of every other kind, indeed," he said.

b

"Isn't the cause of all this that, so far as ruling and being ruled are concerned, each of the parts in him minds its own business?"

"That and nothing else is the cause."

"Are you still looking for justice to be something different from this power which produces such men and cities?"

"No, by Zeus," he said. "I'm not."

"Then that dream of ours has reached its perfect fulfillment. I mean our saying that we suspected that straight from the beginning of the city's founding, through some god, we probably hit upon an origin and model for justice."   c

"That's entirely certain."

"Thus, Glaucon, it was after all a kind of phantom of justice – that's also why it is helpful – its being right for the man who is by nature a shoemaker to practice shoemaking and do nothing else, and for the carpenter to practice carpentry, and so on for the rest."

"It looks like it."

"And in truth justice was, as it seems, something of this sort; however, not with respect to a man's minding his external business, but with respect to what is within, with respect to d what truly concerns him and his own. He doesn't let each part in him mind other people's business or the three classes in the soul meddle with each other, but really sets his own house in good order and rules himself; he arranges himself, becomes his own friend, and harmonizes the three parts, exactly like three notes in a harmonic scale, lowest, highest and middle. And if there are some other parts in between, he binds them together and becomes entirely e one from many, moderate and harmonized. Then, and only then, he acts, if he does act in some way – either concerning the acquisition of money, or the care of the body, or something political, or concerning private contracts. In all these actions he believes and names a just and fine action one that preserves and helps to produce this condition, and wisdom the knowledge that supervises this action; while he believes and names an unjust action one that undoes this condition, and lack of learning, in its turn, the opinion that supervises this action." 444a

"Socrates," he said, "what you say is entirely true."

"All right," I said. "If we should assert that we have found the just man and city and what justice really is in them, I don't suppose we'd seem to be telling an utter lie."

"By Zeus, no indeed," he said.

"Shall we assert it then?"

"Let's assert it."

"So be it," I said. "After that, I suppose injustice must be considered."

"Plainly."

"Mustn't it, in its turn, be a certain faction among those three – a meddling, interference, b and rebellion of a part of the soul against the whole? The purpose of the rebellious part is to rule in the soul although this is not proper, since by nature it is fit to be a slave to that which belongs to the ruling class. Something of this sort I suppose we'll say, and that the confusion and wandering of these parts are injustice, licentiousness, cowardice, lack of learning, and, in sum, vice entire."

"Certainly," he said, "that is what they are."

"Then," I said, "as for performing unjust actions and being unjust and, again, doing just c things, isn't what all of them are by now clearly manifest, if injustice and justice are also manifest?"

"How so?"

"Because," I said, "they don't differ from the healthy and the sick; what these are in a body, they are in a soul."

"In what way?" he said.

"Surely healthy things produce health and sick ones sickness."

"Yes."

444d   "Doesn't doing just things also produce justice and unjust ones injustice?"

"Necessarily."

"To produce health is to establish the parts of the body in a relation of mastering, and being mastered by, one another that is according to nature, while to produce sickness is to establish a relation of ruling, and being ruled by, one another that is contrary to nature."

"It is."

"Then, in its turn," I said, "isn't to produce justice to establish the parts of the soul in a relation of mastering, and being mastered by, one another that is according to nature, while to produce injustice is to establish a relation of ruling, and being ruled by, one another that is contrary to nature?"

"Entirely so," he said.

"Virtue, then, as it seems, would be a certain health, beauty and good condition of a soul, e and vice a sickness, ugliness and weakness."

"So it is."

"Don't fine practices also conduce to the acquisition of virtue and base ones to vice?"

"Necessarily."

"So, as it seems, it now remains for us to consider whether it is profitable to do just things, 445a practice fine ones, and be just – whether or not one's being such remains unnoticed; or whether it is profitable to do injustice and be unjust – provided one doesn't pay the penalty and become better as a result of punishment."

"But Socrates," he said, "that inquiry looks to me as though it has become ridiculous by now. If life doesn't seem livable with the body's nature corrupted, not even with every sort of food and drink and every sort of wealth and every sort of rule, will it then be livable when b the nature of that very thing by which we live is confused and corrupted, even if a man does whatever else he might want except that which will rid him of vice and injustice and will enable him to acquire justice and virtue? Isn't this clear now that all of these qualities have manifested their characters in our description?"

"Yes, it is ridiculous," I said. "But all the same, since we've come to the place from which we are able to see most clearly that these things are so, we mustn't weary."

"Least of all, by Zeus," he said, "must we shrink back."

c   "Now come here," I said, "so you too can see just how many forms vice, in my opinion, has; those, at least, that are worth looking at."

"I am following," he said. "Just tell me."

"Well," I said, "now that we've come up to this point in the argument, from a lookout as it were, it looks to me as though there is one form for virtue and an unlimited number for vice, but some four among them are also worth mentioning."

"How do you mean?"

"There are," I said, "likely to be as many types of soul as there are types of regimes possessing distinct forms."

"How many is that?"

d   "Five of regimes," I said, "and five of soul."

"Tell me what they are," he said.

"I say that one type of regime would be the one we've described, but it could be named in two ways," I said. "If one exceptional man arose among the rulers, it would be called a kingship, if more, an aristocracy."

"True," he said.

"Therefore," I said, "I say that this is one form. For whether it's many or one who arise, none of the city's laws that are worth mentioning would be changed, if that rearing and e education we described were made use of."

"It's not likely," he said.

[. . .]

Book V

"So, next, as it seems, we must try to seek out and demonstrate what is badly done in cities 473b today, and thereby keeps them from being governed in this way, and with what smallest change – preferably one, if not, two, and, if not, the fewest in number and the smallest in power – a city would come to this manner of regime."

"That's entirely certain," he said. c

"Well, then," I said, "with one change – not, however, a small or an easy one, but possible – we can, in my opinion, show that it would be transformed."

"What change?" he said.

"Well here I am," I said, "coming to what we likened to the biggest wave. But it shall be said regardless, even if, exactly like a gurgling wave, it's going to drown me in laughter and ill repute. Consider what I am going to say."

"Speak," he said.

"Unless," I said, "the philosophers rule as kings or those now called kings and chiefs genuinely and adequately philosophize, and political power and philosophy coincide in the same d place, while the many natures now making their way to either apart from the other are by necessity excluded, there is no rest from ills for the cities, my dear Glaucon, nor I think for human kind, nor will the regime we have now described in speech ever come forth from e nature, insofar as possible, and see the light of the sun. This is what for so long was causing my hesitation to speak: seeing how very paradoxical it would be to say. For it is hard to see that in no other city would there be private or public happiness."

And he said, "Socrates, what a phrase and argument you have let burst out. Now that it's said, you can believe that very many men, and not ordinary ones, will on the spot throw 474a off their clothes, and stripped for action, taking hold of whatever weapon falls under the hand of each, run full speed at you to do wonderful deeds. If you don't defend yourself with speech and get away, you'll really pay the penalty in scorn."

"Isn't it you," I said, "that's responsible for this happening to me?"

"And it's a fine thing I'm doing," he said. "But no, I won't betray you, and I'll defend you with what I can. I can provide good will and encouragement; and perhaps I would answer you more suitably than another. And so, with the assurance of such support, try to show b the disbelievers that it is as *you* say."

"It must be tried," I said, "especially since you offer so great an alliance. It's necessary, in my opinion, if we are somehow going to get away from the men you speak of, to distinguish for them whom we mean when we dare to assert the philosophers must rule. Thus, when they have come plainly to light, one will be able to defend oneself, showing that it is by nature fitting for them both to engage in philosophy and to lead a city, and for the rest c not to engage in philosophy and to follow the leader."

"It would be high time," he said, "to distinguish them."

"Come, now, follow me here, if we are somehow or other to set it forth adequately."

"Lead," he said.

"Will you need to be reminded," I said, "or do you remember that when we say a man loves something, if it is rightly said of him, he mustn't show a love for one part of it and not for another, but must cherish all of it?"

474d   "I need reminding, as it seems," he said. "For I scarcely understand."

"It was proper for another, Glaucon, to say what you're saying," I said. "But it's not proper for an erotic man to forget that all boys in the bloom of youth in one way or another put their sting in an erotic lover of boys and arouse him; all seem worthy of attention and delight. Or don't you people behave that way with the fair? You praise the boy with a snub nose by calling him 'cute'; the hook-nose of another you say is 'kingly'; and the boy between these

e   two is 'well proportioned'; the dark look 'manly'; and the white are 'children of gods.' And as for the 'honey-colored,' do you suppose their very name is the work of anyone other than a lover who renders sallowness endearing and easily puts up with it if it accompanies the bloom of youth? And, in a word, you people take advantage of every excuse and employ

475a   any expression so as to reject none of those who glow with the bloom of youth."

"If you want to point to me while you speak about what erotic men do," he said, "I agree for the sake of the argument."

"And what about this?" I said. "Don't you see wine-lovers doing the same thing? Do they delight in every kind of wine, and on every pretext?"

"Indeed, they do."

"And further, I suppose you see that lovers of honor, if they can't become generals, are

b   lieutenants, and if they can't be honored by greater and more august men, are content to be honored by lesser and more ordinary men because they are desirers of honor as a whole."

"That's certainly the case."

"Then affirm this or deny it: when we say a man is a desirer of something, will we assert that he desires all of that form, or one part of it and not another?"

"All," he said.

"Won't we also then assert that the philosopher is a desirer of wisdom, not of one part and not another, but of all of it?"

"True."

"We'll deny, therefore, that the one who's finicky about his learning, especially when he's

c   young and doesn't yet have an account of what's useful and not, is a lover of learning or a philosopher, just as we say that the man who's finicky about his food isn't hungry, doesn't desire food, and isn't a lover of food but a bad eater."

"And we'll be right in denying it."

"But the one who is willing to taste every kind of learning with gusto, and who approaches learning with delight, and is insatiable, we shall justly assert to be a philosopher, won't we?"

d   And Glaucon said, "Then you'll have many strange ones. For all the lovers of sights are in my opinion what they are because they enjoy learning; and the lovers of hearing would be some of the strangest to include among philosophers, those who would never be willing to go voluntarily to a discussion and such occupations but who – just as though they had hired out their ears for hearing – run around to every chorus at the Dionysia, missing none in the cities or the villages. Will we say that all these men and other learners of such things

e   and the petty arts are philosophers?"

"Not at all," I said, "but they are like philosophers."

"Who do you say are the true ones?" he said.

"The lovers of the sight of the truth," I said.

"And that's right," he said. "But how do you mean it?"

"It wouldn't be at all easy to tell someone else. But you, I suppose, will grant me this."

"What?"

"Since fair is the opposite of ugly, they are two."

"Of course." 476a

"Since they are two, isn't each also one?"

"That is so as well."

"The same argument also applies then to justice and injustice, good and bad, and all the forms; each is itself one, but, by showing themselves everywhere in a community with actions, bodies, and one another, each looks like many."

"What you say," he said, "is right."

"Well, now," I said, "this is how I separate them out. On one side I put those of whom you were just speaking, the lovers of sights, the lovers of arts, and the practical men; on the other, those whom the argument concerns, whom alone one could rightly call philosophers." b

"How do you mean?" he said.

"The lovers of hearing and the lovers of sights, on the one hand," I said, "surely delight in fair sounds and colors and shapes and all that craft makes from such things, but their thought is unable to see and delight in the nature of the fair itself."

"That," he said, "is certainly so."

"Wouldn't, on the other hand, those who are able to approach the fair itself and see it by itself be rare?"

"Indeed they would." c

"Is the man who holds that there are fair things but doesn't hold that there is beauty itself and who, if someone leads him to the knowledge of it, isn't able to follow – is he, in your opinion, living in a dream or is he awake? Consider it. Doesn't dreaming, whether one is asleep or awake, consist in believing a likeness of something to be not a likeness, but rather the thing itself to which it is like?"

"I, at least," he said, "would say that a man who does that dreams."

"And what about the man who, contrary to this, believes that there is something fair itself and is able to catch sight both of it and of what participates in it, and doesn't believe that d what participates is it itself, nor that it itself is what participates – is he, in your opinion, living in a dream or is he awake?"

"He's quite awake," he said.

"Wouldn't we be right in saying that this man's thought, because he knows, is knowledge, while the other's is opinion because he opines?"

"Most certainly."

"What if the man of whom we say that he opines but doesn't know, gets harsh with us and disputes the truth of what we say? Will we have some way to soothe and gently e persuade him, while hiding from him that he's not healthy?"

"We surely have to have a way, at least," he said.

"Come, then, and consider what we'll say to him. Or do you want us to question him in this way – saying that if he does know something, it's not begrudged him, but that we would be delighted to see he knows something – but tell us this: Does the man who knows, know something or nothing? You answer me on his behalf."

"I'll answer," he said, "that he knows something."

"Is it something that *is* or *is not*?"

477a   "That *is*. How could what *is not* be known at all?"

"So, do we have an adequate grasp of the fact – even if we should consider it in many ways – that what *is* entirely, is entirely knowable; and what in no way *is*, is in every way unknowable?"

"Most adequate."

"All right. Now if there were something such as both to be and not to be, wouldn't it lie between what purely and simply *is* and what in no way *is*?"

"Yes, it would be between."

"Since knowledge depended on what *is* and ignorance necessarily on what *is not*, mustn't we also seek something between ignorance and knowledge that depends on that which is in

b   between, if there is in fact any such thing?"

"Most certainly."

"Do we say opinion is something?"

"Of course."

"A power different from knowledge or the same?"

"Different."

"Then opinion is dependent on one thing and knowledge on another, each according to its own power."

"That's so."

"Doesn't knowledge naturally depend on what *is*, to know of what is that it is and how it is? However, in my opinion, it's necessary to make this distinction first."

"What distinction?"

c   "We will assert that powers are a certain class of beings by means of which we are capable of what we are capable, and also everything else is capable of whatever it is capable. For example, I say sight and hearing are powers, if perchance you understand the form of which I wish to speak."

"I do understand," he said.

"Now listen to how they look to me. In a power I see no color or shape or anything of the sort such as I see in many other things to which I look when I distinguish one thing from

d   another for myself. With a power I look only to this – on what it depends and what it accomplishes; and it is on this basis that I come to call each of the powers a power; and that which depends on the same thing and accomplishes the same thing, I call the same power, and that which depends on something else and accomplishes something else, I call a different power. What about you? What do you do?"

"The same," he said.

"Now, you best of men, come back here to knowledge again. Do you say it's some kind of power, or in what class do you put it?"

"In this one," he said, "as the most vigorous of all powers."

e   "And what about opinion? Is it among the powers, or shall we refer it to some other form?"

"Not at all," he said. "For that by which we are capable of opining is nothing other than opinion."

"But just a little while ago you agreed that knowledge and opinion are not the same."

"How," he said, "could any intelligent man count that which doesn't make mistakes the same as that which does?"

478a   "Fine," I said, "and we plainly agree that opinion is different from knowledge."

"Yes, it is different."

"Since each is capable of something different, are they, therefore, naturally dependent on different things?"

"Necessarily."

"Knowledge is presumably dependent on what *is*, to know of what *is* that it is and how it is?"

"Yes."

"While opinion, we say, opines."

"Yes."

"The same thing that knowledge knows? And will the knowable and the opinable be the same? Or is that impossible?"

"On the basis of what's been agreed to, it's impossible," he said. "If different powers are naturally dependent on different things and both are powers – opinion and knowledge – and each is, as we say, different, then on this basis it's not admissible that the knowable and the b opinable be the same."

"If what *is*, is knowable, then wouldn't something other than that which *is* be opinable?"

"Yes, it would be something other."

"Then does it opine what *is not*? Or is it also impossible to opine what *is not*? Think about it. Doesn't the man who opines refer his opinion to something? Or is it possible to opine, but to opine nothing?"

"No, it's impossible."

"The man who opines, opines some one thing?"

"Yes."

"But further, that which *is not* could not with any correctness be addressed as some one thing but rather nothing at all." c

"Certainly."

"To that which *is not*, we were compelled to assign ignorance, and to that which *is*, knowledge."

"Right," he said.

"Opinion, therefore, opines neither that which *is* nor that which *is not*."

"No, it doesn't."

"Opinion, therefore, would be neither ignorance nor knowledge?"

"It doesn't seem so."

"Is it, then, beyond these, surpassing either knowledge in clarity or ignorance in obscurity?"

"No, it is neither."

"Does opinion," I said, "look darker than knowledge to you and brighter than ignorance?"

"Very much so," he said.

"And does it lie within the limits set by these two?" d

"Yes."

"Opinion, therefore, would be between the two."

"That's entirely certain."

"Weren't we saying before that if something should come to light as what *is* and what *is not* at the same time, it lies between that which purely and simply *is* and that which in every way *is not*, and that neither knowledge nor ignorance will depend on it, but that which in its turn comes to light between ignorance and knowledge?"

"Right."

"And now it is just that which we call opinion that has come to light between them."

"Yes, that is what has come to light."

478e "Hence, as it seems, it would remain for us to find what participates in both – in *to be* and *not to be* – and could not correctly be addressed as either purely and simply, so that, if it comes to light, we can justly address it as the opinable, thus assigning the extremes to the extremes and that which is in between to that which is in between. Isn't that so?"

"Yes, it is."

"Now, with this taken for granted, let him tell me, I shall say, and let him answer – that
479a good man who doesn't believe that there is anything fair in itself and an *idea* of the beautiful itself, which always stays the same in all respects, but does hold that there are many fair things, this lover of sights who can in no way endure it if anyone asserts the fair is one and the just is one and so on with the rest. 'Now, of these many fair things, you best of men,' we'll say, 'is there any that won't also look ugly? And of the just, any that won't look unjust? And of the holy, any that won't look unholy?'"

b "No," he said, "but it's necessary that they look somehow both fair and ugly, and so it is with all the others you ask about."

"And what about the many doubles? Do they look any less half than double?"

"No."

"And, then, the things that we would assert to be big and little, light and heavy – will they be addressed by these names any more than by the opposites of these names?"

"No," he said, "each will always have something of both."

"Then is each of the several manys what one asserts it to be any more than it is not what one asserts it to be?"

"They are like the ambiguous jokes at feasts," he said, "and the children's riddle about the
c eunuch, about his hitting the bat – with what and on what he struck it. For the manys are also ambiguous, and it's not possible to think of them fixedly as either being or not being, or as both or neither."

"Can you do anything with them?" I said. "Or could you find a finer place to put them than between being and not to be? For presumably nothing darker than not-being will come to light so that something could *not be* more than it; and nothing brighter than being will
d come to light so that something could *be* more than it."

"Very true," he said.

"Then we have found, as it seems, that the many beliefs of the many about what's fair and about the other things roll around somewhere between not-being and being purely and simply."

"Yes, we have found that."

"And we agreed beforehand that, if any such thing should come to light, it must be called opinable but not knowable, the wanderer between, seized by the power between."

"Yes, we did agree."

e "And, as for those who look at many fair things but don't see the fair itself and aren't even able to follow another who leads them to it, and many just things but not justice itself, and so on with all the rest, we'll assert that they opine all these things but know nothing of what they opine."

"Necessarily," he said.

"And what about those who look at each thing itself – at the things that are always the same in all respects? Won't we say that they know and don't opine?"

"That too is necessary."

"Won't we assert that these men delight in and love that on which knowledge depends, and the others that on which opinion depends? Or don't we remember that we were saying 480a that they love and look at fair sounds and colors and such things but can't even endure the fact that the fair itself is something?"

"Yes, we do remember."

"So, will we strike a false note in calling them lovers of opinion rather than lovers of wisdom? And will they be very angry with us if we speak this way?"

"No," he said, "that is, if they are persuaded by me. For it's not lawful to be harsh with what's true."

"Must we, therefore, call philosophers rather than lovers of opinion those who delight in each thing that is itself?"

"That's entirely certain."

Book VI

[. . .]

"Now, then, as it seems, it turns out for us that what we are saying about lawgiving is best 502c if it could come to be, and that it is hard for it to come to be; not, however, impossible."

"Yes," he said, "that's the way it turns out."

"Now that this discussion has after considerable effort reached an end, mustn't we next speak about what remains – in what way and as a result of what studies and practices the saviors will take their place within our regime for us and at what ages each will take up each d study?"

"Indeed we must," he said.

"It hasn't," I said, "turned out to have been very wise of me to have left aside previously the unpleasantness about the possession of women, nor to have left aside procreation, as well as the institution of the rulers either. I did so because I knew that the wholly and completely true institution is a thing both likely to arouse resentment and hard to bring into being. But, as it was, the necessity of going through these things nonetheless arose. Well, what particularly concerns women and children has been completed, but what concerns the e rulers must be pursued as it were from the beginning. We were saying, if you remember, that they must show themselves to be lovers of the city, tested in pleasures and pains, and 503a that they must show that they don't cast out this conviction in labors or fears or any other reverse. The man who's unable to be so must be rejected, while the one who emerges altogether pure, like gold tested in fire, must be set up as ruler and be given gifts and prizes both when he is alive and after he has died. These were the kinds of things that were being said as the argument, covering its face, sneaked by, for fear of setting in motion what now b confronts us."

"What you say is quite true," he said. "I do remember."

"My friend, I shrank from saying what has now been dared anyhow," I said. "And let's now dare to say this: philosophers must be established as the most precise guardians."

"Yes, let it be said," he said.

"Then bear in mind that you'll probably have but a few. For the parts of the nature that we described as a necessary condition for them are rarely willing to grow together in the same place; rather its many parts grow forcibly separated from each other."

503c   "How do you mean?" he said.

"You know that natures that are good at learning, have memories, are shrewd and quick and everything else that goes along with these qualities, and are as well full of youthful fire and magnificence – such natures don't willingly grow together with understandings that choose orderly lives which are quiet and steady. Rather the men who possess them are carried away by their quickness wherever chance leads and all steadiness goes out from them."

"What you say is true," he said.

"And, on the other hand, those steady, not easily changeable dispositions, which one would

d be inclined to count on as trustworthy and which in war are hard to move in the face of fears, act the same way in the face of studies. They are hard to move and hard to teach, as if they had become numb; and they are filled with sleep and yawning when they must work through anything of the sort."

"That's so," he said.

"But we are saying that this nature must participate in both in good and fair fashion, or it mustn't be given a share in the most precise education, in honor, or in rule."

"Right," he said.

"Don't you suppose this will be rare?"

"Of course."

e   "Then it must be tested in the labors, fears, and pleasures we mentioned then; and moreover – what we passed over then but mention now – it must also be given gymnastic in many studies to see whether it will be able to bear the greatest studies, or whether it will

504a turn out to be a coward, as some turn out to be cowards in the other things."

"Well, that's surely the proper way to investigate it," he said. "But exactly what kinds of studies do you mean by the greatest?"

"You, of course, remember," I said, "that by separating out three forms in the soul we figured out what justice, moderation, courage, and wisdom each is."

"If I didn't remember," he said, "it would be just for me not to hear the rest."

"And also what was said before that?"

"What was it?"

b   "We were, I believe, saying that in order to get the finest possible look at these things another and longer road around would be required, and to the man who took it they would become evident, but that proofs on a level with what had been said up to then could be tacked on. And you all said that that would suffice. And so, you see, the statements made at that time were, as it looks to me, deficient in precision. If they were satisfactory to you, only you can tell."

"They were satisfactory to me, within measure," he said. "And it looks as though they were for the others too."

c   "My friend," I said, "a measure in such things, which in any way falls short of that which *is*, is no measure at all. For nothing incomplete is the measure of anything. But certain men are sometimes of the opinion that this question has already been adequately disposed of and that there is no need to seek further."

"Easygoingness," he said, "causes quite a throng of men to have this experience."

"Well," I said, "it's an experience a guardian of a city and of laws hardly needs."

"That's likely," he said.

"Well then, my comrade," I said, "such a man must go the longer way around and labor

d no less at study than at gymnastic, or else, as we were just saying, he'll never come to the end of the greatest and most fitting study."

"So these aren't the greatest," he said, "but there is something yet greater than justice and the other things we went through?"

"There is both something greater," I said, "and also even for these very virtues it won't do to look at a sketch, as we did a while ago, but their most perfect elaboration must not be stinted. Or isn't it ridiculous to make every effort so that other things of little worth be as precise and pure as can be, while not deeming the greatest things worth the greatest e precision?"

"That's a very worthy thought," he said. "However, as to what you mean by the greatest study and what it concerns, do you think anyone is going to let you go without asking what it is?"

"Certainly not," I said. "Just ask. At all events, it's not a few times already that you have heard it; but now you are either not thinking or have it in mind to get hold of me again and cause me trouble. I suppose it's rather the latter, since you have many times heard that the 505a *idea* of the good is the greatest study and that it's by availing oneself of it along with just things and the rest that they become useful and beneficial. And now you know pretty certainly that I'm going to say this and, besides this, that we don't have sufficient knowledge of it. And, if we don't know it and should have ever so much knowledge of the rest without this, you know that it's no profit to us, just as there would be none in possessing something in the absence of the good. Or do you suppose it's of any advantage to possess everything b except what's good? Or to be prudent about everything else in the absence of the good, while being prudent about nothing fine and good?"

"No, by Zeus," he said. "I don't."

"And, further, you also know that in the opinion of the many the good is pleasure, while in that of the more refined it is prudence."

"Of course."

"And, my friend, that those who believe this can't point out what kind of prudence it is, but are finally compelled to say 'about the good.' "

"And it's quite ridiculous of them," he said.

"Of course, it is," I said, "if they reproach us for not knowing the good, and then speak c as though we did know. For they say it is prudence about the good as though we, in turn, grasped what they mean when they utter the name of the good."

"Very true," he said.

"And what about those who define pleasure as good? Are they any less full of confusion than the others? Or aren't they too compelled to agree that there are bad pleasures?"

"Indeed they are."

"Then I suppose the result is that they agree that the same things are good and bad, isn't it?"

"Of course." d

"Isn't it clear that there are many great disputes about it?"

"Of course."

"And what about this? Isn't it clear that many men would choose to do, possess, and enjoy the reputation for things that are opined to be just and fair, even if they aren't, while, when it comes to good things, no one is satisfied with what is opined to be so but each seeks the things that *are*, and from here on out everyone despises the opinion?"

"Quite so," he said.

"Now this is what every soul pursues and for the sake of which it does everything. The soul divines that it is something but is at a loss about it and unable to get a sufficient grasp e of just what it is, or to have a stable trust such as it has about the rest. And because this is so, the soul loses any profit there might have been in the rest. Will we say that even those 506a best men in the city, into whose hands we put everything, must be thus in the dark about a thing of this kind and importance?"

"Least of all," he said.

"I suppose, at least," I said, "that just and fair things, when it isn't known in what way they are good, won't have gotten themselves a guardian who's worth very much in the man who doesn't know this. I divine that no one will adequately know the just and fair things themselves before this is known."

"That's a fine divination of yours," he said.

b   "Won't our regime be perfectly ordered if such a guardian, one who knows these things, oversees it?"

"Necessarily," he said. "But now, Socrates, do you say that the good is knowledge, or pleasure, or something else beside these?"

"Here's a real man!" I said. "It's been pretty transparent all along that other people's opinions about these things wouldn't be enough for you."

"It doesn't appear just to me, Socrates," he said, "to be ready to tell other people's con-
c victions but not your own when you have spent so much time occupied with these things."

"And what about this?" I said. "Is it your opinion that it's just to speak about what one doesn't know as though one knew?"

"Not at all as though one knew," he said; "however, one ought to be willing to state what one supposes, as one's supposition."

"What?" I said. "Haven't you noticed that all opinions without knowledge are ugly? The best of them are blind. Or do men who opine something true without intelligence seem to you any different from blind men who travel the right road?"

"No," he said.

"Do you want to see ugly things, blind and crooked, when it's possible to hear bright and
d fair ones from others?"

"No, in the name of Zeus, Socrates," said Glaucon. "You're not going to withdraw when you are, as it were, at the end. It will satisfy us even if you go through the good just as you went through justice, moderation and the rest."

"It will quite satisfy me too, my comrade," I said. "But I fear I'll not be up to it, and in my eagerness I'll cut a graceless figure and have to pay the penalty by suffering ridicule. But,
e you blessed men, let's leave aside for the time being what the good itself is – for it looks to me as though it's out of the range of our present thrust to attain the opinions I now hold about it. But I'm willing to tell what looks like a child of the good and most similar to it, if you please, or if not, to let it go."

"Do tell," he said. "Another time you'll pay us what's due on the father's narrative."

507a   "I could wish," I said, "that I were able to pay and you were able to receive it itself, and not just the interest, as is the case now. Anyhow, receive this interest and child of the good itself. But be careful that I don't in some way unwillingly deceive you in rendering the account of the interest fraudulent."

"We'll be as careful as we possibly can," he said. "Just speak."

"Yes," I said, "as soon as I've come to an agreement and reminded you of the things stated here earlier and already often repeated on other occasions."

b   "What are they?" he said.

"We both assert that there are," I said, "and distinguish in speech, many fair things, many good things, and so on for each kind of thing."

"Yes, so we do."

"And we also assert that there is a fair itself, a good itself, and so on for all the things that we then set down as many. Now, again, we refer them to one *idea* of each as though the *idea* were one; and we address it as that which really *is*."

"That's so."

"And, moreover, we say that the former are seen but not intellected, while the *ideas* are intellected but not seen."

"That's entirely certain."

"With what part of ourselves do we see the things seen?" c

"With the sight," he said.

"Isn't it with hearing," I said, "that we hear the things heard, and with the other senses that we sense all that is sensed?"

"Of course."

"Have you," I said, "reflected on how lavish the craftsman of the senses was in the fabrication of the power of seeing and being seen?"

"Not very much," he said.

"Well consider it in this way. Is there a need for another class of thing in addition to hearing and sound in order that the one hear and the other be heard – a third thing in the absence of which the one won't hear and the other won't be heard?" d

"No," he said.

"I suppose," I said, "that there are not many other things, not to say none, that need anything of the kind. Or can you tell of any?"

"Not I," he said.

"Don't you notice that the power of seeing and what's seen do have such a need?"

"How?"

"Surely, when sight is in the eyes and the man possessing them tries to make use of it, and color is present in what is to be seen, in the absence of a third class of thing whose nature is specifically directed to this very purpose, you know that the sight will see nothing and the e colors will be unseen."

"What class of thing are you speaking of?" he said.

"It's that which you call light," I said.

"What you say is true," he said.

"Then the sense of sight and the power of being seen are yoked together with a yoke that, by the measure of an *idea* by no means insignificant, is more honorable than the yokes 508a uniting other teams, if light is not without honor."

"But, of course," he said, "it's far from being without honor."

"Which of the gods in heaven can you point to as the lord responsible for this, whose light makes our sight see in the finest way and the seen things seen?"

"The very one you and the others would also point to," he said. "For it's plain your question refers to the sun."

"Is sight, then, naturally related to this god in the following way?"

"How?"

"Neither sight itself nor that in which it comes to be – what we call the eye – is the sun." b

"Surely not."

"But I suppose it is the most sunlike of the organs of the senses."

"Yes, by far."

"Doesn't it get the power it has as a sort of overflow from the sun's treasury?"

"Most certainly."

"And the sun isn't sight either, is it, but as its cause is seen by sight itself?"

"That's so," he said.

"Well, then," I said, "say that the sun is the offspring of the good I mean – an offspring the good begot in a proportion with itself: as the good is in the intelligible region with respect 508c to intelligence and what is intellected, so the sun is in the visible region with respect to sight and what is seen."

"How?" he said. "Explain it to me still further."

"You know," I said, "that eyes, when one no longer turns them to those things over whose colors the light of day extends but to those over which the gleams of night extend, are dimmed and appear nearly blind as though pure sight were not in them."

"Quite so," he said.

d "But, I suppose, when one turns them on those things illuminated by the sun, they see clearly and sight shows itself to be in these same eyes."

"Surely."

"Well, then, think that the soul is also characterized in this way. When it fixes itself on that which is illumined by truth and that which *is*, it intellects, knows, and appears to possess intelligence. But when it fixes itself on that which is mixed with darkness, on coming into being and passing away, it opines and is dimmed, changing opinions up and down, and seems at such times not to possess intelligence."

"Yes, that's the way it seems."

e "Therefore, say that what provides the truth to the things known and gives the power to the one who knows, is the *idea* of the good. And, as the cause of the knowledge and truth, you can understand it to be a thing known; but, as fair as these two are – knowledge and truth – if you believe that it is something different from them and still fairer than they, your 509a belief will be right. As for knowledge and truth, just as in the other region it is right to hold light and sight sunlike, but to believe them to be sun is not right; so, too, here, to hold these two to be like the good is right, but to believe that either of them is the good is not right. The condition which characterizes the good must receive still greater honor."

"You speak of an overwhelming beauty," he said, "if it provides knowledge and truth but is itself beyond them in beauty. You surely don't mean it is pleasure."

"Hush, Glaucon," I said. "But consider its image still further in this way."

b "How?"

"I suppose you'll say the sun not only provides what is seen with the power of being seen, but also with generation, growth, and nourishment although it itself isn't generation."

"Of course."

"Therefore, say that not only being known is present in the things known as a consequence of the good, but also existence and being are in them besides as a result of it, although the good isn't being but is still beyond being, exceeding it in dignity and power."

c And Glaucon, quite ridiculously, said, "Apollo, what a demonic excess."

"You," I said, "are responsible for compelling me to tell my opinions about it."

"And don't under any conditions stop," he said, "at least until you have gone through the likeness with the sun, if you are leaving anything out."

"But, of course," I said, "I am leaving out a throng of things."

"Well," he said, "don't leave even the slightest thing aside."

"I suppose I will leave out quite a bit," I said. "But all the same, insofar as it's possible at present, I'll not leave anything out willingly."

"Don't," he said.

"Well, then," I said, "conceive that, as we say, these two things *are*, and that the one is d king of the intelligible class and region, while the other is king of the visible. I don't say 'of the heaven' so as not to seem to you to be playing the sophist with the name. Now, do you have these two forms, visible and intelligible?"

"I do."

"Then, take a line cut in two unequal segments, one for the class that is seen, the other for the class that is intellected – and go on and cut each segment in the same proportion. Now, in terms of relative clarity and obscurity, you'll have one segment in the visible part for images. I mean by images first shadows, then appearances produced in water and in all e close-grained, smooth, bright things, and everything of the sort, if you understand." 510a

"I do understand."

"Then in the other segment put that of which this first is the likeness – the animals around us, and everything that grows, and the whole class of artifacts."

"I put them there," he said.

"And would you also be willing," I said, "to say that with respect to truth or lack of it, as the opinable is distinguished from the knowable, so the likeness is distinguished from that of which it is the likeness?"

"I would indeed," he said. b

"Now, in its turn, consider also how the intelligible section should be cut."

"How?"

"Like this: in one part of it a soul, using as images the things that were previously imitated, is compelled to investigate on the basis of hypotheses and makes its way not to a beginning but to an end; while in the other part it makes its way to a beginning that is free from hypotheses; starting out from hypothesis and without the images used in the other part, by means of forms themselves it makes its inquiry through them."

"I don't," he said, "sufficiently understand what you mean here."

"Let's try again," I said. "You'll understand more easily after this introduction. I suppose c you know that the men who work in geometry, calculation, and the like treat as known the odd and the even, the figures, three forms of angles, and other things akin to these in each kind of inquiry. These things they make hypotheses and don't think it worthwhile to give any further account of them to themselves or others, as though they were clear to all. Beginning d from them, they go ahead with their exposition of what remains and end consistently at the object toward which their investigation was directed."

"Most certainly, I know that," he said.

"Don't you also know that they use visible forms besides and make their arguments about them, not thinking about them but about those others that they are like? They make the arguments for the sake of the square itself and the diagonal itself, not for the sake of the diagonal they draw, and likewise with the rest. These things themselves that they mold and e draw, of which there are shadows and images in water, they now use as images, seeking to see those things themselves, that one can see in no other way than with thought." 511a

"What you say is true," he said.

"Well, then, this is the form I said was intelligible. However, a soul in investigating it is compelled to use hypotheses, and does not go to a beginning because it is unable to step out above the hypotheses. And it uses as images those very things of which images are made by the things below, and in comparison with which they are opined to be clear and are given honor."

511b   "I understand," he said, "that you mean what falls under geometry and its kindred arts."

    "Well, then, go on to understand that by the other segment of the intelligible I mean that which argument itself grasps with the power of dialectic, making the hypotheses not beginnings but really hypotheses – that is, steppingstones and springboards – in order to reach what is free from hypothesis at the beginning of the whole. When it has grasped this, argument now depends on that which depends on this beginning and in such fashion goes

c back down again to an end; making no use of anything sensed in any way, but using forms themselves, going through forms to forms, it ends in forms too."

    "I understand," he said, "although not adequately – for in my opinion it's an enormous task you speak of – that you wish to distinguish that part of what is and is intelligible contemplated by the knowledge of dialectic as being clearer than that part contemplated by what are called the arts. The beginnings in the arts are hypotheses; and although those who behold their objects are compelled to do so with the thought and not the senses, these men – because

d they don't consider them by going up to a beginning, but rather on the basis of hypotheses – these men, in my opinion, don't possess intelligence with respect to the objects, even though they are, given a beginning, intelligible; and you seem to me to call the habit of geometers and their likes thought and not intelligence, indicating that thought is something between opinion and intelligence."

    "You have made a most adequate exposition," I said. "And, along with me, take these four affections arising in the soul in relation to the four segments: intellection in relation to

e the highest one, and thought in relation to the second; to the third assign trust, and to the last imagination. Arrange them in a proportion, and believe that as the segments to which they correspond participate in truth, so they participate in clarity."

    "I understand," he said. "And I agree and arrange them as you say."

Book VII

514a "Next, then," I said, "make an image of our nature in its education and want of education, likening it to a condition of the following kind. See human beings as though they were in an underground cave-like dwelling with its entrance, a long one, open to the light across the whole width of the cave. They are in it from childhood with their legs and necks in bonds

b so that they are fixed, seeing only in front of them, unable because of the bond to turn their heads all the way around. Their light is from a fire burning far above and behind them. Between the fire and the prisoners there is a road above, along which see a wall, built like the partitions puppet-handlers set in front of the human beings and over which they show the puppets."

    "I see," he said.

    "Then also see along this wall human beings carrying all sorts of artifacts, which project

c above the wall, and statues of men and other animals wrought from stone, wood, and every

515a kind of material; as is to be expected, some of the carriers utter sounds while others are silent."

    "It's a strange image," he said, "and strange prisoners you're telling of."

    "They're like us," I said. "For in the first place, do you suppose such men would have seen anything of themselves and one another other than the shadows cast by the fire on the side of the cave facing them?"

    "How could they," he said, "if they had been compelled to keep their heads motionless

b throughout life?"

"And what about the things that are carried by? Isn't it the same with them?"

"Of course."

"If they were able to discuss things with one another, don't you believe they would hold that they are naming these things going by before them that they see?"

"Necessarily."

"And what if the prison also had an echo from the side facing them? Whenever one of the men passing by happens to utter a sound, do you suppose they would believe that anything other than the passing shadow was uttering the sound?"

"No, by Zeus," he said. "I don't."

"Then most certainly," I said, "such men would hold that the truth is nothing other than c the shadows of artificial things."

"Most necessarily," he said.

"Now consider," I said, "what their release and healing from bonds and folly would be like if something of this sort were by nature to happen to them. Take a man who is released and suddenly compelled to stand up, to turn his neck around, to walk and look up toward the light; and who, moreover, in doing all this is in pain and, because he is dazzled, is unable to make out those things whose shadows he saw before. What do you suppose he'd say if d someone were to tell him that before he saw silly nothings, while now, because he is somewhat nearer to what *is* and more turned toward beings, he sees more correctly; and, in particular, showing him each of the things that pass by, were to compel the man to answer his questions about what they are? Don't you suppose he'd be at a loss and believe that what was seen before is truer than what is now shown?"

"Yes," he said, "by far."

"And, if he compelled him to look at the light itself, would his eyes hurt and would he e flee, turning away to those things that he is able to make out and hold them to be really clearer than what is being shown?"

"So he would," he said.

"And if," I said, "someone dragged him away from there by force along the rough, steep, upward way and didn't let him go before he had dragged him out into the light of the sun, wouldn't he be distressed and annoyed at being so dragged? And when he came to the 516a light, wouldn't he have his eyes full of its beam and be unable to see even one of the things now said to be true?"

"No, he wouldn't," he said, "at least not right away."

"Then I suppose he'd have to get accustomed, if he were going to see what's up above. At first he'd most easily make out the shadows; and after that the phantoms of the human beings and the other things in water; and, later, the things themselves. And from there he could turn to beholding the things in heaven and heaven itself, more easily at night – looking at the light of the stars and the moon – than by day – looking at the sun and sunlight." b

"Of course."

"Then finally I suppose he would be able to make out the sun – not its appearances in water or some alien place, but the sun itself by itself in its own region – and see what it's like."

"Necessarily," he said.

"And after that he would already be in a position to conclude about it that this is the source of the seasons and the years, and is the steward of all things in the visible place, and is in a c certain way the cause of all those things he and his companions had been seeing."

"It's plain," he said, "that this would be his next step."

"What then? When he recalled his first home and the wisdom there, and his fellow prisoners in that time, don't you suppose he would consider himself happy for the change and pity the others?"

"Quite so."

"And if in that time there were among them any honors, praises, and prizes for the man who is sharpest at making out the things that go by, and most remembers which of them 516d are accustomed to pass before, which after, and which at the same time as others, and who is thereby most able to divine what is going to come, in your opinion would he be desirous of them and envy those who are honored and hold power among these men? Or, rather, would he be affected as Homer says and want very much 'to be on the soil, a serf to another man, to a portionless man,' and to undergo anything whatsoever rather than to opine those things and live that way?"

e "Yes," he said, "I suppose he would prefer to undergo everything rather than live that way."

"Now reflect on this too," I said. "If such a man were to come down again and sit in the same seat, on coming suddenly from the sun wouldn't his eyes get infected with darkness?"

"Very much so," he said.

"And if he once more had to compete with those perpetual prisoners in forming judg- 517a ments about those shadows while his vision was still dim, before his eyes had recovered, and if the time needed for getting accustomed were not at all short, wouldn't he be the source of laughter, and wouldn't it be said of him that he went up and came back with his eyes corrupted, and that it's not even worth trying to go up? And if they were somehow able to get their hands on and kill the man who attempts to release and lead up, wouldn't they kill him?"

"No doubt about it," he said.

"Well, then, my dear Glaucon," I said, "this image as a whole must be connected with what b was said before. Liken the domain revealed through sight to the prison home, and the light of the fire in it to the sun's power; and, in applying the going up and the seeing of what's above to the soul's journey up to the intelligible place, you'll not mistake my expectation, since you desire to hear it. A god doubtless knows if it happens to be true. At all events, this is the way the phenomena look to me: in the knowable the last thing to be seen, and that c with considerable effort, is the *idea* of the good; but once seen, it must be concluded that this is in fact the cause of all that is right and fair in everything – in the visible it gave birth to light and its sovereign; in the intelligible, itself sovereign, it provided truth and intelligence – and that the man who is going to act prudently in private or in public must see it."

"I, too, join you in supposing that," he said, "at least in the way I can."

"Come, then," I said, "and join me in supposing this, too, and don't be surprised that the men who get to that point aren't willing to mind the business of human beings, but rather d that their souls are always eager to spend their time above. Surely that's likely, if indeed this, too, follows the image of which I told before."

"Of course it's likely," he said.

"And what about this? Do you suppose it is anything surprising," I said, "if a man, come from acts of divine contemplation to the human things, is graceless and looks quite ridiculous when – with his sight still dim and before he has gotten sufficiently accustomed to the surrounding darkness – he is compelled in courts or elsewhere to contest about the e shadows of the just or the representations of which they are the shadows, and to dispute about the way these things are understood by men who have never seen justice itself?"

"It's not at all surprising," he said.

"But if a man were intelligent," I said, "he would remember that there are two kinds of 518a disturbances of the eyes, stemming from two sources – when they have been transferred from light to darkness and when they have been transferred from darkness to light. And if he held that these same things happen to a soul too, whenever he saw one that is confused and unable to make anything out, he wouldn't laugh without reasoning but would go on to consider whether, come from a brighter life, it is in darkness for want of being accustomed, or whether, going from greater lack of learning to greater brightness, it is dazzled by the greater brilliance. And then he would deem the first soul happy for its condition and its life, b while he would pity the second. And, if he wanted to laugh at the second soul, his laughing in this case would make him less ridiculous himself than would his laughing at the soul which has come from above out of the light."

"What you say is quite sensible," he said.

"Then, if this is true," I said, "we must hold the following about these things: education is not what the professions of certain men assert it to be. They presumably assert that they put into the soul knowledge that isn't in it, as though they were putting sight into blind eyes." c

"Yes," he said, "they do indeed assert that."

"But the present argument, on the other hand," I said, "indicates that this power is in the soul of each, and that the instrument with which each learns – just as an eye is not able to turn toward the light from the dark without the whole body – must be turned around from that which *is coming into being* together with the whole soul until it is able to endure looking at that which *is* and the brightest part of that which *is*. And we affirm that this is the good, don't we?" d

"Yes."

"There would, therefore," I said, "be an art of this turning around, concerned with the way in which this power can most easily and efficiently be turned around, not an art of producing sight in it. Rather, this art takes as given that sight is there, but not rightly turned nor looking at what it ought to look at, and accomplishes this object."

"So it seems," he said.

"Therefore, the other virtues of a soul, as they are called, are probably somewhat close to those of the body. For they are really not there beforehand and are later produced by e habits and exercises, while the virtue of exercising prudence is more than anything somehow more divine, it seems; it never loses its power, but according to the way it is turned, it becomes useful and helpful or, again, useless and harmful. Or haven't you yet reflected 519a about the men who are said to be vicious but wise, how shrewdly their petty soul sees and how sharply it distinguishes those things toward which it is turned, showing that it doesn't have poor vision although it is compelled to serve vice; so that the sharper it sees, the more evil it accomplishes?"

"Most certainly," he said.

"However," I said, "if this part of such a nature were trimmed in earliest childhood and its ties of kinship with becoming were cut off – like leaden weights, which eating and such b pleasures as well as their refinements naturally attach to the soul and turn its vision downward – if, I say, it were rid of them and turned around toward the true things, this same part of the same human beings would also see them most sharply, just as it does those things toward which it now is turned."

"It's likely," he said.

"And what about this? Isn't it likely," I said, "and necessary, as a consequence of what was said before, that those who are without education and experience of truth would never be

519c adequate stewards of a city, nor would those who have been allowed to spend their time in education continuously to the end – the former because they don't have any single goal in life at which they must aim in doing everything they do in private or in public, the latter because they won't be willing to act, believing they have emigrated to a colony on the Isles of the Blessed while they are still alive?"

"True," he said.

"Then our job as founders," I said, "is to compel the best natures to go to the study which we were saying before is the greatest, to see the good and to go up that ascent; and, when

d they have gone up and seen sufficiently, not to permit them what is now permitted."

"What's that?"

"To remain there," I said, "and not be willing to go down again among those prisoners or share their labors and honors, whether they be slighter or more serious."

"What?" he said. "Are we to do them an injustice, and make them live a worse life when a better is possible for them?"

e "My friend, you have again forgotten," I said, "that it's not the concern of law that any one class in the city fare exceptionally well, but it contrives to bring this about for the whole city, harmonizing the citizens by persuasion and compulsion, making them share with one

520a another the benefit that each class is able to bring to the commonwealth. And it produces such men in the city not in order to let them turn whichever way each wants, but in order that it may use them in binding the city together."

"That's true," he said. "I did forget."

"Well, then, Glaucon," I said, "consider that we won't be doing injustice to the philosophers who come to be among us, but rather that we will say just things to them while compelling them besides to care for and guard the others. We'll say that when such men come

b to be in the other cities it is fitting for them not to participate in the labors of those cities. For they grow up spontaneously against the will of the regime in each; and a nature that grows by itself and doesn't owe its rearing to anyone has justice on its side when it is not eager to pay off the price of rearing to anyone. 'But you we have begotten for yourselves and for the rest of the city like leaders and kings in hives; you have been better and more

c perfectly educated and are more able to participate in both lives. So you must go down, each in his turn, into the common dwelling of the others and get habituated along with them to seeing the dark things. And, in getting habituated to it, you will see ten thousand times better than the men there, and you'll know what each of the phantoms is, and of what it is a phantom, because you have seen the truth about fair, just, and good things. And thus, the city will be governed by us and by you in a state of waking, not in a dream as the many cities nowadays are governed by men who fight over shadows with one another and form

d factions for the sake of ruling, as though it were some great good. But the truth is surely this: that city in which those who are going to rule are least eager to rule is necessarily governed in the way that is best and freest from faction, while the one that gets the opposite kind of rulers is governed in the opposite way.'"

"Most certainly," he said.

"Do you suppose our pupils will disobey us when they hear this and be unwilling to join in the labors of the city, each in his turn, while living the greater part of the time with one another in the pure region?"

e "Impossible," he said. "For surely we shall be laying just injunctions on just men. However, each of them will certainly approach ruling as a necessary thing – which is the opposite of what is done by those who now rule in every city."

"That's the way it is, my comrade," I said. "If you discover a life better than ruling for those who are going to rule, it is possible that your well-governed city will come into being. 521a For here alone will the really rich rule, rich not in gold but in those riches required by the happy man, rich in a good and prudent life. But if beggars, men hungering for want of private goods, go to public affairs supposing that in them they must seize the good, it isn't possible. When ruling becomes a thing fought over, such a war – a domestic war, one within the family – destroys these men themselves and the rest of the city as well."

"That's very true," he said.

"Have you," I said, "any other life that despises political offices other than that of true b philosophy?"

"No, by Zeus," he said. "I don't."

"But men who aren't lovers of ruling must go to it; otherwise, rival lovers will fight."

"Of course."

"Who else will you compel to go to the guarding of the city than the men who are most prudent in those things through which a city is best governed, and who have other honors and a better life than the political life?"

"No one else," he said.

"Do you want us now to consider in what way such men will come into being and how c one will lead them up to the light, just as some men are said to have gone from Hades up to the gods?"

"How could I not want to?" he said.

"Then, as it seems, this wouldn't be the twirling of a shell but the turning of a soul around from a day that is like night to the true day; it is that ascent to what *is* which we shall truly affirm to be philosophy."

"Most certainly."

15

Parmenides

The *Parmenides* is a remarkable dialogue, apparently written somewhat later in Plato's career, as he mulled over several problems with his earlier theory of Forms. In this dialogue, a youthful Socrates meets with the two great masters from Elea, Parmenides and Zeno, and by all appearances, Plato has the elder of these two, Parmenides, subject Plato's own theory of Forms (articulated and defended by Socrates) to tough criticism, for which Socrates finds he has no adequate reply. Scholars are not all convinced that the theory presented by Socrates in this dialogue really is the same one that Plato had Socrates defend in dialogues such as the *Phaedo* and the *Republic*. But in dialogues we know to be later than the *Parmenides*, it does appear as if the presentation of Plato's theory of Forms is quite different from its presentations in these other works. If so, the *Parmenides* may have a very special place in the history of philosophy as a work of admirable philosophical integrity, as Plato subjects his earlier views to devastating criticisms.

According to Antiphon, Pythodorus said that Zeno and Parmenides once came to Athens for the Great Panathenaea. Parmenides was then well along in years and quite grey, a dis-
127b tinguished-looking man of perhaps sixty-five. Zeno was about forty, handsome and tall. It was said he had been Parmenides' favorite. He said they stayed at Pythodorus's house in Ceramicus, outside the city walls, and Socrates came there with a number of others, eager
   c to hear a reading of Zeno's treatise, which Zeno and Parmenides had brought to Athens for the first time. Socrates was then quite young. Well, Zeno himself read to them, but Parmenides, as it happened, was out. Pythodorus said he came in with Parmenides and
   d Aristoteles, who was later one of the Thirty Tyrants, when the reading of the arguments was very nearly finished, and they heard only a small part of the remaining treatise. As for himself, however, he'd heard Zeno read it before. When the reading was finished, Socrates
   e asked to hear the hypothesis of the first argument again. When it was read, he asked, What does this mean, Zeno? If things which are, are many, then it must follow that the same things are both like and unlike, but that is impossible; for unlike things cannot be like nor like things unlike. Isn't that your claim?
   It is, said Zeno.

Then if it is impossible for unlike things to be like and like things unlike, it is surely also impossible for there to be many things; for if there were many, they would undergo impossible qualifications. Isn't this the point of your arguments, to contend, contrary to everything generally said, that there is no plurality? And don't you suppose that each of your arguments is a proof of just that, so that you in fact believe you've given precisely as many proofs that there is no plurality as there are arguments in your treatise? Is that what you mean, or have I failed to understand you? 128a

No, said Zeno, you've grasped the point of the whole treatise.

I gather, Parmenides, said Socrates, that Zeno here wishes to associate himself with you not only by other marks of friendship, but also by his book. For he's written to much the same effect as you, but by changing tactics he tries to mislead us into thinking he's saying something different. In your poems, you say the All is one, and you provide fine and excellent proofs of this. He, on the other hand, says it is not many, and himself also provides b proofs great in multitude and magnitude. So you say one, he says not many, and each so speaks that though there is no difference at all in what you mean, what you say scarcely seems the same. That's why what you've said appears quite beyond the rest of us.

Yes, Socrates, said Zeno. But you haven't wholly perceived the truth about my treatise. To be sure, you pick up the scent of the arguments and follow their trail like a young Spartan c hound. But you overlook this at the outset: the treatise is not so thoroughly pretentious as to have been written with the motive you allege, disguised for the public as a great achievement. What you mention is incidental. The real truth is that it's a defense of Parmenides' argument, directed against those who try to ridicule it on the ground that, if it is one, many d absurd and inconsistent consequences follow. This treatise then is a retort to those who assert the many, and pays them back in kind with interest; its purpose is to make clear that their own hypothesis – that plurality is, when followed out far enough – suffers still more absurd consequences than the hypothesis of there being one. I wrote it when I was young, in this sort of spirit of controversy, and after it was written someone stole it, so I wasn't allowed to decide whether or not it should see the light of day. So that's what you overlook, Socrates: e you suppose it was written by an older man zealous of reputation, not by a young man fond of controversy. Though as I said, you did not misrepresent it.

Why, I accept that, said Socrates. What you say is no doubt true. But tell me: do you not acknowledge that there exists, alone by itself, a certain character of likeness, and again, another 129a character opposite it, what it is to be unlike; and that you and I and the other things we call many get a share of these two things? And that things that get a share of likeness become like in the respect and to the degree that they get a share; things that get a share of unlikeness become unlike; and things that get a share of both become both? Even if all things get a share of both, opposite as they are, and by having a share of both they are both like and unlike themselves, what is surprising in that? If someone were to show that things that are b just like become unlike, or just unlike, like, no doubt that would be a portent. But I find nothing strange, Zeno, if he shows that things which get a share of both undergo both qualifications, nor if someone shows that all things are one by reason of having a share of the one, and that those very same things are also many by reason of having a share of multitude. But if he shows that what it is to be one is many, and the many also actually one, that will surprise me. The same is true of all other things in like manner. If someone should c show that the kinds and characters in themselves undergo these opposite qualifications, there is reason for surprise. But what is surprising if someone shall show that I am one and many?

When he wishes to show I am many, he says that my right side is one thing and my left another, that my front is different from my back, and my upper body in like manner different from my lower; for I suppose I have a share of multitude. To show that I am one, he'll 129d say I am one man among the seven of us, since I also have a share of the one. So he shows both are true. Now, if someone should undertake to show that sticks and stones and things like that are many, and the same things one, we'll grant he has proved that something is many and one, but not that the one is many or the many one; he has said nothing out of the ordinary, but a thing on which we all agree. But I should be filled with admiration, Zeno, said Socrates, if someone were first to distinguish separately, alone by themselves, the characters just mentioned – likeness and unlikeness, for example, multitude and the one, rest

e and motion, and all such similar things – and then should show that these things among themselves can be combined and distinguished. You have no doubt dealt manfully with the former issue. But, as I say, I would admire it much more if someone could show that this same perplexity is interwoven in all kinds of ways among the characters themselves – that 130a just as you and Parmenides have explained in the things we see, so it proves too in what we apprehend by reflection.

As Socrates was speaking, Pythodorus said he expected Parmenides and Zeno to be annoyed at every word. Instead, they paid close attention to him, and from time to time glanced at each other and smiled as if in admiration. When Socrates finished, Parmenides expressed

b this. Socrates, he said, your impulse toward argument is admirable. Now tell me: do you yourself thus distinguish, as you say, certain characters themselves separately by themselves, and separately again the things that have a share of them? And do you think that likeness itself is something separate from the likeness which we have, and again one and many and all the others you just heard Zeno mention?

Yes, I do, said Socrates.

And of this sort too? said Parmenides. For example, a certain character of just, alone by itself, and of beautiful and good and again all such as these?

Yes, he said.

c Well, is there a character of man separate from us and all such as we are, a certain character of man by itself, or of fire or water too?

I have often been in perplexity, Parmenides, he said, about whether one should speak about them as about the others, or not.

And what about these, Socrates – they would really seem ridiculous: hair and mud and dirt, for example, or anything else which is utterly worthless and trivial. Are you perplexed

d whether or not one should say that there is a separate character for each of these too, a character that again is other than the sorts of things we handle?

Not at all, said Socrates. Surely these things are just what we see them to be: it would be too absurd to suppose that something is a character of them. Still, I sometimes worry lest what holds in one case may not hold in all; but then, when I take that stand, I retreat, for fear of tumbling undone into depths of nonsense. So I go back to the things we just said have characters, and spend my time dealing with them.

e You are still young, Socrates, said Parmenides, and philosophy has not yet taken hold of you as I think it one day will. You will despise none of these things then. But as it is, because of your youth, you still pay attention to what people think. Now tell me this: do you think, as you say, that there are certain characters, of which these others here have a share and get 131a their names? As, for example, things that get a share of likeness become like, of largeness large, of beauty and justice beautiful and just?

Yes, certainly, said Socrates.

Then does each thing that gets a share get a share of the whole character, or of a part? Or would there be any kind of sharing separate from these?

Surely not, Socrates replied.

Then does it seem to you that the whole character, being one, is in each of the many?

What prevents it, Parmenides? said Socrates.

So being one and the same, it will be present at once and as a whole in things that are b many and separate, and thus it would be separate from itself.

No, it would not, he said, at least if it were like one and the same day, which is in many different places at once and nonetheless not separate from itself. If it were in fact that way, each of the characters could be in everything at once as one and the same.

Very neat, Socrates, he said. You make one and the same thing be in many different places at once, as if you'd spread a sail over a number of men and then claimed that one thing as a whole was over many. Or isn't that the sort of thing you mean to say?

Perhaps, he said.   c

Now, would the whole sail be over each man, or part of it over one and part over another?

Part.

So the characters themselves are divisible, Socrates, he said, and things that have a share of them would have a share of parts of them; whole would no longer be in each, but part of each in each.

Yes, so it appears.

Then are you willing to say that the one character is in truth divided for us, Socrates, and will still be one?

Not at all, he said.

No, for consider, he said: if you divide largeness itself, and each of the many large things is to be large by a part of largeness smaller than largeness itself, won't that appear unreasonable? d

Of course, he said.

Well then, suppose something is to have a given small part of the equal. Will the possessor be equal to anything by what is smaller than the equal itself?

Impossible.

But suppose one of us is to have a part of the small. The small will be larger than this part of it, because it is part of itself, and thus the small itself will be larger. But that to which the part subtracted is added will be smaller but not larger than before.   e

Surely that couldn't happen, he said.

Then in what way, Socrates, he said, will the others get a share of the characters for you, since they cannot get a share part by part nor whole by whole?

Such a thing, it seems to me, is difficult, emphatically difficult, to determine, he said.

Really? Then how do you deal with this?

What's that?

I suppose you think that each character is one for some such reason as this: when 132a some plurality of things seems to you to be large, there perhaps seems to be some one characteristic that is the same when you look over them all, whence you believe that the large is one.

True, he said.

What about the large itself and the other larges? If with your mind you should look over them all in like manner, will not some one large again appear, by which they all appear to be large?

It seems so.

So another character of largeness will have made its appearance, alongside largeness itself and the things which have a share of it; and over and above all those, again, a different one, 132b by which they will all be large. And then each of the characters will no longer be one for you, but unlimited in multitude.

But Parmenides, said Socrates, may it not be that each of the characters is a thought of these things, and it pertains to it to come to be nowhere else except in souls or minds? For in that way, each would be one, and no longer still undergo what was just now said.

Well, he said, is each of the thoughts one, but a thought of nothing?

No, that's impossible, he said.

A thought of something, then?

Yes.

Of something that is, or is not?

c   Of something that is.

Is it not of some one thing which that thought thinks as being over all, as some one characteristic?

Yes.

Then that which is thought to be one will be a character, ever the same over all?

Again, it appears it must.

Really? Then what about this, said Parmenides: in virtue of the necessity by which you say that the others have a share of characters, doesn't it seem to you that either each is composed of thoughts and all think, or that being thoughts they are unthought?

But that, he said, is hardly reasonable.

d   Still, Parmenides, he said, this much is quite clear to me: these characters stand, as it were, as paradigms fixed in the nature of things, but the others resemble them and are likenesses of them, and this sharing that the others come to have of characters is nothing other than being a resemblance of them.

Then if something resembles the character, he said, is it possible for that character not to be like what has come to resemble it, just insofar as it has been made like it? Is there any device by which what is like is not like to what is like?

There is not.

e   But what is like necessarily has a share of one and the same character as what it is like?

Yes.

But will not that of which like things have a share so as to be like be the character itself?

Certainly.

So it is not possible for anything to be like the character, nor the character like anything else. Otherwise, another character will always make its appearance alongside the character, 133a and should that be like something, a different one again, and continual generation of a new character will never stop, if the character becomes like what has a share of itself.

You're quite right.

So the others do not get a share of characters by likeness. Rather, one must look for something else by which they get a share.

So it seems.

Do you see, then, Socrates, he said, how great the perplexity is, if someone distinguishes as characters things that are alone by themselves?

Yes indeed.

Rest assured, he said, that you've hardly yet even begun to grasp how great the per- b
plexity is, if you're going to assume that each character of things which are is one, ever
marking it off as something.

How so? he said.

There are many other difficulties, he said, but the greatest is this. If someone should say
that it doesn't even pertain to the characters to be known if they are such as we say they must
be, one could not show him he was wrong unless the disputant happened to be a man of wide
experience and natural ability, willing to follow full many a remote and laborious demonstration. Otherwise, the man who compels them to be unknowable would be left unconvinced. c

Why is that, Parmenides? said Socrates.

Because, Socrates, I suppose that you and anyone else who assumes that the nature and
reality of each thing exists as something alone by itself would agree, first of all, that none of
them exists in us.

No, for how would it still be alone by itself? said Socrates.

You're right, he said. And further, as many of the characteristics as are what they are relative to each other have their nature and reality relative to themselves, but not relative to
things among us – likenesses, or whatever one assumes they are – of which we have a share d
and are in each case named after them. But things among us, though they are of the same
name as those, are again relative to themselves but not to the characters, and it is to themselves but not to those that as many as are so named refer.

How do you mean? said Socrates.

Take an example, said Parmenides. If one of us is a master or slave of someone, he is
surely not a slave of master by itself, what it is to be master, nor is a master the master of e
slave by itself, what it is to be slave. Being a man, we are both these of a man. Mastership
itself is what it is of slavery itself, and slavery in like manner slavery itself of mastership
itself. Things in us do not have their power and significance relative to things there, nor
things there relative to us. Rather, as I say, things there are themselves of and relative to
themselves, and in like manner things among us are relative to themselves. Or don't you 134a
understand what I mean?

Of course I do, said Socrates.

And furthermore, he said, knowledge itself, what it is to be knowledge, would be knowledge of what is there, namely, what it is to be real and true?

Of course.

And again each of the branches of knowledge which is would be knowledge of what it is
to be each of the things which are. Not so?

Yes.

But wouldn't knowledge among us be knowledge of the truth and reality among us? And
wouldn't it again follow that each branch of knowledge among us is knowledge of each of
the things that are among us? b

Necessarily.

Moreover, as you agree, we do not have the characters themselves, nor can they be
among us.

Of course not.

But the kinds themselves, what it is to be each thing, are known, I take it, by the
character of knowledge itself?

Yes.

Which we do not have.

No.

So none of the characters is known by us, since we do not have a share of knowledge itself.

It seems not.

So what it is to be beautiful itself, and the good, and everything we at this point accept 134c as being characteristics themselves, is for us unknowable.

Very likely.

Consider then whether the following is still more remarkable.

What is it?

You'd say, I take it, that if indeed there is a certain kind of knowledge by itself, it is much more exact than knowledge among us. So too of beauty, and all the rest.

Yes.

Then if indeed anything else has a share of knowledge itself, wouldn't you deny that anyone but god has the most exact knowledge?

Necessarily.

d Then will it also be possible for the god, having knowledge itself, to know things among us? Why shouldn't it be?

Because, Socrates, said Parmenides, we agreed that those characters do not have the power they have relative to things among us, nor things among us relative to those, but each relative to themselves.

Yes, we agreed to that.

Then if the most exact mastership by itself and the most exact knowledge by itself are in the god's realm, mastership there would never master things among us here, nor would know-
e ledge there know us or anything where we are. In like manner, we do not rule there by our authority here, and we know nothing divine by our own knowledge. By the same account, again, those there are not our masters, and have no knowledge of human things, being gods.

But surely, said Socrates, it would be too strange an account, if one were to deprive the gods of knowing.

And yet, Socrates, said Parmenides, these difficulties and many more still in addition nec-
135a essarily hold of the characters, if these characteristics of things that are exist, and one is to distinguish each character as something by itself. The result is that the hearer is perplexed and contends that they do not exist, and that even if their existence is conceded, they are necessarily unknowable by human nature. In saying this, he thinks he is saying something significant and, as we just remarked, it's astonishingly hard to convince him to the contrary. Only a man of considerable natural gifts will be able to understand that there is a certain kind of each thing, a nature and reality alone by itself, and it will take a man more remarkable
b still to discover it and be able to instruct someone else who has examined all these difficulties with sufficient care.

I agree with you, Parmenides, said Socrates. You're saying very much what I think too.

Nevertheless, said Parmenides, if in light of all the present difficulties and others like them, Socrates, one will not allow that there are characters of things that are, and refuses to distinguish as something a character of each single thing, he will not even have anything
c to which to turn his mind, since he will not allow that there is a characteristic, ever the same, of each of the things that are; and so he will utterly destroy the power and significance of thought and discourse. I think you are only too aware of that sort of consequence.

True, he replied.

What will you do about philosophy, then? Which way will you turn while these things are unknown?

For the moment, at least, I am not really sure I see.

No, because you undertake to mark off something beautiful and just and good and each one of the characters too soon, before being properly trained. I realized that yesterday, when d I heard you discussing here with Aristoteles. Believe me, your impulse toward argument is noble and indeed divine. But train yourself more thoroughly while you are still young; drag yourself through what is generally regarded as useless, and condemned by the multitude as idle talk. Otherwise, the truth will escape you.

16

Timaeus

The *Timaeus* is the only work of Plato's that was continuously available in the West, and influenced many thinkers – including arguably Plato's most famous student, Aristotle – in several areas of philosophy and science. The dialogue is represented as a discussion held on the day after the conversation represented in the *Republic*, but the subject matter here is not politics and moral psychology, but cosmology, biology, and metaphysics. Plato approaches these subjects as a rationalist rather than as an empiricist. He recognizes that the questions he asks and seeks to answer cannot be answered with certainty, and represents his own views as, at best, only probable. But the source of his views is his own ability to reason logically. In this, Aristotle's more empiricist approach strikes us as the more scientific one. But Plato's influence on Aristotle, even so, is evident, and the imagination with which Plato approaches these most challenging subjects is magnificent.

27c TIMAEUS: That, Socrates, is what all do, who have the least portion of wisdom: always, at the outset of every undertaking, small or great, they call upon a god. We who are now to discourse about the universe – how it came into being, or perhaps had no beginning of existence – must, if our senses be not altogether gone astray, invoke gods and goddesses with a prayer that our discourse throughout may be above all pleasing to them and in consequence
d satisfactory to us. Let this suffice, then, for our invocation of the gods; but we must also call upon our own powers, so that you may follow most readily and I may give the clearest expression to my thought on the theme proposed.

We must, then, in my judgment, first make this distinction: what is that which is always real and has no becoming, and what is that which is always becoming and is never real? That
28a which is apprehensible by thought with a rational account is the thing that is always unchangeably real; whereas that which is the object of belief together with unreasoning sensation is the thing that becomes and passes away, but never has real being. Again, all that becomes must needs become by the agency of some cause; for without a cause nothing can come to be. Now whenever the maker of anything looks to that which is always unchanging and uses a model of that description in fashioning the form and quality of his work, all
b that he thus accomplishes must be good. If he looks to something that has come to be and uses a generated model, it will not be good.

So concerning the whole Heaven or World – let us call it by whatsoever name may be most acceptable to it[1] – we must ask the question which, it is agreed, must be asked at the outset of inquiry concerning anything: Has it always been, without any source of becoming; or has it come to be, starting from some beginning? It has come to be; for it can be seen and touched and it has body, and all such things are sensible; and, as we saw, c sensible things, that are to be apprehended by belief together with sensation, are things that become and can be generated. But again, that which becomes, we say, must necessarily become by the agency of some cause. The maker and father of this universe it is a hard task to find, and having found him it would be impossible to declare him to all mankind. Be that as it may, we must go back to this question about the world: After which of the two models did its builder frame it – after that which is always in the same unchanging state, or after 29a that which has come to be? Now if this world is good and its maker is good, clearly he looked to the eternal; on the contrary supposition (which cannot be spoken without blasphemy), to that which has come to be. Everyone, then, must see that he looked to the eternal; for the world is the best of things that have become, and he is the best of causes. Having come to be, then, in this way, the world has been fashioned on the model of that which is comprehensible by rational discourse and understanding and is always in the same state.

Again, these things being so, our world must necessarily be a likeness of something. Now b in every matter it is of great moment to start at the right point in accordance with the nature of the subject. Concerning a likeness, then, and its model we must make this distinction: an account is of the same order as the things which it sets forth – an account of that which is abiding and stable and discoverable by the aid of reason will itself be abiding and unchangeable (so far as it is possible and it lies in the nature of an account to be incontrovertible and irrefutable, there must be no falling short of that); while an account of what is made in the c image of that other, but is only a likeness, will itself be but likely, standing to accounts of the former kind in a proportion: as reality is to becoming, so is truth to belief. If then, Socrates, in many respects concerning many things – the gods and the generation of the universe – we prove unable to render an account at all points entirely consistent with itself and exact, you must not be surprised. If we can furnish accounts no less likely than any other, we must be content, remembering that I who speak and you my judges are only human, and consequently it is fitting that we should, in these matters, accept the likely story and look for d nothing further.

SOCRATES: Excellent, Timaeus; we must certainly accept it as you say. Your prelude we have found exceedingly acceptable; so now go on to develop your main theme.

TIMAEUS: Let us, then, state for what reason becoming and this universe were framed by him who framed them. He was good; and in the good no jealousy in any matter can ever e arise. So, being without jealousy, he desired that all things should come as near as possible to being like himself. That this is the supremely valid principle of becoming and of the order of the world, we shall most surely be right to accept from men of understanding. Desiring, 30a then, that all things should be good and, so far as might be, nothing imperfect, the god took over all that is visible – not at rest, but in discordant and unordered motion – and brought it from disorder into order, since he judged that order was in every way the better

Now it was not, nor can it ever be, permitted that the work of the supremely good should be anything but that which is best. Taking thought, therefore, he found that, among things that are by nature visible, no work that is without intelligence will ever be better than one b

---

1 'Heaven' is used throughout the dialogue as a synonym of *cosmos*, the entire world, not the sky.

that has intelligence, when each is taken as a whole, and moreover that intelligence cannot be present in anything apart from soul. In virtue of this reasoning, when he framed the universe, he fashioned reason within soul and soul within body, to the end that the work he accomplished might be by nature as excellent and perfect as possible. This, then, is how we must say, according to the likely account, that this world came to be, by the god's providence, in very truth a living creature with soul and reason.

30c

This being premised, we have now to state what follows next: What was the living creature in whose likeness he framed the world ? We must not suppose that it was any creature that ranks only as a species; for no copy of that which is incomplete can ever be good. Let us rather say that the world is like, above all things, to that Living Creature of which all other living creatures, severally and in their families, are parts. For that embraces and con-

d tains within itself all the intelligible living creatures, just as this world contains ourselves and all other creatures that have been formed as things visible. For the god, wishing to make this world most nearly like that intelligible thing which is best and in every way complete, fashioned it as a single visible living creature, containing within itself all living things whose

31a nature is of the same order.

Have we, then, been right to call it one Heaven, or would it have been true rather to speak of many and indeed of an indefinite number? One we must call it, if we are to hold that it was made according to its pattern. For that which embraces all the intelligible living creatures that there are, cannot be one of a pair; for then there would have to be yet another Living Creature embracing those two, and they would be parts of it; and thus our world would be more truly described as a likeness, not of them, but of that other which would

b embrace them. Accordingly, to the end that this world may be like the complete Living Creature in respect of its uniqueness, for that reason its maker did not make two worlds nor yet an indefinite number; but this Heaven has come to be and is and shall be hereafter one and unique.

Now that which comes to be must be bodily, and so visible and tangible; and nothing can be visible without fire, or tangible without something solid, and nothing is solid without earth. Hence the god, when he began to put together the body of the universe, set about making it of fire and earth. But two things alone cannot be satisfactorily united without a third; for

c there must be some bond between them drawing them together. And of all bonds the best is that which makes itself and the terms it connects a unity in the fullest sense; and it is of the nature of a continued geometrical proportion to effect this most perfectly. For when-

32a ever, of three numbers, the middle one between any two that are either solids (cubes?) or squares is such that, as the first is to it, so is it to the last, and conversely as the last is to the middle, so is the middle to the first, then since the middle becomes first and last, and again the last and first become middle, in that way all will necessarily come to play the same part towards one another, and by so doing they will all make a unity.

b   Now if it had been required that the body of the universe should be a plane surface with no depth, a single mean would have been enough to connect its companions and itself; but in fact the world was to be solid in form, and solids are always conjoined, not by one mean, but by two. Accordingly the god set water and air between fire and earth, and made them, so far as was possible, proportional to one another, so that as fire is to air, so is air to water, and as air is to water, so is water to earth, and thus he bound together the frame of a world visible and tangible.

c   For these reasons and from such constituents, four in number, the body of the universe was brought into being, coming into concord by means of proportion, and from these it acquired

Love,[1] so that coming into unity with itself it became indissoluble by any other save him who bound it together.

Now the frame of the world took up the whole of each of these four; he who put it together made it consist of all the fire and water and air and earth, leaving no part or power of any one of them outside. This was his intent: first, that it might be in the fullest measure a living d being whole and complete, of complete parts; next, that it might be single, nothing being 33a left over, out of which such another might come into being; and moreover that it might be free from age and sickness. For he perceived that, if a body be composite, when hot things and cold and all things that have strong powers beset that body and attack it from without, they bring it to untimely dissolution and cause it to waste away by bringing upon it sickness and age. For this reason and so considering, he fashioned it as a single whole consisting of all these wholes, complete and free from age and sickness.

And for shape he gave it that which is fitting and akin to its nature. For the living creat- b ure that was to embrace all living creatures within itself, the fitting shape would be the figure that comprehends in itself all the figures there are; accordingly, he turned its shape rounded and spherical, equidistant every way from centre to extremity – a figure the most perfect and uniform of all; for he judged uniformity to be immeasurably better than its opposite.

And all round on the outside he made it perfectly smooth, for several reasons. It had no c need of eyes, for nothing visible was left outside; nor of hearing, for there was nothing outside to be heard. There was no surrounding air to require breathing, nor yet was it in need of any organ by which to receive food into itself or to discharge it again when drained of its juices. For nothing went out or came into it from anywhere, since there was nothing: it was designed to feed itself on its own waste and to act and be acted upon entirely by itself and d within itself; because its framer thought that it would be better self-sufficient, rather than dependent upon anything else.

It had no need of hands to grasp with or to defend itself, nor yet of feet or anything that would serve to stand upon; so he saw no need to attach to it these limbs to no purpose. For he assigned to it the motion proper to its bodily form, namely that one of the seven which 34a above all belongs to reason and intelligence; accordingly, he caused it to turn about uniformly in the same place and within its own limits and made it revolve round and round; he took from it all the other six motions and gave it no part in their wanderings. And since for this revolution it needed no feet, he made it without feet or legs.

All this, then, was the plan of the god who is for ever for the god who was sometime to be. According to this plan he made it smooth and uniform, everywhere equidistant from its b centre, a body whole and complete, with complete bodies for its parts. And in the centre he set a soul and caused it to extend throughout the whole and further wrapped its body round with soul on the outside; and so he established one world alone, round and revolving in a circle, solitary but able by reason of its excellence to bear itself company, needing no other acquaintance or friend but sufficient to itself. On all these accounts the world which he brought into being was a blessed god.

Now this soul, though it comes later in the account we are now attempting, was not made by the god younger than the body; for when he joined them together, he would not have c suffered the elder to be ruled by the younger. There is in us too much of the casual and

---

1 A reference to the Love of Empedocles' system. But there is no contrary principle in Plato's scheme, and hence no periodic destruction of the world.

random,[2] which shows itself in our speech; but the god made soul prior to body and more venerable in birth and excellence, to be the body's mistress and governor.

[...]

51d If we could see our way to draw a distinction of great importance in few words, that would best suit the occasion. My own verdict, then, is this. If intelligence and true belief are two different kinds, then these things – Forms that we cannot perceive but only think of – certainly exist in themselves; but if, as some hold, true belief in no way differs from intelligence, then all the things we perceive through the bodily senses must be taken as the most certain real-
e ity. Now we must affirm that they are two different things, for they are distinct in origin and unlike in nature. The one is produced in us by instruction, the other by persuasion; the one can always give a true account of itself, the other can give none; the one cannot be shaken by persuasion, whereas the other can be won over; and true belief, we must allow, is shared by all mankind, intelligence only by the gods and a small number of men.

52a This being so, we must agree that there is, first, the unchanging Form, ungenerated and indestructible, which neither receives anything else into itself from elsewhere nor itself enters into anything else anywhere, invisible and otherwise imperceptible; that, in fact, which think-ing has for its object.

Second is that which bears the same name and is like that Form; is sensible; is brought into existence; is perpetually in motion, coming to be in a certain place and again vanishing out of it; and is to be apprehended by belief involving perception.

Third is Space, which is everlasting, not admitting destruction; providing a situation for
b all things that come into being, but itself apprehended without the senses by a sort of bastard reasoning, and hardly an object of belief.

This, indeed, is that which we look upon as in a dream and say that anything that is must needs be in some place and occupy some room, and that what is not somewhere in earth or heaven is nothing. Because of this dreaming state, we prove unable to rouse ourselves and to draw all these distinctions and others akin to them, even in the case of the waking
c and truly existing nature, and so to state the truth: namely that, whereas for an image, since not even the very principle on which it has come into being belongs to the image itself, but it is the ever moving semblance of something else, it is proper that it should come to be *in* something else, clinging in some sort to existence on pain of being nothing at all, on the other hand that which has real being has the support of the exactly true account, which declares that, so long as the two things are different, neither can ever come to be in the other in such
d a way that the two should become at once one and the same thing and two.

2 Because we are not wholly rational, but partly subject to those wandering causes which, 'being devoid of intelligence, produce their effects casually and without order' (46e).

Part IV

Aristotle (385/4–322 BCE)

Introduction

Aristotle was born in 385/4 BCE in Stagira, a small city in Macedonia. His father, Nicomachus, was court physician to Amyntas III of Macedon, and his father's intellectual influence seems evident in Aristotle's empiricism – his insistence on generating his theories from origins in what we can experience in sense perception and through observation, rather than in pure contemplation and reasoning. At the age of 18 (in 367/6 BCE) Aristotle was sent to Athens for his higher education – to the famous school led by Plato, the Academy. He stayed at the Academy for almost 20 years – until the death of Plato, in fact (in 348/7 BCE), no doubt in the interim "graduating" from the ranks of student to become a member of the faculty there.

After Plato's death, Plato's nephew Speucippus was elected or appointed leader of the Academy, and the relationship between Speucippus (or perhaps other members of the Academy) and Aristotle may not have been especially friendly. At any rate, Aristotle then left Athens and went to Assos, on the coast of Asia Minor (now Turkey), where he spent three years writing extensively on biological subjects. He then went to the island of Lesbos for a year, where he met his own great student, Theophrastus, but then returned to Macedonia in 343 to become the tutor to the 13-year-old crown prince, later to become known as Alexander the Great. In 336 this arrangement came to an end, when Alexander was recalled to Macedon to replace his father (who had been murdered) on the throne of Macedon.

Aristotle then returned to Athens in 335 BCE, by which time Xenocrates of Chalcedon was in charge of the Academy. Within a year of his return, Aristotle had founded his own rival school in Athens, called the Lyceum (so named because it was founded at the gymnasium attached to the temple of Apollo Lyceus, or Apollo of the Lycian people), apparently drawing away many of the more distinguished faculty from the Academy in the process. Because instruction at the Lyceum was given within the *peripatos* or covered portico of the gymnasium, Aristotle's school became known as Peripatetic, and his disciples as the Peripatetics. Ever true to his intellectual origins, Aristotle focused the studies at the Lyceum on biology and history.

But because he was not a native Athenian, Aristotle could not own land, and this left the status of the Lyceum somewhat unsteady. Moreover, as Alexander's conquests became even more threatening to the Greek world, the anti-Macedonian sentiment thereby stirred up some-times targeted Aristotle himself, given his origins and connections to the Macedonian court. In fact, Aristotle's own relationship with Alexander had chilled considerably – one of Aristotle's relatives was accused of instigating an assassination plot against Alexander and either hanged or died in prison before he could be tried. Alexander is said to have held Aristotle responsible for his relative's treachery, and contemplated revenge against the philosopher, but was distracted from the project by his invasion of India.

Alexander himself died in 323 BCE, and a wave of anti-Macedonian sentiment led to Aristotle finding himself, as Socrates had two generations before, on trial for impiety in Athens. Aristotle decided he would not allow Athens to "sin twice against Philosophy," and so withdrew to his homeland, where he lived only another year, dying at the age of 62 or 63 in 322 BCE.

Only about 25 percent of the works that we know were written by Aristotle have survived. The full corpus seems to have included a set of popular or what are called "exoteric" works, some of which were dialogues (after the fashion of Plato's own works). These are almost entirely lost to us, and what survives from this body of work is mainly fragments. In addi-tion to these are other works that seem to have been mainly intended as lecture notes – a fact which may help to explain Aristotle's somewhat pedantic style. Roughly 3,000 pages of these have survived. Since antiquity, they have been divided into three groups: (1) logical writings (the Organon); (2) writings in various areas of natural science; and (3) writings in the areas of ethics and political theory. This division of the Aristotelian corpus goes back to Plato's Academy, and was repeated in later generations (especially by the Stoics), who used it to order Aristotle's body of work. The actual body of work actually defies this classifica-tion system, however, as Aristotle took on more subjects than these divisions recognize: his *Metaphysics* ("After the *Physics*") – named for its position in the ordering of Aristotle's works in antiquity, and which has now given its name to the philosophical area it addresses – is positioned between the scientific and ethical works; his *Poetics* and *Rhetoric*, which also have no place in the canonical ordering, were placed after all of the others.

The first of these groups, the Organon (from the Greek word for "instrument"), includes the *Categories*, *On Interpretation*, *Prior Analytics*, *Posterior Analytics*, *Topics*, and *Sophistical Refutations*. The general focus of these works is on scientific demonstration – the way in which we display or prove why things that have a certain sort of nature necessarily have the prop-erties they have. This display consists in what Aristotle calls the syllogism (literally, a scheme of reasoning). In the case of scientific reasoning, this will take the form of two premises ("All As are B" and "All Bs are C") from which a conclusion is validly derived ("All As are C"). In his logical works, Aristotle explores and considers all of the varieties (and some fallacious variants) of these sorts of reasonings.

In the second group are the works on the natural sciences. These begin with the *Physics*, which lays out Aristotle's general conception of natural science, and which covers topics we would now regards as within the areas of physics, chemistry, and biology. Also included in this group are works on meteorology, psychology (human and animal), geology, zoology, botany, optics, and mechanics. At the end of this second group (or after it) is the *Metaphysics*, which Aristotle regarded as a distinct science from these others, because, as he says, its sub-ject matter is being in and of itself (being qua being), as opposed to being a particular kind of thing. This work also includes Aristotle's theology of a God whose perfection allows only self-contemplation.

In the third group are the works of ethics and applied ethics – Aristotle's conception of the practical sciences. These works include two versions of what may have been intended as a single work in ethics (the *Ethics* dedicated to Eudemus, or *Eudemian Ethics*, and the *Ethics* dedicated to Nicomachus – not Aristotle's father, but his son – the *Nicomachean Ethics*), as well as the *Politics* (which seems to have been patched together out of different pieces). These ethical works, according to Aristotle, were also scientific – no less than the *Physics* – for in his view, ethics is founded upon human nature, and one aspect of human nature is our distinct "final cause," or that for the sake of which all of our activities are undertaken, which Aristotle recognizes as *eudaimonia*, which is typically translated (somewhat misleadingly) as "happiness," and which many scholars now prefer to translate as "flourishing." The study of ethics, for Aristotle, is thus included in the general scientific study of human nature, and articulates what it is for human beings to realize their highest aims as human beings. The study of politics, similarly, is about how states can be constituted in such a way as to facilitate (or frustrate) the project of human flourishing.

Finally, the *Rhetoric* and *Poetics* give accounts of what Aristotle calls "productive sciences," because they are about how to produce something, rather than a scientific analysis of some natural entity. Rhetoric produces speeches, and poetics produces tragedy.

Because so much of what is left of Aristotle's work derives from lecture notes, the style of his prose seems to many readers to be somewhat awkward and incomplete. Like most lecturers, Aristotle almost certainly intended to provide many more details or examples when he actually gave the lecture, but of course his extemporaneous remarks have not survived along with the material he prepared in writing. He often refers to other works (lectures) that are lost, and rarely does a single work – usually compiled by ancient or more recent editors – state clearly all of Aristotle's views on the subject. Another aspect of Aristotle's writing can sometimes confuse readers, as well: he often proceeds dialectically – first surveying and criticizing others' views before stating and arguing for his own. Give the fragmentary nature of some of the writings that have survived, it is sometimes difficult to tell whether a view Aristotle is discussing is his own, or another's, where the subsequent criticism is now lost.

The scope of Aristotle's work also presents special challenges to modern readers. By now, the modern sciences and other disciplines have become much more distinct than they were in Aristotle's time. Indeed, it is fair to say that Aristotle was the *founder* of many of the sciences and disciplines that are now independently organized. Because of the modern divisions of disciplines, we tend to try to understand Aristotle's own work in these areas in isolation from his work in other areas – just as we now study biology completely separately from, say, political theory or literary criticism. Standing, as he did, at the origins of many of our modern disciplines, however, Aristotle did not – or at least did not always – regard them as distinct and separate in the ways that we now do. Failure to see the connections Aristotle saw between what we now regard as different areas often leads to misinterpretation of his work.

Aristotle's works are now generally organized on the basis of the two volumes assembled by Immanuel Bekker in 1831 (volume 1 contains pages 1–789; volume 2 contains pages 790–1462). In Bekker's edition – now followed by all copies of the Greek texts – each page is divided into two columns (labeled a and b), each 30 to 35 lines long. The Greek text now mostly used has been re-edited more recently and published in the Oxford Classical Texts series, but it continues to use the page and column identifications of Bekker's text. Hence, standard forms of reference to Aristotle's work list a page number (between 1 and 1462), a column letter (a or b), followed by a line number (between 1 and 35). Some works are also divided into "books" (which are identified in order by letters of the Greek alphabet, but now often represented by Roman numerals) and "chapters" (which are usually listed in Arabic numerals) and these are also usually included in citations. Hence, a reference *Physics* A. [or Roman I] 1.184a10–12 refers to the first book (*alpha*), first chapter, on the left column of page 184, lines 10 through 12 (which appear in the first volume of Bekker's edition).

17

Categories

The *Categories* is widely recognized as one of Aristotle's earliest works – if not actually the very first of his published works. It is included as the first of a group of works called the "Organon" (or "instrument"), the collection of Aristotle's treatises on logic. It is called the *Categories* from the Greek word *katēgoria*, meaning predicables, or what can be attributed to something. Aristotle regards the sensible individual as the most basic reality (or "substance" – *ousia*), to which all predicates can be attributes. In this selection, Aristotle discusses the various senses of substance, and the categories of things that can be attributed to them.

1

Things are named equivocally if only the name applied to them is common but the expres- 1a sion of the *substance* [i.e., the definition] corresponding to that name is different for each of the things, as in the case of a man and a picture when each is called 'animal'. For only the name is common to these, but the expression of the *substance* corresponding to that name differs for each; for if one were to state what it is to be an animal, he would give a different 5 definition for each of them.

Things are named univocally if both the name applied to them is common and the expres- sion of the *substance* corresponding to that name is the same for each of the things, as in the case of 'animal' when applied to a man and to an ox. For a man and an ox may be called by the common name 'animal', and the expression of the *substance* [corresponding to that name] is the same for both; for if one were to state for each of them what it is to be an 10 animal, he would give the same definition.

Things are derivatively named if they are called by a name which is borrowed from another name but which differs from it in ending. For example, a man may be called 'grammarian', and this name is borrowed from 'grammar'; and he may be called 'brave', and this name is 15 borrowed from 'bravery'.

2

Of expressions, some are composite but others are not composite. For example, 'man runs' and 'man conquers' are composite, but 'man', 'ox', 'runs', and 'conquers' are not composite.

20   Of things, (1) some are said of a subject but are not present in any subject. For example, man is said of an individual man, which is the subject, but is not present in any subject. (2) Others are present in a subject but are not said of any subject (a thing is said to be present

25   in a subject if, not belonging as a part to that subject, it is incapable of existing apart from the subject in which it is). For example, a particular point of grammar is present in the soul, which is the subject, but is not said of any subject, and a particular whiteness is present in a body (for every color is in a body), which is the subject, but is not said of any subject. (3)

1b   Other things, again, are said of a subject and are also present in a subject. For example, *knowledge* is present in the soul, which is the subject, and is said of a subject, e.g., of grammar. Finally, (4) there are things which are neither present in a subject nor said of a subject, such

5   as an individual man and an individual horse; for, of things such as these, no one is either present in a subject or said of a subject. And without qualification, that which is an individual and numerically one is not said of any subject, but nothing prevents some of them from being present in a subject; for a particular point of grammar is present in a subject but is not said of any subject.

3

10 When one thing is predicable of another as of a subject, whatever is said of the predicate will be said of the subject also. For example, 'man' is predicable of an individual man, and 'animal' of 'man' [or of man]; accordingly, 'animal' would be predicable of an individual

15 man also, for an individual man is both a man and an animal.

    The differentiae of genera which are different and not subordinate one to the other are themselves different in kind, as in the case of 'animal' and 'science'. For the differentiae of 'animal' are 'terrestrial', 'two-footed', 'feathered', 'aquatic', etc., and none of these is a

20 differentia of 'science'; for no science differs from another by being two-footed. But if one genus comes under another, nothing prevents both genera from having differentiae which are the same; for a higher genus is predicable of a genus coming under it, and so all the differentiae of the predicate [the higher genus] will be differentiae of the subject [the lower genus] also.

4

25 Expressions which are in no way composite signify either a substance, or a quantity, or a quality, or a relation, or somewhere, or at some time, or being in a position, or possessing [or having], or acting, or being acted upon. To speak sketchily, examples of a [name signifying a] substance are 'a man' and 'a horse'; of a quantity, 'a line two cubits long' and 'a line three cubits long'; of a quality, 'the white' and 'the grammatical'; of a relation,

2a 'a double', 'a half', and 'the greater'; of somewhere, 'in the Lyceum' and 'in the Agora'; of at some time, 'yesterday' and 'last year'; of being in a position, 'lies' and 'sits'; of possessing, 'is shod' and 'is armed'; of acting, 'cuts' and 'burns'; of being acted upon, 'is cut' and 'is burned'.

5   Each of the above, when by itself, is not expressed as an affirmation or a denial, but an affirmation or a denial is formed only if such expressions are combined; for every affirmation and every denial is thought to be either true or false, whereas no expression which

10 is in no way composite, such as 'a man' or 'white' or 'runs' or 'conquers', is either true or false.

5

A substance, spoken of in the most fundamental, primary, and highest sense of the word, is that which is neither said of a subject nor present in a subject; e.g., an individual man or an individual horse. Secondary substances are said to be (a) those to which, as species, belong substances which are called 'primary', and also (b) the genera of those species. For example, 15 an individual man comes under the species man, and the genus of this species is animal; so both man and animal are said to be secondary substances.

It is evident from what has been said that, of things said of a subject, it is necessary for 20 both the name and the definition [corresponding to that name] to be predicable of that subject. For example, man is said of an individual man, which is a subject; so the name 'man', too, is predicable [of the individual man], for one would predicate 'man' of an individual man. And the definition of man, too, would be predicable of the individual man; for an 25 individual man is a man and also an animal. Thus both the name and the corresponding definition would be predicable of the subject.

Of things which are present in a subject, in most cases neither the name nor the definition corresponding to that name is predicable of the subject. In some cases, however, sometimes nothing prevents the name from being predicable of the subject, but the 30 definition [corresponding to that name] cannot be predicable of that subject. For example, white is present in a body, which is the subject, and [the name 'white'] is predicable of that subject (for that body is called 'white'); but the definition of white will never be predicable of that body.

Everything except primary substances is either said of a subject which is a primary sub- 35 stance or is present in a subject which is a primary substance; and this becomes evident if particular cases are taken. For example, 'animal' is predicable of man, and hence it would be predicable of an individual man also; for if it were not predicable of any individual man, 2b neither would it be predicable of man at all. Again, color is present in body, and hence it would be present in an individual body also; for if it were not present in any individual body, neither would it be present in body at all. Thus everything except primary substances is either said of a subject which is a primary substance or is present in a subject which is a primary 5 substance. Accordingly, if primary substances did not exist, it would be impossible for any of the others to exist.

Of secondary substances, the species is to a higher degree a substance than a genus of it, for it is closer to a primary substance than a genus of it is. For if one were to state what a given primary substance is, he would give something which is more informative and more appropriate to that substance by stating its species than by stating a genus of it. Of an indi- 10 vidual man, for example, he would give more information by calling him 'man' than by calling him 'animal'; for the name 'man' is more proper to the individual man than the name 'animal', whereas the name 'animal' is more common than 'man'. Again, in the case of an individual tree, he will give more information by calling it 'tree' than by calling it 'plant'.

Moreover, primary substances are said to be substances in the highest degree because they 15 underlie all the rest and all the rest are either predicable of or present in primary substances. Now the relation of primary substances to all the rest is similar to that of a species [of a primary substance] to a genus of it, since the species underlies the genus; for a genus is 20 predicable of a species of it, whereas a species is not predicable of a genus of it. So in view of this, too, a species [of a primary substance] is a substance to a higher degree than a genus of it. But of the species themselves which are not genera of lower species, no one of

them is a substance to a higher degree than another; for you will not give a more appropri-
25 ate account of the subject by calling an individual man 'man' than by calling an individual
horse 'horse'. And in a similar way, of primary substances, no one of them is a substance
to a higher degree than another; for an individual man is not a substance to a higher degree
than an individual ox.

30 Of all things other than primary substances, it is reasonable that only the species and the
genera [of primary substances] should be called 'secondary substances', for of all the predicates these alone [as predicates] indicate a primary substance. For, if one is to state what an
individual man is, it is by stating the species or a genus of it that he will say something which
is appropriate to him, and he will give more information by saying that he is a man than by
35 saying that he is an animal. Anything else that he might say of him, e.g., that he is white or
that he runs or any other such thing, would be remote from him. Thus it is reasonable that,
of all things other than primary substances, only the species and the genera [of primary
substances] should be called 'substances'.

3a Moreover, it is because they underlie all other things that primary substances are called
'substances' in the most fundamental sense. In fact, just as primary substances are [thus] related
to all other things, so the species and genera of primary substances are related to all other
things [except primary substances], for all these are predicable of those species and genera.
5 Thus if we call an individual man 'grammatical', this predicate will apply also to [the species]
man and to [the genus] animal; and similarly with all other cases.

It is common to all substances that none of them is present in a subject. For a primary
substance is neither present in a subject nor said of a subject; and as for secondary substances,
10 it is evident from what follows also that they are not present in a subject. For man is said
of an individual man, who is the subject, but is not present in a subject; for man is not
present in an individual man. Similarly, animal, too, is said of an individual man, who is the
15 subject, but animal is not present in an individual man. Again, of a thing present in a subject, sometimes nothing prevents the name [of that thing] from being predicable of the subject in which the thing is present, but the corresponding definition of the thing cannot be
predicable of that subject. Of a secondary substance, on the other hand, both the name
and the definition are predicable of the corresponding subject; for we would predicate of an
20 individual man both the definition of man and that of animal. Thus a substance is not a thing
which is present in a subject.

Now this fact is not a property of substances since the differentia [of a substance], too, is
not present in a subject; for terrestrial and two-footed are said of man, who is the subject,
25 but are not present in a subject, for they are not present in man. The definition of a differentia, too, is predicable of that of which the differentia is said; for example, if terrestrial is
said of man, the definition of terrestrial will be predicable of man also, for man is terrestrial.

Let us not be confused by the thought that the parts of a substance are in the whole sub-
30 stance as if present in a subject and be forced to say that those parts are not substances; for
we said earlier that by 'being present in a subject' we do not mean existing as parts which
belong to some whole.

It is a mark of substances and [their] differentiae that all things are univocally named from
35 them; for all the predicates corresponding to them are predicable either of individuals or of
species. First, since a primary substance is not said of a subject, the corresponding predicate
cannot be predicable of anything. As for secondary substances, the species is predicable of
the individuals, and the genus is predicable both of the species and of the individuals. The
3b differentiae [of substances], too, are likewise predicable of the species as well as of the

individuals. Again, primary substances admit of the definition of their species and the definition of their genera, and a species [of a substance] admits of the definition of its genus; for whatever is said of the predicate will be said of the subject also. Similarly, both the species 5 and the individuals admit of the definition of the differentia. But things were stated to be univocally named if both the name is common and the definition corresponding to that name is the same; hence all things are univocally named from a substance or a differentia [of a substance].

Every substance is thought to indicate a *this*. Now in the case of primary substances there 10 is no dispute, and it is true that a primary substance indicates a *this*; for what is exhibited is something individual and numerically one. But in the case of a secondary substance, though the manner of naming it appears to signify in a similar way a *this*, as when one uses 'a man' 15 or 'an animal', this is not true, for [such a name] signifies rather a sort of quality; for the subject is not just one [in an unqualified way], as in the case of a primary substance, but man or animal is said of many things. Nevertheless, such a [name] does not signify simply a quality, as 'white' does; for 'white' signifies a quality and nothing more, whereas a species 20 or a genus [of a primary substance] determines the quality of a substance, for it signifies a substance which is qualified in some way. But the determination in the case of a genus is wider in application than that in the case of a species, for he who uses the name 'animal' includes more things than he who uses the name 'man'.

Another mark of a substance is that it has no contrary. For what would be the contrary 25 of a primary substance, e.g., of an individual man or of an individual animal? There can be none. Nor can there be a contrary of man or of animal. This mark, however, is not a property of substances but is common to many other things also, for example, to quantities; for there can be no contrary to a line two cubits long or three cubits long, nor to the number 30 ten, nor to any other such thing, though one might say that much is the contrary of little and that great is the contrary of small. But of a definite quantity there can be no contrary.

Again, no substance is thought to admit of variation of degree. By this I mean not that one [kind of] substance cannot be more of a substance or less of a substance than another 35 (for it has already been stated that this is the case), but that each substance, *as such*, is not said to admit of variation of degree. For example, if that substance is a man, he cannot be more of a man or less of a man, whether he is compared with himself [at different times] or with another man; for one man is not more of a man than another man, unlike one white thing which may be more white, or less white, than another white thing, or one beautiful 4a thing which may be more beautiful, or less beautiful, than another beautiful thing. Now the same thing may admit of variation of degree [but with respect to quality]; a body which is white, for example, may be [truly] said to be more white now than before, and a body which is hot may be [truly] said to be more hot [at one time than at another]. But a substance [as 5 such] is never [truly] said to vary in degree; for neither is a man [truly] said to be more of a man now than before, nor is this the case with any of the other [kinds of] substances. Accordingly, a substance [as such] does not admit of variation of degree.

The mark most proper to a substance is thought to be that, while remaining numerically 10 one and the same, it admits of contraries. In other words, of all things other than [primary] substances, there is no one which, being numerically one [and the same], can be shown to admit of contraries. A color, for example, being numerically one and the same, cannot be black and white; nor can an *action*, which is numerically one and the same, be both vicious 15 and virtuous; and similarly with other things which are not substances. But a substance, being numerically one and the same, admits of contraries. An individual man, for example, being

20 [numerically] one and the same, becomes at one time light but at another dark in color, at one time warm but at another cold, at one time vicious but at another virtuous.

No such thing appears to apply to any of the other things, although one might object and maintain that a statement or an opinion admits of contraries. For the same statement is thought 25 to be [sometimes] true and [sometimes] false; for example, if the statement 'that man is sitting' is true, the same statement will be false after that man gets up. The same applies to opinions; for if one's opinion that a man is sitting is true, then the same opinion of the same man will be false after that man gets up. Yet even if we were to allow this to be so, still the manner in which it happens here differs from that in the other case; for in the other case it 30 is by a change in themselves that substances admit of contraries, for it is by changing himself (i.e., by altering) that a man became warm from cold, or dark from light, or virtuous from vicious. It is likewise with the other substances, for it is by a change in itself that each 35 of them admits of contraries. But in themselves, statements and opinions keep on being immovable in every way, and they admit of contraries only when the things [signified by them] 4b have moved; for the statement 'that man is sitting' keeps on being the same in itself, but it is said to be first true and then false only when the thing [i.e., that man] has moved; and the same applies to opinions. Thus, at least in the manner indicated, only substances have the 5 property of admitting of contraries in virtue of their own change. So if one accepts also these qualifications, then it would not be true to say that statements and opinions admit of contraries; for it is not by receiving any contraries in themselves that they are said to admit of contraries but by the fact that some other things [i.e., substances] have been affected in this 10 manner, since a statement is now true and later false not by admitting in itself now one contrary and later another but because what is signified is a fact now but not later. In fact, neither a statement nor an opinion can be moved in an unqualified way by anything, so they cannot admit of contraries if they cannot be affected. But as for substances, it is by receiving the contraries in themselves that they are said to admit of contraries; for [animals] become 15 sick and healthy, light and dark, and they are said to admit of contraries when they themselves receive them. Accordingly, it is only a substance that, being the same and numerically one, has the property of admitting contraries in virtue of its own change.

Let so much be said concerning substances.

18

On Interpretation

In this selection from the second work of his Organon, Aristotle considers how we apply truth conditions to statements about the future. Consider something that actually will happen tomorrow, but which seems like something that might *not* happen (Aristotle's example is a sea fight – it certainly *seems* as if those involved *could* simply decide not to fight, but instead to flee): is a reference to tomorrow's sea fight that is made in advance (for example, today) true? If it is true, does that mean that the future is determined? If it is not determined, how could it *already be true*?

9

In the case of that which exists or has occurred, it is necessary for the corresponding affirmation or its denial to be true, or to be false. And in the case of two contradictories with a 30 universal subject universally taken, or with an individual subject, it is always necessary for one of them to be true and the other false, as we stated,[1] but if the subject is a universal without being universally taken, there is no such necessity, and we stated this fact too. Concerning future particulars, on the other hand, the situation is not similar.

First, if every affirmation and every denial is either true or false, then it is necessary for 35 every object, too, either to be or not to be. Accordingly, if one man says that something will be the case while another man denies this, then clearly it is necessary for just one of them to be speaking truly if an affirmation or a denial is either true or false, for in such cases both will not exist at the same time. For if it were true to say that a thing is white (or not white), 18b it would be necessary for the thing to be white (or not white), and if it is white (or not white), then it would be true to affirm that it is (or to deny it); and if the thing is not as stated, the statement is false, and if the statement is false, the thing is not as stated. Accordingly, either the affirmation or the denial must be true, or must be false. 5

If so, [it would appear that] nothing occurs by chance or in either of two ways; nor will it so occur in the future or fail to so occur, but everything [will occur, or will fail to occur], of necessity and not in either of two ways. For either he who affirms a future event will

---

1 17b29.

speak truly or he who denies it; otherwise the event would be just as likely to occur as not to occur, for that which may occur in either of two ways does not occur or will not occur in one way more than in the other.

10   Again, if a thing is white now, it was true to say earlier that it would be white; so concerning an event which has taken place, it was always true to say 'it is' or 'it will be'. And if it was always true to say 'it is' or 'it will be', the event was not of such a nature as not to be or not to come to be; and if it was not of such a nature as not to occur, it was impossible

15 for it not to occur; and if it was impossible for it not to occur, it was necessary for it to occur. So [it appears that] all future events will occur of necessity. Hence nothing will come to be in either of two ways or by chance, for if it will occur by chance, it will not occur of necessity.

Further, one cannot [truly] say of an event that neither the affirmation nor the denial is true, i.e., that the event will neither occur nor fail to occur. Otherwise, if the affirmation is

20 false, the denial [will] not [be] true, and if the denial is false, it turns out that the affirmation [will] not [be] true. In addition, if it is true to say [of a thing] that it is white and large, both [these attributes] will have to belong [to the thing], and if [it is true to say that] they will belong [to the thing] tomorrow, then they will [have to] belong to it tomorrow. But if an event will neither occur nor fail to occur tomorrow, there would be no happening

25 [tomorrow] in either of two ways, e.g., a sea fight would neither have to occur nor have to fail to occur tomorrow.

These and other such absurdities would indeed result, if of every affirmation and its denial, whether with a universal subject taken universally or with an individual subject, it were necessary for one of the opposites to be true and the other false, and if, of things in

30 the process of becoming, that which would be or which would come to be could not he in either of two ways but of necessity only one of them, in which case there would be no need to deliberate or take *action* with the expectation that, if we act in a certain way, a certain result will come about, but if we do not, it will not come about. For nothing prevents one man from saying now that a certain event will occur ten thousand years hence, and another from saying that the event will not occur; and so that alternative [occurrence or non-occurrence],

35 of which it was at one time true to state that it will come to be, would of necessity come to be [at a later time]. Further, neither would it make any difference whether some men make the contradictory statements or not, for it is clear that things would be such even if neither the affirmation nor the denial were stated; for events would, or would not, occur

19a not because we have affirmed or denied them, and [they would occur, or not occur,] no less if we had said so ten thousand years earlier rather than any other period of time. So if at all times things were such that [a definite] one of two contradictory statements [about the future] would be true, then what that statement says would of necessity come to be, and each [future] occurrence would always be such as to come to be of necessity. For that of which someone

5 stated truly that it will be would not be of such a nature as to fail to occur, and of [such] an occurrence it was always true to say [earlier] that it will be.

Now these things are impossible; for we observe that principles of things which will occur

10 arise both from deliberations and from *actions*, and that, in general, objects which do not exist always in *actuality* have alike the potentiality of existing and of not existing; and objects which may be or may not be may also come to be or may not come to be. It is clear, too, that there are many objects which have such [a nature]. For example, this coat has the potentiality of being cut to pieces [at a certain time later] but may wear out before being so cut.

15 Similarly, it has the potentiality of not being so cut; for if it did not have this potentiality, it

could not have the potentiality of wearing out before. Such is also the case with the other kinds of generations which are said to possess such potentiality. It is evident, then, that it is not of necessity that all things exist or are in the process of coming to be; in some cases a thing may come to be in either of two ways, in which case the affirmation of each alternat- 20 ive is no more true than the denial of it, whereas in other cases one of the two alternatives is more likely to occur and in most cases it does occur, but the less likely alternative may still come to be [*actually*].

Now when a thing exists, it does so of necessity, and when a nonbeing does not exist, it is of necessity that it does not exist; but it is not of necessity that every existing thing exists 25 or that every nonbeing does not exist. For it is not the same for a thing to exist of necessity when it exists and for that thing to exist of necessity without qualification, and similarly with nonbeing. The same remarks apply to any two contradictories also. Thus everything of neces- sity either is or is not, and everything of necessity will either be or not be; but one cannot [always truly] state that a definite one of the two alternatives is or will be of necessity. I mean, for example, that a sea fight will of necessity either take place tomorrow or not; but 30 a sea fight will not necessarily take place tomorrow, nor will it necessarily fail to take place either, though it will of necessity either take place tomorrow or fail to take place. So since statements are true in a way which is similar to the corresponding facts, it is clear that if objects are such that they may turn out in either of two ways or may admit contraries, the two contradictory statements corresponding to them are of necessity related in a similar 35 manner. And such indeed is the case with objects which do not always exist or which are not always nonexistent. For though one of the two contradictories concerning these objects must be true (or false), it is not [definitely] the affirmation, nor [definitely] the denial, that will be true but either one of them; and one of them may be more likely to be true, but not already true (or already false) at the time [when a man states it]. Clearly, then, it is not 19b necessary in the case of every affirmation and its opposite denial [concerning future particulars] that one of them be [definitely] true and the other [definitely] false; for the situation with objects which do not exist but have the potentiality of existing and of not existing is not like that of existing things, but as we have stated.

19

Physics

The Greek title of this work is *Phusikēs*, which really means "On Nature," by which Aristotle means any scientific explanation. Aristotle begins with the distinction between what is natural (which has a principle of change or remaining the same in itself), and what is an artifact (which is the result of human action). According to Aristotle's account in this selection, anything that is natural (and, to the extent that they are created out of natural things, also things that are artifacts) can be explained in a scientific way according to four different sorts of explanatory principles – Aristotle's so-called "four causes": matter, form, efficient cause, and final cause. In fact, as you will see, only one of these "causes" is really what we would call "cause" – the efficient cause, or, as Aristotle puts it, "that from which a change or coming to rest first begins." The other three, according to Aristotle, also supply scientific explanations of things (by which he means explanations we can know to be true), and would supply (in the above order) answers to the questions: "From what is it made?," "What is it?," and "What does it do?" (or, in some cases, "To what does it aim?").

Book II

1

192b Of things, some exist by nature, others through other causes. Animals and their parts exist
10   by nature, and so do plants and the simple bodies, for example, earth, fire, air, and water; for we say that these and other such exist by nature. Now all the things mentioned appear to differ from things which are composed not by nature. All things existing by nature appear
15   to have in themselves a principle of motion and of stand-still, whether with respect to place or increase or decrease or alteration. But a bed or a garment or a thing in some other similar genus, insofar as each of them is called by a similar predicate and in virtue of existing by art, has no natural tendency in itself for changing; but insofar as it happens to be made
20   of stone or earth or to be a composite of these, it has such a tendency and only to that extent. So nature is a principle and a cause of being moved or of rest in the thing to which it belongs primarily and in virtue of that thing, but not accidentally. I say "not accidentally" in view of the
25   fact that the same man may cause himself to become healthy by being a doctor; however,

it is not in virtue of becoming healthy that he has the medical art, but it is an accident that the same man is both a doctor and becoming healthy, and on account of this, the one is at times separate from the other. Similarly, each of the other things produced has in itself no principle of producing, but in certain cases [in most cases] such a principle is in another thing or is outside of the thing produced, as in the case of a house and other manufactured prod- 30 ucts, while in the remaining cases it is in the thing itself but not in virtue of that thing, that is, whenever it is an accident in the thing that causes the production in it.

We have stated, then, what nature is. Things which have such a principle are said to have a nature; and they are all substances, for each of them is a subject, and nature exists always in a subject. And they and whatever essentially belongs to them are said to exist according 35 to nature, as, for example, the upward locomotion of fire; for this [locomotion] is not nature, nor does it have a nature, but it exists by nature or according to nature.   193a

We have stated, then, what nature is and what exists by nature and according to nature. As far as trying to prove that nature exists, this would be ridiculous, for it is evident that there are many such things; and to try to prove what is evident through what is not evident is a mark of a man who cannot *judge* what is known through itself from what is known not 5 through itself. That this can take place is clear; for a man born blind may form syllogisms concerning colors, but such a man must be using mere names without conceiving the corresponding things.

Some think that the nature or *substance* of a thing existing by nature is the first constituent 10 which is in the thing and which in itself is without shape, like wood in the case of a bed or bronze in a bronze statue. (According to Antiphon, a sign of this is the fact that if one plants a bed and the moistened wood acquires the power of sending up a shoot, what will result is not a bed but wood, thus showing that the arrangement of the parts according to custom or art belongs to the object planted by accident, but that the substance is that which persists 15 while it is acted upon continuously.) And if each of these is also related to another object in the same way, say bronze and gold to water, bones and wood to earth, and similarly with any others, then it is that other object which is the nature and the *substance* of those things. 20 It is in view of this that some say that the nature of all things is earth; others, that it is fire; others, air; others, water; others, some of these; and others, all of them. For whatever each thinker believed to be of this sort, whether only one object or more than one, he posited this or these as being all that is substance, but all other things as being affections or posses- 25 sions or dispositions of substances, and also this or these as being eternal (for they said that there is no change from one of them to something else), but the other things [he posited] as being in generation and destruction a countless number of times.

In one way, then, nature is said to be the first underlying matter in things which have in themselves a principle of motion or of change, but in another it is said to be the *shape* or 30 form according to formula; for just as we call "art" that which exists in virtue of art and is artistic, so we call "nature" that which exists in virtue of nature and is natural. Neither in the former case would we say that a thing has something in virtue of art or that there is art if the thing is only potentially a bed but has not yet the form of a bed, nor is it so in things 35 which are *composites* by nature; for that which is potentially flesh or bone has not yet its 193b nature or does not yet exist by nature until it acquires the form according to the formula by which [form] we state what flesh or bone is when we define it. Thus, in another way, the nature of things which have in themselves a principle of motion would be the *shape* or form, which does not exist separately from the thing except according to formula. As for the com- 5 *posite* of the two, e.g., a man, this is not nature, but [we say] it exists by nature.

Indeed, the form is a nature to a higher degree than the matter; for each thing receives a name when it exists in actuality rather than when it exists potentially. Moreover, it is from a man that a man is generated, but a bed is not generated from a bed (and in view of this

10 they say that nature is not the shape but the wood, since, if it buds, what is generated is wood and not a bed); so if in the latter case it is the art, in the former too it is the form that should be nature, for it is from a man that a man is generated. Again, when we speak of nature as being a generation, this is a process toward nature [as a form]; for the term "nature" as signifying a process is not like the term "doctoring". The latter term signifies a process

15 toward health, not toward the art of doctoring, for doctoring which begins from the art of doctoring cannot be a process toward the art of doctoring; but nature [as a process] is not related to nature [as a form] in the same way, for from something the growing object proceeds to something or grows into something. Into what does it grow? Not into that from which it begins but into that toward which it proceeds. Thus it is the *form* that is nature. "*Form*" or "nature", it may be added, has two senses, for privation, too, is in a way a form;

20 but whether there is a privation or a contrary in an unqualified generation or not must be considered later.

[. . .]

3

194b Having made these distinctions, we should next examine the causes, their kinds and number. Since our *inquiry* is for the sake of understanding, and we think that we do not

20 understand a thing until we have acquired the *why* of it (and this is to acquire the first cause), clearly we should do this as regards generation and destruction and every physical change so that, with an understanding of their principles, we may try to refer to them each of the things we seek.

In one sense, "a cause" means (1) that from which, as a constituent, something is generated;

25 for example, the bronze is a cause of the statue, and the silver, of the cup, and the genera of these [are also causes].

In another, it means (2) the form or the pattern, this being the formula of the essence, and also the genera of this; for example, in the case of the octave, the ratio 2:1, and, in general, a number and the parts in the formula.

30 In another, it means (3) that from which change or coming to rest first begins; for example, the adviser is a cause, and the father is the cause of the baby, and, in general, that which acts is a cause of that which is acted upon, and that which brings about a change is a cause of that which is being changed.

Finally, it means (4) the end, and this is the final cause [that for the sake of which]; for example, walking is for the sake of health. Why does he walk? We answer, "In order to be

35 healthy"; and having spoken thus, we think that we have given the cause. And those things which, after that which started the motion, lie between the beginning and the end, such as

195a reducing weight or purging or drugs or instruments in the case of health, all of them are for the sake of the end; and they differ in this, that some of them are operations while others are instruments.

The term "cause", then, has about so many senses. And since they [the causes] are spoken

5 of in many ways, there may be many nonaccidental causes of the same thing; for example, in the case of a statue, not with respect to something else but qua a statue, both the art of

sculpture and the bronze are causes of it, though not in the same manner, but the bronze as matter and the art as the source of motion. There may be also causes of each other; for example, exercise is a cause of good physical condition, and good physical condition is a cause of exercise, although not in the same manner, but good physical condition as an end, while 10 exercise as a principle of motion. Again, the same thing may be a cause of contraries, for if one thing, when present, is the cause of another, then the first, when absent, is sometimes also said to be the cause of the contrary of the second; for example, we say that the absence of the pilot was the cause of the capsizing, while his presence was the cause of safety.

All of the causes just mentioned fall into four most evident types. For, the letters of the 15 syllables, the matter of manufactured articles, fire and all such in the case of bodies, the parts of the whole, the hypotheses of the conclusion – in all of these there are causes in the sense that they are *that of which* the latter consists; and in these, those first mentioned in each case are causes in the sense that they are the underlying subject, as in the case of the parts, but 20 each of the others is a cause in the sense of essence, and this is the whole or the composition or the form. As for the seed and the doctor and the adviser and, in general, that which acts, all these are causes in the sense of the source of change or of standstill or of motion. Finally, each of the rest is a cause as the end or the good of the others; for that for the sake of which the others exist or are done tends to be the best or their end. Let there be no dif- 25 ference here between calling this "the good" or "the apparent good".

These, then, are the causes and their number in kind; but their modes are numerically many, although when summarized they too are fewer. For causes are spoken of in many ways, and even within the same kind one cause may be prior or posterior to another; for example, 30 the cause of health is the doctor or the artist, and the cause of the octave is the ratio 2:1 or a number, and whatever includes each is always a cause. Again, there are accidental causes and their genera; for example, Polyclitus as a cause of a statue is distinct from a sculptor as a cause, since the sculptor is by accident Polyclitus. Also, whatever includes the accident would 35 be a cause; for example, a man, or, in general, an animal, would be a cause of the statue. 195b Even of accidents, some are more remote or more near than others; for example, this would be the case if the white or the musical were to be called "a cause" of the statue.

Of all causes, both those said to be *proper* and those said to be accidental, some are said to be causes in the sense of being in potentiality, others in *actuality*; for example, the cause 5 of the house to be built is the builder and of the house that is being built the builder who is building. Similar remarks will apply to the things caused by the causes already listed; for example, the cause may be a cause of this statue or of a statue or of a portrait in general, and it may be a cause of this bronze or of bronze or of matter in general. Similar remarks may be made in the case of accidents. Again, both accidental and *proper* causes and also the 10 objects caused may be spoken of in combination; for example, not Polyclitus, nor the sculptor, but Polyclitus the sculptor.

However, all these are six in number, and each is spoken of in two ways. For as a cause or an object caused each may be stated as a particular or as a genus of a particular; as an accident or as a genus of an accident; in combination or singly taken; and in each of these 15 either in *actuality* or in virtue of its potentiality. And there is this difference, that causes which are in *actuality* and are taken as individuals exist, or do not exist, at the same time as the things of which they are the causes, for example, as in the case of this doctor who is healing and this man who is being healed, and this builder who is building and that building which is being built. But with respect to potentiality this is not always so; for the house is 20 not destroyed at the same time as the builder.

We should always seek the ultimate cause of each thing, as in other cases; for example, a man builds in view of the fact that he is a builder, and a builder builds in virtue of his art
25 of building; accordingly, this latter is the prior cause. It is likewise with all other cases. Moreover, causes generically given should be stated of effects generically given, and particular causes, of particular effects; for example, a sculptor [in general] of a statue [in general], and this sculptor of this statue. Also potential causes should be stated of potential effects, and causes in *actuality* of effects in *actuality*.

Let this, then, be a sufficient description of the number of causes and the manner in which
30 they are causes.

[. . .]

196b 5

10 To begin, then, since we observe that some things come to be always in the same way and others [come to be] for the most part, it is evident that luck as a cause and what comes to be by luck are none of those things, neither of what is necessary or eternal nor of what is for the most part. But since of things that come to be there exist, besides these, also others,
15 which all say exist by luck, it is evident that luck or chance does exist; for we grant that such things do come to be by luck and that things which come to be by luck are of such a kind.

Of things that come to be, some do so for the sake of something [else] but others do not; and of the former, some come to be according to *choice* and others not so, but both these
20 are for the sake of something; so it is clear that, besides things which exist necessarily or for the most part, there are also others to which final cause may belong. Things to which final cause belongs may be done by *thought* or by nature. Now when such things come to be by accident, we say that they do so by luck; for just as being exists either essentially or by
25 accident, so may a cause exist. In the case of a house, for example, a cause which is essential is the art of building, but one that is accidental is the white or the musical. Thus the essential cause of something is definite, but the accidental cause is indefinite, for a great many accidents may belong to a thing.

30 As it was stated, then, when this happens in things for the sake of which there is genera-tion, then it is said to happen by *chance*[1] or by luck. The difference between these two will be specified later,[2] but for the present it is evident that both belong to things for the sake of something. For example, a man engaged in collecting contributions would have gone to a
35 certain place for the sake of getting the money, had he known; but he went there not for the sake of this, and it is by accident that he got the money when he went there; and this
197b happened neither for the most part whenever he went there, nor of necessity. And the end, which is getting the money, is not a cause present in him, but it is something done by *choice* or by *thought*, and he is then said to have gone there by luck; but if he had gone there by *choice* and for the sake of this, whether he was getting the money always or for the most
5 part, then he would have done so not by luck.

It is clear, then, that luck is an accidental cause of things done according to *choice* and for the sake of something; and so both *thought* and luck are concerned with the same thing, for *choice* is not without *thought*.

1 The word translated "chance" in italics is *automaton* and indicates a kind of "chance" (no italics, *tuchē*) in which no choice is possible.
2 197a36–198a13.

Now the causes of things which might come to be by luck are of necessity indefinite. In view of all this, (a) luck seems to be something indefinite or not revealed to man, and (b) 10 there is a sense in which nothing would seem to come to be by luck; for both these opinions are right, since there is a good reason for them. For what comes to be by luck does so in a qualified sense, namely, in virtue of an accident, and it is as an accident that luck is a cause; but as a cause without qualification, it is a cause of no thing. For example, of a house the builder is the cause, but accidentally it is the flute player; and in going to a place and get- 15 ting the money, but not doing so for the sake of getting the money, the accidental causes might be a great many, such as wishing to see someone or following someone or avoiding someone or going to see a play. And it is right to say that luck is contrary to reason; for reason is of what is always or for the most part, while luck is present in events which are 20 outside of these. So, since such causes are indefinite, luck too is indefinite.

In some cases, however, one might raise the problem of whether a cause as luck may not be any chance thing whatever, as in the case of health, for example, whether the wind or the heat from the sun is such a cause but not the purge; for, of accidental causes, some are 25 nearer [to the effects] than others.

Luck is called "good" when the result is good, but "bad" when the result is bad; and it is called "good fortune" and "misfortune" when its goodness and badness, respectively, are of considerable magnitude. In view of this, even if great goodness or badness is missed by a little, we are said to have been fortunate or unfortunate; for the small difference seems negligible, and *so thought* regards good fortune or misfortune as if attained. Further, it is with 30 good reason that good fortune has no certainty, for luck has no certainty; for what comes to be by luck does so neither always nor for the most part.

As we stated, both luck and *chance* are causes, but accidental; and they are among things which come to be neither without qualification nor for the most part, and for the sake of 35 something.

[. . .]

7

It is clear, then, that there are causes and that there are as many [in kind] as we have stated; 198a for the *why* of things includes just so many [in kind]. For the *why* is referred either (a) ultimately 15 to the whatness in the case of what is immovable, as in mathematics (for it is ultimately referred to the definition of a straight line or of commensurability or of something else), or (b) to the first mover – for example: Why did they declare war? Because they were raided – or (c) to a final cause: [in declaring war] for the sake of ruling the enemy, or (d) to matter, 20 as in things generated. Evidently, then, the causes are those stated and are as many in number.

Since the causes are four, it is the task of the physicist to understand all of them; and as a physicist he should state the *why* by referring it to all of them – the matter, the form, the mover, and the final cause. The last three often amount to one; for both the whatness and 25 the final cause are one, and the first source of motion is the same in kind as these (for man begets man), and, in general, this is so in the case of a movable mover. But a mover that is not movable is not a cause within physics, for it moves without having in itself motion or a principle of motion but is immovable. Accordingly, there are three disciplines: one con- 30 cerning immovable things, a second concerning things which are in motion but are indestructible, and a third concerning destructible things.

The *why*, then, is given by being referred to matter, to the whatness, and to the first mover, for in generations causes are sought mostly in this manner: "What comes after what?", "What
35 was the first thing that acted or was acted upon?", and at each step always in this way. Now the principles that cause physical motion are two: One of these is not physical, for it has no
198b principle of motion in itself, and such is that which moves another without itself being moved, as in the case of that which is completely immovable and primary among all; and such is also the whatness or the *form*, for this is the end or final cause. So since nature is a final cause, we should also understand this [cause]. So the *why* must be given in all [four] ways,
5 namely, (1) that this must follow from that (the phrase "this from that" to be taken either without qualification or for the most part); (2) that if this is to be, then that will be (as in the case of premises, from which conclusions follow); (3) that this was the essence; and (4) because it is better in this way (not without qualification, but relative to the *substance*[3] of each thing).

8

10 We must discuss first (a) why nature is a cause for the sake of something; then (b) how necessity exists in physical things, for all thinkers make reference to this cause by saying, for example, that since the hot and the cold and each of such things are by nature of such-and-such a kind, certain other things must exist or come to be (for even if they mention some
15 other cause – one of them mentions *Friendship* and *Strife*,[4] another mentions *Intelligence*[5] – they just touch upon it and let it go at that).

The following question arises: What prevents nature from acting, not for the sake of something or for what is better, but by necessity, as in the case of rain, which does not
20 fall in order that wheat may grow. For, one may say, what goes up must be cooled, and the resulting cold water must come down, and when this takes place, the growth of corn just happens; similarly, if a man's wheat is spoiled on the threshing floor, rain did not fall for the sake of spoiling the wheat, but this just happened. So what should prevent the parts in nature, too, from coming to be of necessity in this manner, for example, the front teeth of neces-
25 sity coming out sharp and so fit for tearing but the molars broad and useful for grinding food, not however for the sake of this but by coincidence? A similar question arises with the other parts in which final cause seems to exist. If so, then whenever all the parts came together
30 as if generated for the sake of something, the wholes which by *chance* were fitfully composed survived, but those which came together not in this manner, like the man-faced offspring of oxen mentioned by Empedocles,[6] perished and still do so.

This is the argument, then, or any other such, that might cause a *difficulty*. Yet it is impos-
35 sible for things to come to be in this manner; for the examples cited and all things by nature come to be either always or for the most part, but none of those by luck or *chance* do so
199a likewise. It is not during the winter that frequent rain is thought to occur by luck or by coincidence, but during the summer, nor frequent beat during the summer, but during the winter. So if these be thought to occur either by coincidence or for the sake of some-
5 thing and if they cannot occur by coincidence or by chance, then they occur for the sake of

3 "Substance" in italics refers to the form or essence of a substance (no italics).
4 Empedocles.
5 Anaxagoras.
6 H. Diels and W. Kranz, *Die Fragmente der Vorsokratiker*, 6th edn. (Berlin, 1952) (DK), 31B61.

something. Besides, those who use the preceding arguments, too, would admit that all such things exist by nature. There is, then, final cause in things which come to be or exist by nature.

Moreover, in that which has an end, a prior stage and the stages that follow are done for the sake of that end. Accordingly, these are done in the manner in which the nature of the 10 thing disposes them to be done; and the nature of the thing disposes them to be done in the manner in which they are done at each stage, if nothing obstructs. But they are done for the sake of something; so they are by nature disposed to be done for the sake of something. For example, if a house were a thing generated by nature, it would have been generated in a way similar to that in which it is now generated by art. So if things by nature were to be generated not only by nature but also by art, they would have been generated just as they are by nature disposed to be generated. So one stage is for the sake of the next. In general, 15 in some cases art completes what nature cannot carry out to an end, in others, it imitates nature. Thus, if things done according to art are for the sake of something, clearly also those according to nature are done for the sake of something; for the later stages are similarly related to the earlier stages in those according to art and those according to nature.

This is most evident in those of the other animals which make things neither by art nor 20 by having inquired or deliberated about them; and from this latter fact arise discussions by some thinkers about the problem of whether spiders and ants and other such animals work by intellect or by some other power. If we go a little further in this direction, we observe that in plants, too, parts appear to be generated which contribute to an end, for example, 25 leaves for the sake of protecting the fruit. So if it is both by nature and for the sake of some-thing that the swallow makes its nest and the spider its web and that plants grow leaves for the sake of fruit and send their roots not up but down for the sake of food, it is evident that there exists such a cause in things which come to be or exist by nature. And since nature 30 may be either matter or *form*, and it is the latter that may be an end while all the rest are for the sake of an end, it is *form* that would be a cause in the sense of a final cause.

Now error occurs even with respect to things produced according to art; for example, a grammarian did not write correctly and a doctor did not give the right medicine; so clearly 35 this may occur also in things that come to be according to nature. If then there are (a) things 199b produced according to art in which there is a right final cause and (b) also things done erroneously when the final cause has been aimed at but failed, a similar situation would exist also in natural things, and monstrosities in these would be failures of final causes. So too must have been the case in the original formation of the offspring of oxen, if they could not 5 attain a certain limit or end; for there must have been some corruption in the source from which their generation started, like that in the seed nowadays. We might add, too, that the seed must have come into being first and not the animals all at once, and the expression "first the wholenatured"[7] meant the seed. And final cause exists also in plants, though it is 10 less capable of being articulated. So did olive-headed offspring of vines come into being just as man-faced offspring did from oxen, or not? It would seem absurd; but they must have, if indeed this was also the case in animals. Again, any chance thing might otherwise be gen-erated from a seed.

In general, he who asserts this rejects things existing by nature as well as nature itself. For 15 what exists by nature is a thing which, having started from some principle in itself, finally arrives by a continuous motion at a certain end; and neither is the end the same from every principle, nor does any chance end come to be from a given principle, but from the same

7 Empedocles (DK 31B6712).

principle the same end comes to be, if nothing obstructs. As for the final cause or what acts
20 for the sake of the final cause, it might take place by luck. (For example, we say "the stranger
came by luck and departed after paying the ransom" if he would have come for the sake of
doing this [had he known], not that he came for the sake of this; and this happened by
25 accident, for luck is an accidental cause, as we stated earlier.[8]) But if it takes place always or
for the most part, it is not an accident nor does it come to be by luck; and in natural things
it takes place always, if nothing obstructs.

It is absurd to think that nothing comes to be for the sake of something if the moving
cause is not observed deliberating (and we may add, even art does not deliberate); and if the
ship-building art were in the wood, it would have produced results similar to those produced
30 by nature. So if there is a final cause in art, so also in nature. This is most clearly seen in a
doctor who heals himself; nature is like that.

It is evident, then, that nature is a cause and that it is a cause also in this manner, namely,
for the sake of something.

9

35 As for that which is necessary, does it exist by hypothesis or also simply? Nowadays it is
200a thought that what exists by necessity does so in generation, as if one were to consider the
wall as having been constructed by necessity, since what is heavy travels down by its nature
and what is light travels up by its nature, and so the stones and the foundations are down,
5 then earth right above because it is lighter, and finally wood at the very top since it is the
lightest. However, although a wall is not constructed without these, still it is constructed
not because of these (except in the sense that they are causes as matter) but for the sake of
sheltering or preserving certain things. Similarly, in all other cases in which there is a final
cause, although what is generated could not have been generated without a nature which
10 is necessary for it, still it is not because of what is necessary (except as a material cause) but
for the sake of something. For example, why is a saw such-and-such? So that this may come
to be or for the sake of this. But this final cause cannot come to be unless the saw is made
of iron. So if there is to be a saw capable of doing this work, it is necessary that it be made
of iron. What is necessary, then, exists by hypothesis and not as an end; for it exists in
matter, while final cause is in the formula.

15 The necessary in mathematics is in some way parallel to that in things generated according to nature. Since this is what a straight line is, it is necessary for a triangle to have its
angles equal to two right angles, but the converse is not the case; but if the angles of a
triangle were not equal to two right angles, neither would a straight line be what it is said
to be. In things generated for the sake of something, this parallelism proceeds in a reverse
20 manner. If the end will exist or exists, what precedes it also will exist or exists; but if what
precedes the end will not or does not exist, then, just as in the other case the starting-point
is not what it is posited to be if the conclusion is not true, so here, the end or final cause
will not or does not exist if what precedes it will not or does not exist. The final cause here,
we may add, is also a starting-point, not of *action*, but of reasoning; but in the other case
[e.g., in mathematics], it is the whatness that is the starting-point of reasoning, for no *actions*
25 exist there. Thus, if there is to be a house, certain things must be made or be available or
exist (or the matter in general, which is for the sake of something, such as bricks and stones

8 196b10–27.

in the case of a house); but the end does not exist because of these things, except in the sense that they are a cause as matter, nor will the house come to be because of these. In general, then, if there are no stones, there can be no house, and if there is no iron, there can be no saw; whereas in mathematics, if the angles of the triangle are not equal to two right angles, the principles from which the equality to two right angles follows cannot be such as are posited.

It is evident, then, that the necessary in natural things is what we call "matter" and also 30 the motions of matter. We may also add that both causes must be stated by the physicist, and the final cause more so than the cause as matter, for it is the former which is the cause of the latter, not the latter, of the end; and we may also add that the end is the final cause and that the starting-point is the definition or the formula, as in the case of things produced 35 according to art. For example, if a house is such-and-such a thing, such other things must 200b be produced or be available; and so in the case of a man: If he is such-and-such, then such other things must be or come to be, and if these, then such others likewise. Perhaps the necessary exists also in the formula; for, if one has defined the operation of sawing as being 5 such-and-such an act of division, then this cannot take place unless the saw has teeth of such-and-such a kind, and these cannot be of such-and-such a kind unless they are made of iron. Indeed, even in formulas there are some parts which are parts as if they were the matter of these formulas.

20

On the Soul

In this work, Aristotle applies the general principles he laid out in his *Physics* to living things in general – or to put it in the Greek way, to things that were "ensouled," things that had souls. Aristotle begins with a definition of "soul," and in the following selections considers many problems of the relations between soul and body and what it means for a single individual to have both. He discovers a hierarchy of psychological attributes, placing cognitive function at the top of the hierarchy. Sense perception is an example of cognitive functioning, and this function we share with all other animals.

Book I

1

402a We regard knowing to be noble and honorable, and one kind of it to be more so than another either by virtue of its accuracy or because its objects are better and more wonderful; and for both these *reasons* it is reasonable that we should give a primary place to the inquiry con-
5 cerning the soul. It is thought, too, that the knowledge of the soul contributes greatly to every kind of truth, and especially to [that about] nature; for the soul is as it were the principle of animals.

   Now we seek to investigate and to know, first, both the nature and the *substance* of the soul and, secondly, its attributes, some of which are thought to be proper *attributes* of the
10 soul while others are thought to belong through the soul to animals also.[1] But to attain any conviction concerning the soul is in every way one of the most difficult things. For although the inquiry here is common to that in many other [sciences] also, I mean the inquiry into the *substance* and the whatness of the subject, one might think that there is some one method applicable to every subject whose *substance* we wish to know, as in the case of proper attributes,
15 which are known [by the method] of demonstration. If so, one should inquire what that method

---

1 That is to composites of body and soul. "Attributes" (with italics) translates the words *pathos* or *pathēma*. These are, roughly, states of a subject, one type of "attribute" (without italics).

is. But if there is not some one and a common method of coming to know the whatness of things, the matter becomes even more difficult; for we would then have to determine the manner [of inquiry] to be used for each subject. And even if it were evident what that manner is, whether a demonstration or a division or some other method, we are still faced with many problems and uncertainties as to what we should use as starting-points in the inquiry; 20 for different sciences proceed from different principles, as in the case of numbers and of planes.

First, perhaps it is necessary to determine the genus under which the soul falls and the whatness of the soul, that is, whether it is a *this* and a substance, or a quality, or a quantity, or falls under some other of the categories already distinguished; and further, whether it is 25 one of those things which exist potentially or is rather an actuality, for this makes no small difference.

Again, we should consider if the soul is divisible into parts or has no parts, and whether 402b every [kind of] soul is homogeneous or not, and if not homogeneous, whether souls differ in species or in genus; for those who nowadays discuss and make inquiries about the soul seem to limit their investigations to the human soul. We should be careful, too, not to over- 5 look the problem of whether there is a single definition for the soul, such as the soul of an animal, or a different definition for each (e.g., for a horse, a dog, a man, and a god) wherein an animal, taken universally, is either nonexistent or posterior; and similarly for anything which might have a common predicate. Again, if there are not many souls but only parts [of a soul in each thing], there is the problem of whether the inquiry into the whole soul 10 should precede or follow that into the parts of it. And with regard to the parts, too, it is difficult to determine which of them are by their nature distinct from one another. There is also the problem of whether the inquiry into the parts should precede or follow that into their functions, e.g., whether the inquiry into the intellect should precede or follow that into thinking [as an activity], whether the inquiry into the sentient part should precede or follow that into sensing [as an activity], and similarly in the case of the other parts. And if the inquiry into the functions should precede that into the parts, one might still raise the problem whether 15 the inquiry into the objects to which those functions are directed should precede that of the corresponding parts, e.g., whether the sensible object should be sought before the sentient part of the soul, and whether the object of thought should be sought before the thinking [part].

It seems that not only is the knowledge of a *substance's* whatness useful to the investigation of the causes of the attributes of that *substance* (as in mathematics, in which knowledge of the whatness of straightness and curvature and a line and a plane are useful in perceiving the number of right angles to which the sum of the triangle's angles is equal), but, conversely, 20 [knowledge of] the attributes [of the *substance* of a thing] contributes a considerable part to the knowledge of the whatness [of that *substance*]; for whenever we can give an account of all or most of the obvious attributes of a thing, we are in the best position to formulate its *substance*. For the starting point of every demonstration is the whatness of a thing; so if a 25 *definition* fails to make us know by inference those attributes or even facilitate a conjecture 403a about them, then clearly it is in every case so stated as to be dialectical or empty.

The *attributes* of the soul, too, give rise to a problem. Are they *attributes* of that which has the soul also, or is there any one of them which is proper to the soul? This problem must 5 be settled, but it is not easy.

Now in most cases it appears that [such *attributes*] cannot exist unless the body is being affected or is acting, as in anger, courage, *desire*, and sensation in general. Thinking, most of all, seems to be proper to the soul; but if this, too, is a species of imagination or incapable

of existing without imagination, then it, too, could not exist without a body. Accordingly,
10 if there is any function or affection of the soul proper to the soul, the soul can be separated
[from the body], but if no function or [affection] is proper to the soul, the soul could not be
separated from the body but would be just like the straight. The straight qua straight has
many attributes, e.g., it touches a bronze sphere at a point; but the straight as something
15 separated [in existence from a body] cannot so touch it, for it is inseparable [from a body]
since it exists always with a body.

Now it seems that all the *attributes* of the soul, e.g., temper, good temper, fear, pity, courage,
also gladness and love and hate, exist with the body; for the body is being affected simultaneously with these. This is indicated by the fact that sometimes when strong or striking
20 affections occur, we are not at the same time irritated or afraid, but at times when the
affections are weak or obscure, we are moved, and the body is agitated in a manner similar
to that when we are angry. Again, a more evident example is the fact that we become afraid
even if there is no [external] cause of fear.

25 If such be the case, it is clear that the *attributes* of the soul are things whose formulae include
matter. So the corresponding definitions will be as follows: anger, for instance, is a certain
motion of such a body or bodily part or faculty of that body, caused by such and such a
mover for the sake of such and such an end. And because of these facts, it becomes evident
that it belongs to the physicist to investigate the soul, either every [kind of] soul or such
[which is inseparable from a body]. Accordingly, a physicist and a dialectician would define
30 each [*attribute* of such a soul] in a different way. For instance, in stating what anger is, the
dialectician would say that it is a desire to retaliate by causing pain, or something of this
sort, whereas a physicist would say that it is the rise in temperature of the blood or heat
403b round the heart. Thus the latter would state the matter, the former would state the form
and formula; for the formula is the form of the thing, but that form must be in such and
such a matter if it is to exist. It is like the case of a house. Its formula is such as this: a
5 covering which tends to prevent its contents from being destroyed by wind or rain or
scorching heat, but another would speak of it as being stones and bricks and timber; still
another would speak of it as being the form in these materials for the sake of such and such
an end.

Which of the above three [definitions] will the physicist give? Is it the one concerned with
the matter but overlooks the formula, or the one concerned with the formula only? Is it not
rather the one which includes both [the matter and the formula]? Then what should we call
each of the other two [thinkers]? Should we not say (1) that there is no [scientist] who is
10 concerned [only] with the *attributes* of matter which are inseparable and is concerned with
them qua separable, (2) but that it is the physicist who is concerned with all [the attributes]
which are functions or *attributes* of such and such a body or matter; and, of the things which
are investigated not qua such attributes, (3) that it is the artist who is concerned with some
[*attributes*], e.g., the carpenter or the physician, if those things happen to be [works of art],
15 (4) that it is the mathematician who is concerned with inseparable *attributes* but by abstrac-
tion and not qua *attributes* of such and such a body, and (5) that it is the first philosopher
who is concerned with [things] insofar as they are separate?

But let us return to the point from which we digressed. We were saying that the *attributes*
of the soul qua such [*attributes*], as in the case of temper and fear, are inseparable from the
physical matter of animals and are not like a line or a plane.

[. . .]

Book II

1

The doctrines concerning the soul handed down to us by our predecessors have been 412a3
sufficiently discussed. Let us then turn to another starting point, as it were, and try to determine what the soul is and what would be its most common formula. 5

Now one genus of things we call "substance," but (1) one kind under this we regard as
matter, which taken by itself is not a *this*, (2) another as *shape* and form, in virtue of which
something is directly called "a *this*," (3) and a third, the composite of the above two kinds.
Matter exists as potentiality; form exists as actuality, but in two senses: e.g., (a) as *knowledge*, 10
and (b) as the exercise of *knowledge*.[2]

Bodies are thought to be substances most of all, especially natural bodies; for the latter
are the principles of all the rest. Of natural bodies, some possess life but others do not; and
by "life" we mean self-nourishment and growth and deterioration of that body. So every 15
natural body which partakes of life would be a substance of the composite kind. And since
there exists such a kind of body (for it has life), the soul would not be a body; for a body
is not something which belongs to a subject but exists rather as a subject or as matter.
Accordingly, the soul must be a substance as the form of a natural body potential with life, 20
and [such] substance is an actuality. So the soul is the actuality of such a body.

But actuality is spoken of in two ways, as in the case of *knowledge* and as in the case of
the exercise of *knowledge*. Evidently, the soul is an actuality as in the case of *knowledge*; for
sleeping and being awake depend on the existence of soul, and being awake is analogous to 25
the exercise of *knowledge*, whereas sleeping is analogous to having [*knowledge*] but not
exercising it. Now in the same individual the *knowledge* of a thing is prior in generation to
the exercise of that *knowledge*. In view of this, the soul is the first actuality of a natural body
with the potentiality of having life; and a body of this kind would be one which has organs. 412b
The parts of plants, too, are organs, but they are entirely simple; e.g., the leaf shelters the
rind and the rind shelters the fruit, and the roots are analogous to the mouth, for both of
these take in food. If, then, there is something common to be said about every [kind of]
soul, this would be: "the first actuality of a natural body which has organs". And in view of 5
this, one should not inquire whether the soul and the body are one or not, just as one should
not ask whether the wax and its shape or, in general, the matter of each thing and that of
which it is the matter are one or not; for, although the terms "one" and "being" have many
senses, the dominant sense is that of actuality.

We have now stated universally what the soul is: with respect to its formula, it is a *sub-* 10
stance, and this is the essence in such and such a body, as in the case of instruments. For
example, if an axe were a natural body, its *substance* would be its essence, and this would
be its soul; and if that essence were removed, there would no longer be an axe, except by
equivocation. Now [the essence with the body], here, is an axe; but the soul is the essence
and the formula not of such a body, but of such a natural body which has in itself the 15
principle of moving and of stopping.

What has just been said should be observed in the parts [of a living body] also. If the eye
were an animal, its vision would be its soul; for vision is the eye's *substance* with respect to

2 "Knowledge" (with italics) translates the Greek word *episteēmē*, and refers to scientific knowledge or
understanding.

20 [the eye's] formula. The eye itself is the matter for vision; and if [vision] departs, there is no eye any longer, except equivocally, as in the case of the eye in a statue or a painting. What was stated of the part [the eye] should be taken to apply to the whole living body, for there is an analogy; this part is to that part [in the case of the eye] as the sentient power as a whole

25 is to the whole sentient body qua such. Thus, that which is potentially living is not that which has lost the soul but that which possesses it. As for the seed or the fruit, it is potentially such and such a body. Now being awake as an actuality is like seeing or cutting, but the soul as

413a [a first] actuality is like vision and the power of the instrument [i.e., of the axe]; and the body is that which exists as potentiality. And just as the eye is its vision with its pupil, so the animal is its soul with its body.

It is not unclear, then, that the soul, or parts of it if by its nature it has parts, cannot
5 be separated from the body; for the actualities in some [living things] are those of the parts themselves. But nothing prevents some actualities from being separable, because they are not actualities of any body. Further, it is not clear whether the soul as the actuality of the
10 body is like the sailor of the boat.

In outline, then, let the above distinctions and sketch concerning the soul suffice for the present.

2

Since what is clear and more known with respect to formula arises from what is unclear but more evident [to us], let us try, by the use of such [method], to go over the soul once more;
15 for the formula which defines the soul should not only make us know the fact, as most definitions do, but also include and make evident the cause. Formulae which are given as definitions nowadays are like conclusions. For instance, what is squaring [of an oblong rectangle]? It is the [construction of an] equilateral rectangle which is equal in area to an oblong rectangle. Now such a definition is a formula of the conclusion. But if a definition states that squaring an oblong rectangle is finding the mean proportional of the sides of that rectangle, it states
20 the cause of the thing.

As a starting-point of our inquiry, then, let us state that an animate thing is distinguished from an inanimate thing by living. The term "living" has many senses; but let us say that a thing is living even if it has in itself only one of the following: the intellect, the power of sensation, the power of producing motion and of stopping with respect to place, the power
25 of moving with respect to nutrition, that of deterioration, and that of growth. Thus all plants, too, are thought to be living; for they appear to possess in themselves such a power and a principle through which they grow and deteriorate in contrary directions, for those which are constantly nourished and continue to live grow [and deteriorate] not only upwards with-
30 out doing so downwards, but alike in both directions, indeed in every direction, and they do so as long as they are able to take in food.

Now the power of nutrition can exist apart from the other powers, but in mortal beings none of the other powers can exist apart from this power. This fact is evident in plants; for
413b no power other than that of nutrition belongs to them. Accordingly, living belongs to [all] living things because of this principle, but it belongs to animals primarily because of the power of sensation; for even those beings which have no power to be in motion or go to another place but have the power of sensation are called "animals" and not only "living things". Of
5 the sentient powers, that of touch is primary; and just as the nutritive power can exist apart from that of touch or any other power of sensation, so the power of touch can exist apart

from any of the other powers of sensation. By "power of nutrition" we mean such part of the soul of which plants partake also; all animals, however, are observed to have the power of touch. As for the cause of each of these facts, it will be discussed later.[3]

    At present let us say only so much, that the soul is the principle of the [functions] already stated and that it is defined by the power of nutrition or of sensation or of *thinking* or of producing motion. Whether each of these powers is a soul or a part of a soul, and, if a part, whether it is such as to be separable only in definition or also in place, are problems to be faced. In the case of certain powers the solution is not difficult to perceive; in the case of some others, there are difficulties. For just as in the case of some plants, when each is divided and the parts are separated, each part appears to continue to live, as if the soul of each such plant is actually one but potentially many, so in the case of some insects, when cut into parts, other kinds of soul are observed to continue to live. For each part has both the power of sensation and that of locomotion, and if the power of sensation, it has also the powers of imagination and of desire; for whenever there is sensation, there is also pleasure and pain, and whenever these exist, *desire* too must exist. With regard to the intellect or the speculative faculty, it is not yet evident; but this seems to be a different genus of soul, and [perhaps] it alone can be separated [from the body], just as that which is eternal [can be separated] from that which is destructible. As for the other parts of the soul, it is evident from what we have said that they are not separable, in spite of what some thinkers say. But it is evident that they are distinct in definition; for the essence of a sentient power is distinct from the essence of a power of forming opinions, if indeed sensing and forming opinions are distinct, and similarly with each of the other powers mentioned. Further, some animals have all the powers mentioned and some have only some of them, but some [living things] have only one power; and it is from this fact that the differentiae of animals arise. As for the cause of this fact, it will be considered later.[4] Almost the same remarks apply to the powers of sensation; for some animals have all of them, others have some of them, and certain animals have only the one most necessary, and this is the power of touch.

    Now the expression "that by which we live or sense" has two meanings, just like the expression "that by which we *know*" (in which the word "that" may mean either *knowledge* or the soul, for we speak of *knowing* by one or by the other) and similarly for the expression "that by which we are healthy" (in which "that" may mean either health or a part of the body, or even the whole body). Further, of these meanings, *knowledge* or health is a *form* or a form of some kind or a formula and, as it were, the *actuality* of the receptive subject, which is the subject which *knows* [in the case of *knowing*] but the subject which is healthy in the case of health (for the *actuality* of that which can act is thought to be in the subject which is affected or is [so] disposed). Accordingly, since the soul is primarily that by which we live or sense or *think*, it would be the formula or the form but not the matter or the subject [of the living thing]. For, as we have already stated,[5] the term "substance" has three meanings, i.e., form, matter, and the composite of these two; and of these three, matter is potentiality, but form is actuality. So since the living thing is the composite of the two, it is not the body that is the actuality of the soul, but the soul that is the actuality of the body, and of a certain [kind of] body. And, because of this, those who think that the soul does not exist without a body or is not a body of any sort have the right belief. For the soul is not a body but something

10

15

20

25

30

414a

5

10

15

20

---

3 434b32–3.

4 434a22–435b28.

5 412a6–9.

of a body, and, because of this, it exists in a body. But it exists in such and such a body and not as the earlier thinkers thought; they fitted it to a body without further specifying what that body is or what kind of a body it is, although there is no evidence that any chance body

25 can receive any chance soul. According to reason, too, the case is such as the following: each thing's actuality by its nature can exist [only] with the [kind of] potentiality which belongs to that thing or with its appropriate matter.

It is evident from the above remarks, then, that the soul is a certain actuality or formula of that which has the potentiality of being such and such a thing.

3

30 Of the soul's powers mentioned above,[6] namely, those of nutrition, desire, sensation, locomotion, and *thinking*, some living things possess all, as we said,[7] others some, and others only one. Plants possess the power of nutrition only, other living things possess this and also

414b the power of sensation. Those which possess the power of sensation have the appetitive power also. For the species of desire are *desire* and temper and wish, and all animals have at least one power of sensation, that of touch; but that which has sensation has also pleasure and

5 pain and is affected by pleasurable and painful objects, and, if so, it has *desire* also, since *desire* is a desire for the pleasurable. Further, [all animals] have the power of sensing food. Food is sensed by touch, since all animals are nourished by dry and moist and hot and cold objects, all of which are sensed by touch; but the other sensible objects are sensed by touch only

10 indirectly; for sounds and colors and odors contribute nothing to food, whereas flavors are a species of tangible [qualities]. Hunger and thirst are *desires*, hunger being a *desire* for dry and hot objects, and thirst for cold and moist objects; and flavor is a sort of seasoning of these objects. These facts will be made clear later,[8] but at present let us say so much, that

15 those animals which have [the power of] touch have [the power of] desire also. As for imagination, it is not clear; but it will be examined later.[9] Some animals possess also the power of locomotion, and others, i.e., men and perhaps beings such as men or even more honorable than men, possess also the power of *thinking* and an intellect.

20 It is clear [from the above discussion], then, that a single formula for a soul could be given in the same manner as for a figure; for neither does a figure exist apart from the triangle [and the quadrilateral] and the rest [of the species of figures], nor does a soul exist apart from the [kinds of] souls listed above. A common formula for a figure, too, can be given which will fit all [kinds of] figures, but it will not be proper to any [one kind]; and similarly in the

25 case of the [kinds of] soul mentioned above. In view of this, it is ridiculous to seek a common formula which will apply to these or other such cases but fail to be proper to things or appropriate to each ultimate species, but not seek one which is proper to a thing or appropriate to each species.

30 There is a parallelism in the [kinds of] figures and in the [kinds of] soul; for in both figures and animate things there is a succession in which that which is prior exists always potentially in that which is posterior. For instance, the triangle exists [potentially] in the quadrilateral, and the nutritive power exists [potentially] in the sentient power, and so one must seek the

---

6 413a22–5

7 413b32–3

8 Bk. III, ch. 12.

9 Bk. III, chs. 3, 11.

whatness of each kind. For instance, "What is the soul of a plant?", "What is the soul of man?", "What is the soul of a nonrational animal?". The *reason* why [the powers of the soul] are related in such succession is a matter which requires consideration;[10] for the sentient power 415a cannot exist without the nutritive power, but the latter power can exist without the former, as it does in plants. Again, without the sense of touch none of the other senses can exist; but the sense of touch can exist without any of the other senses, for there are many animals which have neither vision nor a sense of hearing nor a sense of smell at all. Again, of living 5 things which have the power of sensation, some have the power of locomotion but others do not. Finally, some living things – very few – have [also] the power of judging and of *thinking*; for, of mortal beings, those which have the power of judging have all the other powers also, but those which have one of the latter powers do not all have the power of judging, 10 and, of the latter, some do not even have imagination while others live only by imagination. Concerning the speculative intellect, its discussion is of another kind.[11]

It is clear, then, that the formula most appropriate to each of these [powers] is also the formula of each [kind of] soul.

4

One who intends to make an inquiry into the kinds of soul must first grasp the whatness of each kind and then proceed to what follows or what other things should be sought. On the 15 other hand, if one is to state what each of these is, e.g., what the thinking or the sentient or the nutritive power is, prior to this he should state what thinking or sensing [or taking in food] is; for activities or *actions* are prior in formula to the corresponding powers. If so, then, again, since the objects to which the activities are directed should be investigated before the 20 activities, for the same *reason* those objects (e.g., food, sensible object, object of thought) would have to be determined first.

First, then, we should discuss food and reproduction; for the nutritive soul exists in the other kinds of soul and is the primary and most common power of souls, and it is in virtue of this [power] that living belongs to all living things. The function of this soul is to repro- 25 duce and to use food. For the most natural function of living things which are perfect and neither defective nor generated by chance is to produce another thing like itself (e.g., an animal produces an animal [of the same kind], and a plant likewise a plant) in order that they may partake of the eternal and the divine as far as they can; for all [living things] 'desire' 415b [the eternal and the divine], and it is for the sake of this that those which *act* according to nature do so. The expression "that for the sake of which", of course, has two senses: (a) that which is done, and (b) that for which it is done. Accordingly, since [such] living things cannot share in the eternal and the divine continuously (because no destructible thing, which is the same and numerically one, can last forever), they partake of the eternal and the 5 divine only as far as they can, some sharing in these more, others doing so less; and what lasts forever is not that which is [numerically one and] the same, but something like it, i.e., something which is one not numerically but in species.

The soul is the cause and the principle of a living body. Now the terms "cause" and "principle" have many senses, and, similarly, the soul is a cause in the three specified senses of

10 Bk. III, chs. 12–13.
11 Bk. III, chs. 4–6.

10 "cause"; for it is a cause as a source of motion, and as a final cause, and as the *substance* of an animate body.

Clearly, it is a cause as the *substance* [of an animate body]; for the cause of the existence of each thing is the *substance* of that thing, existence in living things is life, and the cause and principle [in living things] is the soul. Further, the formula of that which exists potentially is its actuality.

15 It is evident that the soul is a cause as final cause also. For just as the intellect acts for the sake of something, so does nature, and nature's end is a final cause. Such [end] in animals is the soul and [is an end] according to their nature; for all natural bodies are instruments 20 of the soul, and, as in the case of animals, so in the case of plants, [natural bodies] exist for the sake of their soul. And, [as already stated], "that for the sake of which" has two senses: (a) that which is done, and (b) that for which it is done.

Finally, the soul is also a cause as a source of motion with respect to place, but such power does not exist in all living things. Alteration and growth, too, exist [in living things] by virtue 25 of their soul; for sensation is thought to be a species of alteration, and no thing without soul can have sensations. Similar remarks apply to growth and deterioration; for no thing can by its nature grow or deteriorate without taking in food, and no thing can be nourished unless it shares in life.

21

Metaphysics

This work is really more a collection of essays than a single unified work. The original title of the work meant only "after the *Physics*," but "metaphysics" has come to be the name of the field it first sought to define and explicate. In these essays, Aristotle seeks to discern whether there can be a science of things, not as they are by nature, and not in the mathematical sense, but rather just in virtue of being things at all – that is, just in virtue of their being qua being. If there can be such a science, it would be the most general and basic of all sciences, as being (or being something) is shared by everything that any science studies. Aristotle here defends the claim that there can be such a science, and he attempts to articulate its first principles – but scholars continue to debate the details of Aristotle's positions. In the following selections, Aristotle criticizes the accounts of being given by his predecessors, especially Plato. Aristotle also considers the question of whether the science of being qua being is really the same as the science of substance. Finally, he identifies the science of being qua being (which he also calls the science of first principles or causes and the science of wisdom) with theology, the science of god or gods, and seeks to show that all nature depends upon a divine unmoved mover.

Book I (= **A**)

1

All men by nature desire understanding. A sign of this is their liking of sensations; for, even 980a apart from the need of these for other things, they are liked for their own sake, and of all sensations those received by means of the eyes are liked most. For, not only for the sake of doing something else, but even if we are not going to do anything else, we prefer, as one 25 might say, seeing to the other sensations. The cause of this is the fact that, of all the sensations, seeing makes us know in the highest degree and makes clear many differences in things.

By nature, animals are born with the power of sensation, and from sensation memory comes into being in some of them but not in others. Because of this, animals which can remember 980b are more prudent or more teachable than animals which cannot remember. Of the former,

those which cannot hear sounds are prudent but cannot be taught, such as the bee or any
25 other species of animals like it, but those which can hear can also be taught.

All animals, except men, live with the aid of appearances and memory, and they participate but little in experience; but the race of men lives also by art and judgment. In men,
experience comes into being from memory; for many memories of the same thing result in
981a the capacity for one experience. And experience seems to be almost similar to science and
art, but science and art come to men through experience; for, as Polus rightly says, "experience made art, but inexperience, luck."[1]
5 Now art comes into being when out of many notions from experience we form one
universal belief concerning similar facts. For, to have a belief that when Callias was having
this disease this benefited him, and similarly with Socrates and many other individuals, is a
10 matter of experience; but to have a belief that this benefited all persons of a certain kind
who were having this sickness, such as the phlegmatic or the bilious or those burning with
high fever, is a matter of art.

Experience does not seem to differ from art where something is to be done; in fact, we
observe that men of experience succeed more than men who have the theory but have no
15 experience. The cause of this is that experience is knowledge of individuals but art is universal knowledge, and all *actions* and productions deal with individuals. The doctor does not
cure 'a man' universally taken, except accidentally, but Callias or Socrates or someone else
20 to whom also the essence of man happens to belong. If, then, someone without experience
has the theory and knows the universal but is ignorant of the individual included under this
universal, he will often fail to cure; for it is rather the individual that is curable. Nevertheless,
25 we regard understanding and comprehension as belonging to art more than to experience,
and we believe that artists are wiser than men of experience; and this indicates that wisdom
is attributed to men in virtue of their understanding rather than their experience, inasmuch
as men of understanding know the cause but men of experience do not. For men of experi-
30 ence know the fact but not the *why* of it; but men of art know the *why* of it or the cause. It
is because of this that we regard also the master-artists of a given craft as more honorable,
981b as possessing understanding to a higher degree, and as wiser than the manual workers, since
the former know the causes of the things produced, but the latter are like certain inanimate
things which act but do so without understanding that action, as in the case of fire which
burns. Inanimate things bring about the effects of their actions by some nature, while
5 manual workers do so through habit which results by practicing. Thus, master-artists are considered wiser not in virtue of their ability to do something but in virtue of having the theory
and knowing the causes. And in general, a sign of a man who understands is the ability to
teach, and because of this we regard art more than experience to be science; for those who
have the art can teach, but those who do not have it cannot teach. Again, we do not con-
10 sider any of the sensations to be wisdom, although these are the most authoritative in the
knowledge of individuals; but they do not tell us the *why* of anything, as for example why
fire is hot, but only the fact that it is hot.

The first who arrived at any art that went beyond the ordinary sensations was probably
15 admired by men, not only because there was some usefulness in the objects arrived at, but
also as being wise and superior to others. As more arts were arrived at, some for the necessities of life and others as the only ends of *activity*, those who arrived at the arts for the latter purpose were always believed to be wiser than those who did so for the former because

---

1 See Plato, *Gorgias* 448c, 462b–c.

their sciences were not instrumental to something else. Now when all such arts were 20 already developed, the sciences concerned neither with giving pleasure to others nor with the necessities of life were discovered, and first in such places where men had leisure. Accordingly, it was in Egypt that the mathematical arts were first formed, for there the priestly class was allowed leisure.   25

In the *Ethics*[2] we have stated the difference between art and science and the others which come under the same genus. But the purpose of our present discussion is to bring out this: all men believe that what is called "wisdom" is concerned with the first causes and prin- ciples; so that, as stated before, a man of experience seems to be wiser than a man who has 30 any of the sensations, a man of art wiser than a man of experience, a master-artist wiser than a manual worker, and theoretical sciences to be wisdom to a higher degree than productive 982a sciences. Clearly, then, wisdom is a science of certain causes and principles.

2

Since this is the science we are seeking, we must inquire what are the kinds of causes and 5 principles whose science is wisdom. If we were to go over the beliefs which we have about the wise man, this might perhaps make the answer more evident. We believe (a) first, that the wise man *knows* all things in a manner in which this is possible, not, however, *knowing* them individually; (b) second, that a wise man can acquire knowledge of what is hard and 10 not easy for any man to know (ability to have sensations is common to all, and therefore easy, but not a mark of wisdom); (c) third, that he who is more accurate and more able to teach the causes in each science is wiser; (d) fourth, that of the sciences, the one pursued for its own sake and for the sake of understanding is wisdom to a higher degree than the one 15 pursued for the sake of what results from it; (e) fifth, that the superior science is wisdom to a higher degree than the subordinate science, for the wise man must not be placed in rank by another but must set the ordering, and he must not obey another but must be obeyed by the less wise.

These, then, are the beliefs in kind and in number which we have concerning wisdom 20 and wise men. Of the attributes listed, that of *knowing* all things must belong to him who has universal *knowledge* in the highest degree; for he understands in a sense all the underlying subjects. And the most universal things are on the whole the hardest for men to know, for they are most removed from sensations.[3] Also, the most accurate of the sciences are those 25 which are concerned mostly with the first causes, for the sciences with fewer principles are more accurate than those which use additional principles; for example, arithmetic is more accurate than geometry. Moreover, the science which investigates causes is more capable of teaching than the one which does not; for those who teach are those who state the causes of each thing. Further, to understand things or *know* them for their own sake belongs in the 30 highest degree to the science of that which is *known* in the highest degree; for he who pur- sues *knowing* for its own sake will pursue most of all the science taken in the highest degree, and such is the science of that which is *knowable* in the highest degree; and that which is 982b *knowable* in the highest degree is that which is first or the causes, for it is because of these and from these that the other things are known, and not these because of the underlying subjects. Finally, the supreme science, and superior to any subordinate science, is the one 5

2 *Nicomachean Ethics* 1139b14–1141b8.
3 See *Posterior Analytics* 100a3–6.

which knows that for the sake of which each thing must be done, and this is the good in each case, and, in general, the highest good in the whole of nature.

From all that has been said, then, it is evident that the name which is sought applies to the same science; for it is this science which must investigate the first principles and causes, 10 and the good or final cause is one of the causes.

That it is not a productive science is also clear from those who began to philosophize, for it is because of wondering that men began to philosophize and do so now. First, they wondered at the *difficulties* close at hand; then, advancing little by little, they discussed *difficulties* 15 also about greater matters, for example, about the changing attributes of the Moon and of the Sun and of the stars, and about the generation of the universe. Now a man who is perplexed and wonders considers himself ignorant (whence a lover of myth, too, is in a sense a philosopher, for a myth is composed of wonders), so if indeed they philosophized in order 20 to avoid ignorance, it is evident that they pursued science in order to understand and not in order to use it for something else. This is confirmed by what happened; for it was when almost all the necessities of life were supplied, both for comfort and leisure, that such think- 25 ing began to be sought. Clearly, then, we do not seek this science for any other need; but just as a man is said to be free if he exists for his own sake and not for the sake of somebody else, so this alone of all the sciences is free, for only this science exists for its own sake.

Accordingly, the possession of this science might justly be regarded as not befitting man; 30 for human nature is servile in many ways, and so, as Simonides says, "God alone should have this prerogative," and it would be unworthy of a *man* not to seek the science proper to his nature. If, then, there is something in what the poets say and the Deity is by nature 983a jealous, he would most probably be so in this case, and all men of intellectual eminence would be unfortunate. But neither is it possible for the Deity to be jealous (nay, according to the proverb, "bards tell many a lie"), nor need we suppose that there is a science more honor- 5 able than this one. For the most divine science is the most honorable, and a science would be most divine in only two ways: if God above all would have it, or if it were a science of divine objects. This science alone happens to be divine in both ways; for God is thought by all to be one of the causes and a principle, and God alone or in the highest degree would 10 possess such a science. Accordingly, all the other sciences are more instrumental than this, but none is better.

However, the acquisition of this science must in a sense bring us to a state which is contrary to that when we began our inquiries. For all men begin, as we said, by wondering that things are as they are when the cause has not been investigated, as in the case of marionettes or of the solstices or of the incommensurability of the diagonal of a square with respect to 15 its side; for all seem to wonder at the fact that no least unit of magnitude exists which can measure both the side and the diagonal of a square. But we must end with the contrary and, according to the proverb, the better state, as is also the case in these instances when one has 20 learned the cause; for nothing would make a geometrician wonder so much as this, namely, if a diagonal were to be commensurable with the side of a square.

We have stated, then, the nature of the science we are seeking, and the aim of our concern and of our entire *inquiry*.

3

It is evident, then, that we must acquire *knowledge* of the first causes (for we say that we 25 understand each thing when we think that we know its first cause), and causes are spoken of in four senses. In one sense, we say that *the substance* or the essence is a cause (for the *why* leads us back to the ultimate formula, and the first *why* is a cause and a principle); in another, it is the matter or the underlying subject; in a third, the source which begins motion; 30 and in a fourth, the cause opposite to the previous, namely, the final cause or the good (for this is the end of every generation and every motion). We have investigated these causes sufficiently in the *Physics*;[4] however, let us examine the contributions of others before us who 983b attempted the investigation of being and philosophized about truth. For clearly they, too, speak of certain principles and causes, and so there will be some profit in our present *inquiry* if we go over what they say; for either we shall discover some other genus of cause, or we 5 shall be more convinced of those we just stated.

Most of those who first philosophized regarded the material kinds of principles as the principles of all things; for that of which things consist, and the first from which things come to be and into which they are finally resolved after destruction (this being the per- 10 sisting *substance* of the thing, while the thing changes in its affections), this they say is the element and the principle of things; and because of this they think that nothing is generated and nothing perishes, since such a nature is always preserved. Just as in the case of Socrates when he becomes noble or musical, we do not say that he is generated in the full sense, 15 nor that he perishes in the full sense if he loses these habits, because Socrates himself as an underlying subject still persists, so it is in the other cases; for there must be some nature, either one or more than one, which is preserved and from which the others are generated.

[. . .]

6   987a

After the philosophies named came the system of Plato, which followed these philosophies 30 in many respects but also had its own peculiarities distinguishing it from the philosophy of the Italians. For, having in his youth become familiar first with Cratylus and the Heraclitean doctrines (that all sensible things are always in a state of flux and that no science of them exists), he continued to believe these even in his later years. Now Socrates was engaged in 987b the study of ethical matters, but not at all in the study of nature as a whole, yet in ethical matters he sought the universal and was the first to fix his *thought* on definitions. Plato, on the other hand, taking into account the *thought* of Socrates, came to the belief that, because sensible things are always in a state of flux, such inquiries were concerned with other things 5 and not with the sensibles; for there can be no common definition of sensible things when these are always changing. He called things of this other sort "Ideas" and believed that sensible things exist apart from Ideas and are named according to Ideas. For the many sensibles which have the same name exist by participating in the corresponding Forms. The only change 10 he made was to use the name "participation"; for the Pythagoreans say that things exist by imitating numbers, but Plato, changing the name, says that things exist by participating in the Forms. As to what this imitation of or participation in the Forms might be, they left this an open question.

Further, he says that besides the sensible things and the Forms, and between these, there 15 exist the Mathematical Objects, differing from the sensible things in being eternal and

4 *Physics* Bk. II, chs. 3, 7.

immovable, and from the Forms in that there are many alike whereas the Form itself corresponding to these is only one.

20 Since the Forms are the causes of all other things, he thought the elements of the Forms are the elements of all things. As matter, the *Great* and the *Small* are the principles; as *substance*, it is the *One*. For from the *Great* and the *Small* and by participation in the *One* come the Forms, and these are Numbers.

25 In saying that the *One* is a substance, and not that it is something else of which "one" is predicated, he spoke like the Pythagoreans, and like them he believed that the Numbers are the causes of the *substance* of all other things. But he was unlike the Pythagoreans, (a) in making the *Infinite* not one principle but a *Dyad*, consisting of the *Great* and the *Small*, (b) in saying that the Numbers exist apart from the sensible things and not that these are numbers, and (c) in positing the Mathematical Objects between the Numbers and the sensible things; and this is peculiar to him. Now Plato, unlike the Pythagoreans, posited the *One* and

30 the Numbers as existing apart from things and introduced the Forms because he was making logical inquiries (for earlier thinkers had no knowledge of dialectics), and he made the other nature a *Dyad* because the Numbers, except those which are first, could be generated

988a with natural ease from it as from some plastic material. Yet what really happens is the contrary; for this sort of generation is not reasonable. For these thinkers make many things out of the matter, and the Form generates only once; but what we observe is that from one piece of matter one table is made, while he who puts the form upon the matter, although

5 he is one, makes many tables. The relation of the male to the female is similar, for the female is impregnated by one copulation, while the male impregnates many females. But these are imitations of those principles.

This, then, is how Plato described the causes we are seeking. It is evident from what has

10 been said that he uses only two causes, the cause of the whatness and the cause according to matter (for the Forms are causes of the whatness of the other things, and the cause of the whatness of the Forms is the *One*). It is also evident what the underlying matter is, in virtue of which the Forms are predicated of the sensible things, and the *One* is predicated of the Forms; this is the *Dyad*, or the *Great* and the *Small*. Further, he assigned the cause of good-

15 ness and the cause of evil to the elements, one to each of them, just as some of the earlier philosophers (for example, Empedocles and Anaxagoras) sought to do.

[...]

9

Let us leave the Pythagoreans for the present, for to have touched upon them as much as

990b we did is sufficient. Those who posited the Ideas as causes, first, in seeking to find the causes of the things about us, introduced other things equal in number to these, as if a man who wished to count but, thinking that he could not do so with the few things at hand, created

5 more. In seeking the causes of these things, they proceeded from these to the Forms, which are about equal to or not less than these; for, there exists a Form having the same name as that which is predicated of many sensibles, of substances as well as of non-substances, and of these things as well as of eternal things.

Yet none of the ways which are used to show that the Forms exist appears convincing; for,

10 from what is laid down, in some cases a syllogism is not necessarily formed, and in others it follows that there will be Forms even of things of which we think that no Forms exist. For, according to the arguments from the sciences there will be Forms of all things of which there

are sciences; according to the "one predicated of many" argument there will be Forms even of denials; and according to the argument, that we can think of something which has been destroyed, there will be Forms of destructible things, for an image of what has been destroyed can exist. 15

Again, of the most accurate statements, some posit Ideas of relations, yet we deny that a genus of relations exists by itself, and others speak of the *third man*. And in general, the statements concerning the Forms discard those things whose existence we prefer to the existence of the Ideas; for what follows is that Number is first and not the *Dyad*, that the relative 20 is prior to that which exists by itself, and all other conclusions which, drawn by some believers in the doctrine of Ideas, are contrary to the principles of that doctrine.

Again, according to the belief in virtue of which we say that Ideas exist, there will be Forms not only of substances but also of many other things (for not only of a substance is a con- 25 cept one but also of any other thing, and not only of substances are there sciences but also of other things; and a countless number of other such difficulties follow).

According to what necessarily follows and the doctrine of Forms, if Forms can be shared, only of substances must there be Ideas; for Ideas are not shared as attributes, but each Idea 30 must be shared in this sense, namely, qua not being said of a subject. I mean, for example, that if a double participates in Double Itself, it does so also in eternity, but as in an attribute, for eternity is an attribute of the Double. Accordingly, the Forms will be of substances; and 991a the same names signify substances whether applied to these things or to the Ideas, otherwise, what will be the meaning of saying that there exists something apart from the many things here, the one over the many? And if each Idea and the things that participate in it have the same form, there will be something common to all; for, why should the form of two be one and the same in the perishable two's and the many eternal Two's any more than 5 in Two Itself and any perishable two? But if that form is not the same for all, they would be equivocally named, and this would be similar to calling both Callias and a piece of wood "a man", although we observe nothing common in them.

Above all, one might go over the difficulties raised by this question: What do the Forms contribute to the eternal things among the sensibles or to those which are generated and 10 destroyed? For, they are not the causes of motion or of any other change in them. And they do not in any way help either towards the *knowledge* of the other things (for, they are not the *substances* of them, otherwise they would be in them) or towards their existence (for they are not constituents of the things which share in them). It might perhaps seem that they are causes in the way in which whiteness is a cause when it is blended in the white thing. But 15 this argument, first used by Anaxagoras and then by Eudoxus and some others, can easily be upset; for it is easy to collect many statements contradicting such a doctrine. Moreover, all other things do not come to be from the Forms in any of the usual senses of "from." And 20 to say that the Forms are patterns and that the other things participate in them is to use empty words and poetic metaphors. For, if we look up to the Ideas, what will their function be? Any chance thing may be or become like another thing even without being copied from it, so that, whether Socrates exists or not, a man like Socrates might be born. Likewise, it is 25 clear that this might be the case even if there were to be an eternal Socrates. Moreover, there will have to be many patterns of the same thing, and so many Forms; of a man, for example, there will be Animal, Two-footed, and at the same time Man Himself. Also, Forms will be patterns not only of sensible things but also of other Forms; for example, this is how the 30 genus will be related to a species of it among the Forms. Thus, the same Form will be both a pattern and a copy. 991b

Again, it would seem impossible for a *substance* to exist apart from that of which it is the *substance*. Accordingly, how could the Ideas, being the *substances* of things, exist apart from

them? In the *Phaedo*[5] this is stated in this manner: The Forms are the causes of the existence
5 as well as of the generation of things. But even if the Forms do exist, still no thing which
participates in something is generated unless there is a mover. And many other things are
generated, such as a house or a ring, of which we[6] say no Forms exist. Clearly, then, also
the rest may be generated by such causes as the ones which produce the two things just
mentioned.

10   Again, if the Forms are Numbers, how will they be causes? Is it in view of this, that the
things themselves are other numbers, for example, that one man is this number, Socrates is
that number, and Callias is another? Why then are the Numbers causes of the latter? If the
former are eternal but the latter are not, this difference too would not account for it at all.
On the other hand, if it is in view of this, that the things about us are ratios of numbers, like
a harmony, clearly there is still some one thing in each of the numbers which form that ratio.
15 If this thing then is the matter, it is evident that the Numbers themselves will be certain
ratios of something to something else. I mean, for example, that if Callias is a numerical ratio
of fire and earth and water and air, his Idea too will be a Number of certain underlying things;
and Man Himself, whether it is a Number of a sort or not, will still be a numerical Ratio
20 and not just a Number. Because of all this, then, none of these will be just a Number.

Again, from many numbers one number is formed, but how can one Form be formed
from many Forms? And if it is not from them but from the Units in them that a Number is
formed, such as 10,000 for example, how are the Units related to each other in the Number
formed? Many absurdities will follow whether the Units (a) are all alike in kind, or (b) are
25 not alike in kind, either in the sense that, prior to the formation of this Number, the Units
of each Number are alike in kind but not alike in kind with those of any other Number, or
in the sense that no one Unit is alike in kind with any other Unit. For, having no attributes,
with respect to what will the Units differ? These alternatives are neither reasonable nor in
agreement with our thinking.

Again, these thinkers must set up another genus of number as the subject of arithmetic,
30 and also other genera, all of which are simply called "Intermediate Objects" by some of them.
But how is this to be done, and from what principles will these objects come? Or, why will
these be between the things about us and the Ideas? Again, each of the Units in Two is
992a generated from a prior *Dyad*, although this is impossible. Again, why is a Number, taken as
a whole, one?

Again, in addition to what has been said, if the Units are different, these thinkers should
5 have spoken like those who say that the elements by are four or two, for each of those thinkers
does not call the elements by a common name, such as "body", but calls them, "fire" and
"earth", whether body is common to both fire and earth or not; but as it is, these thinkers
speak of the *One* as if it were homogenous, like fire, or like water. But if this is so, the Numbers
will not be substances; but it is clear that, if there is a *One Itself* and this is a principle, the
10 term "one" is used in many senses, for no other way is possible.

When we wish to reduce substances to their principles, we posit lengths as being formed
from the *Long* and *Short* (a sort of species of the *Great* and *Small*), planes from the *Wide* and
Narrow, and bodies from the *Deep* and *Shallow*. But then, how will a plane have a line, or a
15 solid have a line and a plane? The *Wide* and *Narrow* is a genus distinct from the *Deep* and

---

5 See *Phaedo* 100c–E.

6 Here Aristotle is speaking as a member of Plato's Academy, though he does not endorse all of Plato's
views.

Shallow. Accordingly, just as a number does not belong to these, in view of the fact that the *Many* and *Few* is distinct from them, so it is clear that none of the higher will belong to any of the lower. Nor yet is the *Wide* a genus of the *Deep*, for then the body would have been a species of the plane. Further, from what principles are the points, which are present in magnitudes, generated? Even Plato was struggling against this genus of things as being geometrical suppositions, and he called the point "principle of a line"; however, he often posited the indivisible lines as this genus, although such lines must have limits. Thus, if from an argument the existence of a line follows, from the same argument follows also the existence of a point.

In general, although philosophy seeks the cause of visible things, we have left out such a cause (for we say nothing about the cause which begins change), and thinking that we state the *substances* of these things, we assert the existence of other *substances*; but as to how the latter are *substances* of the former, our statements say nothing, for "participation", as we said,[7] means nothing. Nor do the Forms touch upon that which we observe in the sciences to be indeed the cause, for whose sake each intellect and each nature acts, and which we claim to be one of the principles; but philosophy has become mathematics for modern thinkers, although they say that mathematics should be studied for the sake of other things.[8]

Moreover, one would come to the belief that the underlying substance as matter is too mathematical, and that it is a predicate and a differentia of a substance and of matter rather than matter, that is, I am speaking of the *Great* and the *Small*; and this is like the *Rare* and the *Dense*, of which the natural philosophers speak as being the first differentiae of the underlying subject, for these are species of *Excess* and *Deficiency*. As for motion, if the *Great* and the *Small* are motion, it is clear that the Forms will be moved; if not, whence did motion come? Indeed, the whole inquiry into nature is discarded.

Also, what seems to be easy is not done, namely, to show that all things are one; for, if we grant all their assumptions, what follows from the examples they use is not that all things are one but that there is a *One Itself*. And even this is not shown, unless we grant that the universal is a genus; but this is impossible in some cases.

Nor are there any arguments to show how Lengths and Planes and Solids, which come after the Numbers, exist or will exist, or what power they have; for these can neither be Forms (for they are not Numbers), nor Intermediates (for these are Mathematical Objects), nor yet destructible, but they appear to be another and a fourth genus of objects.

In general, the search for the elements of all beings, without distinguishing the many senses of the term "being", makes discovery impossible, especially if the manner of proceeding is by seeking the kinds of elements out of which things are composed. For it is indeed impossible to find the elements out of which acting, being acted upon, or straightness are composed, but if at all, those of substances alone can be found; consequently, it is not true to think that one is seeking or has found the elements of all things. And how would one be taught the elements of all things? Clearly, it is not possible for him to start with previous knowledge of them. For, just as a man who is learning geometry, although he may have previous understanding of other things, has no previous knowledge at all of what that science is concerned with and what he is about to learn, so it is also in other cases; so if there is a science of all things, as some say, he who is learning it could have no previous knowledge of it at all, although all instruction received proceeds by means of previous knowledge

---

7 991b20–2.

8 See *Republic* vii. 531D, 533B–D.

of some or all of the elements, whether by means of demonstration or by means of definition; for one must have prior understanding of the elements from which a definition is to be formed and these must be known; and learning by induction proceeds similarly. But 993a if, on the other hand, the science under consideration happens to be innate, it is strange that we are not aware of possessing the best of all sciences.

Again, how will one know in that science the elements out of which its objects are composed, and how will this be made clear? This, too, presents a *difficulty*, for there might be
5 disagreement, as there is about certain syllables; for some say that *za* is composed of *s*, *th*, and *a*, but others say that it is a distinct sound and is none of those which are known. Moreover, how could one come to know the objects of sensation without the corresponding power of sensation? But if indeed the elements of which things are composed are the same for all, one should be able to do so, as one does in the case of the composite sounds which have
10 elements proper to sound.

[. . .]

Book II (= α)

1

30 The investigation of truth is in one sense difficult, in another easy. A sign of this is the fact
993b that neither can one attain it adequately, nor do all fail, but each says something about the nature of things; and while each of us contributes nothing or little to the truth, a considerable amount of it results from all our contributions. Thus, if the truth seems to be like the
5 door in the proverb "Who would miss it?", in this sense it would be easy; but to have some of the whole truth and not be able to attain the part we are aiming at, this indicates that it is difficult. Perhaps the cause of this difficulty, which may exist in two ways, is in us and not
10 in the facts. For as the eyes of bats are to the light of day, so is the intellect of our soul to the objects which in their nature are most evident of all.

It is just to be grateful not only to those with whose opinions we might agree, but also to those who have expressed rather superficial opinions; for the latter, too, have contributed something, namely, they have handed down for us the habit of thinking. If there had been
15 no Timotheus, we would not have much lyric poetry; and if there had been no Phrynis, there would have been no Timotheus. The same may be said of those who spoke about the truth; for some of them handed down to us certain doctrines, but there were others before who caused them to be what they were.

20 It is also right for philosophy to be called "a science of truth". For the end of a theoretical science is truth, but the end of a practical science is performance; for even if practical scientists examine how things are, they investigate what is relative to something else and what exists at the moment, and not what is eternal. Now we do not understand a truth without its cause; also, of things to which the same predicate belongs, the one to which it belongs
25 in the highest degree is that in virtue of which it belongs also to the others. For example, fire is the hottest of whatever is truly called "hot", for fire is the cause of hotness in the others. Likewise, therefore, that is most true which is the cause of truth in whatever is posterior to it. Accordingly, the principles of eternal things are of necessity always the most true; for they are true not merely sometimes, nor is there anything which is the cause of their

existence, but they are the cause of the existence of the other things; accordingly, as each 30
thing is related to its existence, so is it related to its truth.

[. . .]

Book IV (= Γ)

1

There is a science which investigates being qua being and what belongs essentially to it. This 1003a
science is not the same as any of the so-called "special sciences"; for none of those sciences
examines universally being qua being, but, cutting off some part of it, each of them investigates the attributes of that part, as in the case of the mathematical sciences. Now since we 25
are seeking the principles and the highest causes, clearly these must belong to some nature
in virtue of itself. If, then, also those who were seeking the elements of things were seeking
these principles, these elements too must be elements of being, not accidentally, but qua 30
being. Accordingly, it is of being qua being that we, too, must find the first causes.

2

The term "being" is used in many senses, yet not equivocally, but all of these are related to
something which is one and a single nature. It is like everything that is called "healthy", which 35
is related to health by preserving health, or by producing health, or by being a sign of health,
or by being receptive of health. And what is called "medical" is similarly related to the medical 1003b
art; for it is so called by possessing the medical art, or by being naturally adapted for it, or
by being something done by it. And we can find other terms which are used in the same
way as "healthy" and "medical". Thus, also "being" is used in many senses, but all of these 5
are related to one principle, for some are called "being" in view of the fact that they are substances, others by being *attributes* of substances, others by being on their way to becoming
substances, or else by being destructions or privations or qualities of substances, or productive or generative either of substances or of whatever is related to substances, or negations
of any of these or of substances. On account of this, we even say that nonbeing *is* nonbeing. 10
   Now, just as there is one science of all that is healthy, so it is with the others. For not
only does the investigation of objects which are named according to one nature belong to
one science, but also of objects which are named in relation to one nature; for the latter,
too, are in some sense named according to one nature. Clearly, then, the investigation of all 15
things qua things belongs to one science. Now in every case a science is concerned mainly
with that which is first, both as that on which the others depend, and as that through which
the others are named. Accordingly, if this is a substance, it is of substances that the philosopher should possess the principles and the causes.
   For each genus of things there is both one power of sensation and one science; grammar, 20
for example, which is one science, investigates all kinds of speech. Accordingly, it belongs
to one generic science to investigate all the kinds of being, and it belongs also to one specific
science to investigate each kind of being.
   If, now, being and unity are the same and are one nature in the sense that they follow
each other in the same way in which a principle and a cause do, but not in the sense that

25 they are signified by one formula (however, it makes no difference even if we were to believe the latter; in fact, it would be even more suitable), seeing that *one man* and *being a man* and *a man* are the same and that the added word in "one man exists" does not make it signify something other than what "a man exists" does (this is clear from the fact that unity and

30 being are not separated in generation or in destruction), and similarly with "unity", then it is evident that the same thing is indicated by the addition of any one of these, and what is one is not distinct from what is a being. Moreover, the *substance* of each individual is one not by accident, and similarly it is essentially a being; so that there are as many kinds of being

35 as there are of unity. And the investigation of the whatness of these belongs to the same generic science; I mean, for example, the investigation of sameness and likeness and the

1004a others of this sort as well as of their opposites. And nearly all the contraries are referred to this principle. Let us regard these as having been investigated in the *Collection of Contraries*.[9] And there are as many parts of philosophy as there are substances, so that there must be

5 among them a first and one which follows; for there are immediate genera which have being and unity. Therefore, the corresponding sciences will follow these genera. For the philosopher is like the so-called mathematician, for also mathematics has parts, and in it there is a first and a second science and others which follow.

10 Since it belongs to one science to investigate opposites, and plurality is opposed to unity, and since it belongs to one science to investigate also denial and privation because unity is investigated in both ways, that is, with respect to its denial as well as to its privation (for we say that something does not exist either without qualification or in some genus; thus, in the

15 former case, from the denial of unity no differentia is added to it, for the denial of it is its absence; but in privation there is also an underlying nature of which the privation is asserted); to repeat, since plurality is opposed to unity, it belongs to the same science to know also the opposites of the kinds of unity which we mentioned, for example, otherness and unlikeness and inequality and all the others which are named either according to these or

20 according to plurality and unity. One of them is contrariety, for contrariety is a kind of difference, and difference is a kind of otherness. Since, then, "unity" has many senses, all these will also have many senses, yet it belongs to one science to know them all; for terms belong to different sciences not if they just have many meanings, but if neither are they asserted of one nature nor have their formulae reference to one nature. Now since all things are

25 referred to that which is primary, as for example all things which are called "one" are referred to what is primarily one, we must say that the case is similar with sameness and otherness and the contraries; so that after distinguishing the various senses of each, we must give a similar account of how the others are related to that which is primary in each category; for

30 some are referred to what is primary in the sense that they possess it, others in the sense that they produce it, and others in other such ways.

It is evident, then, that it belongs to one science to discuss these things as well as substance (this was one of the problems we listed);[10] and so, it is the philosopher's task to be

1004b able to investigate all of them. For if it is not the philosopher, then who will examine whether Socrates and sitting Socrates are the same, or if a given contrary has only one contrary to it, or what is a contrary, or the various senses of the term "contrary"? And similarly with all other such questions.

9 Perhaps a lost work.
10 995b18–27.

Since, then, these are essential *attributes* of unity qua unity and of being qua being, but 5 not qua numbers or qua lines or qua fire, clearly it belongs to this science also to know both the whatness of these and their attributes. And those who inquire into these matters err not in the sense that they do not philosophize, but in not considering substances, of which they comprehend nothing, as prior to attributes. For just as there are proper *attributes* of num- 10 bers qua numbers, such as oddness and evenness, commensurability and equality, excess and deficiency, whether these belong to numbers essentially or in relation to one another, and likewise other proper *attributes* belonging to solids, whether motionless or in motion, and whether without weight or with weight, so there are proper *attributes* belonging to being 15 qua being, and it is the task of the philosopher to examine the truth about these. A sign of this is the following: dialecticians and sophists put on the same appearance as the philosopher (for sophistry only appears to be wisdom, and dialecticians discuss everything) since being 20 is common to all. But clearly they discuss all things because these are *proper* to philosophy. Now sophistry and dialectics busy themselves with the same genus of things as philosophy, but philosophy differs from dialectic in the manner of its capacity, and from sophistry in the kind of life *chosen*. Dialectics is tentative concerning things which philosophy knows, 25 sophistry makes the appearance of knowing without knowing.

Again, one of the two columns of contraries is a privation, and all objects are referred to being and not-being, and to unity and plurality; for example, rest is referred to unity, motion to plurality. Now almost all thinkers agree that things and substances are composed of con- 30 traries; at any rate, all say that the principles are contraries, some positing the *Odd* and the *Even*,[11] others the *Hot* and *Cold*,[12] others the *Limit* and the *Unlimited*,[13] others *Friendship* and *Strife*.[14] All the other objects, too, appear to be referred to unity and plurality (let us assume this reference), and the principles posited by the other thinkers fall indeed entirely under these 1005a as if these were their genera. So it is evident also from this discussion that it belongs to one science to investigate being qua being; for all these objects are either contraries or composed of contraries, and the principles of contraries are unity and plurality. And these belong to one science, whether they are named according to one nature or not; perhaps the truth is 5 that they are not so named. But even if "unity" has many meanings, the other meanings are stated by being referred to the primary meaning, and likewise for the contraries of these; and even if being or unity is not universal and the same or not separable when applied to all things (as perhaps it is not), still some things are referred to one primary object and the 10 others to those which follow the primary. Because of this, it is not the task of the geometer to investigate what a contrary is, or completeness, or being, or unity, or sameness, or otherness, except by hypothesis.

It is clear, then, that it belongs to one science to investigate being qua being and whatever belongs to it qua being, and that the same science investigates not only substances, 15 but also whatever belongs to substances, both the attributes mentioned and also priority and posteriority, genus and species, whole and part, and the others of this sort.

[. . .]

11 Pythagoreans.
12 Perhaps Parmenides.
13 Platonists.
14 Empedocles.

Book VI (= E)

1

1025b We are seeking the principles and causes of things, but clearly, qua things. For there is a cause of health and of good physical condition, and there are principles and elements and
5 causes of mathematical objects, and in general, every science which proceeds by *thinking* or which participates in *thought* to some extent is concerned with causes and principles, whether these are very accurate or rather simplified. But all these sciences, marking off some being or some genus, conduct their investigations into this part of being, although not into
10 unqualified being nor into their part of being qua being, and they say nothing concerning whatness; but starting from the whatness of their subject, which [whatness] in some sciences is made clear by sensation but in others is laid down by hypothesis, they thus proceed to demonstrate more or less rigorously the essential attributes of their genus. Consequently, it
15 is evident by such induction from these sciences that there is no demonstration of *substance* or of whatness but that these are made known in some other way. Similarly, they say nothing as to the existence or non-existence of the genus they investigate, and this is because it belongs to the same power of *thought* to make known both the whatness and the existence of a genus.

Now physical science, too, happens to be concerned with some genus of being (for it is
20 concerned with such a substance which has in itself a principle of motion and of rest), and it is clear that this science is neither practical nor productive. For in productive sciences the principle of a thing produced is in that which produces, whether this is intellect or art or some power, and in practical sciences the principle of *action* is in the doer, and this is *choice*; for that which is done and that which is *chosen* are the same thing. Thus, if every *thought* is
25 practical or productive or theoretical, physics would be a theoretical science, and theoretical about such being as can be moved, and about *substances* which according to formula are for the most part nonseparable only.

We must not fail to notice how the essence and the formula of an object of physics exists,
30 for inquiry without this leads nowhere. Now of things defined and of the whatness of things, some are considered in the manner in which snubness exists, others in the manner in which concavity exists. These differ by the fact that "snubness" is *understood* with matter (for a snub is a concave nose) but "concavity" without sensible matter. If, then, all physical things are
1026a named in a manner like the snub (as for example a nose, an eye, a face, flesh, bone, and in general an animal, and also a leaf, a root, a bark, and in general a plant; for what is signified by the formula of each of these is not without motion but always has matter), it is clear how we must seek and define the whatness in physical things and why it belongs to the physi-
5 cist to investigate even some part of the soul, namely, that which does not exist without matter. From what has been said, then, it is evident that physics is a theoretical science.

Mathematics, too, is a theoretical science; but whether its objects are immovable and separate is not at present clear. It is clear, however, that some mathematical sciences inves-
10 tigate their objects qua immovable and qua separate. But if there is something which is eternal and immovable and separate, the knowledge of it evidently belongs to a theoretical science, not however to physics (for physics is concerned with certain movable things) nor to mathematics, but to a science which is prior to both. For physics is concerned with sep-arable but not immovable things, and mathematics is concerned with some immovable things
15 although perhaps not separable but as in matter. The first science, however, is concerned

with things which are both separate and immovable. Now all causes must be eternal, and these most of all; for these are the causes of what is visible among things divine. Hence, there should be three theoretical philosophies, mathematics, physics, and theology. For it is clear that if the divine is present anywhere, it would be present in a nature of this sort, and 20 the most honorable science should be concerned with the most honorable genus of things. So, the theoretical sciences are to be preferred over the other sciences, but theology is to be preferred over the other theoretical sciences.

One might raise the question whether first philosophy is in any way universal or is concerned merely with some genus and some one nature. In the case of the mathematical 25 sciences, their objects are not all treated in the same manner; geometry and astronomy are concerned with some nature, but universal mathematics is common to all. Accordingly, if there were no substances other than those formed by nature, physics would be the first science; but if there is an immovable substance, this would be prior, and the science of it would be first philosophy and would be universal in this manner, in view of the fact that it 30 is first. And it would be the concern of this science, too, to investigate being qua being, both what being is and what belongs to it qua being.

[. . .]

Book VII (= **Z**)

1   1028a

The term "being" is used in several senses, as we pointed out previously[15] in our account of 10 the various senses of terms. In one sense, it signifies whatness and a *this*; in another, it signifies a quality or a quantity or one of the others which are predicated in this way. Although "being" is used in so many senses, it is evident that of these the primary sense is whatness, and used in this sense it signifies a substance. For when we state that this has some quality, we say 15 that it is good or bad but not that it is three cubits long or a man; but when we state what it is, we say that it is a man or a God but not white or hot or three cubits long. The others are called "beings" in view of the fact that they are quantities of being which is spoken of in this primary sense, or qualities of it, or affections of it, or something else of this kind. Because of this, one might even raise the problem whether walking, being healthy, sitting, 20 and the others of this kind are beings or not beings; for by nature each of these does not exist by itself and cannot be separated from a substance, but rather, if anything, it is that which walks or that which sits or that which is healthy that is a being. These latter appear 25 to be beings to a higher degree, because there is something definite in each of them, namely, the underlying subject; and this is the substance and the individual, which is indicated in the corresponding predication, for we do not use the terms "the good" and "that which sits" without including the substance. It is clear, then, that each of the others exists because 30 substances exist. Thus, being in the primary sense, not in a qualified sense but without qualification, would be a substance.

Now the term "primary" ["first", or "prior to all others"] is used in many senses, yet a substance is primary in every sense: in formula, in knowledge, and in time. For of the other

15 1017a7–b9.

categories no one is separable, but only substance. And in formula, too, substance is primary;
35 for in the formula of each of the other categories the formula of a substance must be present. And we think we understand each thing to the highest degree when we know, for
1028b example, what a man is or what fire is, rather than their quality or their quantity or their whereness, and even of these latter, we understand each when we know what a quantity is or what a quality is. And indeed the inquiry or perplexity concerning what being is, in early times and now and always, is just this: What is a substance? For it is this that some assert
5 to be one,[16] others more than one, and some say that it is finite,[17] while others that it is infinite.[18] And so we, too, must speculate most of all, and first of all, and exclusively, so to say, concerning being which is spoken of in this sense. What is being?

2

Substance is thought to belong most evidently to bodies; and so we say that animals and
10 plants and their parts are substances, and also the natural bodies, such as fire and water and earth and each one of this sort, and also parts of these, and composites of these (either of parts or of all of them), such as the heavens and its parts, the stars and the Moon and the Sun. We must inquire whether these alone are substances or also others, or some of these
15 and some others, or none of these but some others.

Some thinkers are of the opinion that the limits of bodies are substances, such as surfaces and lines and points and units, and that they are substances to a higher degree than bodies or solids. Moreover, some think that no such as the ones just mentioned exist, but only sensible objects; but others think that such do exist, and that they are many and are eternal and
20 are beings to a higher degree, as in the case of Plato, who posits two [kinds of] substances, the Forms and the Mathematical Objects, and also the sensible bodies as the third kind. Speusippus spoke of yet a greater number [of kinds] of substances, and of distinct principles for each kind; he starts from the *One* as a principle for numbers, posits another principle for magnitudes, still another for soul, and in this manner he extends the kinds of substances.
25 Still others say that the Forms and the Numbers have the same nature, and that from these follow all the others, such as the lines, the planes, and so on, all the way down to the substances of the universe and the sensible substances.

Concerning these matters we must examine what is stated well and what is not, which are the substances, whether there are other substances besides the sensible or not and how
30 these exist, whether there exist separate substances other than sensible substances or not, and if yes, then why such exist and how. But first, we must sketch out what a substance is.

3

The term "substance" is spoken of, if not in more, still in four main senses; for the essence
35 is thought to be the substance of an individual, and the universal, and the genus, and fourthly the underlying subject. The subject is that of which the others are said, but the subject itself
1029a is not said of anything else. And so we must describe first the subject; for the primary subject is thought to be a substance in the highest degree.

16 e.g. Eleatics.
17 e.g. Pythagoreans, Empedocles.
18 e.g. Anaxagoras.

In one sense, the subject is said to be the matter; in another sense, it is said to be the *form*;[19] in a third, it is said to be the composite of these. By "matter" I mean, for instance, bronze; by "*form*", the shape of its outward appearance; and by "the composite of these", the statue as a *composite*. Thus, if the form is prior to matter and is a being to a higher degree than matter, for the same reason it will be prior to the composite of form and matter.

We have now stated sketchily what a substance is, that it is that which is not said of a subject but of which the others are said. But we must not state it only in this manner, as this is not enough. The statement itself is not clear, and further, matter becomes a substance. For if this is not a substance, we are at a loss as to what else is a substance. If the others are taken off, nothing appears to remain. For, of the others, some are affections and actions and potencies of bodies, while length and width and depth are quantities and not substances (for a quantity is not a substance), but that to which as first these belong is a substance to a higher degree. Yet if length and width and depth are removed, we observe nothing left, unless there is something bounded by these; so matter alone must appear to be a substance, if we inquire in this manner. By "matter" I mean that which in itself is not stated as being the whatness of something, nor a quantity, nor any of the other senses of "being". For there is something of which each of these is a predicate, whose being is other than that of each of the predicates; for all the others are predicates of a substance, while a substance is a predicate of matter. Thus, this last is in itself neither a whatness nor a quantity nor any of the others; and it is not a denial of any of these, for even a denial belongs to something accidentally.

From what has been said, it follows that matter is a substance. But this is impossible; for to be separable and a *this* is thought to belong most of all to a substance. Accordingly, the form or the *composite* would seem to be a substance to a higher degree than matter. The *composite* substance, that is, the composite of matter and *shape*, may be laid aside; for it is posterior and clear. Matter, too, is in a sense evident. But we must examine the third, for this is the most perplexing.

It is agreed that there exist substances among the sensibles, so we must first inquire into the sensibles. For, it is useful to proceed from the less to the more known. Instruction is acquired by all in this manner: through the less known by nature to the more known by nature; and just as in *actions*, in which the purpose is to start from what is good to each individual and make good to each individual that which is good in general, so here, the purpose is to start from what is more known to the individual and proceed to make known to the individual what is known by nature. Now what is known and first to each individual is often known slightly and has little or no being. Nevertheless, from what is poorly knowable but knowable to oneself one must make an effort to know what is generally knowable, proceeding, as we stated, from what is knowable to oneself.

[. . .]

Book XII (= Λ)

6

Since three kinds of substances were named,[20] two of them physical and one immovable, we should discuss the latter, in view of the fact that there must be some eternal substance which

---

19 "Form" (with italics) translates *morphē*; "form" (without italics) translates *eidos*. The words are often used synonymously, though *morphē* is usually used for a physical shape.
20 1069a30.

is immovable. For substances are the first of all things, and if they are all destructible, all
5   things are destructible. But it is impossible for motion either to be generated or to be destroyed;
for it always existed. The same applies to time; for if there is no time, neither can there be
a *before* and an *after* in time. And so motion, too, is continuous in the same manner as time
10 is; for either motion and time are the same, or time is an *attribute* of motion. But motion
cannot be continuous except with respect to place, and of this motion, only the one which
is circular.

Moreover, if there is a thing which can move other things or can act upon them but which
will not *actually* do so, then there will be no motion; for that which has a potency may not
be *actualizing* it. So there is no gain even if we posit eternal substances, like those who posit
15 the Forms, unless there is in them a principle which can cause a change. But even such a
principle is not enough (nor is any substance other than the Forms), for, if this principle will
not be in activity, there will be no motion. Moreover, if the substance of such a principle is
a potency, still this is not enough even if this principle is in activity, for motion will not be
eternal; for that which exists potentially may not be existing [*actually*]. Hence, there must
20 be a principle of such a kind that its *substance* is *actuality*. Moreover, such substances must
be without matter; for they must be eternal, if indeed something else is also eternal. They
must exist, then, as *actualities*.

Yet there is a *difficulty*; for it seems that whatever exists in *actuality* also has the potency
for it, but that whatever has a potency need not *actualize* it, and so potency seems to be
25 prior to *actuality*. But if this is so, nothing will exist; for something may have the potency to
be and still not be. And indeed, the same impossibility follows from the statements of the
theologians who generate the universe from *Night*, or of the physicists who say that all things
were together.[21] For how will anything be moved if no cause exists in *actuality*? Matter itself
30 will certainly not move itself, but carpentry will move it; and neither the menses nor the
earth will move themselves, but the seeds will act on the earth and the semen on the menses.

This is why some thinkers, like Leucippus[22] and Plato,[23] posit eternal activity; for they say
that motion is eternal. But they do not state why this exists nor which it is, nor yet its man-
35 ner or the cause of it. For nothing is moved at random, but there must always be something, just as it is at present with physical bodies which are moved in one way by nature but
in another by force or by the intellect or by something else. Then again, which of them is
1072a first? For this makes a great difference. Plato cannot even state what it is that he sometimes
considers to be the principle, that is that which moves itself;[24] for, as he himself says, the
soul came after,[25] and it is generated at the same time as the universe.

Now to regard potency as prior to *actuality* is in one sense right and in another sense not
right; and we have already stated[26] how this is so. That *actuality* is prior is confirmed by
5   Anaxagoras (for *Intelligence* according to him exists in *actuality*), by Empedocles (who posits
Friendship and *Strife*), and by others, such as Leucippus, who say that motion always exists.
If so, then *Chaos* or *Night* did not exist for an infinite time, but the same things existed always,
whether passing through cycles or in some other way, if indeed *actuality* is prior to potency.

21 Anaxagoras.
22 See *On the Heavens* 300b8.
23 *Timaeus* 30A.
24 *Phaedrus* 245C; *Laws* 894E.
25 *Timaeus* 34B.
26 1071b22–6.

So if the same things always take place in cycles, there must be something, say A, which always remains and is in activity in the same way. But if there is to be generation and destruction, there must be something else, say B, which is always in activity now in one way and now in another. So it is necessary for it to be active in one way according to itself and in another according to something else; then the latter is either still another thing, say C, or the first thing. Surely, it must be the first thing; for otherwise C would still be its own cause and the cause of B. So it is better to say that it is the first, for it is this that is the cause of being in activity always in the same way, and it is something else that is the cause of being in activity in another way; and so it is evident that that which is always active in distinct ways requires two causes. And, in fact, it is in this way that motions take place. So why should we seek other principles?

7

Since the account given in this manner is possible, and if it were not, the universe would have been generated from *Night* or from the *togetherness of all things* or from nonbeing, the *difficulties* may be regarded as solved, and so there is something which is always moved with an unceasing motion, which is circular; and this is clear not only by arguments but also from the facts. So, the first heaven must be eternal; and further, there is also something which this moves. And since that which is moved and is a mover is thus an intermediate, there is something which causes motion without being moved, and this is eternal, a substance, and an *actuality*. And this is the way in which the object of desire or the intelligible object moves, namely, without itself being moved. Of these, the primary objects are the same; for the object of *desire* is that which *appears* to be noble, and the primary object of wish is that which is noble. We desire because it seems rather that it seems because we desire; and thinking *is* the starting-point. Now the intellect is moved by the intelligible, and things which are intelligible in virtue of themselves are in one of the two columns of opposites; and of these, substances are primary, and of substances, that which is simple and in *actuality* is primary. Oneness is not the same as the simple; for "one" signifies a measure, but "simple" signifies the manner in which something exists. Moreover, both the noble and that which is chosen for its own sake are in the same column of opposites; and that which is primary is always the best, or by analogy so.

1072b

That the final cause exists in immovable things is clear by distinguishing the two meanings of "final cause". For the final cause may be (a) for some thing or (b) that for the sake of which, and of these the one may exist but the other may not; and it [the final cause] causes motion as something which is loved, and that which is moved moves the others. If, then, something is moved, it can be otherwise than as it is; so even if the primary locomotion exists as an *actuality*, still that which is moved qua being moved can be otherwise with respect to place, even if not with respect to its *substance*.[27] And since there is some mover which causes motion but is itself immovable and exists as *actuality*, this can in no way be otherwise than as it is. Now of all changes locomotion is primary, and of locomotions the circular is primary; and it is this motion which the immovable mover causes. This mover, then, exists of necessity; and if so, then nobly, and as such, it is a first principle. For "necessity" has the following senses: (a) by force, which is contrary to a thing's tendency, (b) that without which the good is impossible, and (c) that which cannot be otherwise but exists without qualification.

---

27 "Substance" (with italics) refers to the form or essence of a "substance" (no italics).

Such, then, is the principle upon which depends the heaven and nature. And its *activity* is
15 like the best which we can have but for a little while. For it exists in this manner eternally
(which is impossible for us), since its *actuality* is also pleasure. And it is because of this [activ-
ity] that being awake, sensing, and thinking are most pleasant, and hopes and memories are
pleasant because of these. Now thinking according to itself is of the best according to itself,
20 and thinking in the highest degree is of that which is best in the highest degree. Thus, in
partaking of the intelligible, it is of Himself that the Intellect is thinking; for by apprehend-
ing and thinking it is He Himself who becomes intelligible, and so the Intellect and its intelligible object are the same. For that which is capable of receiving the intelligible object and
the *substance* is the intellect, and the latter is in *actuality* by possessing the intelligible object;
so that the possession of the intelligible is more divine than the potency of receiving it,
and the contemplation of it is the most pleasant and the best. If, then, the manner of God's
25 existence is as good as ours sometimes is, but eternally, then this is marvelous, and if it is
better, this is still more marvelous; and it is the latter. And life belongs to God, for the
actuality of the intellect is life, and He is *actuality*; and His *actuality* is in virtue of itself a life
which is the best and is eternal. We say that God is a living being which is eternal and the
30 best; so life and continuous duration and eternity belong to God, for this is God.

Those who believe, as the Pythagoreans[28] and Speusippus[29] do, that the most noble and
the best are not in the principle, because the principles of plants and of animals are also causes
but nobility and completeness are in what comes from them, do not think rightly. For the
35 seed comes from other things which are prior and complete, and that which is first is not
1073a the seed but the complete thing. One might say, for example, that prior to the seed is the
man, not the man who comes from this seed but the man from whom this seed comes.

It is evident from what has been said that there exists a substance which is eternal and
5 immovable and separate from sensible things. It has also been shown that this substance cannot have any magnitude but is without parts and indivisible. For it causes motion for an
infinite time, but no finite thing has infinite potency. Since every magnitude is either infinite
or finite, this substance cannot have a finite magnitude because of what we said, and it can-
10 not be infinite in view of the fact that there exists no infinite magnitude at all. Moreover, it
cannot be affected or altered; for all the other motions are posterior to locomotion. It is clear,
then, why these facts are so.

8

We should not neglect to consider whether we should posit one such substance or more
15 than one, and if the latter, how many; but with regard to the statements made by other thinkers,
we should mention the fact that concerning the number of such substances they said nothing that can be even *clearly* stated. The doctrine of Ideas does not inquire specifically into
this problem, for those who speak of the Ideas speak of them as Numbers, and concerning
20 Numbers they sometimes speak as if these were infinite but at other times as if they were
limited to ten;[30] but as to why there should be so many Numbers, nothing is stated seriously
enough to amount to a demonstration. We, however, should discuss this problem by starting with the assumptions and distinctions already made.

28 See 1075a36.
29 See 1028b21, 1091a34–6, 1092a11–15.
30 *Physics* 206b32–3.

Now the principle and the first of beings is immovable, both in virtue of itself and accidentally, and it causes the primary motion, which is eternal and one. But since that which 25 is moved must be moved by something, and the first mover is of necessity immovable in virtue of itself, and an eternal motion must be caused by an eternal being and one motion by one being, and since we also observe that, besides the simple locomotion of the universe which we say is caused by the first and immovable substance, there are other locomotions 30 (those of the planets) which are eternal (for a body with a circular motion is eternal and is never at rest, and we have shown this in the *Physics*[31]), then each of these locomotions, too, must be caused by a substance which is in virtue of itself immovable and eternal. For a star is by its nature an eternal substance, and the mover is eternal and prior to that which is moved, 35 and that which is prior to a substance must be a substance. So it is evident that there must be as many substances as there are locomotions and that in their nature they are eternal and immovable in virtue of themselves and without magnitude, and the cause of this has been stated earlier.[32]   1073b

It is evident, then, that the movers are substances, and that of these there is a first, a second etc., according to the same order as the locomotions of the stars. Now as regards the number of locomotions, this should be the concern of the mathematical science which is closest to philosophy, and this is astronomy; for it is this science which is concerned with 5 the investigation of sensible but eternal substances, while the others, such as arithmetic and geometry, are not concerned with any substances. That there are many locomotions of heavenly bodies is evident also to those who have studied the matter to some extent; for each of the planets has more than one locomotion. But as to the number of these, we may 10 for the present give an indication by quoting what some mathematicians are saying, so that there may be in our thought a belief in some definite number; as for the rest, we should partly investigate ourselves and partly inquire from those who investigate the subject, and if those who are investigating this subject have opinions contrary to those just stated, we 15 should respect both views but accept the more accurate.

Eudoxus held that each of the locomotions of the Sun and of the Moon is in three spheres, of which the first is that of the fixed stars, the second along the circle which bisects the Zodiac, 20 and the third along the circle inclined across the breadth of the Zodiac, but the circle along which the Moon moves is inclined at a greater angle than that along which the Sun moves. The motion of each of the planets is in four spheres, and of these the first and second are the same as those in the previous case (for the locomotion of the sphere of the fixed stars 25 belongs to all the spheres, and that of the sphere next under it which moves along the circle bisecting the Zodiac belongs to all), the poles of the third sphere of each planet are in the circle bisecting the Zodiac, and the locomotion of the fourth sphere is in the circle 30 inclined at an angle to the equator of the third; and the poles of the third sphere are different for different planets, except for Venus and Mercury which have the same poles.

Callippus posited the same position of the spheres as that held by Eudoxus, that is, with respect to the order of the intervals, but while he assigned to Jupiter and Saturn the same number of spheres as Eudoxus did, he thought that two more spheres should be added to 35 the Sun and also to the Moon, if one is to account for the observed phenomena, and one more to each of the other planets.

---

31 *Physics* Bk. VIII, chs. 8, 9.
32 1073a5–11.

1074a   But if all the spheres combined are to account for the observed phenomena, there must be other spheres for each planet, one less in number than those assigned to it, which would counteract these and restore to the same position the first sphere of the star which in each
5   case is next in order below; for only thus can the motion of the combined spheres produce the motion of the planets. Since, then, the spheres in which the planets are carried are eight for Jupiter and Saturn and twenty-five for the others, and of these only those need not be counteracted in which the lowest-situated planet is carried, the spheres which counteract those
10   of the first two planets will be six, those of the next four planets will be sixteen, and the total number of spheres which includes both those which carry the planets and the ones which counteract those spheres will be fifty-five. If we are not to add to the Moon and to the Sun the motions we mentioned,[33] all the spheres will be forty-seven. Let, then, this be the
15   number of spheres, and if so, it is reasonable to believe that the immovable substances or principles are also as many. As to what is necessarily the case, this may be left to more competent thinkers.

If there can be no locomotion which does not contribute to the locomotion of a star, and if moreover every nature or substance which is unaffected and which in virtue of itself attains
20   its best should be regarded as an end, then there can be no other nature besides those mentioned, but this must be the number of substances. For if there were others, they would be movers as ends of locomotions; but there can be no other locomotions besides those mentioned. And in view of the heavenly bodies which are in locomotion, this is a reasonable
25   belief. For if each thing that carries something does so by nature for the sake of that which is carried, and every locomotion is likewise for the sake of something which is so moved, no locomotion can exist for its own sake or for the sake of another locomotion, but each must exist for the sake of a star. For if every locomotion exists for the sake of another locomotion, the latter too will exist for the sake of a third; and so, since it is impossible to
30   proceed to infinity, the end of each locomotion in the heavens must be some of the divine bodies which are so moved there.

It is evident that there is only one heaven. For if there are more than one, like men, the principle for each will be one in species but many in number. But things which are many in number have matter; for the formula is one and the same for the many, as in the case of
35   the formula of a man, while Socrates is only one. But the primary essence has no matter, for it is actuality. Thus, the first immovable mover is one both in formula and in number; and so, that which is always and continuously in motion is only one. Hence, there is only one heaven.

1074b   The ancients of very early times bequeathed to posterity in the form of a myth a tradition that the heavenly bodies are gods and that the divinity encompasses the whole of nature. The rest of the tradition has been added later as a means of persuading the masses and as
5   something useful for the laws and for matters of expediency; for they say that these gods are like men in form and like some of the other animals, and also other things which follow from or are similar to those stated. But if one were to separate from the later additions the first point and attend to this alone (namely, that they thought the first substances to be gods),
10   he might realize that this was divinely spoken and that, while probably every art and every philosophy has often reached a stage of development as far as it could and then again has perished, these doctrines about the gods were saved like relics up to the present day. Anyway, the opinion of our forefathers and of the earliest thinkers is evident to us to just this extent.

33 1073b35–1074a4.

9

Certain problems arise with regard to The Intellect [God]; for He seems to be the most divine 15 of things manifest to us, yet there are certain difficulties as to how He can exist as such. For if He is not thinking of anything, why the veneration of Him? He is like a man who sleeps. And if He is thinking, but what decides this thinking is something else (for the *substance* of that which decides thinking is not thinking, but a potency), then He cannot be the best sub- 20 stance. For it is because of [the act of] thinking that honor belongs to Him. Moreover, whether His *substance* is intellect or thinking, of what does He think? Either He thinks of Himself or of something else; and if something else, then either always of the same thing or sometimes of one thing and sometimes of another. But does it make any difference or not whether He is thinking of that which is noble rather than of any chance thing? Would it not be absurd 25 to be *thinking* of certain things? Clearly, then, He is thinking of that which is most divine and most honorable, and He is not changing; for change would be for the worse, and this change would then be a motion.

First, then, if He were not thinking but a potency, it is reasonable that the continuity of His thinking would be fatiguing Him. Moreover, it is clear that something else would be more honorable than The Intellect, namely, the object of thought; for to think or thinking 30 may belong even to that which thinks of the worst objects, so that if this is to be avoided (for there are even things which it is better not to see than to see), Thinking would not be the best of things. It is of Himself, then, that The Intellect is thinking, if He is the most excellent of things, and so Thinking is the thinking of Thinking.

But it appears that *knowledge* and sensation and opinion and *thought* are always of other 35 objects, and only incidentally of themselves. Moreover, if thinking and being thought are distinct, in virtue of which of these does goodness belong to The Intellect? For to be think-ing and to be an object of thought are not the same. Or is it not that in some cases *know-* 1075a *ledge* and its object are the same? In the productive sciences, this object is the *substance* or the essence but without the matter, in the theoretical sciences it is the formula and the thinking. Accordingly, since the intellect and the object of thought are not distinct in things which have no matter, the two will be the same, and so both thinking and the object of 5 thought will be one.

Further, there remains the problem whether the object of Thinking is composite; for if so, Thinking would be changing in passing from one part of the whole to another part. Is it not the case that what has no matter is indivisible, like the human intellect, or even that which is thinking of a composite object in an interval of time? For it does not possess good-ness in this part or in that part but possesses the highest good in the whole, though it is dis-tinct from it. It is in this manner that Thinking is the thinking of Himself through all eternity. 10

10

We must also inquire in which of two ways the nature of the whole has the good and the highest good, whether as something separate and by itself, or as the order of its parts. Or does it have it in both ways, as in the case of an army? For in an army goodness exists both in the order and in the general, and rather in the general; for it is not because of the order 15 that he exists, but the order exists because of him. Now all things are ordered in some way, water-animals and birds and plants, but not similarly; and they do not exist without being related at all to one another, but they are in some way related. For all things are ordered in

relation to one thing. It is as in a household, in which the freemen are least at liberty to
20 act at random but all or most things are ordered, while slaves and wild animals contribute
little to the common good but for the most part act at random; for such is the principle of
each of these, which is their nature. I mean, for example, that all these must come together
if they are to be distinguished; and this is what happens in other cases in which all the mem-
25 bers participate in the whole.

We must not fail to notice how many impossible or absurd results face those who speak
otherwise, what sort of views are put forward by subtler thinkers, and what sort of views
are faced with the least difficulties. Now all thinkers posit all things as coming from contraries. But neither "all things" nor "from contraries" is right. Nor do these thinkers say, of
30 things to which contraries belong, how those things are composed of contraries; for contraries cannot be acted upon by each other. For us, however, the problem is reasonably solved
by the positing of a third object. But these thinkers posit one of the contraries as being matter, as in the case of those who posit the *Unequal* as the matter for the *Equal* or those who
regard the *Many* as the matter for the *One*.[34] This difficulty, too, is solved in the same manner; for the matter, for us, is not contrary to anything. Moreover, for these thinkers all things
35 except the *One* will participate in badness, for *Bad Itself* is one of the two elements. As for
the other thinkers,[35] they do not even regard the principles as being the *Good* and the *Bad*;
yet in all things the good is in the highest degree a principle. Now the former thinkers rightly
1075b regard the *Good* as a principle, but they do not say how it is a principle, whether as an end
or as a mover or as form.

Empedocles, too, speaks absurdly, for he posits *Friendship* as the good; and as a principle,
it is posited both as a mover (for it brings things together), and as matter (for it is a part of
the *Blend*). Indeed, even if the same thing happens to be a principle both as matter and as a
5 mover, nevertheless to be matter is not the same as to be a mover. In which sense, then, is
Friendship a good? It is also absurd that *Strife* should be indestructible, since *Strife*, for him,
is the nature of the bad. Anaxagoras posits the *Good* as a principle in the sense of a mover,
since for him *Intelligence* moves things; but it moves for the sake of something, so that the
Good should be something else (unless it is so posited in another sense, as used by us; for,
10 the medical art is in some sense health). It is also absurd that he should posit no contrary of
the *Good* or of *Intelligence*. As a matter of fact, all those who posit contraries do not use them,
unless we reshape their views into a system.

Again, no one states why some things are destructible but others are indestructible; for
all things are posited by these thinkers as being composed of the same principles. Again, some
15 thinkers posit things as coming from nonbeing; others, to avoid this necessity, say that all
things are one.

Again, no one states why there will always be generation and what is the cause of generation. And those who posit two principles need another principle which is more authoritative. And those who posit the Forms also need a more authoritative principle; for why did
20 things participate in the Forms or do so now? And for all other thinkers there must be something which is the contrary of wisdom or of the most honorable science; but for us this is
not necessary, for there is nothing contrary to that which is first. For, in all cases, contraries
have matter which is potentially these contraries, and ignorance, which is the contrary of
knowledge, should be of the contrary object; but there is nothing contrary to what is first.

34 Those in Plato's Academy.
35 Pythagoreans and Speusippus. See 1072b32–4.

Again, if there were nothing besides the sensible things, there would be no principle or order 25
or generation or heavenly objects, but of a principle there would always be another principle, as all the theologians and the physicists say. And if the Forms or Numbers were to
exist, they would not be the causes of anything; or if they were, at least not of motion.
Again, how can magnitude or what is continuous come from things which have no magnitude? For no number, either as a mover or as a form, can make what is continuous. Moreover, no contrary is just a potency of acting or of moving, for it would then be possible for 30
it not to exist, and besides, action is posterior to the potency of it; and if so, no things would
be eternal. But there are such; so some of their premises must be rejected. We have stated
how this should be done.[36]

Again, in virtue of what is a number one, or a soul, or a body, or in general, each form 35
or thing? No one says anything at all; nor can any of them say anything, unless they do in
the way we do, that it is the mover that makes each one. As for those who assert that
Mathematical Numbers are first,[37] and following these, posit one kind of substances after another
with distinct principles for each kind, they represent the substances of the universe as a 1076a
plurality of unrelated parts (for substances of one kind, whether existing or not, contribute
nothing to those of another kind) and with many principles; but things do not wish to be
governed badly. *"The rule of many is not good; let one the ruler be."*[38]

36 1071b19–20.
37 Speusippus. See 1028b27, 1090b13–20.
38 Homer, *Iliad* II. 204.

22

Nicomachean Ethics

Of the two ethical works that have survived, the *Eudemian Ethics* and the *Nicomachean Ethics*, the latter is generally regarded as the more sophisticated and finished work, and far more widely studied. Even today, it continues to be counted as one of the most important works in the field of ethics. Unlike the ethical theories formulated in modernity, Aristotle's theories in the *Nicomachean Ethics* regard the primary bearer of value to be neither actions themselves, nor their consequences, nor does he seek to establish a set of rules through which we might establish decision-making procedures for which courses of action we should follow (or avoid). Instead Aristotle's perspective understands ethics as the science of explaining and evaluating human action in virtue of the more primary value of the characterological traits that inform and motivate what we do. Aristotle's focus, accordingly, is on what he calls *aretē* (virtue or excellence), and good action thus becomes whatever the virtuous person would do in a given circumstance. The highest good for human beings, and thus the aim of all that we do, Aristotle says, is *eudaimonia* (happiness or flourishing). Virtue, then, will consist in activity that conforms to rationality (since, plainly, an irrational pursuit of our ultimate goal would not be well designed to obtain that goal). Among the virtues, some pertain to actions and emotions; these Aristotle calls the "ethical" virtues. Others pertain to the ways in which we engage the intellect itself, in theoretical or contemplative activities; these are the "intellectual" virtues, and the very best of human lives, according to Aristotle, are those in which these are fully realized.

Book I

1

1094a Every art and every *inquiry*, and similarly, every *action* and every intention is thought to aim at some good; hence men have expressed themselves well in declaring the good to be that at which all things aim.[1] But there appears to be a difference among the ends; for some are

1 Perhaps a reference to Eudoxus, a member of Plato's Academy. See 1172b10–15. But cf. Plato, *Meno* 78ʙ; *Gorgias* 468ʙ as well.

activities, others are products apart from the [activities which produce them]. Whenever there are ends apart from the *actions* [which produce them], the products are by nature better than 5 the corresponding activities.

Since there are many kinds of *actions* and arts and sciences, the corresponding ends are many also; for the end of the medical [science] is health, that of shipbuilding is a ship, that of strategy is victory, and that of economics is wealth. Whenever a number of such [sciences] come under a single faculty (as bridle-making and all other arts concerned with the equip- 10 ment of horses come under horsemanship, and as this [science] and every military *action* comes under strategy, and similarly in the case of other [sciences] which come under another [sciences]), in every case the end of the architectonic [science] is preferable to the ends of the subordinate [sciences], for the latter ends are pursued for the sake of the former end. It makes 15 no difference whether the ends of the *actions* are the activities themselves or something other than those activities, as in the case of the sciences just mentioned.

Now if of things we do there is an end which we wish for its own sake whereas the other things we wish for the sake of this end, and if we do not choose everything for the sake of something else (for in this manner the process will go on to infinity and our desire will be 20 empty and vain), then clearly this end would be the good and the highest good. Will not the knowledge of it, then, have a great influence on our way of life, and would we not [as a consequence] be more likely to attain the desired end, like archers who have a mark to aim at? If so, then we should try to grasp, in outline at least, what that end is and to which 25 of the sciences or faculties it belongs. It would seem to belong to the one which is most authoritative and most architectonic. Now politics appears to be such; for it is this which regulates what sciences are needed in a state and what kind of sciences should be learned 1094b by each [kind of individuals] and to what extent. The most honored faculties, too, e.g., strategy and economics and rhetoric, are observed to come under this [faculty]. And since this faculty uses the rest of the practical sciences and also legislates what men should do and what 5 they should abstain from doing, its end would include the ends of the other faculties; hence this is the end which would be the good for mankind. For even if this end be the same for an individual as for the state, nevertheless the end of the state appears to be greater and more complete to attain and to preserve; for though this end is dear also to a single individual, it appears to be more noble and more divine to a race of men or to a state. 10

Our *inquiry*, then, has as its aim these ends, and it is a political *inquiry*; and it would be adequately discussed if it is presented as clearly as is proper to its subject-matter; for, as in hand-made articles, precision should not be sought for alike in all discussions. Noble and just things, with which politics is concerned, have so many differences and fluctuations that they 15 are thought to exist only by custom and not by nature. Good things, too, have such fluctuations because harm has come from them to many individuals; for some men even perished because of wealth, others because of bravery. So in discussing such matters and in using [premises] concerning them, we should be content to indicate the truth roughly and in out- 20 line, and when we deal with things which occur for the most part and use similar [premises] for them, [we should be content to draw] conclusions of a similar nature. The listener, too, should accept each of these statements in the same manner; for it is the mark of an educated man to seek as much precision in things of a given genus as their nature allows, for to accept 25 persuasive arguments from a mathematician appears to be [as improper as] to demand demonstrations from a rhetorician.

Now a man judges well the things he knows [well], and it is of these that he is a good judge; so a good judge in a subject is one who is educated in that subject, and a good judge 1095a without qualification is one who is educated in every subject. In view of this, a young man is not a proper student of [lectures on] politics; for he is inexperienced in *actions* concerned with human life, and discussions proceed from [premises concerning those *actions*] and deal with [those *actions*]. Moreover, being disposed to follow his passions, he will listen in vain

5 and without benefit, since the end of such discussions is not knowledge but *action*. (And it makes no difference whether he is young in age or youthful in character, for his deficiency arises not from lack of time but because he lives and pursues things according to passion.) For knowledge about such matters in such a man, as in those who are incontinent, becomes

10 unprofitable; but in those who form their desires and *act* according to [right] reason, it becomes very beneficial.

Let so much, then, be taken as a preface concerning (a) the kind of student, (b) the manner in which the discussion of the subject should be accepted, and (c) the subject of the *inquiry* which is before us.

2

To resume, since all knowledge and every intention desire some good, let us discuss what

15 is that which is aimed at by politics and what is the highest of all goods achievable by *action*. Most people are almost agreed as to its name; for both ordinary and cultivated people call it "happiness", and, both regard living well and *acting* well as being the same as being happy.

20 But there is disagreement as to what happiness is, and the account of it given by ordinary people is not similar to that given by the wise. For some regard it as something obvious or apparent, such as pleasure or wealth or honor, while others regard it as something else; and often the same man changes his mind about it, for when suffering from disease he regards it as being health, when poor as being wealth, and when he becomes conscious of his ignor-

25 ance he admires those who discuss something great and beyond his comprehension. Again, some [the Platonists] held that besides these particular goods there exists something by itself [*Goodness*, as an Ideal] and that it is this [Idea] which causes these particulars to be good.

To examine all the doctrines would perhaps be rather fruitless, but it is sufficient to exam-

30 ine only those which are most prevalent or are thought to be based on some reason. Let us also not forget that arguments from principles differ from those which lead to principles. Plato, too, was right when he raised this problem and inquired whether the right way to

1095b proceed is from the principles or towards the principle,[2] e.g., whether in a stadium the right procedure is from the judges to the goal or vice versa. One should begin, of course, from what is familiar; but things are familiar in two ways, for some are familiar relative to us while others are familiar without qualification. Probably we should begin from things which are familiar relative to us. Accordingly, he who is to listen effectively to lectures concerning noble

5 and just things and, in general, to subjects dealt with by politics should be brought up well in ethical habits; for the beginning [here] is the fact, and if this fact should appear to be adequate, there will be no further need of the why of it. Such a man either has or can easily get principles. As for him who lacks both, let him listen to the words of Hesiod:

10   That man's completely best who of himself
                             Thinks of all things, . . . and he is also good
                             Who trusts a good advisor; but the man

2 *Republic* 511B.

Who neither for himself can think nor, listening,
Takes what he hears to heart, this man is useless.³

3

Let us continue the discussion from the point at which we digressed. It is not unreasonable
that what men regard the good or happiness to be seems to come from their ways of living. 15
Thus ordinary people or those who are most vulgar regard it as being pleasure, and in
view of this they like a life of sensual pleasure. Now there are thee kinds of life which stand
out most; the one just mentioned, the political, and thirdly the contemplative. Ordinary people appear to be quite slavish in choosing deliberately a life of beastly pleasures, but their 20
view has support because many men of means share the tastes of Sardanapalus.⁴ Men of culture and *action* seek a life of honor; for the end of political life is almost this. But this good
appears rather superficial to be what is sought; for it is thought to depend on those who
bestow rather than on those who receive honor, whereas we have a strong inner sense that 25
the good is something which belongs to the man who possesses it and cannot be taken away
from him easily. Further, men seem to pursue honor in order to assure themselves that they
are good; at least, they seek to be honored (a) by men of prudence, and (b) among those
who know them, and (c) on the basis of their virtue. Clearly, then, virtue, according to these,
is superior to the other goods. And perhaps one might even regard this more than any other 30
good to be the end of political life. But this too appears to be rather incomplete, for it seems
that a man may have virtue even when he is asleep, or when he goes through life without
acting, or, besides these, when one meets with the greatest sufferings and misfortunes; but 1096a
no one would regard a man living in this manner as being happy, unless he wishes to uphold
a paradox. But enough of this subject, for it has been sufficiently treated in periodicals. The
third kind of life is the theoretical, which we shall examine later.⁵ 5

As for the life of a money-maker, it is one of tension; and clearly the good sought is not
wealth, for wealth is instrumental and is sought for the sake of something else. So one might
rather regard as ends those mentioned above, for they are liked for their own sake. Yet they,
too, do not appear to be the highest good, although many arguments have been used to
support them. So let the discussion of these be left aside. 10

[. . .]

5

1097a

Let us return to the good which we are seeking and inquire what it might be. It appears to 15
be different in different *actions* or arts; for in medical art it is different from that in strategy
and similarly from that in any of the rest of the arts. What then is the good in each? Is it
not that for the sake of which the rest are done? This is health in the medical art, victory in
strategy, a house in architecture, something else in another art, and in every *action* or 20
intention it is the end; for it is for the sake of this that the rest are done by all men. So if
there is some one end of all the things that are done, this would be the good achievable by

3 Hesiod, *Works and Days* 293, 295–7.
4 An Assyrian king who lived luxuriously, according to Greek legend.
5 1177a12–1178a8, 1178a22–1179a32.

action, but if there are many ends, these would be the corresponding goods. Thus by taking a different course the argument arrives at the same thing. But we must try to state this more clearly.

Since the ends appear to be many, and since we choose some of them (e.g., wealth, flutes, and instruments in general) for the sake of others, it is clear that not all ends are complete; but the highest good appears to be something which is complete. So if there is only one end which is complete, this will be the good we are seeking, but if there are many, the most complete of these will be that good. Now what we maintain is this: that which is pursued for its own sake is more complete than that which is pursued for the sake of something else, and that which is chosen but never chosen for the sake of something else is more complete than other things which, though chosen for their own sake, are also chosen for the sake of this; and that which is complete without any qualification is that which is chosen always for its own sake and never for the sake of something else. Now happiness is thought to be such an end most of all, for it is this that we choose always for its own sake and never for the sake of something else; and as for honor and pleasure and intellect and every virtue, we choose them for their own sake (for we might choose each of them when nothing else resulted from them), but we also choose them for the sake of happiness, believing that through these we shall be happy. But no one chooses happiness for the sake of these, nor, in general, for the sake of some other thing.

The result appears to be still the same if we proceed from self-sufficiency, for the perfect good is thought to be self-sufficient. By "self-sufficient" we do not mean an individual who leads just a solitary life, but one with parents and children and a wife and, in general, with friends and fellow-citizens as well, since man is by nature political. Some limit, however, should be set to these, for if we extend them to include one's ancestors, descendants, and friends of friends, these will proceed to infinity; but we shall examine this later.[6] Now we posit the self-sufficient to be that which taken by itself makes one's way of life worthy of choice and lacking in nothing; and such we consider happiness to be. Moreover, we posit happiness to be of all things the most worthy of choice and not capable of being increased by the addition of some other good, since if it were capable of being increased by the addition even of the least of the goods, the result would clearly be more worthy of choice; for the result would exceed [the original, i.e., happiness], and the greater of two goods is always more worthy of choice. It appears, then, that happiness is something perfect and self-sufficient, and it is the end of things we do.

6

Perhaps to say that happiness is the highest good is something which appears to be agreed upon; what we miss, however, is a more explicit statement as to what it is. Perhaps this might be given if the function of man is taken into consideration. For just as in a flute-player or a statue-maker or any artist or, in general, in anyone who has a function or an *action* to perform the goodness or excellence lies in that function, so it would seem to be the case in a man, if indeed he has a function. But should we hold that, while a carpenter and a shoe-maker have certain functions or *actions* to perform, a man has none at all but is by nature without a function? Is it not more reasonable to posit that, just as an eye and a hand and a

6 Ch. 11.

foot and any part of the body in general appear to have certain functions, so a man has some function other than these? What then would this function be?

Now living appears to be common to plants as well as to men; but what we seek is proper to men alone. So let us leave aside the life of nutrition and of growth. Next there would be 1098a the life of sensation; but this, too, appears to be common also to a horse and an ox and all animals. There remains, then, the life of *action* of a being who has reason. Of that which has reason, (a) one part has reason in the sense that it may obey reason, (b) the other part has it in the sense that it possesses reason or in the sense that it is *thinking*. Since we speak of 5 part (b), too, in two senses, let us confine ourselves to the life with reason in activity [i.e., to the process of *thinking*], for it is this sense which is thought to be more important. Accordingly, if the function of a man is an activity of the soul according to reason or not without reason, and if the function of a man is generically the same as that of a good man, like that of a lyre-player and a good lyre-player, and of all others without qualification, when excellence 10 with respect to virtue is added to that function (for the function of a lyre-player is to play the lyre while that of a good lyre-player is to play it well, and if so, then we posit the function of a man to be a certain kind of life, namely, activity or *actions* of the soul with reason, and of a virtuous man we posit these to be well and nobly done; so since each thing is performed 15 well according to its proper virtue), then the good for a man turns out to be an activity of the soul according to virtue, and if the virtues are many, then according to the best and most complete virtue. And we should add 'in a complete life', for one swallow does not make a spring, nor does one day; and so too one day or a short time does not make a man blessed 20 or happy.

7

Let this, then, be the outline of the good [for a man], for perhaps we should first make a sketch and later fill in the details. When a good outline has been made, it would seem that anyone could go forward and articulate the parts, for time is a good discoverer and helper in such matters. It is in this way that the arts advanced, for anyone can add what is lacking. 25 We should also recall what has been stated previously:[7] precision should not be sought alike in all cases, but in each case only as much as the subject-matter allows and as much as is proper to the *inquiry*. Thus a carpenter and a geometer make inquiries concerning the right 30 angle in different ways; for the first does it as much as is useful for his work, while the second inquires what it is or what kind of thing it is, since his aim is to contemplate the truth. We should proceed likewise in other situations and not allow side lines to dominate the main task. Again, we should not demand the cause in all things alike, but in some cases it is sufficient 1098b to indicate the fact well, as is also the case with principles; and the fact is first and is a principle. Now some principles are perceived by induction, others are observed by sensation, others are acquired by some kind of habituation, and others in some other way. So we should try to present each according to its nature and should make a serious effort to describe them 5 well, for they have a great influence on what follows; for a principle is thought to be more than half of the whole, and through it many of the things sought become apparent also.

[. . .]

7 1094b11–27.

Book II

1

Since virtues are of two kinds, intellectual and ethical, an intellectual virtue originates and grows mostly by teaching, and in view of this it requires experience and time, whereas an ethical virtue is acquired by habituation (ethos), as is indicated by the name 'ethical', which varies slightly from the name 'ethos'. From this fact it is also clear that none of the ethical virtues arises in us by nature [at birth], for no thing which exists by nature can be changed

20 into something else by habituation; e.g., no stone, which moves downwards by nature, can be changed by being habituated to move upwards, even if one were to keep on throwing it up countless of times, nor can fire be similarly made to move downwards, nor can anything else with some other attribute existing by nature be made to change that attribute by habituation. Hence virtues arise in us neither by nature nor contrary to nature; but by our

25 nature we can receive them and perfect them by habituation.

Again, of things which come to us by nature, we first bring along the powers and later exhibit the corresponding activities. This indeed is clear in the case of sensations; for it is

30 not by seeing often or hearing often that we acquired the corresponding power of sensation, but conversely: we used the power after we possessed it, we did not come to possess it after using it. In the case of the virtues, on the other hand, we acquire them as a result of prior activities; and this is like the case of the arts, for that which we are to perform by art after learning, we first learn by performing, e.g., we become builders by building and

1103b lyre-players by playing the lyre. Similarly, we become just by doing what is just, temperate by doing what is temperate, and brave by doing brave deeds. This is confirmed also by what happens in states. For it is by making citizens acquire certain habits that legislators make them good, and this is what every legislator wishes, but legislators who do not do

5 this well are making a mistake; and good government differs from bad government in this respect.

Again, it is from the same *actions* and because of the same *actions* that every virtue comes into being or is destroyed, and similarly with every art; for it is by playing the lyre well or badly that men become good or bad lyre players, respectively. In the case of architects

10 and all the rest, too, the situation is analogous; for men become good architects by building houses well, and bad architects by building houses badly. For if such were not the case, there would have been no need for a teacher, but all would have become good or bad artists.

Such indeed is the case with virtues also; for it is by our *actions* with other men in trans-

15 actions that we are in the process of becoming just or unjust, and it is by our *actions* in dangerous situations in which we are in the process of acquiring the habit of being courageous or afraid that we become brave or cowardly, respectively. It is likewise with *desires* and with anger; for, by behaving in one way or in the contrary way in corresponding situations, some men become temperate or intemperate, good-tempered or irascible. In short, it is by sim-

20 ilar activities that habits are developed in men; and in view of this, the activities in which men are engaged should be of [the right] quality, for the kinds of habits which develop follow the corresponding differences in those activities. So in acquiring a habit it makes no small difference whether we are *acting* in one way or in the contrary way right from our

25 early youth; it makes a great difference, or rather all the difference.

2

Since our present study is not for the sake of contemplation, like the other theoretical inquiries – for we are inquiring what virtue is, not in order [just] to know it, but in order to become good, since otherwise there would be no benefit from that inquiry – we should examine certain things about *actions*, namely, how they should be done, for these are the principal [causes] 30 also of the formation of the kinds of habits, as we have already stated. Now to *act* according to right reason is commonly accepted, and let it be assumed here; later there will be a discussion concerning right reason,[8] both as to what it is and how it is related to the other virtues. But first, let us agree on that other matter, namely, that all statements concerning 1104a matters of *action* should be made sketchily and not with precision, for, as we said at first, our demands of statements should be in accordance with the subject-matter of those statements; in matters concerning *action* and expediency, as in those of health, there is no uni- 5 formity. And if such is the universal statement, a statement concerning particulars will be even less precise; for these do not come under any art or precept, but those who are to *act* must always consider what is proper to the occasion, as in medical art and in navigation. Yet even though our present statement is of such a nature, we should try to be of some help. 10

First, then, let us perceive this, that it is the nature of such things [ethical virtues] to be destroyed by deficiency as well as by excess, as we observe in the case of strength and of health (for we should use as evidence what is apparent for the sake of what is obscure), for both excess and deficiency in exercise destroy strength; and similarly, when too much or too 15 little drink or food is taken, it destroys health, but when the amount is proportionate, it produces or increases or preserves health. Such is the case also with temperance and bravery and the other [ethical] virtues; for a man who flees from and fears everything and never stands 20 his ground becomes a coward, but he who fears nothing at all but proceeds against all dangers becomes rash, and, similarly, a man who indulges in all [bodily] pleasures and abstains from none becomes intemperate, but he who avoids them all, like a boor, becomes 25 a sort of insensible man; for temperance and bravery are destroyed by excess as well as by deficiency, but they are preserved by moderation (or the mean).

Furthermore, not only is each virtue generated, or grows, or is destroyed from the same and by the same [kind of *actions*], but also the activities [according to each virtue] will depend on that same [virtue], for such is the case with other things which are more apparent, as 30 with strength; for not only does strength come into being by taking much nourishment and undergoing many exertions, but it is also the strong man who is most able to do such things. Such too is the case with the virtues; for by abstaining from [excessive bodily] pleasures we become temperate, and, in turn, when we have become temperate we are most able to abstain 35 from such pleasures. And similarly with bravery; for by becoming habituated to show con- 1104b tempt for and endure what is fearful we become brave, and when we have become brave we are most able to endure what is fearful.

As a sign of what habits are we may consider the pleasures and pains which accompany our actions; for a man who abstains from [excessive] bodily pleasures and enjoys doing so 5 is temperate, but a man who is oppressed by so doing is intemperate, and he who faces danger and enjoys it or at least is not pained by so doing is brave, but he who is pained by so doing is a coward. Thus ethical virtue is concerned with pleasures and pains; for we do what is bad for the sake of pleasure, and we abstain from doing what is noble because of pain. In 10

8 Bk. VI, ch. 13.

view of this, we should be brought up from our early youth in such a way as to enjoy and be pained by the things we should, as Plato says,⁹ this is the right education.

Again, since virtues are concerned with *actions* and passions, and since every *action* and
15 every passion is accompanied by pleasure or pain, then for this *reason*, too, virtues would be concerned with pleasures and pains. This is indicated also by punishment, which is inflicted by means of pains; for punishment is a sort of cure, and cures by their nature are effected by means of contraries. Again, as we said before, every habit of the soul has a nature which
20 is related to and is concerned with those things by which it becomes by nature worse or better; but a habit becomes bad because of pleasures and pains, that is, by pursuing or avoiding pleasures or pains either when one should not, or at a time when he should not, or in the manner in which he should not, or in some other way contrary to that specified by [right] reason. It is in view of this that some thinkers even define the virtues as being certain states without feeling or as states of rest; but they do not define them well, for they define them
25 in an unqualified way and do not specify them by adding "in the manner in which they should or should not, or at the time when they should" or whatever other qualifications are needed. We assume, then, that such virtue is concerned with pleasures and pains and disposes us to do what is best, while vice disposes us to do the contrary.

That virtues and vices are concerned with the same things [pleasures and pains] may become
30 apparent to us also from the following. There are three objects which we choose, the noble, the expedient, and the pleasant, and there are three contrary objects which we avoid, the disgraceful, the harmful, and the painful; and a good man is apt to *succeed* in all of these,
35 while a bad man is apt to be mistaken, especially about pleasure, for pleasure is common to
1105a animals also and accompanies all objects of choice, for also the noble and the expedient appear to be pleasant. Again, pleasure has been from infancy with us all; so it is difficult to rub off this feeling, ingrained as it is in our life. We also regulate our *actions*, some of us more and
5 others less, by pleasure and pain. Because of this, then, it is necessary for our whole study to be concerned with pleasures and pains; for to enjoy or be pained rightly or wrongly has no small effect on our *actions*. Again, as Heraclitus says, it is more difficult to fight against pleasure than to fight against temper, and of that which is more difficult one can always acquire
10 an art or a virtue; for excellence, too, is better in that which is more difficult to achieve. So because of this, too, the whole study of virtue or of politics is concerned with pleasures and pains; for he who uses these well will become good, but he who uses them badly will become bad.

Let it be affirmed, then, that virtue is concerned with pleasures and pains, that it grows by those *actions* by which it is in the process of coming into being but is destroyed if those
15 *actions* are not done in this manner, and that its activity is concerned with the same *actions* as those from which it came to be.

[. . .]

5

Concerning virtue we should state not only this, that it is a habit, but also the kind of habit
15 it is. It should be noted that every virtue (a) makes that of which it is the virtue be well disposed and (b) makes it perform its function well; e.g., the virtue of an eye both makes the

---

9 *Euthydemus* 279A–B; *Laws* 743E.

eye a good eye and makes it perform its function well, for it is by the virtue of the eye that we see well. Similarly, the virtue of a horse makes (a) the horse a good horse and also (b) good at running and carrying its rider and facing the enemy. So if such is the case in every 20 instance, the virtue of a man, too, would be the habit from which he becomes good and performs his function well. How this can be done has already been stated,[10] but it may become evident also if we view the kind of nature possessed by virtue. Now in everything which is 25 continuous and divisible it is possible to take an amount which is greater than or less than or equal to the amount required, and the amounts taken may be so related either with respect to the thing itself or in relation to us; and the equal is a mean between excess and deficiency. By 'the mean', in the case of the thing itself, I mean that which lies at equal intervals from 30 the extremes, and this mean is just one thing and is the same for everyone; but, when related to us, it neither exceeds nor falls short [of what is proper to each of us], and this is neither just one thing nor the same for everyone. For example, if ten is many and two is few, then six is taken as the mean with respect to the thing itself, for six exceeds two and is exceeded by ten by equal amounts; and this is the mean according to an arithmetic proportion. But 35 the mean relative to us should not be taken in this manner; for if ten pounds are too much 1106b and two pounds are too little for someone to eat, the trainer will not [necessarily] order six pounds, since this is perhaps too much or too little for the one who is to take it; for Milo[11] it is too little, but for a beginner in athletics it is too much. It is likewise in running and wrestling. And this is the way in which every scientist avoids excess and deficiency but seeks 5 and chooses the mean, not the mean with respect to the thing itself but the one in relation to a given person.

If, then, this is the manner in which every science performs its function well, namely, by keeping an eye on the mean and working towards it (whence arises the usual remark concerning excellent works, that nothing can be subtracted from or added to them, since both 10 excess and deficiency destroy the excellence in them while the mean preserves it), and if, as is our manner of saying, it is with an eye on this that good artists do their work, and if virtue, like nature, is more precise and better than any art, then virtue would be aiming at the mean. 15 I am speaking here of ethical virtue, for it is this which is concerned with feelings and *actions*, in which there is excess, deficiency, and moderation. For example, we may have the feelings of fear, courage, *desire*, anger, pity, and any pleasure or pain in general either more or less than we should, and in both cases this is not a good thing; but to have these feelings at 20 the right times and for the right things and towards the right men and for the right purpose and in the right manner, this is the mean and the best, and it is precisely this which belongs to virtue. In *actions*, too, there is excess, deficiency, and moderation in a similar manner. Now an [ethical] virtue is concerned with feelings and *actions*, in which excess and deficiency 25 are errors and are blamed, while moderation is a *success* and is praised; and both *success* and praise belong to virtue. Virtue, then, is a kind of moderation, at least having the mean as its aim. Also, a man may make an error in many ways (for evil, as the Pythagoreans conjectured, belongs to the infinite, while goodness belongs to the finite), but he may *succeed* in 30 one way only; and in view of this, one of them is easy but the other hard. It is easy to miss the mark but hard to hit it. So it is because of these, too, that excess and deficiency belong to vice, but moderation to virtue.

For men are good in one way, bad in many. 35

10 1104a11–27.
11 A famous wrestler.

6

[Ethical] virtue, then, is a habit, disposed toward *action* by deliberate choice, being at the
1107a mean relative to us, and defined by reason and as a prudent man would define it. It is a
mean between two vices, one by excess and the other by deficiency; and while some of the
vices exceed while the others are deficient in what is right in feelings and *actions*, virtue finds
5 and chooses the mean. Thus, according to its *substance* or the definition stating its essence,
virtue is a mean [of a certain kind], but with respect to the highest good and to excellence,
it is an extreme.

Not every *action* nor every feeling, however, admits of the mean, for some of them have
10 names which directly include badness, e.g., such feelings as malicious gladness, shameless-
ness, and envy, and, in the case of *actions*, adultery, theft, and murder; for all of these and
others like them are blamed for being bad, not [just] their excesses or deficiencies.
15 Accordingly, one is never right in performing these but is always mistaken; and there is no
problem of whether it is good or not to do them, e.g., whether to commit adultery with the
right woman, at the right time, in the right manner, etc., for to perform any of these is without qualification to be mistaken. If this were not so, we would be maintaining that in *acting*
20 unjustly or in a cowardly way or intemperately, too, there is moderation and excess and
deficiency; for according to such a view there would be also a moderation of excess and of
deficiency, an excess of excess, and a deficiency of deficiency. But just as there is no excess
or deficiency of temperance or of bravery, because the mean is in a certain way an extreme,
so, too, there is no moderation or excess or deficiency in the vices mentioned above
25 but only a mistake, regardless of the manner in which one *acts*; for, universally, there is no
moderation of excess or of deficiency, nor an excess or a deficiency of moderation.

7

We must not only state this universally, however, but also apply it to particular cases; for,
30 among statements about *actions*, those which are [more] universal are rather empty while
those which are [more] particular tend to be more true; for *actions* deal with particulars, and
it is with these that our statements should be in harmony. So let us consider each of these
virtues and vices from our table.
1107b With regard to fear and courage, the mean is bravery. He who exceeds in not fearing has
no name (many virtues and vices have no names), but he who exceeds in courage is rash;
and he who exceeds in fear and is deficient in courage is a coward.
5 With regard to pleasures and pains – not all of them [but mainly of the bodily senses],
and less with regard to pains than with regard to pleasures – the mean is temperance while
the excess is intemperance. Men deficient with regard to pleasures hardly exist, and for this
reason such men happen to have no name; but let them be called 'insensible'.
With regard to giving and taking property, the mean is generosity, while the excess and
10 deficiency are, respectively, wastefulness and stinginess. Excess and deficiency in these two
vices are present in contrary ways; for the wasteful man exceeds in giving away and is deficient
in taking, while the stingy man exceeds in taking but is deficient in giving away. (At present
15 we are giving a sketchy and summary account of these, and this is sufficient; later[12] we shall
specify them more precisely.) With regard to property there are also certain other dispositions.

12 1119b22–1122a17.

The mean is munificence, for a munificent man differs from a generous man in that he deals with large amounts, while a generous man deals with small amounts [also]. The excess in large donations is extravagance or conspicuous consumption, and the deficiency is meanness; but these vices differ from the vices opposed to generosity, and the manner in which 20 they differ will be stated later.[13]

With regard to honor and dishonor, the mean is high-mindedness, the excess is said to be a sort of vanity, and the deficiency is low-mindedness. And just as generosity was said to be related to munificence by being concerned with smaller amounts, so too there is a virtue 25 which is concerned with smaller honors and is similarly related to high-mindedness, which is concerned with great honors; for it is possible to desire honor as one should, or more than one should, or less than one should. Now he who exceeds in his desires is called 'ambitious', he who is deficient is called 'unambitious', but he who desires honor in moderation has no name. The dispositions too are nameless, except for that of the ambitious man, which is called 30 'ambition'. It is in view of this lack of name that those who are at the extremes claim to be in the middle position; and we, too, sometimes call the moderate man 'ambitious' but sometimes 'unambitious', and sometimes we praise the ambitious man but sometimes 1108a the unambitious. The *reason* why we do this will be stated later;[14] for the present, let us continue with the other habits in the manner already proposed.

With regard to anger, too, there is excess, deficiency, and moderation. These habits are 5 almost nameless, but since we say that the moderate man is good-tempered, let us call the mean 'good temper'. As for the extremes, let the man who exceeds be called 'irascible' and the corresponding vice 'irascibility', and let the man who is deficient be called 'inirascible' and the corresponding deficiency 'inirascibility'.

There are three other moderations which have some likeness towards each other yet dif- 10 fer from each other; for all of them are concerned with associations among men as they speak or *act* but differ in that one is concerned with truth about oneself while the other two are concerned with what is pleasurable, and of these two, one is exhibited in amusement while the other in all situations of life. So we should consider these, too, in order to observe better that moderation is praiseworthy in all cases while the extremes are neither right nor praise- 15 worthy but worthy of blame. Now most of these habits, too, have no names, but we should try, as in the other cases, to introduce names ourselves in order to make our point clear and easy to follow.

With regard to truth, then, the moderate man is a sort of truthful man and the mean may 20 be called 'truthfulness'; but pretense which exaggerates is boastfulness and the possessor of it is boastful, while pretense which understates is self-depreciation and the possessor of it is self-depreciatory.

With regard to what is pleasant in amusing others, the moderate man is witty and the corresponding disposition is wit, but the disposition which tends to exceed is buffoonery and the possessor of it is a buffoon, while he who is deficient is a sort of boor and the 25 corresponding habit is boorishness.

With regard to what is pleasant in the other manner, the one found in [all] situations of life, the man who is pleasant as he should be is friendly and the mean is friendliness; but he who behaves excessively is complaisant, if he does this not for the sake of anything else, but is a flatterer, if he does it for his personal benefit, while he who is deficient

13 1122a20–b18.
14 1108b11–26.

30 and is unpleasant in all situations is a quarrelsome sort of man or a man hard to get along with.

There are moderations in feelings, too, and in what concerns feelings. Thus a sense of shame is not a virtue, but a man with a sense of shame is praised also; for here, too, one man is said to be moderate, i.e., he who has a sense of shame, another behaves excessively, 35 like the abashed man who is ashamed of everything, and a third is deficient or is not ashamed at all, and he is called 'shameless'.

1108b   As for righteous indignation, it is a mean between envy and malicious gladness. These dispositions are concerned with pain and pleasure felt at the fortunes of others for a man with righteous indignation is pained by the undeserved good fortune of others, an envious 5 man, who exceeds, is pained by the good fortune of all others, and a man who is maliciously glad is so deficient in being pained as to be even joyful at the good fortunes of others. These will be discussed elsewhere at the proper time.[15]

As for justice, since the term 'justice' does not have only one meaning, we shall, after discussing the other habits, distinguish those meanings and state the manner in which each 10 of them is a mean;[16] and in a similar manner we shall discuss also the rational virtues.[17]

[. . .]

Book X

[. . .]

1176a 6

30 After a discussion of the virtues and friendship and pleasures, what remains is a sketchy dis-cussion of happiness, since this is what we posited as the end of whatever is human. Our discussion will be shorter if we review what has already been stated.

We have said[18] that happiness is not a disposition; for otherwise it might-belong also to a 35 man who sleeps all his life and so lives like a plant, or to a man who suffers the greatest of 1176b misfortunes. So since this is not satisfactory but happiness should be posited as being rather an activity of some sort, as we have stated earlier,[19] and since some activities are necessary and are chosen for the sake of something else while others [are chosen just] for their own sake, it is clear that happiness should be posited as chosen for its own sake and not for the 5 sake of something else, for happiness has no need of anything else but is self-sufficient.

Activities which are chosen for their own sake are those from which nothing else is sought beyond them. Now such are thought to be the *actions* in accordance with virtue, for doing what is noble or good is something chosen for its own sake. And such, too, are thought to be the amusements, which are pleasant, since they are chosen not for the sake of something 10 else; for men are harmed rather than benefited by them, when they neglect their bodies and

15 Bk. III, ch. 6–Bk. IV, ch. 8.
16 Bk. V.
17 Bk. VI.
18 1095b31–1096a2, 1098b31–1099a7.
19 See n. 18.

the acquisition of property. Most people who are regarded as happy resort to pastimes such as these; and this is the reason why witty men are highly favored by tyrants, for they offer the kind of pleasure which tyrants aim at, and tyrants need such men. So these pastimes are 15 thought to contribute to happiness because it is in these that men in despotic positions spend their time.

But perhaps the apparent happiness of such men is no sign that they are really happy, for virtue and thought, from which good activities arise, do not depend on despotic power; and the fact that such men, who have never tasted pure and liberal pleasure, resort to bodily 20 pleasures is no *reason* for regarding these pleasures as being more choiceworthy, for children too regard the things they value as being the best. It is with good reason, then, that just as different things appear to be of value to children and to men, so different things appear to be of value to bad men and to *good* men. Accordingly, as we have often stated,[20] things which are both valuable and pleasant are those which appear such to a good man. The activity 25 most choiceworthy to each man, then, is the one in accordance with his own disposition, and so the activity most choiceworthy to a virtuous man would be the one which proceeds according to virtue. Consequently, happiness is not found in amusement, for it would be also absurd to maintain that the end of man is amusement and that men work and suffer all their life for the sake of amusement. For, in short, we choose everything for the sake of some- 30 thing else, except happiness, since happiness is the end of a man. So to be serious and work hard for the sake of amusement appears foolish and very childish, but to amuse oneself for the sake of serious work seems, as Anarchasis put it, to be right; for amusement is like relax-ation, and we need relaxation since we cannot keep on working hard continuously. Thus 35 amusement is not the end, for it is chosen for the sake of serious activity. 1177a

A happy life, on the other hand, is thought to be a life according to virtue; and it proceeds with seriousness but does not exist in amusement. And we speak of serious things as being better than those which are humorous or amusing, and we speak of the activity of the better part of a man or of a better man as being always better; and the activity of what is 5 better is superior and so makes one more happy. Any man, even one with a slavish nature, can indulge in the bodily pleasures no less than the best man, but no one would attribute happiness to a man with a slavish nature, unless he attributes to him also a way of life which is human; for happiness is not found in such pastimes but in activities according to virtue, 10 as we have already stated.[21]

7

Since happiness is an activity according to virtue, it is reasonable that it should be an activ-ity according to the highest virtue; and this would be an activity of the best part of man. So whether this be intellect or something else which is thought to rule and guide us by its nature and to have comprehension of noble and divine objects, being itself divine or else the most 15 divine part in us, its activity according to its proper virtue would be perfect happiness. That this activity is contemplative has already been mentioned; and this would seem to be in agree-ment both with our previous remarks[22] and with the truth.

---

20 1113a22–33.
21 1098a16.
22 1097a25–b21, 1099a7–21, 1173b15–19, 1174b20–23, 1175b36–1176a3.

20   (1) This activity is the highest of all since the intellect (a) is the best of the parts in us and (b) is concerned with the best of the known objects.

    (2) It is the most continuous of our activities; for (a) we are more able to be engaged continuously in theoretical activity than to perform any *action* continuously, and (b) we think that pleasure should be intermingled with happiness; and it is agreed that the most pleasant of our virtuous activities is the one in accordance with wisdom. Indeed, philosophy is

25 regarded as possessing pleasures which are wonderful in purity as well as in certainty, and it is reasonable for men who have understanding to pass their time more pleasantly than those who [merely] inquire.

    (3) What goes by the name 'self-sufficiency', too, would apply to theoretical activity most of all; for although wise men and just men and all the rest have need of the necessities of

30 life, when they are all sufficiently provided with them, a just man needs others towards whom and with whom he will *act* justly, and similarly in the case of a temperate man, a brave man, and each of the others, while a wise man is able to theorize even if he were alone, and the wiser he is, the more he can do so by himself. Perhaps it is better for him to have colleagues;

1177b but still, he is the most self-sufficient of all.

    (4) This activity alone is thought to be loved for its own sake; for nothing results from it except contemplation itself, while from practical activities we gain for ourselves, either more or less, other things besides the *action* itself.

5   (5) Happiness is thought to depend on leisure; for we toil for the sake of leisurely activity, and we are at war for the sake of peaceful activity. Now the activities of the practical virtues are concerned with political or military matters, and the *actions* concerning these matters are thought to be toilsome. Military *actions* are altogether toilsome; for no reason-

10 able man chooses to wage a war for its own sake or to prepare for a war for its own sake; for if a man were to make enemies of his friends for the sake of fighting or killing, he would be regarded as utterly bloodthirsty. The activity of a man in politics, too, is toilsome and aims at something other than itself, namely, power or honor or, at any rate, at one's own

15 or the citizens' happiness, which is different from the political [*action* itself] and is clearly sought as an activity which is different.

    So if political and military *actions* among virtuous *actions* stand out in fineness and greatness and, being toilsome, are aimed at some other end but are not chosen for their own sake, whereas the activity of the intellect, being theoretical, is thought to be superior in

20 seriousness and to aim at no other end besides itself but to have its own pleasure which increases that activity, then also self-sufficiency and leisure and freedom from weariness (as much as are possible for man) and all the other things which are attributed to a blessed man appear to exist in this activity. This, then, would be the perfect happiness for man, if extended to

25 the full length of life, for none of the attributes of happiness is incomplete.

    Such a life, of course, would be above that of a man, for a man will live in this manner not insofar as he is a man, but insofar as he has something divine in him; and the activity of this divine part of the soul is as much superior to that of the other kind of virtue as that

30 divine part is superior to the composite soul of a man. So since the intellect is divine relative to a man, the life according to this intellect, too, will be divine relative to human life. Thus we should not follow the recommendation of thinkers who say that those who are men should think only of human things and that mortals should think only of mortal things, but we should try as far as possible to partake of immortality and to make every effort to live according to the best part of the soul in us; for even if this part be of small measure, it

1178a surpasses all the others by far in power and worth. It would seem, too, that each man is this part, if indeed this is the dominant part and is better than the other parts; so it would be strange if a man did not choose the life proper to himself but that proper to another. And what was stated earlier[23] is appropriate here also: that which is by nature proper to each thing 5 is the best and most pleasant for that thing. So for a man, too, the life according to his intellect is the best and most pleasant, if indeed a man in the highest sense is his intellect. Hence this life, too, is the happiest.

8

The life according to the other kind of virtue is happy in a secondary way, since the activities according to that virtue are concerned with human affairs; for it is according to the virtues 10 which relate one man to another that we perform just and brave and other *actions* relating to contracts and needs and all other sorts, observing in each case what is fitting with regard to our passions. All these appear to be concerned with human affairs. Some of them are thought to result even from the body, and the virtue of character is thought to be in 15 many ways closely associated with the passions.

Prudence, too, is bound up with ethical virtue, and ethical virtue is bound up with prudence, if indeed the principles of prudence are in accordance with ethical virtues and the rightness of the ethical virtues is in accordance with prudence. Since these ethical virtues are connected with the passions also, they would be concerned with the composite nature of man; and 20 the virtues of that composite are concerned with human affairs. So the life and happiness in accordance with these virtues, too, would be human.

The virtue of the intellect, on the other hand, is separated [from the passions]; and let this much be said about this virtue, for detailed accuracy about it would take us beyond our present purpose. We might add, too, that this virtue would seem to require external resources only to a small extent, or less than ethical virtue does; for if granting that both kinds of virtue 25 require the necessities of life equally, even if a statesman's effort concerning the body and other such things is greater than that of the theoretical thinker (for there would be little difference here), still there will be much difference in what their activities require. For a generous man will need property for his generous *actions*, and so will a just man if he is to reciprocate for the services done to him (for wishes are not clearly seen, and even unjust 30 men pretend that they wish to *act* justly); and a brave man will need power, if he is to perform an *action* according to virtue, while a temperate man will need the means, for how else can he manifest himself as being a temperate man rather than one of the others [i.e., stingy or wasteful]?

Disagreement arises as to whether the more important part of virtue is intention or the 35 corresponding *actions*, since virtue depends on both. Clearly, perfection of virtue depends 1178b on both. As for *actions*, they require many things, and more of these are required if the *actions* are greater and nobler. A theoretical thinker, on the other hand, requires none of such things, at least for his activity, and one might say that these even obstruct theoretical activity; but insofar as he is a man and lives with many others, he will choose to *act* according to 5 [ethical] virtue, so he will need such things to live as a man.

That perfect happiness is contemplative activity would be evident also from the following. We regard the gods as being most blessed and happy; but what kind of *actions* must we attribute to them? Are they just *actions*? Will they not appear ridiculous if they are regarded 10

23 1169b33–1176b26.

as making contracts and returning deposits and all other such things? Are they brave *actions*? Are they to be regarded as facing dangers and risking their lives for something noble? Are they generous *actions*? But whom will they give gifts to? It would be absurd, too, if they are regarded as using money or some such thing. And what would their temperate *actions* be? Is it not vulgar to praise them for not having bad *desires*? If we were to go through all of these ethical virtues, all praises or honors concerning the corresponding *actions* would appear trivial and unworthy of the gods. Yet all believe that the gods are living and in activity, for surely we cannot regard them as being asleep like Endymion. So if *action*, and production even more so, are omitted from their lives, is not contemplation the only activity left?

The activity of a god, then, which surpasses all other activities in blessedness, would be contemplative. Consequently, of human activities, too, that which is closest in kind to this would be the happiest. A sign of this is the fact that none of the other animals share in happiness but are completely deprived of such activity; for while the entire life of the gods is blessed, the life of men exists as a sort of likeness of such [blessed] activity, but none of the other animals is happy since none of them shares in contemplation. So while contemplation endures, happiness does so also, and those who are more contemplative are more happy also, not in virtue of some other attribute but in virtue of contemplation, for contemplation is by its nature honorable. Happiness, then, would be a kind of contemplation.

9

Being human, however, a man will need external resources also; for his nature is not self-sufficient for contemplation but he needs a healthy body and nourishment and other services. Still, we must not think that the man who is to be happy will need many and great external goods if he cannot be blessed without them; for self-sufficiency and *action* do not depend on the excess of them, and one can do noble things even if he is not a ruler of land and sea since he can *act* according to virtue even with moderate means. This can be plainly seen from the fact that private citizens are thought to do *good* deeds no less than those in power, but even more. So it is enough if one has as much as that [i.e., moderate means], for the life of a man whose activity proceeds according to virtue will be happy.

Perhaps Solon, too, expressed it well when he spoke of happy men as being those who were moderately supplied with external means but who have performed the noblest *actions* – so he thought – and have lived a temperate life; for it is possible for one to *act* as he should with moderate possessions. Anaxagoras, too, seems to have regarded the happy man to be neither wealthy nor in a position of power, when he said that he would not be surprised if a happy man appeared strange to most men, for they judge a man by externals since these are the only things they perceive. The opinions of the wise, then, seem to be in harmony with our arguments. But while these opinions, too, carry some conviction, still the truth concerning practical matters is judged by what men do and how they live, for it is these that carry authority. So we should examine the statements which we have already made by referring them to the deeds and the lives of men, and we should accept them as true if they harmonize with the facts but should regard them merely as arguments if they clash with those facts.

Now he who proceeds in his activities according to his intellect and cultivates his intellect seems to be best disposed and most dear to the gods; for if the gods had any care for human matters, as they are thought to have, it would be also reasonable that they should take joy in what is best and most akin to themselves (this would be man's intellect) and should reward those who love and honor this most, as if they cared for their friends and were *acting* rightly and nobly. Clearly, all these attributes belong to the wise man most of all; so 30 it is he who would be most dear to the gods, and it is also reasonable that he would be the most happy of men. Thus if we view the matter in this manner, it is again the wise man who would be the most happy of men.

10

If we have sufficiently discussed in a sketchy manner these matters and the virtues, and also friendship and pleasure, should we think that we achieved what we have intended to do, or, 35 as the saying goes, is the end in practical matters not speculation and knowledge but rather 1179b *action*? With regard to virtue, to be sure, it is not enough to know what it is, but we should try to acquire and use it or try to become good in some other way. Now if arguments alone were enough to make us *good*, they would with justice, according to Theognis, have brought 5 us many and great rewards, and we should have obtained these. As a matter of fact, however, while arguments appear to have an effect in exhorting and stimulating the liberally-minded among young men and might cause the character of those who come from high lineage and are truly lovers of what is noble to be possessed of virtue, they cannot exhort ordinary men to do good and noble deeds, for it is the nature of these men to obey not a 10 sense of shame but fear, and to abstain from what is bad not because this is disgraceful but because of the penalties which they would receive, since by leading a life of passion such men pursue the corresponding pleasures and the means to them but avoid the opposite pains, having no conception of what is noble and truly pleasant as they have never tasted it. What 15 argument, then, would reform these men? It is not possible or not easy to remove by argument the long-standing habits which are deeply rooted in one's character. So when all the means through which we can become *good* are available, perhaps we should be content if we were to get some share of virtue. 20

Some think that men become good by nature, others think that they do so by habituation, still others, by teaching. Now it is clear that nature's part is not in our power to do anything about but is present in those who are truly fortunate through some divine cause. Perhaps argument and teaching, too, cannot reach all men, but the soul of the listener, like 25 the earth which is to nourish the seed, should first be cultivated by habit to enjoy or hate things properly; for he who lives according to passion would neither listen to an argument which dissuades him nor understand it, and if he is disposed in this manner, how can he be persuaded to change? In general, passion seems to yield not to argument but to force. So one's character must be somehow predisposed towards virtue, liking what is noble and 30 disliking what is disgraceful.

But it is difficult for one to be guided rightly towards virtue from an early age unless he is brought up under such [i.e., right] laws; for a life of temperance and endurance is not pleasant to most people, especially to the young. For this reason the nurture and pursuits of the young should be regulated by laws, for when they become habitual they are not painful. 35 Getting the right nurture and care while young, however, is perhaps not sufficient; but since 1180a young men should pursue and be habituated to these also when they have become adults, laws would be needed for these too, and, in general, laws would be needed for man's entire life, for most people obey necessity rather than argument, and penalties rather than what is 5 noble. In view of this, some think[24] that legislators (a) should urge men to pursue virtue and

24 Cf. Plato, *Laws* 718B ff.

should exhort them to act for the sake of what is noble, expecting those who are well on their way in their habits of acting well to follow the advice, (b) should impose punishments and penalties on those who disobey and are of inferior nature, and (c) should banish per-

10 manently those who are incurable;[25] for they think that a man who is *good* and lives with a view to what is noble will obey reason, while a bad man who desires [just bodily] pleasures should be punished by pain like a beast of burden. And for this reason they also say that the pains inflicted should be those which are most contrary to the pleasures these men love. So

15 if, as already stated,[26] the man who is to be good should be well nurtured and acquire the proper habits so that he may live in *good* pursuits and neither willingly nor unwillingly do what is bad, these [proper habits] would be attained by those who live according to intel-lect and an order which is right and has effective strength. Now paternal command possesses

20 neither strength nor necessity, nor in general does that of a single man, unless he be a king or some such person; but the law has compelling power and is an expression issuing from a sort of prudence and intellect. And while we are hostile to those who oppose our impulses, even if these men are right, we do not feel oppressed by the law when it ordains us to do what is *good*. [. . .]

1181b   Since our predecessors left the subject of lawgiving without scrutiny, perhaps it is better if we make a greater effort to examine it, and especially the subject concerning constitutions

15 in general, so that we may complete as best as we can the philosophy concerning human affairs. First, then, let us try to go over those parts which have been stated well by our pre-decessors, then from the constitutions we have collected let us investigate what kinds of things tend to preserve or destroy the states or each of the forms of government and why some

20 states are well while others are badly administered; for, after having investigated these mat-ters, perhaps we would also be in a better position to perceive what form of government is best, how each form of government should be ordered, and what laws and customs each should use. So let us start to discuss these.

---

25 Cf. Plato, *Protagoras* 325A.
26 1179b31–1180a5.

23

Politics

Although obviously intended as a continuation of the *Nicomachean Ethics*, the *Politics* has not come down to us in a clear and unified condition, and scholars continue to debate how to order its different books, chapters, and sections – and even whether some parts of what is now included in the work belong to it at all. Even so, the work that comes to us in its present form makes clear many of the applications of Aristotle's ethical theory to the political realm. Our word "politics" comes from the Greek word *polis*, which referred to a fully independent and sovereign political state, which actually contained only a single city and its immediate environs (hence the translation "city-state"). "Political science," then, for Aristotle, was the science that studied how the *polis* came into being, and the role it played and the various forms it might take in helping (or hindering) human beings in the pursuit of *eudaimonia* (happiness or flourishing). Aristotle proposes his own ideas on how states should be organized, on what a citizen's proper roles consist in, and on how a *polis* should provide education to its citizens.

Book I

1

We observe that every state is a sort of association, and that every association is formed for 1252a
the sake of some good (for all men always *act* in order to attain what they think to be good).
So it is clear that, while all associations aim at some good, the association which aims in the
highest degree and at the supreme good is the one which is the most authoritative and includes 5
all the others. Now this is called "a state," and it is a political association.

Those who think[1] that a statesman, a king, a ruler of a household, and a master of slaves
are all the same do not speak well, for they hold that these [rulers] differ not in kind but
with respect to the number of their subjects. Thus they regard a master as a ruler of few, a 10
householder as a ruler of a somewhat greater number, and a statesman or a king as a ruler

---

1 Plato, *Statesman* 258E–259D.

of a still greater number, as if there were no difference between a large household and a
15 small state; and [they distinguish] a king from a statesman [only] in this, that the first is the
sole authority of the state but the second rules and is ruled in turn according to the truths
of political science.

Now these views are not true, and this will be clear if we examine what has just been said
according to our usual method of inquiry. For, just as in every other discipline it is necessary to analyze a composite subject into its elements, which are the smallest parts of the
20 whole, so by looking closely at the elements of a state, we will be better placed to observe
how these elements differ from one another and, if possible, to grasp something about each
of the above-mentioned arts [royal art, political art, etc.].

2

If one were to look at the growth of things from their beginning, one would also be, as in
25 other disciplines, in the best position to speculate on these matters. First, there must be a
union of those who cannot exist without each other, that is, a union of male and female for
the sake of procreation (and the tendency in men, as in the other animals and in plants, to
30 leave behind their own kind is natural and not the result of deliberate choice). Second, there
must be a union of that which by nature can rule and that which [by nature should be] ruled,
for the sake of their preservation; for that which can foresee by *thought* is by nature a ruler
or by nature a master, whereas that which [cannot foresee by *thought* but] can carry out the
orders with the body is by nature a subject or a slave. In view of this, the master and the
slave have the same interest [i.e., preservation].

1252b   Now there is a distinction by nature between the female and the slave. For nature is never
niggardly like the smiths who make the Delphian knife: she makes a thing to serve only one
thing, for an instrument can best accomplish its task by serving one and not many functions.
5 Yet among the barbarians the female and the slave are placed in the same rank; and the
reason for this is the fact that they do not have rulers by nature but their association consists
of slaves, both male and female. It is in view of this that poets say,

"It is meet that Greeks should rule barbarians,"[2]

implying that a barbarian and a slave are the same by nature. Out of these two associations
10 [male-female, master-slave] a household is formed first, and Hesiod was right when he said,

"First a house and a wife and an ox for the plough,"[3]

for a poor man uses an ox instead of a house slave. An association formed by nature for the
daily needs of life, then, is a household, and its members are called by Charondas "companions
15 of the hearth," and by Epimenides the Cretan "companions of the manger." But the first
association formed from many households for other than daily needs is the village, and the
most natural form of a village seems to be a colony of a household, comprised of the children and grandchildren, those who are called by some "suckled with the same milk"; and
it is in view of this that the first states were at first ruled by kings, (and nations are still so

2 Euripides, *Iphigenia in Aulis* 1400–1.
3 *Works and Days*, 405.

governed nowadays), for they were formed of persons [already] governed by kings. For every 20
household is ruled royally by the eldest, so the [early] colonies, too, were similarly ruled
because of their kinship. And this is Homer's meaning [concerning the Cyclopes] when he
says,[4] "each of them rules over children and wife," for they lived in scattered groups, as in
ancient times. And it is because of this, too, that all men say that the Gods are ruled by kings,
for men were ruled by kings in ancient days, and are still so ruled now; just as the forms of 25
the Gods were thought to resemble those of men, so were the living habits of the Gods.

Finally, a complete association composed of many villages is a state, an association which
(a) has reached the limit of every self-sufficiency, so to speak, (b) was formed for the sake
of living, but (c) exists for the sake of living well. For this reason, every state exists by nature, 30
if indeed the first associations too existed by nature; for the latter associations have the state
as their end, and nature is the end [of becoming]. For the kind of thing which a subject becomes
at the end of a generation is said to be the nature of that subject, as in the case of a man or
a horse or a house. Besides, the final cause or the end is the best, and the self-sufficiency [of
an association] is the end and the best.   1253a

From the above remarks, then, it is evident that a state exists by nature and that man is
by nature a political animal; but [he] who exists outside a state because of [his] nature and
not by luck is either [bad] or superior to man: [he] is like the man denounced by Homer[5]
as being "tribeless, lawless, heartless." In addition, such a [man] by [his] nature *desires* war 5
inasmuch as [he] is solitary, like an isolated piece in a game of draughts. It is clear, then,
why man is more of a political animal than a bee or any other gregarious animal; for nature,
as we say, does nothing in vain, and man alone of all animals has the power of reason.   10

Voice, of course, serves as a sign of the painful and the pleasurable, and for this reason it
belongs to other animals also; for the nature of these advances only up to the point of sensing the painful and the pleasurable and of communicating these to one another. But speech
serves to make known what is beneficial or harmful, and so what is just or unjust; for what 15
is proper to man compared to the other animals is this: he alone has the sense of what is
good or evil, just or unjust, and the like, and it is an association of beings with this sense
which makes possible a household and a state. Further, a state is prior by nature to a household or each man, since the whole is of necessity prior to each of its parts. For if the whole 20
[man] ceases to exist, his foot or hand will exist only equivocally, and such a hand will then
be like a hand made of stone. Indeed every part, such as [a hand or a foot], is defined by its
function or power, so if the [power and the function] are lacking, one should not say that
what remains is the same as a hand unless one uses the term "hand" equivocally.

It is clear, then, that a state exists by nature and is prior to each [of its parts]; for if each man 25
is not self-sufficient when existing apart from a state, he will be like a part when separated
from the whole; and one who cannot associate with others or does not need association with
others because of self-sufficiency is no part of a state but is either a brute or a God.

Now there is a natural tendency in all men to form such an association [i.e., a state], and 30
he who was the first to do so was the cause of the greatest good; for just as man when per-
fected is the best of all animals, so he is the worst of all when separated from law and judgement. For the most cruel injustice is the one which has weapons to carry it out; and a man,
born with weapons [e.g., speech, hands, ability to reason, etc.] to be used with prudence and
virtue, can misuse these [weapons through folly and vice] for contrary ends most of all. For 35

4 *Odyssey* IX. 114.
5 *Iliad* IX. 63.

this reason, a man without virtue can be the most unholy, the most savage, and the worst [of animals] for lust and gluttony. Justice, on the other hand, is political [i.e., belongs to the state]; for judgment about matters requiring justice, that is, the discernment of what is just, is the principle of ordering in a political association.

[. . .]

Book II

1

1260b27 Since our intention is to investigate the political association which is the best for all those who are able to lead the ideal life, we should examine also the [forms of] government of
30 both those states which are said to be well-managed and any other forms which some thinkers happen to consider as being well constituted, so that (a) we may observe what is right or useful and, in seeking some form other than those above, (b) we should be regarded as using this method not altogether because we wish to appear ingenious, but because the existing
35 forms of government are not well framed.

We should begin our inquiry with what is first by nature. Now all citizens must participate either (a) in all things, or (b) in none at all, or (c) in some things but not in others.
40 Evidently, it is impossible for them to have nothing in common, for a government is an association of some kind, and the citizens of a state must first of all have a common place; for
1261a a state must exist in one place, and its citizens are those who participate in one state. Then is it better for the citizens of a state which is to be well managed to share in all things that
5 can be shared or to share in some but not in others? It is possible for the citizens of a state, as in Plato's *Republic*, to have children and wives and property in common; for *Socrates* in the *Republic* holds that children and wives and possessions should be common [to all]. So we are faced with the problem of whether it is better for children and wives and possessions to be kept as they are now [i.e., private] or to be [common] according to the law laid down in the *Republic*.[6]

2

10 There are many difficulties in the theory that wives should be common to all *men*, and the *reason* given by *Socrates* for instituting such a law does not appear to follow from his arguments. Further, [the community of women] as a means to the end of the state, as *Socrates* describes it, becomes impossible; and as to the steps to be taken, no specification is made. I
15 am speaking of the hypothesis made by *Socrates* that the best state is the one which has the highest unity. It is indeed evident that as a state tends to become more of a unity, it eventually ceases to be a state; for a state is by its nature a plurality of a certain sort, and in proceeding to a greater unity, it will first become a household, which in turn will become
20 one man. For we would regard a household as having more unity than a state, and a man as having more unity than a household. So even if one were able to bring about that unity, it should not be done, for it would be the ruin of the state.

6 *Republic* IV. 423E, V. 457C, 462B.

Again, a state is not only a plurality of men, but also of men of different kinds; for men who are similar do not make a state. Thus a state is distinct from a military alliance. For [the latter] is useful by virtue of its quantity, even if the members of that alliance are [not] the 25 same in kind, and such alliance is by nature made for the sake of numerical assistance, just as a greater weight pulls down the scale more. It is in such a manner, too, that a state differs from a nation in which a multitude of people live not in scattered villages but as the Arcadians do. Thus if a unity is to be formed out of many, these should differ in kind. 30

In view of the above, it is indeed reciprocal equality which preserves the states, as already stated in the *Ethics*,[7] since this must be the case even among men who are free and equal; for it is not possible for all such men to rule at the same time: they must take their turn by changing at the end of each year or period or according to some other order of sequence. And it is indeed in this manner that eventually all of them partake of rule, as if shoemakers 35 and carpenters were to exchange occupations and not the same men be always shoemakers and carpenters. On the other hand, since a political association is better if [in view of the differences in kind of its members] it functions like [an association of trades which differ in kind], it is clearly better for the same [citizens] to be the rulers, whenever this is possible. But whenever this is not possible because all its [citizens] are by nature equal, then, whether ruling 1261b be a good or a bad thing, it is at the same time just that all should so partake of rule, that those who succeed in rule imitate by turns in a similar way those who ruled at first; for, in this way, some rule and others are ruled in turn, as if becoming different. If indeed rule occurs 5 in this manner, [the same] citizens hold different kinds of offices.

It is evident from the above remarks, then, that a state is by nature not a unity of the type which some thinkers assert, and that what is said to be the greatest good of a state is really the ruin of that state; yet surely the good of each thing is that which preserves it. From another point of view, too, it is evident that to seek in a state a very strong unity is not to seek what 10 is better for it; for a household is more self-sufficient for its individuals than an individual [without any association], and a state is [likewise] more self-sufficient than a household, and it is whenever an association of a multitude attains self-sufficiency [without qualification] that a state exists. So if, indeed, that which is more self-sufficient is more preferable, then that which has less unity would be more preferable. 15

3

Moreover, even if the best association is considered as being the one which has the highest unity, such unity does not appear to be demonstrated from the argument that all the citizens of a state will be using the expressions "mine" and "not mine" at the same time; for *Socrates* considers such use to be a sign of the state's perfect unity.[8] 20

Now the term "all" here can have two senses. If "all" means each separately, then *Socrates* might be more likely to achieve what he wishes; for each *man* will call [only] his own child "my son," [only his own] wife "my wife," and similarly with property or any other thing which happens to be so related to him. But *men* who have wives and children in common 25 would not speak of using these terms in this manner; they would say "all," but not in the sense that each *man* [and only he]. Similarly with possessions; they would belong to all [taken together] but not to each *man* [and to him alone]. It is evident, then, that there is a fallacy

7 1132b31–4.
8 See *Republic* V. 462c.

in the use of the term "all"; for each of the terms "all," "both," "odd," and "even" has two
30 senses, and in discussions they may lead to eristic syllogisms.

In view of this fact, to say that all *men* possess the same things is in one sense [i.e., each separately] a fine thing yet impossible, but in another sense [i.e., all taken together] it does not lead to harmony at all; and, if [the expression is used in the collective sense] it leads to harm in another way, for that which is common to the greatest number of men is given the least care. Each man pays most attention to what is his own, but less attention to what is
35 common, or else, as much as contributes to his own interest. For each man, besides other reasons, thinks that others will take care of the matter and so pays less attention to it, as in domestic duties where many servants sometimes do a job worse than a few servants [would]. Thus a citizen will have [let us say] one thousand sons, not as being his very own, but each of them being equally the son of any chance father, with the result that each son
1262a will be equally given little attention. Further, in saying "mine" of each son (be these one thousand or some other number) who does good deeds or the reverse, each [father] will be
5 using the term "mine" or so-and-so's fractionally and with hesitation; for he cannot know whether he happened to have a son or whether a son by him has survived. But is it better for each father to use the term "mine" in this manner and apply it to two thousand or some greater number of sons in this manner or rather in the manner in which it is now done in states? For nowadays the same person is called "son" by one man, "brother" by another,
10 "nephew" or "relative" by still another, whether he be a blood relative or connected by his marriage or that of a blood relative, and "clansman" or "tribesman" by someone else. It is certainly better to be a nephew of a *man* in the usual sense than to be his son in Plato's sense.
15 Moreover, nor is it possible for some persons to escape recognizing their own brothers or children or fathers or mothers; for resemblances which offspring have to their begetters must convince some of them of their relation to one another. Indeed, according to some who are making explorations of other parts of the Earth, this is happening; for they say that
20 in some parts of upper Libya the women are common to men but that the children born can be distinguished by their resemblances [to their parents]. And there are women (as well as females of other animals, e.g., mares and cows) who have a strong natural tendency to bring forth offspring which resemble their parents, as in the case of the Pharsalian mare which was named "the Just Mare."

4

25 Again, those who advocate the establishment of such association cannot easily avoid such evils as assaults, voluntary and involuntary homicides, fights, and verbal abuses, all of which are unholy when directed against fathers and mothers and other close relatives, although not as unholy when committed against others. Moreover, these must occur even more often
30 against relatives when the agents are not aware of their relation to them than when they are aware; and whenever they have occurred, those who are aware of their relation can make the customary expiations, but those who are not aware cannot do so.

It is also strange that [*Socrates*[9] in the *Republic*], after making [all young *men*] common sons of older *men*, should bar only lovers from having intimate relations, but permit love and other
35 intimate gestures which are most unbecoming between father and son and between brother and brother, seeing that even love alone between these is [most unbecoming]. It is again

9 *Republic* III. 403A–C.

strange that [Plato] should forbid intimate relations for no *reason* other than the intensity of its pleasure but regard such relations between father and son or between brothers as making no difference. It seems that having common wives and common children would be more 40 useful to farmers than to the guardians, for in this way there would be less friendship among 1262b the farmers, who as subjects should be obedient and not seek revolutionary changes.

In general, such laws must lead to consequences which are contrary to those to which rightly posited laws ought to lead, and contrary to the *reason* [i.e., the purpose] for which 5 *Socrates* thinks that these should be the regulations concerning children and wives. For we regard friendship [among citizens] to be the greatest good in a state[10] (since it is least likely to cause rebellion), and *Socrates* praises particularly the state's unity, which is thought to 10 be, as he himself says, the function of friendship, like that in the *Symposium*,[11] where Aristophanes, speaking of two lovers, is made to say that, because of their excessive love, they *desire* to grow together and become one. But the occurrence of this would necessitate the destruction of both of them, or else of one of them; and the kind of association [which *Socrates* advocates] in a state would necessitate a diluted sort of friendship, in which the words 15 "my father", "my son," and the like would be uttered with the weakest feeling of friendship. For just as a small quantity of sweet wine mingled with much water is hardly perceptible in the blend, so too the use of names based on such kind of kinship, whether made by a father towards his [countless] sons or by a son toward his [countless] fathers or by a brother towards 20 his [countless] brothers, [would hardly be perceptible and] must arouse the least family care in such a state [as that in Plato's *Republic*]. For there are two things which, most of all, make a man show concern and affection: (a) that the thing be his own, and (b) that the thing be dear to him; but neither of these can belong to men who are governed in such a state.

Moreover, the manner in which children born to farmers and artisans are transferred to 25 guardians and those born to guardians are transferred to farmers and artisans,[12] too, will cause much confusion; besides, all parents must know what they give and to whom and what they take and from whom. And the evils mentioned previously,[13] such as assaults, [illicit] love affairs, and homicides must occur even more [under these circumstances]; for children 30 given by guardians to others will no longer address the guardians as fathers or mothers or brothers or children, and the same will apply to children given by the others to guardians, and so they will not hesitate to commit evil *actions* by *reason* of kinship.

Concerning the community of wives and children, then, let the things specified above suffice. 35

5

Our next concern is to examine the manner in which property should be arranged for citizens who are to be best governed, namely, whether property should be commonly owned or not; and this problem may be considered even apart from laws posited about wives and 40 children. In other words, even if wives and children are not common but in a condition such 1263a as it now exists in all [states], is it not better for the ownership of property and its use to be common? There are three alternatives: (a) the plots of ground are privately owned, but the crops are brought into the common stock for consumption (which is done by some nations),

10 *Nicomachean Ethics* 1155a22–8.
11 Plato, *Symposium* 191A, 192C.
12 *Republic* III. 415B–E, 423C–D.
13 1262a22–40.

5 (b) conversely, the land is commonly owned and cultivated but the crops are distributed and used privately (this manner of sharing is said to be done by some barbarians), and (c) both the plots and the use of the crops are common.

When those who cultivate the land are a class distinct [from the citizens, like the farmers 10 or slaves], the manner of handling the situation is different and easier.[14] But when the [citizens] themselves cultivate the land, many troubles arise with respect to what is provided; for if rewards and labors are not proportional, those who labor more and receive less will necessarily raise complaints against those who labor less but are rewarded or receive more. 15 In general, of all human relations, living together or participating in common endeavors is the most difficult, especially when such [i.e., rewards and toils] are the issues. This is clearly shown by travelling partners; for almost all of them quarrel with each other over everyday 20 and trivial matters. Again, we are most angry over such things especially with servants, whom we employ most frequently to do the daily chores. These, then, and other such difficulties arise when property is common.

The manner in which property is now held, if also enhanced with the right customs and laws, would be far better; for it will have the goodness of both systems. By "goodness of 25 both systems" I mean the goodness which arises when the use of property is partly common and partly private; for property should be in some respect common, but in general private. For, when each attends to his own property, men will not complain against one another [in matters of property], and they will produce more since each will be paying special attention to what he regards as being his own; and because of virtue, the use of property 30 will be according to the proverb "common are the possessions of friends."

Even in our time some states subscribe to these [principles], thus suggesting that such arrangement is not impossible; and especially in well-administered states some of these things actually exist and others might be added. For [in these states] each has his own property, yet he makes available a part of it to his friends and another part for common use. In Sparta, 35 for example, men use one another's slaves and horses and dogs as if they owned them; and whenever they need provisions on a journey, they are likewise supplied from the fields in the country-side.

Evidently, then, it is better to make property private but its use common; and to make men so disposed as to regard property in this manner is a function proper to the legislator. Further, 40 to regard property as one's own gives a man immense pleasure; for it is indeed natural and 1263b not in vain for each man to love himself. Selfishness is justly censured, but it is not the [same as] love of oneself; it is rather the excessive love of oneself, like the excessive love of money, 5 for every man loves such things, so to speak.[15] Moreover, to do favors to and help friends or strangers or comrades gives one the greatest of pleasure, and this can happen only when property is private. Now these things do not happen to those who posit an excessively unified state. Besides, these thinkers evidently destroy the functions of two virtues, (a) temperance 10 towards women (for to refrain from having relations with another *man's* wife because of temperance is a fine attitude), and (b) generosity, which is concerned with how property should be used (for, according to them, no man will appear to be generous or ever perform a generous *action*, seeing that the function of generosity depends on the use of [one's own] property).

---

14 See 1330a25–31.

15 See *Nicomachean Ethics* 1168b13–1169b2.

Legislation such as [Plato's] might seem to be attractive and benevolent; for the listener 15
accepts it gladly, thinking that some wonderful feeling of friendship will arise in all, especially when the evils in the existing forms of government, such as lawsuits about contracts 20
and convictions for perjury and flatteries of the wealthy, are denounced as arising because
property is not common. But these evils arise because of human wickedness and not because
property is not common; for quarrels are observed to arise even among those who own common property and share in it, and to a much greater degree, although few of them are observed 25
because those with common property are few relative to those who have private property.

Again, in adopting a system of common property, it is just to take into account not only
the evils which will be avoided but also the good things which will be lost. The kind of life
one leads in such a system appears to be utterly impossible. The *reason* why *Socrates* [in the 30
Republic] was led astray should be held to be his wrong hypothesis.[16] For both households
and states should be unities in some sense, but not in every sense. There is a point beyond
which a state [in becoming more unified] will no longer be a state, and also a point beyond
which, while remaining a state, it will be close to losing its nature and becoming an inferior
state. It is like harmony when passing into unison, or rhythm reduced to a single metrical 35
foot. But a state, as stated previously, being a multitude, should be made a unity because of
a common education; and it is absurd that [a lawgiver] who intends to introduce a kind of
education and holds that this education will make the state virtuous should think that measures such as the above [e.g., Plato's] will be the correct ones and not those which have to
do with the [right] customs and philosophy and [good] laws, like those which the law-givers 40
of Sparta and Crete, who brought people together in matters of possessions by the practice
of communal dining.   1264a

We should also not ignore this very fact, namely, that if [Plato's proposals] were well taken,
they would not have escaped men's notice over periods of time, indeed, over a great many
years; for almost all things have been discovered, although some of them were not brought
together, while others are known [to be well-stated] but are not used.   5

[Plato's form of government] would become most evident if one were to observe the actual
construction of the government; for [Plato] would not be able to form the state without distributing and separating its members, some into groups for communal meals, some into clans,
and others into tribes. What would then follow by law is nothing other than that the guardians
would not be farming – a thing which the Spartans are trying to bring about nowadays.   10

Moreover, *Socrates* did not state, nor is it easy to state, the manner in which the citizens
will participate in the government as a whole; and although the multitude of citizens
[excluding the guardians] constitute almost the whole state, he said nothing specifically about
them at all. He did not state whether the property of the farmers will be common also or 15
private, and whether their wives and children will be private or also common.

If the farmers are likewise to have all things in common, in what way will they differ from
the guardians, or what will they get by submitting to their rule, or for what other reason
will they submit, unless the rulers make deals with them as in Crete, where the slaves were 20
allowed the same [rights] in other respects as the rest [of the citizens] but were barred from
gymnastic exercises and possession of arms? If, on the other hand, the institutions [of
property and marriage] are such as they are in other states, what manner of association will
exist among them? For two states will exist of necessity in one state, each of them being 25

16 1261a18.

inconsistent with the other. For Plato makes the guardians like a garrison, but the farmers and the artisans and the rest [like] citizens. As for accusations and lawsuits and all other such evils which, according to *Socrates*,[17] exist in other states, all of them will exist among these [citizens] also.

30   Now *Socrates* maintains that, because of a good education, the [citizens] will have no need of many regulations about the city or the market or others of this sort;[18] yet he limits education to the guardians. Further, he allows the farmers to be owners of property, provided that they pay a tribute [to the state];[19] but under this condition they will probably be much
35   more troublesome and filled with arrogance than the Helots [serfs of Sparta] or the Penestae [serfs of Thessaly] or the slaves in other states.[20] Anyway, whether these matters [common property and wives] must or must not be treated for the farmers also, and what the consequences would be, namely, what their government and education and laws should be, nothing has been specified [in the *Republic*]. In fact, it is not easy to find out (although it is
40   a matter of no small importance) what the character of these farmers should be, if the association of the guardians is to be preserved.

1264b   Again, if *Socrates* makes the women common but the property private, who will manage the house of each farmer while he is out working on his farm? And who will manage the house even if the farmers have both the women and the property in common? It is also absurd
5   to compare men to the other animals and say that women should do the same kind of work as *men*,[21] for these animals have no houses to take care of.

It is also dangerous to set up rulers in the manner in which *Socrates* does; for he makes them keep their rule for life. This system causes discord even among those who have noth-
10   ing of worth to speak of, and certainly much more so among *men* who are high-spirited or have warlike tendencies. Evidently, *Socrates* must have the same rulers rule for life; for [according to him] God mingles the golden element in the souls of the same men for life and does not take them away from the souls of some and place them in the souls of others. He says "God mingles at birth gold in some, silver in others, and brass and iron in those who are to
15   become artisans and farmers, respectively."[22]

Again, *Socrates* deprives the guardians even of happiness yet he says that the lawgiver should make the whole state happy.[23] But it is impossible for the whole to be happy unless most or all or some of the parts are happy; for the happiness of a whole is not related to the happiness of its parts in the same way as, for example, the evenness of a number is related to the
20   evenness of its parts. Evenness may belong to a number [e.g., to 6] but to none of its parts [e.g., to each unit of 6], but this is impossible in the case of happiness. And if the guardians are not happy, who of the others would be? Certainly not the artisans or the multitude of vulgar people.

According to what *Socrates* says in Plato's *Republic*, then, the difficulties just mentioned
25   follow, and also others which are no less great.

[. . .]

17 *Republic* V. 464–5.
18 *Republic* IV. 425D.
19 *Republic* V. 464C.
20 1269a36.
21 *Republic* V. 451 ff.
22 *Republic* III. 415A.
23 *Republic* IV. 419–20.

Book III

[. . .]

6

Having settled these things, let us consider next whether we should posit only one or many 1278b
forms of government, and if many, what they are and how many there are, and what the
differences among them are.

A government is the arrangement of the various offices of a state, and especially of the
most authoritative of all the others, for the authority over each of the others is the ruling 10
body, and this is [the main part of] the government. I mean, for example, that the authority in popular governments is the common people, whereas in oligarchies it is the few [wealthy];
so we speak of these two governments as being different, and we may speak of the other
forms of government in the same way. 15

First, let us lay down the purpose for which a state has been formed and also the kinds
of rule which govern men and their social life. Now we have stated also at the start of this
treatise,²⁴ where we described household management and the rule of a master, that men
are by nature political animals, and for this reason, even when they have no need of each 20
other's help, they desire no less to live with each other; and, moreover, common expediency brings them together to the extent that it contributes to the good life of each. In fact,
the good life is the end in the highest degree for all men taken together and for each of them
taken separately; and they come together for the sake of mere living also (for perhaps there 25
is in [mere] living itself something fine), and they maintain their political association even
for the sake of mere living, as long as life's hardships are not excessive. Clearly, most men
cling to life at the cost of enduring many ills, which shows that there is some contentment
and a natural sweetness in mere living. 30

It is easy, surely, to distinguish the various modes of rule, and we have also described
them often in *Public Writings*.²⁵ The rule of the master, although when truly exercised is to
the interest of both the slave by nature and the master by nature, is nevertheless primarily 35
to the interest of the master but indirectly to the interest of the slave; for it cannot be preserved when the slave perishes. But the rule over a wife and children and the entire household, also called "household management," whether exercised for the sake of those ruled or
for the sake of something common to both the ruler and the ruled, is essentially for the sake 40
of those ruled (for we observe this also in the other arts, e.g., in the medical arts and in gym- 1279a
nastics) but indirectly it might be for the sake of the rulers themselves (for nothing prevents
the game trainer of boys to be himself one of the trainees, just as in the case of the pilot of
a ship, who is always one of the sailors). The game trainer or the pilot, then, is aiming at 5
the good of those who are ruled, and whenever he himself happens to become one of those
he rules, he shares in that benefit but indirectly; for the pilot in the first case, although a
pilot, is one of those who are sailing, and the trainer in the second case, although a trainer,
is one of those who are trained. So in the political rule, too, whenever the state consists of
citizens in virtue of their equality and similarity, the citizens expect to rule [and be ruled] in 10
turn. Formerly, as was natural, they expected someone, say A, to take his turn in serving
others and then again someone else, say B, to look after A's good just as earlier A looked

---

24 1253a2–3.
25 It is not clear to which of Aristotle's (lost) writings he is referring.

after B's interest. Nowadays, however, because of the benefits received from public revenues for holding office, those who rule wish to do so continuously; it's as if rulers who were dis-
15 posed to sickness happen to be kept always healthy while in office, for perhaps this is the assumption on which they are seeking office.

It is evident, then, that the forms of government which aim at the common interest happen to be right with respect to what is just without qualification; but those forms which
20 aim only at the interest of the rulers are all erroneous and deviations from the right forms, for they are despotic, whereas a state is an association of freemen.

7

Having settled these matters, we shall next examine the forms of government, their number and what each of them is, starting first with the right forms, for when these have
25 been described, the deviations from them, too will become evident.

The terms "government" and "ruling body" are [generically] the same in meaning, the ruling body being the authoritative part of a state, and this part must be either one ruler or few or the majority; and whenever the ruling body, whether one or few or the majority, rules for the common interest, the corresponding form of government is necessarily right,
30 but whenever the ruling body rules for its own interest, whether it be one ruler or few or the majority, the corresponding form of government is a deviation from the right form. For we should say that either those who do not partake [of benefits] are not citizens, or that they [as citizens] should get a share of those benefits.

We usually employ the name "kingship" for a monarchy which aims at the common inter-
35 est, the name "aristocracy" for a government by the few but more than one, either because the rulers are the best *men*, or because they aim at the best interest of the state or of those who participate in it, and the common name πολιτεία [i.e., "democracy"] for a government by the many if it governs for the common interest. And there is a good reason for this
40 [use of language]; for it is possible for one *man* or a few to excel in virtue but very difficult
1279b for the majority to become perfect in every virtue, unless this be military virtue, which is most likely to exist in the majority. It is in view of this that, in this form of government, the military men have the greatest authority and those who share in the government are those who possess arms.
5 Of governments which deviate from the right forms, tyranny is opposed to kingship, oligarchy is opposed to aristocracy, and people's rule is opposed to democracy. For tyranny is a monarchy which aims at the interest of the monarch [only], oligarchy aims at the interest of the prosperous [only], people's rule aims at the interest of the poor [only], but none of
10 them aims at the common interest.

8

But we should state what each of the above governments is at greater length, for there are some difficulties; and it is appropriate for one, who makes a philosophical inquiry into a subject but does not attend only to the practical side of it, not to overlook or omit anything but
15 to bring out the truth concerning each point.

As already stated, tyranny is a monarchy, and its rule is despotic over the political association; oligarchy is a government ruled by those who possess [much] property; people's rule, on the contrary, is a government ruled by those who do not possess much property but are needy.

Now the first difficulty is concerned with the specification [of these forms of government]. 20
For if [in deviant states] it is in a people's rule that the majority has authority but this majority were to be [not needy but] prosperous, and, similarly, if it is in an oligarchy that the few
have authority but those few happen to be [not prosperous but] needy and stronger, one
would think that the definitions of the various governments have not been framed well. 25
Moreover, if one classifies the forms of government by combining fewness with prosperity
and majority with need and describes an oligarchy as a government in which the prosperous who are few hold the offices and a people's rule as a government in which the needy 30
who are the majority have them, another difficulty arises. For what name shall we give to
the other two governments we have just described, that is, that in which the ruling majority are prosperous and that in which the ruling minority are needy, if indeed there can be
no form of government other than the six we mentioned? So the argument seems to indicate that the number of those who rule, whether few or the majority, is an accident, and 35
that fewness and majority are not differentiae of an oligarchy and of a people's rule, respectively, just because everywhere the prosperous happen to be few and the needy happen to
be a majority. The difference between people's rule and oligarchy is that between poverty 40
and wealth. So the government in which few or the majority hold office because of wealth 1280a
must be an oligarchy, and that in which the poor, whether few or many, hold office must
be a people's rule, although it happens [always or most of the time], as already stated, that
the rulers in an oligarchy are few whereas those in a people's rule are the majority; for those
who are prosperous are [usually] few, but sharing in freedom belongs to all, and it is because
of prosperity and freedom that disputes arise between the wealthy and the free as to the 5
form of government.

Part V

Diogenes the Cynic (404–323 BCE)

Introduction

Diogenes the Cynic was from Sinope, a Greek colony on the Black Sea, but was forced into exile either because his father, or he himself, was caught adulterating money. He eventually ended up in Athens, where his bizarre behavior and challenging views were revered by some, and reviled by others. No doubt partly because of his bestial habits, he came to be called (perhaps originally by Plato) "The Dog" (kuōn), so "Cynic" actually means "Dog." As the following passages show, Diogenes did not mind being called by this name at all. He died the same year as Alexander the Great, with whom he enjoyed some acquaintance.

24

Diogenes Laertius, *Life of Diogenes*

24. He was very violent in expressing his haughty disdain of others. He said that the *scholê* (school) of Euclides was *cholê* (gall). And he used to call Plato's *diatribê* (discussions) *katatribê* (disguise). It was also a saying of his that the Dionysian games were a great marvel to fools; and that the demagogues were the ministers of the multitude. He used likewise to say, "that when in the course of his life he beheld navigators, and physicians, and philosophers, he thought man the wisest of all animals; but when again he beheld interpreters of dreams, and sooth-sayers, and those who listened to them, and men puffed up with glory or riches, then he thought that there was not a more foolish animal than man." [. . .]

26. [. . .] Sotion too, in his fourth book, states, that the Cynic made the following speech to Plato: Diogenes once asked him for some wine, and then for some dried figs; so he sent him an entire jar full; and Diogenes said to him, "Will you, if you are asked how many two and two make, answer twenty? In this way, you neither give with any reference to what you are asked for, nor do you answer with reference to the question put to you." He used also to ridicule him as an interminable talker.

27. When he was asked where in Greece he saw virtuous men; "Men," said he, "nowhere; but I see good boys in Lacedaemon [Sparta]." On one occasion, when no one came to listen to him while he was discoursing seriously, he began to whistle. And then when people flocked round him, he reproached them for coming with eagerness to folly, but being lazy and indifferent about good things. [. . .] He used to express his astonishment at the gram-marians for being desirous to learn everything about the misfortunes of Ulysses, and being ignorant of their own. He used also to say, "The musicians fitted the strings to the lyre pro-perly, but left all the habits of their soul ill-arranged."

28. And, "Mathematicians kept their eyes fixed on the sun and moon, and overlooked what was under their feet." "Orators were anxious to speak justly, but not at all about acting so." Also, "Misers blamed money, but were preposterously fond of it." He often condemned those who praise the just for being superior to money, but who at the same time are eager them-selves for great riches. He was also very indignant at seeing men sacrifice to the Gods to procure good health, and yet at the sacrifice eating in a manner injurious to health. [. . .]

29. He would frequently praise those who were about to marry, and yet did not marry; or who were about to take a voyage, and yet did not take a voyage; or who were about to

engage in affairs of state, and did not do so; and those who were about to rear children, yet did not rear any; and those who were preparing to take up their abode with princes, and yet did not take it up. [. . .] Hermippus, in his "Sale of Diogenes," says that he was taken prisoner and put up to be sold, and asked what he could do; and he answered, "Govern men." And so he bade the crier "give notice that if any one wants to purchase a master, there is one here for him." [. . .]

30. When Xeniades bought him, he said to him that he ought to obey him even though he was his slave; for that a physician or a pilot would find men to obey them even though they might be slaves. And Eubulus says, in his essay entitled, "The Sale of Diogenes," that he taught the children of Xeniades, after their other lessons, to ride, and shoot, and sling, and dart. And then in the Gymnasium he did not permit the trainer to exercise them after the fashion of athletes, but exercised them himself to just the degree sufficient to give them a good colour and good health.

31. And the boys retained in their memory many sentences of poets and prose writers, and of Diogenes himself; and he used to give them a concise statement of everything in order to strengthen their memory; and at home he used to teach them to wait upon themselves, contenting themselves with plain food, and drinking water. And he accustomed them to cut their hair close, and to eschew ornament, and to go without tunics or shoes, and to keep silent, looking at nothing except themselves as they walked along. He used, also, to take them out hunting; and they paid the greatest attention and respect to Diogenes himself, and spoke well of him to their parents. And the same author affirms that he grew old in the household of Xeniades, and that when he died he was buried by his sons. And that while he was living with him, Xeniades once asked him how he should bury him, and he said, "On my face."

32. When he was asked why, he said, "Because, in a little while, everything will be turned upside down." And he said this because the Macedonians were already attaining power, and becoming a mighty people from having been very inconsiderable. Once, when a man had conducted him into a magnificent house, and had told him that he must not spit, after hawking a little, he spit in his face, saying that he could not find a worse place. [. . .] They also relate that Alexander said that if he had not been Alexander, he should have liked to be Diogenes. [. . .]

34. Once, when some strangers wished to see Demosthenes, he stretched out his middle finger, and said, "This is the great demagogue of the Athenian people." [. . .]

35. Another of his sayings was that most men were within a finger's breadth of being mad. If, then, any one were to walk along, stretching out his middle finger, he will seem to be mad; but if he puts out his fore finger, he will not be thought so. [. . .]

37. On one occasion he saw a child drinking out of his hands, and so he threw away the cup which belonged to his wallet, saying, "That child has beaten me in simplicity." He also threw away his spoon, after seeing a boy, when he had broken his vessel, take up his lentils with a crust of bread. [. . .] Once he saw a woman falling down before the gods in an unbecoming attitude; he, wishing to cure her of her superstition, as Zoilus of Perga tells us, came up to her, and said, "Are you not afraid, O woman, to be in such an indecent attitude, when some god may be behind you, for every place is full of him?" [. . .]

38. Once, while he was sitting in the sun in the Craneum, Alexander was standing by, and said to him, "Ask any favour you choose of me." And he replied, "Cease to shade me from the sun." [. . .]

41. A man once struck him with a beam, and then said, "Take care." "What," said he, "are you going to strike me again?" He used to say that the demagogues were the servants of the

people; and garlands the blossoms of glory. Having lighted a candle in the day time, he said, "I am looking for a man." On one occasion he stood under a fountain, and as the bystanders were pitying him, Plato, who was present, said to them, "If you wish really to show your pity for him, come away;" intimating that he was only acting thus out of a desire for notoriety. [. . .]

46. Once at a banquet, some of the guests threw him bones, as if he had been a dog; so he, as he went away, put up his leg against them as if he had been a dog in reality. [. . .]

53. When Plato was discoursing about his "ideas," and using the nouns "tableness" and "cupness;" "I, O Plato!" interrupted Diogenes, "see a table and a cup, but I see no tableness or cupness." Plato made answer, "That is natural enough, for you have eyes, by which a cup and a table are contemplated; but you have not intellect, by which tableness and cupness are seen." [. . .]

54. When asked what wine he liked to drink, he said, "That which belongs to another." [. . .]

56. When asked why people give to beggars and not to philosophers, he said, "Because they think it possible that they themselves may become lame and blind, but they do not expect ever to turn out philosophers." [. . .]

60. Once Alexander the Great came and stood by him, and said, "I am Alexander, the great king." "And I," said he, "am Diogenes the dog." And when he was asked to what actions of his it was owing that he was called a dog, he said, "Because I fawn upon those who give me anything, and bark at those who give me nothing, and bite the rogues." [. . .]

63. When he was asked what advantage he had derived from philosophy, he replied, "If no other, at least this, that I am prepared for every kind of fortune." The question was put to him what countryman he was, and he replied, "A Citizen of the world." [. . .]

64. He used to say that those who utter virtuous sentiments but do not do them, are no better than harps, for that a harp has no hearing or feeling. [. . .]

67. He used to say that those who were in love were disappointed in regard of the pleasure they expected.

68. When he was asked whether death was an evil, he replied, "How can that be an evil which we do not feel when it is present?" When Alexander was once standing by him, and saying, "Do not you fear me?" He replied, "No; for what are you, a good or an evil?" And as he said that he was good, 'Who, then," said Diogenes, "fears the good?" He used to say, that education was, for the young sobriety, for the old comfort, for the poor riches, and for the rich an ornament." [. . .]

69. On one occasion he was asked, what was the most excellent thing among men; and he said, "Freedom of speech." [. . .] He was in the habit of doing everything in public, whether in respect of Demeter or Aphrodite;[1] and he used to put his conclusions in this way to people: "If there is nothing absurd in dining, then it is not absurd to dine in the market-place. But it is not absurd to dine, therefore it is not absurd to dine in the market-place." [. . .]

70. He used to say, that there were two kinds of exercise: that, namely, of the mind and that of the body; and that the former of these created in the mind such quick and agile phantasies at the time of its performance, as very much facilitated the practice of virtue; but that one was imperfect without the other, since the health and vigour necessary for the practice

1 [Editor's note] "In respect of Demeter," meaning Diogenes would eat in public (considered very bad manners by the Greeks); "in respect of Aphrodite" meaning that Diogenes would perform sex acts (presumably masturbation) in public – even worse manners! – NS.

of what is good, depend equally on both mind and body. And he used to allege as proofs of this, and of the ease which practice imparts to acts of virtue, that people could see that in the case of mere common working trades, and other employments of that kind, the artisans arrived at no inconsiderable accuracy by constant practice; and that any one may see how much one flute player, or one wrestler, is superior to another, by his own continued practice. And that if these men transferred the same training to their minds they would not labour in a profitless or imperfect manner.

71. He used to say also, that there was nothing whatever in life which could be brought to perfection without practice, and that that alone was able to overcome every obstacle; that, therefore, as we ought to repudiate all useless toils, and to apply ourselves to useful labours and to live happily, we are only unhappy in consequence of most exceeding folly. For the very contempt of pleasure, if we only inure ourselves to it, is very pleasant; and just as they who are accustomed to live luxuriously, are brought very unwillingly to adopt the contrary system; so they who have been originally inured to that opposite system, feel a sort of pleasure in the contempt of pleasure. [...]

72. He also argued about the law, that without it there is no possibility of a constitution being maintained; for without a city there can be nothing orderly, but a city is an orderly thing; and without a city there can be no law; therefore law is order. And he played in the same manner with the topics of noble birth, and reputation, and all things of that kind, saying that they were all veils, as it were, for wickedness; and that that was the only proper constitution which consisted in order. Another of his doctrines was that all women ought to be possessed in common; and he said that marriage was a nullity, and that the proper way would be for every man to live with her whom he could persuade to agree with him. And on the same principle he said, that all people's sons ought to belong to every one in common.

73. And there was nothing intolerable in the idea of taking anything out of a temple, or eating any animal whatever, and that there was no impiety in tasting even human flesh; as is plain from the habits of foreign nations; and he said that this principle might be correctly extended to every case and every people. For he said that in reality everything was a combination of all things. For that in bread there was meat, and in vegetables there was bread, and so there were some particles of all other bodies in everything, communicating by invisible passages and evaporating. [...]

Part VI

Epicurus (341–270 BCE) and Epicureanism

Introduction

Epicurus was an Athenian citizen, but was actually born on the Aegean island of Samos (barely a mile off the coast of Asia Minor, now Turkey), where the Athenians set up a colony not long before Epicurus was born. After an early education under a philosopher trained at Plato's Academy, he moved on, in his youth, to Athens itself (in 323 BCE, the year Aristotle left Athens for the last time), where he joined the Academy, which was then under the directorship of Xenocrates. He did not remain there long, however; his family soon after moved to Colophon on the Greek mainland, and Epicurus joined them there, where he studied the atomist philosophy of Democritus under a teacher named Nausiphanes. He then moved on to Mytilene, on the island of Lesbos, and later to Lampsacus on the Hellespont, setting up schools in both places. In 307/6 BCE, he purchased a home in Athens, where he established another school, which came to be known as "The Garden," as it was held in the garden of his home.

Epicurus was a phenomenally prolific writer: Diogenes Laertius reports that he wrote more than any of the other philosophers – about 300 scrolls (which scholars estimate would be around 3,600 pages, of which less than 3 percent has survived). The main corpus of his surviving work consists of three letters, two on cosmological or physical issues (*Letter to Herodotus* and *Letter to Pythocles*) and one on ethics (*Letter to Menoeceus*), and two collections of sayings (the *Vatican Collection* – known as such for the location of the original manuscript – and the *Principal Doctrines*). In addition to these, some fragments of his work *On Nature* have been uncovered in excavations at Herculaneum (which was buried in the famous eruption of Mount Vesuvius in 79 CE); these excavations have also uncovered fragments of other Epicurean writers, most notably Philodemus of Gadara in Syria (*c.*110–40 BCE).

The other main source for Epicurean philosophy is the Roman philosopher Lucretius (Titus Lucretius Carus), who lived in the first half of the first century BCE, whose poem *On the Nature of Things* has survived, but about whom we know surprisingly little.

The influence of his early training in atomist philosophy continued strongly in Epicurus' own philosophy. But Epicurus and his followers considerably extended the atomism of his predecessor, Democritus, using it, as well, as the basis of all of his other doctrines. In the

Epicurean view, the fear of death and the related fear of divine retribution in the afterlife for our wrongdoing were two of the most significant impediments to living well. To address these problems, the Epicureans applied their theory of atomism. To take an example from Lucretius, once one understands that all is atoms and void, colliding and coming apart randomly, one can be free of the fear of death – for death simply means the dissolution of the atoms of which we are (temporarily) composed, and to fear death would be as irrational, in the Epicurean view, as to find fearsome what occurred before we were born. Nothing could happen to *us* in either instance, because we did not (or will not) exist at that time. And since the very conception of a god, according to the Epicureans, was that of a being having a blessed existence, and no such being would disturb their own blessed condition by becoming involved with beings like us, we needn't worry about what the gods might do to us.

As Plato and Aristotle had observed, all animals desire to obtain pleasure and to avoid pain. But Plato and Aristotle argued against the hedonists of their day. Epicurus, however, identified the good with pleasure, and the best possible life with the life that contained the most pleasure, which he understood not in terms of a positive condition, but rather as the privation and elimination of psychological or physical pain. Now, some pain is inevitable in a human life, but other pains we can be free of simply by recognizing that the desires that give rise to them are neither natural nor necessary. So, for example, the desires for wealth and honor are ones we can do without – and if we do eliminate these desires, we thereby eliminate the pains associated with the frustration of such desires, when we cannot satisfy them. The ideal life, accordingly, avoids any involvement in the sorts of human activities that are ordinarily dedicated to such desires, and thereby comes to be marked by calm restraint and an absence of fear.

Epicureanism had great influence in antiquity. One mark of this influence is in the way it was vilified by other schools of philosophy (and later particularly the Christians) – for its hedonism, for its view that human beings did not survive death, and for its view that the organization of the cosmos was essentially random, and for its view of divinity as either non-existent or uncaring.

25

Epicurus, *Letters* and *Principal Doctrines*

The *Letter to Herodotus* offers a brief statement of Epicurus' views about nature. The *Letter to Menoeceus* does the same for his ethical views. The *Principal Doctrines* is a collection of Epicurus' sayings about human life and how we can avoid unnecessary suffering and become calm and without fear (and, as a result, happier). Each work was apparently intended for non-specialist readers. The point of these works is to provide their readers with the basic means by which to incorporate Epicurean teachings into their lives. Epicurus' more technically sophisticated works (which were almost certainly considerable) have been lost.

Letter to Herodotus

(37) First, then, Herodotus, we must grasp the things which underlie words, so that we may have them as a reference point against which to judge matters of opinion, inquiry and puzzlement, and not have everything undiscriminated for ourselves as we attempt infinite chains of proofs, or have words which are empty. (38) For the primary concept corresponding to each word must be seen and need no additional proof, if we are going to have a reference point for matters of inquiry, puzzlement and opinion. Second, we should observe everything in the light of our sensations, and in general in the light of our present focusings whether of thought or of any of our discriminatory faculties, and likewise also in the light of the feelings which exist in us, in order to have a basis for sign-inferences about evidence yet awaited and about the non-evident.

Having grasped these points, we must now observe, concerning the non-evident, first of all that nothing comes into being out of what is not. For in that case everything would come into being out of everything, with no need for seeds. (39) Also, if that which disappears were destroyed into what is not all, all things would have perished, for lack of that into which they dissolved. Moreover, the totality of things was always such as it is now, and always will be, since there is nothing into which it changes, and since beside the totality there is nothing which could pass into it and produce the change.

Moreover, the totality of things is bodies and void. That bodies exist is universally witnessed by sensation itself, in accordance with which it is necessary to judge by reason that which is non-evident, as I said above; (40) and if place, which we call 'void', 'room', and 'intangible substance', did not exist, bodies would not have anywhere to be or to move through in the way they are observed to move. Beyond these [i.e. body and void] nothing can even be thought of, either by imagination or by analogy with what is imagined, as completely substantial things we call accidents and properties of these.

Moreover, of bodies some are compounds, others the constituents of those compounds. (41) The latter must be atomic [literally 'uncuttable'] and unalterable – if all things are not going to be destroyed into the non-existent but be strong enough to survive the dissolution of the compounds – full in nature, and incapable of dissolution at any point of in any way. The primary entities, then, must be atomic kinds of bodies.

Moreover, the totality of things is infinite. For that which is finite has an extremity, and that which is an extremity is viewed as next to some further thing. Therefore having no extremity it has no limit. And not having a limit it would be infinite [literally 'unlimited'] and not finite. Indeed, the totality of things is infinite both in the number of the bodies and in the magnitude of the void. (42) For if the void were infinite but the bodies finite, the bodies would not remain anywhere but would be traveling scattered all over the infinite void, for lack of the bodies which support and marshal them by buffering. And if the void were finite, the infinite bodies would not have anywhere to be. In addition, these bodies which are atomic and full, from which compounds are formed and into which they are dissolved, have unimaginably many differences of shape. For it is not possible for as many varieties as there are to arise from the same shapes if these are of an imaginable number. For each species of shape, also, the number of atoms of the same kind is absolutely infinite; but in the number of their differences they are not absolutely infinite, just unimaginably many, if one is not going to expand them to absolute infinity in their sizes too.

(43) The atoms move continuously for ever, some separating a great distance from each other, others keeping up their vibration on the spot whenever they happen to get trapped by their interlinking or imprisoned by atoms which link up. (44) For the nature of the void brings this about by separating each atom off by itself, since it is unable to lend them any support; and their own solidity causes them as a result of their knocking together to vibrate back, to whatever distance their interlinking allows them to recoil from the knock. There is no beginning to this, because atoms and void are eternal. [. . .]

(46) Moreover, there are delineations which represent the shapes of solid bodies and which in their fineness of texture are far different from things evident. For it is not impossible that such emanations should arise in the space around us, or appropriate conditions for the production of their concavity and fineness of texture, or effluences preserving the same sequential arrangement and the same pattern of motion as they had in the solid bodies. These delineations we call 'images'. Moreover, the lack of obstruction from colliding bodies makes motion through the void achieve any imaginable distance in an unimaginable time. For it is collision and non-collision that take on the resemblance of slow and fast. (47) Nor, on the other hand, does the moving body itself reach a plurality of places *simultaneously* in the periods of time seen by reason. That is unthinkable. And when in perceptible time this body arrives in company with others from some point or other in the infinite, the distance which it covers will not be one from any place from which we may imagine its travel. For that will resemble [cases involving] collision – even if we do admit such a degree of speed of motion as a result of non-collision. This too is a useful principle to grasp. Next, that the images are of unsurpassed fineness is uncontested by anything evident. Hence they also have unsurpassed speed, having every passage commensurate with themselves, in addition to the fact that infinitely

many of them suffer no collision or few collisions, whereas many, indeed infinitely many, atoms suffer immediate collision.   (48) Also that the creation of the images happens as fast as thought. For there is a continuous flow from the surface of bodies – not revealed by diminution in their size, thanks to reciprocal replenishment – which preserves for a long time the positioning and arrangement which the atoms had in the solid body, even if it is also sometimes distorted; and formations of them in the space around us, swift because they do not need to be filled out in depth; and other ways too in which things of this kind are produced. For none of this is contested by our sensations from external objects to us in such a way as to bring back co-affections too.   (49) And we must indeed suppose that it is on the impingement of something from outside that we see and think of shapes. For external objects would not imprint their own nature, of both colour and shape, by means of the air between us and them, or by means of rays or of any effluences passing from us to them, as effectively as they can through certain delineations penetrating us form objects, sharing their colour and shape, of a size to fit into our vision or thought, and traveling at high speed,   (50) with the result that their unity and continuity then results in the impression, and preserves their co-affection all the way from the object because of their uniform bombardment from it, resulting from the vibration of the atoms deep in the solid body. And whatever impression we get by focusing our thought or senses, whether of shape or of properties, that is the shape of the solid body, produced through the image's concentrated succession or after-effect.

But falsehood and error are always located in the opinion which we add.   (51) For the portrait-like resemblance of the impressions which we gain either in sleep or through certain other focusings of thought or of the other discriminatory faculties, to the things we call existent and true, would not exist if the things with which we come into contact were not themselves something. And error would not exist if we did not also get a certain other process within ourselves, one which, although casually connected, possesses differentiation. It is through this that, if it is unattested or contested, falsehood arises, and if attested or uncontested, truth.

(52) This doctrine too, then, is a very necessary one to grasp, so that the criteria based on self-evident impressions should not be done away with, and so that falsehood should not be treated as equally established and confound everything. Hearing too results from a sort of wind traveling from the object which speaks, rings, bangs, or produces an auditory sensation in whatever way it may be. This current is dispersed into similarly-constituted particles. These at the same time preserve a certain co-affection in relation to each other, and a distinctive unity which extends right to the source, and which usually causes the sensory recognition appropriate to that source, and which usually causes the sensory recognition appropriate to that source, or, failing that, just reveals what is external to us.   (53) For without a certain co-affection brought back from the source to us such sensory recognition could not occur. We should not, then, hold that the air is shaped by the projected voice, or likewise by the other things classed with voice. For the air will be much less adequate if this is an effect imposed on it by the voice. Rather we should hold that the impact which occurs inside us when we emit out voice immediately squeezes out certain particles constitutive of a wind current in a way which produces the auditory feeling in us. We must suppose that smell, too, just like hearing, would never cause and feeling if there were not certain particles traveling away from the object and with the right dimensions to stimulate this sense, some kinds being disharmonious and unwelcome, others harmonious and welcome.

(54) Moreover, the atoms themselves must be considered to exhibit no quality of things evident, beyond shape, weight, size and the necessary concomitants of shape. For all quality

changes. But the atoms do not change at all, since something solid and indissoluble must survive the dissolution of the compounds to ensure that the changes are not into, or out of, the non-existent, but result from transpositions within many things, and in other cases from additions and subtractions of certain things. Hence those things which do not admit of [internal] transposition must be indestructible, and must lack the nature of that which changes. And their own peculiar masses and shapes must survive since this is actually necessary. (55) After all, also in familiar objects which have their shape altered by shaving, it can be ascertained that in the matter which undergoes change, as it is left, shape remains whereas the qualities do not remain but vanish from the entire body. So these properties which are left are sufficient to bring about the differences of the compounds, given the necessity for *some* things to be left and not be destroyed into the non-existent.

We must not adopt, either, the view that every size is to be found among the atoms, lest it be contested by things evident. On the other hand, we must suppose that there are *some* variations of size, for this addition with yield better explanations of the events reported by out feelings and senses. (56) But the existence of *every* size is not useful with respect to the differences of qualities. Indeed, we ourselves ought to have experienced how a visible atom might occur.

Furthermore, we must not consider that the finite body contains an infinite number of bits, nor bits with no [lower] limit to size. Therefore not only must we deny *cutting* into smaller and smaller parts to infinity, so that we do not make everything weak and be compelled by our conceptions of complex entities to grind away existing things and waste them away into non-existence, but also we must not consider that in finite bodies there is *traversal* to infinity, not even through smaller and smaller parts. (57) For, first, it is impossible to conceive how [there could be traversal], once someone says that something contains an infinite number of bits or bits with no [lower] limit to size. Second, how could this magnitude still be finite? For obviously these infinitely many bits are themselves of some size, and however small they may be the magnitude consisting of them would also be infinite. And third, since the finite body has an extremity which is distinguishable, even if not imaginable as existing *per se*, one must inevitably think of what is in sequence to it as being of the same kind, and by proceeding forward in sequence it must be possible, to that extent, to reach infinity in thought.

(58) As for the minimum in sensation, we must grasp that it is neither or the same kind as that which admits of traversal, nor entirely unlike it; but that while having a certain resemblance to traversable things it has no distinction of parts. Whenever because of the closeness of the resemblance we thing we are going to make a distinction in it – one part on this side, the other on that – it must be the same magnitude that confronts us. We view these minima in sequence, starting from the first, neither all in the same place nor touching parts with parts, but merely in their own peculiar way providing the measure of magnitudes – more for a larger magnitude, fewer for a smaller one.

This analogy, we must consider, is followed also by the minimum in the atom. (59) In its smallness, obviously, it differs from the one viewed through sensation, but it follows the same analogy. For even the claim that the atom has size is one which we made in accordance with the analogy of things before our eyes, merely projecting something small onto a larger scale. We must also think of the minimum uncompounded limits as providing out of themselves in the first instance the measure of lengths for both greater and smaller magnitudes, using our reason to view that which is invisible. For the resemblance which they bear to changeable things is sufficient to establish this much; but a process of composition out of minima with their own movement is an impossibility.

(60) Moreover in speaking of the infinite we must not use 'up' or 'down' with the implication that they are top or bottom, but with the implication that from wherever we stand it is possible to protract the line above our heads to infinity without the danger of this ever seeming so to us, or likewise the line below us (in what is conceived to stretch to infinity simultaneously both upwards and downwards in relation to the same point). For this [i.e. that there should be a top and bottom] is unthinkable. Therefore it is possible to take as one motion that which is conceived as upwards to infinity, and as one motion that which is conceived as downwards to infinity, even if that which moves from where we are towards the places above our heads arrives ten thousand times at the feet of those above, or at the heads of those below, in the case of that which moves downwards from where we are. For each of the two mutually opposed motions is none the less, as a whole, conceived as being to infinity.

(61) Moreover the atoms must be of equal velocity whenever they travel through the void and nothing collides with them. For neither will the heavy ones move faster than the small light ones, provided nothing runs into them; nor will the small ones move faster than the larger ones, through having all their trajectories commensurate with them, at any rate when the large ones are suffering no collision either. Nor will either their upwards motion or sideways motion caused by knocks [be quicker], or those downwards because of their individual weights. For however far along either kind of trajectory it gets, for that distance it will move as fast as thought, until it is in collision, either through some external cause or through its own weight in relation to the force of the impacting body.   (62) Now it will also be said in the case of compounds that one atom is faster than another, where they are in fact of equal velocity, because the atoms in the complexes move in a single direction even in the shortest continuous time, although it is not single in the periods of time seen by reason; but they frequently collide, until the continuity of their motion presents itself to the senses. [. . .]

(63) The next thing to see – referring it to the sensations and feelings, since that will provide the strongest confirmation – is that the soul is a finestructured body diffused through the whole aggregate, most strongly resembling wind with a certain blending of heat, and resembling wind in some respects but heat in others. But there is that part which differs greatly also from wind and heat themselves in its fineness of structure, a fact which makes it the more liable to co-affection with the rest of the aggregate. All this is shown by the soul's powers, feelings, mobilities and thought processes, and by those features of it whose loss marks our death.

We must grasp too that the soul has the major share of responsibility for sensation. (64) On the other hand, it would not be in possession of this if it were not contained in some way by the rest of the aggregate. And the rest of the aggregate, having granted this responsibility to the soul, itself too receives from the soul a share of this kind of accidental attribute – though not all those which the soul possesses. That is why when the soul has been separated from it the rest of the aggregate does not have sensation. For we saw that it does not have this power as its own intrinsic possession, but grants it to a second thing, which shares its moment of birth and which, by means of the power brought to perfection in it, instantly produces the accidental property of sensation as a result of the process and bestows it both on itself and, as I said, on the rest of the aggregate, owing to their contiguity and co-affection.

(65) Hence too the soul, so long as it remains in [the rest of the aggregate], will never lose sensation through the separation of some other part: whatever of the soul itself is destroyed

too when all or part of the container disintegrates will, so long as it remains, have sensation. But the rest of the aggregate, when either all or part of it remains does not have sensation following the separation of however many atoms it takes to make up the nature of the soul.

Moreover, when the whole aggregate disintegrates the soul is dispersed and no longer has the same powers, or its motions. Hence it does not possess sensation either.   (66) For it is impossible to think of it perceiving while not in this organism, and moving with these motions when what contains and surrounds it are not of the same as those in which it now has these motions.   (67) Another point to appreciate is this. The 'incorporeal', according to the prevailing usage of the word, is applied to that which can be thought of *per se*. But it is impossible to think of the incorporeal *per se* except as void. And void can neither act nor be acted upon, but merely provides bodies with motion through itself. Consequently those who say that the soul is incorporeal are talking non sense. For if it were like that it would be unable to act or be acted upon in any way, whereas as a matter of fact both these accidental properties are self-evidently discriminable in the soul.   (68) Now as for the shapes, colours, sizes, weights and other things predicated of a body as permanent attributes – belonging either to all bodies or to those which are visible, and knowable in themselves through sensation – we must not hold that they are *per se* substances; that is inconceivable.   (69) Nor, at all, that they are non-existent. Nor that they are some distinct incorporeal things accruing to the body. Nor that they are parts of it; but that the whole body cannot have its own permanent nature consisting *entirely* of the sum total of them, in an amalgamation like that when a larger aggregate is composed directly of particles, either primary ones or magnitudes smaller than such-and-such a whole, but that it is only in the way I am describing that it has its own permanent nature consisting of the sum total of them. And these things have all their own individual ways of being focused on and distinguished, yet with the whole complex accompanying them and at no point separated from them, but with the body receiving its predication according to the complex conception.

(70) Now there often also accidentally befall bodies, and impermanently accompany them, things which will neither exist at the invisible level nor be incorporeal. Therefore by using the name in accordance with its general meaning we make it clear that 'accidents' have neither the nature of the whole which we grasp collectively through its complex [of attributes] and call 'body', nor that of the permanent concomitants without which body cannot be thought of. They can get their individual names through certain ways of being focused on, in concomitance with the complex (71) but just whenever they are each seen to become attributes of it, accidents being impermanent concomitants. And we should not banish this self-evident thing from the existent, just because it does not have the nature of the whole of which it becomes an attribute – 'body', as we also call it – nor that of the permanent concomitants. Nor should we think of them as *per se* entities: that is inconceivable too, for either these or the permanent attributes. But we should think of all the accidents of bodies as just what they seem to be, and not a permanent concomitants or as having the status of a *per se* nature either. They are viewed in just the way that sensation itself individualizes them.

(72) Now another thing that it is important to appreciate forcefully is this. We should not inquire into time in the same way as other things, which we inquire into in an object by referring them to familiar preconceptions. But the self-evident thing in virtue of which we articulate the words 'long time' and 'short time', conferring a uniform cycle on it, must itself be grasped by analogy. And we should neither adopt alternative terminology for it as being better – we should use that which is current – nor predicate anything else of it as having the same essence as this peculiar thing – for this too is done by some – but we must merely

work out empirically what we associate this peculiarity with and tend to measure it against. (73) After all, it requires no additional proof but merely empirical reasoning, to see that with days, nights, and fractions thereof, and likewise with the presence and absence of feelings, and with motions and rests, we associate a certain peculiar accident, and that it is, conversely, as belonging to these things that we conceive that entity itself, in virtue of which we use the word 'time'.

In addition to what was said earlier, we must suppose that the worlds and every limited compound which bears a close resemblance to the things we see, has come into being from the infinite: all these things, the larger and the smaller alike, have been separated off from it as a result of individual entanglements. And all disintegrate again, some faster some slower, and through differing kinds of causes. [. . .]

(75) We must take it that even nature was educated and constrained in many different ways by actual states of affairs, and that its lessons were later made more accurate, and augmented with new discoveries by reason – faster among some people, slower among others, and in some ages and eras, owing to <individual needs, by greater leaps>, in others by smaller leaps. Thus names too did not originally come into being by coining, but men's own natures underwent feelings and received impressions which varied peculiarly from tribe to tribe, and each of the individual feelings and impressions caused them to exhale breath peculiarly, according also to the racial differences from place to place. (76) Later, particular coinings were made by consensus within the individual races, so as to make the designations less ambiguous and more concisely expressed. Also, the men who shared knowledge introduced certain unseen entities, and brought words for them into usage. <Hence some> men gave utterance under compulsion, and others chose words rationally, and it is thus, as far as the principal cause is concerned, that they achieved self-expression.

Among celestial phenomena movement, turning, eclipse, rising, setting and the like should not be thought to come about through the ministry and present or future arrangements of some individual who at the same time possesses the combination of total blessedness and imperishability. (77) For trouble, concern, anger and favour are incompatible with blessedness, but have their origin in weakness, fear and dependence on neighbours. Nor should we think that beings which are at the same time conglomerations of fire possess blessedness and voluntarily take on these movements. But we must observe all the majesty associated with all the names which we apply to such conceptions, if they give rise to no belief conflicting with majesty. Otherwise the conflict itself will give rise to the greatest mental disquiet. [. . .]

Letter to Menoeceus

Epicurus to Menoeceus, greeting.

Let no one be slow to seek wisdom when he is young nor weary in the search thereof when he is grown old. For no age is too early or too late for the health of the soul. And to say that the season for studying philosophy has not yet come, or that it is past and gone, is like saying that the season for happiness is not yet or that it is now no more. Therefore, both old and young ought to seek wisdom, the former in order that, as age comes over him, he may be young in good things because of the grace of what has been, and the latter in order that, while he is young, he may at the same time be old, because he has no fear of the things which are to come. So we must exercise ourselves in the things which bring happiness, since, if that be present, we have everything, and, if that be absent, all our actions are directed toward attaining it.

Those things which without ceasing I have declared unto thee, those do, and exercise thyself therein, holding them to be the elements of right life. First believe that god is a living being immortal and blessed, according to the notion of a god indicated by the common sense of mankind; and so believing, thou shalt not affirm of him ought that is foreign to his immortality or that agrees not with blessedness, but shalt believe about him whatever may uphold both his blessedness and his immortality. For verily there are gods, and the knowledge of them is manifest; but they are not such as the multitude believe, seeing that men do not steadfastly maintain the notions they form respecting them. Not the man who denies the gods worshipped by the multitude, but he who affirms of the gods what the multitude believes about them is truly impious. For the utterances of the multitude about the gods are not true preconceptions but false assumptions; hence it is that the greatest evils happen to the wicked and the greatest blessings happen to the good from the hand of the gods, seeing that they are always favourable to their own good qualities and take pleasure in men like unto themselves, but reject as alien whatever is not of their kind.

Accustom thyself to believe that death is nothing to us, for good and evil imply sentience, and death is the privation of all sentience; therefore a right understanding that death is nothing to us makes the mortality of life enjoyable, not by adding to life an illimitable time, but by taking away the yearning after immortality. For life has no terrors for him who has thoroughly apprehended that there are no terrors for him in ceasing to live. Foolish, therefore, is the man who says that he fears death, not because it will pain when it comes, but because it pains in the prospect. Whatsoever causes no annoyance when it is present, causes only a groundless pain in the expectation. Death, therefore, the most awful of evils, is nothing to us, seeing that, when we are, death is not come, and, when death is come, we are not. It is nothing, then, either to the living or to the dead, for with the living it is not and the dead exist no longer. But in the world, at one time men shun death as the greatest of all evils, and at another time choose it as a respite from the evils in life. The wise man does not deprecate life nor does he fear the cessation of life. The thought of life is no offense to him, nor is the cessation of life regarded as an evil. And even as men choose of food not merely and simply the larger portion, but the more pleasant, so the wise seek to enjoy the time which is most pleasant and not merely that which is longest. And he who admonishes the young to live well and the old to make a good end speaks foolishly, not merely because of the desirableness of life, but because the same exercise at once teaches to live well and die well. Much worse is he who says that it were good not to be born, but when once one is born to pass with all speed through the gates of Hades. For if he truly believes this, why does he not depart from life? It were easy for him to do so, if once he were firmly convinced. If he speaks only in mockery, his words are foolishness, for those who hear believe him not.

We must remember that the future is neither wholly ours nor wholly not ours, so that neither must we count upon it as quite certain to come nor despair of it as quite certain not to come.

We must also reflect that of desires some are natural, others are groundless; and that of the natural some are necessary as well as natural, and some natural only. And of the necessary desires some are necessary if we are to be happy, some if the body is to be rid of uneasiness, some if we are even to live. He who has a clear and certain understanding of these things will direct every preference and aversion toward securing health of body and tranquillity of mind, seeing that this is the sum and end of a blessed life. For the end of all our actions is to be free from pain and fear, and, when once we have attained all this, the tempest of the soul is laid; seeing that the living creature has no need to go in search of something that is lacking, nor to look for anything else by which the good of the soul and of the body will be fulfilled. When we are pained because of the absence of pleasure, then, and then only, do we feel the need of pleasure. Wherefore we call pleasure the alpha and omega of a blessed life. Pleasure is our first and kindred good. It is the starting point of every choice and of every aversion, and to it we come back, inasmuch as we make feeling the rule by which to judge of every good thing. And since pleasure is our first and native good, for that reason we do not choose every pleasure whatsoever, but ofttimes pass over many pleasures when a greater annoyance ensues from them. And ofttimes we consider pains superior to pleasures when submission to the pains for a long time brings us as a consequence a greater pleasure. While therefore all pleasure because it is naturally akin to us is good, not all pleasure is choice-worthy, just as all pain is an evil and yet not all pain is to be shunned. It is, however, by measuring one against another, and by looking at the conveniences and inconveniences, that all these matters must be judged. Sometimes we treat the good as an evil, and the evil, on the contrary, as a good. Again, we regard independence of outward things as a great good, not so as in all cases to use little, but so as to be contented with little if we have not much, being honestly persuaded that they have the sweetest enjoyment of luxury who stand least in need of it, and that whatever is natural is easily procured and only the vain and worthless hard to win. Plain fare gives as much pleasure as a costly diet, when once the pain of want has been removed, while bread and water confer the highest possible pleasure when they are brought to hungry lips. To habituate one's self, therefore, to simple and inexpensive diet supplies all that is needful for health, and enables a man to meet the necessary requirements of life without shrinking, and it places us in a better condition when we approach at intervals a costly fare and renders us fearless of fortune.

When we say, then, that pleasure is the end and aim, we do not mean the pleasures of the prodigal or the pleasures of sensuality, as we are understood to do by some through ignorance, prejudice, or wilful misrepresentation. By pleasure we mean the absence of pain in the body and of trouble in the soul. It is not an unbroken succession of drinking bouts and of revelry, not sexual love, not the enjoyment of the fish and other delicacies of a luxurious table, which produce a pleasant life; it is sober reasoning, searching out the grounds of every choice and avoidance, and banishing those beliefs through which the greatest tumults take possession of the soul. Of all this the beginning and the greatest good is prudence. Wherefore prudence is a more precious thing even than philosophy; from it spring all the other virtues, for it teaches that we cannot lead a life of pleasure which is not also a life of prudence, honor, and justice; nor lead a life of prudence, honor, and justice, which is not also a life of pleasure. For the virtues have grown into one with a pleasant life, and a pleasant life is inseparable from them.

Who, then, is superior in thy judgement to such a man? He holds a holy belief concerning the gods, and is altogether free from the fear of death. He has diligently considered the end fixed by nature, and understands how easily the limit of good things can be reached and attained, and how either the duration or the intensity of evils is but slight. Destiny, which some introduce as sovereign over all things, he laughs to scorn, affirming rather that some things happen of necessity, others by chance, others through our own agency. For he sees that necessity destroys responsibility and that chance or fortune is inconstant; whereas our own actions are free, and it is to them that praise and blame naturally attach. It were better, indeed, to accept the legends of the gods than to bow beneath that yoke of destiny which the natural philsophers have imposed. The one holds out some faint hope that we may escape if we honor the gods, while the necessity of the naturalists is deaf to all entreaties. Nor does he hold chance to be a god, as the world in general does, for in the acts of a god there is no disorder; nor to be a cause, though an uncertain one, for he believes that no good or evil is dispensed by chance to men so as to make life blessed, though it supplies the starting-point of great good and great evil. He believes that the misfortune of the wise is better than the prosperity of the fool. It is better, in short, that what is well judged in action should not owe its successful issue to the aid of chance.

Exercise thyself in these and kindred precepts day and night, both by thyself and with him who is like unto thee; then never, either in waking or in dream, wilt thou be disturbed; but wilt live as a god among men. For man loses all semblance of mortality by living in the midst of immortal blessings.

Principal Doctrines

1. A blessed and eternal being has no trouble himself and brings no trouble upon any other being; hence he is exempt from movements of anger and partiality, for every such movement implies weakness.

2. Death is nothing to us; for the body, when it has been resolved into its elements, has no feeling, and that which has no feeling is nothing to us.

3. The magnitude of pleasure reaches its limit in the removal of all pain. When pleasure is present, so long as it is uninterrupted, there is no pain either of body or of mind or of both together.

4. Continuous pain does not last long in the flesh; on the contrary, pain, if extreme, is present a very short time, and even that degree of pain which barely outweighs pleasure in the flesh does not last for many days together. Illnesses of long duration even permit of an excess of pleasure over pain in the flesh.

5. It is impossible to live a pleasant life without living wisely and well and justly, and it is impossible to live wisely and well and justly without living pleasantly. Whenever any one of these is lacking, when, for instance, the man is not able to live wisely, though he lives well and justly, it is impossible for him to live a pleasant life.

6. In order to obtain security from other men any means whatsoever of procuring this was a natural good.

7. Some men have sought to become famous and renowned, thinking that thus they would make themselves secure against their fellow-men. If, then, the life of such persons really was secure, they attained natural good; if, however, it was insecure, they have not attained the end which by nature's own prompting they originally sought.

8. No pleasure is in itself evil, but the things which produce certain pleasures entail annoyances many times greater than the pleasures themselves.

9. If all pleasure had been capable of accumulation, – if this had gone on not only by recurrence in time, but all over the frame or, at any rate, over the principal parts of man's nature, there would never have been any difference between one pleasure and another, as in fact there is.

10. If the objects which are productive of pleasures to profligate persons really freed them from fears of the mind, – the fears, I mean, inspired by celestial and atmospheric phenomena,

the fear of death, the fear of pain; if, further, they taught them to limit their desires, we should never have any fault to find with such persons, for they would then be filled with pleasures to overflowing on all sides and would be exempt from all pain, whether of body or mind, that is, from all evil.

11. If we had never been molested by alarms at celestial and atmospheric phenomena, nor by the misgiving that death somehow affects us, nor by neglect of the proper limits of pains and desires, we should have had no need to study natural science.

12. It would be impossible to banish fear on matters of the highest importance, if a man did not know the nature of the whole universe, but lived in dread of what the legend tells us. Hence without the study of nature there was no enjoyment of unmixed pleasures.

13. There would be no advantage in providing security against our fellow-men, so long as we were alarmed by occurrences over our heads or beneath the earth or in general by whatever happens in the boundless universe.

14. When tolerable security against our fellow-men is attained, then on a basis of power sufficient to afford support and of material prosperity arises in most genuine form the security of a quiet private life withdrawn from the multitude.

15. Nature's wealth at once has its bounds and is easy to procure; but the wealth of vain fancies recedes to an infinite distance.

16. Fortune but seldom interferes with the wise man; his greatest and highest interests have been, are, and will be, directed by reason throughout the course of his life.

17. The just man enjoys the greatest peace of mind, while the unjust is full of the utmost disquietude.

18. Pleasure in the flesh admits no increase when once the pain of want has been removed; after that it only admits of variation. The limit of pleasure in the mind, however, is reached when we reflect on the things themselves and their congeners which cause the mind the greatest alarms.

19. Unlimited time and limited time afford an equal amount of pleasure, if we measure the limits of that pleasure by reason.

20. The flesh receives as unlimited the limits of pleasure; and to provide it requires unlimited time. But the mind, grasping in thought what the end and limit of the flesh is, and banishing the terrors of futurity, procures a complete and perfect life, and has no longer any need of unlimited time. Nevertheless it does not shun pleasure, and even in the hour of death, when ushered out of existence by circumstances, the mind does not lack enjoyment of the best life.

21. He who understands the limits of life knows how easy it is to procure enough to remove the pain of want and make the whole of life complete and perfect. Hence he has no longer any need of things which are not to be won save by labor and conflict.

22. We must take into account as the end all that really exists and all clear evidence of sense to which we refer our opinions; for otherwise everything will be full of uncertainty and confusion.

23. If you fight against all your sensations, you will have no standard to which to refer, and thus no means of judging even those judgments which you pronounce false.

24. If you reject absolutely any single sensation without stopping to discriminate with respect to that which awaits confirmation between matter of opinion and that which is already present, whether in sensation or in feelings or in any presentative perception of the mind, you will throw into confusion even the rest of your sensations by your groundless belief and so you will be rejecting the standard of truth altogether. If in your ideas based upon opinion

you hastily affirm as true all that awaits confirmation as well as that which does not, you will not escape error, as you will be maintaining complete ambiguity whenever it is a case of judging between right and wrong opinion.

25. If you do not on every separate occasion refer each of your actions to the end prescribed by nature, but instead of this in the act of choice or avoidance swerve aside to some other end, your acts will not be consistent with your theories.

26. All such desires as lead to no pain when they remain ungratified are unnecessary, and the longing is easily got rid of, when the thing desired is difficult to procure or when the desires seem likely to produce harm.

27. Of all the means which are procured by wisdom to ensure happiness throughout the whole of life, by far the most important is the acquisition of friends.

28. The same conviction which inspires confidence that nothing we have to fear is eternal or even of long duration, also enables us to see that even in our limited conditions of life nothing enhances our security so much as friendship.

29. Of our desires some are natural and necessary; others are natural, but not necessary; others, again, are neither natural nor necessary, but are due to illusory opinion. [Epicurus regards as natural and necessary desires which bring relief from pain, as *e.g.* drink when we are thirsty; while by natural and not necessary he means those which merely diversify the pleasure without removing the pain, as *e.g.* costly viands; by the neither natural nor necessary he means desires for crowns and the erection of statues in one's honor.][1]

30. Those natural desires which entail no pain when not gratified, though their objects are vehemently pursued, are also due to illusory opinion; and when they are not got rid of, it is not because of their own nature, but because of the man's illusory opinion.

31. Natural justice is a symbol or expression of expediency, to prevent one man from harming or being harmed by another.

32. Those animals which are incapable of making covenants with one another, to the end that they may neither inflict nor suffer harm, are without either justice or injustice. And those tribes which either could not or would not form mutual covenants to the same end are in like case.

33. There never was an absolute justice, but only an agreement made in reciprocal intercourse in whatever localities now and again from time to time, providing against the infliction or suffering of harm.

34. Injustice is not in itself an evil, but only in its consequence, viz. the terror which is excited by apprehension that those appointed to punish such offences will discover the injustice.

35. It is impossible for the man who secretly violates any article of the social compact to feel confident that he will remain undiscovered, even if he has already escaped ten thousand times; for right on to the end of his life he is never sure he will not be detected.

36. Taken generally, justice is the same for all, to wit, something found expedient in mutual intercourse; but in its application to particular cases of locality or conditions of whatever kind, it varies under different circumstances.

37. Among the things accounted just by conventional law, whatever in the needs of mutual intercourse is attested to be expedient, is thereby stamped as just, whether or not it be the same for all; and in case any law is made and does not prove suitable to the expediencies of mutual intercourse, then this is no longer just. And should the expediency which is expressed

1 The bracketed remarks are by an ancient commentator.

by the law vary and only for a time correspond with the prior conception, nevertheless for the time being it was just, so long as we do not trouble ourselves about empty words, but look simply at the facts.

38. Where without any change in circumstances the conventional laws, when judged by their consequences, were seen not to correspond with the notion of justice, such laws were not really just; but wherever the laws have ceased to be expedient in consequence of a change in circumstances, in that case the laws were for the time being just when they were expedient for the mutual intercourse of the citizens, and subsequently ceased to be just when they ceased to be expedient.

39. He who best knew how to meet fear of external foes made into one family all the creatures he could; and those he could not, he at any rate did not treat as aliens; and where he found even this impossible, he avoided all intercourse, and, so far as was expedient, kept them at a distance.

40. Those who were best able to provide themselves with the means of security against their neighbors, being thus in possession of the surest guarantee, passed the most agreeable life in each other's society; and their enjoyment of the fullest intimacy was such that, if one of them died before his time, the survivors did not lament his death as if it called for commiseration.

26

Lucretius, *On the Nature of Things*

Unlike the other works in this collection, the original language of *On the Nature of Things* is Latin, and the author is Roman, not Greek. In the following selections from this considerable work, Lucretius (Titus Lucretius Carus) summarizes the main aspects of Epicurean philosophy, including its materialism (in the form of atomism), its rejection of the immortality of the soul, and its insistence that the fear of death is irrational and that religious superstition is a source of human misery.

Book I

[...]

50 For the rest, turn open ears and a sharp mind
    set free from cares to the true system of philosophy,
    so that you do not despise and abandon my gifts to you,
    set out with constant eagerness, before they are understood.
    For I am beginning to set out for you the deepest workings
55 of the heavens and the gods, and to reveal the first beginnings[1] of things
    out of which nature creates all things, and increases and maintains them,
    and into which nature dissolves them again once they have perished.
    These we are accustomed, in setting forth our account, to call
    "matter" and "the generating bodies of things" and to name them
60 "the seeds of things," and to use the term "first bodies" for them,
    because all things exist from these first beginnings.[2]
    It used to be that human life, polluted, was lying

---

1 "The first beginnings" = *primordia*, one of the Latin terms Lucretius uses for "atoms." Lucretius never uses the Greek term *atomoi* ("atoms") in the poem.
2 As just noted, Lucretius does not transliterate Epicurus' Greek term for atom (*atomos*, literally "unable to be cut") into Latin, but instead uses a number of different Latin terms to get at the idea.

in the dirt before our eyes, crushed by the weight of religion,
which stretched out its head on display from the regions of heaven,
threatening mortals from above with its horrible-looking face. 65
It was a Greek man[3] who first dared to raise his mortal eyes
against religion, and who first fought back against it.
Neither the stories about the gods, nor thunderbolts, nor the sky
with its threatening rumbles held him back, but provoked
all the more the fierce sharpness of his mind, so that he desired 70
to be the first to shatter the imprisoning bolts of the gates of nature.
As a result the vital force of his mind was victorious,
and he traveled far beyond the flaming walls of the world
and trekked throughout the measureless universe in mind and spirit.
As victor he brings back from there the knowledge of what can come to be, 75
what cannot, in short, by what process each thing
has its power limited, and its deep-set boundary stone.
And so the tables are turned. Religion lies crushed
beneath our feet, and his victory raises us to the sky.
I am afraid of one thing in all this: that you might think 80
that you are starting on the first steps of an unholy system of thought,
and are walking the path of crime. On the contrary, it has happened too often
that this so-called religion has produced criminal and unholy actions.
Thus was the case at Aulis when the chosen leaders of the Greeks,
the first among men, foully defiled the altar 85
of the virgin goddess of the crossroads[4] with the blood of Iphianassa.[5]
As soon as the sacrificial headband was wreathed about her virgin locks
with its streamers flowing down equally from both her cheeks,
and as soon as she saw her father standing in mourning before the altar,
with his attendants beside him concealing the iron blade, 90
and the citizens pouring forth tears at the sight of her,
speechless with fear she sank in her knees and fell to the ground.
Nor was it a help to the wretched girl at such a moment
that she had been the first child to call the king "father."
She was lifted up by men's hands and led trembling 95
to the altar, not so that she might be greeted by the loud-ringing
marriage hymn when the solemn wedding rite was finished,
but that the chaste girl might be slaughtered unchastely at the very point
of marriage, a grieving victim, by the sacrificial stroke of her father.
All this so that a happy and auspicious departure might be granted to the fleet. 100
Such great evils could religion make seem advisable.
Even you today at some time or other will be overcome

---

3 Epicurus (341–271 BC), the founder of Epicureanism and the philosophical hero of Lucretius' poem.
4 "Virgin goddess of the crossroads" = Diana (Artemis in Greek).
5 Iphianassa is the name Homer used for Iphigenia, the daughter of Agamemnon and Clytemnestra.
Artemis forced Agamemnon and the Greeks to sacrifice Iphigenia before the Greeks could sail to Troy
at the beginning of the Trojan War. The story of her sacrifice was retold in many 5th c. BC Greek tragedies,
including Euripides' *Iphigenia at Aulis*, and Aeschylus' *Agamemnon*.

by the fearful words of seers and try to desert us.
Why not, since so many are the dreams they can now

105   invent for you which can overturn the guiding principles of your life
and throw all your fortunes into complete confusion with fear!
And deservedly so. For if people saw that there is a fixed limit
to oppressive cares, with some reason they would be strong enough
to fight back against religious beliefs and the threats of seers.

110   As it is, there is no means of resisting, no power,
since death must bring with it the fear of eternal punishment.
For people do not know what the nature of the soul is.
Is it born, or does it work its way into us as we are being born?
Does it perish when we do, torn apart by death,

115   or does it go to see the shades of Orcus[6] and its desolate pits?
Or does it work its way by divine aid into other creatures,
as our Ennius[7] proclaimed? He was the first to bring down
a crown of everlasting foliage from lovely Mount Helicon[8]
to become famous throughout the Italian tribes of people.

120   And yet moreover Ennius still sets forth
in his everlasting verses that there really are regions of Acheron,
where neither our souls nor our bodies remain,
but certain kinds of shades pale in wondrous ways.
He recalls how from that region the shade of Homer, forever

125   blooming, rose before him and began to shed salty
tears, setting out in words the nature of things.
Therefore we must not only give a correct account of celestial
matters, explaining in what way the wanderings of the sun
and moon occur and by what power things happen on earth.

130   We must also take special care and employ keen reasoning
to see where the soul and the nature of the mind come from,
and what it is that meets our minds and terrifies us when
we are awake and suffering from disease, and when we are buried in sleep,
so that we seem to hear and see face to face people

135   who have already met death and whose bones the earth embraces.
Nor does it escape my thought that it is difficult to throw light
upon the obscure discoveries of the Greeks in Latin verses,
especially since we must use new words for many things
because of the poverty of our language and the newness of the subject matter.

140   But still it is your excellence and the pleasure of the sweet friendship
I hope to have with you that urges me to undergo hardship
however great and to keep my watch in the quiet of the night
as I try to find the right words and poem with which at last
I might be able to hold a clear light up to your mind

145   that will allow you to see deeply into obscure matters.

6 "The shades of Orcus" = the underworld.
7 Ennius (239–169 BC) was one of the greatest early Roman poets.
8 Mt. Helicon, located in Boeotia in Greece, was the home of the Muses.

Therefore this fear and darkness of the mind must be shattered
apart not by the rays of the sun and the clear shafts
of the day but by the external appearance and inner law of nature.
Its first principle will take its starting point for us as follows:
nothing ever comes to be from nothing through divine intervention.[9]   150
The reason that fear so dominates all mortals is
because they see many things happen on earth and in the heavens
the causes of whose activities they are able in no way
to understand, and they imagine they take place through divine power.
For which reason, when we see that nothing can be created from nothing,   155
then we will more correctly perceive what we are after:
the source from which each thing is created, and the way
each thing happens without divine intervention.
For if things came to be from nothing, every kind of thing
could be born from all things, and nothing would need a seed.   160
Men might sprout from the sea and the scaly race
of fishes from the earth, and birds might hatch from the sky.
Cattle and other livestock, and every kind of beast,
with uncertain birth would inhabit farms and wilderness alike.
Trees would not consistently produce the same fruit,   165
but they would change, and all trees could bear all fruit.
Since there would not be generating bodies for each thing,
how could there be a fixed and constant mother for things?
But now, since all things are created from fixed seeds,
each thing is born and emerges into the shores of light   170
from the source of the matter and first bodies of each thing.
And thus all things are unable to be born from all things,
because there is a separate power present in fixed things.
And why do we see roses in the spring, grain in the heat,
or vines bursting forth in response to autumn's call?   175
Is it not because whatever is created becomes visible
in its own time when fixed seeds have flowed together,
while favorable seasons are at hand and the lively earth safely
brings forth tender things into the shores of light?
But if they came to be from nothing, they would suddenly spring forth   180
at random periods of time and during unsuitable parts of the year,
seeing that there would be no first beginnings which would be able
to be kept apart from generating union at an unfavorable time.
Nor further, in order for things to increase, would there need to be time
for seeds to come together, if they were able to grow from nothing.   185
For tiny babies would suddenly become young adults,
and trees would rise up and leap from the earth in an instant.
It is obvious that none of these things happens, since everything

9 This is the first major law of Epicurean physics: Nothing can come to be out of nothing. Cf. Epicurus'
Letter to Herodotus 38 ("First, nothing comes into being out of what does not exist"). Lucretius' words
in 150, "through divine intervention," appear to be his own addition.

increases little by little, as is fitting for fixed seed,
190   and preserves their kind as they increase. Thus you can recognize
that each thing grows and is nourished from its own matter.
In addition, without dependable rains each year
the earth is unable to produce its joy-bringing crops,
nor is the nature of living creatures, if deprived of food,
195   able to reproduce its race and safeguard its life.
You should thus believe all the more that many bodies are common
to many things, as we see letters are common to words,
rather than that anything is able to exist without first beginnings.
Next, why was nature unable to produce men
200   so large that they could cross the ocean by walking through the shallows,
rip apart huge mountains with their bare hands,
and succeed in living through many ages of living creatures,
unless it is because fixed matter has been assigned to things
for their growth, from which it is determined what is able to come to be?
205   So it must be confessed that nothing is able to come from nothing,
since things have a need for seed by which they all can,
when created, be brought forth into the soft breezes of the air.
Finally, since we see that cultivated lands are better than uncultivated,
and produce better crops when they are cared for by our hands,
210   it is clear that there exist in the earth the first beginnings of things
which we stir into being when we turn over the fertile clods
with a plough and work the soil of the earth from deep down.
But if there were not first beginnings, you would see everything
come to be much better on its own without our efforts.
215   Next is this: nature dissolves each thing back
into its particles and does not destroy things into nothing.[10]
For if anything were mortal in all its parts, each thing
would perish by being snatched suddenly from before our eyes.
For no need would exist for a force that was able to arrange
220   the destruction of the parts of each thing and dissolve its structure.
But as it is, since each thing is composed out of eternal seed,
until a force is present that hammers apart the thing with a blow
or penetrates within through empty spaces and dissolves it,
nature does not allow the destruction of anything to be seen.
225   And if time annihilates whatever it removes through the aging process,
consuming all the matter, from where would Venus restore
the living race each according to kind, or from where
does earth the sweet artificer nourish and increase them
once restored, providing them with food each according to kind?
230   From where would internal springs and external, far-off rivers
supply the sea? From where would the sky feed the stars?

10 This is the second major law of Epicurean physics: Nothing can be destroyed into nothing, or every-thing would cease to be. Cf. Epicurus' *Letter to Herodotus* 39 ("And if what disappears had perished into what is not, all things would have perished, since what they were dissolved into does not exist.").

For infinite time gone by and the passing days
ought to have consumed everything that has a mortal structure.
But if in this duration and time gone by there have been
things from which this sum of things is restored and exists,   235
they are without any doubt endowed with an immortal nature.
Therefore everything cannot be changed back into nothing.
Next, the same force and cause would destroy everything
indiscriminately, unless they were held together by an eternal stuff
entangled to a lesser or greater degree in its interconnections with itself   240
Indeed a mere touch would undoubtedly be a sufficient cause
of death, especially seeing that there would be nothing with eternal body
whose texture a special force would be required to dissolve.
But as things are, since there are various interconnections
of the first beginnings with themselves and matter is everlasting,   245
things persist with their bodies sound, until a force found
sufficiently strong to overcome their textures meets them.
Thus not one thing returns to nothing, but all things
when they split apart return to the first bodies of matter.
Lastly, the rains pass away, when father sky   250
sends them down into the lap of mother earth.
But glistening crops erupt and branches turn green on trees,
while the trees themselves grow and are weighed down by fruit.
Hence further our race and the race of beasts are fed,
hence we see glad cities flower with children   255
and lush forests everywhere sing with young birds.
Hence cows exhausted by their fat lay their bodies
down on the joyful pasture and the glistening moisture of milk
drips from their distended udders. Hence new calves
play and frolic on shaky limbs in the soft grass,   260
their tender young minds drunk on pure milk.
Thus all things that are visible do not perish completely,
since nature remakes one thing from another, nor does she allow
anything to be born unless it is aided by another's death.
Come now, since I have shown that things cannot be created from nothing,   265
and likewise that once created they cannot be reduced to nothing,
lest by any chance you still begin to doubt my words,
since you cannot see the first beginnings of things with your eyes,
let me remind you besides that there are bodies which you must admit
exist in things and yet are not able to be seen.   270
First, when the force of the wind is whipped up it lashes
at the sea, overwhelming huge ships and scattering the clouds.
Rushing along at times with a quick whirlwind it strews
the plains with great trees and attacks the mountain tops
with forest-cracking blasts. So the wind with its shrill howling   275
rages wildly, shrieking savagely and moaning with menace.
It is therefore beyond doubt that there are invisible bodies of wind
which sweep over the sea, the lands, and the clouds of the sky,

buffeting them and snatching them up in a sudden whirlwind.
280　They flow along and breed destruction in the same way
as when the soothing nature of water is carried off suddenly
in an overflowing river, when it has been swollen after heavy rains
by a tremendous rush of water coming off the high mountains.
It tosses shattered branches from the forests and whole trees,
285　and not even sturdy bridges can withstand the sudden force
of the approaching water. Stirred up by the heavy rains,
the river rushes against the pilings with effective force.
It wreaks a deafening havoc and beneath its waves it rolls
huge rocks, rushing against whatever opposes its flow.
290　Therefore so too should the blasts of wind be carried along,
which, whenever they have spread out in any direction
like a powerful river, drive things before them and rush at them
with constant force, and now and then in a twisting gust
they seize them and quickly carry them off in a spinning whirlwind.
295　Therefore again and again there are invisible bodies of wind,
since they have been found to rival mighty rivers in what
they do and in how they act, and rivers have bodies we can see.
Second, we experience the different kinds of smells things have,
but nonetheless we never see the smells coming to our noses.
300　We do not see warm heat, nor can we apprehend
cold with our eyes, nor are we in the habit of seeing voices.
But it must be that all these things are bodily
by nature, since they are able to set the sense organs in motion.
For nothing is able to touch or be touched except body.
305　Third, clothes hung along the wave-beaten shore
grow damp, but they dry when spread out in the sun.
But we neither see how the dampness of the water settled on them,
nor again how it was forced out owing to the heat.
This shows that the moisture is split up into small
310　particles that the eye is in no way able to see.
Fourth, as the sun completes its journey year after year
a ring on the finger grows thinner beneath with wear,
the fall of water-drops hollows out a stone, the curved
iron plow of a farmer shrinks imperceptibly in the fields,
315　and we see that people's feet today are wearing down
the stone surfaces of the street. Then too near the gates of the city
bronze statues extend right hands thinned
by the frequent touch of those who pass by and greet them.
These then we see diminish, since they have been worn away.
320　But the jealous nature of vision blocks our seeing which
bodies move away at any given time.
Finally, whatever time and nature gradually add
to things, compelling them to grow in due measure,
no sharpness of vision, no matter how it strains, is able to see.
325　Moreover, neither when things age by the wasting of time,

nor when rocks overhanging the sea are eaten away by the devouring
salt are you able to see at the time what they are losing.
This is proof that nature conducts her business with invisible bodies.
But all things are not held packed tightly
together everywhere by the nature of body, for there is void in things.   330
Understanding this will be useful to you in many matters.
It will prevent you from wandering around, always doubting and seeking
after the nature of reality, and from lacking faith in my words.
Therefore there exists intangible space, void, and emptiness.
If void did not exist, there is no way things   335
would be able to move. For that which is the natural role[11] of body,
to roll in the way and obstruct, would be present at all times
for all things. Therefore nothing would be able
to move forward, because nothing would provide a beginning of yielding.
Yet now through the oceans and lands and the heights of heaven   340
we see before our eyes many things move by many
means and in various ways. If void did not exist,
these things would not only be deprived of and lack
restless motion, but would never have been brought to birth at all,
since everywhere matter would be still, packed tightly together.   345
Besides, however solid things might be thought to be,
nevertheless you may tell their bodies are loose-knit from this:
in rocks in caves the liquid moisture of water seeps
and trickles through, and everything weeps with plentiful drops.
Food is distributed into every part of an animal's body.   350
Trees grow and bear fruit at the proper time,
because food is distributed throughout all the parts of trees,
from the deepest roots, through the trunks, and throughout all the branches.
Voices travel through walls and fly across closed-off
rooms in houses, stiffening cold penetrates to the bone.   355
These things you would never see happen in any way
unless there were empty spaces through which individual bodies pass.
And next, why do we see that some things exceed
others in weight, although they are no different in size?
For if there is the same amount of body in a ball of wool   360
as there is in a ball of lead, it is fair to suppose they weigh
the same, since it is the role of body to press everything downward.
But in contrast it is the nature of the void to persist without weight.
Therefore whatever is equal in size but is observed to be lighter
without doubt shows that it possesses more void.   365
But in contrast the heavier thing declares that there is more body in it
and that it has within much less empty space.
Therefore it is certain that what we have been searching for with keen
reasoning, what we call void, exists, mixed in things.

11 "Role . . . roll" is an attempt to get at Lucretius' play on words with *officium* ("duty, function, job,
role") and *officere* ("to block, get in the way").

370　In order that what some assert in these matters not be able
　　　to lead you from the truth, I feel compelled to outstrip their argument.
　　　They say that water yields to scaly creatures as they strive
　　　and opens fluid paths, because fish leave spaces
　　　behind them where the waters as they yield are able to flow together.
375　So too they say that other things are able to move
　　　among themselves and change place, although all is full.
　　　This all has of course been accepted on false reasoning.
　　　For where can the scaly creatures go forward after all,
　　　if water does not give space? Furthermore where will the waves
380　be able to give place, when the fish will not be able to go?
　　　Therefore either all bodies must be deprived of motion,
　　　or it must be admitted that void is mixed in things, from which
　　　source each thing takes its first beginning of motion.
　　　Finally, if two broad bodies suddenly leap
385　apart from their union, it is of course necessary that air fill
　　　up all the void which is created between the bodies.
　　　Yet however fast the breezes circulate with which the air
　　　flows together, still the entire space would never be able
　　　to be filled up at one time. For the air must
390　occupy each space in succession, before all are occupied.
　　　But if someone by chance should happen to think that this occurs
　　　when the bodies leap apart because the air compresses itself,
　　　he errs. For then a vacuum is created which did not exist
　　　before and likewise a vacuum is filled which existed before,
395　nor is air able to be condensed in any such way
　　　nor, if it could, could it, I think, without void
　　　contract into itself and gather its parts into one.
　　　Wherefore although you delay by raising many objections,
　　　it is nevertheless necessary to admit that void is present in things.
400　And moreover by relating many arguments to you I am able
　　　to scrape together trust in these words of mine.
　　　But these little traces are enough for a keen intellect,
　　　and by their means you are able to discover the rest on your own.
　　　For just as dogs often find with their noses the resting places,
405　covered by foliage, of a wild beast that roams the mountains,
　　　as soon as they set to work on the sure traces of its path,
　　　so you yourself on your own will be able in such cases
　　　to see one thing from another and to work your way into every
　　　dark hiding place and drag back the truth from them.
410　But if you show hesitation or turn aside a little from your task,
　　　I am able to promise this clearly to you, Memmius:
　　　such large draughts from deep fountains will my sweet
　　　tongue pour out from my well-stocked mind
　　　that I am afraid that slow-moving old age will creep
415　through our limbs and dissolve the bonds of life in both of us
　　　before the whole abundant supply of arguments in my poem

on any particular point has been sent flying through your ears.
But now to return to weave in words what I have begun:
the nature of the universe, then, as it is in itself, is made
up of two things; for there are bodies and void. 420
Bodies are located in the void and move in it this way and that.
For ordinary perception declares by itself that body exists.
Unless trust in perception is firmly founded and flourishes,
in the case of hidden things there will be nothing to which we can refer
to prove anything at all with the reasoning power of the mind. 425
Then again if there were no place and space, which we call void,
bodies would never be able to have location nor to travel
at all in this way and that in any direction.
This is what I have already showed you a little while ago.[12]
In addition to this, there is nothing you are able to name which is distinct 430
and separated off apart from all body and the void,
which can be discovered to be some third type of nature.
For whatever will exist, this will have to be something itself.
Now if it will be subject to touch, no matter how light and tiny,
it will, by an increase either great or at least small, if it does exist, 435
increase the number of body and be part of the sum of the whole.
But if it will not be subject to touch, and is able from no side
to stop anything which is traveling from passing through it,
it will of course be what we call empty void.
In addition, whatever will exist by itself either will act on something 440
or will have to suffer other things acting upon it,
or will be such that things are able to exist and move in it.
But nothing is able to act or be acted upon without body,
nor again to provide place unless what is void and empty.
Therefore besides void and bodies there can remain by itself 445
among the number of things no third nature
that could come and make contact with our senses at any time
or that anyone might be able to grasp with the reasoning power of the mind.
For all things that have a name, either you will find that they are properties
of these two things or you will see that they are accidents of them. 450
A property is that which is never able to be disjoined
and separated off without a fatally harmful disintegration,
as weight is to rocks, heat to fire, fluidity is to water,
tangibility to all bodies, and intangibility to void.
Slavery, on the other hand, and poverty and wealth, 455
freedom, war, peace, and other things at whose
arrival and departure the nature of things remains unharmed,
we are accustomed to call, as is right, accidents.
Time likewise does not exist independently, but from things themselves
comes a sense of what has happened in ages past, then what 460
thing looms before us, and then further what will follow.

12 1.335–45, 370–83.

No one, it must be confessed, senses time through itself,
separated off from the motion and the quiet immobility of things.
Indeed when they say the daughter of Tyndareus[13] was raped and the Trojan
465   peoples were subdued in war, we must beware that they do not accidentally
force us to admit that these things exist on their own
just because an age which is past and can't be called back
took away these races of men, whose accidents these were.
For whatever will have happened will be able to be called an accident,
470   on the one hand of the lands, on the other of the regions of space themselves.
Indeed if there had been no material for things, nor place
and space, in which all things are carried out,
never would the fire, fanned by love for the beautiful shape
of Tyndareus' daughter, glistening in the Phrygian heart of Alexander,
475   have ignited the glowing contests of savage war,
nor unbeknownst to the Trojans would the wooden horse have set fire
to Pergama by giving birth to Greeks at night.
You can see, then, that absolutely all things that occur
never are nor exist through themselves as body does,
480   nor are they spoken of in the same sense as void is,
but rather so that you can rightly call them events
of body and place, in which all things are carried on.

[. . .]

Book II

Sweet it is, when the wind whips the water on the great sea,
to gaze from the land upon the great struggles of another,
5   not because it is a delightful pleasure for anyone to be distressed,
but because it is sweet to observe those evils which you lack yourself.
Sweet, too, to gaze upon the great contests of war
staged on the plains, when you are free from all danger.
But nothing is more delightful than to possess sanctuaries
10   which are lofty, peaceful, and well fortified by the teachings of the wise.
From there you can look down upon others and see them lose
their way here and there and wander, seeking a road through life,
struggling with their wits, striving with their high birth,
exerting themselves night and day with outstanding effort
to rise to the level of the greatest wealth and to have mastery over things.
O wretched minds of men, o blind hearts!
15   In what darkness of life and in what great dangers
this little span of time is spent! Don't you see
that nature cries out for nothing except that somehow
pain be separated and absent from the body, and that she enjoy in the mind
pleasant feelings, and be far from care and fear?

13 Helen of Troy.

Therefore we see that there is need for very little   20
for our bodily nature, just enough to take away pain
and also to spread out many delights before us;
nor does nature itself ever ask for anything more pleasing,
if there are no golden statues of youths in the halls,
holding fire-bearing torches in their right hands,   25
so illumination can be supplied for banquets at nighttime,[14]
if the house does not gleam with silver and shine with gold,
and if the gilded and paneled roof timbers do not resound with the lyre,
when nevertheless people lie in groups on the soft grass
beside a stream of water beneath the branches of a tall tree   30
and at little expense delightfully tend to their bodies,
especially when the weather smiles and the seasons of the year
sprinkle the green-growing grass with flowers.
Nor do hot fevers leave the body more quickly,
if you lie on embroidered cloth and blushing purple sheets,   35
than if you have to recuperate under common cloth.
Wherefore since neither wealth nor high birth nor the glory of ruling
do our body any good at all, so it remains,
that they cannot be thought to benefit our mind at all either.
Unless by chance when you see your legions seething about   40
on the Campus Martius[15] as they rouse pretend images of war,
well supported by reinforcements and a force of cavalry,
decked out in arms and all equally spirited,[16]
then these things chase fear-produced and frightened
religious superstitions from the mind, and fears of death   45
then leave your heart unoccupied and free from care.
But if we see that these things are ridiculous and frivolous,
and in truth the fears of men and the cares that follow them
neither fear the clash of arms nor fierce weapons,
and boldly walk among kings and those who have power over things,   50
and do not stand in awe of the gleam of gold
nor the shining brilliance of a purple-colored garment,
why do you doubt that all of this power belongs to reason,
especially since all life struggles in the darkness?
For just like children who tremble and fear everything   55
in the dark night, so we are afraid in the light sometimes
of things that ought to be no more feared than
the things that children tremble at and imagine will happen.
Therefore this fear and darkness of the mind must be shattered
apart not by the rays of the sun and the clear shafts   60
of the day but by the external appearance and inner law of nature.

---

14 Lines 24–6 echo Homer, *Odyssey* VII. 100–2.

15 The phrase *per loca campi*, literally "throughout the surface of the plain," probably refers to the Campus Martius ("Field of Mars"), a large field by the Tiber River in Rome that the Romans used for exercise and military practice.

16 There are textual difficulties with both lines 42 and 43.

Now come, I will explain with what motion the generating bodies
of matter generate different things, and destroy what has been generated,
and by what force they are compelled to do this, and what
65   velocity of voyaging through the vast void has been assigned to them.
You remember to give yourself over to my words.
For certainly matter does not cohere to itself close-packed,
since we see each thing decrease and observe all
things flowing away, so to speak, with the length of time,
70   and old age taking them away from our sight.
But nevertheless the sum of things is seen to remain safe,
because whatever bodies are lost from one thing
diminish what they depart, and increase that to which they have come.
They force the former to deteriorate, but the latter on the contrary to flourish,
75   nor do they remain there. So the sum of things is renewed
always, and mortal creatures live by mutual exchange.
Some races increase, others are diminished,
and in a short time the generations of living creatures change
and like runners pass on the torch of life.

[. . .]

Book III

From shadows so sheer you[17] were the first who was able to cast
such clear light and illuminate all that makes life worthwhile:
it is you I follow, O glory of the Greek race, and now
in the tracks you have laid down I fix my firm footprints,
5   not so much eager to compete with you, but because from love
I desire to imitate you. For why would a swallow contend with
swans, or what can young goats with their shaky legs
accomplish in a race to match the powerful energy of a horse?
You are our father, the discover of how things are, you supply us
10   with a father's precepts, and from your pages, o illustrious one,
just as bees sample everything in the flower-strewn meadow,
so we too feed upon all of your golden words,
golden they are, and always worthy of eternal life.
For as soon as your philosophy, sprung from your divine mind,
15   begins to give voice to the nature of things,
the mind's terrors dissipate, the walls of the world
dissolve, I see things carried along through the whole void.
The divinity of the gods appears, and their quiet dwelling-places,
which neither winds buffet nor clouds soak with violent
20   rains, nor does snow formed from biting frost, falling
white, disturb them, but an always cloudless atmosphere

17 Lucretius addresses Epicurus.

spreads over them and smiles with light diffused in all directions.[18]
Nature, moreover, supplies all their needs, nor does anything
nibble away at their peace of mind[19] at any time.
But in contrast, never do the regions of Acheron appear,[20]   25
nor does the earth prevent from being seen all the things
which are carried along through the void below beneath our feet.
Then, from these things a kind of divine rapture
and shivering awe seizes me, because in this way nature
by your power has been uncovered and laid open in all directions.   30
And since I have shown of what sort are the beginnings
of all things,[21] and how, differing in their various shapes,
they fly around on their own, stirred up by eternal motion,
and how from them all things are able to be created,
next after these things it appears that the nature of the mind   35
and soul[22] must now be made clear in my verses,
and the fear of Acheron must be thrown violently out the door.
This fear throws human life into deep and utter confusion,
staining everything with the black darkness of death,
and leaves no pleasure clear and pure.   40
For although people often assert that sickness and a bad reputation
are more to be feared than the infernal regions of death,
and that they know the nature of the mind is made up of blood,
or maybe of wind, if by chance they want it that way,
and further, that they have no need at all of our philosophy,   45
you can tell from the following that they proclaim all this to gain
praise rather than because the idea itself is thought to be true:
These same people, exiled from their country and banished far
from the sight of humans, befouled by some awful crime,
inflicted in short with every trouble, continue living,   50
and wherever these wretched people go they sacrifice to their ancestors,
and slaughter black cattle and send down offerings
to the shades below, and in intense situations turn
their minds much more intensely to religion.
Wherefore it is more effective to gauge a person in times   55
of doubt and danger, and to learn what they are like in adversity.
For then at last real voices are extracted from the bottom
of the heart and the mask is ripped off: reality remains.
So too, greed and blind burning after elected office,
which coerce wretched people to go beyond the boundaries   60
of what is right, and at times as allies in crime and accomplices

18 Lucretius' description of the residences of the gods are based on Homer, *Odyssey* VI. 42–6.
19 "Peace of mind" is a translation of *animi pacem*, the Latin translation of the Greek *ataraxia*, the goal
of Epicurean philosophy.
20 "Regions of Acheron" = "hell." Acheron was one of the rivers of hell.
21 "Beginnings of all things" = atoms.
22 "Mind" = *mens*, "soul" = *anima*. Lucretius distinguishes the mind and the soul in his account.

they exert themselves night and day with outstanding effort
to rise to the level of the greatest wealth – these lacerations of life
are nourished in no small way by the fear of death.

65   For low social standing and bitter poverty nearly always
seem to be far removed from a calm and pleasant life,
and to be a kind of loitering, so to speak, before the gates of death.
This is why people, attacked by false fears,
desiring to escape far away and to withdraw themselves far away,

70   amass wealth through civil bloodshed and in their greed double
their riches, piling up slaughter on slaughter.
Unmercifully they rejoice in the sad death of a brother
and they disdain and fear eating with their relatives.[23]
In a similar way, often as a result of the same fear,

75   envy taunts them that before their very eyes he is powerful,
he is the center of attention, who parades in official glory,[24]
while they whine that they themselves are mired in obscurity.
Some perish to acquire a statue or good name.
And often through fear of death such a great hatred of life

80   and of seeing the light grabs hold of human beings,
that they inflict death on themselves with a sad heart,
forgetting that this fear is the source of their cares.
It convinces one to abuse honor, another to burst
the ties of friendship, and in short to abandon responsible conduct.[25]

85   For these days people often betray their country
and dear parents, trying to escape the regions of Acheron.
For just like children who tremble and fear everything
in the dark night, so we are afraid in the light sometimes
of things that ought to be no more feared than

90   the things that children tremble at and imagine will happen.
Therefore this fear and darkness of the mind must be shattered
apart not by the rays of the sun and the clear shafts
of the day but by the external appearance and inner law of nature.

[...]

And the mind is better at keeping the doors of life locked
and a better master over life than the power of the soul is.
For without the intelligence and mind no part of the soul
can reside in the limbs for even a tiny part of time,

400   but follows easily as its companion and departs into the breezes,
and leaves the chilly limbs in the coolness of death.
But a person remains in life whose intelligence and mind remains.
However lacerated the trunk is, with its limbs cut off all around,

23 i.e., they are afraid of being poisoned.
24 The reference in "official glory" is to the dress of Roman magistrates.
25 "Responsible conduct" = *pietas*, a key Roman virtue, which meant something like "the care and duty one owed to one's parents, family, friends, and state."

although the soul has been snatched off and removed from the limbs,
the person lives on and takes in life-sustaining ethereal breezes.   405
But if not the entire soul, but a great part of it, has been taken
from a person, still he remains alive and hangs on.
It is just as when the eye has been lacerated all over: if the pupil remains
uninjured, the living power of sight stands firm,
provided only that you do not destroy the whole orb of the eye,   410
cutting around the pupil and leaving it all alone:
for this also could not occur without the destruction of both.[26]
But if this tiny middle part of the eye is eaten away,
its light immediately sets and darkness falls,
although the shining orb is not otherwise injured.   415
In such an arrangement the soul and mind are bound forever.
Now come, so that you might learn that the minds and light souls
of living creatures are born and subject to death,
I will proceed to set out my poem, sought for so long
and discovered with such sweet labor, so as to be worthy of your way of life.   420
You, take care to link both of these[27] with one name,
and when I go on to mention, for example, the soul,
showing that it is mortal, understand that I also mean the mind,
inasmuch as it is a single unit and an interconnected entity.

[. . .]

Death is nothing to us nor does it concern us at all,[28]   830
inasmuch as the nature of the mind has been shown to be mortal.
And just as in time gone by we felt no distress
at the Carthaginians rushing from all sides to attack[29]
when all things were shattered by the tremendous tumult of war,
shuddering and rocking beneath the lofty regions of the sky,   835
and were in doubt as to which of the two[30] it must fall
to rule over all peoples on both land and sea,
so too, when we will no longer exist, when there will be a destruction
of the body and soul from which we have been joined together,
surely nothing at all will be able to happen to us,   840
who will not exist then, nor move our senses,
not even if the earth be mixed with the sea, and the sea with the sky.
And even if the nature of the mind and power of the soul
have feeling after they have been dragged out of our body,

26 "Both" = the pupil and rest of the eye.
27 "Both of these" = the mind and soul.
28 Lucretius here begins the third and final section of Book III with a Latin translation of Epicurus'
famous saying, "Death is nothing to us." See Epicurus, *Letter to Menoeceus* 124–7 and *Principal Doctrine* 2.
29 Lucretius here describes Hannibal's invasion of Italy during the Second Punic War (219–202 BC).
He is apparently adapting a famous passage from the Roman epic poet Ennius.
30 i.e., to either the Romans or Carthaginians.

845   still this is nothing to us, who consist of the conjunction and connection
of body and soul joined tightly together as one.
Nor, if passing time should collect our matter
after death and restore it again as it is now situated
and for a second time the light of life be given to us,

850   would it still matter at all to us even if this happened,
when once the memory of ourselves has been broken apart.
And even now it makes no difference to us about who we were
before, nor does pain from those former selves affect us now.
For when you look back at the whole past extent

855   of boundless time, and then at how various are
the motions of matter, you could easily come to believe this,
that these same seeds out of which we are now made
have been arranged before in the same order as they are now.
Nor nevertheless can we recover this with our remembering mind,

860   because a break in existence has been interposed and far and wide
all the motions have wandered off all over from the senses.
For if by chance someone is going to do badly and suffer
in the future, the person who could do poorly must exist at that
time too. Since death precludes this, and prevents

865   the existence of him for whom these troubles could be assembled,
we may know that there is nothing for us to fear in death,
nor can a person who does not exist become miserable nor at all
does it matter whether he now will have been born at any time,
when immortal death takes away mortal life.

870   And so when you see a person getting angry that
after death it will happen that either he will rot once his body is buried,
or that he will be finished by flames or the jaws of fierce beasts,
you may know he does not ring true and that there exists beneath the surface
some invisible goad in his mind, however much he himself denies

875   that he believes that he will possess any sort of sensation in death.
For he does not, I think, grant what he professes nor its premises,[31]
nor does he root himself up and throw himself out of life,
but he makes something of himself survive without realizing it.
For when each person while still alive imagines what will happen

880   when birds and wild beasts tear his body apart in death,
he himself takes pity on himself – for he does not separate himself from it,[32]
nor does he sufficiently remove himself from the cast-out corpse and
he imagines that it is him and he infects it with his own feelings as he stands by.
This is why he gets angry that he has been made mortal

885   and he does not see that in real death there will be no other self
who will be alive and able to grieve for himself now bereft of himself,
and who standing can weep for himself lying there as he is mangled or burnt.

---

31 "What he professes" = that he will not have sensation after death; "its premises" = that the soul
perishes with the body.
32 i.e., from his corpse.

For if in death it is a disaster to be shredded by the jaws and teeth
of wild animals, I do not understand why it is not awful
to be placed on the fire and begin to burn over hot flames,   890
or to be placed in honey and be suffocated and to grow rigid
frigidly, resting on the smooth surface of ice-cold rock,
or to be flattened from above, ground down by the weight of the earth.
"Now, now never again will your joyful home or wonderful
wife receive you, nor will your sweet children   895
race to snatch kisses and touch your heart with silent sweetness.
Nor will you be able to provide protection for your flourishing affairs
and those close to you. Miserably for miserable you," they say,
"one awful day takes away all the many prizes of life."
On this topic they do not add this: "Nor does a desire   900
for these things then any longer weigh upon you."
If they kept this clearly in mind and followed it out in words,
they would free themselves from great mental anguish and fear.
"Yes you, just as you are now asleep in death, so you will
be for what remains of time, freed from all bitter sorrows.   905
But we nearby have wept inconsolably for you turned to
ashes on the horrifying pyre, and no day will
come to remove eternal grief from our hearts."
Then we must inquire of this man the following: What
is so bitter, if it all comes down to sleep and repose,   910
that someone could waste away in eternal grief?
Thus, indeed, people often act when they recline at table
and hold their glasses and shade their brows with garlands,
as they say from their hearts, "Such enjoyment is fleeting for poor mortals.
Soon it will be over, and it will never be recoverable later."   915
As if in death this will be the foremost of their troubles,
that parching thirst should burn and scorch the miserable creatures,
or that longing for some other thing should settle on them.
For no one misses himself or his life,
when both his mind and body equally rest in sleep.   920
For all we care, sleep could be everlasting on these
terms, and no longing for ourselves affects us.
And yet those first bodies then do not stray
very far at all from the motions that bring sensation,
when a person is roused from sleep and pulls himself together.   925
Therefore we should think that death is much less to us,
if anything can be less than what we see is nothing.
For a greater turmoil and disruption of matter occurs
at death and no one wakes up and gets up
whom the cold break in existence has once overtaken.   930
And next suppose that the nature of things should suddenly raise
her voice and herself thus scold anyone of us about this:
"What is so troublesome to you, o mortal, that you indulge too much in
anxious lamentations? Why do you groan and bewail death?

935 For if your past and former life was pleasing to you
and all its blessings have not flowed out and perished
thanklessly, as if they were gathered in a vessel full of holes,
why do you not depart like a banqueter who is sated with life,
and embrace untroubled quiet with a calm mind, you fool?

940 But if those things which you enjoyed have been poured out and perished,
and life is hateful, why do you seek to add more,
which again will perish badly and pass away thanklessly?
Why not rather put an end to life and trouble?[33]
Moreover, there is nothing I can devise and invent for you

945 which will please you: all things are always the same.
Even if your body is not yet withered nor your limbs
worn and feeble, still all things remain the same,
even if you proceed to conquer all ages
by living, and even more, if you never are going to die."

950 What do we respond, except that nature is setting out
a just charge and with her words is pleading a true case?
But if now someone older and more advanced in years should complain
and wretchedly lament his death more than is right, would she not
call out even more deservedly and protest with a sharp voice?

955 "Get your tears out of here, you ingrate, and cease your complaints.
You have enjoyed all the prizes of life and are withering away.
But since you always want what is absent, and despise what is present,
your life has slipped away, incomplete and unsatisfying,
and death has unexpectedly taken his stand by your head

960 before you could depart satisfied and full of good things.
But now give up everything not suited to your age, and with a calm
mind yield to your years – come on! – it must happen."[34]
Justly she would plead, I think, and justly rebuke and reprove.
For old things, pushed out by new things, always

965 yield, and one thing must always be built up out of others.
Nothing is handed over to the underworld and black Tartarus.
Matter is needed so that later generations may grow, and yet they all,
once they have finished their life, will follow you, and so no less
than you have they passed away before now, and will pass away.

970 Thus one thing will never stop arising from another,
and life is a permanent possession of no one, but on loan to all.
Consider likewise how the vast expanse of time
gone by before we were born has been nothing to us.
Therefore nature holds this up for us as a mirror

975 of future time after our death finally comes.
Does anything appear frightening in this, does anything seem

33 Epicurus had taken a generally dim view of suicide, believing that the true Epicurean should almost always be able to find more pleasure in life than pain. He did allow suicide as an option, however, in extreme cases.

34 There is a textual problem with this line.

distressing, isn't it more calming than any sleep?
And certainly these things which are said to exist
in the depths of Acheron are all present in this life of ours.
There is no wretched Tantalus who, as the story goes, is numbed   980
by empty terror and fears the boulder hanging in the air;
rather it is in this life that empty fear of the gods crushes
mortals, who fear the fall chance furnishes for each.
Neither is there a Tityos lying in Acheron whom birds
root around in nor at all are they able to keep finding   985
something in his huge chest to probe forever.
However much he stretches out with the vast projection
of his body – say he not only covers nine acres
with his extended limbs, but the circle of the entire world –
still he will not be able to endure eternal pain,   990
nor provide food from his own body forever.
But Tityos is here among us, and winged creatures[35]
tear at him as he lies in love, and anxious anguish consumes him,
or cares carve him up with some other desire.
Sisyphus, too, is here in life before our eyes,   995
he who thirsts to seek the rods and awesome axes[36]
from the people and always goes away defeated and dejected.
For to seek power, which is empty and never really attained,
and always to undergo harsh labors in the process,
this is to struggle to push up the face of a mountain   1000
a stone which rolls still yet again from the highest summit
and rapidly seeks the level areas of the even plain.[37]
Next, always to feed the insatiable nature of the mind
and to fill it with good things and never satisfy it,
as the seasons of the year do for us, when they return   1005
round and bear their produce and various delights,
and yet we are never filled with the fruits of life,
this, I think, is what people recall: that girls,[38] in the flower
of their age, gather liquid into a vessel full of holes
which yet is unable to be filled in any way at all.   1010
Cerberus and the Furies, moreover, and the absence of light,
Tartarus belching forth terrifying heat,
these neither exist anywhere nor can they exist at all.
But in this life there exists remarkable fear of punishment
for remarkable misdeeds, and paying the price of crime,   1015

35 The Latin word translated "winged creature" (*volucres*) is the same word Lucretius uses in 984 to name the birds eating Tityos. The winged creatures that attack contemporary Tityoses here on earth are not birds, though, but the *Erotes*, or winged Cupids.
36 The rods (*fasces*) and axes (*secures*) were symbols of power for Roman elected officials.
37 Lucretius again plays on words: just as the rock seeks the level areas of the even plain (*campi*), so the unsuccessful candidate returns to the Campus Martius in Rome to try again for election.
38 The girls are the Danaids, condemned to try to gather water in sieves forever.

prison and a horrible casting down from the rock,[39]
whippings, executioners, the rack, pitch, hot-plates, torches.
And even if these are absent, still the mind, aware of its misdeeds,
fears in anticipation and goads and stings itself with whips,
1020 and fails to see meanwhile what the limit of its troubles
can be and what the end of its punishments will be at last,
and it fears that these same things will grow even greater in death.
The life of fools at last becomes hell here on earth.
This too you might tell yourself sometimes:
1025 "Even good Ancus left the light of day behind with his eyes,[40]
and he was much better in many ways than you, you reprobate.
Since then, many other kings and those who have power
over things have died, who governed great peoples.
And even that man himself, who once built a road
1030 across the great sea,[41] and let his legions go on a journey over the deep,
and taught his infantry to go over the salt waters,
and with his cavalry spurned and pranced upon waves' crashing, even he
saw the light slip away and poured out his soul from his dying body.
The descendant of the Scipios,[42] thunderbolt of war, terror of Carthage,
1035 gave his bones to the earth just as if he had been an ordinary household
slave. Add the discoverers of the sciences and the arts.
Add the companions of the daughters of Helicon,[43] over whom Homer had singular
supremacy, though even he went to sleep with the same repose as the others.
Next, after ripe old age warned Democritus
1040 that the motions of memory in his mind were slowing down,
he himself voluntarily directed his life in the direction of death.
Epicurus[44] himself died when the light of his life ran its course,
he who surpassed the human race in intellect and overwhelmed
everyone else, as the ethereal sun does the stars when it has risen.
1045 Will you then really be hesitant and angry at dying?
Life is even now almost dead to you while you are alive and alert,
you who waste the greater part of your years in sleep
and snore wide awake and never stop seeing dreams
and possess a mind plagued by empty fear, and who are unable

---

39 Lucretius refers to Roman forms of torture. With the word "prison" (*carcer*) Lucretius probably refers to the state prison located near the Roman Forum. The rock (*saxum*) refers to the Tarpeian Rock, a spot in Rome from which criminals were thrown.

40 In this line Lucretius is quoting the Roman poet Ennius. Ancus was the fourth king of Rome, regularly called "good."

41 Lucretius here describes the Persian King Xerxes' bridging of the Hellespont in 480 BC when he was leading an expedition against the Greeks.

42 "The descendant of the Scipios" is probably a reference to Scipio Africanus the Elder, who defeated the Carthaginian general Hannibal at Zama in 202 BC during the Second Punic War. The phrase could also apply, however, to Scipio Aemilianus Africanus the Younger, who defeated Carthage decisively in 146 BC in the Third Punic War.

43 The daughters of Helicon are the Muses.

44 This is the only place in the poem where Lucretius mentions Epicurus by name.

often to discover what the matter is with yourself, when in a drunken   1050
haze, you wretch, you are everywhere oppressed by many cares,
drifting and wandering with aimless missteps of the mind."
If people were able, just as they are seen to sense
that there is a weight on their minds because it wears them out by its heaviness,
to understand from what causes each thing happens   1055
and from what source such a mound of misery exists in their hearts,
not at all would they lead their lives as we now usually see them,
each not knowing what he wants for himself, and always seeking
to change location, as if he could put down his burden.
The man who is sick and tired of his home   1060
often leaves his mansion, and then suddenly returns,
since he feels things are not at all better outdoors.
Driving his imported ponies he races to his country villa
at top speed, as if rushing to bring help to a house on fire.
He immediately starts yawning when he touches the threshold of his villa,   1065
or goes off into a heavy sleep and just tries to forget,
or dashing off again he seeks to return to the city.
Thus each person flees himself, but he cannot, of course,
escape the one he flees, but clings to him unwillingly and hates him
because he is sick and does not understand the cause of his disease.   1070
If he understood this well, each would now drop other things
and be eager above all to understand the nature of things,
since what is at stake is the state of all time to come,
not just of one hour, the state in which mortals must
remain for the whole period which remains after death.   1075
Moreover, what destructive desire of life is so great
that it forces us to shake anxiously in times of doubt and danger?
Assuredly there is an unalterable limit of life for mortals,
and it is impossible for us to avoid death and not pass away.
Besides, we are involved and live always among the same things,   1080
and no new pleasure is ever hammered out by living.
But while what we desire is absent, it seems to surpass other things.
Afterwards, having attained this, we desire something else and the same
thirst for life holds us, our mouths always agape.
What fortune the years to come may bring us is uncertain,   1085
or what chance may bear us, or what end awaits us.
And by extending our life we will not subtract one jot at all
from the time we will be dead, nor can we take away anything
so that by chance we might be able to be dead for less long.
Accordingly, grant that you complete as many ages as you wish by living,   1090
still no less at all will everlasting death await you,
nor will he who makes an end to his life from today's light
not exist from that moment any less than he,
who passed away many months and years before.

Part VII

Stoics and Stoicism

Introduction

Both Stoicism and Skepticism (to which we turn in part VIII of this book) came out of developments within Plato's Academy after his death in 347/6 BCE. Plato's first successor in the Academy was Speucippus (c.410–339 BCE), followed by Xenocrates (396–314 BCE), and then Polemo (c.355–276/5 BCE), who held the position for over 40 years. During his lengthy tenure, Polemo trained two men who became founders of their own very influential schools of philosophy, Arcesilaus (316/15–241/40 BCE), who founded the school known as the Skeptics within the Academy itself and later became its head, and Zeno of Citium on Cyprus (c.334/3–262/1 BCE), who founded a rival school in the Stoics, who became at least as influential in the ancient world as the Platonists.

Zeno is said to have offered his teachings in the Stoa Poecile (the "Painted Porch" of the Athenian Agora) – hence, the name "Stoics." Zeno's successors were Cleanthes of Assos (c.302–230 BCE), followed by Chrysippus of Soli (c.280–207 BCE). These three together are known as the leaders of the Old Stoa. Then followed those counted as the Middle Stoa, including especially Panaetius of Rhodes (c.185–109 BCE) and Posidonius of Apamea (c.135–c.51 BCE), and then those of the Late Stoa, who included Seneca (c.50–130 CE), Musonius Rufus (c.30–100 CE), Epictetus (c.50–130 CE), and Marcus Aurelius (121–80 CE). These three phases of Stoicism recognized some shifting in various positions, but nonetheless persisted with significant coherence in the basic doctrines of the philosophical movement. Given the nature of this collection, the following selections will emphasize this coherence rather than the less significant disputes within the school.

The most basic view presented in Stoicism is that human beings should "live in agreement with nature." In some sense, this same claim could easily have been made by Plato or Aristotle – and indeed by the Epicureans. But the Stoics' conception of nature was very different from these others, and accordingly, so was the ethics that derived from the idea of living in accordance with nature. Like the Epicureans, the Stoics were materialists, believing that nature consisted only of three-dimensional bodies interacting with each other. Thus, they rejected the Platonist conception of the real as consisting of incorporeal realities (Plato's Forms), and also Aristotle's understanding of nature as in some way depending upon the incorporeal (Formal and Final Causes, as well as the categories). For the Stoics, incorporeals such as space, time, void, and predicables or meanings of terms and propositions, were real – but only as subsisting in material things, and hence as completely dependent upon corporeal entities. To become wise, then, for a Stoic, was to come to comprehend the structure and arrangement of corporeal nature, all of which they regarded as necessary and immutable. Hence, the Stoics were hard determinists.

Stoic logic, then, is the study of the rational structure of nature, and what rules of reasoning can be deduced from the immutable and necessary laws of nature. Stoic ethics, recognizing the necessity of nature, seeks the most orderly adjustment of one's own psychology to the way the world actually is, and always will be – as it *must* be. As a later critic put it, Stoic ethics can be represented by the example of a dog tied to a wagon. If the wagon moves and the dog wishes to follow, the dog does well, for what is in his power (the adjustment of his own psychological reactions to accord with the uncontrollable forces of nature) and necessity are aligned. But if the dog wishes not to follow, he will be dragged along by the cart anyway. The Stoic Sage, therefore, aligns his will to the necessities of nature and wills all and only what will occur anyway, independent of his will. This is why the Stoic Sage will feel neither pity nor remorse – for both are examples of wishing that what happened of necessity should not happen, or should not have happened.

27

Diogenes Laertius on Stoicism

The following fragments are selected from Diogenes Laertius' *Lives and Opinions of Eminent Philosophers* [DL] VII, which begins with a review of the life of Zeno, but then goes on to provide the best summary that has come down to us of Stoic philosophy generally. As Diogenes puts it, "I have decided to give a general account of all the Stoic doctrines in the life of Zeno because he is the founder of the School" (DL VII.38). For the purposes of this collection, I have included selections from the section on ethics and the section on physical doctrines.

Part I   Ethical Doctrines

84. The ethical branch of philosophy [the Stoics] divide as follows: (1) the topic of impulse; (2) the topic of things good and evil; (3) that of the passions; (4) that of virtue; (5) that of the end; (6) that of primary value and of actions; (7) that of duties or the befitting; and (8) of inducements to act or refrain from acting. [. . .]

85. An animal's first impulse, say the Stoics, is to self-preservation, because nature from the outset endears it to itself, as Chrysippus affirms in the first book of his work *On Ends*: his words are, "The dearest thing to every animal is its own constitution and its consciousness thereof"; for it was not likely that nature should estrange the living thing from itself or that she should leave the creature she has made without either estrangement from or affection for its own constitution. We are forced then to conclude that nature in constituting the animal made it near and dear to itself; for so it comes to repel all that is injurious and give free access to all that is serviceable or akin to it.

As for the assertion made by some people that pleasure is the object to which the first impulse of animals is directed, it is shown by the Stoics to be false.

86. For pleasure, if it is really felt, they declare to be a by-product, which never comes until nature by itself has sought and found the means suitable to the animal's existence or constitution; it is an aftermath comparable to the condition of animals thriving and plants in full bloom. And nature, they say, made no difference originally between plants and animals, for she regulates the life of plants too, in their case without impulse and sensation, just as also certain processes go on of a vegetative kind in us. But when in the case of animals

impulse has been superadded, whereby they are enabled to go in quest of their proper aliment, for them, say the Stoics, Nature's rule is to follow the direction of impulse. But when reason by way of a more perfect leadership has been bestowed on the beings we call rational, for them life according to reason rightly becomes the natural life. For reason supervenes to shape impulse scientifically.

87. This is why Zeno was the first (in his treatise *On the Nature of Man*) to designate as the end "life in agreement with nature" (or living agreeably to nature), which is the same as a virtuous life, virtue being the goal towards which nature guides us. So too Cleanthes in his treatise *On Pleasure* [. . .] Again, living virtuously is equivalent to living in accordance with experience of the actual course of nature, as Chrysippus says in the first book of his *De finibus*; for our individual natures are parts of the nature of the whole universe.

88. And this is why the end may be defined as life in accordance with nature, or, in other words, in accordance with our own human nature as well as that of the universe, a life in which we refrain from every action forbidden by the law common to all things, that is to say, the right reason which pervades all things, and is identical with this Zeus, lord and ruler of all that is. And this very thing constitutes the virtue of the happy man and the smooth current of life, when all actions promote the harmony of the spirit dwelling in the individual man with the will of him who orders the universe. Diogenes then expressly declares the end to be to act with good reason in the selection of what is natural. Archedemus says the end is to live in the performance of all befitting actions.

89. By the nature with which our life ought to be in accord, Chrysippus understands both universal nature and more particularly the nature of man, whereas Cleanthes takes the nature of the universe alone as that which should be followed, without adding the nature of the individual.

And virtue, he holds, is harmonious disposition, choice-worthy for its own sake and not from hope or fear or any external motive. Moreover, it is in virtue that happiness consists; for virtue is the state of mind which tends to make the whole of life harmonious. When a rational being is perverted, this is due to the deceptiveness of external pursuits or sometimes to the influence of associates. For the starting-points of nature are never perverse. [. . .]

94. Good in general is that from which some advantage comes, and more particularly what is either identical with or not distinct from benefit. From this it follows that virtue itself and whatever partakes of virtue is called good in these three senses – namely, as being (1) the source from which all benefit results; or (2) that in respect of which benefit results, e.g., the virtuous act; or (3) that by the agency of which benefit results, e.g., the good man who partakes in virtue.

Another particular definition of good which they give is "the natural perfection of a natural being *qua* rational." To this answers virtue and, as being partakers in virtue, virtuous acts and good men; as also its supervening accessories, joy and gladness and the like.

95. So with evils: either they are vices, folly, cowardice, injustice, and the like; or things which partake of vice, including vicious acts and wicked persons as well as their accompaniments, despair, moroseness, and the like.

Again, some goods are goods of the mind and others external, while some are neither mental nor external. The former include the virtues and virtuous acts; external goods are such as having a good country or a good friend, and the prosperity of such. Whereas to be good and happy oneself is of the class of goods neither mental nor external.

96. Similarly of things evil some are mental evils, namely, vices and vicious actions; others are outward evils, as to have a foolish country or a foolish friend and the unhappiness

of such; other evils again are neither mental nor outward, e.g. to be yourself bad and unhappy . . .

97. The virtues (they say) are goods of the nature at once of ends and of means. On the one hand, in so far as they cause happiness they are means, and on the other hand, in so far as they make it complete, and so are themselves part of it, they are ends. Similarly of evils some are of the nature of ends and some of means, while others are at once both means and ends. Your enemy and the harm he does you are means; consternation, abasement, slavery, gloom, despair, excess of grief, and every vicious action are of the nature of ends. Vices are evils both as ends and as means, since in so far as they cause misery they are means, but in so far as they make it complete, so that they become part of it, they are ends. [. . .]

101. And they say that only the morally beautiful is good. [. . .] They hold, that is that virtue and whatever partakes of virtue consists in this; which is equivalent to saying that all that is good is beautiful, or that the term "good" has equal force with the term "beautiful," which comes to the same thing. "Since a thing is good, it is beautiful; now it is beautiful, therefore it is good." They hold that all goods are equal and that all good is desirable in the highest degree and admits of no lowering or heightening of intensity. Of things that are, some, they say, are good, some are evil, and some neither good nor evil (that is, morally indifferent).

102. Goods comprised the virtues of prudence, justice, courage, temperance, and the rest; while the opposites of these are evil, namely folly, injustice, and the rest. Neutral (neither good nor evil, that is) are all those things which neither benefit nor harm a man: such as life, health, pleasure, beauty, strength, wealth, fair fame and noble birth, and their opposites, death disease, pain ugliness, weakness, poverty, ignominy, low birth, and the like. [. . .]

103. For, say they, such things (as life, health, and pleasure) are not in themselves goods, but are morally indifferent, though falling under the species or subdivision "things preferred." For as the property of hot is to warm, not to cool, so the property of good is to benefit, not to injure; but wealth and health do no more benefit than injury, therefore neither wealth nor health is good. Further, they say that that is not good of which both good and bad use can be made; but of wealth and health both good and bad use can be made; therefore wealth and health are not goods. [. . .]

Chrysippus in his work *On Pleasure*, den[ies] that pleasure is a good [. . .]; for some pleasures are disgraceful, and nothing disgraceful is good.

104. To benefit is to set in motion or sustain in accordance with virtue; whereas to harm is to set in motion or sustain in accordance with vice.

The term "indifferent" has two meanings: in the first it denotes the things which do not contribute either to happiness or to misery, as wealth, fame, health, strength, and the like; for it is possible to be happy without having these, although, if they are used in a certain way, such use of them tends to happiness or misery. In quite another sense those things are said to be indifferent which are without the power of stirring inclination or aversion; e.g. the fact that the number of hairs on one's head is odd or even or whether you hold out your finger straight or bent. But it was not in this sense that the things mentioned above were termed indifferent, they being quite capable of exciting inclination or aversion.

105. Hence of these latter some are taken by preference, others are rejected, whereas indifference in the other sense affords no ground for either choosing or avoiding.

Of things indifferent, as they express it, some are "preferred" others "rejected." Such as have value, they say, are "preferred," while such as have negative, instead of positive, value are "rejected." Value they define as, first, any contribution to harmonious living, such as attaches to every good; secondly, some faculty or use which indirectly contributes to the life according to nature: which is as much as to say "any assistance brought by wealth or health towards living a natural life"; thirdly, value is the full equivalent of an appraiser, as fixed by an expert acquainted with the facts. [. . .]

106. Thus things of the preferred class are those which have positive value, e.g. amongst mental qualities, natural ability, skill, moral improvement, and the like; among bodily qualities, life, health, strength, good condition, soundness of organs, beauty, and so forth; and in the sphere of external things, wealth, fame, noble birth, and the like. To the class of things "rejected" belong, of mental qualities, lack of ability, want of skill, and the like; among bodily qualities, death, disease, weakness, being out of condition, mutilation, ugliness, and the like; in the sphere of external things, poverty, ignominy, low birth, and so forth. But again there are things belonging to neither class; such as not preferred, neither are they rejected. [. . .]

111. The main or most universal emotions [. . .] constitute four great classes, grief, fear, desire or craving, pleasure. They hold the emotions to be judgments, as is stated by Chrysippus in his treatise *On The Passions*: avarice being a supposition that money is a good, while the case is similar with that money is a good, while the case is similar with drunkenness and profligacy and all the other emotions.

And grief or pain they hold to be an irrational mental contraction. Its species are pity, envy, jealousy, rivalry, heaviness, annoyance, distress, anguish, distraction. Pity is grief felt at undeserved suffering; envy, grief at others' prosperity; jealousy, grief at the possession by another of that which one desires for oneself; rivalry, pain at the possession by another of what one has oneself. [. . .]

113. Desire or craving is irrational appetency, and under it are ranged the following states: want, hatred, contentiousness, anger, love, wrath, resentment. [. . .] Hatred is a growing and lasting desire or craving that it should go ill with somebody [. . .]; anger a craving or desire to punish one who is thought to have done you an undeserved injury. The passion of love is a craving from which good men are free; for it is an effort to win affection due to the visible presence of beauty.

115. And as there are said to be certain infirmities in the body, as for instant gout and arthritic disorders, so too there is in the soul love of fame, love of pleasure, and the like. By infirmity is meant disease accompanied by weakness; and by disease is meant a fond imagining of something that seems desirable. And as in the body there are tendencies to certain maladies such as colds and diarrhoea, so it is with the soul, there are tendencies like enviousness, pitifulness, quarrelsomeness, and the like. . . .

117. Now they say that the wise man is passionless, because he is not prone to fall into such infirmity. But they add that in another sense the term apathy is applied to the bad man, when, that is, it means that he is callous and relentless. Further, the wise man is said to be free from vanity; for he is indifferent to good or evil report. However, he is not alone in this, there being another who is also free from vanity, he who is ranged among the rash, and that is the bad man. Again, they tell us that all good men are austere or harsh, because they neither have dealings with pleasure themselves nor tolerate those who have. The term harsh is applied, however, to others as well, and in much the same sense as a wine is said to be harsh when it is employed medicinally and not for drinking at all.

118. Again, the goods are genuinely in earnest and vigilant for their own improvement, using a manner of life which banishes evil out of sight and makes what good there is in things appear. At the same time they are free from pretence; for they have stripped off all pretence or "make-up" whether in voice or in look. Free too are they from all business cares, declining to do anything which conflicts with duty. They will take wine, but not get drunk. [. . . .]

Nor indeed will the wise man ever feel grief; seeing that grief is irrational contraction of the soul, as Apollodorus says in his *Ethics*.

119. They are also, it is declared, godlike; for they have a something divine within them; whereas the bad man is godless. And yet of this word – godless or ungodly – there are two senses, one in which it is the opposite of the term "godly," the other denoting the man who ignores the divine altogether: in this latter sense, as they note, the term does not apply to every bad man. The good, it is added are also worshippers of God; for they have acquaintance with the rites of the gods, and piety is the knowledge of how to serve the gods. Further, they will sacrifice to the gods and they keep themselves pure; for they avoid all acts that are offences against the gods, and the goods think highly of them: for they are holy and just in what concerns the gods. The wise too are the only priests; for they have made sacrifices their study, as also the building of temples purifications and all the other matters appertaining to the gods.

120. The Stoics approve also of honouring parents and brothers in the second place after the gods. They further maintain that parental affection for children is natural in the good, but not to the bad. [. . .]

121. Again, the Stoics say that the wise man will take part in politics, if nothing hinders him [. . .] since thus he will restrain vice and promote virtue. Also (they maintain) he will marry [. . .] and beget children. Moreover, they say that the wise man will never form mere opinions, that is to say, he will never give assent to anything that is false [. . .]

They declare that he alone is free and bad men are slaves, freedom being power of independent action, whereas slavery is privation of the same. [. . .]

125. They hold that the virtues involve one another, and that the possessor of one is the possessor of all, inasmuch as they have common principles. [. . .]

126. For if a man be possessed of virtue, he is at once able to discover and to put into practice what he ought to do. Now such rules of conduct comprise rules for choosing, enduring, staying, and distributing; so that if a man does some things by intelligent choice, some things with fortitude, some thing by way of just distribution, and some steadily, he is at once wise, courageous, just, and temperate. And each of the virtues has a particular subject with which it deals, as for instance, courage is concerned with things that must be endured, practical wisdom with acts to be done, acts from which one must abstain, and those which fall under neither head. Similarly each of the other virtues is concerned with its own proper sphere. To wisdom are subordinate good counsel and understanding; to temperance, good discipline and orderliness; to justice, equality and fair-mindedness; to courage, constancy and vigour.

127. It is a tenet of theirs that between virtue and vice that there is nothing intermediate, whereas according to the Peripatetics there is, namely, the state of moral improvement. For, say the Stoics, just as a stick must be either straight or crooked, so a man must be either just or unjust. Nor again are there degrees of justice and injustice; and the same rule applies to the other virtues. Further, while Chrysippus holds that virtue can be lost, Cleanthes maintains that it cannot. According to the former it may be lost in consequence of drunkenness or melancholy; the latter takes it to be inalienable owing to the certainty of our mental apprehension. And virtue in itself they hold to be worthy of choice for its own sake. At all events we are ashamed of bad conduct as if we knew that nothing is really good but the morally beautiful. Moreover, they hold that it is in itself sufficient to ensure well-being. [. . .]

128. Another tenet of theirs is the perpetual exercise of virtue, as held by Cleanthes and his followers. For virtue can never be lost, and the good man is always exercising his mind, which is perfect. Again, they say that justice, as well as law and right reason, exists by nature

and not by convention [. . .] Neither do they think that the divergence of opinion between philosophers is any reason for abandoning the study of philosophy, since at that rate we should have to give up life altogether. [. . .]

It is their doctrine that there can be no question of right as between man and the lower animals, because of their unlikeness. [. . .]

130. Of the three kinds of life, the contemplative, the practical, and the rational, they declare that we ought to choose the last, for that a rational being is expressly produced by nature for contemplation and for action. They tell us that the wise man will for reasonable cause make his own exit from life, on his country's behalf or for the sake of his friends, or if he suffers intolerable pain, mutilation, or incurable disease.

131. It is also their doctrine that amongst the wise there should be a community of wives with free choice of partners. [. . .] Under such circumstances we shall feel paternal affection for all the children alike, and there will; be an end of the jealousies arising from adultery. The best form of government they hold to be a mixture of democracy, kingship, and aristocracy (or rule of the best).

Such, then, are the statements they make in their ethical doctrines, with much more besides, together with their proper proofs: let this, however, suffice for a statement of them in a summary and elementary form.

Part II   Physical Doctrines

132. Their physical doctrine they divide into sections (1) about bodies; (2) about principles; (3) about elements; (4) about the gods; (5) about bounding surfaces and space whether filled or empty. This is a division into species; but the generic division is into three parts, dealing with (i.) the universe; (ii.) the elements; (iii.) the subject of causation.

The part dealing with the universe admits, they say, of division into two: for with one aspect of it the mathematicians also are concerned, in so far as they treat questions relating to the fixed stars and the planets, e.g. whether the sun is or is not just so large as it appears to be, and the same about the moon, the question of their revolutions, and other inquiries of the same sort.

133. But there is another aspect or field of cosmological inquiry, which belongs to the physicists alone: this includes such questions as what the substance of the universe is, whether the sun and the stars are made up of form and matter, whether the world has had a beginning in time or not, whether it is animate or inanimate, whether it is destructible or indestructible, whether it is governed by providence, and all the rest. They part concerned with causation, again, is itself subdivided into two. And in one of its aspects medical inquiries have a share in it, in so far as it involves investigation of the ruling principle of the soul and the phenomena of soul, seeds, and the like. Whereas the other part is claimed by the mathematicians also, e.g. how vision is to be explained, what causes the image on the mirror, what is the origin of clouds, thunder, rainbows, halos, comets, and the like.

134. They hold that there are two principles in the universe, the active principle and the passive. The passive principle, then, is a substance without quality, i.e. matter, whereas the active is the reason inherent in this substance, that is God. [. . .]

There is a difference, according to them, between principles and elements; the former being without generation or destruction, whereas the elements are destroyed when all things are resolved into fire. Moreover, the principles are incorporeal and destitute of form, while the elements have been endowed with form.

135. Body is [...] as that which is extended in three dimensions, length, breadth, and depth. This is also called solid body. But surface is the extremity of a solid body, or that which has length and breadth only without depth. [...] A line is the extremity of a surface or length without breadth, or that which has length alone. A point is the extremity of a line, the smallest possible mark or dot.

God is one and the same with Reason, Fate, and Zeus; he is also called by many other names.

136. In the beginning he was by himself; he transformed the whole of substance through air into water, and just as in animal generation the seed has a moist vehicle, so in cosmic moisture God, who is the seminal reason of the universe, remains behind in the moisture as such an agent, adapting matter to himself with a view to the next stage of creation. Thereupon he created first of all the four elements, fire, water, air, earth. An element is defined as that from which particular things first come to be at their birth and into which they are finally resolved.

137. The four elements together constitute unqualified substance or matter. Fire is the hot element, water the moist, air the cold, earth the dry. Not but what the quality of dryness is also found in the air. Fire has the uppermost place; it is also called aether, and in it the sphere of the fixed stars is first created; then come the sphere of the planets, next to that the air, then the water, and lowest of all the earth, which is at the centre of all things.

The term universe or cosmos is used by them in three senses: (1) of God himself, the individual being whose quality is derived from the whole of substance; he is indestructible and ingenerable, being the artificer of this orderly arrangement, who at stated periods of time absorbs into himself the whole of substance and again creates it from himself.

138. (2) Again, they give the name of cosmos to the orderly arrangement of the heavenly bodies in itself as such; and (3) in the third place to that whole of which these two are parts. [...]

140. The world, they say, is one and finite, having a spherical shape, such a shape being the most suitable for motion. [...] Outside of the world is diffused the infinite void, which is incorporeal. By incorporeal is meant that which, though capable of being occupied by body, is not so occupied. The world has no empty space within it, but forms one united whole. This is a necessary result of the sympathy and tension which binds together things in heaven and earth. [...]

141. Time too is incorporeal, being the measure of the world's motion. And time past and time future are infinite, but time present is finite. They hold that the world must come to an end, inasmuch as it had a beginning, on the analogy of those things which are understood by the senses. And that of which the parts are perishable is perishable as a whole. Now the parts of the world are perishable, seeing that they are transformed one into the other. Therefore the world itself is doomed to perish. Moreover, anything is destructible if it admits of deterioration; therefore the world is so, for it is first evaporated and again dissolved into water.

The world, they hold, comes into being when its substance has first been converted from fire through air into moisture and then the coarser part of the moisture has condensed as earth, while that whose particles are fine has been turned into air, and this process of rarefaction goes on increasing till it generates fire. Thereupon out of these elements animals and plants and all other natural kinds are formed by their mixture. [...]

147. The deity, say them, is a living being, immortal, rational, perfect or intelligent in happiness, admitting nothing evil [into him], taking providential care of the world and all that therein is, but he is not of human shape. He is, however, the artificer of the universe and, as it were, the father of all, both in general and in that which is called many names according to its various powers. [...]

148. The substance of God is declared by Zeno to be the whole world and the heaven, as well as by Chrysippus in his first book *Of the Gods*. [. . .] Now the term Nature is used by them to mean sometimes that which holds the world together, sometimes that which causes terrestrial things to spring up. Nature is defined as a force moving of itself, producing and preserving in being its offspring in accordance with seminal principles within definite periods, and effecting results homogeneous with their sources.

149. Nature, they hold, aims both at utility and at pleasure, as is clear from the analogy of human craftsmanship. That all things happen by fate or destiny is maintained by Chrysippus in his treatise *De fato*. [. . .] Fate is defined as an endless chair of causation, whereby things are, or as the reason or formula by which the world goes on. What is more, they say that divination in all its forms is a real and substantial fact, if there is really Providence. And they prove it to be actually a science on the evidence of certain results. [. . .]

150. The primary matter they make the substratum of all things: so Chrysippus in the first book of his *Physics*, and Zeno. By matter is meant that out of which anything whatsoever is produced. Both substance and matter are terms used in a twofold sense according as they signify (1) universal or (2) particular substance or matter. The former neither increases nor diminishes, while the matter of particular things both increases and diminishes. Body according to them is substance which is finite. [. . .] Matter can also be acted upon, as the same author says, for if it were immutable, the things which are produced would never have been produced out of it. Hence the further doctrine that matter is divisible *ad infinitum*. Chrysippus says that the divisible is not *ad infinitum*, but itself infinite; for there is nothing infinitely small to which the division can extend. But nevertheless the division goes on without ceasing.

151. Hence, again, their explanation of the mixture of two substances is, according to Chrysippus in the third book of his *Physics*, that they permeate each other through and through, and that the particles of the one do not merely surround those of the other or lie beside them. Thus, if a little drop of wine be thrown into the sea, it will be equally diffused over the whole sea for a while and then will be blended with it. [. . .]

28

Epictetus, *Manual*[1]

Epictetus (*c*.50–130 CE), as noted in the introduction to part VII, was from the group of Stoics called the Late Stoa. Epictetus was, in early life, a slave in a Roman household, but was eventually freed by his master. He then studied with the Late Stoic teacher Musonius Rufus, and taught Stoic philosophy in Rome until the Emperor Domitian (Titus Flavius Domitianus) banished the philosophers from Rome in 89 CE (apparently, on the ground that he thought they helped to foment rebellion against his rule). In exile, Epictetus set up a school in Nicopolis at Epirus, in the northwest of Greece, where he attracted many students from the Roman upper class.

The *Manual* (also known as the *Handbook*) of Epictetus was intended to provide a popular summary of Stoic ethical doctrine, and was excerpted in antiquity from Epictetus' longer work, the *Discourses*. At the heart of his Stoicism is his view that we live in a universe wholly determined by divine law or necessity. Since we cannot possibly change the way anything will happen in the universe, we must strive instead to gain control over what we *can* control, namely, our own reactions to the way things happen. We must not only learn to accept fatalistically what we cannot change, however; we must also strive to discover what we can about the operations of the universe, so as to be able to predict the way things will occur, and also to rid ourselves of the false opinions that are the source of all irrational desires, which make us miserable.

1. Of all existing things some are in our power, and others are not in our power. In our power are thought, impulse, will to get and will to avoid, and, in a word, everything which is our own doing. Things not in our power include the body, property, reputation, office, and, in a word, everything which is not our own doing. Things in our power are by nature free, unhindered, untrammelled; things not in our power are weak, servile, subject to hindrance, dependent on others. Remember then that if you imagine that what is naturally slavish is free, and what is naturally another's is your own, you will be hampered, you will mourn, you will be put to confusion, you will blame gods and men; but if you think that only your

---

1 This "handbook" of Epictetus' principles was probably compiled by Arrian, and contains an excellent summary of the master's thought.

own belongs to you, and that what is another's is indeed another's, no one will ever put compulsion or hindrance on you, you will blame none, you will accuse none, you will do nothing against your will, no one will harm you, you will have no enemy, for no harm can touch you.

Aiming then at these high matters, you must remember that to attain them requires more than ordinary effort; you will have to give up some things entirely, and put off others for the moment. And if you would have these also – office and wealth – it may be that you will fail to get them, just because your desire is set on the former, and you will certainly fail to attain those things which alone bring freedom and happiness.

Make it your study then to confront every harsh impression with the words, 'You are but an impression, and not at all what you seem to be'. Then test it by those rules that you possess; and first by this – the chief test of all – 'Is it concerned with what is in our power or with what is not in our power?' And if it is concerned with what is not in our power, be ready with the answer that it is nothing to you.

2. Remember that the will to get promises attainment of what you will, and the will to avoid promises escape from what you avoid; and he who fails to get what he wills is unfortunate, and he who does not escape what he wills to avoid is miserable. If then you try to avoid only what is unnatural in the region within your control, you will escape from all that you avoid; but if you try to avoid disease or death or poverty you will be miserable.

Therefore let your will to avoid have no concern with what is not in man's power; direct it only to things in man's power that are contrary to nature. But for the moment you must utterly remove the will to get; for if you will to get something not in man's power you are bound to be unfortunate; while none of the things in man's power that you could honourably will to get is yet within your reach. Impulse to act and not to act, these are your concern; yet exercise them gently and without strain, and provisionally.

3. When anything, from the meanest thing upwards, is attractive or serviceable or an object of affection, remember always to say to yourself, 'What is its nature?' If you are fond of a jug, say you are fond of a jug; then you will not be disturbed if it be broken. If you kiss your child or your wife, say to yourself that you are kissing a human being, for then if death strikes it you will not be disturbed.

4. When you are about to take something in hand, remind yourself what manner of thing it is. If you are going to bathe put before your mind what happens in the bath – water pouring over some, others being jostled, some reviling, others stealing; and you will set to work more securely if you say to yourself at once: 'I want to bathe, and I want to keep my will in harmony with nature,' and so in each thing you do; for in this way, if anything turns up to hinder you in your bathing, you will be ready to say, 'I did not want only to bathe, but to keep my will in harmony with nature, and I shall not so keep it, if I lose my temper at what happens'.

5. What disturbs men's minds is not events but their judgements on events. For instance, death is nothing dreadful, or else Socrates would have thought it so. No, the only dreadful thing about it is men's judgement that it is dreadful. And so when we are hindered, or disturbed, or distressed, let us never lay the blame on others, but on ourselves, that is, on our own judgements. To accuse others for one's own misfortunes is a sign of want of education; to accuse oneself shows that one's education has begun; to accuse neither oneself nor others shows that one's education is complete.

6. Be not elated at an excellence which is not your own. If the horse in his pride were to say, 'I am handsome', we could bear with it. But when you say with pride, 'I have a handsome

horse', know that the good horse is the ground of your pride. You ask then what you can call your own. The answer is – the way you deal with your impressions. Therefore when you deal with your impressions in accord with nature, then you may be proud indeed, for your pride will be in a good which is your own.

7. When you are on a voyage, and your ship is at anchorage, and you disembark to get fresh water, you may pick up a small shellfish or a truffle by the way, but you must keep your attention fixed on the ship, and keep looking towards it constantly, to see if the Helmsman calls you; and if he does, you have to leave everything, or be bundled on board with your legs tied like a sheep. So it is in life. If you have a dear wife or child given you, they are like the shellfish or the truffle, they are very well in their way. Only, if the Helmsman call, run back to your ship, leave all else, and do not look behind you. And if you are old, never go far from the ship, so that when you are called you may not fail to appear.

8. Ask not that events should happen as you will, but let your will be that events should happen as they do, and you shall have peace.

9. Sickness is a hindrance to the body, but not to the will, unless the will consent. Lameness is a hindrance to the leg, but not to the will. Say this to yourself at each event that happens, for you shall find that though it hinders something else it will not hinder you.

10. When anything happens to you, always remember to turn to yourself and ask what faculty you have to deal with it. If you see a beautiful boy or a beautiful woman, you will find continence the faculty to exercise there; if trouble is laid on you, you will find endurance; if ribaldry, you will find patience. And if you train yourself in this habit your impressions will not carry you away.

11. Never say of anything, 'I lost it', but say, 'I gave it back'. Has your child died? It was given back. Has your wife died? She was given back. Has your estate been taken from you? Was not this also given back? But you say, 'He who took it from me is wicked'. What does it matter to you through whom the Giver asked it back? As long as He gives it you, take care of it, but not as your own; treat it as passers-by treat an inn.

12. If you wish to make progress, abandon reasonings of this sort: 'If I neglect my affairs I shall have nothing to live on'; 'If I do not punish my slave, he will be wicked.' For it is better to die of hunger, so that you be free from pain and free from fear, than to live in plenty and be troubled in mind. It is better for your slave to be wicked than for you to be miserable. Wherefore begin with little things. Is your drop of oil spilt? Is your sup of wine stolen? Say to yourself, 'This is the price paid for freedom from passion, this is the price of a quiet mind.' Nothing can be had without a price. When you call your slave, reflect that he may not be able to hear you, and if he hears you, he may not be able to do anything you want. But he is not so well off that it rests with him to give you peace of mind.

13. If you wish to make progress, you must be content in external matters to seem a fool and a simpleton; do not wish men to think you know anything, and if any should think you to be somebody, distrust yourself. For know that it is not easy to keep your will in accord with nature and at the same time keep outward things; if you attend to one you must needs neglect the other.

14. It is silly to want your children and your wife and your friends to live for ever, for that means that you want what is not in your control to be in your control, and what is not your own to be yours. In the same way if you want your servant to make no mistakes, you are a fool, for you want vice not to be vice but something different. But if you want not to be disappointed in your will to get, you can attain to that.

Exercise yourself then in what lies in your power. Each man's master is the man who has authority over what he wishes or does not wish, to secure the one or to take away the other. Let him then who wishes to be free not wish for anything or avoid anything that depends on others; or else he is bound to be a slave.

15. Remember that you must behave in life as you would at a banquet. A dish is handed round and comes to you; put out your hand and take it politely. It passes you; do not stop it. It has not reached you; do not be impatient to get it, but wait till your turn comes. Bear yourself thus towards children, wife, office, wealth, and one day you will be worthy to banquet with the gods. But if when they are set before you, you do not take them but despise them, then you shall not only share the gods' banquet, but shall share their rule. For by so doing Diogenes and Heraclitus and men like them were called divine and deserved the name.

16. When you see a man shedding tears in sorrow for a child abroad or dead, or for loss of property, beware that you are not carried away by the impression that it is outward ills that make him miserable. Keep this thought by you: 'What distresses him is not the event, for that does not distress another, but his judgement on the event.' Therefore do not hesitate to sympathize with him so far as words go, and if it so chance, even to groan with him; but take heed that you do not also groan in your inner being.

17. Remember that you are an actor in a play, and the Playwright chooses the manner of it: if he wants it short, it is short; if long, it is long. If he wants you to act a poor man you must act the part with all your powers; and so if your part be a cripple or a magistrate or a plain man. For your business is to act the character that is given you and act it well; the choice of the cast is Another's.

18. When a raven croaks with evil omen, let not the impression carry you away, but straightway distinguish in your own mind and say, 'These portents mean nothing to me; but only to my bit of a body or my bit of property or name, or my children or my wife. But for me all omens are favourable if I will, for, whatever the issue may be, it is in my power to get benefit therefrom.'

19. You can be invincible, if you never enter on a contest where victory is not in your power. Beware then that when you see a man raised to honour or great power or high repute you do not let your impression carry you away. For if the reality of good lies in what is in our power, there is no room for envy or jealousy. And you will not wish to be praetor, or prefect or consul, but to be free; and there is but one way to freedom – to despise what is not in our power.

20. Remember that foul words or blows in themselves are no outrage, but your judgement that they are so. So when any one makes you angry, know that it is your own thought that has angered you. Wherefore make it your first endeavour not to let your impressions carry you away. For if once you gain time and delay, you will find it easier to control yourself.

21. Keep before your eyes from day to day death and exile and all things that seem terrible, but death most of all, and then you will never set your thoughts on what is low and will never desire anything beyond measure.

22. If you set your desire on philosophy you must at once prepare to meet with ridicule and the jeers of many who will say, 'Here he is again, turned philosopher. Where has he got these proud looks?' Nay, put on no proud looks, but hold fast to what seems best to you, in confidence that God has set you at this post. And remember that if you abide where you are, those who first laugh at you will one day admire you, and that if you give way to them, you will get doubly laughed at.

23. If it ever happen to you to be diverted to things outside, so that you desire to please another, know that you have lost your life's plan. Be content then always to be a philosopher; if you wish to be regarded as one too, show yourself that you are one and you will be able to achieve it.

24. Let not reflections such as these afflict you: 'I shall live without honour, and never be of any account'; for if lack of honour is an evil, no one but yourself can involve you in evil any more than in shame. Is it your business to get office or to be invited to an entertainment?

Certainly not.

Where then is the dishonour you talk of? How can you be 'of no account anywhere', when you ought to count for something in those matters only which are in your power, where you may achieve the highest worth?

'But my friends,' you say, 'will lack assistance.'

What do you mean by 'lack assistance'? They will not have cash from you and you will not make them Roman citizens. Who told you that to do these things is in our power, and not dependent upon others? Who can give to another what is not his to give?

'Get them then,' says he, 'that we may, have them.'

If I can get them and keep my self-respect, honour, magnanimity, show the way and I will get them. But if you call on me to lose the good things that are mine, in order that you may win things that are not good, look how unfair and thoughtless you are. And which do you really prefer? Money, or a faithful, modest friend? Therefore help me rather to keep these qualities, and do not expect from me actions which will make me lose them.

'But my country,' says he, 'will lack assistance, so far as lies in me.'

Once more I ask, What assistance do you mean? It will not owe colonnades or baths to you. What of that? It does not owe shoes to the blacksmith or arms to the shoemaker; it is sufficient if each man fulfils his own function. Would you do it no good if you secured to it another faithful and modest citizen?

'Yes.'

Well, then, you would not be useless to it.

'What place then shall I have in the city?'

Whatever place you can hold while you keep your character for honour and self-respect. But if you are going to lose these qualities in trying to benefit your city, what benefit, I ask, would you have done her when you attain to the perfection of being lost to shame and honour?

25. Has some one had precedence of you at an entertainment or a levee or been called in before you to give advice? If these things are good you ought to be glad that he got them; if they are evil, do not be angry that you did not get them yourself. Remember that if you want to get what is not in your power, you cannot earn the same reward as others unless you act as they do. How is it possible for one who does not haunt the great man's door to have equal shares with one who does, or one who does not go in his train equality with one who does; or one who does not praise him with one who does? You will be unjust then and insatiable if you wish to get these privileges for nothing, without paying their price. What is the price of a lettuce? An obol perhaps. If then a man pays his obol and gets his lettuces, and you do not pay and do not get them, do not think you are defrauded. For as he has the lettuces so you have the obol you did not give. The same principle holds good too in conduct. You were not invited to someone's entertainment? Because you did not give the host the price for which he sells his dinner. He sells it for compliments, he sells it for attentions.

Pay him the price then, if it is to your profit. But if you wish to get the one and yet not give up the other, nothing can satisfy you in your folly.

What! you say, you have nothing instead of the dinner?

Nay, you have this, you have not praised the man you did not want to praise, you have not had to bear with the insults of his doorstep.

26. It is in our power to discover the will of Nature from those matters on which we have no difference of opinion. For instance, when another man's slave has broken the wine-cup we are very ready to say at once, 'Such things must happen'. Know then that when your own cup is broken, you ought to behave in the same way as when your neighbour's was broken. Apply the same principle to higher matters. Is another's child or wife dead? Not one of us but would say, 'Such is the lot of man'; but when one's own dies, straightway one cries, 'Alas! miserable am I'. But we ought to remember what our feelings are when we hear it of another.

27. As a mark is not set up for men to miss it, so there is nothing intrinsically evil in the world.

28. If any one trusted your body to the first man he met, you would be indignant, but yet you trust your mind to the chance comer, and allow it to be disturbed and confounded if he revile you; are you not ashamed to do so?

29.[2] In everything you do consider what comes first and what follows, and so approach it. Otherwise you will come to it with a good heart at first because you have not reflected on any of the consequences, and afterwards, when difficulties have appeared, you will desist to your shame. Do you wish to win at Olympia? So do I, by the gods, for it is a fine thing. But consider the first steps to it, and the consequences, and so lay your hand to the work. You must submit to discipline, eat to order, touch no sweets, train under compulsion, at a fixed hour, in heat and cold, drink no cold water, nor wine, except by order; you must hand yourself over completely to your trainer as you would to a physician, and then when the contest comes you must risk getting hacked, and sometimes dislocate your hand, twist your ankle, swallow plenty of sand, sometimes get a flogging, and with all this suffer defeat. When you have considered all this well, then enter on the athlete's course, if you still wish it. If you act without thought you will be behaving like children, who one day play at wrestlers, another day at gladiators, now sound the trumpet, and next strut the stage. Like them you will be now an athlete, now a gladiator, then orator, then philosopher, but nothing with all your soul. Like an ape, you imitate every sight you see, and one thing after another takes your fancy. When you undertake a thing you do it casually and half-heartedly, instead of considering it and looking at it all round. In the same way some people, when they see a philosopher and hear a man speaking like Euphrates (and indeed who can speak as he can?), wish to be philosophers themselves.

Man, consider first what it is you are undertaking; then look at your own powers and see if you can bear it. Do you want to compete in the pentathlon or in wrestling? Look to your arms, your thighs, see what your loins are like. For different men are born for different tasks. Do you suppose that if you do this you can live as you do now – eat and drink as you do now, indulge desire and discontent just as before? Nay, you must sit up late, work hard, abandon your own people, be looked down on by a mere slave, be ridiculed by those who meet you, get the worst of it in everything – in honour, in office, in justice, in every possible thing.

2 Cf. Epictetus, *Discourses*, III, ch. xv.

This is what you have to consider: whether you are willing to pay this price for peace of mind, freedom, tranquillity. If not, do not come near; do not be, like the children, first a philosopher, then a tax-collector, then an orator, then one of Caesar's procurators. These callings do not agree. You must be one man, good or bad; you must develop either your Governing Principle, or your outward endowments; you must study either your inner man, or outward things – in a word, you must choose between the position of a philosopher and that of a mere outsider.

30. Appropriate acts are in general measured by the relations they are concerned with. 'He is your father.' This means you are called on to take care of him, give way to him in all things, bear with him if he reviles or strikes you.

'But he is a bad father.'

Well, have you any natural claim to a good father? No, only to a father.

'My brother wrongs me.'

Be careful then to maintain the relation you hold to him, and do not consider what he does, but what you must do if your purpose is to keep in accord with nature. For no one shall harm you, without your consent; you will only be harmed, when you think you are harmed. You will only discover what is proper to expect from neighbour, citizen, or praetor, if you get into the habit of looking at the relations implied by each.

31. For piety towards the gods know that the most important thing is this: to have right opinions about them – that they exist, and that they govern the universe well and justly – and to have set yourself to obey them, and to give way to all that happens, following events with a free will, in the belief that they are fulfilled by the highest mind. For thus you will never blame the gods, nor accuse them of neglecting you. But this you cannot achieve, unless you apply your conception of good and evil to those things only which are in our power, and not to those which are out of our power. For if you apply your notion of good or evil to the latter, then, as soon as you fail to get what you will to get or fail to avoid what you will to avoid, you will be bound to blame and hate those you hold responsible. For every living creature has a natural tendency to avoid and shun what seems harmful and all that causes it, and to pursue and admire what is helpful and all that causes it. It is not possible then for one who thinks he is harmed to take pleasure in what he thinks is the author of the harm, any more than to take pleasure in the harm itself. That is why a father is reviled by his son, when he does not give his son a share of what the son regards as good things; thus Polynices and Eteocles were set at enmity with one another by thinking that a king's throne was a good thing. That is why the farmer, and the sailor, and the merchant, and those who lose wife or children revile the gods. For men's religion is bound up with their interest. Therefore he who makes it his concern rightly to direct his will to get and his will to avoid, is thereby making piety his concern. But it is proper on each occasion to make libation and sacrifice and to offer first-fruits according to the custom of our fathers, with purity and not in slovenly or careless fashion, without meanness and without extravagance.

32. When you make use of prophecy remember that while you know not what the issue will be, but are come to learn it from the prophet, you do know before you come what manner of thing it is, if you are really a philosopher. For if the event is not in our control, it cannot be either good or evil. Therefore do not bring with you to the prophet the will to get or the will to avoid, and do not approach him with trembling, but with your mind made up, that the whole issue is indifferent and does not affect you and that, whatever it be, it will be in your power to make good use of it, and no one shall hinder this. With confidence then

approach the gods as counsellors, and further, when the counsel is given you, remember whose counsel it is, and whom you will be disregarding if you disobey. And consult the oracle, as Socrates thought men should, only when the whole question turns upon the issue of events, and neither reason nor any art of man provides opportunities for discovering what lies before you. Therefore, when it is your duty to risk your life with friend or country, do not ask the oracle whether you should risk your life. For if the prophet warns you that the sacrifice is unfavourable, though it is plain that this means death or exile or injury to some part of your body, yet reason requires that even at this cost you must stand by your friend and share your country's danger. Wherefore pay heed to the greater prophet, Pythian Apollo, who cast out of his temple the man who did not help his friend when he was being killed.

Lay down for yourself from the first a definite stamp and style of conduct, which you will maintain when you are alone and also in the society of men. Be silent for the most part, or, if you speak, say only what is necessary and in a few words. Talk, but rarely, if occasion calls you, but do not talk of ordinary things – of gladiators, or horse-races, or athletes, or of meats or drinks – these are topics that arise everywhere – but above all do not talk about men in blame or compliment or comparison. If you can, turn the conversation of your company by your talk to some fitting subject; but if you should chance to be isolated among strangers, be silent. Do not laugh much, nor at many things, nor without restraint.

Refuse to take oaths, altogether if that be possible, but if not, as far as circumstances allow.

Refuse the entertainments of strangers and the vulgar.[3] But if occasions arise to accept them, then strain every nerve to avoid lapsing into the state of the vulgar. For know that, if your comrade has a stain on him, he that associates with him must needs share the stain, even though he be clean in himself.

For your body take just so much as your bare need requires, such as food, drink, clothing, house, servants, but cut down all that tends to luxury and outward show.

Avoid impurity to the utmost of your power before marriage, and if you indulge your passion, let it be done lawfully. But do not be offensive or censorious to those who indulge it, and do not be always bringing up your own chastity. If some one tells you that so and so speaks ill of you, do not defend yourself against what he says, but answer, 'He did not know my other faults, or he would not have mentioned these alone.'

It is not necessary for the most part to go to the games; but if you should have occasion to go, show that your first concern is for yourself; that is, wish that only to happen which does happen, and him only to win who does win, for so you will suffer no hindrance. But refrain entirely from applause, or ridicule, or prolonged excitement. And when you go away do not talk much of what happened there, except so far as it tends to your improvement. For to talk about it implies that the spectacle excited your wonder.

Do not go lightly or casually to hear lectures; but if you do go, maintain your gravity and dignity and do not make yourself offensive. When you are going to meet any one, and particularly some man of reputed eminence, set before your mind the thought, 'What would Socrates or Zeno have done?' and you will not fail to make proper use of the occasion.

When you go to visit some great man, prepare your mind by thinking that you will not find him in, that you will be shut out, that the doors will be slammed in your face, that he will pay no heed to you. And if in spite of all this you find it fitting for you to go, go and bear what happens and never say to yourself, 'It was not worth all this'; for that shows a vulgar mind and one at odds with outward things.

---

3 i.e., those untrained in philosophy.

In your conversation avoid frequent and disproportionate mention of your own doings or adventures; for other people do not take the same pleasure in hearing what has happened to you as you take in recounting your adventures.

Avoid raising men's laughter; for it is a habit that easily slips into vulgarity, and it may well suffice to lessen your neighbour's respect.

It is dangerous too to lapse into foul language; when anything of the kind occurs, rebuke the offender, if the occasion allow, and if not, make it plain to him by your silence, or a blush or a frown, that you are angry at his words.

34. When you imagine some pleasure, beware that it does not carry you away, like other imaginations. Wait a while, and give yourself pause. Next remember two things: how long you will enjoy the pleasure, and also how long you will afterwards repent and revile yourself. And set on the other side the joy and self-satisfaction you will feel if you refrain. And if the moment seems come to realize it, take heed that you be not overcome by the winning sweetness and attraction of it; set in the other scale the thought how much better is the consciousness of having vanquished it.

35. When you do a thing because you have determined that it ought to be done, never avoid being seen doing it, even if the opinion of the multitude is going to condemn you. For if your action is wrong, then avoid doing it altogether, but if it is right, why do you fear those who will rebuke you wrongly?

36. The phrases, 'It is day' and 'It is night', mean a great deal if taken separately, but have no meaning if combined. In the same way, to choose the larger portion at a banquet may be worth while for your body, but if you want to maintain social decencies it is worthless. Therefore, when you are at meat with another, remember not only to consider the value of what is set before you for the body, but also to maintain your self-respect before your host.

37. If you try to act a part beyond your powers, you not only disgrace yourself in it, but you neglect the part which you could have filled with success.

38. As in walking you take care not to tread on a nail or to twist your foot, so take care that you do not harm your Governing Principle. And if we guard this in everything we do, we shall set to work more securely.

39. Every man's body is a measure for his property, as the foot is the measure for his shoe. If you stick to this limit, you will keep the right measure; if you go beyond it, you are bound to be carried away down a precipice in the end; just as with the shoe, if you once go beyond the foot, your shoe puts on gilding, and soon purple and embroidery. For when once you go beyond the measure there is no limit.

40. Women from fourteen years upwards are called 'madam' by men. Wherefore, when they see that the only advantage they have got is to be marriageable, they begin to make themselves smart and to set all their hopes on this. We must take pains then to make them understand that they are really honoured for nothing but a modest and decorous life.

41. It is a sign of a dull mind to dwell upon the cares of the body, to prolong exercise, eating, drinking, and other bodily functions. These things are to be done by the way; all your attention must be given to the mind.

42. When a man speaks evil or does evil to you, remember that he does or says it because he thinks it is fitting for him. It is not possible for him to follow what seems good to you, but only what seems good to him, so that, if his opinion is wrong, he suffers, in that he is the victim of deception. In the same way, if a composite judgement which is true is thought to be false, it is not the judgement that suffers, but the man who is deluded about it. If you

act on this principle you will be gentle to him who reviles you, saying to yourself on each occasion, 'He thought it right.'

43. Everything has two handles, one by which you can carry it, the other by which you cannot. If your brother wrongs you, do not take it by that handle, the handle of his wrong, for you cannot carry it by that, but rather by the other handle – that he is a brother, brought up with you, and then you will take it by the handle that you can carry by.

44. It is illogical to reason thus, 'I am richer than you, therefore I am superior to you', 'I am more eloquent than you, therefore I am superior to you.' It is more logical to reason, 'I am richer than you, therefore my property is superior to yours', 'I am more eloquent than you, therefore my speech is superior to yours.' You are something more than property or speech.

45. If a man washes quickly, do not say that he washes badly, but that he washes quickly. If a man drinks much wine, do not say that he drinks badly, but that he drinks much. For till you have decided what judgement prompts him, how do you know that he acts badly? If you do as I say, you will assent to your apprehensive impressions and to none other.

46. On no occasion call yourself a philosopher, nor talk at large of your principles among the multitude, but act on your principles. For instance, at a banquet do not say how one ought to eat, but eat as you ought. Remember that Socrates had so completely got rid of the thought of display that when men came and wanted an introduction to philosophers he took them to be introduced; so patient of neglect was he. And if a discussion arise among the multitude on some principle, keep silent for the most part; for you are in great danger of blurting out some undigested thought. And when someone says to you, 'You know nothing', and you do not let it provoke you, then know that you are really on the right road. For sheep do not bring grass to their shepherds and show them how much they have eaten, but they digest their fodder and then produce it in the form of wool and milk. Do the same yourself; instead of displaying your principles to the multitude, show them the results of the principles you have digested.

47. When you have adopted the simple life, do not pride yourself upon it, and if you are a water-drinker do not say on every occasion, 'I am a water-drinker.' And if you ever want to train laboriously, keep it to yourself and do not make a show of it. Do not embrace statues. If you are very thirsty take a good draught of cold water, and rinse your mouth and tell no one.

48. The ignorant man's position and character is this: he never looks to himself for benefit or harm, but to the world outside him. The philosopher's position and character is that he always look to himself for benefit and harm.

The signs of one who is making progress are: he blames none, praises none, complains of none, accuses none, never speaks of himself as if he were somebody, or as if he knew anything. And if any one compliments him he laughs in himself at his compliment; and if one blames him, he makes no defence. He goes about like a convalescent, careful not to disturb his constitution on its road to recovery, until it has got firm hold. He has got rid of the will to get, and his will to avoid is directed no longer to what is beyond our power but only to what is in our power and contrary to nature. In all things he exercises his will without strain. If men regard him as foolish, or ignorant he pays no heed. In one word, he keeps watch and guard on himself as his own enemy, lying in wait for him.

49. When a man prides himself on being able to understand and interpret the books of Chrysippus, say to yourself, 'If Chrysippus had not written obscurely this man would have had nothing on which to pride himself.'

What is my object? To understand Nature and follow her. I look then for some one who interprets her, and having heard that Chrysippus does I come to him. But I do not understand his writings, so I seek an interpreter. So far there is nothing to be proud of. But when I have found the interpreter it remains for me to act on his precepts; that and that alone is a thing to be proud of. But if I admire the mere power of exposition, it comes to this – that I am turned into a grammarian instead of a philosopher, except that I interpret Chrysippus in place of Homer. Therefore, when some one says to me, 'Read me Chrysippus', when I cannot point to actions which are in harmony and correspondence with his teaching, I am rather inclined to blush.

50. Whatever principles you put before you, hold fast to them as laws which it will be impious to transgress. But pay no heed to what any one says of you; for this is something beyond your own control.

51. How long will you wait to think yourself worthy of the highest and transgress in nothing the clear pronouncement of reason? You have received the precepts which you ought to accept, and you have accepted them. Why then do you still wait for a master, that you may delay the amendment of yourself till he comes? You are a youth no longer, you are now a full-grown man. If now you are careless and indolent and are always putting off, fixing one day after another as the limit when you mean to begin attending to yourself, then, living or dying, you will make no progress but will continue unawares in ignorance. Therefore make up your mind before it is too late to live as one who is mature and proficient, and let all that seems best to you be a law that you cannot transgress. And if you encounter anything troublesome or pleasant or glorious or inglorious, remember that the hour of struggle is come, the Olympic contest is here and you may put off no longer, and that one day and one action determines whether the progress you have achieved is lost or maintained.

This was how Socrates attained perfection, paying heed to nothing but reason, in all that he encountered. And if you are not yet Socrates, yet ought you to live as one who would wish to be a Socrates.

52. The first and most necessary department of philosophy deals with the application of principles; for instance, 'not to lie'. The second deals with demonstrations; for instance, 'How comes it that one ought not to lie?' The third is concerned with establishing and analysing these processes; for instance, 'How comes it that this is a demonstration? What is demonstration, what is consequence, what is contradiction, what is true, what is false?' It follows then that the third department is necessary because of the second, and the second because of the first. The first is the most necessary part, and that in which we must rest. But we reverse the order: we occupy ourselves with the third, and make that our whole concern, and the first we completely neglect. Wherefore we lie, but are ready enough with the demonstration that lying is wrong.

53. On every occasion we must have these thoughts at hand,

> Lead me, O Zeus, and lead me, Destiny,
> Whither ordainèd is by your decree.
> I'll follow, doubting not, or if with will
> Recreant I falter, I shall follow still.
>
> Cleanthes

> Who rightly with necessity complies
> In things divine we count him skilled and wise.
>
> Euripides, Fragment 965

Well, Crito, if this be the gods' will, so be it.

Plato, *Crito*, 43d

Anytus and Meletus have power to put me to death, but not to harm me.

Plato, *Apology*, 30c

Part VIII

Skeptics and Skepticism

Introduction

Skepticism has come to be understood as a position of doubt in relation to some subject. Philosophical or epistemic skepticism is the view that human beings do not actually have knowledge. But these positions are entirely compatible with contemporary skeptics continuing to hold beliefs – even strongly held beliefs – about the relevant subjects, and even to suppose that certain beliefs about these subjects can be highly justified, such that the opposing belief would be unjustified, even to the point of irrationality.

Ancient Skepticism, however, took a very different position – according to the ancient Skeptics, not only was knowledge impossible for human beings, strongly held beliefs were regarded as ill advised, for Skeptics held that most of human suffering derived from what they derisively called Dogmatism: holding on to beliefs too strongly, such that if those beliefs should prove to be false, or if the evidence for them should be undermined, the Dogmatic would suffer distress. The aim of the ancient Skeptic, therefore, was not, as with modern skeptics, an increase of epistemic humility towards one or more subjects – it was, instead, as far as possible to suspend belief altogether, or at least to refuse to hold any belief with confidence of its truth, or as adequately justified.

Also unlike modern skepticism, ancient Skepticism was really a philosophy of *life* – it sought to explicate how we should approach the project of attaining the best possible life for humans. In the case of Skepticism, the best life was the one most free of the disturbance of dogmatically held beliefs. The Skeptical Sage would instead go through life as free from convictions as he possibly could. In this way, the Skeptics overturned entirely the Platonic and Aristotelian hope that adequate education and knowledge could help one to secure a good life. Instead, the Skeptics argued, the good life would only be available to those who recognized that they knew nothing, and who not only did not seek such knowledge, but did their best not even to pass judgment on any subject.

According to Diogenes Laertius, *Lives and Opinions of Eminent Philosophers* (DL IX.71), the Skeptics traced their philosophy all the way back to Homer, on the ground that Homer managed to give different answers at different times, and thus prevented his readers from drawing any dogmatic conclusions about his views. The Skeptics also counted as forebears any other philosophers or literary figures they took (sometimes quite tendentiously) as claiming that knowledge was difficult for human beings to obtain.

The actual truth of the development of Skepticism, however, probably leads back to Pyrrho of Elis (*c.*360–*c.*270 BCE). The difficulty of this hypothesis is that – as with Pythagoras and Socrates before him – Pyrrho seems not to have written anything, or if he did, we know nothing of it. His most famous student, Timon of Phlius (*c.*325–235 BCE), was a prolific writer, however, and though only fragments of his own works survive, they allow us to piece together a picture of his master's teachings. Pyrrho – apparently quite strikingly – was not only very critical of all of the thinkers and literary figures generally regarded by the Greeks as wise, he also sought to live "non-dogmatically," to such a degree that his unwillingness to be convinced by anything actually led him to take extraordinary risks (with precipices, dogs, and other dangers, the perception of which he regarded as inadequate to warrant any judgment) to such an extent that his disciples would have to go to great pains to keep him from coming to harm (DL IX.62). They must have been remarkably conscientious, if so, for Pyrrho is reported to have lived to be nearly 90 (DL IX.62).

The Pyrrhonian tradition of Skepticism perhaps found its most important advocate somewhat later in antiquity, in Aenesidemus of Knossos (first century BCE), who revived Pyrrhonism in his now lost works, *Modes of Inducing Suspension of Judgment* and *Pyrrhonian Discourses*. We can piece some of the main themes of these works together from the testimony of Diogenes Laertius, to whom they were available.

A rather different school of Skeptical philosophy formed in Plato's Academy, four generations after Plato's death. As noted in the introduction to part VII above, one of the two famous students of Polemo (*c.*355–276/5 BCE), who headed the Academy for over 40 years, was Arcesilaus of Pitane (316/15–241/40 BCE), who later became the head of the Academy himself and turned it into a school of and for Skeptics. Arcesilaus' Skeptical tendencies continued under Carneades of Cyrene (214–129/8 BCE), his pupil Clitomachus of Carthage (187/6–110/9 BCE), and Philo of Larissa (158–84 BCE). This group, known as the Academic Skeptics, interpreted Plato as claiming that knowledge was not possible for embodied human beings, though it might be possible for disembodied souls (before birth or after death). The Academic Skeptics were not opposed to holding beliefs, and even described criteria by which beliefs might become justified, and thus rationally held, but insisted that the true Skeptic should always regard himself as a "searcher for wisdom." This more relaxed view of the advisability of making judgments led the great historian of Skepticism, Sextus Empiricus (second century CE), to call the Academic Skeptics "Skeptics in name only." For Sextus, the only *true* Skeptics were the Pyrrhonists.

29

Diogenes Laertius, *Life of Pyrrho*

In his *Life of Pyrrho*, Diogenes begins with what he knows or has heard about Pyrrho's actual life, but then moves on to the views of the whole school of philosophy that came to be known as Pyrrhonian Skepticism (as opposed to the Academic Skepticism taught at the school Plato founded). In this selection, the main argumentative strategies of the Pyrrhonians are enumerated, and the ethical philosophy that flows from these strategies is explained.

74. The Skeptics persevered in overthrowing all the dogmas of every sect, while they themselves asserted nothing dogmatically; and contented themselves with expressing the opinions of others, without affirming anything themselves, not even that they did affirm nothing; so that even discarded all positive denial; for to say, "We affirm nothing," was to affirm something. "But we," said they, "enunciate the doctrines of others, to prove our own perfect indifference; it is just as if we were to express the same thing by a simple sign." So these words, "We affirm nothing," indicate the absence of all affirmation, just as other propositions, such as, "Not more one thing than another,"

75. "Every reason has a corresponding reason opposed to it," and all such maxims indicate a similar idea. [. . .]

76. "Prudence has not existence, any more than it has no existence." Accordingly, then, expression, as Timon says in his *Python*, indicates nothing more than an absence of all affirmation, or of all assent of the judgment.

Also the expression, "Every reason has a corresponding reason," etc., does in the same manner indicate the suspension of the judgment; for if, while the facts are different, the expressions are equipollent, it follows that a man must be quite ignorant of the real truth.

Besides this, to this assertion there is a contrary assertion opposed, which, after having destroyed all others, turns itself against itself, and destroys itself, resembling, as it were, those cathartic medicines which, after they have cleansed the stomach, then discharge themselves and are got rid of.

77. And so the dogmatic philosophers say, that all these reasonings are so far from over-turning the authority of reason that they confirm it. To this the Skeptics reply that they only employ reason as an instrument, because it is impossible to overturn the authority of

reason, without employing reason; just as if we assert that there is no such thing as space, we must employ the word "space," but that not dogmatically, but demonstratively; and if we assert that nothing exists according to necessity, it is unavoidable that we must use the word "necessity." The same principle of interpretation did they adopt; for they affirmed that facts are not by nature such as they appear to be, but that they only seem such; and they said, that what they doubt is not what they think, for their thoughts are evident to themselves, but the reality of the things which are only made known to them by their sensations.

78. The Pyrrhonean system, then, is a simple explanation of appearances, or of notions of every kind, by means of which, comparing one thing with another, one arrives at the conclusion, that there is nothing in all these notions, but contradiction and confusion; as Aenesidemus says in his Introduction to Pyrrhonism. As to the contradictions which are found in those speculations, when they have pointed out in what way each fact is convincing, they then, by the same means, take away all belief from it; for they say that we regard as certain, those things which always produce similar impressions on the senses, those which are the offspring of habit, or which are established by the laws, and those too which give pleasure or excite wonder.

79. And they prove that the reasons opposite to those on which our assent is founded are entitled to equal belief.

The difficulties which they suggest, relating to the agreement subsisting between what appears to the senses, and what is comprehended by the intellect, divide themselves into ten modes of argument, according to which the subject and object of our knowledge is incessantly changing. And these ten modes Phyrrho lays down in the following manner.

The first relates to the difference which one remarks between the sentiments of animals in respect of pleasure, and pain, and what is injurious, and what is advantageous; and from this we conclude, that the same objects do not always produce the same impressions; and that the fact of this difference ought to be a reason with us for suspending our judgment. For there are some animals which are produced without any sexual connexion, as those which live in the fire, and the Arabian Phoenix, and worms.

80. Others again are engendered by copulation, as men and others of that kind; and some are composed in one way, and others in another; on which account they also differ in their senses, as for instance, hawks are very keen-sighted; dogs have a most acute scent. It is plain, therefore, that the things seen produce different impressions on those animals which differ in their power of sight. So, too, young branches are eagerly eaten by the goat, but are bitter to mankind; and hemlock is nutritious for the quail, but, deadly to man; and pigs eat their own dung, but a horse does not.

The second mode refers to the nature and idiosyncracies of men. According to Demophon, the steward of Alexander used to feel warm in the shade, and to shiver in the sun.

81. And Andron, the Argive, as Aristotle tells us, travelled through the dry parts of Libya, without once drinking. Again, one man is fond of medicine, another of farming, another of commerce; and the same pursuits are good for one man, and injurious to another; on which account, we ought to suspend our opinions.

The third mode is that which has for its object the difference of the organs of sense. Accordingly, an apple presents itself to the sight as yellow, to the taste as sweet, to the smell as fragrant; and the same form is seen, in very different lights, according to the differences of mirrors. It follows, therefore, that what is seen is just as likely to be something else as the reality.

82. The fourth refers to the dispositions of the subject, and the changes in general to which it is liable. Such as health, sickness, sleep, waking, joy, grief, youth, old age, courage, fear,

want, abundance, hatred, friendship, warmth, cold, easiness of breathing, oppression of the respiratory organs, and so on. The objects, therefore, appear different to us according to the disposition of the moment; for, even madmen are not in a state contrary to nature. For, why are we to say that of them more than of ourselves? For we too look at the sun as if it stood still. Theon, of Tithora, the Stoic, used to walk about in his sleep; and a slave of Pericles' used, when in the same state, to walk on the top of the house.

83. The fifth mode is conversant with laws, and established customs, and belief in mythical traditions, and the conventions of art, and dogmatical opinions. This mode embraces all that relates to vice, and to honesty; to the true, and to the false; to the good, and to the bad; to the Gods, and to the production, and destruction of all visible objects. Accordingly, the same action is just in the case of some people, and unjust in that of others. And good in the case of some, and bad in that of others. On this principle we see that the Persians do not think it unnatural for a man to marry his daughter; but among the Greeks it is unlawful. Again, the Massagetae, as Eudoxus tells us in the first book of his Travels over the World, have their women in common; but the Greeks do not. And the Cilicians delight in piracy, but the Greeks avoid it.

84. So again, different nations worship different Gods; and some believe in the providence of God, and others do not. The Egyptians embalm their dead, and then bury them; the Romans burn them; the Paeonians throw them into the lakes. All these considerations show that we ought to suspend our judgment.

The sixth mode has reference to the promiscuousness and confusion of objects; according to which nothing is seen by us simply and by itself; but in combination either with air, or with light, or with moisture, or with solidity, or heat, or cold, or motion, or evaporation or some other power. Accordingly, purple exhibits a different hue in the sun, and in the moon, and in a lamp. And our own complexions appear different when seen at noonday and at sunset.

85. And a stone which one cannot lift in the air, is easily displaced in the water, either because it is heavy itself and is made light by the water, or because it is light in itself and is made heavy by the air. So that we cannot positively know the peculiar qualities of anything, just as we cannot discover oil in ointment.

The seventh mode has reference to distances, and position, and space, and to the objects which are in space. In this mode one establishes the fact that objects which we believe to be large, sometimes appear small; that those which we believe to be square, sometimes appear round; that those which we fancy even, appear full of projections; those which we think straight, seem bent; and those which we believe to be colourless, appear of quite a different complexion.

86. Accordingly, the sun, on account of its distance from us, appears small. The mountains too, at a distance, appear airy masses and smooth, but when beheld close, they are rough. Again, the sun has one appearance at his rise, and quite a different one at midday. And the same body looks very different in a wood from what it does on plain ground. So too, the appearance of an object changes according to its position as regards us; for instance, the neck of a dove varies as it turns. Since then, it is impossible to view these things irrespectively of place and position, it is clear that their real nature is not known.

The eighth mode has respect to the magnitudes or quantities of things; or to the heat or coldness, or to the speed or slowness, or to the paleness or variety of colour of the subject. For instance, a moderate quantity of wine when taken invigorates, but an excessive quantity weakens. And the same is the case with food, and other similar things.

87. The ninth depends upon the frequency, or rarity, or strangeness of the thing under consideration. For instance, earthquakes excite no wonder among those nations with whom they are of frequent occurrence; nor does the sun, because he is seen every day.

The ninth mode is called by Favorinus, the eighth, and by Sextus and Aenesidemus, the tenth; and Sextus calls the tenth the eighth, which Favorinus reckons the tenth as the ninth in order.

The tenth mode refers to the comparison between one thing and another; as, for instance, between what is light and what is heavy; between what is strong and what is weak; between what is greater and what is less; what is above and what is below. For instance, that which is on the right, is not on the right intrinsically and by nature, but it is looked upon as such in consequence of its relation to something else; and if that other thing be transposed, then it will no longer be on the right.

88. In the same way, a man is spoken of as a father, or brother, or relation to some one else; and day is called so in relation to the sun; and everything has its distinctive name in relation to human thought: therefore, those things which are known in relation to others, are unknown of themselves.

And these are the ten modes. [. . .]

That which refers to the disagreement of opinions, shows that all the questions which philosophers propose to themselves, or which people in general discuss, are full of uncertainty and contradiction. [. . .]

90. These Skeptics then deny the existence of any demonstration, of any test of truth, of any signs, or causes, or motion, or learning, and of anything as intrinsically or naturally good or bad. For every demonstration, say they, depends either on things which demonstrate themselves, or on principles which are indemonstrable. If on things which demonstrate themselves, then these things themselves require demonstration; and so on *ad infinitum*. If on principles which are indemonstrable, then, the very moment that either the sum total of these principles or even one single one of them, is incorrectly urged, the whole demonstration falls instantly to pieces. But if any one supposes, they add, that there are principles which require no demonstration, that man deceives himself strangely, not seeing that it is necessary for him in the first place to establish this point, that they contain their proof in themselves.

91. For a man cannot prove that there are four elements, [from the mere fact that] there are four elements.

Besides, if particular proofs are denied in a complex demonstration, it must follow that the whole demonstration is also incorrect. Again, if we are to know that an argument is really a demonstrative proof, we must have a test of truth; and in order to establish a test, we require a demonstrative proof; and these two things must be devoid of every kind of certainty, since they bear reciprocally the one on the other.

How then is any one to arrive at certainty about obscure matters, if one is ignorant even how one ought to attempt to prove them? For what one is desirous to understand is not what the appearance of things is, but what their nature and essence is.

They show, too, that the dogmatic philosophers act [like simpletons]; for the conclusions which they draw from their hypothetical principles, are not scientific truths but mere suppositions; and that, in the same manner, one might establish the most improbable propositions.

92. They also say that those who pretend that one ought not to judge of things by the circumstances which surround them, or by their accessories, but that one ought to take their nature itself as one's guide, do not perceive that, while they pretend to give the precise

measure and definition of everything, if the objects present such and such an appearance, that depends solely on their position and relative arrangement. They conclude from thence, that it is necessary to say that everything is true, or that everything is false. For if certain things only are true, how is one to recognize them? Evidently it will not be the senses which judge in that case of the objects of sensation, for all appearances are equal to the senses; nor will it be the intellect, for the same reason. But besides these two faculties, there does not appear to be any other test or criterion at all: So, say they, if we desire to arrive at any certainty with respect to any object which comes under either sense or intellect, we must first establish those opinions which are laid down previously [by others] as bearing on those objects. For some people have denied this doctrine, and others have overturned that; it is therefore indispensable that they should be judged of either by the senses or by the intellect. And the authority of each of these faculties is contested.

93. It is therefore impossible to form a positive judgment of the operations of the senses and of the intellect; and if the contest between the different opinions compels us to a neutrality, then the measure which appeared proper to apply, to the appreciation of all those objects is at the same time put an end to, and one must fix a similar valuation on everything.

Perhaps our opponent will, say, "Are then appearances trustworthy or deceitful?"

We answer that, if they are trustworthy, the other side has nothing to object to those to whom the contrary appearance presents itself. For, as he who says that such and such a thing appears to him is trustworthy, so also is he who says that the contrary appears to him. And if appearances are deceitful, then they do not deserve any confidence when they assert what appears to them to be true.

94. We are not bound then to believe that a thing is true, merely because it obtains assent. For all men do not yield to the same reasons; and even the same individual does not always see things in the same light. Persuasion often depends on external circumstances, on the authority of the speaker, on his ability, on the elegance of his language, on habit, or even on pleasure.

They also, by this train of reasoning, suppress the criterion of truth. Either the criterion has been decided on, or it has not. And if it has not, it does not deserve any confidence, and it cannot be of any use at all in aiding us to discern truth from falsehood. If, on the other hand, it has been decided on, it then enters into the class of particular things which require a criterion, and in that case to judge and to be judged amount to the same thing; the criterion which judges is itself judged of by something else, that again by a third criterion, and so on *ad infinitum*.

95. Add to this, say they, the fact that people are not even agreed as to the nature of the criterion of truth; some say that man is the criterion, others that it is the senses which are so; one set places reason in the van, another class rely upon cataleptic perception.

As to man himself, he disagrees both with himself and with others, as the diversity of laws and customs proves. The senses are deceivers, and reason disagrees with itself. Cataleptic perception is judged of by the intellect, and the intellect changes in various manners; accordingly, we can never find any positive criterion, and in consequence, truth itself wholly eludes our search.

96. They also affirm that there are no such things as signs; for if there are signs, they argue they must be such as are apprehended either by the senses or by the intellect. Now, there are none which are apprehended by the senses, for everything which is apprehended by the senses is general, while a sign is something particular. Moreover, any object which is apprehended by the senses has an existence of its own, while signs are only relative. Again,

signs are not apprehended by the intellect, for in that case they would be either the visible manifestation of a visible thing, or the invisible manifestation of an invisible thing, or the invisible sign of a visible thing; or the visible sign of an invisible thing. But none of all these cases are possible; there are therefore no such things as signs at all.

There is therefore no such thing as a visible sign of a visible thing, for that which is visible has no need of a sign. Nor, again, is there any invisible sign of an invisible thing; for when anything is manifested by means of another thing, it must become visible. On the same principle there is no invisible sign of a visible object; for that which aids in the perception of something else must be visible.

97. Lastly, there is no visible manifestation of an invisible thing; for as a sign is something wholly relative, it must be perceived in that of which it is the sign; and that is not the case. It follows, therefore, that none of those things which are not visible in themselves admit of being perceived; for one considers signs as things which aid in the perception of that which is not evident by itself.

They also wholly discard, and, as far as depends on them, overturn the idea of any cause, by means of this same train of reasoning. Cause is something relative. It is relative to that of which it is the cause.

98. But that which is relative is only conceived, and has no real existence. The idea of a cause then is a pure conception; for, inasmuch as it is a cause, it must be a cause of something; otherwise it would be no cause at all. In the same way as a father cannot be a father, unless there exists some being in respect of whom one gives him the title of father; so too a cause stands on the same ground. For, supposing that nothing exists relatively to which a cause can be spoken of; then, as there is no production, or destruction, or anything of that sort, there can likewise be no cause. However, let us admit that there are such things as causes. In that case then, either a body must be the cause of a body, or that which is incorporeal must be the cause of that which is incorporeal. Now, neither of these cases is possible; therefore, there is no such thing as cause. In fact, one body cannot be the cause of another body, since both bodies must have the same nature; and if it be said that one is the cause, inasmuch as it is a body, then the other must be a cause for the same reason.

99. And in that case one would have two reciprocal causes; two agents without any passive subject.

Again, one incorporeal thing cannot be the cause of another incorporeal thing for the same reason. Also, an incorporeal thing cannot be the cause of a body, because nothing that is incorporeal can produce a body. Nor, on the other hand, can a body be the cause of anything incorporeal, because in every production there must be some passive subject matter; but, as what is incorporeal is by its own nature protected from being a passive subject, it cannot be the object of any productive power. There is, therefore, no such thing as any cause at all. From all which it follows, that the first principles of all things have no reality; for such a principle, if it did exist, must be both the agent and the efficient cause.

Again, there is no such thing as motion. For whatever is moved, is moved either in the place in which it is, or in that in which it is not. It certainly is not moved in the place in which it is, and it is impossible that it should be moved in the place in which it is not; therefore, there is no such thing as motion at all.

100. They also denied the existence of all learning. If, said they, anything is taught, then either that which does exist is taught in its existence or that which does not exist is taught in its non-existence; but that which does exist is not taught in its existence (for the nature of all existent things is visible to all men, and is known by all men); nor is that which does

not exist, taught in its non-existence, for nothing can happen to that which does not exist, so that to be taught cannot happen to it.

Nor again, say they, is there any such thing as production. For that which is, is not produced, for it exists already; nor that which is not, for that does not exist at all. And that which has no being nor existence at all, cannot be produced.

101. Another of their doctrines is that there is no such thing as any natural good, or natural evil. For if there be any natural good, or natural evil, then it must be good to everyone, or evil to everyone; just as snow is cold to everyone. But there is no such thing as one general good or evil which is common to all beings; therefore, there is no such thing as any natural good, or natural evil. For either one must pronounce everything good which is thought so by anyone whatever, or one must say that it does not follow that everything which is thought good is good. Now, we cannot say that everything which is thought good is good, since the same thing is thought good by one person (as, for instance, pleasure is thought good by Epicurus) and evil by another (as it is thought evil by Antisthenes); and on this principle the same thing will be both good and evil. If, again, we assert that it does not follow that everything which is thought good is good, then we must distinguish between the different opinions; which it is not possible to do by reason of the equality of the reasons adduced in support of them. It follows that we cannot recognize anything as good by nature. [. . .]

102. And the dogmatical philosophers arguing against them, say that they also adopt spurious and pronounce positive dogmas. For where they think that they are refuting others they are convicted, for in the very act of refutation, they assert positively and dogmatize. For when they say that they define nothing, and that every argument has an opposite argument, they do here give a positive definition, and assert a positive dogma.

103. But they reply to these objectors; as to the things which happen to us as men, we admit the truth of what you say; for we certainly do know that it is day, and that we are alive; and we admit that we know many other of the phaenomena of life. But with respect to those things as to which the dogmatic philosophers make positive assertions, saying that they are comprehended, we suspend our judgment on the ground of their being uncertain; and we know nothing but the passions; for we confess that we see, and we are aware that we comprehend that such a thing is the fact; but we do not know how we see, or how we comprehend. Also, we state in the way of narrative, that this appears white, without asserting positively that it really is so. And with respect to the assertion, "We define nothing," and other sentences of that sort, we do not pronounce them as dogmas.

104. For to say that is a different kind of statement from saying that the world is spherical; for the one fact is not evident, while the other statements are mere admissions.

While, therefore, we say that we define nothing, we do not even say that as a definition.

Again, the dogmatic philosophers say that the Skeptics overthrow all life, when they deny everything of which life consists. But the Skeptics say that they are mistaken; for they do not deny that they see, but that they do not know how it is that they see. For, say they, we assert what is actually the fact, but we do not describe its character. Again, we feel that fire burns, but we suspend our judgment as to whether it has a burning nature.

105. Also we see whether a person moves, and that a man dies; but how these things happen we know not. Therefore, say they, we only resist the uncertain deductions which are put by the side of evident facts. For when we say that an image has projections, we only state plainly what is evident; but when we say that it has not projections, we no longer say what appears evident, but something else. [. . .]

107. Lastly, the Skeptics say, that the chief good is the suspension of the judgment which tranquillity of mind follows, like its shadow, as Timon and Aenesidemus say.

108. For that we need not choose these things, or avoid those which all depend on ourselves: but as to those things which do not depend upon us, but upon necessity, such as hunger, thirst, and pain, those we cannot avoid; for it is not possible to put an end to them by reason.

But when the dogmatic philosophers object that the Skeptic, on his principles, will not refuse to kill his own father, if he is ordered to do so; so that they answer, that they can live very well without disquieting themselves about the speculations of the dogmatic philosophers, but suspend their judgment in all matters which do not refer to living and the preservation of life. Accordingly, say they, we avoid some things, and we seek others, following custom in that; and we obey the laws.

Some authors have asserted that the chief good of the Stoics is impassability; others say that it is mildness and tranquility.

30

Sextus Empiricus, *Outlines of Pyrrhonism*

In this selection, Sextus gives his own versions of how a real Skeptic (that is, a Pyrrhonian) manages to suspend belief, even in the face of what might first appear to be compelling evidence for some belief.

1.31–9

(1) Broadly speaking, this [suspension of judgement about everything] comes about because of the setting of things in opposition. We oppose either appearances to appearances, or ideas to ideas, or appearances to ideas. (2) We oppose appearances to appearances when we say 'The same tower seems round from a distance but square from near by.' (3) We oppose ideas to ideas when someone establishes the existence of providence from the orderliness of the things in the heavens and we oppose to this the frequency with which the good fare badly and the bad prosper, thereby deducing the non-existence of providence. (4) We oppose ideas to appearances in the way in which Anaxagoras opposed to snow's being white the consideration: snow is frozen water, and water is black, therefore snow is black too. (5) On a different scheme, we oppose sometimes present things to present things, as in the cases just given, but sometimes present things to past and future things. For example, when someone presents us with an argument for a thesis which we cannot refute, we reply, 'Just as before the founder of the school you follow was born the school's thesis did not yet seem sound, but was an objective natural fact, likewise it is possible that the very opposite thesis to the one you have just argued is an objective natural fact but does not yet appear so to us. Hence it is premature to assent to the thesis which appears powerful to us at the present moment.

[. . .]

1.40–61

(1) The first argument we mentioned was the one according to which depending on the difference between animals the same objects do not produce the same impressions. We infer this from their different modes of generation and the variety of their bodily make-up. (2) The point about modes of generation is that some animals are generated asexually, some

sexually; and of those generated asexually some are generated from fire, such as the tiny creatures that appear in ovens, others from putrescent water, such as mosquitoes . . . Of those generated sexually, some have homogeneous parents, like the majority of animals, others have heterogeneous parents, as mules do . . . It is likely, then, that the generative dissimilarities and divergences should produce great contrasts in the way the animals are affected, bringing in their wake incompatibility, incongruity and conflict. (3) Another potential source of conflict among impressions depending on the disparity between animals is the difference in the principal bodily parts, especially those whose natural function is to discriminate and to perceive. People with jaundice say that those things are yellow which appear white to us, and people with bloodshot eyes call them blood-red. Since, then, with animals too, some have yellow eyes, some bloodshot, some white, some of other colours, it is likely, I think, that they register colours in different ways . . . (4) The same argument applies to the other senses. How could the tactile processes of shelled, fleshy, prickly, feathered, and scaly creatures be called similar? How could hearing be called alike in creatures with the narrowest auditory ducts and those with the widest, or in those with hairy and those with bare ears, considering that even our own auditory processes are different when we block our ears from when we leave them alone? . . . (5) Just as the same food when digested becomes here a vein, here an artery, here a bone, here a sinew, and so on, revealing different capacities depending on the differences in the parts which absorb it . . . , so too it is likely that external objects are perceived differently according to the different structures of the animals undergoing the impressions. (6) A more self-evident understanding of the matter can be obtained from animals' choices and avoidances. Perfume seems delightful to men but unbearable to beetles and bees. Olive oil is beneficial to men, but is sprinkled to exterminate wasps and bees. Sea water, if drunk, is unpleasant and poisonous to men, but delicious and drinkable for fish. Pigs get more pleasure from wallowing in foul-smelling sewage than in clear pure water . . . If the same things are unpleasant to some animals but pleasant to others, and pleasant and unpleasant depend on impressions, the animals are receiving different impressions from objects. (7) If the same things appear unalike depending on the difference between animals, we will be able to say how the object is perceived by us, but will suspend judgement as to how it is in its own nature. For we ourselves will not be able to adjudicate between our own impressions and those of other animals: we are ourselves parties to the disagreement, and hence in need of an adjudicator, rather than capable of judging for ourselves. (8) Besides, we cannot judge our impressions superior to those found in irrational animals either without proof or with proof. For in addition to the possibility that proof does not exist, as we will note later, the so-called proof must itself be either apparent to us or non-apparent. If it is non-apparent, we will not propound it with confidence. But if it is apparent to us, since our inquiry is about what is apparent to animals and proof is apparent to us, who are animals, it will itself in so far as it is apparent be subject to inquiry as to its truth . . . (9) If, then, impressions differ depending on the divergences between animals, and there is no way of adjudicating between them, it is necessary to suspend judgement about external objects.

1.79–91

(1) Such is the first mode of suspending judgement. The second, as we said, is that derived from the difference between men. For even if one hypothetically grants that men are more credible than the irrational animals, we will find inducements to suspend judgement even so far as concerns our own differences. (2) Now man is said to have two constituents, namely

soul and body, and we differ from each other in respect of both. In respect of the body, we differ both in form and in our individual mixtures. For the body of a Scythian differs from the body of an Indian in form. This divergence is, it is said, the result of different predomin- ance of humours. And in accordance with different predominance of humours impressions also differ, as we established in the first argument . . . (3) Such are the differences of our individual mixtures that some men digest beef more easily than rock-fish, and get an upset stomach from a drop of Lesbian wine. There was reportedly an old Attic woman who could swallow thirty drams of hemlock without ill-effect. Lysis also used to take four drams of opium without upset. Demophon, Alexander's butler, shivered in the sun or in the bath but felt warm in the shade . . . (4) Since (if we may make do with listing a few of the many cases recorded by the doctrinaire writers) the divergence between men with regard to their bodies is so great, it is likely that they also differ from each other with regard to their actual souls. For the body is a sort of outline sketch of the soul, as is also shown by the science of physiognomics. (5) But the strongest indication of men's great and limitless mental differ- ences is the disagreement between what the doctrinaire thinkers say, especially about what to choose and what to avoid . . . (6) Since, then, choice and avoidance lie in pleasure and dis- pleasure, and pleasure and displeasure lie in sensation and impression, when some people choose what others avoid the natural consequence is for us to infer that they are not moved in even similar ways by the same things, since if they were they would have the same choices or avoidances. (7) But if the same things move us differently depending on the difference between men, that too might reasonably induce us to suspend judgement. Perhaps we are capable of saying how each object appears, with respect to each human difference, but not of asserting what its power is, with respect to its own nature. (8) For we will trust either all men, or some. If all, we will be attempting the impossible and accepting contradictories. If some, let them tell us whose view we are to assent to. The Platonist will say Plato's, the Epicurean Epicurus', and the others likewise. And by this inarbitrable dispute they will once again bring us round to suspension of judgement. (9) Anyone who says that we should assent to the *majority* opinion is accepting a childish idea. Nobody is capable of approaching all the men in the world and calculating what is the majority opinion. It is possible that in some tribes unknown to us things rare among us are found in the majority of people, while attributes which belong to the majority of us are rare . . . (10) Certain self-satisfied people, the doctri- naire thinkers, say that in judging things they should rate *themselves* above other men. We know the absurdity of this evaluation. They are, after all, themselves parties to the disagreement, and if their way of judging between appearances is to give themselves precedence they are, by entrusting the judgement to themselves, begging the question. But even so, in order to achieve the suspension of judgement by focusing the argument on a single man, such as their dream-figure the wise man, we adopt the third mode.

1.91–8

(1) This is how we label the mode which derives from the difference between the senses. That the senses are at variance with each other is pre-evident. (2) Pictures seem to the sense of sight to have concavities and convexities, but not to the touch. Honey seems pleasant to the tongue on some things, but unpleasant to the eyes, so that whether it is absolutely pleas- ant or unpleasant is impossible to say. Likewise perfume: it delights the sense of smell, but displeases that of taste . . . (3) Hence what each of these is like as regards its nature we will be unable to say. What we can say is how it appears on each occasion. (4) . . . Each of the

sense-objects which appear to us seems to make a complex impression on us. For example, the apple strikes us as smooth, pleasant-smelling, sweet and yellow. Consequently it is not evident whether it really has these and only these qualities; or whether it has a single quality, but appears different according to the different structures of the sense-organs; or whether it has more qualities than those apparent but some of them do not strike us. (5) The idea that it has a single quality can be worked out on the basis of our earlier remarks . . . (6) Our argument for the apple's having more qualities than those apparent to us is as follows. Let us imagine someone who from birth has had the senses of touch, smell and taste, but has lacked hearing and sight. He will start out believing in the existence of nothing visible or audible, but only of the three kinds of quality which he can register. It is therefore a possibility that we too, having only our five senses, only register from the qualities belonging to the apple those which we are capable of registering. But it may be that there objectively exist other qualities, and that these are the objects of further sense-organs which we do not share, so that we do not register the corresponding sense-objects either. (7) Someone will reply that nature made the senses co-extensive with the range of sense-objects. What *kind* of nature, in view of the great inarbitrable disagreement among the doctrinaire thinkers about natural existence? For anyone arbitrating the very question whether nature exists would, if he were a layman, according to them be unreliable. But if he is a philosopher, he will be a party to the disagreement, and himself subject to judgement, not a judge.

1.100–13

(1) In order also to be able to end up suspending judgement by focusing the argument on each individual sense, or even without reference to the senses, we adopt in addition the fourth mode. This is the one which we say depends on 'situations', a word which we use for 'dispositions'. We say that it is observed in the natural or unnatural state, in being awake or asleep, and depending on age, on motion or rest, on hating or liking, on want or satiety, on intoxication or sobriety, on predispositions, on confidence or fear, or on depression or elation. (2) For example, things strike us differently depending on whether our state is natural or unnatural, because those who are deranged or possessed seem to hear the voices of spirits, while we do not . . . And the same honey appears sweet to me but bitter to those with jaundice. (3) If someone says that it is an intermingling of certain bodily humours that produces, in those in an unnatural state, improper impressions deriving from objects, we must reply that since the healthy also have mixtures of humours, it is possible that external objects are in their nature such as they appear to people in the so-called 'unnatural' state, and that these mixtures make them appear different to the healthy. For to assign a power of distorting objects to one set of mixtures, while denying it to the other set, is artificial. Indeed, just as the healthy are in a state which is natural for the healthy but unnatural for the sick, so too the sick are in a state which is unnatural for the healthy but natural for the sick. So we should have faith in the sick too, as being relatively speaking, in a natural state. (4) . . . The point about 'depending on age' is that the same air seems chilly to the aged but mild to the youthful, and the same colour dull to the elderly but strong to the youthful . . . Things appear different 'depending on motion or rest' because things which we see as stationary when we are standing we think are moving when we sail past them . . . 'Depending on intoxication or sobriety': things we think infamous when sober appear not at all infamous to us when we are drunk. 'Depending on predispositions': the same wine appears dry to those who have just eaten dates or dried figs, but sweet to those who have been tasting nuts or

chick-peas . . . (5) Given that there is also such a great disparity depending on dispositions, and that men are differently disposed on different occasions, while it is perhaps easy to say how each object appears to each person, it is by no means easy to say what the object is like. For the disparity is inarbitrable: its arbitrator is either in some of the dispositions we have mentioned, or in no disposition whatsoever. Now to say that he is in absolutely no disposition – neither healthy nor sick, neither moving nor stationary, of no age, and likewise lacking the other dispositions – is completely incoherent. But if he is going to arbitrate our impressions while himself in some disposition, he is a party to the disagreement, and in any case he is not a neutral judge of external objects, his viewpoint being obscured by the dispositions he is in.

1.118–20

(1) The fifth mode is the one depending on positions, distances and locations. For according to each of these factors too the same things appear different. (2) For example, the same colonnade seen from one end appears tapering, and seen from the centre appears completely symmetrical. The same ship appears small and stationary from far off, large and moving from near by. The same tower appears round from far off but square from near by. These are examples depending on distances. (3) Examples depending on locations are that the light of a lantern appears dim in sunlight but bright in the dark, and that the same oar appears bent in water but straight when out of the water . . . (4) Examples depending on positions are that the same picture appears flat when lying on its back but at a certain angle seems to have concavities and convexities; and that pigeons' necks seem differently coloured depending on the angle of inclination.

1.124–8

(1) The sixth mode is the one based on admixtures, by which we deduce that since no object strikes us entirely by itself, but along with something, it may perhaps be possible to say what the mixture compounded out of the external object and the thing perceived with it is like, but we would not be able to say what the external object is like by itself. (2) That nothing external strikes us by itself, but always along with something, and that, depending on this, it is perceived as different, is I think pre-evident. Our colour appears one way in warm air, another in the cold, and we would not be able to say what our colour is like in its nature, but just how it is perceived along with each of these accompaniments. The same sound appears one way when accompanied by a rarefied atmosphere, another way when accompanied by a dense atmosphere. Smells are more pungent in a bath-house or in sunshine than in chilly air. And the body is light when immersed in water, but heavy when in air. (3) To pass on from external admixture, our eyes have membranes and liquids in them. Hence visible objects, since they are not seen without these, will not be accurately grasped. For what we are registering is the mixture, and that is why jaundice-sufferers see everything as yellow and those with bloodshot eyes see everything as blood-red . . . (4) Nor does the mind [register external objects accurately], especially since its guides the senses make mistakes. It may also be that it itself adds some admixture of its own to the reports of the senses. For we see certain fluids belonging to each of the regions in which the doctrinaire thinkers believe that the commanding-faculty is located – be it the brain, the heart, or whatever part of the animal one may care to put it in. (5) So according to this mode too we see that, being unable to say anything about the nature of external objects, we are forced to suspend judgement about it.

1.129–32

(1) The seventh mode, as we said, is the one which depends on the quantities and configurations of the objects. By 'configurations' we mean quite generally their composition. This is another mode according to which we are clearly forced to suspend judgement about the nature of things. (2) For example, filings of goatshorn, when perceived simply and not in composition, appear white, but composed in the actual horn they are perceived as black . . . Isolated grains of sand appear rough, but composed as a heap they produce a smooth sensory effect . . . (3) Wine drunk in moderation invigorates us, but taken in larger quantities incapacitates the body. And food likewise displays different powers depending on the quantity. Often through heavy consumption it purges the body with indigestion and diarrhoea. (4) Here too, then, we will be able to describe the quality of powdered horn and of the composite of many filings . . . , and in the cases of the sand . . . and the wine and the food to describe their relative qualities. But we will not be able to describe the nature of the things in itself, thanks to the disparity among impressions which depend on composition.

1.135–40

(1) The eighth mode is the one derived from relativity, on the basis of which we deduce that, since all things are relative, we will suspend judgement about what things exist absolutely and in nature. (2) It must be recognized that here, as elsewhere, we use 'are' loosely, to stand for 'appear', so that what we say is tantamount to 'all things are relative in appearance'. (3) This has two senses. One is in relation to the judging subject, since the external object being judged appears in relation to the judging subject. The other is in relation to the things perceived with it, like right in relation to left. (4) That all things are relative we have also argued earlier: so far as concerns the judging subject, that each thing is relative in appearance to the particular animal, the particular man, and the particular sense, and also to the particular situation; so far as concerns the things perceived with them, that each thing is relative in appearance to the particular admixture, the particular location, the particular composition, the particular quantity, and the particular position. (5) It can also be specifically deduced that all things are relative, as follows. Are differentiated things different from relative things, or not? If not, they too are relative. But if they are different, since everything different is relative, being called different in relation to that from which it differs, differentiated things are relative. (6) Also, of existing things, some are *summa genera* according to the doctrinaire thinkers, others *infimae species*, and yet others genera and species. And all of these are relative. Therefore all things are relative . . . (7) Even someone who denies that all things are relative *eo ipso* confirms that all things are relative. For by his means of opposing us he shows that 'All things are relative' is relative to us, and not universal. (8) It remains to add that, in view of our proof that all things are relative, it is clear that we will not be able to say what each object is like in its own nature and absolutely, but just how it appears in its relativity. It follows that we should suspend judgement about the nature of things.

1.141–4

(1) Here now is some explanation of the mode which we listed as ninth, the one depending on regularity or rarity of meeting. (2) The sun is much more astonishing than a comet, but because we see the sun regularly but the comet rarely, we are so astonished at the comet

as to think it a portent, but not at the sun. If, on the other hand, we imagine the appearance and setting of the sun as rare, and the sun as all at once illuminating the whole world, then suddenly casting it all into shade, we might expect to witness immense astonishment at it . . . (3) Also, rare things seem precious, whereas familiar and plentiful things do not. If we imagine water as a rarity, how much more precious it would appear to us than all the things that are thought precious. Or if we imagine gold simply scattered over the earth like stones, to whom could we expect it to be precious or worth hoarding? (4) Since, then, the same things seem astonishing or precious at some times but not at others, depending on regularity or rarity of confrontation, we reason that we will perhaps be able to say how each of them appears with regular or rare confrontation, but cannot baldly state what each of the external objects is like by itself. Hence this is another mode that leads us to suspend judgement about them.

1.145–63

(1) The tenth mode, which is also the most relevant to ethics, is the one depending on ways of life, customs, laws, legendary beliefs, and doctrinaire opinions. (2) A 'way of life' is a choice of lifestyle or of a certain behaviour adopted by one or many people, such as Diogenes [the Cynic] or the Spartans. (3) A law is a written agreement within the body politic, infringement of which incurs punishment. A custom, or convention (which is the same thing), is the acceptance of a certain behaviour in common between many people, infringement of which does not necessarily incur punishment. For example, not to commit adultery is a law, whereas not to have sexual intercourse in public is (for us) a custom. (4) A legendary belief is the acceptance of unhistorical and fictional events. A good example is the legends about Cronos, which induce many people to believe them. (5) A doctrinaire opinion is the acceptance of something which seems to be confirmed through analogical reasoning or through some proof, for example that as elements of existing things there are atoms, homogeneous substances, minima, or whatever. (6) We oppose each of these sometimes to itself, sometimes to each of the others. (7) For example, we oppose custom to custom as follows. Some Ethiopians tattoo their babies, but we do not. Persians think it proper to wear lurid ankle-length clothing, while we think it improper. And Indians have sexual intercourse in public, while most other races think it shameful. (8) We oppose law to law as follows . . . In Scythian Tauri, there was a law that foreigners should be sacrificed in propitiation of Artemis, while here human sacrifice is banned. (9) We oppose way of life to way of life when we oppose that of Diogenes to that of Aristippus, or that of the Spartans to that of the Italians. (10) We oppose legendary belief to legendary belief when we observe that in some places legend makes Zeus the father of men and gods, but in other places Ocean, quoting 'Ocean who begat the gods, and Tethys their mother' [Homer, *Iliad* XIV. 201]. (11) We oppose doctrinaire opinions to each other when we observe that some people declare that there is one element, others infinitely many; some say that the soul is mortal, others immortal; some say that our affairs are governed by divine providence, others that they are unprovidential. (12) We also oppose custom to the other things. For example to law, when we say that among the Persians intercourse beween males is customary, whereas among the Romans it is prohibited by law . . . (13) Custom is opposed to way of life when most men go indoors to have intercourse with their wives, while Crates [the Cynic] did it with Hipparchia in public . . . (14) Custom is opposed to legendary belief when the legends say that Cronos ate his own children, while our custom is to take care of children. And it is conventional among us to

revere the gods as good and impervious to harm, whereas the poets introduce gods who sustain wounds and bear grudges against each other. (15) Custom is opposed to doctrinaire opinion when our custom is to pray for blessings from the gods, whereas Epicurus says that divinity pays no attention to us . . . (16) We could have taken many more examples of each of the oppositions mentioned, but this will suffice as a summary. It just remains to add that since this mode too reveals such a great disparity among things, we will not be able to say what each object is like in its nature, but just how it appears in relation to this way of life, to this law, to this custom, and so on for each of the others. Therefore this is another mode which makes it necessary for us to suspend judgement about the nature of external objects. (17) That then is how, by means of the ten modes, we end up suspending judgement.

[. . .]

1.180–5

(1) Aenesidemus presents eight modes in accordance with which he thinks that he criticizes every doctrinaire causal theory and exposes it as defective. (2) The first, he says, is one according to which the whole class of causal theory, dealing as it does with non-apparent matters, does not have agreed attestation from things apparent. (3) The second is one according to which often, although the object of investigation has a plentiful variety of causal explanations available, some people choose a single kind of causal explanation for it. (4) Third is one according to which, when dealing with things which come about in an order, they expound causal explanations for them which display no order. (5) According to the fourth mode, they take the way apparent things come about and think they have grasped how non-apparent things come about. For although the non-apparent things *may* be effected in a way similar to apparent things, it is also possible that they are not, but in their own distinctive way. (6) According to the fifth, practically all base their causal theories on their own hypotheses about the elements, and not on some common and agreed methods. (7) According to the sixth, they often adopt findings obtained by their own hypotheses while rejecting equally convincing findings to the opposite effect. (8) According to the seventh, they often expound causal explanations which conflict not only with things apparent but also with their own hypotheses. (9) According to the eighth, the things thought to be apparent and the things subject to inquiry are often equally problematic, so that their demonstrations have their premises and their conclusions equally problematic. (10) It is not impossible, he says, that some people's errors in causal theory also accord with some mixed modes, dependent on those just listed.

31

Sextus Empiricus, *Against the Professors*

This selection gives a sample of Sextus' criticism of dogmatic philosophy, and explains several of the ways in which Academic Skepticism differed from Pyrrhonian Skepticism. Sextus considers the view of the Academic Skeptics of a criterion by which plausibility is given to beliefs, and argues that this makes them more Platonists than Skeptics. Sextus, a Pyrrhonian himself, argues that the true Skeptic denies that any belief can be more plausible than any another.

7.159–65

(1) On the subject of the criterion, Carneades marshalled arguments not only against the Stoics but also against all previous philosophers. (2) His first argument, aimed against all of them jointly, is one on the basis of which he establishes that there is not, in an unqualified sense, any criterion of truth – not reason, not sensation, not impression, not any other existing thing. For all of these alike deceive us. (3) His second argument is one on the basis of which he shows that even if this criterion does exist, it is not independent of the way we are affected by what is self-evident. (4) For since the animal differs from inanimate things by its sensory capacity, it will be entirely through this capacity that it registers both itself and external things. Sensation which is unmoved, unaffected and unaltered is not sensation at all, and is incapable of registering anything: it is when it is altered, and affected in some way in accordance with the impingement of things which are self-evident, that it reveals objects. (5) Therefore it is in the way that the soul is affected as a result of self-evidence that the criterion must be sought. This affection must be capable of revealing itself and the object which produced it in us. Such an affection is nothing other than the impression. Hence we should say that an impression is a sort of affection belonging to the animal, capable of presenting both itself and that which is distinct from itself. (6) For example, when (as Antiochus puts it) we look at something, we have our vision in a certain condition, and not in the same condition as we had it in before the act of seeing. But on the basis of this kind of alteration we register two things: one, the alteration itself, i.e. the impression, the other the thing which produced the alteration in us, i.e. the object seen. Similarly too with the other senses. Hence just as light shows up both itself and all the things in it, so too the impression, as the prime

mover of the animal's knowledge, must in the manner of light both show up itself and be capable of revealing the self-evident object that caused it. (7) But because it does not always reveal what is truly there, but often deceives us and is at variance with the things which transmitted it, like incompetent messengers, a necessary consequence is that we cannot allow every impression to be a criterion of truth, but just, if any, the true impression. (8) Then since, once again there is no true impression of such a kind that it could not turn out to be false, but for every apparently true impression an indiscernible false one is found, the criterion will turn out to consist in an impression which spans true and false. But the impression which spans both of these is not cognitive, and, not being cognitive, will not be a criterion either. (9) Given that no impression is criterial [or 'judgemental'], reason could not be a criterion either, since it is derived from impression. This is plausible. For the object being judged must first appear to it, and nothing can appear without irrational sensation. (10) Therefore neither irrational sensation nor reason is a criterion.

[. . .]

7.166–75

(1) These were the arguments which Carneades set out in full as a strategy against the other philosophers, to prove the non-existence of the criterion. But since he himself too has some criterion demanded of him for the conduct of life and the attainment of happiness, he is virtually compelled, as far as he himself is concerned, to adopt a position on this by taking as his criterion both the 'convincing' impression and the one which is simultaneously convincing, undiverted and thoroughly explored. (2) What the difference is between these must be briefly indicated. The impression is an impression of something, i.e., both of that from which it arises and of that in which it arises: the former is, for instance, the external object of sensation, and the latter, say, a man. Being of this kind, it would have two dispositions, one relative to the impressor, the other relative to the person experiencing the impression. Now in regard to its disposition relative to the impressor, it is either true or false – true when it is in agreement with the impressor, and false when it is not in agreement. But in regard to its disposition relative to the person experiencing the impression, one impression is apparently true and the other not apparently true; of these, the apparently true is called 'manifestation' by the Academics, and 'convincingness' and 'convincing impression', while the not apparently true is called 'non-manifestation' and 'unconvincing impression'. For neither what appears immediately false, nor what is true but does not appear so to us, is of a nature to convince us. (3) Of these impressions, the one which is apparently false and not apparently true is to be ruled out and is not the criterion. (4) Of the apparently true impressions, one kind is dim, e.g. in the case of those whose apprehension of something is confused and not distinct, owing to the smallness of the thing observed or the length of the distance or even the weakness of their vision; the other kind, along with appearing true, is additionally characterized by the intensity of its appearing true. Of these again, the dim and feeble impression could not be a criterion; for since it does not clearly indicate either itself or its cause, it is not of a nature to convince us or to pull us to assent. But the impression which appears true and fully manifests itself is the criterion of truth according to Carneades and his followers. (5) As the criterion, it has a considerable breadth; and by admitting of degrees, it includes some impressions which are more convincing and striking in their form than others. Convincingness, for our present purpose, has three senses: first, what both is and appears true; secondly, what

is actually false but appears true; and thirdly, <what appears> true, <which is> common to them both. Hence the criterion will be the impression which appears true – also called 'convincing' by the Academics – but there are times when it actually turns out false, so that it is necessary actually to use the impression which is common on occasion to truth and falsehood. Yet the rare occurrence of this one, I mean the impression which counterfeits the truth [i.e. the second], is not a reason for distrusting the impression [i.e. the third] which tells the truth for the most part. For both judgements and actions, as it turns out, are regulated by what holds for the most part.

7.176–84

(1) Such then is the first and general criterion of Carneades and his followers. But since an impression never stands in isolation but one depends on another like links in a chain, a second criterion will be added which is simultaneously convincing and undiverted. E.g. someone who takes in an impression of a man necessarily also gets an impression of things to do with the man and with the extraneous circumstances – things to do with him like his colour, size, shape, motion, conversation, dress, foot-wear; and external circumstances like atmosphere, light, day, sky, earth, friends and everything else. So whenever none of these impressions diverts us by appearing false, but all with one accord appear true, our belief is all the greater. For we believe that this is Socrates from his having all his usual features – colour, size, shape, conversation, cloak, and his being in a place where there is no one indiscernible from him . . . (2) When Menelaus left the image of Helen (which he brought from Troy as Helen) on his ship, and disembarked on the island of Pharos, he saw the true Helen; but though he took in a true impression from her, he still did not believe an impression of that kind since he was diverted by another one, in virtue of which he *knew* he had left Helen on the ship. That is what the undiverted impression is like; and it too seems to have breadth, since one such impression is found to be more undiverted than another. (3) Still more credible than the undiverted impression, and the one which makes judgement most perfect, is the impression which combines being undiverted with also being thoroughly explored. Its features must next be explained. In the case of the undiverted impression, it is merely required that none of the impressions in the concurrence should divert us by appearing false but all should be ones which appear true and are not unconvincing. But in the case of the concurrence which involves the thoroughly explored impression, we meticulously examine each impression in the concurrence, in the way that happens at government assemblies, when the people cross-examine every candidate for political office or the judiciary, to see whether he is worthy to be entrusted with the office or the position of judge. (4) Thus . . . we make judgements about the properties of each of the items pertaining to the place of the judgement: the subject judging, in case his vision is faint . . . ; the object judged, in case it is too small; the medium of the judgement, in case the atmosphere is murky; the distance, in case it is too far . . . ; the place, in case it is too vast; the time, in case it is too short; the character, in case it is observed to be insane; and the activity, in case it is unacceptable. (5) For all of these in turn become the criterion – the convincing impression, and the one which is simultaneously convincing and undiverted, and in addition the one which is simultaneously convincing and undiverted and thoroughly explored. For this reason, as in everyday life when we are investigating a small matter we question a single witness, but in the case of a larger one several, and in a still more crucial matter we cross-question each of the witnesses from the mutual corroboration provided by the others – so, say Carneades and his followers, in

matters of no importance we make use of the merely convincing impression, but in weightier matters the undiverted impression as a criterion, and in matters which contribute to happiness the thoroughly explored impression.

[. . .]

9.139–41

(1) If, then, there are gods, they are animals. And if they are animals, they have sensation, since every animal is thought of as an animal in virtue of its sharing in sensation. (2) But if they have sensation, they are also affected by bitter and sweet. For it is not the case that while registering sense-objects through some other sense they do not do so also through that of taste. (3) Hence simply to strip god of this or any other sense is quite unconvincing, for if man has more senses than god he will be superior to god, whereas, as Carneades said, god ought to have, as well as these five senses which we all have, the additional evidence of further senses, so as to be able to register more things, rather than be deprived of the five. (4) Therefore we must say that god has some sense of taste, through which he registers taste-objects. But if he registers through the sense of taste, he is affected by sweet and bitter. And if he is affected by sweet and bitter, he will be pleased by some things and displeased by others. But if he is displeased by some things, he will be vulnerable to distress and to change for the worse. If so, he is perishable. (5) Hence if there are gods, they are perishable. Therefore there are no gods.

[. . .]

9.182–4

(1) There are also some arguments posed by Carneades in the manner of the Sorites. They were written up by his colleague Clitomachus, who took them to be very weighty and effective, and they take the following form. (2) 'If Zeus is a god, . . . Posidon too, being his brother, will be a god. But if Posidon is a god, the [river] Achelous too will be a god. And if the Achelous is, so is the Nile. If the Nile is, so are all rivers. If all rivers are, streams too would be gods. If streams were, torrents would be. But streams are not. Therefore Zeus is not a god either. But if there were gods, Zeus too would be a god. Therefore there are no gods.' (3) Again, 'If the sun is a god, day too would be a god (for day is nothing but the sun above the earth). And if day is a god, so will the month be (for it is a compound of days). And if the month is a god, the year too would be a god (for the year is a compound of months). But not the last. Therefore not the first either.'

[. . .]

Part IX

Neoplatonism

Introduction

After Plato's death his Academy soon entered a period in which the so-called Academic Skeptics ran the school. But, starting in the first century BCE and continuing through the second century CE, several members of the Academy and other noteworthy thinkers from around the Greek world aligned themselves with the Stoics and Peripatetics (see the introductions to parts IV and VII above for details) and sought to reclaim Platonic philosophy from the Skeptics. This group of philosophers is now known as the "Middle Platonists," and it was from within this group that a powerful new understanding of Platonic philosophy emerged, now called "Neoplatonism," first advanced by Plotinus (204/5–70 CE), then followed by his disciple (and biographer), Porphyry (234–c.305 CE), then Porphyry's disciple, Iamblichus (c.245–325 CE), and then, later, perhaps the most important Neoplatonist other than Plotinus himself, Proclus (412–85 CE). This section includes selections from both Plotinus and Proclus.

After Imablichus, two schools of Neoplatonism became established: one in Athens, and one in Alexandria, Egypt. The Athenian school was eventually forcibly closed by the Byzantine emperor Justinian in 529 CE, scattering the school's members into exile in Persia. The Alexandrian school survived somewhat longer, but eventually perished in the Muslim conquest in the seventh century CE. Even though Christianity and Islam sought to destroy Greek philosophy, the influence of Neoplatonism in particular is plain enough in the theologies of both religions, especially through the writings of Proclus.

The main doctrines of Neoplatonism are these: (1) There is a single first principle, which they called either "the One" or "the Good." This first principle provides the ultimate explanation of everything. (2) In addition to the One, however, is Intellect (*Nous*), which forever desires absolute union with the One, and which forever achieves this in the only way it can, which is via contemplation of the realm of Forms. (3) Soul (*Psychē*) they understood not as the principle of life, as it had been conceived by the earlier Greeks, but as the principle of desire, which they said strives always for the One or the Good. Intellect serves as the instrument of the One to provide the structure of reality; Soul serves as the instrument of the One and Intellect ensuring that all things strive towards some goal that is beyond themselves.

32

Plotinus, *Enneads*

Plotinus (204/5–70 CE) wrote nothing until he was 50 years old. But then he began to write a series of philosophical essays, intended to explicate and derive further consequences from Platonic philosophy. These essays were collected by Plotinus' student and biographer Porphyry (234–c.305 CE), who classified them roughly according to subject and then arranged them in six "Enneads" or groups of nine. It is not at all clear why he found this the appropriate arrangement. The *Enneads* cover every topic of Greek philosophy except for politics. *Enneads* I covers ethics and aesthetics; II and III discuss physics and cosmology; the theory of soul is provided in IV; and V and VI cover logic, epistemology, and metaphysics. The density of his style may derive not only from the transcendence of his subject matter, but also from the fact that the writings themselves may have been intended as lectures, and these he never revised because of his struggles with poor eyesight.

The following selections are *Enneads* I.6 (On Beauty), IV.8 (The Descent of the Soul), V.1 (The Three Primal Hypostases); and VI.9 (The Good or The One).

I.6   Beauty

1. Chiefly beauty is visual. Yet in word patterns and in music (for cadences and rhythms are beautiful) it addresses itself to the hearing as well. Dedicated living, achievement, character, intellectual pursuits are beautiful to those who rise above the realm of the senses; to such ones the virtues, too, are beautiful. Whether the range of beauty goes beyond these will become clear in the course of this exposition.

What makes bodily forms beautiful to behold and has one give ear to sounds because they are "beautiful"? Why is it that whatever takes its rise directly from the soul is, in each instance, beautiful? Is everything beautiful with the one same beauty, or is there a beauty proper to the bodily and another to the bodiless? What, one or many, is beauty?

Some things, as the virtues, are themselves beautiful. Others, as bodily forms, are not themselves beautiful but are beautiful because of something added to them: the same bodies are seen to be at times beautiful, at other times not, so that to be body is one thing and to be beautiful is something else again.

Now what this something is that is manifest in some bodily forms we must inquire into first. Could we discover what this is – what it is that lures the eyes of onlookers, bends them to itself, and makes them pleased with what they see – we could "mount this ladder" for a wider view.

On every side it is said that visual beauty is constituted by symmetry of parts one with another and with the whole (and, in addition, "goodly coloration"); that in things seen (as, generally speaking, in all things else) the beautiful simply is the symmetrical and proportioned. Of necessity, say those who hold this theory, only a composite is beautiful, something without parts will never be beautiful; and then, they say, it is only the whole that is beautiful, the parts having no beauty except as constituting the whole.

However, that the whole be beautiful, its parts must be so, too; as beautiful, it cannot be the sum of ugliness: beauty must pervade it wholly. Further: colors, beautiful hues as those of the sun, this theory would rule out; no parts, therefore no symmetry, therefore no beauty. But is not gold beautiful? And a single star by night? It is the same with sound: the simple tone would be proscribed, yet how often each of the sounds that contribute to a beautiful ensemble is, all by itself, beautiful. When one sees the same face, constant in its symmetry, now beautiful and now not, is it not obvious that beauty is other than symmetry, that symmetry draws its beauty from something else?

And what of the beauty of dedicated lives, of thought expressed? Is symmetry here the cause? Who would suggest there is symmetry in such lives, or in laws, or in intellectual pursuits?

What symmetry is there in points of abstract thought? That of being accordant with one another? There may be accord, even complete agreement, where there is nothing particularly estimable: the idea that "temperance is folly" fits in with the idea that "justice is naïve generosity"; the accord is perfect.

Then again, every virtue is a beauty of The Soul – more authentically beautiful than anything mentioned so far. The Soul, it is true, is not a simple unity. Yet neither does it have quantitative numerical symmetry. What yardstick could preside over the balancing and interplay of The Soul's potencies and purposes?

Finally, in what would the beauty of that solitary, The Intelligence, consist?

2. Let us, then, go back to the beginning and determine what beauty is in bodily forms.

Clearly it is something detected at a first glance, something that the soul – remembering – names, recognizes, gives welcome to, and, in a way, fuses with. When the soul falls in with ugliness, it shrinks back, repulses it, turns away from it as disagreeable and alien. We therefore suggest that the soul, being what it is and related to the reality above it, is delighted when it sees any signs of kinship or anything that is akin to itself, takes its own to itself, and is stirred to new awareness of whence and what it really is.

But is there any similarity between loveliness here below and that of the intelligible realm? If there is, then the two orders will be – in this – alike. What can they have in common, beauty here and beauty there? They have, we suggest, this in common: they are sharers of the same Idea.

As long as any shapelessness that admits of being patterned and shaped does not share in reason or in Idea, it continues to be ugly and foreign to that above it. It is utter ugliness since all ugliness comes from an insufficient mastery by form and reason, matter not yielding at every point to formation in accord with Idea. When Idea enters in, it groups and arranges what, from a manifold of parts, is to become a unit; contention it transforms into collaboration, making the totality one coherent harmoniousness, because Idea is one and one as well (to the degree possible to a composite of many parts) must be the being it informs.

In what is thus compacted to unity, beauty resides, present to the parts and to the whole. In what is naturally unified, its parts being all alike, beauty is present to the whole. Thus there is the beauty craftsmanship confers upon a house, let us say, and all its parts, and there is the beauty some natural quality may give to a single stone.

3. The beauty, then, of bodily forms comes about in this way – from communion with the intelligible realm. Either the soul has a faculty that is peculiarly sensitive to this beauty – one incomparably sure in recognizing what is kin to it, while the entire soul concurs – or the soul itself reacts without intermediary, affirms a thing to be beautiful if it finds it accordant with its own inner Idea, which it uses as canon of accuracy.

What accordance can there be between the bodily and the prior to the bodily? That is like asking on what grounds an architect, who has built a house in keeping with his own idea of a house, says that it is beautiful. Is it not that the house, aside from the stones, is inner idea stamped upon outer material, unity manifest in diversity? When one discerns in the bodily the Idea that binds and masters matter of itself formless and indeed recalcitrant to formation, and when one also detects an uncommon form stamped upon those that are common, then at a stroke one grasps the scattered multiplicity, gathers it together, and draws it within oneself to present it there to one's interior and indivisible oneness as concordant, congenial, a friend. The procedure is not unlike that of a virtuous man recognizing in a youth tokens of a virtue that is in accord with his own achieved goodness.

The beauty of a simple color is from form: reason and Idea, an invasion of incorporeal light, overwhelm the darkness inherent in matter. That is why fire glows with a beauty beyond all other bodies, for fire holds the rank of Idea in their regard. Always struggling aloft, this subtlest of elements is at the last limits of the bodily. It admits no other into itself, while all bodies else give it entry; it is not cooled by them, they are warmed by it; it has color primally, they receive color from it. It sparkles and glows like an Idea. Bodies unable to sustain its light cease being beautiful because they thus cease sharing the very form of color in its fullness.

In the realm of sound, unheard harmonies create harmonies we hear because they stir to an awareness of beauty by showing it to be the single essence in diversity. The measures in music, you see, are not arbitrary, but fixed by the Idea whose office is the mastering of matter.

This will suffice for the beauties of the realm of sense, which – images, shadow pictures, fugitives – have invaded matter, there to adorn and to ravish wherever they are perceived.

4. But there are beauties more lofty than these, imperceptible to sense, that the soul without aid of sense perceives and proclaims. To perceive them we must go higher, leaving sensation behind on its own low level.

It is impossible to talk about bodily beauty if one, like one born blind, has never seen and known bodily beauty. In the same way, it is impossible to talk about the "luster" of right living and of learning and of the like if one has never cared for such things, never beheld "the face of justice" and temperance and seen it to be "beyond the beauty of evening or morning star." Seeing of this sort is done only with the eye of the soul. And, seeing thus, one undergoes a joy, a wonder, and a distress more deep than any other because here one touches truth.

Such emotion all beauty must induce – an astonishment, a delicious wonderment, a longing, a love, a trembling that is all delight. It may be felt for things invisible quite as for things you see, and indeed the soul does feel it. All souls, we can say, feel it, but souls that are apt for love feel it especially. It is the same here as with bodily beauty. All perceive it. Not all are stung sharply by it. Only they whom we call lovers ever are.

5. These lovers of beauty beyond the realm of sense must be made to declare themselves.

What is your experience in beholding beauty in actions, manners, temperate behavior, in all the acts and intents of virtue? Or the beauty in souls? What do you feel when you see that you are yourselves all beautiful within? What is this intoxication, this exultation, this longing to break away from the body and live sunken within yourselves? All true lovers experience it. But what awakens so much passion? It is not shape, or color, or size. It is the soul, itself "colorless," and the soul's temperance and the hueless "luster" of its virtues. In yourselves or others you see largeness of spirit, goodness of life, chasteness, the courage behind a majestic countenance, gravity, the self-respect that pervades a temperament that is calm and at peace and without passion; and above them all you see the radiance of The Intelligence diffusing itself throughout them all. They are attractive, they are lovable. Why are they said to be beautiful? "Because clearly they are beautiful and anyone that sees them must admit that they are true realities." What sort of realities? "Beautiful ones." But reason wants to know why they make the soul lovable, wants to know what it is that, like a light, shines through all the virtues.

Let us take the contrary, the soul's varied ugliness, and contrast it with beauty; for us to know what ugliness is and why it puts in its appearance may help us attain our purpose here.

Take, then, an ugly soul. It is dissolute, unjust, teeming with lusts, torn by inner discord, beset by craven fears and petty envies. It thinks indeed. But it thinks only of the perishable and the base. In everything perverse, friend to filthy pleasures, it lives a life abandoned to bodily sensation and enjoys its depravity. Ought we not say that this ugliness has come to it as an evil from without, soiling it, rendering it filthy, "encumbering it" with turpitude of every sort, so that it no longer has an activity or a sensation that is clean? For the life it leads is dark with evil, sunk in manifold death. It sees no longer what the soul should see. It can no longer rest within itself but is forever being dragged towards the external, the lower, the dark. It is a filthy thing, I say, borne every which way by the allurement of objects of sense, branded by the bodily, always immersed in matter and sucking matter into itself. In its trafficking with the unworthy it has bartered its Idea for a nature foreign to itself.

If someone is immersed in mire or daubed with mud, his native comeliness disappears; all one sees is the mire and mud with which he is covered. Ugliness is due to the alien matter that encrusts him. If he would be attractive once more, he has to wash himself, get clean again, make himself what he was before. Thus we would be right in saying that ugliness of soul comes from its mingling with, fusion with, collapse into the bodily and material: the soul is ugly when it is not purely itself. It is the same as with gold that is mixed with earthy particles. If they are worked out, the gold is left and it is beautiful; separated from all that is foreign to it, it is gold with gold alone. So also the soul. Separated from the desires that come to it from the body with which it has all too close a union, cleansed of the passions, washed clean of all that embodiment has daubed it with, withdrawn into itself again – at that moment the ugliness, which is foreign to the soul, vanishes.

6. For it is as was said of old: "Temperance, courage, every virtue – even prudence itself – are purifications." That is why in initiation into the mystery religions the idea is adumbrated that the unpurified soul, even in Hades, will still be immersed in filth because the unpurified loves filth for filth's sake quite as swine, foul of body, find their joy in foulness. For what is temperance, rightly so called, but to abstain from the pleasures of the body, to reject them rather as unclean and unworthy of the clean? What else is courage but being unafraid of death, that mere parting of soul from body, an event no one can fear whose happiness lies in being his own unmingled self? What is magnanimity except scorn of earthly

things? What is prudence but the kind of thinking that bends the soul away from earthly things and draws it on high?

Purified, the soul is wholly Idea and reason. It becomes wholly free of the body, intellective, entirely of that intelligible realm whence comes beauty and all things beautiful. The more intellective it is, the more beautiful it is. Intellection, and all that comes from intellection, is for the soul a beauty that is its own and not another's because then it is that the soul is truly soul. That is why one is right in saying that the good and the beauty of the soul consist in its becoming godlike because from the divinity all beauty comes and all the constituents of reality. Beauty is genuine reality; ugliness, its counter. Ugliness and evil are basically one. Goodness and beauty are also one (or, if you prefer, the Good and Beauty). Therefore the one same method will reveal to us the beauty-good and the ugliness-evil.

First off, beauty is the Good. From the Good, The Intelligence draws its beauty directly. The Soul is, because of The Intelligence, beautiful. Other beauties, those of action or of behavior, come from the imprint upon them of The Soul, which is author, too, of bodily beauty. A divine entity and a part, as it were, of Beauty, The Soul renders beautiful to the fullness of their capacity all things it touches or controls.

7. Therefore must we ascend once more towards the Good, towards there where tend all souls.

Anyone who has seen it knows what I mean, in what sense it is beautiful. As good, it is desired and towards it desire advances. But only those reach it who rise to the intelligible realm, face it fully, stripped of the muddy vesture with which they were clothed in their descent (just as those who mount to the temple sanctuaries must purify themselves and leave aside their old clothing), and enter in nakedness, having cast off in the ascent all that is alien to the divine. There one, in the solitude of self, beholds simplicity and purity, the existent upon which all depends, towards which all look, by which reality is, life is, thought is. For the Good is the cause of life, of thought, of being.

Seeing, with what love and desire for union one is seized – what wondering delight! If a person who has never seen this hungers for it as for his all, one that has seen it must love and reverence it as authentic beauty, must be flooded with an awesome happiness, stricken by a salutary terror. Such a one loves with a true love, with desires that flame. All other loves than this he must despise and all that once seemed fair he must disdain.

Those who have witnessed the manifestation of divine or supernal realities can never again feel the old delight in bodily beauty. What then are we to think of those who see beauty in itself, in all its purity, unencumbered by flesh and body, so perfect is its purity that it transcends by far such things of earth and heaven? All other beauties are imports, are alloys. They are not primal. They come, all of them, from it. If then one sees it, the provider of beauty to all things beautiful while remaining solely itself and receiving nothing from them, what beauty can still be lacking? This is true and primal beauty that graces its lovers and makes them worthy of love. This is the point at which is imposed upon the soul the sternest and uttermost combat, the struggle to which it gives its total strength in order not to be denied its portion in this best of visions, which to attain is blessedness. The one who does not attain to it is life's unfortunate, not the one who has never seen beautiful colors or beautiful bodies or has failed of power and of honors and of kingdoms. He is the true unfortunate who has not seen this beauty and he alone. It were well to cast kingdoms aside and the domination of the entire earth and sea and sky if, by this spurning, one might attain this vision.

8. What is this vision like? How is it attained? How will one see this immense beauty that dwells, as it were, in inner sanctuaries and comes not forward to be seen by the profane?

Let him who can arise, withdraw into himself, forego all that is known by the eyes, turn aside forever from the bodily beauty that was once his joy. He must not hanker after the graceful shapes that appear in bodies, but know them for copies, for traceries, for shadows, and hasten away towards that which they bespeak. For if one pursue what is like a beautiful shape moving over water – Is there not a myth about just such a dupe, how he sank into the depths of the current and was swept away to nothingness? Well, so too, one that is caught by material beauty and will not cut himself free will be precipitated, not in body but in soul, down into the dark depths loathed by The Intelligence where, blind even there in Hades, he will traffic only with shadows, there as he did here.

"Let us flee then to the beloved Fatherland." Here is sound counsel. But what is this flight? How are we to "gain the open sea"? For surely Odysseus is a parable for us here when he commends flight from the sorceries of a Circe or a Calypso, being unwilling to linger on for all the pleasure offered to his eyes and all the delight of sense that filled his days. The Fatherland for us is there whence we have come. There is the Father. What is our course? What is to be the manner of our flight? Here is no journeying for the feet; feet bring us only from land to land. Nor is it for coach or ship to bear us off. We must close our eyes and invoke a new manner of seeing, a wakefulness that is the birthright of us all, though few put it to use.

What, then, is this inner vision?

9. Like anyone just awakened, the soul cannot look at bright objects. It must be persuaded to look first at beautiful habits, then the works of beauty produced not by craftsman's skill but by the virtue of men known for their goodness, then the souls of those who achieve beautiful deeds. "How can one see the beauty of a good soul?" Withdraw into yourself and look. If you do not as yet see beauty within you, do as does the sculptor of a statue that is to be beautified: he cuts away here, he smooths it there, he makes this line lighter, this other one purer, until he disengages beautiful lineaments in the marble. Do you this, too. Cut away all that is excessive, straighten all that is crooked, bring light to all that is overcast, labor to make all one radiance of beauty. Never cease "working at the statue" until there shines out upon you from it the divine sheen of virtue, until you see perfect "goodness firmly established in stainless shrine." Have you become like this? Do you see yourself, abiding within yourself, in pure solitude? Does nothing now remain to shatter that interior unity, nor anything external cling to your authentic self? Are you entirely that sole true light which is not contained by space, not confined to any circumscribed form, not diffused as something without term, but ever unmeasurable as something greater than all measure and something more than all quantity? Do you see yourself in this state? Then you have become vision itself. Be of good heart. Remaining here you have ascended aloft. You need a guide no longer. Strain and see.

Only the mind's eye can contemplate this mighty beauty. But if it comes to contemplation purblind with vice, impure, weak, without the strength to look upon brilliant objects, it then sees nothing even if it is placed in the presence of an object that can be seen. For the eye must be adapted to what is to be seen, have some likeness to it, if it would give itself to contemplation. No eye that has not become like unto the sun will ever look upon the sun; nor will any that is not beautiful look upon the beautiful. Let each one therefore become godlike and beautiful who would contemplate the divine and beautiful.

So ascending, the soul will come first to The Intelligence and will survey all the beautiful Ideas therein and will avow their beauty, for it is by these Ideas that there comes all beauty else, by the offspring and the essence of The Intelligence. What is beyond The Intelligence we affirm to be the nature of good, radiating beauty before it.

Thus, in sum, one would say that the first hypostasis is Beauty. But, if one would divide up the intelligibles, one would distinguish Beauty, which is the place of the Ideas, from the Good that lies beyond the beautiful and is its "source and principle." Otherwise one would begin by making the Good and Beauty one and the same principle. In any case it is in the intelligible realm that Beauty dwells.

IV.8 The Descent of The Soul

1. It has happened often.

Roused into myself from my body – outside everything else and inside myself – my gaze has met a beauty wondrous and great. At such moments I have been certain that mine was the better part, mine the best of lives lived to the fullest, mine identity with the divine. Fixed there firmly, poised above everything in the intellectual that is less than the highest, utter actuality was mine.

But then there has come the descent, down from intellection to the discourse of reason. And it leaves me puzzled. Why this descent?

Indeed, why did my soul ever enter my body since even when in the body it remains what it has shown itself to be when by itself?

Heracleitus, who urges the study of this matter, says that "contraries necessarily change into each other." But talking of "the way up and the way down," asserting that "change is repose," that "to make the same efforts and to obey is a wearisome business," he engages in metaphor and is little concerned with explaining himself, feeling perhaps that we should seek out the answers for ourselves as he did for himself.

Empedocles, for his part, says it is ordained that souls at fault descend into this world, that he himself was "fugitive from the divine, to mad discord enslaved." But he is, I fear, no more revealing than Pythagoras; his interpreters, here as elsewhere, find allegory; what is more, he speaks as a poet, and that adds to the obscurity.

But then there is the divine Plato who has had so much that is beautiful to say of the soul.

In the *Dialogues* he frequently treats of the soul's arrival in this world and awakens hope that here will be clarity. Unfortunately, consistency is not his strong point, so it is not easy to catch his meaning. However, everywhere he holds the bodily in low esteem; he deplores the association of soul with body; he says that the soul is enchained and entombed by the body; he considers "high doctrine with challenging implications" the assertion of the mystery religions that the soul when here below is in a prison. What he calls "the cave" seems to me, like the "grotto" of Empedocles, to signify the realm of sense, because for the soul "to break its chains and ascend" from its cave is, he says, to rise "to the intelligible realm." In the *Phaedrus* "the loss of its wings" is cause of the soul's descent; periodically recurring cycles bring the soul back down here after it has gone aloft. Judgments, loss, chance, and necessity drive other souls down into this world. In all these instances Plato deplores the association of soul with body.

Yet, treating of the sense world in the *Timaeus*, he praises it and calls it a "blessed god" and contends The Soul was given it by the goodness of the demiurge so that the sum of things might be possessed of intelligence, which, without The Soul, it could not be. The soul of each of us is dispatched hither for the same reason: if the realm of sense is to be complete, it is necessary that it contain as many kinds of living beings as does the intelligible realm.

2. So seeking in Plato an answer to questions about one's own soul, one is driven to questions about soul in general: How has soul been brought into association with body? Of what sort is this world in which soul (freely or necessarily or in any other way) lives? Did the demiurge do right in making this world? Or as our souls do?

It would seem that our souls, charged with the managing of bodies less perfect than they, had to penetrate into them if they were to manage them truly. For such bodies have a tendency to come apart, their parts struggling to return to their natural places (since everything in the cosmos has its natural place). More than that, such bodies require a knowing management that is both extensive and detailed because they are forever exposed to the assaults of alien bodies, are forever oppressed by wants; they need help, unremittingly, in the multiple adversities that beset them.

The body of The Soul, on the other hand, is perfect. It is complete. It is self-sufficient. It is not subject to influences that prevent its expressing its own nature. It requires, accordingly, only a light control. That is why The Soul remains free of care and molestations, its native disposition intact – "nothing going out, nothing coming in." Hence Plato says that the human soul, when it is with this perfect one, becomes perfect itself and "journeys on high and controls the whole world," and, so long as it does not withdraw (to enter a body, to be attached to something individual), exercises a control as effortless as that of The Soul. That it gives body existence is not necessarily to the soul's hurt: providing for a lower nature does not necessarily prevent the agency that exercises it from remaining itself in a state of perfection. Providence is of two kinds: it is directed to the whole and regulates everything after the fashion of kings, giving orders to be executed by others, or it is involved with detail and operates directly, adapting agent and acted upon one to the other. The Soul, divine, administers the heavens in the first way: transcending them in its highest phases and immanent to them solely in its lowest. One cannot accordingly accuse divinity of having assigned an inferior place to The Soul; it has never been deprived of its native status; this operation, which is not counter to its nature, it always possessed and always will.

In saying that the relation of the souls of the stars to their bodies is the same as that of The Soul of the world to the world (since these starry bodies are encompassed in the circuit of The Soul), Plato also accords the stars their appropriate happiness. Of the two objections against the interaction of soul and body – that it "hinders" the soul's intellective act and that it "fills" the soul with pleasure, "lust," fear – neither holds here. The soul has not penetrated deeply into body and is not dependent on the particular. Body is for it and not it for body. Its body lacks nothing, wants nothing. Hence the soul is free from both desires and fears. Since the starry body is what it is, the soul has no cause for disturbance on its account. Nothing intrudes upon its repose and makes it incline downward, robbing it of the high happiness of contemplation. It is always with the things in the realm above and, empowered and undisturbed, governs the realm of sense.

3. Let us now consider the human soul, which while in the body is subject to ills and suffering, a prey to griefs, lusts, fears, and evils of every kind, whose body is a "chain" or a "tomb" and the realm of sense a "cave" or a "grotto." That it should be thus does not go counter to the preceding; it is simply that the causes of its descent are different.

To begin with, The Intelligence dwells entire within that region of thought we call the intelligible realm, yet it comprises within itself a variety of intellective powers and particular intelligences. The Intelligence is not merely one: it is one and many. In the same way is there both Soul and many souls. From the one Soul proceeds a multiplicity of different souls, as from one and the same genus proceed species of various ranks, some of which are more rational and others (at least in their actual existence) less rational in form.

Again, in the intelligible realm there is The Intelligence, which like some huge organism contains potentially all other intelligences, and there are the individual intelligences, each of them an actuality. Think of a city as having a soul. It would include inhabitants, each of whom would have a soul. The soul of the city would be the more perfect and more powerful. What would prevent the souls of the inhabitants from being of the same nature as the soul of the city? Or, again, take fire, the universal, from which proceed large and small particular fires; all of them have a common essence, that of universal fire – or, rather, all partake of that essence whence proceeds universal fire. The function of The Soul, as intellective, is intellection. But it is not limited to intellection. If it were, there would be no distinction between it and The Intelligence. It has functions besides the intellectual and these, by which it is not simply intelligence, determine its distinctive existence. In directing itself to what is above itself, it thinks. In directing itself to itself, it preserves itself. In directing itself to what is lower than itself, it orders, administers, and governs. The reason for such an existent as The Soul is that the totality of things cannot continue limited to the intelligible so long as a succession of further existents is possible; although less perfect, they necessarily are because the prior existent necessarily is.

4. Thus individual souls are possessed by a desire for the intelligible that would have them return there whence they came, and they possess, too, a power over the realm of sense much in the way that sunshine, although attached to the sun above, does not deny its rays to what is below. If the souls remain in the intelligible realm with The Soul, they are beyond harm and share in The Soul's governance. They are like kings who live with the high king and govern with him and, like him, do not come down from the palace.

Thus far all are in the one same place.

But there comes a point at which they come down from this state, cosmic in its dimensions, to one of individuality. They wish to be independent. They are tired, you might say, of living with someone else. Each steps down into its own individuality.

When a soul remains for long in this withdrawal and estrangement from the whole, with never a glance towards the intelligible, it becomes a thing fragmented, isolated, and weak. Activity lacks concentration. Attention is tied to particulars. Severed from the whole, the soul clings to the part; to this one sole thing, buffeted about by a whole worldful of things, has it turned and given itself. Adrift now from the whole, it manages even this particular thing with difficulty, its care of it compelling attention to externals, presence to the body, the deep penetration of the body.

Thus comes about what is called "loss of wings" or the "chaining" of the soul. Its no longer are the ways of innocence in which, with The Soul, it presided over the higher realms. Life above was better by far than this. A thing fallen, chained, at first barred off from intelligence and living only by sensation, the soul is, as they say, in tomb or cavern pent.

Yet its higher part remains. Let the soul, taking its lead from memory, merely "think on essential being" and its shackles are loosed and it soars.

Souls of necessity lead a double life, partly in the intelligible realm and partly in that of sense, the higher life dominant in those able to commune more continuously with The Intelligence, the lower dominant where character or circumstance are the less favorable. This is pretty much what Plato indicates in distinguishing those of the second mixing bowl: after they have been divided in this way they must, he says, be born. When he speaks of divinity "sowing" souls, he is to be understood as when he has divinity giving orations and speeches; he describes the things contained in the universe as begotten and created and presents as successive what in truth exist in an eternal state of becoming or of being.

5. There is no contradiction between the sowing to birth and the willing descent for the perfection of the whole, between justice and the cave, between necessity and free choice (necessity includes free choice), being in the body being an evil; nor, in the teaching of Empedocles: the flight from God and the wandering and the sin that is justly punished; nor, in that of Heracleitus: the repose that is flight; in general, willing descent that is also unwilling. Everything that becomes worse does so unwillingly, yet when it becomes so through inherent tendency, that submission to the lower can be regarded as a penalty. Then, too, these experiences and acts are determined by an eternal law of nature, so that it may be said, without being either inconsistent or untruthful, that a soul that descends from the world above to some lower being is sent by the divinity; for final effects, however far removed by intermediate effects, are always to be referred back to the starting point.

There are two wrongs the soul commits. The first is its descent; the second, the evil done after arrival here below. The first is punished by the very conditions of its descent. Punishment for the second is passage once more into other bodies, there to remain at greater or less length according to the judgment of its deserts. (The word "judgment" indicates that this takes place as a result of divine law.) If, however, its perversity goes beyond all measure, the soul incurs an even more severe penalty administered by avenging daimons.

Thus, too, The Soul enters body – although its nature is divine and its realm the intelligible. A lesser divinity, it is impelled by the stress of its powers and the attraction of governing the next below it. By voluntary inclination it plunges into this sphere. If it returns quickly, it will have suffered no harm in thus learning of evil and of what sin is, in bringing its powers into manifest play, in exhibiting activities and achievements that, remaining merely potentialities in the intelligible realm, might as well never have been if they were never meant to be actualized: The Soul itself would never really know these suppressed, inhibited potencies. Potencies are revealed by acts, for potencies in themselves are hidden and undetectable and, for all practical purposes, nonexistent. As it is, all now marvel at the inner greatness of The Soul exteriorly revealed in the richness of its acts.

6. The One must not be solely the solitary. If it were, reality would remain buried and shapeless since in The One there is no differentiation of forms. No beings would exist if The One remained shut up in itself. More than that, the multiplicity of beings issued from The One would not exist as they do if there did not issue from The One those beings that are in the rank of souls. Likewise, souls must not play the solitaries, their issue stifled. Every nature must produce its next, for each thing must unfold, seedlike, from indivisible principle into a visible effect. Principle continues unaltered in its proper place; what unfolds from it is the product of the inexpressible power that resides in it. It must not stay this power and, as though jealous, limit its effects. It must proceed continuously until all things, to the very last, have within the limits of possibility come forth. All is the result of this immense power giving its gifts to the universe, unable to let any part remain without its share.

Nothing hinders anything from sharing in the Good to the extent it is able. That statement holds true even for matter. If, on the one hand, matter is assumed to have existed from all eternity, it is impossible that, having existence, it should not have a share in that which, in accord with each receptivity, communicates the Good to all. If, on the other hand, matter is held to be the necessary consequence of anterior causes, it will not be separated from this principle either as though, having graciously given it existence, it was powerless to reach it.

The excellence, the power, and the goodness of the intelligible realm is revealed in what is most excellent in the realm of sense, for the realms are linked together. From the one, self-existent, the other eternally draws its existence by participation and, to the extent it reproduces the intelligible, by imitation.

7. As there are these two realms, the intelligible and that of sense, it is better for the soul to dwell in the intelligible. But, such is its nature, it is necessary that it live also in the realm of sense. Accordingly it occupies only an intermediate rank. Yet there is no cause for complaint that it is not in all respects the highest. By nature divine, it is located at the nethermost limit of the intelligible realm, bordering on the realm of sense, and there gives to the realm of sense something of its own. In turn it is itself affected when, instead of controlling the body without endangering its own security, it lets itself be carried away by an excessive zeal and plunges deep into the body and ceases to be wholly united to The Soul. Yet the soul can rise above this condition again and, turning to account the experience of what it has seen and suffered here below, can better appreciate the life that is above and can know more clearly what is the better by contrast with its opposite. Indeed, knowledge of good is sharpened by experience of evil in those incapable of any sure knowledge of evil unless they have experienced it.

For The Intelligence, to reason discursively is to descend to its lowest level rather than to rise to the level of the existence beyond. But it cannot remain within itself. Of necessity it produces. Of necessity, then, by the very law of its nature, it proceeds to the level of The Soul. It goes no further. Entrusting the later stages of being to The Soul, it returns once more to the intelligible realm.

For The Soul it is much the same. Its lowest act is the realm of sense; its highest, contemplation of the supernal beings.

For individual souls this contemplation is fragmentary and divided by time, so their conversion begins on a lower level. But The Soul never becomes involved in the activities of the lower world. Immune to evil, it comprehends intellectually what is below it while always cleaving to what is above it. Therefore is it able, at one and the same time, to be debtor to what is above and, since as soul it cannot escape touching this sphere, benefactor to what is below.

8. This, now, goes counter to current belief. But let us take our courage in our hands and say it: No soul, not even our own, enters into the body completely. Soul always remains united by its higher part to the intelligible realm. But if the part that is in the realm of sense dominates, or rather becomes dominated and disturbed, it keeps us unaware of what the higher part of the soul contemplates. Indeed we are aware of what the soul contemplates only if the content descends to the level of sensation. We do not know what happens in any part of the soul until it becomes present to the entire soul. (For instance, an appetite does not become known to us as long as it remains in the faculty of desire. We detect it only when we perceive it by interior sense or by the act of judgment, or by both.)

Every soul has a lower part directed towards the bodily and a higher part directed towards the intelligible. The Soul, effortlessly, manages the universe by that part directed towards the bodily. For The Soul governs the bodily not by discursive reasoning, as we do, but by intuition (much as is done in the arts). Individual souls, each of which manages a part of the universe, also have a higher phase. But they are preoccupied with sensation and its impressions. Much they perceive is contrary to nature and troubles and confuses them. This is so because the body in their care is deficient, hedged about with alien influences, filled with desires, deceived in its very pleasures. Yet there is a part of the soul insensitive to the lure of these passing pleasures, whose living is correspondent to its reality.

V.1 The three primal hypostases

1. How is it, then, that souls forget the divinity that begot them so that – divine by nature, divine by origin – they now know neither divinity nor self?

This evil that has befallen them has its source in self-will, in being born, in becoming different, in desiring to be independent. Once having tasted the pleasures of independence, they use their freedom to go in a direction that leads away from their origin. And when they have gone a great distance, they even forget that they came from it. Like children separated from their family since birth and educated away from home, they are ignorant now of their parentage and therefore of their identity.

Our souls know neither who nor whence they are, because they hold themselves cheap and accord their admiration and honor to everything except themselves. They bestow esteem, love, and sympathy on anything rather than on themselves. They cut themselves off, as much as may be, from the things above. They forget their worth. Ignorance of origin is caused by excessive valuation of sense objects and disdain of self, for to pursue something and hold it dear implies acknowledgment of inferiority to what is pursued. As soon as a soul thinks it is worth less than things subject to birth and death, considers itself least honorable and enduring of all, it can no longer grasp the nature and power of the divinity.

A soul in such condition can be turned about and led back to the world above and the supreme existent, The One and first, by a twofold discipline: by showing it the low value of the things it esteems at present, and by informing – reminding! – it of its nature and worth. The second discipline precedes the first and, once made clear, supports the first (which we shall treat elsewhere rather fully).

The second must occupy us now, particularly as it is a prerequisite for the study of that supreme object we desire to know.

It is the soul that desires to know. Therefore the soul must first examine its own nature in order to know itself and decide whether it is capable of such an investigation, has an eye capable of such seeing, and whether such seeking is its function. If the things it seeks are alien to the soul, what good will its seeking do? But, if the soul is akin to them and it seeks them, it can find them.

2. Each should recall at the outset that soul is the author of all living things, has breathed life into them all, on earth, in the air, and in the sea – the divine stars, the sun, the ample heavens. It was soul that brought order into the heavens and guides now its measured revolving. All this it does while yet remaining transcendent to what it gives form, movement, life. Necessarily, it is superior by far to them. They are born or they die to the extent that soul gives or withdraws their life. Soul, because it can "never abandon itself," exists eternally.

Now to understand how life is imparted to the universe and to each individual, the soul must rise to the contemplation of The Soul, the soul of the world. The individual soul, though different from The Soul, is itself no slight thing. Yet it must become worthy of this contemplation: freed of the errors and seductions to which other souls are subject, it must be quiet. Let us assume that quiet too is the body that wraps it round – quiet the earth, quiet the air and the sea, quiet the high heavens. Then picture The Soul flowing into this tranquil mass from all sides, streaming into it, spreading through it until it is luminous. As the rays of the sun lighten and gild the blackest cloud, so The Soul by entering the body of the universe gives it life and immortality; the abject it lifts up. The universe, moved eternally by an intelligent Soul, becomes blessed and alive. The Soul's presence gives value to a universe that before was no more than an inert corpse, water and earth, or rather darksome matter and nonbeing, an "object of horror to the gods," as someone has said.

The Soul's nature and power reveal themselves still more clearly in the way it envelops and rules the world in accordance with its will. It is present in every point of the world's immense mass, animating all its segments, great and small. While two bodies cannot be in the same place and are separated from each other both spatially and otherwise, The Soul is not thus extended. It need not divide itself to give life to each particular individual. Although it animates particular things, it remains whole and is present in its wholeness, resembling in this indivisibility and omnipresence its begetter, The Intelligence. It is through the power of The Soul that this world of multiplicity and variety is held within the bonds of unity. It is through its presence that this world is divine: divine the sun because ensouled; so too the stars. And whatever we are, we are on its account, for "a corpse is viler than a dunghill."

The deities owe their divinity to a cause necessarily their superior. Our soul is the same as The Soul which animates the deities: strip it of all things infesting it, consider it in its original purity, and you will see it to be of equal rank with The Soul, superior to everything that is body. The Body, without the soul, is nothing but earth. If one make fire the basic element, one still needs a principle to give life to its flame. It is the same even if one combines earth and fire, or adds to them water and air as well.

If it is soul that makes us lovable, why is it that we seek it only in others and not in ourselves? You love others because of it. Love, then, yourself.

3. So divine and precious is The Soul, be confident that, by its power, you can attain to divinity. Start your ascent. You will not need to search long. Few are the steps that separate you from your goal. Take as your guide the most divine part of The Soul, that which "borders" upon the superior realm from which it came.

Indeed, in spite of the qualities that we have shown it to have, The Soul is no more than an image of The Intelligence. Just as the spoken word is the image of the word in the soul, The Soul itself is the image of the word in The Intelligence and is the act of The Intelligence by which a further level of existence is produced, for the act of The Intelligence has this further phase, quite as fire contains heat as part of its essence but also radiates heat. Nevertheless, The Soul does not become completely separated from The Intelligence. Partly it remains in it. Although its nature is distinct because it derives from The Intelligence, The Soul is itself an intellective existent: discursive reason is the manifestation of its intellectual capacity. The Soul derives its perfection from The Intelligence, which nourishes it as a father would. But, in comparison with itself, The Intelligence has not endowed The Soul with complete perfection.

Thus The Soul is the hypostasis that proceeds from The Intelligence. Its reason finds its actualization when it contemplates The Intelligence. So contemplating, it possesses the object of its contemplation within itself, as its own, and it is then wholly active. These intellectual and interior activities are alone characteristic of The Soul. Those of a lower kind are due to an alien principle and they are passive rather than active experiences for The Soul. The Intelligence makes The Soul more divine because it is its begetter and grants its presence to it. Nothing separates the two but the difference of their natures. The Soul is related to The Intelligence as matter is to Idea. But this "matter" of The Intelligence is beautiful: it has an intellectual form and is partless.

How great, then, must The Intelligence be if it is greater than The Soul!

4. Greatness of The Intelligence may also be seen in this: We marvel at the magnitude and beauty of the sense world, the eternal regularity of its movement, the divinities – visible and

invisible – that it contains, its daimons, animals, plants. Let us then rise to the model, to the higher reality from which this world derives, and let us there contemplate the whole array of intelligibles that possess eternally an inalienable intelligence and life. Over them presides pure Intelligence, unapproachable wisdom. That world is the true realm of Cronus, whose very name suggests both abundance (*koros*) and intelligence (*nous*). There is contained all that is immortal, intelligent, divine. There is the place of every soul. There is eternal rest.

Since it is in a state of bliss, why should The Intelligence seek change? Since it contains everything, why should it aspire to anything? Since it is perfect, what need has it of development? All its content is perfect, too, so that it is perfect throughout. It contains nothing that is not of the nature of thought – of thought, however, that is not a search but possession. Its happiness does not depend on something else. It is eternally all things in that eternity of which time, which abandons one moment for the next, is only a fleeting image upon the level of The Soul. The Soul's action is successive, divided by the various objects that draw its attention – now Socrates, now a horse, always some particular. The Intelligence, however, embraces all, possesses all in unchanging identity. It "is" alone. And it always has this character of presentness. Future it has not; already it is all it could ever later become. Past it has not; no intelligible entity ever passes away. All it contains exist in an eternal present because they remain identical with themselves, contented, you might say, with their present condition. Singly they are both intelligence and being. Together they form the totality of intelligence and the totality of being. The Intelligence gives existence to Being in thinking it. Being, by being object of thought, gives to The Intelligence its thinking and its existence.

But there must still exist something else that makes The Intelligence think and Being be – their common cause. It is true that The Intelligence and Being exist simultaneously and together and never part. But their oneness – which is simultaneously intelligence and being, thinking and object of thought – is twofold: The Intelligence inasmuch as it thinks, and Being inasmuch as it is the object of thought. Intellection implies difference as well as identity. Therefore the primary terms are "intelligence," "being," "identity," "difference." And to them must be added "movement" and "rest." Movement is implied in the intellective activity of the intelligible realm; rest, in its sameness. Difference is implicit in the distinction between the thinker and the thought because without difference they are reduced to unity and to silence. The objects of thought also require difference in order to be distinguished from one another. Identity is implied in the self-sufficient unity of The Intelligence and in the nature shared in common by all intelligible beings, quite as difference is implied in their being distinguishable. From this multiplicity of these terms come "number" and "quantity," while the proper character of each of them is "quality." From these terms, as from originating principles, everything else proceeds.

5. The Intelligence, manifold and divine, is in The Soul, since The Soul is joined to it, provided The Soul does not will to overstep its bounds and "secede" from it. So close to The Intelligence that it is almost one with it. The Soul is everlastingly vivified.

What established The Intelligence thus?

Its source did, the partless that is prior to plurality, that is the cause both of being and of multiplicity, that is the maker of number.

Number is not the first; one is prior to two and two comes after one. Two, indeterminate in itself, is made determinate by one. When plurality becomes determinate, with a determinacy rather like that of substances, it becomes number. The Soul is number, too, because the primals are not quantitative masses. Masses, the gross in nature, are secondary, for all that sense perception thinks them essences. Nobility of seed or plants consists not in perceptible moisture but in number and seminal reason – both imperceptible.

Number and plurality that are in the intelligible realm are reasons and intelligence. But, in itself, as it were, plurality is indeterminate. The number, however, that comes from it and from The One is form – quite as if all things assumed form in it. The Intelligence is formed differently by The One than it is formed of itself, that is, like sight made actual, for intellection is the seen as seen – the two are one.

6. Some questions remain: How does The Intelligence see? What does it see? How does it exist and issue from The One in order to see?

The soul accepts what is necessarily so, but now it wishes to resolve the problem so often raised by the ancient philosophers: how multiplicity, duality, and number proceeded from The One. Why did The One not remain by itself? Why did it emanate the multiplicity we find characterizing being and that we strive to trace back to The One?

In approaching this problem let us first invoke the divinity. Let us do so not with words but with a lifting of our souls to it and thus to pray alone to the Alone.

To see The One that remains in itself as if in an inner sanctuary, undisturbed and remote from all things, we must first consider the images in the outer precincts, or rather the first one to appear. This seems to be its message: All that is moved must have a goal towards which it is moved. But The One has no goal towards which it is moved. We must, then, not assume it to be moved. When things proceed from it, it must not cease being turned towards itself. (We have to remove from our minds any idea that this is a process like generation in time because here we are treating of eternal realities. We speak metaphorically, in terms of generation, to indicate the causal relations of things eternal and their systematic order.) What is begotten by The One must be said to be begotten without any motion on the part of The One. If The One were moved, the begotten, because of this movement, would have to be ranked third since the movement would be second. The One therefore produces the second hypostasis without assent, or decree, or movement of any kind. How are we to conceive this sort of generation and its relation to its immovable cause? We are to conceive it as a radiation that, though it proceeds from The One, leaves its selfsameness undisturbed, much in the way the brilliance that encircles and is ceaselessly generated by the sun does not affect its selfsame and unchanging existence. Indeed everything, as existing, necessarily produces of its own substance some further existent dependent on its power and image of its existence. Thus fire radiates heat and snow radiates cold. Perfumes provide an especially striking example: as long as they last they send off exhalations in which everything around them shares. What becomes perfect becomes productive. The eternally perfect is eternally productive, and what it produces is eternal, too, although its inferior.

What, then, are we to say of that which is supremely perfect? It produces only the very greatest of the things that are less than it. What is most perfect after it is the second hypostasis, The Intelligence. The Intelligence contemplates The One and needs nothing but The One. The One, however, has no need of The Intelligence. The One, superior to The Intelligence, produces The Intelligence, the best after The One since it is superior to all the others. The Soul is word and deed of The Intelligence just as The Intelligence is word and deed of The One. But in The Soul the word is obscure, for The Soul is only an image of The Intelligence. Therefore The Soul turns itself to The Intelligence, just as, to be The Intelligence, it must contemplate The One. The Intelligence contemplates The One without being separated from it because there is no other existent between the two of them, just as there is none between The Intelligence and The Soul. Begotten always longs for its begetter and loves it; especially is this so when begetter and begotten are solitaries. But when the begetter is the highest Good, the begotten must be so close to it that its only separateness is its otherness.

7. We call The Intelligence image of The One. This we must explain.

It is its image because what is begotten by The One must possess many of its characteristics, be like it as light is like the sun. But The One is not an intellectual principle. How then can it produce an intellectual principle? In turning towards itself The One sees. It is this seeing that constitutes The Intelligence. For what is seen is different from sensation or intelligence. . . . Sensation as line and so on. . . . But the circle is divisible; The One is not.

In The Intelligence there is unity; The One, however, is the power productive of all things. Thought, apportioning itself in accord with this power, beholds all in the power of The One: did it not, it would not be The Intelligence. The Intelligence is aware of its power to produce and even to limit being through that power derived from The One. It sees that being is a part of what belongs to The One and proceeds from it and owes all its force to it, that it achieves being because of The One. The Intelligence sees that, because it becomes multiple when proceeding from The One, it derives from The One (which is indivisible) all the realities it has, such as life and thought, while The One is not any of these things. The totality of beings must come after The One because The One itself has no determinate form. The One simply is one while The Intelligence is what in the realm of being constitutes the totality of beings. Thus The One is not any of the beings The Intelligence contains but the sole source from which all of them are derived. That is why they are "beings"; they are already determined, each with its specific form; a being cannot be indeterminate, but only definite and stable. For intelligible beings such stability consists in the determination and form to which they owe their existence.

The Intelligence of which we speak deserves to be of this lineage and to derive from no other source than the supreme. Once begotten, it begets with it all beings, all the beauty of the Ideas, all the intelligible deities. Full of the things it has begotten, it "devours" them in the sense that it keeps them all, does not allow them to fall into matter or to come under the rule of Rhea. This the mysteries and myths of the gods obscurely hint at: Cronus, the wisest of the gods, was born before Zeus and devoured his children – quite like The Intelligence, big with its conceptions and in a state of satiety. Then, out of his fullness, Cronus begot Zeus. Thus The Intelligence, out of its fullness, begets The Soul. It begets necessarily because it is perfect and, being so great a power, it cannot remain sterile. Here, again, the begotten had to be inferior, an image, and – since it was indeterminate by itself – be determined and formed by the principle that begot it. What The Intelligence begets is a word and substantive reasoning, the being that moves about The Intelligence and is the light of The Intelligence, the ray that springs from it. On the one hand, it is bound to The Intelligence, fills itself with it, enjoys its presence, shares in it, and is itself an intellectual existent. On the other hand, it is in contact with lower beings begetting beings lower than itself. Of these we shall treat later. The sphere of the divine stops here at The Soul.

8. This is the reason why Plato establishes three degrees of reality. He says: "It is in relation to the king of all and on his account that everything exists. . . . In relation to a second, the second class of things exists, and in relation to a third, the third class." Further, he speaks of the "father of the cause," by "cause" meaning The Intelligence because for him The Intelligence is the demiurge. He adds that it is this power that forms the soul in the mixing bowl. The Good, he says, the existent that is superior to The Intelligence and "superior to Being," is the father of the cause, *i.e.*, of The Intelligence. Several times he says that Idea is

Being and The Intelligence. Therefore, he realized that The Intelligence proceeds from the Good and The Soul proceeds from The Intelligence. These, indeed, are not new doctrines; they have been taught from the most ancient times, without, however, being made fully explicit. Our claim is to be no more than interpreters of these earlier doctrines whose antiquity is attested by Plato's writings.

The first philosopher to teach this was Parmenides. He identified Being and The Intelligence and did not place Being among sense objects. "To think," he said, "is the same as to be," and "Being is immobile." Although he adds thought to Being, he denies that Being (since it must remain always the same) has any bodily motion. He compares it to a "well-rounded sphere"; it contains everything and does not draw thought from without but possesses it within. When in his writings he called Being The One, he was criticized because his unity was found to be multiple.

The Parmenides of Plato speaks with greater accuracy. He distinguishes between the first one, which is one in the proper sense, and the second one, which is a multiple one, and a third – The-One-and-the-manifold. Therefore this latter Parmenides also distinguished the three degrees here discussed.

9. Anaxagoras, in teaching the simplicity of pure and unmingled Intelligence, also asserted that The One is primary and separate. But, living too long ago, he did not treat the matter in sufficient detail. Heracleitus also knew The One, eternal and intelligible, for he taught that bodies are in a perpetual process of flux and return. According to Empedocles, "Hate" is the principle of division but "Love" is The One, an incorporeal principle, the elements playing the role of matter.

Aristotle says that the first existent is "separate" and intelligible. But in saying that "it thinks itself," he denies it transcendency. He asserts as well the existence of a plurality of other intelligible entities in a number equal to the heavenly spheres so that each of them has its own principle of motion. He therefore advances a doctrine of intelligible entities that is different from that of Plato. And as he has no valid reason for this change, he appeals to necessity. Even if his reasons were valid, one might well object that it seems more reasonable to suppose that the spheres, as they are coordinated in a single system, are directed towards the one ultimate, the supreme existent. We might also ask whether, for him, intelligible beings derive from one first originating principle or whether there are for them several such principles. If intelligible beings proceed from one principle, their condition will be analogous to that of the sense spheres where one envelops another and one alone – the exterior sphere – dominates all of the others. In this case the primal existent will contain all intelligible entities and be the intelligible realm. The spheres in the realm of sense are not empty, for the first is full of stars and the others, too, have theirs. Similarly, the principles of motion in the intelligible realm will contain many entities, beings that are more real than sense objects. On the other hand, if each of these principles is independent, their interrelation will be subject to chance. How, then, will they unite their actions and converge in producing that single effect which is the harmony of the heavens? Further, what is the basis for the assertion that sense objects in the heavens equal in number their intelligible movers? Finally, why is there a plurality of movers since they are incorporeal and are not separated one from another by matter?

Thus the ancient philosophers who faithfully followed the doctrines of Pythagoras, of his disciples, and of Pherecydes have maintained the existence of the intelligible realm. Some of them have recorded their views in their writing; others orally; others have bothered to do neither.

10. That beyond Being there exists The One we have attempted to prove as far as such an assertion admits of proof. In the second place come Being and The Intelligence; in the third, The Soul.

Now it must be admitted that as these three are in the very nature of things, they also are in us.

My meaning is not that they exist in our sense part (they are separate from sense) but in what is external to sense (understanding "external" in the same way that one says they are "external" to the heavens) – the area, that is, that Plato calls "the man within."

Our soul, too, then, is something divine, its nature different from that of sense. It is essentially like The Soul. Possessing intelligence, it is perfect.

It is necessary to distinguish between the intelligence which reasons and that which furnishes the principles of reasoning. The soul's discursive reasoning needs no bodily organ; it keeps its action pure of the bodily in order to reason purely. Separate from the body, it has no admixture of body. It is no mistake to place it in the first degree of the intelligible. We need not seek to locate it in space; it exists outside space. To be within oneself and exterior to all else and immaterial is to be outside body and the bodily. That is why Plato says, speaking of the cosmos, that the demiurge has The Soul envelop the world "from without." His meaning? A part of The Soul remains in the intelligible realm. Thus, in speaking of the human soul, he says that "it dwells at the top of the body." When he counsels separation of soul from body, he does not mean spatial separation, such as is established by Nature, but that soul must not incline towards body even in imagination but must alienate itself from body. Such separation is achieved by raising to the intelligible realm that lower part of the soul which, established in the realm of sense, is the sole agent that builds up and modifies the body and busies itself with its care.

11. Since discursive reason inquires, "Is this just?" or, "Is that beautiful?" and then decides that a particular object is beautiful or that a certain action is just, there must exist a justice that is immutable and a beauty that is immutable according to which the soul deliberates. Otherwise, how could it reason? Moreover, since the soul reasons only intermittently about such topics, it cannot be discursive reason that continually possesses the idea, say, of justice. Rather must it be intelligence. We must also possess within us the source and cause of intelligence, the divinity, which is not divisible and exists not in a place but in itself. Not in a place, it is found in that multitude of beings capable of receiving it just as if it were divisible – quite as the center of the circle remains in itself while each of the points of the circle contains it and each of the radii touches it. Thus we ourselves, by one of our parts, touch the supreme, unite ourselves to it, and are suspended from it. We establish ourselves in it when we turn towards it.

12. How is it that we who possess in ourselves such great things are not aware of them, that some of us often, and some of us always, fail to actualize these capacities? The realities themselves, The Intelligence and the self-sufficient above it, are "always active." The Soul, too, is always active. As to our own souls, we are not aware of all that goes on in them. Such activities are known only when perceptible by sensation. Unless they attain to sense they are not communicated to the entire soul and thus we are not conscious of them. Yet the faculty of sense perception is only part of man; it is the whole soul with all of its parts that constitutes the man. Each part of the soul is always alert and always engaging in its appropriate function, but we are aware only when there is communication as well as perception.

To grasp what is within us we must turn our perceptive faculties inward, focusing their whole attention there. Just as the person who wants to hear a cherished sound must neglect all others and keep his ears attuned to the approach of the sound he prefers to those he hears about him, so we too must here close our senses to all the noises that assail us (if they are not necessary) and preserve the perceptive power of the soul pure and ready to attend to tones that come from above.

VI.9   The Good or The One

1. It is by The One that all beings are beings.

This is equally true of those that are primarily beings and those that in some way are simply classed among beings, for what could exist were it not one? Not a one, a thing is not. No army, no choir, no flock exists except it be one. No house, even, or ship exists except as the unit, house, or the unit, ship; their unity gone, the house is no longer a house, the ship is no longer a ship. Similarly quantitative continua would not exist had they not an inner unity; divided, they forfeit existence along with unity. It is the same with plant and animal bodies; each of them is a unit; with disintegration, they lose their previous nature and are no longer what they were; they become new, different beings that in turn exist only as long as each of them is a unit. Health is contingent upon the body's being coordinated in unity; beauty, upon the mastery of parts by The One; the soul's virtue, upon unification into one sole coherence.

The Soul imparts unity to all things in producing, fashioning, forming, and disposing them. Ought we then to say that The Soul not only gives unity but is unity itself, The One? No. It bestows other qualities upon bodies without being what it bestows (shape, for instance, and Idea, which are different from it); so also this unity; The Soul makes each being one by looking upon The One, just as it makes man by contemplating the Idea, Man, effecting in the man the unity that belongs to Man.

Each thing that is called "one" has a unity proportionate to its nature, sharing in unity, either more or less, according to the degree of its being. The Soul, while distinct from The One, has greater unity because it has a higher degree of being. It is not The One. It is one, but its unity is contingent. Between The Soul and its unity there is the same difference as between body and body's unity. Looser aggregates, such as a choir, are furthest from unity; the more compact are the nearer; The Soul is nearer still, yet – as all the others – is only a participant in unity.

The fact that The Soul could not exist unless it was one should not, really, lead anyone to think it and The One identical. All other things exist only as units, and none of them is The One; body, for instance, and unity are not identical. Besides, The Soul is manifold as well as one even though it is not constituted of parts; it has various faculties – discursive reason, desire, perception – joined together in unity as by a bond. The Soul bestows unity because it has unity, but a unity received from another source.

2. Granted that being is not identical with unity in each particular thing, might not the totality, Being, be identical with unity? Then upon grasping Being, we would hold The One, for they would be the same. Then, if Being is The Intelligence, The One would also be The Intelligence; The Intelligence, as Being and as The One, would impart to the rest of things both being and, in proportion, unity.

Is The One identical with Being as "man" and "one man" are identical? Or is it the number of each thing taken individually? (Just as one object and another joined to it are spoken of as "two," so an object taken singly is referred to as "one.") In the second case, if number belongs to the class of being, evidently The One will belong in that way, too, and we shall have to discover what kind of being it is. But if unity is no more than a numbering device of the soul, The One has no real existence; but this possibility is eliminated by our previous observation that each object upon losing unity loses existence as well.

Accordingly, we must determine whether being and unity are identical either in each individual object or in their totality.

As the being of each thing consists in multiplicity and The One cannot be multiplicity, The One must differ from Being. Man is animal, rational, and many things besides; and this multiplicity is held together by a bondlike unity. Thus there is a difference between man and unity: man is divisible, unity indivisible. Being, containing all beings, is still more multiple, thus differing from The One even though it is one by participation. Because being possesses life and intelligence, it is not dead. It must be multiple. If it is The Intelligence, it must be multiple – and the more so if it contains the Ideas, because Ideas, individually and in their totality, are a sort of number and are one only in the way in which the universe is one.

In general, then, The One is the first existent. But The Intelligence, the Ideas, and Being are not the first. Every form is multiple and composite, and consequently something derived because parts precede the composite they constitute.

That The Intelligence cannot be primary should be obvious as well from the following. The activity of The Intelligence consists necessarily in intellection. Intelligence, which does not turn to external objects, contemplates what is superior to it; in turning towards itself it turns towards its origin. Duality is implied if The Intelligence is both thinker and thought; it is not simple, therefore not The One. And if The Intelligence contemplates some object other than itself, then certainly there exists something superior to The Intelligence. Even if The Intelligence contemplate itself and at the same time that which is superior to it, it still is only of secondary rank. We must conceive The Intelligence as enjoying the presence of the Good and The One and contemplating it while it is also present to itself, thinks itself, and thinks itself as being all things. Constituting such a diversity, The Intelligence is far from being The One.

Thus The One is not all things because then it would no longer be one. It is not The Intelligence, because The Intelligence is all things, and The One would then be all things. It is not Being because Being is all things.

3. What then is The One? What is its nature?

It is not surprising that it is difficult to say what it is when it is difficult to say even what being is or what form is, although there knowledge has some sort of approach through the forms. As the soul advances towards the formless, unable to grasp what is without contour or to receive the imprint of reality so diffuse, it fears it will encounter nothingness, and it slips away. Its state is distressing. It seeks solace in retreating down to the sense realm, there to rest as upon a sure and firm-set earth, just as the eye, wearied with looking at small objects, gladly turns to large ones. But when the soul seeks to know in its own way – by coalescence and unification – it is prevented by that very unification from recognizing it has found The One, for it is unable to distinguish knower and known. Nevertheless, a philosophical study of The One must follow this course.

Because what the soul seeks is The One and it would look upon the source of all reality, namely the Good and The One, it must not withdraw from the primal realm and sink down to the lowest realm. Rather must it withdraw from sense objects, of the lowest existence, and turn to those of the highest. It must free itself from all evil since it aspires to rise to the Good. It must rise to the principle possessed within itself; from the multiplicity that it was it must again become one. Only thus can it contemplate the supreme principle, The One.

Having become The Intelligence, having entrusted itself to it, committed itself to it, having confided and established itself in it so that by alert concentration the soul may grasp all The Intelligence sees, it will, by The Intelligence, contemplate The One without employing the senses, without mingling perception with the activity of The Intelligence. It must contemplate this purest of objects through the purest of The Intelligence, through that which is supreme in The Intelligence.

When, then, the soul applies itself to the contemplation of such an object and has the impression of extension or shape or mass, it is not The Intelligence that guides its seeing, for it is not the nature of The Intelligence to see such things. From sensation, rather, and from opinion, the associate of sensation, comes this activity. From The Intelligence must come the word of what its scope is. It contemplates its priors, its own content, and its issue. Purity and simplicity characterize its issue and, even more, its content and, most of all, its priors or Prior.

The One, then, is not The Intelligence but higher. The Intelligence is still a being, while The One is not a being because it is precedent to all being. Being has, you might say, the form of being; The One is without form, even intelligible form.

As The One begets all things, it cannot be any of them – neither thing, nor quality, nor quantity, nor intelligence, nor soul. Not in motion, nor at rest, not in space, nor in time, it is "the in itself uniform," or rather it is the "without-form" preceding form, movement, and rest, which are characteristics of Being and make Being multiple.

But if The One is not in motion, why is it not at rest? Because rest or motion, or both together, are characteristic of Being. Again, because what is at rest must be so on account of something distinct from it, rest as such. The One at rest would have the contingent attribute, "at rest," and would be simple no longer.

Let no one object that something contingent is attributed to The One when we call it the first cause. It is to ourselves that we are thereby attributing contingency because it is we who are receiving something from The One while The One remains self-enclosed. When we wish to speak with precision, we should not say that The One is this or that, but revolving, as it were, around it, try to express our own experience of it, now drawing nigh to it, now falling back from it as a result of the difficulties involved.

4. The chief difficulty is this: awareness of The One comes to us neither by knowing nor by the pure thought that discovers the other intelligible things, but by a presence transcending knowledge. When the soul knows something, it loses its unity; it cannot remain simply one because knowledge implies discursive reason and discursive reason implies multiplicity. The soul then misses The One and falls into number and multiplicity.

Therefore we must go beyond knowledge and hold to unity. We must renounce knowing and knowable, every object of thought, even Beauty, because Beauty, too, is posterior to The One and is derived from it as, from the sun, the daylight. That is why Plato says of The One, "It can neither be spoken nor written about." If nevertheless we speak of it and write about it, we do so only to give direction, to urge towards that vision beyond discourse, to point out the road to one desirous of seeing. Instruction goes only as far as showing the road and the direction. To obtain the vision is solely the work of him who desires to obtain it. If he does not arrive at contemplation, if his soul does not achieve awareness of that life that is beyond, if the soul does not feel a rapture within it like that of the lover come to rest in his love, if, because of his closeness to The One, he receives its true light – his whole soul made luminous – but is still weighted down and his vision frustrated, if he does not rise alone but still carries within him something alien to The One, if he is not yet sufficiently unified, if he has not yet risen far but is still at a distance either because of the obstacles of which we have just spoken or because of the lack of such instruction as would have given him direction and faith in the existence of things beyond, he has no one to blame but himself and should try to become pure by detaching himself from everything.

The One is absent from nothing and from everything. It is present only to those who are prepared for it and are able to receive it, to enter into harmony with it, to grasp and to touch it by virtue of their likeness to it, by virtue of that inner power similar to and stemming from The One when it is in that state in which it was when it originated from The One. Thus will The One be "seen" as far as it can become an object of contemplation. Anyone who still lacks faith in these arguments should consider the following:

5. Those who believe that the world of being is governed by luck or by chance and that it depends upon material causes are far removed from the divine and from the notion of The One. It is not such men as these that we address but such as admit the existence of a world other than the corporeal and at least acknowledge the existence of soul. These men should apply themselves to the study of soul, learning among other things that it proceeds from The Intelligence and attains virtue by participating in the reason that proceeds from The Intelligence. Next, they must realize that The Intelligence is different from our faculty of reasoning (the so-called rational principle), that reasoning implies, as it were, separate steps and movements. They must see that knowledge consists in the manifestation of the rational forms that exist in The Soul and come to The Soul from The Intelligence, the source of knowledge. After one has seen The Intelligence, which like a thing of sense is immediately perceived (but which, although it transcends the soul, is its begetter and the author of the intelligible world), one must think of it as quiet, unwavering movement; embracing all things and being all things, in its multiplicity it is both indivisible and divisible. It is not divisible as are the ingredients of discursive reason, conceived item by item. Still its content is not confused either: each element is distinct from the other, just as in science the theories form an indivisible whole and yet each theory has its own separate status. This multitude of co-existing beings, the intelligible realm, is near The One. (Its existence is necessary, as reason demonstrates, if one admits The Soul exists, to which it is superior.) It is nevertheless not the supreme because it is neither one nor simple.

The One, the source of all things, is simple. It is above even the highest in the world of being because it is above The Intelligence, which itself, not The One but like The One, would become The One. Not sundered from The One, close to The One, but to itself present, it has to a degree dared secession.

The awesome existent above, The One, is not a being for then its unity would repose in another than itself. There is no name that suits it, really. But, since name it we must, it may appropriately be called "one," on the understanding, however, that it is not a substance that possesses unity only as an attribute. So, the strictly nameless, it is difficult to know. The best approach is through its offspring, Being: we know it brings The Intelligence into existence, that it is the source of all that is best, the self-sufficing and unflagging begetter of every being, to be numbered among none of them since it is their prior.

We are necessarily led to call this "The One" in our discussions the better to designate "partlessness" while we strive to bring our minds to "oneness." But when we say that it is one and partless, it is not in the same sense that we speak of geometrical point or numerical unit, where "one" is the quantitative principle which would not exist unless substance, and that which precedes substance and being, were there first. It is not of this kind of unity that we are to think, but simply use such things here below – in their simplicity and the absence of multiplicity and division – as symbols of the higher.

6. In what sense, then, do we call the supreme The One? How can we conceive of it?

We shall have to insist that its unity is much more perfect than that of the numerical unit or the geometrical point. For with regard to these, the soul, abstracting from magnitude and numerical plurality, stops indeed at that which is smallest and comes to rest in something indivisible. This kind of unity is found in something that is divisible and exists in a subject other than itself. But "what is not in another than itself" is not in the divisible. Nor is it indivisible in the same sense in which the smallest is indivisible. On the contrary, The One is the greatest, not physically but dynamically. Hence it is indivisible, not physically but dynamically. So also the beings that proceed from it; they are, not in mass but in might, indivisible and partless. Also, The One is infinite not as extension or a numerical series is infinite, but in its limitless power. Conceive it as intelligence or divinity; it is more than that. Compress unity within your mind, it is still more than that. Here is unity superior to any your thought lays hold of, unity that exists by itself and in itself and is without attributes.

Something of its unity can be understood from its self-sufficiency. It is necessarily the most powerful, the most self-sufficient, the most independent of all. Whatever is not one, but multiple, needs something else. Its being needs unification. But The One is already one. It does not even need itself. A being that is multiple, in order to be what it is, needs the multiplicity of things it contains. And each of the things contained is what it is by its union with the others and not by itself, and so it needs the others. Accordingly, such a being is deficient both with regard to its parts and as a whole. There must be something that is fully self-sufficient. That is The One; it alone, within and without, is without need. It needs nothing outside itself either to exist, to achieve well-being, or to be sustained in existence. As it is the cause of the other things, how could it owe its existence to them? And how could it derive its well-being from outside itself since its well-being is not something contingent but is its very nature? And, since it does not occupy space, how can it need support or foundation? What needs foundation is the material mass which, unfounded, falls. The One is the foundation of all other things and gives them, at one and the same time, existence and location; what needs locating is not self-sufficing.

Again, no principle needs others after it. The principle of all has no need of anything at all. Deficient being is deficient because it aspires to its principle. But if The One were to aspire to anything, it would evidently seek not to be The One, that is, it would aspire to that which destroys it. Everything in need needs well-being and preservation. Hence The One cannot aim at any good or desire anything: it is superior to the Good; it is the Good, not for itself, but for other things to the extent to which they can share in it.

The One is not an intellective existence. If it were, it would constitute a duality. It is motionless because it is prior to motion quite as it is prior to thinking. Anyhow, what would it think? Would it think itself? If it did, it would be in a state of ignorance before thinking, and the self-sufficient would be in need of thought. Neither should one suppose it to be in a state of ignorance on the ground that it does not know itself and does not think itself. Ignorance presupposes a dual relationship: one does not know another. But The One, in its aloneness, can neither know nor be ignorant of anything. Being with itself, it does not need to know itself. Still, we should not even attribute to it this presence with itself if we are to preserve its unity.

Excluded from it are both thinking of itself and thinking of others. It is not like that which thinks but, rather, like the activity of thinking. The activity of thinking does not itself think;

it is the cause that has some other being think and cause cannot be identical with effect. This cause, therefore, of all existing things cannot be any one of them. Because it is the cause of good it cannot, then, be called the Good; yet in another sense it is the Good above all.

7. If the mind reels at this, The One being none of the things we mentioned, a start yet can be made, from them to contemplate it.

Do not let yourself be distracted by anything exterior, for The One is not in some one place, depriving all the rest of its presence. It is present to all those who can touch it and absent only to those who cannot. No man can concentrate on one thing by thinking of some other thing; so he should not connect something else with the object he is thinking of if he wishes really to grasp it. Similarly, it is impossible for a soul, impressed with something else, to conceive of The One so long as such an impression occupies its attention, just as it is impossible that a soul, at the moment when it is attentive to other things, should receive the form of what is their contrary. It is said that matter must be void of all qualities in order to be capable of receiving all forms. So must the soul, and for a stronger reason, be stripped of all forms if it would be filled and fired by the supreme without any hindrance from within itself.

Having thus freed itself of all externals, the soul must turn totally inward; not allowing itself to be wrested back towards the outer, it must forget everything, the subjective first and, finally, the objective. It must not even know that it is itself that is applying itself to contemplation of The One.

After having dwelled with it sufficiently, the soul should, if it can, reveal to others this transcendent communion. (Doubtless it was enjoyment of this communion that was the basis of calling Minos "the confidant of Zeus"; remembering, he made laws that are the image of The One, inspired to legislate by his contact with the divine.) If a man looks down on the life of the city as unworthy of him, he should, if he so wishes, remain in this world above. This does indeed happen to those who have contemplated much.

This divinity, it is said, is not outside any being but, on the contrary, is present to all beings though they may not know it. They are fugitives from the divine, or rather from themselves. What they turn from they cannot reach. Themselves lost, they can find no other. A son distraught and beside himself is not likely to recognize his father. But the man who has learned to know himself will at the same time discover whence he comes.

8. Self-knowledge reveals to the soul that its natural motion is not, if uninterrupted, in a straight line, but circular, as around some inner object, about a center, the point to which it owes its origin. If the soul knows this, it will move around this center from which it came, will cling to it and commune with it as indeed all souls should but only divine souls do. That is the secret of their divinity, for divinity consists in being attached to the center. One who withdraws far from it becomes an ordinary man or an animal.

Is this "center" of our souls, then, the principle we are seeking? No, we must look for some other principle upon which all centers converge and to which, only by analogy to the visible circle, the word "center" is applied. The soul is not a circle as, say, a geometrical figure. Our meaning is that in the soul and around about it exists the "primordial nature," that it derives its existence from the first existence especially when entirely separate from the body. Now, however, as we have a part of our being contained in the body, we are like a man whose feet are immersed in water while the rest of his body remains above it. Raising ourselves above the body by the part of us that is not submerged, we are, by our own center, attaching ourselves to the center of all. And so we remain, just as the centers of the great circles coincide with that of the sphere that surrounds them. If these circles were material and not spiritual, center and circumference would have to occupy definite places. But since the souls are of the intelligible realm and The One is still above The Intelligence, we are forced to say that the union of the intellective thinking being with its object proceeds by different means. The intellective thinking being is in the presence of its object by virtue of its similarity and identity, and it is united with its kindred with nothing to separate it from them. Bodies are by their bodies kept from union, but the bodiless are not held by this bodily limitation. What separates bodiless beings from one another is not spatial distance but their own differences and diversities: when there is no difference between them, they are mutually present.

As The One does not contain any difference, it is always present and we are present to it when we no longer contain difference. The One does not aspire to us, to move around us; we aspire to it, to move around it. Actually, we always move around it; but we do not always look. We are like a chorus grouped about a conductor who allow their attention to be distracted by the audience. If, however, they were to turn towards their conductor, they would sing as they should and would really be with him. We are always around The One. If we were not, we would dissolve and cease to exist. Yet our gaze does not remain fixed upon The One. When we look at it, we then attain the end of our desires and find rest. Then it is that, all discord past, we dance an inspired dance around it.

9. In this dance the soul looks upon the source of life, the source of The Intelligence, the origin of Being, the cause of the Good, the root of The Soul.

All these entities emanate from The One without any lessening for it is not a material mass. If it were, the emanants would be perishable. But they are eternal because their originating principle always stays the same; not fragmenting itself in producing them, it remains entire. So they persist as well, just as light persists as long as sun shines.

We are not separated from The One, not distant from it, even though bodily nature has closed about us and drawn us to itself. It is because of The One that we breathe and have our being: it does not bestow its gifts at one moment only to leave us again; its giving is without cessation so long as it remains what it is. As we turn towards The One, we exist to a higher degree, while to withdraw from it is to fall. Our soul is delivered from evil by rising to that place which is free of all evils. There it knows. There it is immune. There it truly lives. Life not united with the divinity is shadow and mimicry of authentic life. Life there is the native act of The Intelligence, which, motionless in its contact with The One, gives birth to gods, beauty, justice, and virtue.

With all of these The Soul, filled with divinity, is pregnant; this is its starting point and its goal. It is its starting point because it is from the world above that it proceeds. It is its goal because in the world above is the Good to which it aspires and by returning to it there its proper nature is regained. Life here below in the midst of sense objects is for the soul a degradation, an exile, a loss of wings.

Further proof that our good is in the realm above is the love innate in our souls; hence the coupling in picture and story of Eros with Psyche. The soul, different from the divinity but sprung from it, must needs love. When it is in the realm above, its love is heavenly; here below, only commonplace. The heavenly Aphrodite dwells in the realm above; here below, the vulgar, harlot Aphrodite.

Every soul is an Aphrodite, as is suggested in the myth of Aphrodite's birth at the same time as that of Eros. As long as soul stays true to itself, it loves the divinity and desires to be at one with it, as a daughter loves with a noble love a noble father. When, however, the soul has come down here to human birth, it exchanges (as if deceived by the false promises of an adulterous lover) its divine love for one that is mortal. And then, far from its begetter, the soul yields to all manner of excess.

But, when the soul begins to hate its shame and puts away evil and makes its return, it finds its peace.

How great, then, is its bliss can be conceived by those who have not tasted it if they but think of earthly unions in love, marking well the joy felt by the lover who succeeds in obtaining his desires. But this is love directed to the mortal and harmful – to shadows – and soon disappears because such is not the authentic object of our love nor the good we really seek. Only in the world beyond does the real object of our love exist, the only one with which we can unite ourselves, of which we can have a part and which we can intimately possess without being separated by the barriers of flesh.

Anyone who has had this experience will know what I am talking about. He will know that the soul lives another life as it advances towards The One, reaches it and shares in it. Thus restored, the soul recognizes the presence of the dispenser of the true life. It needs nothing more. On the contrary, it must renounce everything else and rest in it alone, become it alone, all earthiness gone, eager to be free, impatient of every fetter that binds below in order so to embrace the real object of its love with its entire being that no part of it does not touch The One.

Then of it and of itself the soul has all the vision that may be – of itself luminous now, filled with intellectual light, become pure light, subtle and weightless. It has become divine, is part of the eternal that is beyond becoming. It is like a flame. If later it is weighted down again by the realm of sense, it is like a flame extinguished.

10. Why does a soul that has risen to the realm above not stay there? Because it has not yet entirely detached itself from things here below. Yet a time will come when it will uninterruptedly have vision, when it will no longer be bothered by body. The part of us that sees is not troubled. It is the other part which, even when we cease from our vision, does not cease from its activity of demonstration, proof and dialectic. But the act and faculty of vision is not reason but something greater than, prior and superior to, reason. So also is the object of the vision. When the contemplative looks upon himself in the act of contemplation, he will see himself to be like its object. He feels himself to be united to himself in the way that the object is united to itself; that is to say, he will experience himself as simple, just as it is simple.

Actually, we should not say, "He will see." What he sees (in case it is still possible to distinguish here the seer and the seen, to assert that the two are one would be indeed rash) is not seen, not distinguished, not represented as a thing apart. The man who obtains the vision becomes, as it were, another being. He ceases to be himself, retains nothing of himself. Absorbed in the beyond he is one with it, like a center coincident with another center. While the centers coincide, they are one. They become two only when they separate. It is in this sense that we can speak of The One as something separate.

Therefore is it so very difficult to describe this vision, for how can we represent as different from us what seemed, while we were contemplating it, not other than ourselves but perfect at-oneness with us?

11. This, doubtless, is what is back of the injunction of the mystery religions which prohibit revelation to the uninitiated. The divine is not expressible, so the initiate is forbidden to speak of it to anyone who has not been fortunate enough to have beheld it himself.

The vision, in any case, did not imply duality; the man who saw was identical with what he saw. Hence he did not "see" it but rather was "oned" with it. If only he could preserve the memory of what he was while thus absorbed into The One, he would possess within himself an image of what it was.

In that state he had attained unity, nothing within him or without effecting diversity. When he had made his ascent, there was within him no disturbance, no anger, emotion, desire, reason, or thought. Actually, he was no longer himself; but, swept away and filled with the divine, he was still, solitary, and at rest, not turning to this side or that or even towards himself. He was in utter rest, having, so to say, become rest itself. In this state he busied himself no longer even with the beautiful. He had risen above beauty, had passed beyond even the choir of virtues.

He was like one who, penetrating the innermost sanctuary of a temple, leaves temple images behind. They will be the first objects to strike his view upon coming out of the sanctuary, after his contemplation and communion there not with an image or statue but with what they represent. They are but lesser objects of contemplation.

Such experience is hardly a vision. It is a seeing of a quite different kind, a self-transcendence, a simplification, self-abandonment, a striving for union and a repose, an intentness upon conformation. This is the way one sees in the sanctuary. Anyone who tries to see in any other way will see nothing.

By the use of these images, the wise among the soothsayers expressed in riddles how the divinity is seen. A wise priest, reading the riddle, will, once arrived in the realm beyond, achieve the true vision of the sanctuary. One who has not yet arrived there and knows the sanctuary is invisible, is the source and principle of everything, will also know that by hypostasis is hypostasis seen, and that like alone joins like. He will leave aside nothing of the divine the soul is capable of acquiring. If his vision is not yet complete, he will attend to its completion, which, for him who has risen above all, is The One that is above all. It is not the soul's nature to attain to utter nothingness. Falling into evil it falls, in this sense, into nothingness, but still not complete nothingness. And when it reverses direction, it arrives not at something different but at itself. Thus, when it is not in anything else, it is in nothing but itself. Yet, when it is in itself alone and not in being, it is in the supreme.

We as well transcend Being by virtue of The Soul with which we are united.

Now if you look upon yourself in this state, you find yourself an image of The One.

If you rise beyond yourself, an image rising to its model, you have reached the goal of your journey.

When you fall from this vision, you will, by arousing the virtue that is within yourself and by remembering the perfection that you possess, regain your likeness and through virtue rise to The Intelligence and through wisdom to The One.

Such is the life of the divinity and of divine and blessed men: detachment from all things here below, scorn of all earthly pleasures, the flight of the lone to the Alone.

33

Proclus, *On Evil*

Though originally written in Greek, the only complete edition of this work is the Latin translation of it done by William of Moerbeke (1215–86 CE), though fragments of the Greek text can be found in the writings of Isaac (Sebastocrator) Comnenus (1047–1107 CE). In this selection, Proclus considers the origins of evil – a problem for the Neoplatonists, since they claim that everything derives from The Good. Proclus proposes that the problem of evil can be solved by recognizing evil as absolute non-being – a privation of Good – though, as mixed with particular things in the world, it becomes part of the structure of reality, and thus good.

Introduction

1. What is the nature of evil, and where does it originate? These questions have already been examined by some of our predecessors, who have pursued the theory of evil neither incidentally nor for the sake of other things, but have considered evil in itself, [examining] whether it exists or does not exist, and if it exists, how it exists and from where it has come into being and existence.

5   It is, however, not a bad thing that we too, especially because we have the time for it, summarise the observations rightly made by each of them. We will start, however, with the speculations of the divine Plato on the essence of evil things. For we shall understand more easily the words of those predecessors and we shall always be closer to an understanding of the problems once we have discovered the thought of Plato and, as it were, kindled a light 10 for our subsequent inquiries.

First, we must examine whether evil exists or not; and if it does, whether or not it exists in intelligible things; and if it exists in the sensible realm, whether it exists through a principal cause or not; and if not, whether we should attribute any substantial being to it or whether 15 we should posit its being as completely insubstantial; and if the latter is the case, how it can exist, if its principle is a different one, and from where it begins and up to which point it proceeds; and further, if there is providence, how evil can exist and where it originates. In short, we have to consider all the questions we usually raise in our commentaries.

Above all and before all, we must get a grasp of Plato's doctrine on evil, for if we fall short 20
of this theory, we will give the impression that we have achieved nothing.

Does Evil Exist?

First point of view: evil does not exist

2. The natural starting point for examining these questions should be whether evil belongs
to beings or not. Indeed, how is it possible that something exists which utterly lacks a share
in the principle of beings? For just as darkness cannot participate in light nor vice in virtue,
so is it impossible that evil should participate in the good. Suppose light were the first cause;
then there would be no darkness in the secondary beings – unless it had its origin in chance 5
and came from somewhere other than the principle. Likewise, since the good is the cause
of everything, evil can have no place among beings. [For there are two alternatives.] Either
evil, too, comes from the good – but then the question arises: how can that which has produced the nature of evil still be the cause of all good and fine things? Or evil does not come 10
from the good – but then the good will not be the good of all things nor the principle of all
beings, since the evil established in beings escapes the procession from the good.

In general, if anything, in whatever way it exists, derives its existence from being, and if
that which participates in being must necessarily participate in the One as well – for it is at
the same time being and one, and before it is being it is one – and if it neither was nor will
be permitted to secondary beings to do what they do without the beings above them – for 15
Intellect must act with Life, Life with Being, and everything with the One – then evil again
is subject to one of the following alternatives: either it will absolutely not participate in being,
or it is somehow generated from being and must participate at the same time in the cause
beyond being. And a direct consequence of this argument is the following: either there is no 20
principle, or evil does not exist and has not been generated. For that which has no share in
being is not being, and that which [proceeds] from the first cause is not evil. In both cases,
however, it is mandatory to say that evil is nowhere.

If, then, the good is, as we say, beyond being and is the source of beings – since everything, in whatever way it exists and is generated, strives for the good according to its nature 25
– how then could evil be any one thing among beings, if it is actually excluded from such a
desire? Thus, it is far from true to say that evil exists because 'there must be something that
is completely contrary to the good'. For how could that which is completely contrary [to
something] desire the nature that is contrary to it? Now, it is impossible that there is any 30
being which does not strive for the good, since all beings have been generated and exist because
of that desire and are preserved through it. Hence, if evil is contrary to the good, evil does
not belong to beings.

3. Why should we say more? For if the One and what we call the nature of the good is
beyond being, then evil is beyond non-being itself – I mean absolute non-being, for the good
is better than absolute being. Thus, one of these two implications follows. <Non-being
is either absolutely-not-being or what is beyond being. But it is impossible that evil is beyond superessential non-being, which is the good.> If, <on the other hand> non-being is
absolutely-not-being, then evil even more is not; for evil is even more wraith-like, as the 5
saying goes, than that which absolutely does not exist, since evil is further removed from
the good than non-being. This is what is shown by those who give priority to non-being

over being, evil.[1] However, that which is further removed from the good is more insubstantial than that which is closer; thus, that which is absolutely not has more being than the so-called
10 evil; therefore evil is much more deprived of being than that which is absolutely not.

Besides, if – according to Plato's account – the father of this world not only gives existence to the nature of good things, but also wants evil not to exist anywhere, then how could evil possibly exist, which the demiurge does not want to exist? For it is inconceivable that what he wants is different from what he produces; on the contrary, in divine substances will-
15 ing and making always coincide. Hence, evil is not only not wanted by him, but it is even without existence, not [only] in the sense that he does not produce it – for it is not right even to think this – but in the sense that he even causes it not to exist; for his will was not that evil would not be produced by him, but rather that it would not exist at all. What then
20 could still produce its being when that which brings it to non-being is the father who gives existence to all things? For what would be contrary to him, and from where could it come? Evil agency, indeed, does not spring from him – for this is not right for him – and it would be absurd [to think] that it could originate elsewhere; for everything in the world stems from the father, some things directly from him, as has been said, other things through the proper activity of other beings.

The opposite point of view: evil exists

4. The argument that banishes evil from being could go like this, and along these lines it may sound probable. The argument that gives voice to the opposite viewpoint, however, will require that we first look at the reality of things and declare, with that reality in mind,
5 whether or not evil exists; so we must look at licentiousness itself and injustice and all the other things that we usually call vices of the soul and ask ourselves whether we will accept calling each of them good or evil. For if we admit that each of these [vices] is good, we must necessarily affirm one of the two following: either virtue is not contrary to vice – that is,
10 virtue on the whole is not contrary to vice on the whole, and particular virtues are not contrary to the corresponding vices – or that which opposes the good is not in every respect evil. But what could be more implausible than each one of these positions, or what could be less in accordance with the nature of things?

For the vices oppose the virtues; how they oppose one another becomes clear if one takes a look at human life, in which the unjust are opposed to the righteous, and the licentious
15 to the temperate, and also if one looks at what one might call the discord within souls themselves – for instance, when people lacking continence are drawn by reason in one direction, but forced by passion in the other direction, and in the fight between the two the better is overcome by the worse, but sometimes the worse by the better. For what else is happening in these people than that their souls' temperance is in discord with their licentious
20 manners? What is happening in those who are fighting with anger? Is it not something similar? And what about the other cases of evil in which we perceive our souls to be in discord? Indeed, in general the manifest oppositions between good and evil men exist long before in a hidden way within the souls themselves. And the stupidity and disease of the soul are then extreme when the better part in us and the good rational principles that exist in it are

---

1. Proclus is thinking of people committing suicide to escape from a miserable life; in doing so they prefer non-being to something that is worse (the argument seems to require that death indeed is the end of everything, at least in the mind of the people who argue along these lines).

overcome by worldly, vile passions. But to adduce many more examples would be foolish, 25
would it not?

Now, if vices are contrary to virtues, as we have said, and evil is in every respect contrary
to good – for the nature of the good itself is not so constituted as to be in discord with itself,
but being an offspring of one cause and one henad, it maintains a relation of likeness, unity, 30
and friendship with itself, and the greater goods preserve the lesser goods, and the lesser
goods are beautifully ordered by the more perfect ⁑ then it is absolutely necessary that the
vices be not merely vices (*kakiai*) 'by way of speaking', but each of them must also really be
evil and not just something less good. For the lesser good is not contrary to the greater good,
just as the less hot is not contrary to the more hot nor the less cold to the more cold. Now 35
if it is agreed that the vices of the soul belong to the nature of evil, it will have been demonstrated that evil pertains to beings.

5. And this is not the only reason. Evil is also that which corrupts everything. Indeed, that
this is evil has been shown by Socrates in the *Republic*, where he makes the correct observation that the good of each thing is that which preserves this thing, and that therefore all
things have an appetite for the good. For all things have their being from the good and are
preserved by the good, just as, conversely, non-being and corruption occur on account of 5
the nature of evil. Thus, it is necessary either <that evil exists or> that nothing is corruptive of anything. But in the latter case, 'generation will collapse and come to a halt'; for if
there is nothing corruptive, there can be no corruption; and if there is no corruption, there
can be no generation either, since generation always comes about through the corruption
of something else. And if there is no generation, the whole world will be 'incomplete', 'as 10
it will not contain in itself the mortal classes of animals; and they must exist if the world is
to be sufficiently perfect', says Timaeus. Hence, if the world is to be a 'blessed god', then it
must perfectly preserve a 'similarity' with the 'completely perfect animal'; if this is true, even
'the mortal classes' must complete the universe; and if this is true, there must be generation 15
and corruption; and if this is true, there must be both principles corruptive of beings and
generative principles, and different principles for different classes of beings. For not all things
have their generation or corruption from the same principles. If, then, in the classes that have
been allotted generation there are congenital corruptive principles which destroy the powers 20
of those beings, then evil must also exist. For this is what evil has been said to be, namely,
that which is corruptive of each of the things that are generated in which it exists primarily
and *per se*. Indeed, some things are able to corrupt the soul, others the body, and what is
corrupted is in each case something different. Neither is the mode of corruption the same,
but in the first case it is a corruption of substance, in the other of life; and in the first case 25
substance is led towards non-being and corruption, while in the other case life flees from
being and, in short, to something else that is not. Thus, it will be the same argument that
keeps the whole world perfect and posits evil among beings. And so, evil will not only exist
because of the good, but evil will also be good because of its very being. This, then, may
seem extremely paradoxical, but it will become more clear later. 30

[. . .]

Proclus' own view

8. If, as we have said, one should not only adduce the above arguments but also unfold the
doctrine on the existence of evils from Plato's teaching, what has already been said is

sufficient even for those who are capable only of moderate comprehension. However, as in a court of justice, we should not only listen to the contending parties, but also pass some judgement of our own. Let this then be, if you like, our verdict. To begin with, evil is twofold: on the one hand, pure evil on its own, unmixed with the good; and on the other hand, evil that is not pure nor unmixed with the nature of the good. For the good too [is twofold]: on the one hand, that which is primarily good and as it were the good itself, and nothing else but good – it is neither intellect nor intelligence nor real being; on the other hand, the good that is mixed with other things. And the latter sometimes is not mixed with privation, whereas elsewhere it does have such a mixture. For that which intermittently participates in the primarily good is manifestly entwined with the non-good. Indeed, the same holds for being itself and the nature of being: in the higher realm being is really being and merely being, but in the last beings, being is somehow mixed with non-being. For take that which in one respect is, but in another is not, that which at times is, but is not for countless times, that which is this but is not all other things: how could one say that it is, rather than that it is not, when it is completely filled with non-being?

And non-being itself, too [, is twofold]: on the one hand, that which absolutely does not exist – it is beyond the lowest nature, whose being is accidental – as it is unable to exist either in itself or even accidentally, for that which does not exist at all does not in some respect exist, in another not. On the other hand, [there is] non-being that is together with being, whether you call it privation of being or 'otherness'. The former [i.e. absolute non-being] is in all respects non-being, whereas the latter [i.e. relative non-being] is in the higher realm 'not less than being', as the Eleatic Stranger asserts, but when it is present among the things that sometimes are and sometimes are not, it is weaker than being, but nonetheless even then it is somehow dominated by being.

9. Hence, if someone were to ask whether non-being is or is not, our answer would be that what absolutely does not exist and has no share whatever in being has absolutely no being; however, we would concede to the questioner that what somehow is not, should be counted among beings.

The same reasoning, then, holds for evil, since this is twofold too: on the one hand, that which is exclusively evil; on the other hand, that which is not [exclusively evil], but is mixed with the good. We will rank the former beyond that which absolutely does not exist, inasmuch as the good is beyond being, and the latter among beings, for, because of the mediation of the good, it can no longer remain deprived of being and because of its being it cannot remain deprived of the good. Indeed, it is both being and good. And that which is in all respects evil, being a falling off and as it were a departure from the first good, is of course also deprived of being: for how could it have an entrance into beings if it could not participate in the good? But that which is not in all respects evil, is on the one hand 'contrary' to some good, though not to the good in general; on the other hand, it is ordered and made good because of the pre-eminence of the wholes that are good. And it is evil for those things which it opposes, but depends on other things [i.e. the wholes] as something good. For it is not right that evil oppose the wholes, but all things ought to follow in accordance with justice or not exist at all.

[. . .]

33. If, then, the souls suffer weakness and fall, this is not because of matter, since these [deficiencies] existed already before the bodies and matter, and somehow a cause of evil existed in the souls themselves prior to [their descent into] matter. What else could be the

explanation for the fact that among the souls that follow Zeus some raise the head of the charioteer into the outer region, whereas <others> are incapable and sink down, and are as 5 it were blunted by that spectacle and turn away their eyes? Indeed, how can 'oblivion' of being and 'mischance' and 'heaviness' occur in those souls? For 'the horse that participates in evil becomes heavy and verges to the earth', without there being matter [involved]. Indeed, only after the soul has fallen to earth does it enter into communion with matter and the darkness here below. Up there, however, and prior to matter and darkness, there is [already] 10 weakness and oblivion and evil; for we would not have departed if not out of weakness, since even at a distance we still cling to the contemplation of being.

Hence, if souls are weakened before [they drink from] the cup [of oblivion], and if they come to be in matter and descend into matter after the flight from up there, [it can] no longer [be held that] weakness and evils in general occur in souls because of matter. For what could 15 something do to other things that is itself incapable of doing anything? And also, how could that which on its own is without qualities have the capacity to do something?

Does matter draw souls to itself or are they drawn by themselves and become separated through their own power, or [rather] their own powerlessness? If souls are drawn by themselves, evil for them will consist in an impulse towards the inferior and the desire for it, and 20 not in matter. Indeed, for each thing evil is the flight from the better, and even more is it the flight towards the worse. And because of their weakness such souls suffer what they ought to suffer when they have chosen badly. If, on the other hand, souls are drawn by matter – that is, if we attribute the cause of their generation to the attraction matter exercises upon souls, as something that draws them – where is their self-motion and ability to choose? Or 25 how can one explain why among the souls that are generated in matter, some gaze at intellect and the good, whereas others gaze at generation and matter, if matter draws all of them alike to itself, troubling them and doing violence to them even when they are in the upper regions? These will be the conclusions of the argument: it will compel us to demonstrate not just that matter is not evil, but even, trying to prove what is contrary to the first thesis, that matter is good.

[. . .]

36. Perhaps, then, someone may ask us what our opinion is concerning matter, whether we consider it to be good or evil, and in what respect [we may admit] either of these options. Let this, then, be our decision: that matter is neither good nor evil. For if it is good, it will be a goal, instead of the last of things, and it will be 'that for the sake of which' and desir- 5 able. For all good is like this, since the primary good is the goal, that for the sake of which everything [exists], and the object of desire for all beings.

If, on the other hand, matter is evil, it will be a god and an alternative principle of beings, dissident from the cause of good things, and there will be 'two sources releasing their flow in opposite directions', one the source of good things, the other of evil things. Even for the gods themselves there will not be an unharmed life, nor a life free from mortal toiling, since 10 something for them will be difficult to bear, foreign and troubling as it were.

If, then, matter is neither good nor evil, what will it be in its own right? We should repeat what has been often said about matter, that it is a necessity. Indeed, the nature of good is one thing, that of evil another, and they are contrary to each other. But there is another, a 15 third nature, that is neither simply good nor evil, but necessary. Indeed, evil leads away from the good and flees from its nature; but the necessary is everything it is for the sake of the

good, and it has a relation to the good. And any generation that befalls the necessary, happens because of the good. If then matter exists for the sake of generation, and if no other
20 nature exists for the sake of matter in such a way that we could call it the goal or the good, then we must say that matter is necessary to generation, that it is not evil and that it is produced by divinity as necessary, and that it is necessary for the forms that are incapable of being established in themselves.

For the cause of all good things had to produce not only beings that are good and that
25 are good by themselves, but also the nature that is not absolutely and intrinsically good, but that desires the good and through its desire – and, as it were, by itself – gives other things the possibility of coming into being. Indeed, through its need for good things this nature [i.e. matter] contributes to the creation of the sensibles. For being, too, imparts existence not only to beings, but also to things that desire a participation in Being itself. For those things,
30 being consists in the desire for being. Hence, that which is primarily desirable is one thing; another thing is that which desires this and possesses good through this; yet another thing is everything that is intermediate, which is desirable to some things, but itself desires other things, namely the things that are prior to it and for the sake of which it exists.

37. If we consider matter itself from this perspective, we will see that it is neither good nor evil, but only necessary; in having been produced for the sake of good it is good, but taken on its own it is not good; and as the lowest of beings it is evil – if indeed what is most
5 remote from the good is evil – but taken on its own it is not evil, but necessary, as we have explained.

And in general, it is not true that evil exists on its own anywhere, for there is no unmixed evil, no primary evil. For if evil were contrary to the good in all respects, then, given the fact that the good that is on its own and primary precedes the good in other things, evil,
10 too, has to be twofold: evil itself, and evil in something else.

But if evil is [only] contrary to those goods that have their being in something else, then *a fortiori* evil is in something else and does not exist on its own; neither does the good of which evil is the contrary exist on its own, but it exists only in something else and not separately. Indeed, what would be contrary to the primary good? I do not mean evil, but
15 what else among beings [would be contrary to the primary good]? For all beings exist because of the good and for the sake of the good. But that the contrary exists because of the nature of its contrary, that is impossible; it is rather the case that [because of the latter] the contrary does not exist. For contraries are destroyed by each other. And in general all contraries proceed from a single summit and genus. But what would be the genus of the first good?
20 Indeed, what could be beyond the nature of the good? What among beings could become homogeneous to it? For in that case it would be necessary that there be something else prior to both of them, of which either one of them would be a part. And the good would no longer be the principle of beings. No, the principle of beings would be the principle that is common to both these.

Hence, nothing is contrary to the primary good, and neither to all things that participate
25 in it, but there is only contrariety to things whose participation is not immutable. Of these, however, we have spoken before.

[. . .]

51. Now we have to say what the nature of evil itself is. It will appear, however, to be the most difficult of all things to know the nature of evil in itself, since all knowledge is contact with form and is a form, whereas evil is formless and like a kind of privation. But perhaps

even this will become clear, if we look at the good itself and at the number of good things and 5 thus consider what evil is. For just as the primary good surpasses all things, so evil itself is destitute of all good things – I mean insofar as it is evil – and is a lack and privation of these.

Regarding the good, we have remarked elsewhere on its extension, on the manner in which it exists, and on the orders it possesses. With respect to evil, on the other hand, we should say the following. From the fact that *qua* evil it is a complete privation of goodness, it 10 follows that:

(1)   as evil it is deprived of the fount of good things;
(2.1.1) as unlimited [it is deprived] of the first limit;
(2.1.2) as weakness [it is deprived] of the power that resides there;
(2.1.3) as incommensurate and false and ugly [it is deprived] of 'beauty', 'truth' and 'meas-
        ure' – by which the mixed is produced, and in which the henads of beings reside;
(2.2)   as being unfounded in its own nature, and unstable, it is deprived of 'eternity which 15
        remains in one' – and of the power of eternity; for 'not in the same way' is typic-
        ally said of impotence;
(2.3)   as privation and lifelessness it is deprived of the first monad of forms and of the life
        that is there.

And if evil is destructive, and the cause of division for any being to which it is present, and imperfect, it is deprived of (3) the goodness that perfects complete beings. For the destruc-tive leads from (3.1) being to non-being; the divisive destroys (3.2) the continuity and union 20 of being; and the imperfect prevents each thing from obtaining (3.3) its perfection and natural order.

Moreover, the indefiniteness of the nature of evil is a failure and a deprivation of the (4.1) unitary summit; its barrenness is deprivation of (4.2) the summit of fertility; and its inactivity is deprivation of (4.3) the summit of demiurgy. Withdrawal, and weakness, and 25 indeterminateness, then, consist in the privation of these goods, privation, that is, of the monadic cause, of generative power, and of efficient creation.

But if evil is also the cause of dissimilitude, division, and disorder, it is clearly necessary that it is deprived of (5) assimilative goods, and of (5.1) the indivisible providence of divisible beings, and of the order that exists in the divided beings. Since, however, the good is not lim- 30 ited to this level, but there is also (6) the immaculate class, and the effective and the splendid in its accomplishments, evil then will be ineffectual, dark and material. Or from where will it obtain each of these and similar properties, if not from privations of these good things? For in the higher realm the good things exist primarily; and it is of these higher goods that also the good in us is a part and an image; and the privation of the good in us is evil. As a 35 consequence it is also a privation of those goods, to which, as we claim, the good bears a resemblance.

And why say more, since it is obvious that evil in bodies is not only privation of the good that resides in them, but also of the good that prior to them resides in souls? For the good in bodies consists in being the image of the good in souls. Destruction, therefore, and the privation of form will be nothing other than the falling from intellective power, for form, 40 too, is the offspring of Intellect, and that which produces forms is intellective in substance.

Now, about that which is in every sense evil this much has been said: it is a privation of goods and a deficiency.

[. . .]

Bibliography of Translations Used

Allen, R. E., *The Dialogues of Plato*. New Haven: Yale University Press, 1984, 1991, 1997.

Apostle, Hippocrates G., and Gerson, Lloyd P., *Aristotle: Selected Works*, 3rd edn. Grinnell, IA: The Peripatetic Press, 1991.

Benjamin, Anna S., *Xenophon: Recollections of Socrates* and *Socrates' Defense Before the Jury*. New York: Macmillan, 1985.

Bloom, Allen, *The Republic of Plato*. New York: Basic Books, 1968.

Brickhouse, Thomas C., and Smith, Nicholas D., *The Trial and Execution of Socrates: Sources and Controversies*. New York: Oxford University Press, 2002.

Cornford, F. M., *Plato's Cosmology: The Timaeus of Plato Translated with a Running Commentary*. New York: Humanities Press [Routledge], 1937.

Englert, Walter, *Lucretius: On the Nature of Things*. Newburyport, MA: R. Pullins Company, 2003.

Gallop, David, *Plato, Phaedo*. Oxford: Clarendon Press, 1988.

Hicks, R. D., *Diogenes Laertius: Lives of Eminent Philosophers*, vols. 1 and 2. Loeb Classical Library. Cambridge, MA: Harvard University Press, 1925, 1931.

Long, A. A., and Sedley, D. N., *The Hellenistic Philosophers*, vol. 1. Cambridge: Cambridge University Press, 1987.

O'Brien, Elmer, *The Essential Plotinus*. New York: New American Library, 1964.

Opsomer, Jan, and Steel, Carlos, *Proclus, On the Existence of Evils*. Ithaca, NY: Cornell University Press, 2003.

Saunders, Jason, *Greek and Roman Philosophy after Aristotle*. New York: Free Press [Macmillan], 1966.

Yonge, C. D., *Diogenes Laertius, Lives and Opinions of Eminent Philosophers*. All but the lives of Zeno and Epicurus are now available at <http://classicpersuasion.org/pw/diogenes/>.

Recommended Further Reading (English-Language Sources)

PART I. THE PRESOCRATICS AND SOPHISTS

Guthrie, W. K. C., *A History of Greek Philosophy*, vols. 1 and 2. Cambridge: Cambridge University Press, 1962, 1965.
Guthrie, W. K. C., *The Sophists*. Cambridge: Cambridge University Press, 1971.
Kerferd, G. B., *The Sophistic Movement*. Cambridge: Cambridge University Press, 1981.
Kirk, G. S., Raven, J. E., and Schofield, M., *The Presocratic Philosophers: A Critical History with a Selection of Texts*, 2nd edn. Cambridge: Cambridge University Press, 1995.
Long, A. A., ed., *The Cambridge Companion to Early Greek Philosophy*. Cambridge: Cambridge University Press, 1999.
McKirahan, R. D. Jr., *Philosophy Before Socrates*. Indianapolis: Hackett, 1994.
Mourelatos, A. P. D., ed., *The Pre-Socratics: A Collection of Critical Essays*. Princeton: Princeton University Press, 1993.

PART II. XENOPHON

Bartlett, R. C. ed., *Xenophon, The Shorter Socratic Writings: Apology of Socrates to the Jury, Oeconomicus, and Symposium*. Ithaca, NY: Cornell University Press, 1996.
Cooper, J. M., "Notes on Xenophon's Socrates," in *Reason and Emotion: Essays on Ancient Moral Psychology and Ethical Theory*, pp. 3–28. Princeton: Princeton University Press, 1999.
Vander Waerdt, P. A., ed., *The Socratic Movement*. Ithaca, NY: Cornell University Press, 1994.

PART III. PLATO

EARLY OR SOCRATIC DIALOGUES

Benson, H. H., ed., *Essays on the Philosophy of Socrates*. Oxford: Oxford University Press, 1992.
Brickhouse, T. C., and Smith, N. D., *Plato's Socrates*. Oxford: Oxford University Press, 1994.
Brickhouse, T. C., and Smith, N. D., *The Philosophy of Socrates*. Boulder, CO: Westview Press, 2000.
McPherran, M. L., *The Religion of Socrates*. University Park: Pennsylvania State University Press, 1996.
Prior, W. J., ed., *Socrates: Critical Assessments*, 4 vols. London: Routledge, 1996.
Santas, G. X., *Socrates: Philosophy in Plato's Early Dialogues*. London: Routledge & Kegan Paul, 1979.

Vlastos, G., *Socrates: Ironist and Moral Philosopher*. Ithaca, NY: Cambridge University Press and Cornell University Press, 1991.

Vlastos, G., *Socratic Studies*. Cambridge: Cambridge University Press, 1994.

MIDDLE AND LATE DIALOGUES

Allen, R. E., ed., *Studies in Plato's Metaphysics*. London: Routledge & Kegan Paul, 1965.

Benson, H. H., ed., *A Companion to Plato*. London: Blackwell, 2006.

Irwin, T. I., *Plato's Ethics*. Oxford: Oxford University Press, 1995.

Kraut, R., ed., *The Cambridge Companion to Plato*. Cambridge: Cambridge University Press, 1992.

Patterson, R., *Image and Reality in Plato's Metaphysics*. Indianapolis: Hackett, 1985.

Penner, T., *The Ascent from Nominalism: Some Existence Arguments in Plato's Middle Dialogues*. Dordrecht: D. Reidel, 1987.

Prior, W., *Unity and Development in Plato's Metaphysics*. London: Croom Helm, 1985.

Sayre, K. M., *Plato's Late Ontology: A Riddle Resolved*. Princeton: Princeton University Press.

Smith, N. D., ed., *Plato: Critical Assessments*, 4 vols. London: Routledge, 1998.

Vlastos, G., *Platonic Studies*. 2nd edn. Princeton: Princeton University Press, 1981.

Vlastos, G., ed., *Plato: A Collection of Critical Essays*, 2 vols. Garden City, NY: Anchor Books (Doubleday), 1970.

Wagner, E., ed., *Essays on Plato's Psychology*. Lanham, Maryland: Lexington Books, 2001.

PART IV. ARISTOTLE

Ackrill, J. L., *Aristotle the Philosopher*. Oxford: Oxford University Press, 1981.

Anagnostopoulos, G., ed., *A Companion to Aristotle*. Oxford: Blackwell, 2007.

Barnes, J., *Aristotle*. Oxford: Oxford University Press, 1982.

Barnes, J., ed., *The Cambridge Companion to Aristotle*. Cambridge: Cambridge University Press, 1995.

Barnes, J., Schofield, M., and Sorabji, R., eds., *Articles on Aristotle*, 4 vols. London: Duckworth, 1975–9.

Code, A. D., *The Philosophy of Aristotle*. Boulder, CO: Westview Press, 2004.

Cohen, S. M., *Aristotle on Natural and Incomplete Substance*. Cambridge: Cambridge University Press, 1996.

Cooper, J. M., *Reason and the Human Good in Aristotle*. Cambridge, MA: Harvard University Press, 1975.

Everson, S., *Aristotle on Perception*. Oxford: Oxford University Press, 1997.

Ferejohn, M., *On the Origins of Aristotelian Science*. New Haven: Yale University Press, 1991.

Freudenthal, Gad, *Aristotle's Theory of Material Substance: Heat and Pneuma, Form and Soul*. Oxford: Oxford University Press, 1995.

Gerson, L. P., *Aristotle: Critical Assessments*, 4 vols. London: Routledge, 1999.

Gill, M. L., *Aristotle on Substance: The Paradox of Unity*. Princeton: Princeton University Press, 1989.

Gotthelf, A., and Lennox, J. G., eds., *Philosophical Issues in Aristotle's Biology*. Cambridge: Cambridge University Press, 1987.

Irwin, T. H., *Aristotle's First Principles*. Oxford: Oxford University Press, 1988.

Judson, L., ed., *Aristotle's Physics: A Collection of Essays*. Oxford: Oxford University Press, 1991.

Keyt, D., and Miller, F. D. Jr., eds., *A Companion to Aristotle's Politics*. Oxford: Blackwell, 1991.

Lear, J., *Aristotle and Logical Theory*. Cambridge: Cambridge University Press, 1980.

Lear, J., *Aristotle: The Desire to Understand*. Cambridge: Cambridge University Press, 1988.

Lloyd, G. E. R., *Aristotle: The Growth and Structure of his Thought*. Cambridge: Cambridge University Press, 1968.

McKirahan, R. D. Jr., *Principles and Proofs: Aristotle's Theory of Demonstrative Science*. Princeton: Princeton University Press, 1992.

Nussbaum, M. C., and Rorty, A., eds., *Essays on Aristotle's De Anima*. Oxford: Oxford University Press, 1992.

Ross, D., *Aristotle*, 6th edn. London: Routledge, 1995.

Wedin, M. V., *Mind and Imagination in Aristotle*. New Haven: Yale University Press, 1988.

Witt, C., *Substance and Essence in Aristotle*. Ithaca, NY: Cornell University Press, 1989.

PART V. DIOGENES THE CYNIC

Branham, Bracht, and Goulet-Cazé, Marie-Odile, eds., *The Cynics: The Cynic Movement in Antiquity and its Legacy*. Berkeley: University of California Press, 1996.

Dudley, D. R., *A History of Cynicism from Diogenes to the 6th Century A.D.* Cambridge: Cambridge University Press, 1937.

Navia, Luis E., *Classical Cynicism: A Critical Study*. Westport, CT: Greenwood Press, 1996.

PARTS VI–VIII. HELLENISTIC PHILOSOPHY: EPICURUS AND EPICUREANISM, STOICS AND STOICISM, SKEPTICS AND SKEPTICISM

GENERAL WORKS ON HELLENISTIC PHILOSOPHY

Algra, K., Barnes, J., Mansfeld, J., and Schofield, M., eds., *The Cambridge History of Hellenistic Philosophy*. Cambridge: Cambridge University Press, 2005.

Long, A. A., *Hellenistic Philosophy*. Berkeley: University of California Press, 1986.

Long, A. A., and Sedley, D. N., *The Hellenistic Philosophers*, vol. 1. Cambridge: Cambridge University Press, 1987.

Schofield, M., Burnyeat, M. F. and Barnes, J., *Doubt and Dogmatism: Studies in Hellenistic Epistemology*. Oxford: Clarendon Press, 1980.

EPICURUS AND EPICUREANISM

Annas, J., *Hellenistic Philosophy of Mind*. Berkeley: University of California Press, 1992.

Asmis, E., *Epicurus' Scientific Method*. Ithaca, NY: Cornell University Press, 1984.

Clay, D., *Paradosis and Survival: Three Chapters in the History of Epicurean Philosophy*. Ann Arbor: University of Michigan Press, 1999.

DeWitt, N. W., *Epicurus and his Philosophy*. Minneapolis: University of Minnesota Press, 1954.

Jones, H., *The Epicurean Tradition*. London: Routledge, 1989.

Lillegard, N., *On Epicurus*. Belmont, CA: Wadsworth, 2002.

Mitsis, P., *Epicurus' Ethical Theory: The Pleasures of Invulnerability*. Ithaca, NY: Cornell University Press, 1988.

O'Keefe, T., *Epicurus on Freedom*. Cambridge: Cambridge University Press, 2005.

Rist, J. M., *Epicurus: An Introduction*. Cambridge: Cambridge University Press, 1972.

Warren, J., *Facing Death: Epicurus and his Critics*. Oxford: Oxford University Press, 2004.

STOICS AND STOICISM

Bobzien, S., *Determinism and Freedom in Stoic Philosophy*. Oxford: Clarendon Press, 1998.

Brennan, T., *The Stoic Life: Emotions, Duties, and Fate*. Oxford: Oxford University Press, 2005.

Ierodiakonou, K., ed., *Topics in Stoic Philosophy*. Oxford: Oxford University Press, 1999.

Inwood, B., *The Cambridge Companion to the Stoics*. Cambridge: Cambridge University Press, 2003.

Rist, J. M., *Stoic Philosophy*. Cambridge: Cambridge University Press, 1969.

Sellars, J., *Stoicism*. Berkeley: University of California Press, 2006.

Skeptics and Skepticism

Annas, J., and Barnes, J., *The Modes of Scepticism: Ancient Texts and Modern Interpretations*. Cambridge: Cambridge University Press, 1985.

Bailey, A., *Sextus Empiricus and Pyrrhonean Scepticism*. Oxford: Oxford University Press, 2002.

Barnes, J., *The Toils of Scepticism*. Cambridge: Cambridge University Press, 1990.

Bett, R., *Pyrrho, his Antecedents, and his Legacy*. Oxford: Oxford University Press, 2003.

Burnyeat, M. F., ed., *The Skeptical Tradition*. Berkeley: University of California Press, 1983.

Burnyeat, M. F., and Frede, M., eds., *The Original Sceptics: A Controversy*. Indianapolis: Hackett, 1997.

Hankinson, R. J., *The Sceptics*. London: Routledge, 1995.

PART IX. NEOPLATONISM

Barnes, J., *Porphyry: Introduction*. Oxford. Oxford University Press, 2003.

Blumenthal, H. J., *Plotinus' Psychology*. The Hague: Springer, 1971.

Bussanich, J., *The One and its Relation to Intellect in Plotinus: A Commentary on Selected Texts*. Leiden: Brill, 1997.

Emilsson, E., *Plotinus on Sense-Perception*. Cambridge: Cambridge University Press, 1988.

Gerson, L. P., *Plotinus*. London: Routledge, 1998.

Gerson, L. P., ed., *The Cambridge Companion to Plotinus*. Cambridge: Cambridge University Press, 1996.

O'Meara, D., *Plotinus: An Introduction to the Enneads*. Oxford: Oxford University Press, 1993.

Rist, J., *Plotinus: The Road to Reality*. Cambridge: Cambridge University Press, 1967.

Smith, A., *Porphyry's Place in the Neoplatonic Tradition: A Study in Post-Plotinian Neoplatonism*. The Hague: Springer, 1974.

Whittaker, T., *The Neo-Platonists*, 2nd edn. Cambridge: Cambridge University Press, 1918.

Index

Index compiled by Meg Davies
(Fellow of the Society of Indexers)